spider-man
visionaries
john romita

cover
john romita

cover colors
steve buccellato

interior colors to
amazing spider-man #39-42, 50 and 68-69
vlm

interior colors to
amazing spider-man #108
steve buccellato

interior colors to
amazing spider-man #109
digital chameleon

book design
john "jg" roshell
of comicraft

assistant editor
matty ryan

collections editor
ben abernathy

manufacturing representative
stefano perrone jr.

editor in chief
joe quesada

president
bill jemas

special thanks to
mike farah, ralph macchio
and jessica schwartz

DIFFERENT MEMORIES COME WITH EACH OF THE NINE STORIES YOU ARE ABOUT TO ENJOY. PARTLY BECAUSE THEY SPANNED MORE THAN SIX YEARS WITH A LOT OF TWISTS AND TURNS FOR THESE CHARACTERS WE ALL CARE ABOUT.

AND, BECAUSE THEY BEGAN MY RUN ON THE AMAZING SPIDER-MAN, I WAS INTENT ON KEEPING THE "FLOW" STAN LEE AND STEVE DITKO HAD SET IN MOTION THROUGH THE FIRST 38 ISSUES.

TRYING TO COME UP WITH NEW CHARACTERS GOOD ENOUGH TO STAND UP TO THE CLASSIC VILLAINS AND "STOCK COMPANY" THEY HAD FILLED OUR HEARTS WITH WAS NO EASY CHORE.

A MEMORY-ROLLER COASTER FOR ME AND, I HOPE, PLENTY OF CHILLS AND THRILLS FOR YOU!

JOHN ROMITA
NEW YORK, 2001

SPIDER-MAN® VISIONARIES: JOHN ROMITA. Contains material originally published in magazine form as AMAZING SPIDER-MAN Vol. 1, #'s 39-42, 50, 69, 108 & 109. Published by MARVEL COMICS, a division of MARVEL ENTER-PRISES, INC. Lou Gioia, Executive Vice-President, Publishing; Bob Greenberger, Director Publishing Operations; Stan Lee, Chairman Emeritus. OFFICE OF PUBLICATION: 10 EAST 40TH STREET, NEW YORK, N.Y. 10016. Printed in Canada. First Printing, August 2001. ISBN: 0-7851-0794-0 GST #R127032852. MARVEL COMICS is a division of MARVEL ENTERPRISES, INC. Peter Cuneo, Chief Executive Officer; Avi Arad, Chief Creative Officer. 10 9 8 7 6 5 4 3 2 1

amazing spider-man #39

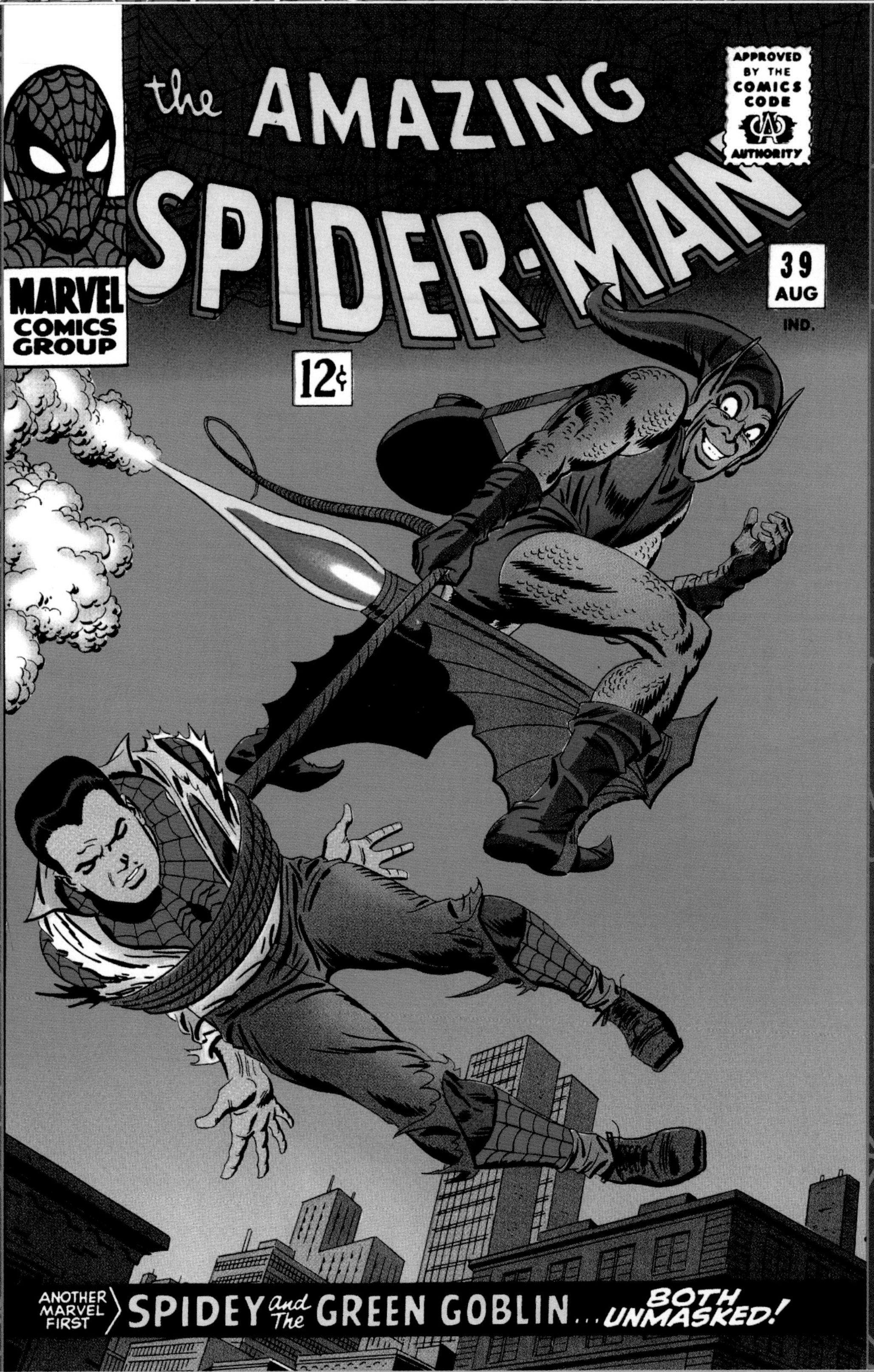
APPROVED BY THE COMICS CODE AUTHORITY
the AMAZING SPIDER-MAN
39
AUG
IND.
MARVEL COMICS GROUP
12¢
ANOTHER MARVEL FIRST
SPIDEY and The GREEN GOBLIN... BOTH UNMASKED!

august 1966

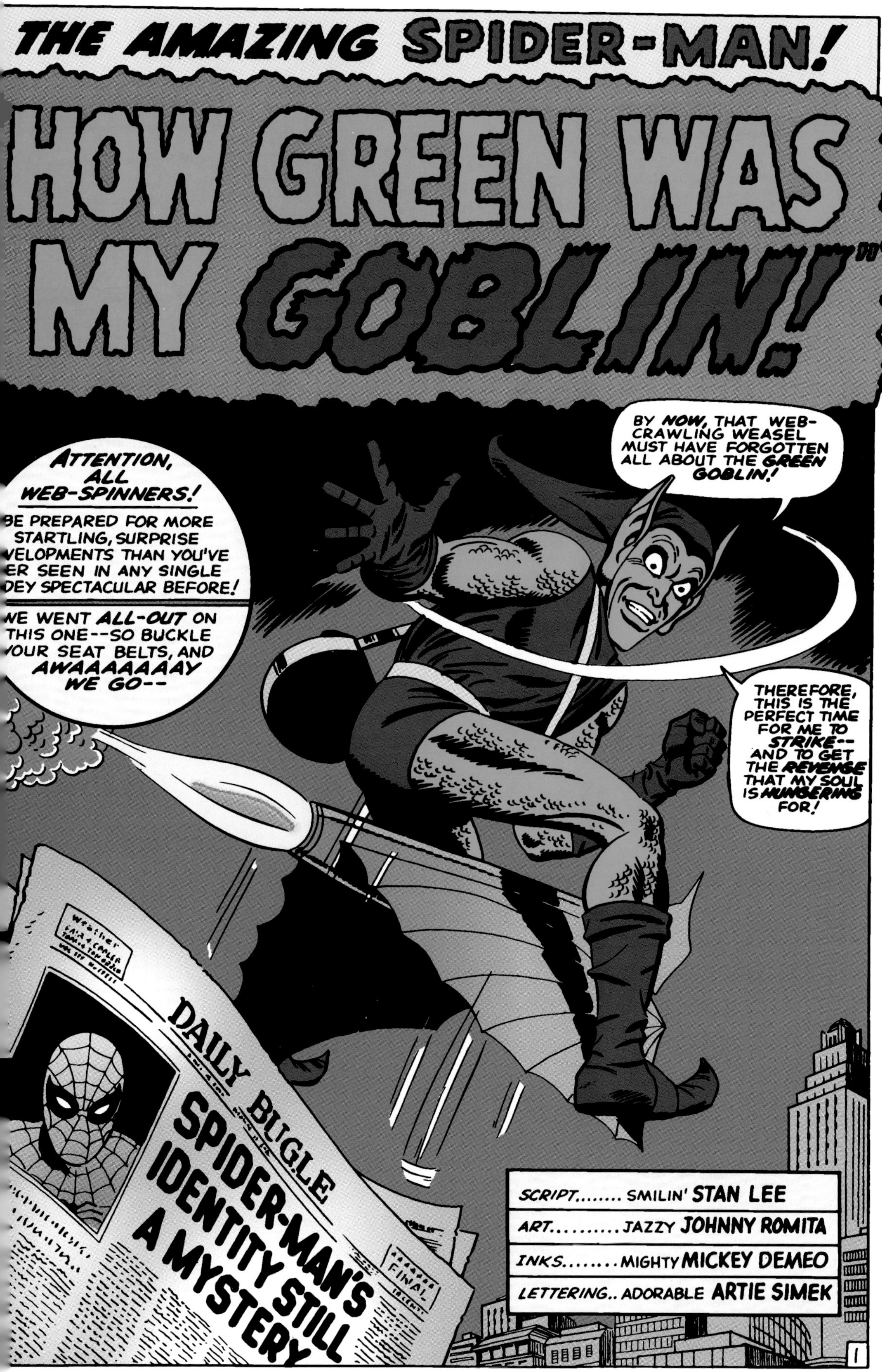

THE AMAZING SPIDER-MAN!
"HOW GREEN WAS MY GOBLIN!"
ATTENTION, ALL WEB-SPINNERS!
BE PREPARED FOR MORE STARTLING, SURPRISE VELOPMENTS THAN YOU'VE ER SEEN IN ANY SINGLE DEY SPECTACULAR BEFORE!
WE WENT ALL-OUT ON THIS ONE--SO BUCKLE OUR SEAT BELTS, AND AWAAAAAAAY WE GO--
BY NOW, THAT WEB-CRAWLING WEASEL MUST HAVE FORGOTTEN ALL ABOUT THE GREEN GOBLIN!
THEREFORE, THIS IS THE PERFECT TIME FOR ME TO STRIKE-- AND TO GET THE REVENGE THAT MY SOUL IS HUNGERING FOR!
DAILY BUGLE
SPIDER-MAN'S IDENTITY STILL A MYSTERY
FINAL
SCRIPT........ SMILIN' STAN LEE
ART.......... JAZZY JOHNNY ROMITA
INKS....... MIGHTY MICKEY DEMEO
LETTERING.. ADORABLE ARTIE SIMEK

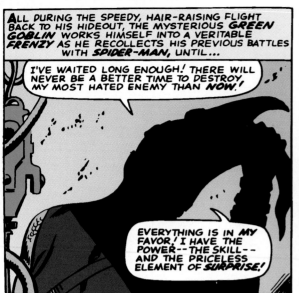

ALL DURING THE SPEEDY, HAIR-RAISING FLIGHT BACK TO HIS HIDEOUT, THE MYSTERIOUS *GREEN GOBLIN* WORKS HIMSELF INTO A VERITABLE *FRENZY* AS HE RECOLLECTS HIS PREVIOUS BATTLES WITH *SPIDER-MAN*, UNTIL...

I'VE WAITED LONG ENOUGH! THERE WILL NEVER BE A BETTER TIME TO DESTROY MY MOST HATED ENEMY THAN *NOW!*

EVERYTHING IS IN *MY* FAVOR! I HAVE THE POWER--THE SKILL-- AND THE PRICELESS ELEMENT OF *SURPRISE!*

BUT, MERELY *DESTROYING* HIM-- SIMPLY *CRUSHING* HIM LIKE A WORM --WILL NOT GIVE ME ENOUGH SATISFACTION!

I MUST DO STILL *MORE* THAN THAT!

FIRST, I'LL *TOY* WITH HIM-- OUTSMART HIM EVERY STEP OF THE WAY--AS ONLY THE *GOBLIN* CAN!

THEN, BEFORE DELIVERING THE *FINAL STROKE,* I'LL ADMINISTER THE MOST *HUMILIATING* BLOW OF ALL--

I'LL LEARN HIS *SECRET IDENTITY,* AND REVEAL IT TO ALL THE WORLD!

THEN-- AND ONLY THEN--I'LL FINISH HIM-- FOREVER!

MY LITTLE BAG OF TRICKS IS FULLY LOADED-- AND MY *STUN BOMBS* ARE MORE POTENT THAN EVER!

IF I DIDN'T *DESPISE* THAT MISERABLE MASKED MISANTHROPE SO MUCH, I'D ALMOST *PITY* HIM--BECAUSE OF WHAT'S IN STORE!

I'VE MODIFIED MY ROCKET-POWERED *FLYING BROOMSTICK* SO THAT IT'S FASTER AND MORE MANEUVERABLE THAN EVER!

HAD I NOT BEEN SO CARELESS--AND SO OVERCONFIDENT IN THE PAST, I COULD HAVE BEATEN SPIDER MAN EVEN *THEN*--

--BUT *NOW*-- THE OUTCOME IS A FOREGON CONCLUSION!

HE HASN'T A *CHANCE*

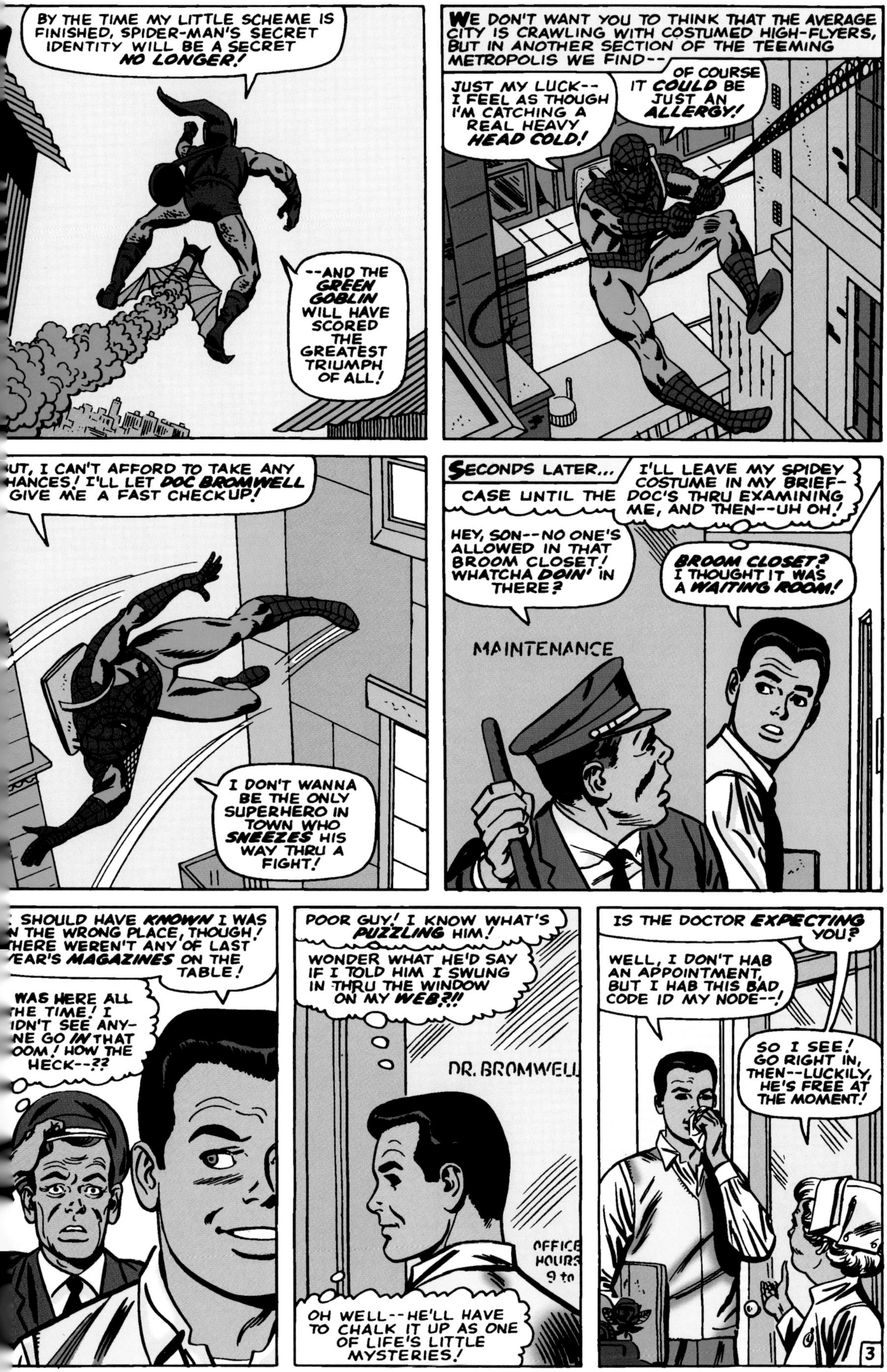
BY THE TIME MY LITTLE SCHEME IS FINISHED, SPIDER-MAN'S SECRET IDENTITY WILL BE A SECRET NO LONGER!
--AND THE GREEN GOBLIN WILL HAVE SCORED THE GREATEST TRIUMPH OF ALL!
WE DON'T WANT YOU TO THINK THAT THE AVERAGE CITY IS CRAWLING WITH COSTUMED HIGH-FLYERS, BUT IN ANOTHER SECTION OF THE TEEMING METROPOLIS WE FIND--
JUST MY LUCK-- I FEEL AS THOUGH I'M CATCHING A REAL HEAVY HEAD COLD!
OF COURSE IT COULD BE JUST AN ALLERGY!
UT, I CAN'T AFFORD TO TAKE ANY HANCES! I'LL LET DOC BROMWELL GIVE ME A FAST CHECKUP!
I DON'T WANNA BE THE ONLY SUPERHERO IN TOWN WHO SNEEZES HIS WAY THRU A FIGHT!
SECONDS LATER...
I'LL LEAVE MY SPIDEY COSTUME IN MY BRIEF-CASE UNTIL THE DOC'S THRU EXAMINING ME, AND THEN--UH OH!
HEY, SON--NO ONE'S ALLOWED IN THAT BROOM CLOSET! WHATCHA DOIN' IN THERE?
BROOM CLOSET? I THOUGHT IT WAS A WAITING ROOM!
MAINTENANCE
SHOULD HAVE KNOWN I WAS N THE WRONG PLACE, THOUGH! THERE WEREN'T ANY OF LAST YEAR'S MAGAZINES ON THE TABLE!
WAS HERE ALL THE TIME! I IDN'T SEE ANY-NE GO IN THAT OOM! HOW THE HECK--??
POOR GUY! I KNOW WHAT'S PUZZLING HIM!
WONDER WHAT HE'D SAY IF I TOLD HIM I SWUNG IN THRU THE WINDOW ON MY WEB?!!
DR. BROMWELL
OFFICE HOURS 9 to
OH WELL--HE'LL HAVE TO CHALK IT UP AS ONE OF LIFE'S LITTLE MYSTERIES!
IS THE DOCTOR EXPECTING YOU?
WELL, I DON'T HAB AN APPOINTMENT, BUT I HAB THIS BAD CODE ID MY NODE--!
SO I SEE! GO RIGHT IN, THEN--LUCKILY, HE'S FREE AT THE MOMENT!
3

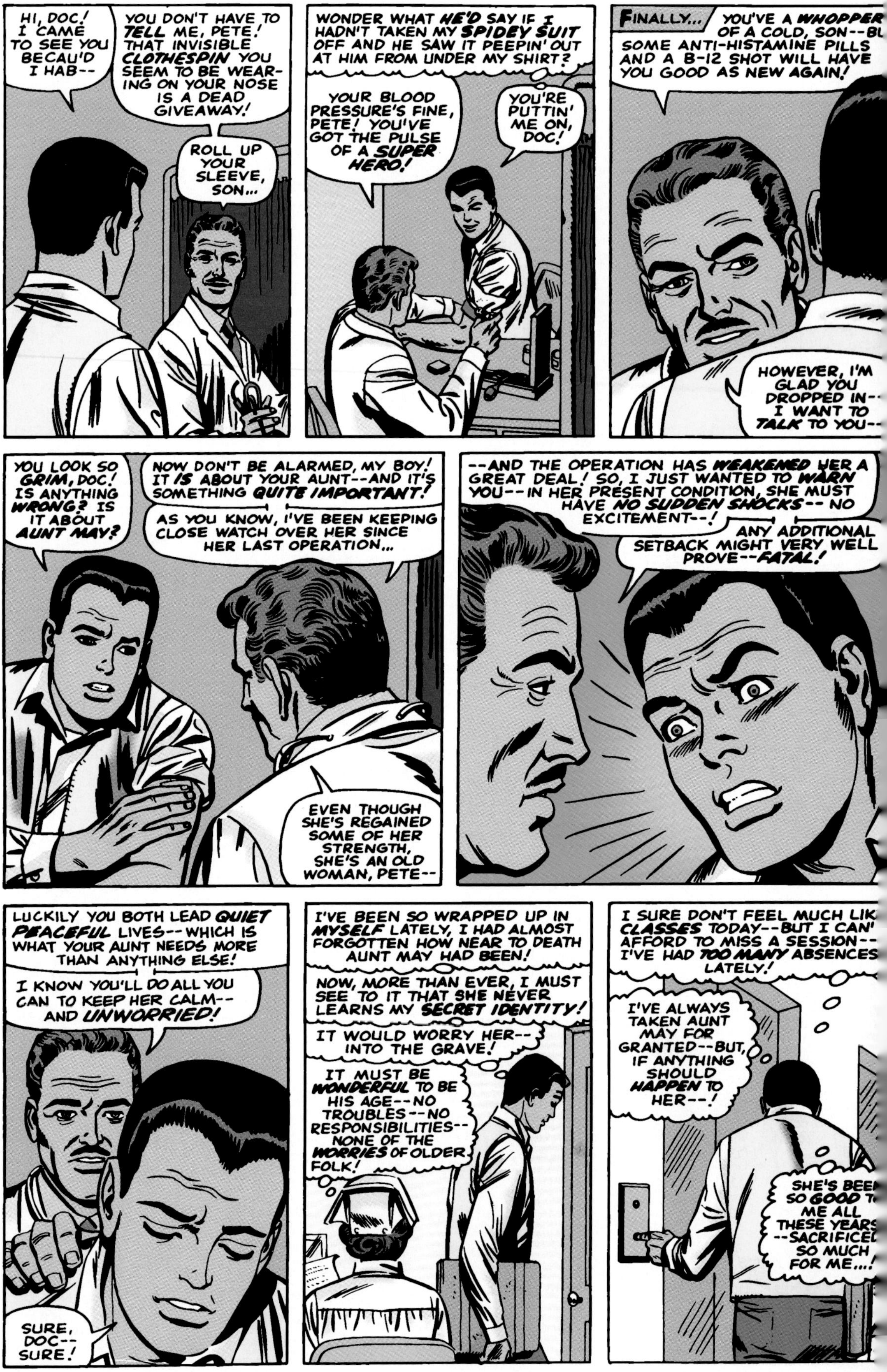

HI, DOC! I CAME TO SEE YOU BECAU'D I HAB--
YOU DON'T HAVE TO TELL ME, PETE! THAT INVISIBLE CLOTHESPIN YOU SEEM TO BE WEARING ON YOUR NOSE IS A DEAD GIVEAWAY!
ROLL UP YOUR SLEEVE, SON...
WONDER WHAT HE'D SAY IF I HADN'T TAKEN MY SPIDEY SUIT OFF AND HE SAW IT PEEPIN' OUT AT HIM FROM UNDER MY SHIRT?
YOUR BLOOD PRESSURE'S FINE, PETE! YOU'VE GOT THE PULSE OF A SUPER HERO!
YOU'RE PUTTIN' ME ON, DOC!
FINALLY...
YOU'VE A WHOPPER OF A COLD, SON--BU SOME ANTI-HISTAMINE PILLS AND A B-12 SHOT WILL HAVE YOU GOOD AS NEW AGAIN!
HOWEVER, I'M GLAD YOU DROPPED IN-- I WANT TO TALK TO YOU--
YOU LOOK SO GRIM, DOC! IS ANYTHING WRONG? IS IT ABOUT AUNT MAY?
NOW DON'T BE ALARMED, MY BOY! IT IS ABOUT YOUR AUNT--AND IT'S SOMETHING QUITE IMPORTANT!
AS YOU KNOW, I'VE BEEN KEEPING CLOSE WATCH OVER HER SINCE HER LAST OPERATION...
EVEN THOUGH SHE'S REGAINED SOME OF HER STRENGTH, SHE'S AN OLD WOMAN, PETE--
--AND THE OPERATION HAS WEAKENED HER A GREAT DEAL! SO, I JUST WANTED TO WARN YOU--IN HER PRESENT CONDITION, SHE MUST HAVE NO SUDDEN SHOCKS--NO EXCITEMENT--!
ANY ADDITIONAL SETBACK MIGHT VERY WELL PROVE--FATAL!
LUCKILY YOU BOTH LEAD QUIET PEACEFUL LIVES--WHICH IS WHAT YOUR AUNT NEEDS MORE THAN ANYTHING ELSE!
I KNOW YOU'LL DO ALL YOU CAN TO KEEP HER CALM--AND UNWORRIED!
SURE, DOC--SURE!
I'VE BEEN SO WRAPPED UP IN MYSELF LATELY, I HAD ALMOST FORGOTTEN HOW NEAR TO DEATH AUNT MAY HAD BEEN!
NOW, MORE THAN EVER, I MUST SEE TO IT THAT SHE NEVER LEARNS MY SECRET IDENTITY!
IT WOULD WORRY HER--INTO THE GRAVE!
IT MUST BE WONDERFUL TO BE HIS AGE--NO TROUBLES--NO RESPONSIBILITIES--NONE OF THE WORRIES OF OLDER FOLK!
I SURE DON'T FEEL MUCH LIK CLASSES TODAY--BUT I CAN' AFFORD TO MISS A SESSION--I'VE HAD TOO MANY ABSENCES LATELY!
I'VE ALWAYS TAKEN AUNT MAY FOR GRANTED--BUT, IF ANYTHING SHOULD HAPPEN TO HER--!
SHE'S BEE SO GOOD T ME ALL THESE YEARS --SACRIFICED SO MUCH FOR ME...!

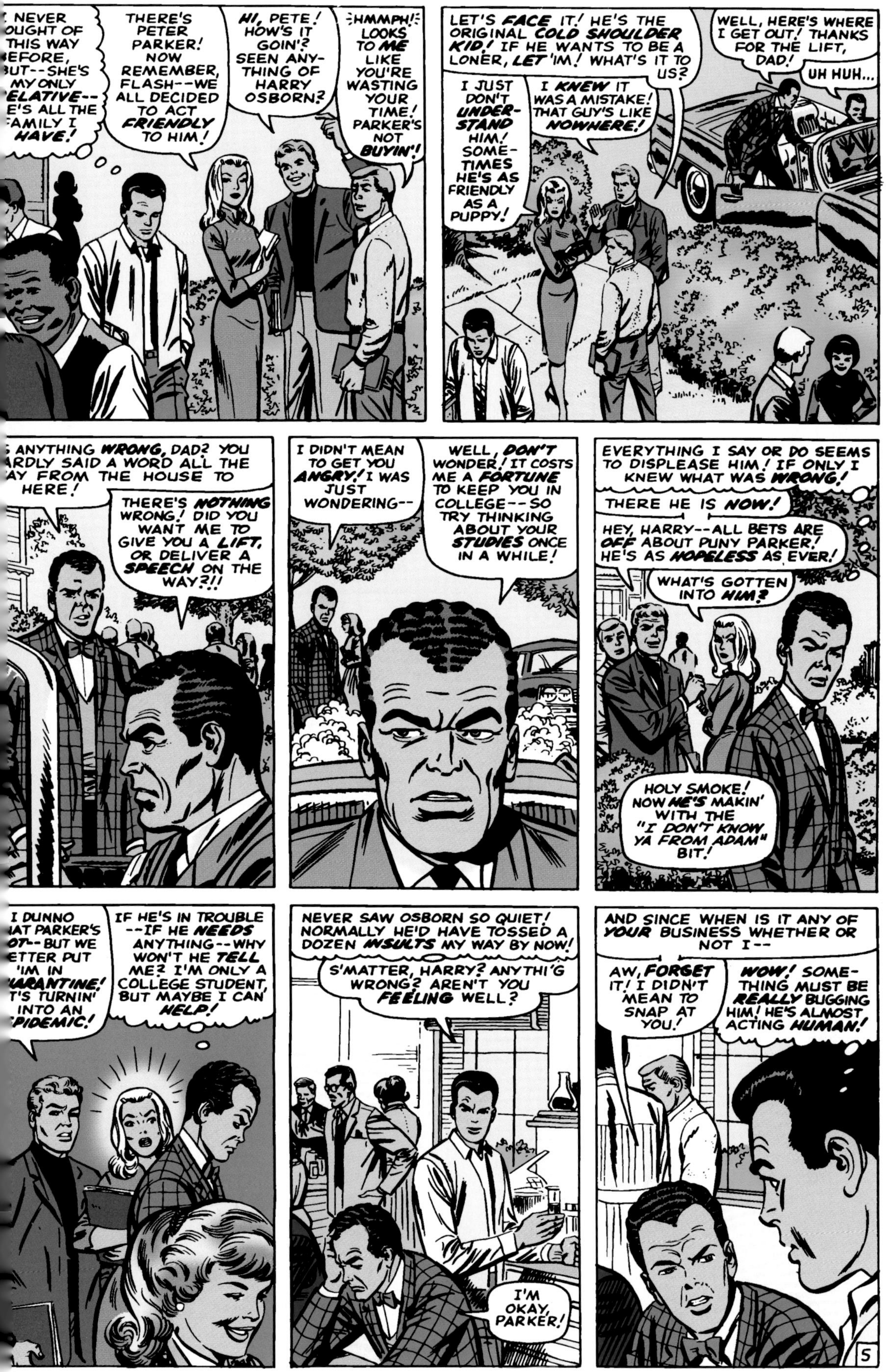

NEVER OUGHT OF THIS WAY BEFORE, BUT--SHE'S MY ONLY RELATIVE-- E'S ALL THE FAMILY I HAVE!
THERE'S PETER PARKER! NOW REMEMBER, FLASH--WE ALL DECIDED TO ACT FRIENDLY TO HIM!
HI, PETE! HOW'S IT GOIN'? SEEN ANYTHING OF HARRY OSBORN?
HMMPH! LOOKS TO ME LIKE YOU'RE WASTING YOUR TIME! PARKER'S NOT BUYIN'!
LET'S FACE IT! HE'S THE ORIGINAL COLD SHOULDER KID! IF HE WANTS TO BE A LONER, LET 'IM! WHAT'S IT TO US?
I JUST DON'T UNDERSTAND HIM! SOMETIMES HE'S AS FRIENDLY AS A PUPPY!
I KNEW IT WAS A MISTAKE! THAT GUY'S LIKE NOWHERE!
WELL, HERE'S WHERE I GET OUT! THANKS FOR THE LIFT, DAD!
UH HUH...
ANYTHING WRONG, DAD? YOU ARDLY SAID A WORD ALL THE AY FROM THE HOUSE TO HERE!
THERE'S NOTHING WRONG! DID YOU WANT ME TO GIVE YOU A LIFT, OR DELIVER A SPEECH ON THE WAY?!!
I DIDN'T MEAN TO GET YOU ANGRY! I WAS JUST WONDERING--
WELL, DON'T WONDER! IT COSTS ME A FORTUNE TO KEEP YOU IN COLLEGE--SO TRY THINKING ABOUT YOUR STUDIES ONCE IN A WHILE!
EVERYTHING I SAY OR DO SEEMS TO DISPLEASE HIM! IF ONLY I KNEW WHAT WAS WRONG!
THERE HE IS NOW!
HEY, HARRY--ALL BETS ARE OFF ABOUT PUNY PARKER! HE'S AS HOPELESS AS EVER!
WHAT'S GOTTEN INTO HIM?
HOLY SMOKE! NOW HE'S MAKIN' WITH THE "I DON'T KNOW YA FROM ADAM" BIT!
I DUNNO HAT PARKER'S OT--BUT WE ETTER PUT 'IM IN UARANTINE! T'S TURNIN' INTO AN PIDEMIC!
IF HE'S IN TROUBLE --IF HE NEEDS ANYTHING--WHY WON'T HE TELL ME? I'M ONLY A COLLEGE STUDENT, BUT MAYBE I CAN HELP!
NEVER SAW OSBORN SO QUIET! NORMALLY HE'D HAVE TOSSED A DOZEN INSULTS MY WAY BY NOW!
S'MATTER, HARRY? ANYTHI'G WRONG? AREN'T YOU FEELING WELL?
I'M OKAY, PARKER!
AND SINCE WHEN IS IT ANY OF YOUR BUSINESS WHETHER OR NOT I--
AW, FORGET IT! I DIDN'T MEAN TO SNAP AT YOU!
WOW! SOMETHING MUST BE REALLY BUGGING HIM! HE'S ALMOST ACTING HUMAN!
5

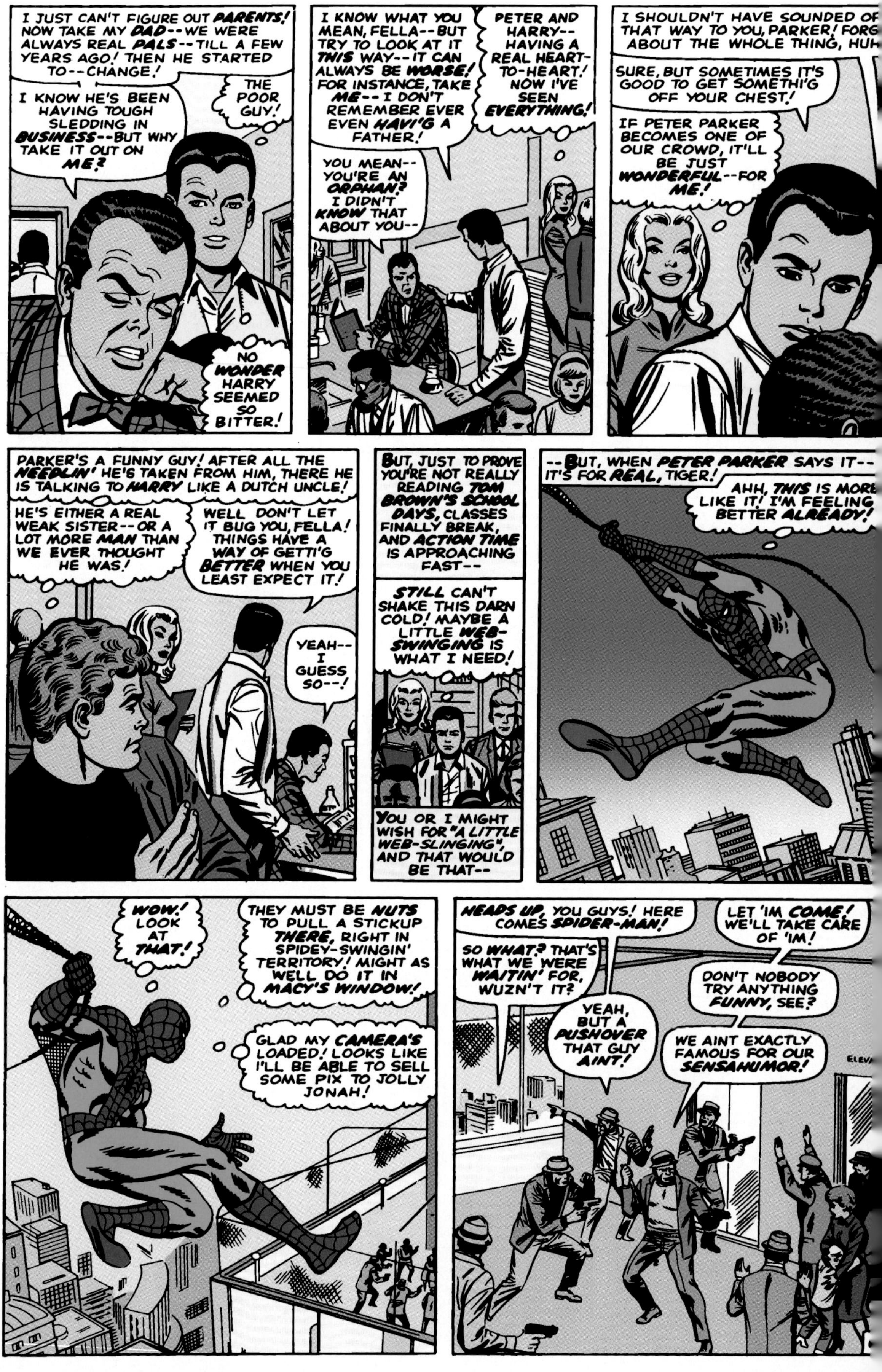

I JUST CAN'T FIGURE OUT PARENTS! NOW TAKE MY DAD--WE WERE ALWAYS REAL PALS--TILL A FEW YEARS AGO! THEN HE STARTED TO--CHANGE!
I KNOW HE'S BEEN HAVING TOUGH SLEDDING IN BUSINESS--BUT WHY TAKE IT OUT ON ME?
THE POOR GUY!
NO WONDER HARRY SEEMED SO BITTER!
I KNOW WHAT YOU MEAN, FELLA--BUT TRY TO LOOK AT IT THIS WAY--IT CAN ALWAYS BE WORSE! FOR INSTANCE, TAKE ME--I DON'T REMEMBER EVER EVEN HAVI'G A FATHER!
PETER AND HARRY--HAVING A REAL HEART-TO-HEART! NOW I'VE SEEN EVERYTHING!
YOU MEAN--YOU'RE AN ORPHAN? I DIDN'T KNOW THAT ABOUT YOU--
I SHOULDN'T HAVE SOUNDED OF
THAT WAY TO YOU, PARKER! FORG
ABOUT THE WHOLE THING, HUH
SURE, BUT SOMETIMES IT'S GOOD TO GET SOMETHI'G OFF YOUR CHEST!
IF PETER PARKER BECOMES ONE OF OUR CROWD, IT'LL BE JUST WONDERFUL--FOR ME!
PARKER'S A FUNNY GUY! AFTER ALL THE NEEDLIN' HE'S TAKEN FROM HIM, THERE HE IS TALKING TO HARRY LIKE A DUTCH UNCLE!
HE'S EITHER A REAL WEAK SISTER--OR A LOT MORE MAN THAN WE EVER THOUGHT HE WAS!
WELL DON'T LET IT BUG YOU, FELLA! THINGS HAVE A WAY OF GETTI'G BETTER WHEN YOU LEAST EXPECT IT!
YEAH--I GUESS SO--!
BUT, JUST TO PROVE YOU'RE NOT REALLY READING TOM BROWN'S SCHOOL DAYS, CLASSES FINALLY BREAK, AND ACTION TIME IS APPROACHING FAST--
STILL CAN'T SHAKE THIS DARN COLD! MAYBE A LITTLE WEB-SWINGING IS WHAT I NEED!
YOU OR I MIGHT WISH FOR "A LITTLE WEB-SLINGING", AND THAT WOULD BE THAT--
--BUT, WHEN PETER PARKER SAYS IT--IT'S FOR REAL, TIGER!
AHH, THIS IS MORE LIKE IT! I'M FEELING BETTER ALREADY!
WOW! LOOK AT THAT!
THEY MUST BE NUTS TO PULL A STICKUP THERE, RIGHT IN SPIDEY-SWINGIN' TERRITORY! MIGHT AS WELL DO IT IN MACY'S WINDOW!
GLAD MY CAMERA'S LOADED! LOOKS LIKE I'LL BE ABLE TO SELL SOME PIX TO JOLLY JONAH!
HEADS UP, YOU GUYS! HERE COMES SPIDER-MAN!
SO WHAT? THAT'S WHAT WE WERE WAITIN' FOR, WUZN'T IT?
YEAH, BUT A PUSHOVER THAT GUY AINT!
LET 'IM COME! WE'LL TAKE CARE OF 'IM!
DON'T NOBODY TRY ANYTHING FUNNY, SEE?
WE AINT EXACTLY FAMOUS FOR OUR SENSAHUMOR!

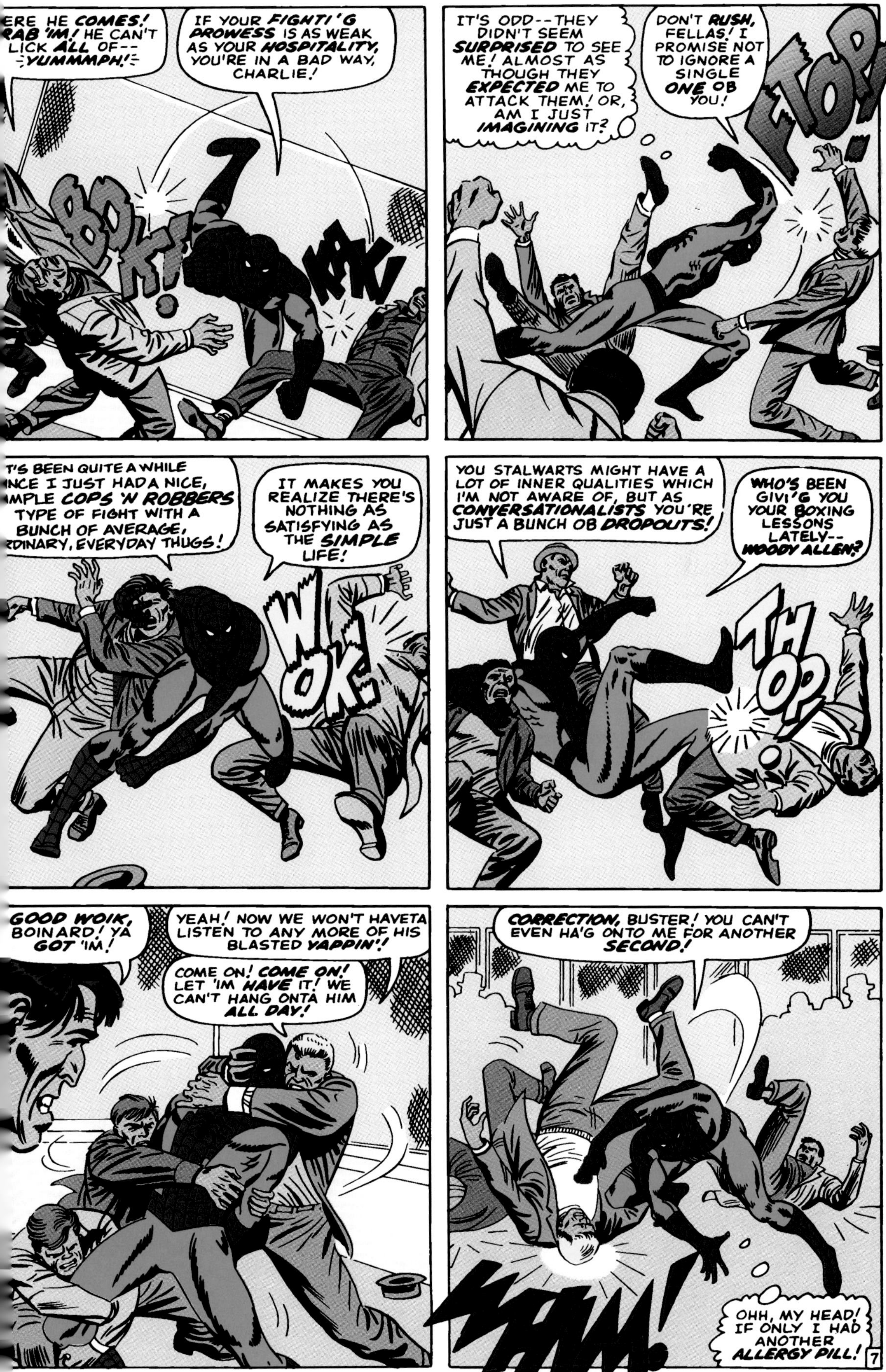

ERE HE COMES! RAB 'IM! HE CAN'T LICK ALL OF-- YUMMMPH!
IF YOUR FIGHTI'G PROWESS IS AS WEAK AS YOUR HOSPITALITY, YOU'RE IN A BAD WAY, CHARLIE!
BOK!
KRAK!
IT'S ODD--THEY DIDN'T SEEM SURPRISED TO SEE ME! ALMOST AS THOUGH THEY EXPECTED ME TO ATTACK THEM! OR, AM I JUST IMAGINING IT?
DON'T RUSH, FELLAS! I PROMISE NOT TO IGNORE A SINGLE ONE OB YOU!
FTOP!
T'S BEEN QUITE A WHILE NCE I JUST HAD A NICE, MPLE COPS 'N ROBBERS TYPE OF FIGHT WITH A BUNCH OF AVERAGE, DINARY, EVERYDAY THUGS!
IT MAKES YOU REALIZE THERE'S NOTHING AS SATISFYING AS THE SIMPLE LIFE!
WHOK!
YOU STALWARTS MIGHT HAVE A LOT OF INNER QUALITIES WHICH I'M NOT AWARE OF, BUT AS CONVERSATIONALISTS YOU'RE JUST A BUNCH OB DROPOUTS!
WHO'S BEEN GIVI'G YOU YOUR BOXING LESSONS LATELY-- WOODY ALLEN?
THOP!
GOOD WOIK, BOINARD! YA GOT 'IM!
YEAH! NOW WE WON'T HAVETA LISTEN TO ANY MORE OF HIS BLASTED YAPPIN'!
COME ON! COME ON! LET 'IM HAVE IT! WE CAN'T HANG ONTA HIM ALL DAY!
CORRECTION, BUSTER! YOU CAN'T EVEN HA'G ONTO ME FOR ANOTHER SECOND!
WHAM!
OHH, MY HEAD! IF ONLY I HAD ANOTHER ALLERGY PILL!

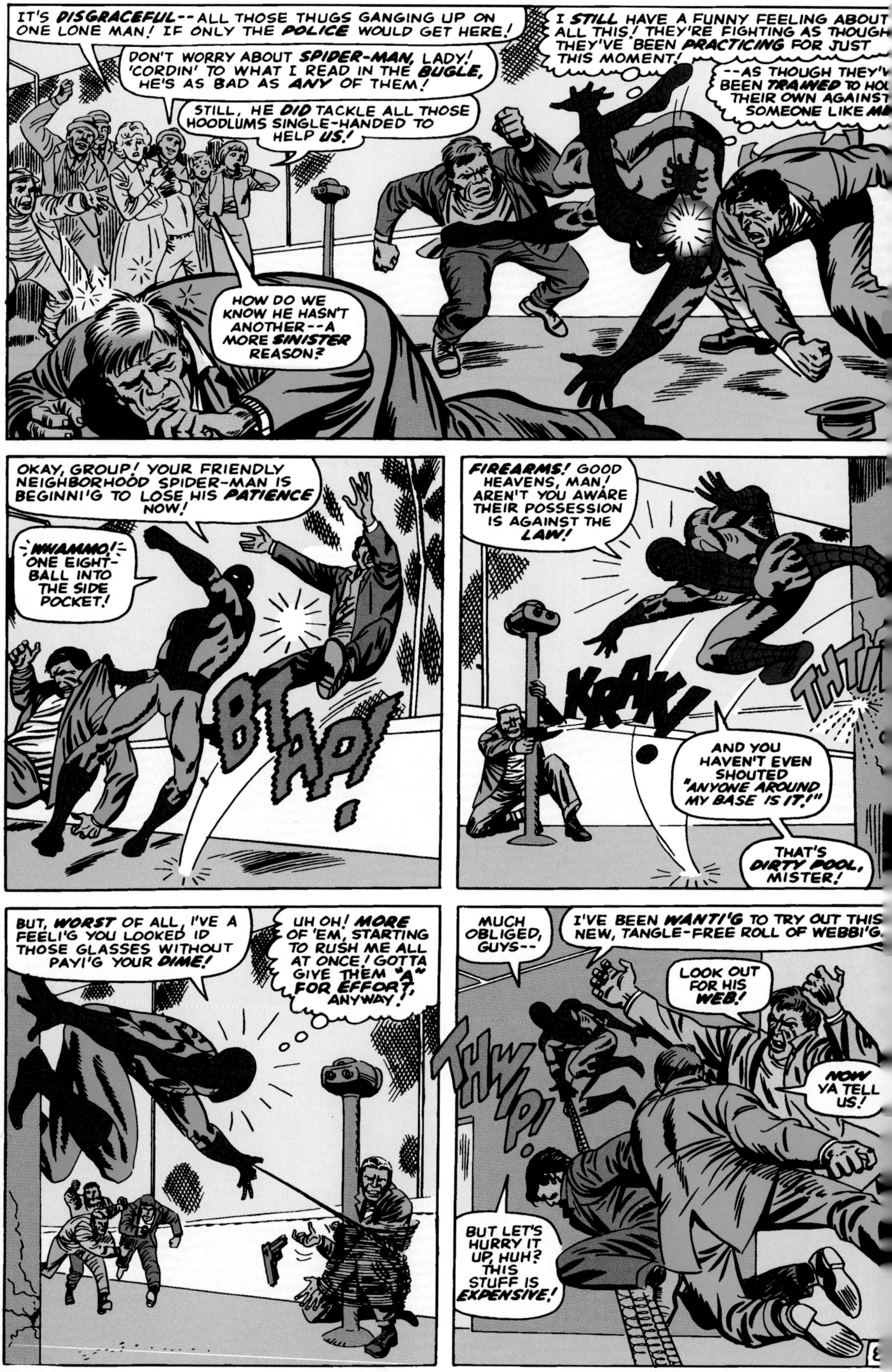
IT'S DISGRACEFUL--ALL THOSE THUGS GANGING UP ON ONE LONE MAN! IF ONLY THE POLICE WOULD GET HERE!
DON'T WORRY ABOUT SPIDER-MAN, LADY! 'CORDIN' TO WHAT I READ IN THE BUGLE, HE'S AS BAD AS ANY OF THEM!
STILL, HE DID TACKLE ALL THOSE HOODLUMS SINGLE-HANDED TO HELP US!
HOW DO WE KNOW HE HASN'T ANOTHER--A MORE SINISTER REASON?
I STILL HAVE A FUNNY FEELING ABOUT ALL THIS! THEY'RE FIGHTING AS THOUGH THEY'VE BEEN PRACTICING FOR JUST THIS MOMENT!
--AS THOUGH THEY'V BEEN TRAINED TO HO THEIR OWN AGAINST SOMEONE LIKE M
OKAY, GROUP! YOUR FRIENDLY NEIGHBORHOOD SPIDER-MAN IS BEGINNI'G TO LOSE HIS PATIENCE NOW!
WHAMMO! ONE EIGHT-BALL INTO THE SIDE POCKET!
BTAPP!
FIREARMS! GOOD HEAVENS, MAN! AREN'T YOU AWARE THEIR POSSESSION IS AGAINST THE LAW!
KRAK!
THTI
AND YOU HAVEN'T EVEN SHOUTED "ANYONE AROUND MY BASE IS IT!"
THAT'S DIRTY POOL, MISTER!
BUT, WORST OF ALL, I'VE A FEELI'G YOU LOOKED ID THOSE GLASSES WITHOUT PAYI'G YOUR DIME!
UH OH! MORE OF 'EM, STARTING TO RUSH ME ALL AT ONCE! GOTTA GIVE THEM "A" FOR EFFORT, ANYWAY!
MUCH OBLIGED, GUYS--
I'VE BEEN WANTI'G TO TRY OUT THIS NEW, TANGLE-FREE ROLL OF WEBBI'G.
THWIP!
LOOK OUT FOR HIS WEB!
NOW YA TELL US!
BUT LET'S HURRY IT UP, HUH? THIS STUFF IS EXPENSIVE!
8

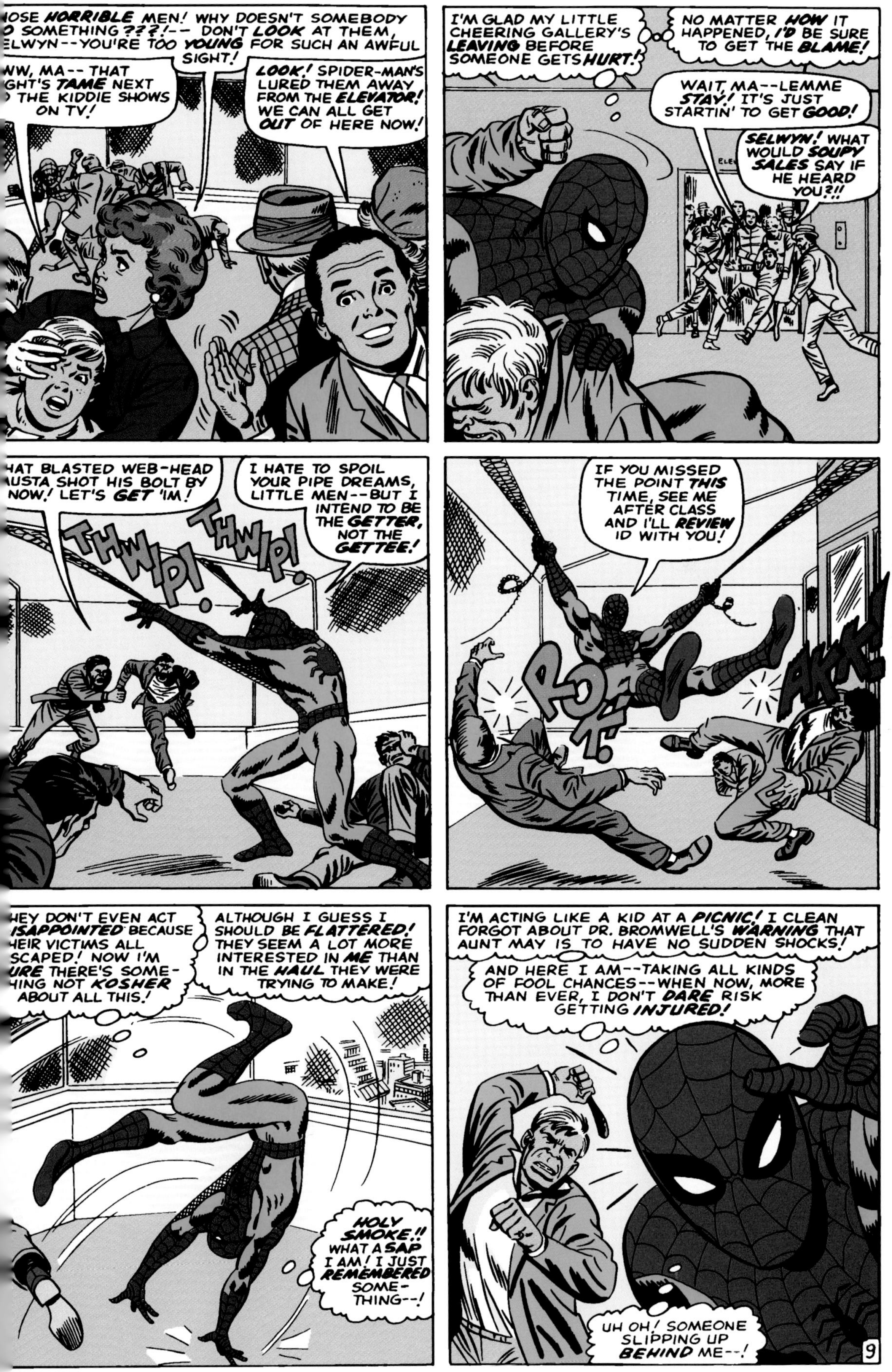

IOSE HORRIBLE MEN! WHY DOESN'T SOMEBODY O SOMETHING???!-- DON'T LOOK AT THEM, ELWYN--YOU'RE TOO YOUNG FOR SUCH AN AWFUL SIGHT!
WW, MA-- THAT GHT'S TAME NEXT THE KIDDIE SHOWS ON TV!
LOOK! SPIDER-MAN'S LURED THEM AWAY FROM THE ELEVATOR! WE CAN ALL GET OUT OF HERE NOW!
I'M GLAD MY LITTLE CHEERING GALLERY'S LEAVING BEFORE SOMEONE GETS HURT!
NO MATTER HOW IT HAPPENED, I'D BE SURE TO GET THE BLAME!
WAIT, MA--LEMME STAY! IT'S JUST STARTIN' TO GET GOOD!
SELWYN! WHAT WOULD SOUPY SALES SAY IF HE HEARD YOU?!!
HAT BLASTED WEB-HEAD AUSTA SHOT HIS BOLT BY NOW! LET'S GET 'IM!
I HATE TO SPOIL YOUR PIPE DREAMS, LITTLE MEN--BUT I INTEND TO BE THE GETTER, NOT THE GETTEE!
THWIP! THWIP!
IF YOU MISSED THE POINT THIS TIME, SEE ME AFTER CLASS AND I'LL REVIEW ID WITH YOU!
ROK!
AKK!
HEY DON'T EVEN ACT ISAPPOINTED BECAUSE HEIR VICTIMS ALL SCAPED! NOW I'M URE THERE'S SOME-HING NOT KOSHER ABOUT ALL THIS!
ALTHOUGH I GUESS I SHOULD BE FLATTERED! THEY SEEM A LOT MORE INTERESTED IN ME THAN IN THE HAUL THEY WERE TRYING TO MAKE!
HOLY SMOKE!! WHAT A SAP I AM! I JUST REMEMBERED SOME-THING--!
I'M ACTING LIKE A KID AT A PICNIC! I CLEAN FORGOT ABOUT DR. BROMWELL'S WARNING THAT AUNT MAY IS TO HAVE NO SUDDEN SHOCKS!
AND HERE I AM--TAKING ALL KINDS OF FOOL CHANCES--WHEN NOW, MORE THAN EVER, I DON'T DARE RISK GETTING INJURED!
UH OH! SOMEONE SLIPPING UP BEHIND ME--!
9

MMMYUMMMPH!

BEEYOK!

UHHH--!

EVEN THOUGH THIS IS A *BALL*, I'VE GOT TO *END* IT QUICKLY, CAN'T TAKE A CHANCE OF ACCIDENTALLY GETTING HURT -- FOR *AUNT MAY'S* SAKE!

WE'LL GET YOU *YET*, MASKED MAN!

SPIDER SENSE -- I *LOVE* YOU!

IT'S *NO USE!* WE *CAN'T* OUT-FIGHT 'IM! WE'VE GOTTA USE THE *GIMMICK!* HURR -- GET THE -- *UNNHHH!*

GIMMICK? WHAT WAS HE *TALKING* ABOUT? WHAT ARE THEY *UP* TO?

THIS IS *IT*, WISE GUY! THAT BLASTED *SPIDER STRENGTH* OF YOURS AINT GONNA HELP YA *NOW!*

CLAM UP, BLACKIE! I'LL GIVE 'IM THE *GIMMICK!*

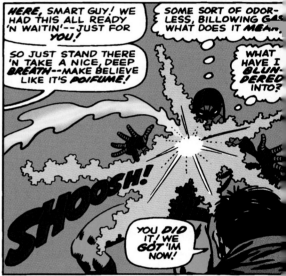

HERE, SMART GUY! WE HAD THIS ALL READY 'N WAITIN' -- JUST FOR *YOU!*

SO JUST STAND THERE 'N TAKE A NICE, DEEP *BREATH* -- MAKE BELIEVE LIKE IT'S *POIFUME!*

SOME SORT OF ODOR-LESS, BILLOWING *GAS* WHAT DOES IT *MEAN*--

WHAT HAVE I *BLUN-DERED* INTO?

SHOOSH!

YOU *DID* IT! WE *GOT* 'IM NOW!

AND, HIGH ABOVE THE SCENE OF BATTLE, A SINISTERLY SMIRKING SPECTATOR SLYLY SPIES UPON THE STARTLED SPIDER-MAN--!

EVERYTHING WENT *PERFECTLY* -- ACCORDING TO PLAN!

MY TRUMPED-UP ROBBERY ATTRACTED HIM -- AS I *KNEW* IT WOULD--!

AND THE *GAS* HE HAS JUST INHALED WILL WEAKEN ALL HIS *SENSES* -- INCLUDING HIS MOST POTENT WEAPON -- HIS *SPIDER SENSE!*

THEN WITH HIS SPIDER SENSE *NOT FUNCTIONING* I'LL BE ABLE TO *HUMBLE* HIM AT WILL!

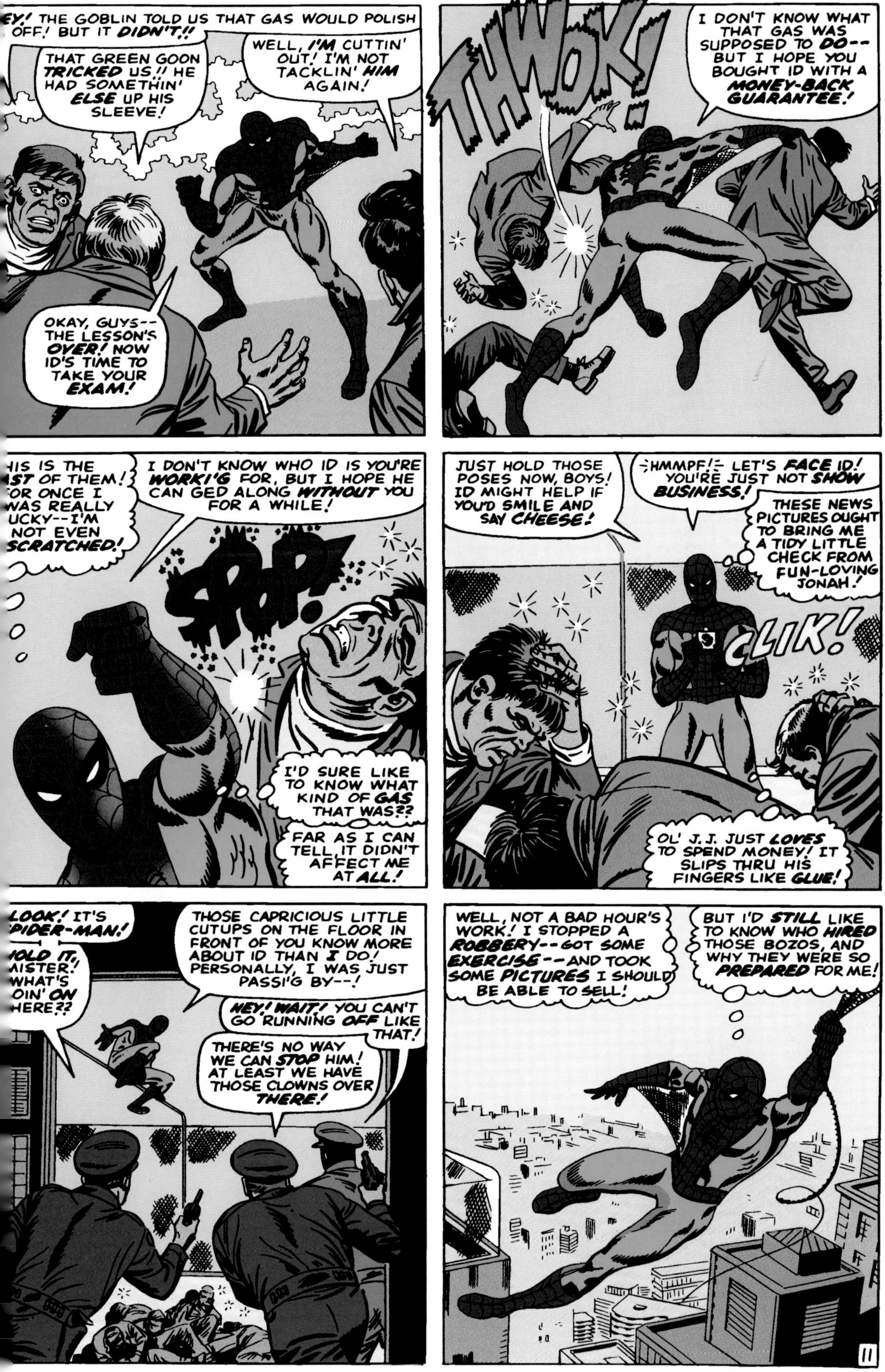
EY! THE GOBLIN TOLD US THAT GAS WOULD POLISH OFF! BUT IT DIDN'T!!
THAT GREEN GOON TRICKED US!! HE HAD SOMETHIN' ELSE UP HIS SLEEVE!
WELL, I'M CUTTIN' OUT! I'M NOT TACKLIN' HIM AGAIN!
OKAY, GUYS-- THE LESSON'S OVER! NOW ID'S TIME TO TAKE YOUR EXAM!
THWOK!
I DON'T KNOW WHAT THAT GAS WAS SUPPOSED TO DO-- BUT I HOPE YOU BOUGHT ID WITH A MONEY-BACK GUARANTEE!
HIS IS THE ST OF THEM! OR ONCE I WAS REALLY UCKY--I'M NOT EVEN SCRATCHED!
I DON'T KNOW WHO ID IS YOU'RE WORKI'G FOR, BUT I HOPE HE CAN GED ALONG WITHOUT YOU FOR A WHILE!
SPOP!
I'D SURE LIKE TO KNOW WHAT KIND OF GAS THAT WAS??
FAR AS I CAN TELL, IT DIDN'T AFFECT ME AT ALL!
JUST HOLD THOSE POSES NOW, BOYS! ID MIGHT HELP IF YOU'D SMILE AND SAY CHEESE!
HMMPF! LET'S FACE ID! YOU'RE JUST NOT SHOW BUSINESS!
THESE NEWS PICTURES OUGHT TO BRING ME A TIDY LITTLE CHECK FROM FUN-LOVING JONAH!
CLIK!
OL' J.J. JUST LOVES TO SPEND MONEY! IT SLIPS THRU HIS FINGERS LIKE GLUE!
LOOK! IT'S PIDER-MAN!
HOLD IT, MISTER! WHAT'S OIN' ON HERE??
THOSE CAPRICIOUS LITTLE CUTUPS ON THE FLOOR IN FRONT OF YOU KNOW MORE ABOUT ID THAN I DO! PERSONALLY, I WAS JUST PASSI'G BY--!
HEY! WAIT! YOU CAN'T GO RUNNING OFF LIKE THAT!
THERE'S NO WAY WE CAN STOP HIM! AT LEAST WE HAVE THOSE CLOWNS OVER THERE!
WELL, NOT A BAD HOUR'S WORK! I STOPPED A ROBBERY--GOT SOME EXERCISE--AND TOOK SOME PICTURES I SHOULD BE ABLE TO SELL!
BUT I'D STILL LIKE TO KNOW WHO HIRED THOSE BOZOS, AND WHY THEY WERE SO PREPARED FOR ME!

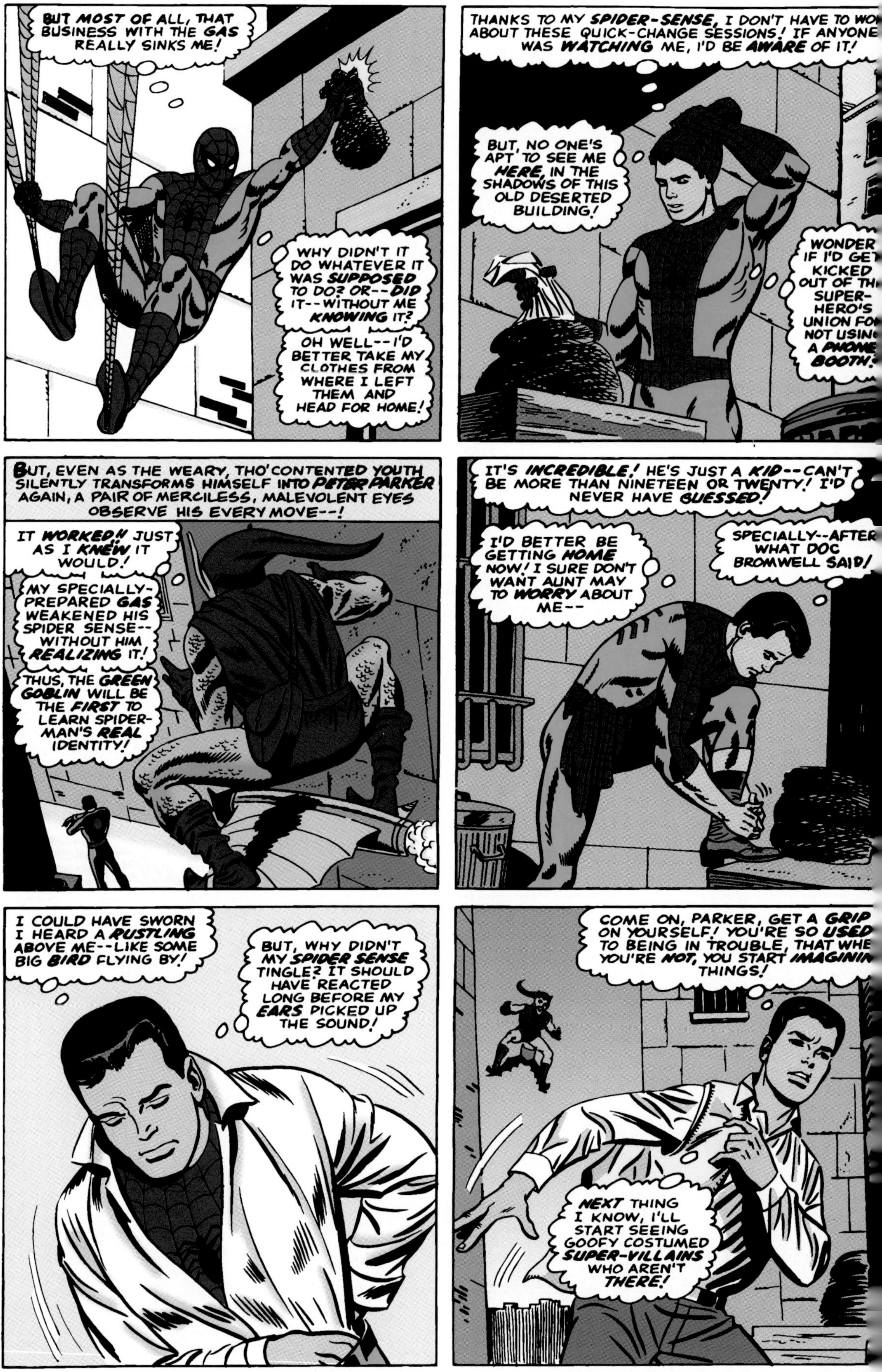
BUT MOST OF ALL, THAT BUSINESS WITH THE GAS REALLY SINKS ME!
WHY DIDN'T IT DO WHATEVER IT WAS SUPPOSED TO DO? OR--DID IT--WITHOUT ME KNOWING IT?
OH WELL--I'D BETTER TAKE MY CLOTHES FROM WHERE I LEFT THEM AND HEAD FOR HOME!
THANKS TO MY SPIDER-SENSE, I DON'T HAVE TO WO ABOUT THESE QUICK-CHANGE SESSIONS! IF ANYONE WAS WATCHING ME, I'D BE AWARE OF IT!
BUT, NO ONE'S APT TO SEE ME HERE, IN THE SHADOWS OF THIS OLD DESERTED BUILDING!
WONDER IF I'D GET KICKED OUT OF TH SUPER-HERO'S UNION FO NOT USIN A PHONE BOOTH!
BUT, EVEN AS THE WEARY, THO' CONTENTED YOUTH SILENTLY TRANSFORMS HIMSELF INTO PETER PARKER AGAIN, A PAIR OF MERCILESS, MALEVOLENT EYES OBSERVE HIS EVERY MOVE--!
IT WORKED!! JUST AS I KNEW IT WOULD!
MY SPECIALLY-PREPARED GAS WEAKENED HIS SPIDER SENSE--WITHOUT HIM REALIZING IT!
THUS, THE GREEN GOBLIN WILL BE THE FIRST TO LEARN SPIDER-MAN'S REAL IDENTITY!
IT'S INCREDIBLE! HE'S JUST A KID--CAN'T BE MORE THAN NINETEEN OR TWENTY! I'D NEVER HAVE GUESSED!
SPECIALLY--AFTER WHAT DOC BROMWELL SAID!
I'D BETTER BE GETTING HOME NOW! I SURE DON'T WANT AUNT MAY TO WORRY ABOUT ME--
I COULD HAVE SWORN I HEARD A RUSTLING ABOVE ME--LIKE SOME BIG BIRD FLYING BY!
BUT, WHY DIDN'T MY SPIDER SENSE TINGLE? IT SHOULD HAVE REACTED LONG BEFORE MY EARS PICKED UP THE SOUND!
COME ON, PARKER, GET A GRIP ON YOURSELF! YOU'RE SO USED TO BEING IN TROUBLE, THAT WHE YOU'RE NOT, YOU START IMAGININ THINGS!
NEXT THING I KNOW, I'LL START SEEING GOOFY COSTUMED SUPER-VILLAINS WHO AREN'T THERE!

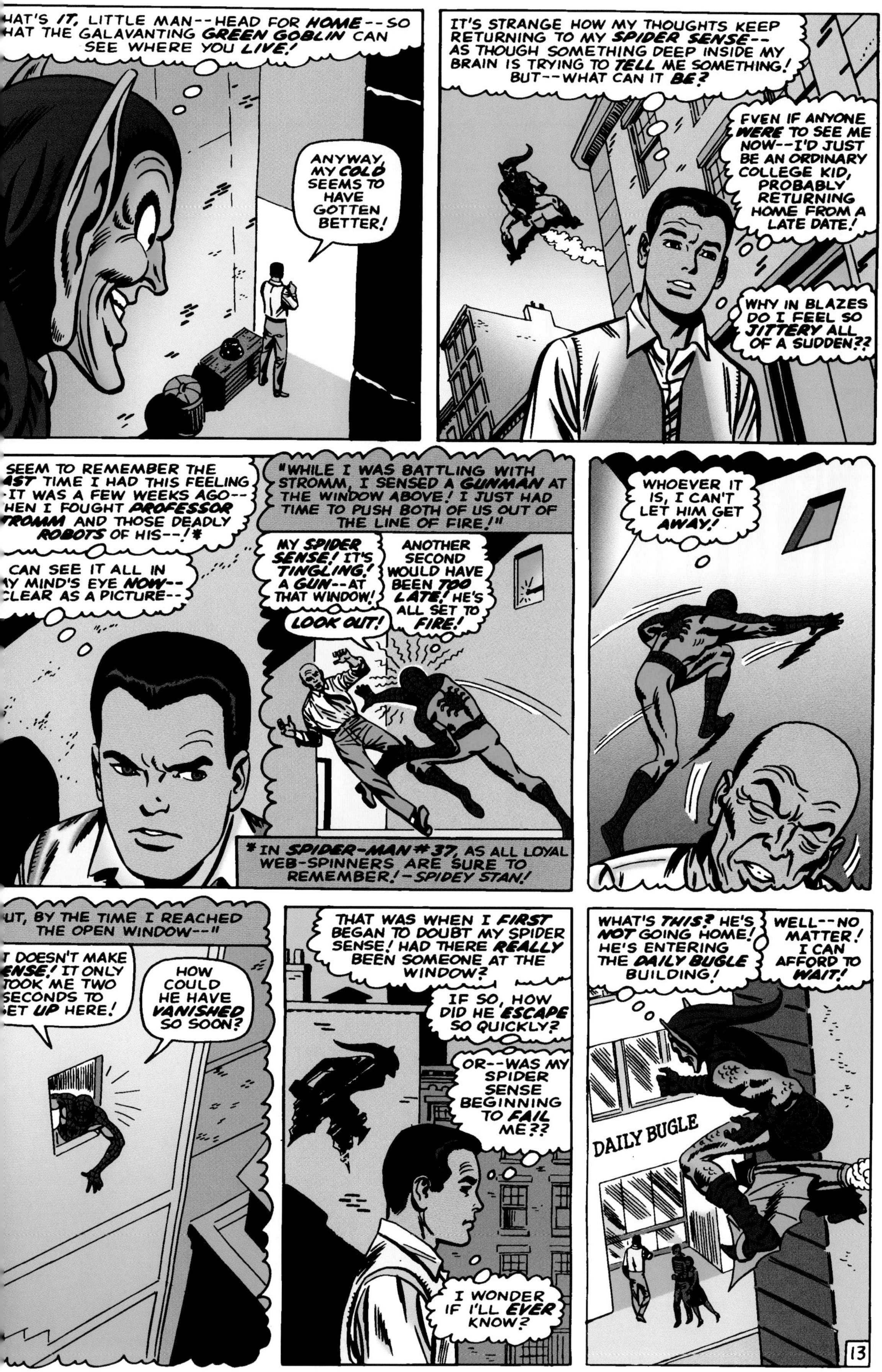

HAT'S IT, LITTLE MAN--HEAD FOR HOME--SO HAT THE GALAVANTING GREEN GOBLIN CAN SEE WHERE YOU LIVE!
ANYWAY, MY COLD SEEMS TO HAVE GOTTEN BETTER!
IT'S STRANGE HOW MY THOUGHTS KEEP RETURNING TO MY SPIDER SENSE--AS THOUGH SOMETHING DEEP INSIDE MY BRAIN IS TRYING TO TELL ME SOMETHING! BUT--WHAT CAN IT BE?
EVEN IF ANYONE WERE TO SEE ME NOW--I'D JUST BE AN ORDINARY COLLEGE KID, PROBABLY RETURNING HOME FROM A LATE DATE!
WHY IN BLAZES DO I FEEL SO JITTERY ALL OF A SUDDEN??
SEEM TO REMEMBER THE AST TIME I HAD THIS FEELING -IT WAS A FEW WEEKS AGO-- HEN I FOUGHT PROFESSOR TROMM AND THOSE DEADLY ROBOTS OF HIS--!*
CAN SEE IT ALL IN Y MIND'S EYE NOW-- CLEAR AS A PICTURE--
"WHILE I WAS BATTLING WITH STROMM, I SENSED A GUNMAN AT THE WINDOW ABOVE! I JUST HAD TIME TO PUSH BOTH OF US OUT OF THE LINE OF FIRE!"
MY SPIDER SENSE! IT'S TINGLING! A GUN--AT THAT WINDOW!
ANOTHER SECOND WOULD HAVE BEEN TOO LATE! HE'S ALL SET TO FIRE!
LOOK OUT!
*IN SPIDER-MAN #37, AS ALL LOYAL WEB-SPINNERS ARE SURE TO REMEMBER! -SPIDEY STAN!
WHOEVER IT IS, I CAN'T LET HIM GET AWAY!
UT, BY THE TIME I REACHED THE OPEN WINDOW--"
T DOESN'T MAKE ENSE! IT ONLY TOOK ME TWO SECONDS TO ET UP HERE!
HOW COULD HE HAVE VANISHED SO SOON?
THAT WAS WHEN I FIRST BEGAN TO DOUBT MY SPIDER SENSE! HAD THERE REALLY BEEN SOMEONE AT THE WINDOW?
IF SO, HOW DID HE ESCAPE SO QUICKLY?
OR--WAS MY SPIDER SENSE BEGINNING TO FAIL ME??
I WONDER IF I'LL EVER KNOW?
WHAT'S THIS? HE'S NOT GOING HOME! HE'S ENTERING THE DAILY BUGLE BUILDING!
WELL--NO MATTER! I CAN AFFORD TO WAIT!
DAILY BUGLE

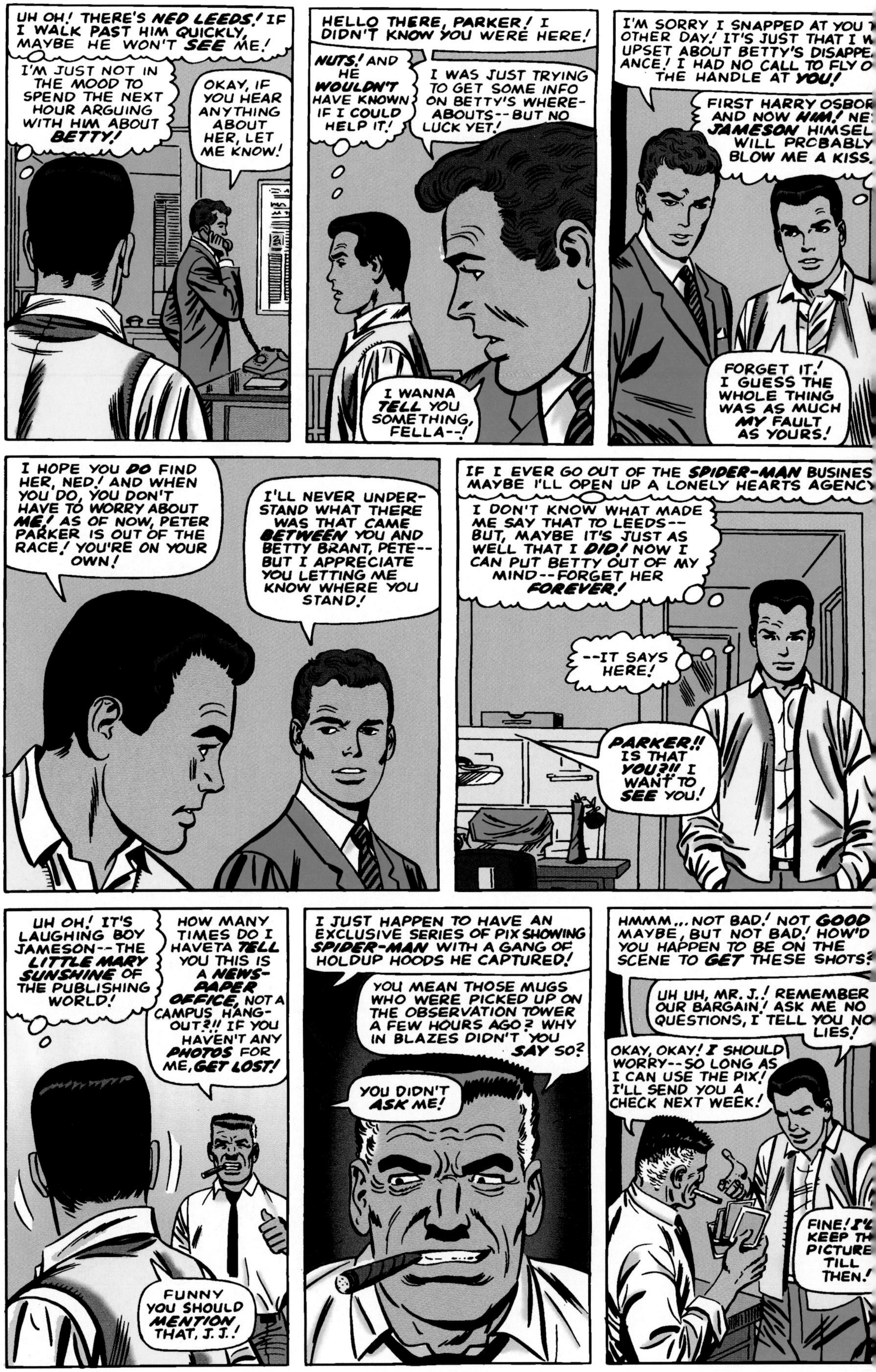
UH OH! THERE'S NED LEEDS! IF I WALK PAST HIM QUICKLY, MAYBE HE WON'T SEE ME!
I'M JUST NOT IN THE MOOD TO SPEND THE NEXT HOUR ARGUING WITH HIM ABOUT BETTY!
OKAY, IF YOU HEAR ANYTHING ABOUT HER, LET ME KNOW!
HELLO THERE, PARKER! I DIDN'T KNOW YOU WERE HERE!
NUTS! AND HE WOULDN'T HAVE KNOWN IF I COULD HELP IT!
I WAS JUST TRYING TO GET SOME INFO ON BETTY'S WHERE-ABOUTS--BUT NO LUCK YET!
I WANNA TELL YOU SOMETHING, FELLA--!
I'M SORRY I SNAPPED AT YOU T OTHER DAY! IT'S JUST THAT I W UPSET ABOUT BETTY'S DISAPPE ANCE! I HAD NO CALL TO FLY O THE HANDLE AT YOU!
FIRST HARRY OSBOR AND NOW HIM! NE JAMESON HIMSEL WILL PROBABLY BLOW ME A KISS.
FORGET IT! I GUESS THE WHOLE THING WAS AS MUCH MY FAULT AS YOURS!
I HOPE YOU DO FIND HER, NED! AND WHEN YOU DO, YOU DON'T HAVE TO WORRY ABOUT ME! AS OF NOW, PETER PARKER IS OUT OF THE RACE! YOU'RE ON YOUR OWN!
I'LL NEVER UNDER-STAND WHAT THERE WAS THAT CAME BETWEEN YOU AND BETTY BRANT, PETE--BUT I APPRECIATE YOU LETTING ME KNOW WHERE YOU STAND!
IF I EVER GO OUT OF THE SPIDER-MAN BUSINES MAYBE I'LL OPEN UP A LONELY HEARTS AGENCY
I DON'T KNOW WHAT MADE ME SAY THAT TO LEEDS--BUT, MAYBE IT'S JUST AS WELL THAT I DID! NOW I CAN PUT BETTY OUT OF MY MIND--FORGET HER FOREVER!
--IT SAYS HERE!
PARKER!! IS THAT YOU?!! I WANT TO SEE YOU!
UH OH! IT'S LAUGHING BOY JAMESON--THE LITTLE MARY SUNSHINE OF THE PUBLISHING WORLD!
HOW MANY TIMES DO I HAVETA TELL YOU THIS IS A NEWS-PAPER OFFICE, NOT A CAMPUS HANG-OUT?!! IF YOU HAVEN'T ANY PHOTOS FOR ME, GET LOST!
FUNNY YOU SHOULD MENTION THAT, J.J.!
I JUST HAPPEN TO HAVE AN EXCLUSIVE SERIES OF PIX SHOWING SPIDER-MAN WITH A GANG OF HOLDUP HOODS HE CAPTURED!
YOU MEAN THOSE MUGS WHO WERE PICKED UP ON THE OBSERVATION TOWER A FEW HOURS AGO? WHY IN BLAZES DIDN'T YOU SAY SO?
YOU DIDN'T ASK ME!
HMMM... NOT BAD! NOT GOOD MAYBE, BUT NOT BAD! HOW'D YOU HAPPEN TO BE ON THE SCENE TO GET THESE SHOTS?
UH UH, MR. J.! REMEMBER OUR BARGAIN! ASK ME NO QUESTIONS, I TELL YOU NO LIES!
OKAY, OKAY! I SHOULD WORRY--SO LONG AS I CAN USE THE PIX! I'LL SEND YOU A CHECK NEXT WEEK!
FINE! I'L KEEP TH PICTURE TILL THEN!

NO PUNK KID HOLDS UP *J. JONAH JAMESON!* YOU CAN *HAVE* YOUR CRUMMY PHOTOS!

THANKS! THE *GLOBE* PAYS MORE THAN *YOU* DO, ANYHOW!

THE *GLOBE!* THEY WOULDN'T *TOUCH* YOUR PIX WITH A TEN-FOOT POLE!

BUT, JUST BECAUSE I *LIKE* YOU TOO MUCH TO LET THEM TURN YOU DOWN, *I'LL* TAKE THOSE SHOTS OFF YOUR HANDS! AND HERE'S YOUR BLASTED *MONEY!!* NOW *GET OUT*--BEFORE I COME TO MY SENSES!

JUST LIKE EVERYONE SAYS, J.J., YOU'RE *ALL HEART!*

SURE! SURE! I'M ALL TANKED UP WITH THE MILK OF HUMAN KINDNESS!

BUT, AS FOR *YOU....!*

YOU CALL YOURSELF A *PHOTOGRAPHER?* HORSE THIEF IS MORE LIKE IT! YOU *ROBBED* ME!! *EVERYBODY* ROBS ME--BECAUSE I'M SO *EASY GOING!*

HE ONLY PAID *HALF* WHAT THE PICTURES ARE WORTH--BUT I SHOULD WORRY!

THIS MONEY'S GONNA LOOK MIGHTY GOOD TO *AUNT MAY*--AND THAT'S ALL I CARE ABOUT!

THANKS TO MY LITTLE *SHOTGUN MIKE,* I HEARD HIM CALL HIMSELF *PETER PARKER!* SO NOW I KNOW HIS *NAME!*

ALAS, POOR SPIDER-MAN! HIS PRECIOUS *IDENTITY* IS A SECRET *NO LONGER!*

IF ONLY I COULD THIS FEELING OF--*DANGER!*

AWW, ALL I PROBABLY NEED IS A GOOD NIGHT'S *SLEEP!* I'M PROBABLY JUST OVERTIRED FROM ALL MY STUDYING AND WEB-SWINGING!

BUT I CAN'T WAIT TO SEE AUNT MAY'S FACE WHEN I GIVE HER THIS CHECK!--I JUST WISH IT COULD BE STILL *MORE!*

FUNNY--I *STILL* FEEL SOMEONE *ELSE* IS NEARBY!

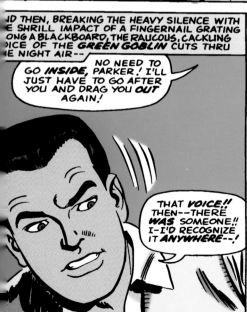

AND THEN, BREAKING THE HEAVY SILENCE WITH THE SHRILL IMPACT OF A FINGERNAIL GRATING ALONG A BLACKBOARD, THE RAUCOUS, CACKLING VOICE OF THE *GREEN GOBLIN* CUTS THRU THE NIGHT AIR--

NO NEED TO GO *INSIDE,* PARKER! I'LL JUST HAVE TO GO AFTER YOU AND DRAG YOU *OUT* AGAIN!

THAT *VOICE!!* THEN--THERE *WAS* SOMEONE!! I-I'D RECOGNIZE IT *ANYWHERE*--!

THE *GREEN GOBLIN!!* YOU--YOU'VE *FOUND* ME!

CORRECT, PARKER! YOUR WEB-SLINGING MASQUERADE IS FINALLY *FINISHED*--

--AND SO ARE *YOU*--*SPIDER MAN!*

15

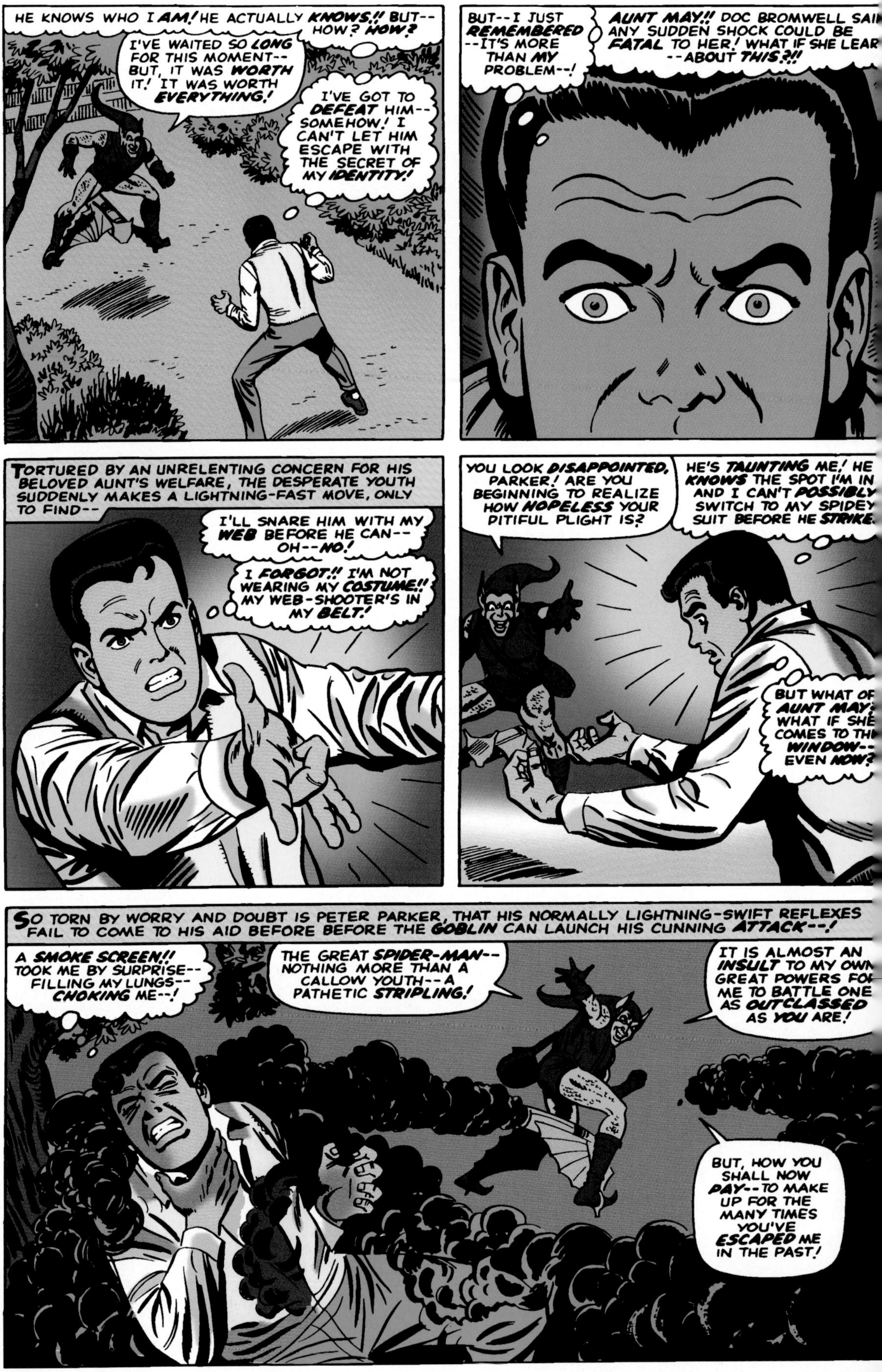
HE KNOWS WHO I AM! HE ACTUALLY KNOWS!! BUT-- HOW? HOW?
I'VE WAITED SO LONG FOR THIS MOMENT-- BUT, IT WAS WORTH IT! IT WAS WORTH EVERYTHING!
I'VE GOT TO DEFEAT HIM-- SOMEHOW! I CAN'T LET HIM ESCAPE WITH THE SECRET OF MY IDENTITY!
BUT--I JUST REMEMBERED --IT'S MORE THAN MY PROBLEM--!
AUNT MAY!! DOC BROMWELL SAI ANY SUDDEN SHOCK COULD BE FATAL TO HER! WHAT IF SHE LEAR --ABOUT THIS?!!
TORTURED BY AN UNRELENTING CONCERN FOR HIS BELOVED AUNT'S WELFARE, THE DESPERATE YOUTH SUDDENLY MAKES A LIGHTNING-FAST MOVE, ONLY TO FIND--
I'LL SNARE HIM WITH MY WEB BEFORE HE CAN-- OH--NO!
I FORGOT!! I'M NOT WEARING MY COSTUME!! MY WEB-SHOOTER'S IN MY BELT!
YOU LOOK DISAPPOINTED, PARKER! ARE YOU BEGINNING TO REALIZE HOW HOPELESS YOUR PITIFUL PLIGHT IS?
HE'S TAUNTING ME! HE KNOWS THE SPOT I'M IN AND I CAN'T POSSIBLY SWITCH TO MY SPIDEY SUIT BEFORE HE STRIKE
BUT WHAT OF AUNT MAY? WHAT IF SHE COMES TO TH WINDOW-- EVEN NOW?
SO TORN BY WORRY AND DOUBT IS PETER PARKER, THAT HIS NORMALLY LIGHTNING-SWIFT REFLEXES FAIL TO COME TO HIS AID BEFORE BEFORE THE GOBLIN CAN LAUNCH HIS CUNNING ATTACK--!
A SMOKE SCREEN!! TOOK ME BY SURPRISE-- FILLING MY LUNGS-- CHOKING ME--!
THE GREAT SPIDER-MAN-- NOTHING MORE THAN A CALLOW YOUTH--A PATHETIC STRIPLING!
IT IS ALMOST AN INSULT TO MY OWN GREAT POWERS FOR ME TO BATTLE ONE AS OUTCLASSED AS YOU ARE!
BUT, HOW YOU SHALL NOW PAY--TO MAKE UP FOR THE MANY TIMES YOU'VE ESCAPED ME IN THE PAST!

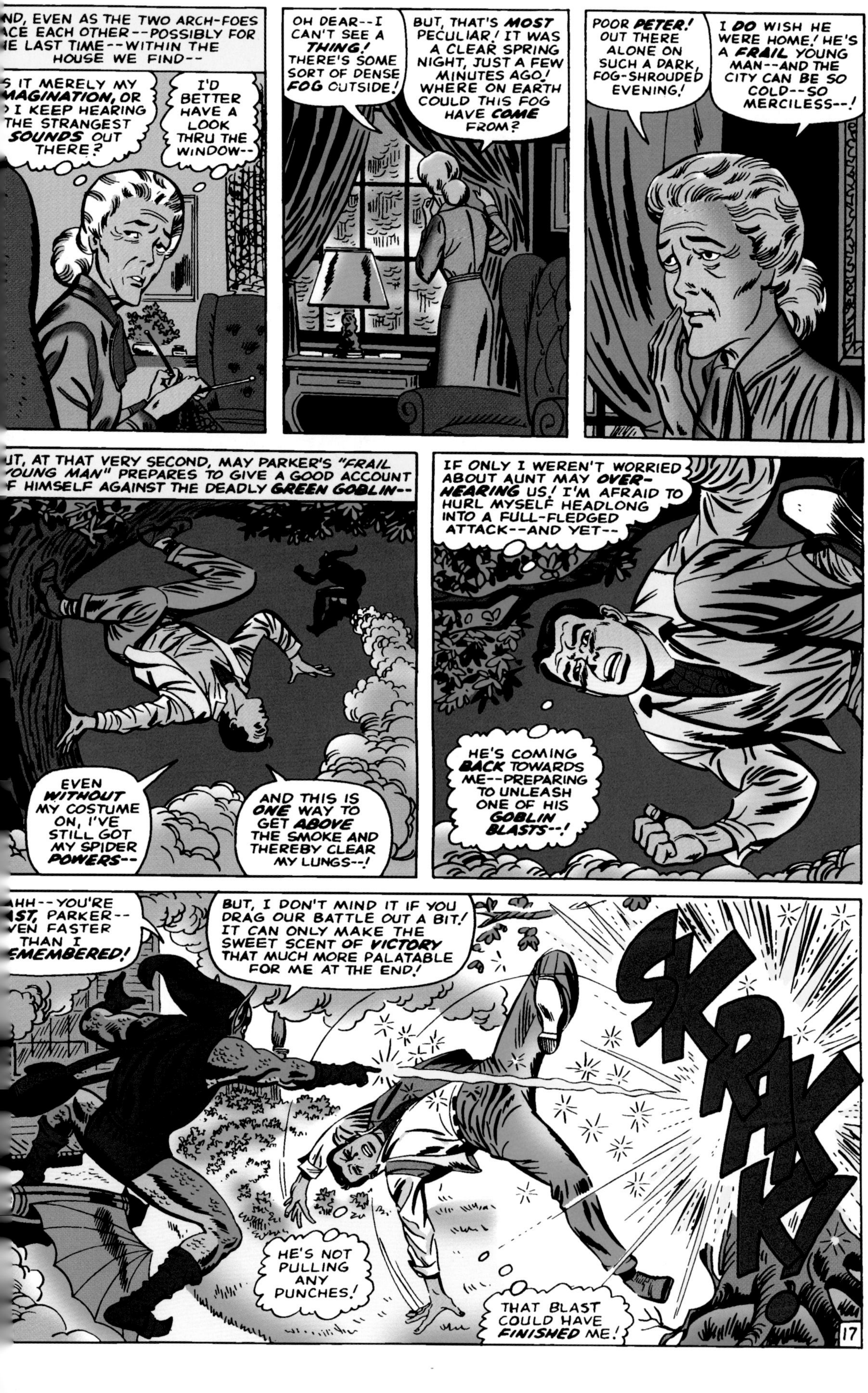
ND, EVEN AS THE TWO ARCH-FOES ACE EACH OTHER--POSSIBLY FOR HE LAST TIME--WITHIN THE HOUSE WE FIND--
S IT MERELY MY MAGINATION, OR I KEEP HEARING THE STRANGEST SOUNDS OUT THERE?
I'D BETTER HAVE A LOOK THRU THE WINDOW--
OH DEAR--I CAN'T SEE A THING! THERE'S SOME SORT OF DENSE FOG OUTSIDE!
BUT, THAT'S MOST PECULIAR! IT WAS A CLEAR SPRING NIGHT, JUST A FEW MINUTES AGO! WHERE ON EARTH COULD THIS FOG HAVE COME FROM?
POOR PETER! OUT THERE ALONE ON SUCH A DARK, FOG-SHROUDED EVENING!
I DO WISH HE WERE HOME! HE'S A FRAIL YOUNG MAN--AND THE CITY CAN BE SO COLD--SO MERCILESS--!
UT, AT THAT VERY SECOND, MAY PARKER'S "FRAIL YOUNG MAN" PREPARES TO GIVE A GOOD ACCOUNT F HIMSELF AGAINST THE DEADLY GREEN GOBLIN--
EVEN WITHOUT MY COSTUME ON, I'VE STILL GOT MY SPIDER POWERS--
AND THIS IS ONE WAY TO GET ABOVE THE SMOKE AND THEREBY CLEAR MY LUNGS--!
IF ONLY I WEREN'T WORRIED ABOUT AUNT MAY OVER-HEARING US! I'M AFRAID TO HURL MYSELF HEADLONG INTO A FULL-FLEDGED ATTACK--AND YET--
HE'S COMING BACK TOWARDS ME--PREPARING TO UNLEASH ONE OF HIS GOBLIN BLASTS--!
AHH--YOU'RE AST, PARKER--VEN FASTER THAN I EMEMBERED!
BUT, I DON'T MIND IT IF YOU DRAG OUR BATTLE OUT A BIT! IT CAN ONLY MAKE THE SWEET SCENT OF VICTORY THAT MUCH MORE PALATABLE FOR ME AT THE END!
SKRAKK!
HE'S NOT PULLING ANY PUNCHES!
THAT BLAST COULD HAVE FINISHED ME!

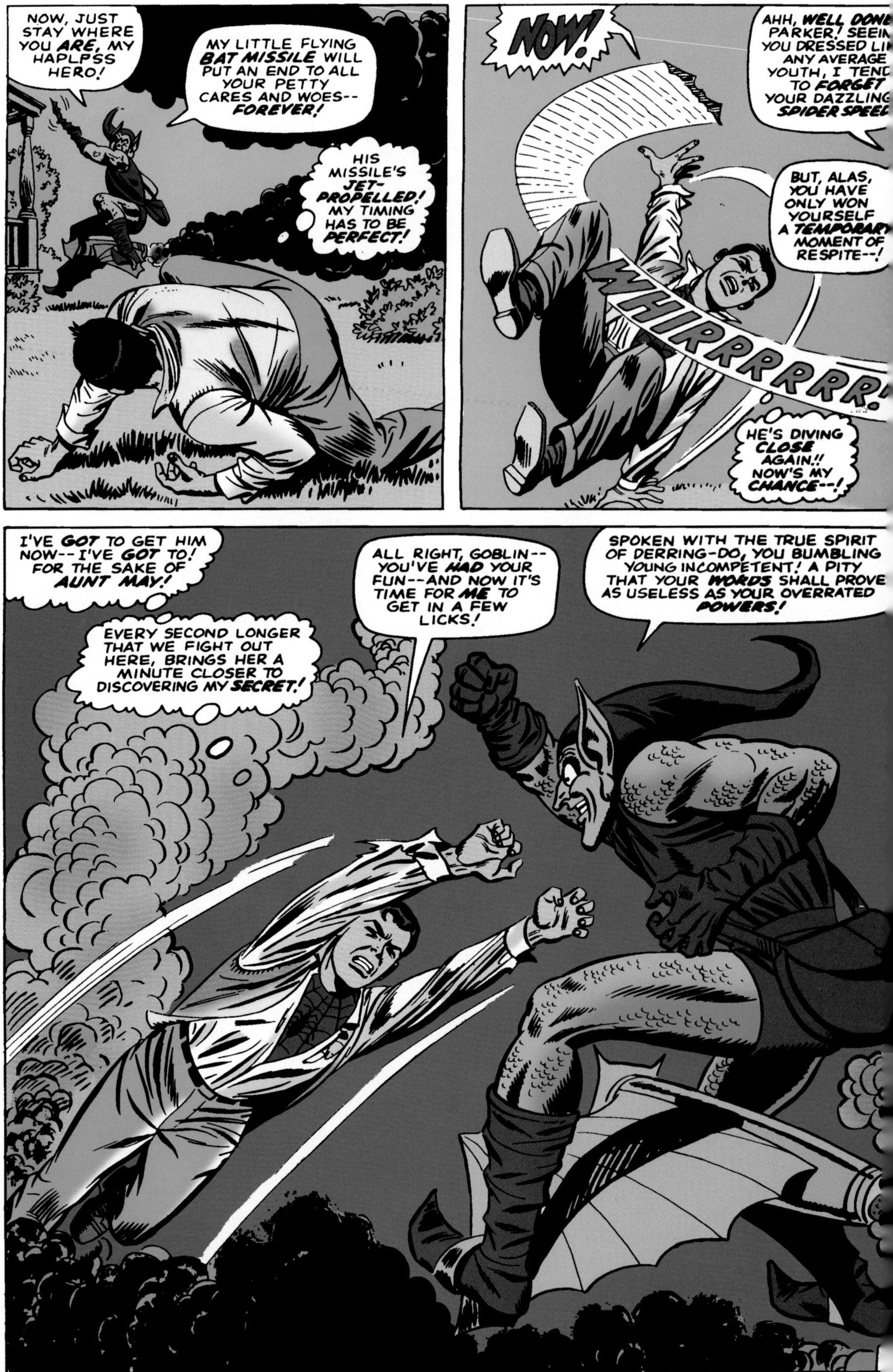

NOW, JUST STAY WHERE YOU ARE, MY HAPLPSS HERO!
MY LITTLE FLYING BAT MISSILE WILL PUT AN END TO ALL YOUR PETTY CARES AND WOES-- FOREVER!
HIS MISSILE'S JET-PROPELLED! MY TIMING HAS TO BE PERFECT!
NOW!
AHH, WELL DONE PARKER! SEEIN YOU DRESSED LI ANY AVERAGE YOUTH, I TEND TO FORGET YOUR DAZZLING SPIDER SPEE
BUT, ALAS, YOU HAVE ONLY WON YOURSELF A TEMPORAR MOMENT OF RESPITE--!
WHIRRRRRRR!
HE'S DIVING CLOSE AGAIN!! NOW'S MY CHANCE--!
I'VE GOT TO GET HIM NOW-- I'VE GOT TO! FOR THE SAKE OF AUNT MAY!
EVERY SECOND LONGER THAT WE FIGHT OUT HERE, BRINGS HER A MINUTE CLOSER TO DISCOVERING MY SECRET!
ALL RIGHT, GOBLIN-- YOU'VE HAD YOUR FUN--AND NOW IT'S TIME FOR ME TO GET IN A FEW LICKS!
SPOKEN WITH THE TRUE SPIRIT OF DERRING-DO, YOU BUMBLING YOUNG INCOMPETENT! A PITY THAT YOUR WORDS SHALL PROVE AS USELESS AS YOUR OVERRATED POWERS!

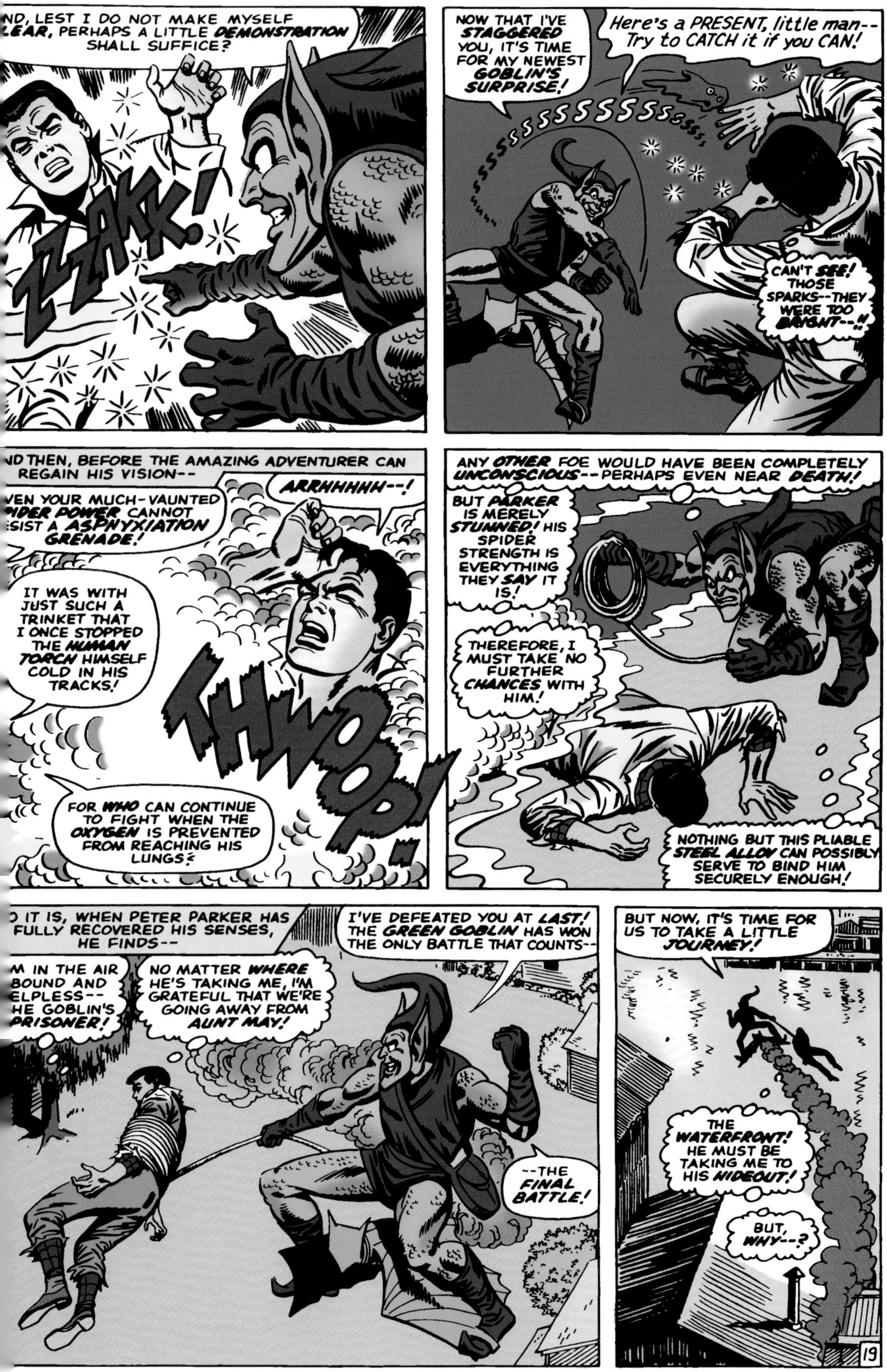
ND, LEST I DO NOT MAKE MYSELF
LEAR, PERHAPS A LITTLE DEMONSTRATION SHALL SUFFICE?
ZZZAKK!
NOW THAT I'VE STAGGERED YOU, IT'S TIME FOR MY NEWEST GOBLIN'S SURPRISE!
Here's a PRESENT, little man-- Try to CATCH it if you CAN!
SSSSSSSSSSSSSSSS
CAN'T SEE! THOSE SPARKS--THEY WERE TOO BRIGHT--!!
ND THEN, BEFORE THE AMAZING ADVENTURER CAN REGAIN HIS VISION--
ARRHHHHH--!
VEN YOUR MUCH-VAUNTED PIDER POWER CANNOT ESIST A ASPHYXIATION GRENADE!
IT WAS WITH JUST SUCH A TRINKET THAT I ONCE STOPPED THE HUMAN TORCH HIMSELF COLD IN HIS TRACKS!
THWOOP!
FOR WHO CAN CONTINUE TO FIGHT WHEN THE OXYGEN IS PREVENTED FROM REACHING HIS LUNGS?
ANY OTHER FOE WOULD HAVE BEEN COMPLETELY UNCONSCIOUS--PERHAPS EVEN NEAR DEATH!
BUT PARKER IS MERELY STUNNED! HIS SPIDER STRENGTH IS EVERYTHING THEY SAY IT IS!
THEREFORE, I MUST TAKE NO FURTHER CHANCES WITH HIM!
NOTHING BUT THIS PLIABLE STEEL ALLOY CAN POSSIBLY SERVE TO BIND HIM SECURELY ENOUGH!
O IT IS, WHEN PETER PARKER HAS FULLY RECOVERED HIS SENSES, HE FINDS--
I'VE DEFEATED YOU AT LAST! THE GREEN GOBLIN HAS WON THE ONLY BATTLE THAT COUNTS--
M IN THE AIR BOUND AND ELPLESS-- HE GOBLIN'S PRISONER!
NO MATTER WHERE HE'S TAKING ME, I'M GRATEFUL THAT WE'RE GOING AWAY FROM AUNT MAY!
--THE FINAL BATTLE!
BUT NOW, IT'S TIME FOR US TO TAKE A LITTLE JOURNEY!
THE WATERFRONT! HE MUST BE TAKING ME TO HIS HIDEOUT!
BUT, WHY--?

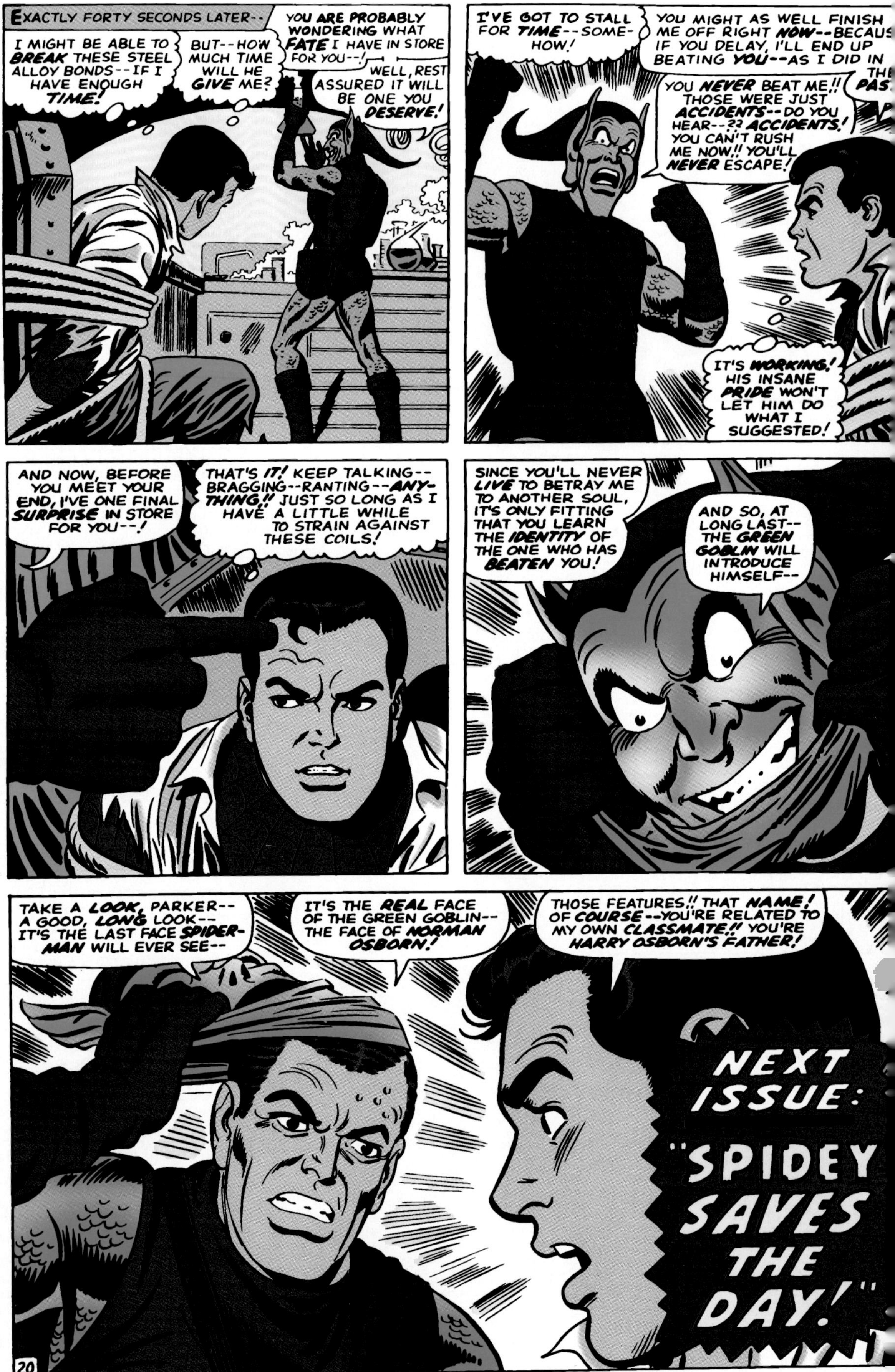
EXACTLY FORTY SECONDS LATER--
I MIGHT BE ABLE TO BREAK THESE STEEL ALLOY BONDS--IF I HAVE ENOUGH TIME!
BUT--HOW MUCH TIME WILL HE GIVE ME?
YOU ARE PROBABLY WONDERING WHAT FATE I HAVE IN STORE FOR YOU--!
WELL, REST ASSURED IT WILL BE ONE YOU DESERVE!
I'VE GOT TO STALL FOR TIME--SOME-HOW!
YOU MIGHT AS WELL FINISH ME OFF RIGHT NOW--BECAUS IF YOU DELAY, I'LL END UP BEATING YOU--AS I DID IN THE PAS
YOU NEVER BEAT ME!! THOSE WERE JUST ACCIDENTS--DO YOU HEAR--?? ACCIDENTS! YOU CAN'T RUSH ME NOW!! YOU'LL NEVER ESCAPE!
IT'S WORKING! HIS INSANE PRIDE WON'T LET HIM DO WHAT I SUGGESTED!
AND NOW, BEFORE YOU MEET YOUR END, I'VE ONE FINAL SURPRISE IN STORE FOR YOU--!
THAT'S IT! KEEP TALKING--BRAGGING--RANTING--ANY-THING!! JUST SO LONG AS I HAVE A LITTLE WHILE TO STRAIN AGAINST THESE COILS!
SINCE YOU'LL NEVER LIVE TO BETRAY ME TO ANOTHER SOUL, IT'S ONLY FITTING THAT YOU LEARN THE IDENTITY OF THE ONE WHO HAS BEATEN YOU!
AND SO, AT LONG LAST--THE GREEN GOBLIN WILL INTRODUCE HIMSELF--
TAKE A LOOK, PARKER--A GOOD, LONG LOOK--IT'S THE LAST FACE SPIDER-MAN WILL EVER SEE--
IT'S THE REAL FACE OF THE GREEN GOBLIN--THE FACE OF NORMAN OSBORN!
THOSE FEATURES!! THAT NAME! OF COURSE--YOU'RE RELATED TO MY OWN CLASSMATE!! YOU'RE HARRY OSBORN'S FATHER!
NEXT ISSUE: "SPIDEY SAVES THE DAY!"
20

amazing spider-man #40

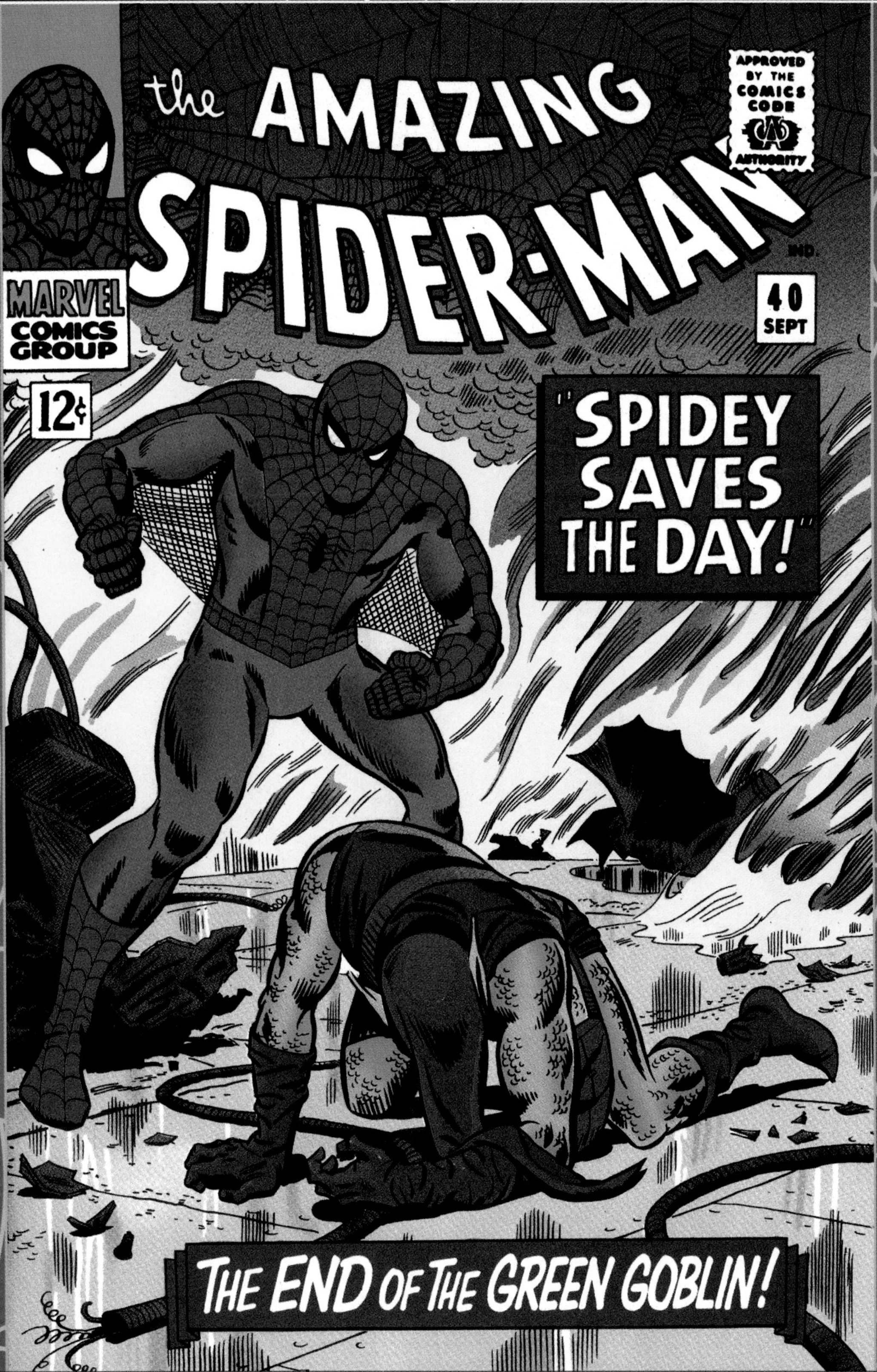

the AMAZING SPIDER-MAN
APPROVED BY THE COMICS CODE AUTHORITY
IND.
MARVEL COMICS GROUP
40 SEPT
12¢
"SPIDEY SAVES THE DAY!"
THE END OF THE GREEN GOBLIN!

september 1966

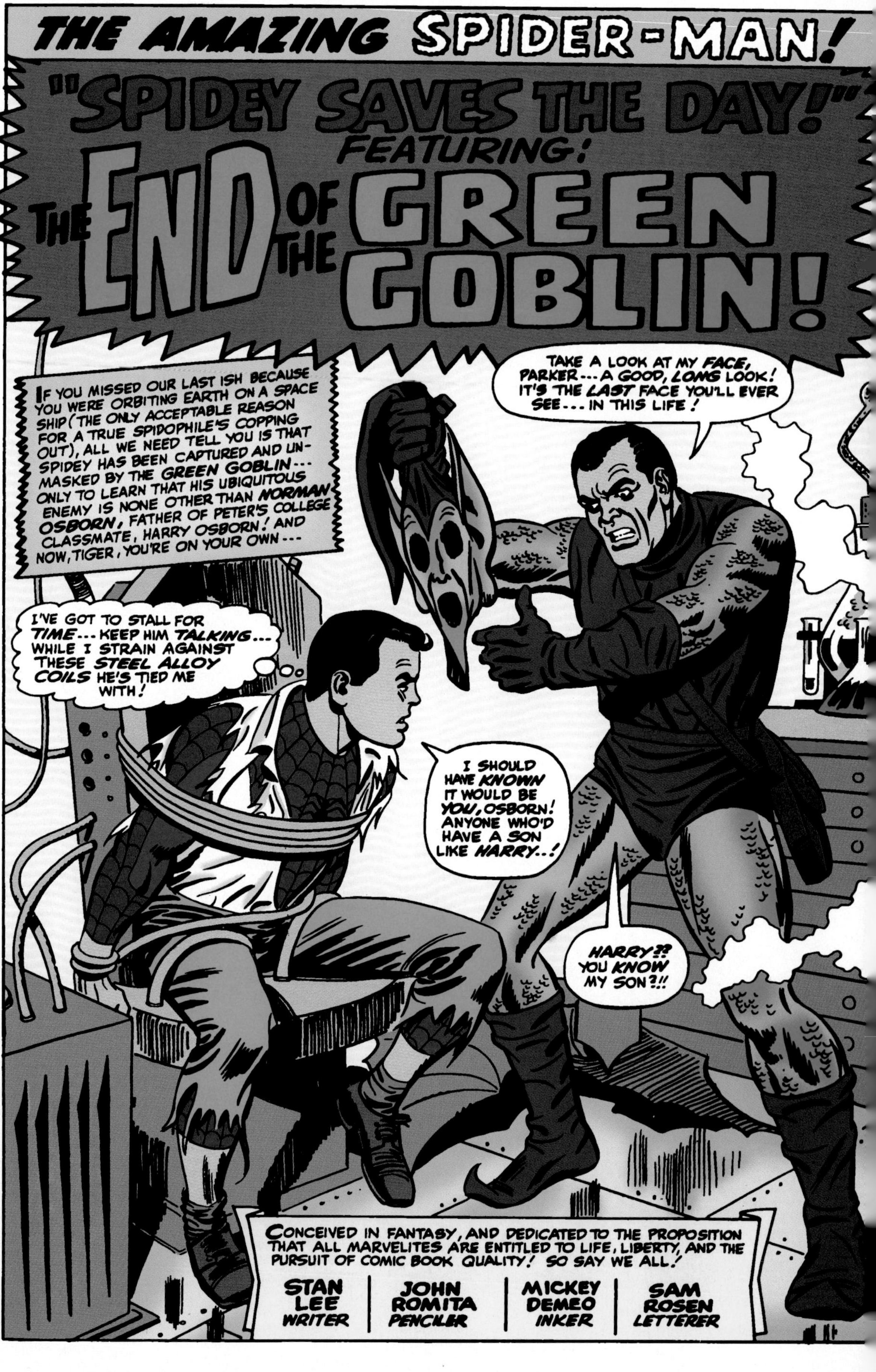
THE AMAZING SPIDER-MAN!
"SPIDEY SAVES THE DAY!" FEATURING!
THE END OF THE GREEN GOBLIN!
IF YOU MISSED OUR LAST ISH BECAUSE YOU WERE ORBITING EARTH ON A SPACE SHIP (THE ONLY ACCEPTABLE REASON FOR A TRUE SPIDOPHILE'S COPPING OUT), ALL WE NEED TELL YOU IS THAT SPIDEY HAS BEEN CAPTURED AND UNMASKED BY THE GREEN GOBLIN... ONLY TO LEARN THAT HIS UBIQUITOUS ENEMY IS NONE OTHER THAN NORMAN OSBORN, FATHER OF PETER'S COLLEGE CLASSMATE, HARRY OSBORN! AND NOW, TIGER, YOU'RE ON YOUR OWN...
TAKE A LOOK AT MY FACE, PARKER... A GOOD, LONG LOOK! IT'S THE LAST FACE YOU'LL EVER SEE... IN THIS LIFE!
I'VE GOT TO STALL FOR TIME... KEEP HIM TALKING... WHILE I STRAIN AGAINST THESE STEEL ALLOY COILS HE'S TIED ME WITH!
I SHOULD HAVE KNOWN IT WOULD BE YOU, OSBORN! ANYONE WHO'D HAVE A SON LIKE HARRY..!
HARRY?? YOU KNOW MY SON?!!
CONCEIVED IN FANTASY, AND DEDICATED TO THE PROPOSITION THAT ALL MARVELITES ARE ENTITLED TO LIFE, LIBERTY, AND THE PURSUIT OF COMIC BOOK QUALITY! SO SAY WE ALL!
STAN LEE WRITER
JOHN ROMITA PENCILER
MICKEY DEMEO INKER
SAM ROSEN LETTERER

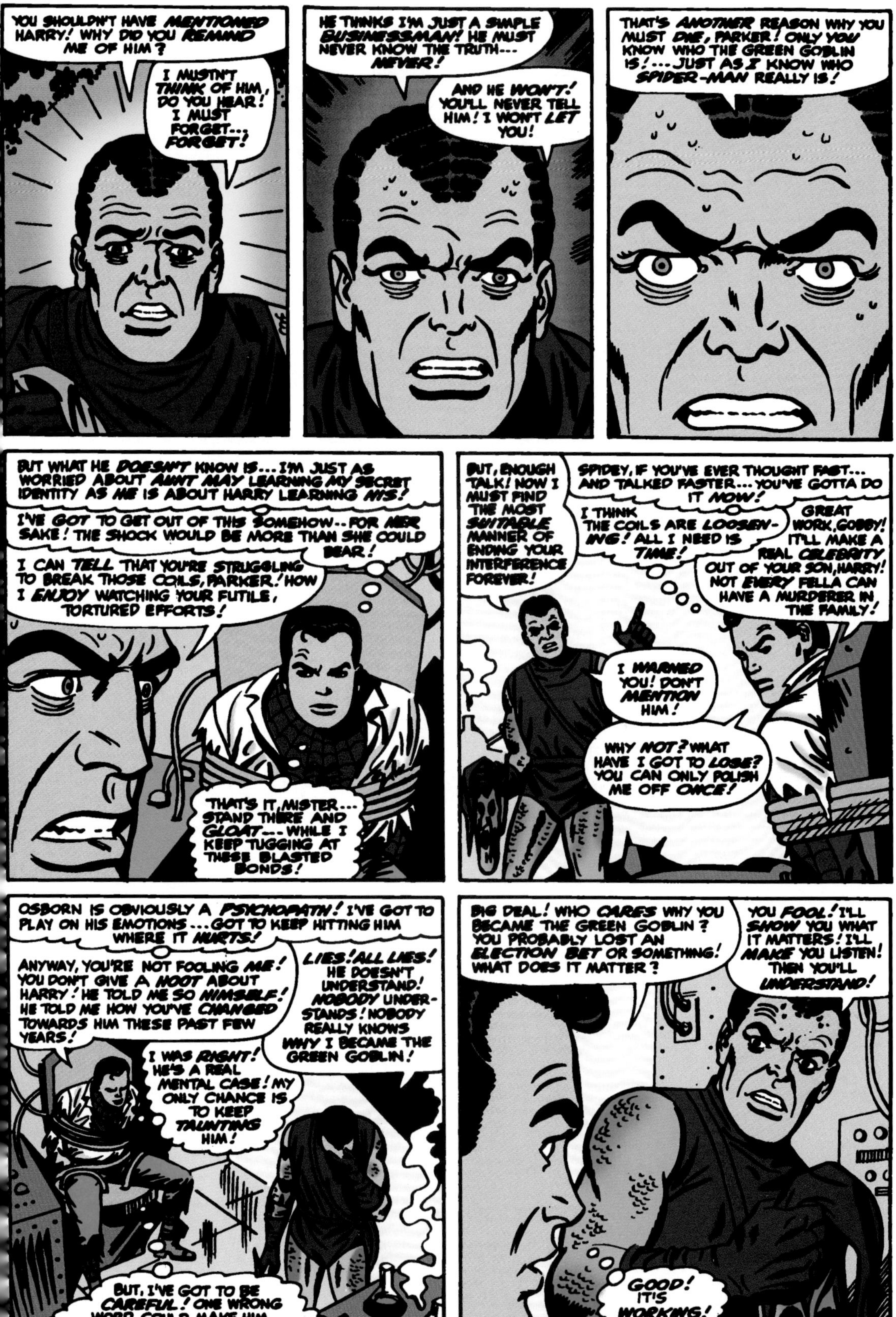
YOU SHOULDN'T HAVE MENTIONED HARRY! WHY DID YOU REMIND ME OF HIM?
I MUSTN'T THINK OF HIM, DO YOU HEAR! I MUST FORGET... FORGET!
HE THINKS I'M JUST A SIMPLE BUSINESSMAN! HE MUST NEVER KNOW THE TRUTH--- NEVER!
AND HE WON'T! YOU'LL NEVER TELL HIM! I WON'T LET YOU!
THAT'S ANOTHER REASON WHY YOU MUST DIE, PARKER! ONLY YOU KNOW WHO THE GREEN GOBLIN IS! ...JUST AS I KNOW WHO SPIDER-MAN REALLY IS!
BUT WHAT HE DOESN'T KNOW IS... I'M JUST AS WORRIED ABOUT AUNT MAY LEARNING MY SECRET IDENTITY AS HE IS ABOUT HARRY LEARNING HIS!
I'VE GOT TO GET OUT OF THIS SOMEHOW -- FOR HER SAKE! THE SHOCK WOULD BE MORE THAN SHE COULD BEAR!
I CAN TELL THAT YOU'RE STRUGGLING TO BREAK THOSE COILS, PARKER! HOW I ENJOY WATCHING YOUR FUTILE, TORTURED EFFORTS!
THAT'S IT, MISTER... STAND THERE AND GLOAT... WHILE I KEEP TUGGING AT THESE BLASTED BONDS!
BUT, ENOUGH TALK! NOW I MUST FIND THE MOST SUITABLE MANNER OF ENDING YOUR INTERFERENCE FOREVER!
SPIDEY, IF YOU'VE EVER THOUGHT FAST... AND TALKED FASTER... YOU'VE GOTTA DO IT NOW!
I THINK THE COILS ARE LOOSEN-ING! ALL I NEED IS TIME!
GREAT WORK, GOBBY! IT'LL MAKE A REAL CELEBRITY OUT OF YOUR SON, HARRY! NOT EVERY FELLA CAN HAVE A MURDERER IN THE FAMILY!
I WARNED YOU! DON'T MENTION HIM!
WHY NOT? WHAT HAVE I GOT TO LOSE? YOU CAN ONLY POLISH ME OFF ONCE!
OSBORN IS OBVIOUSLY A PSYCHOPATH! I'VE GOT TO PLAY ON HIS EMOTIONS... GOT TO KEEP HITTING HIM WHERE IT HURTS!
ANYWAY, YOU'RE NOT FOOLING ME! YOU DON'T GIVE A HOOT ABOUT HARRY! HE TOLD ME SO HIMSELF! HE TOLD ME HOW YOU'VE CHANGED TOWARDS HIM THESE PAST FEW YEARS!
LIES! ALL LIES! HE DOESN'T UNDERSTAND! NOBODY UNDER-STANDS! NOBODY REALLY KNOWS WHY I BECAME THE GREEN GOBLIN!
I WAS RIGHT! HE'S A REAL MENTAL CASE! MY ONLY CHANCE IS TO KEEP TAUNTING HIM!
BUT, I'VE GOT TO BE CAREFUL! ONE WRONG WORD COULD MAKE HIM VIOLENT... AND THEN, BYE-BYE SPIDEY!
BIG DEAL! WHO CARES WHY YOU BECAME THE GREEN GOBLIN? YOU PROBABLY LOST AN ELECTION BET OR SOMETHING! WHAT DOES IT MATTER?
YOU FOOL! I'LL SHOW YOU WHAT IT MATTERS! I'LL MAKE YOU LISTEN! THEN YOU'LL UNDERSTAND!
GOOD! IT'S WORKING!
2.

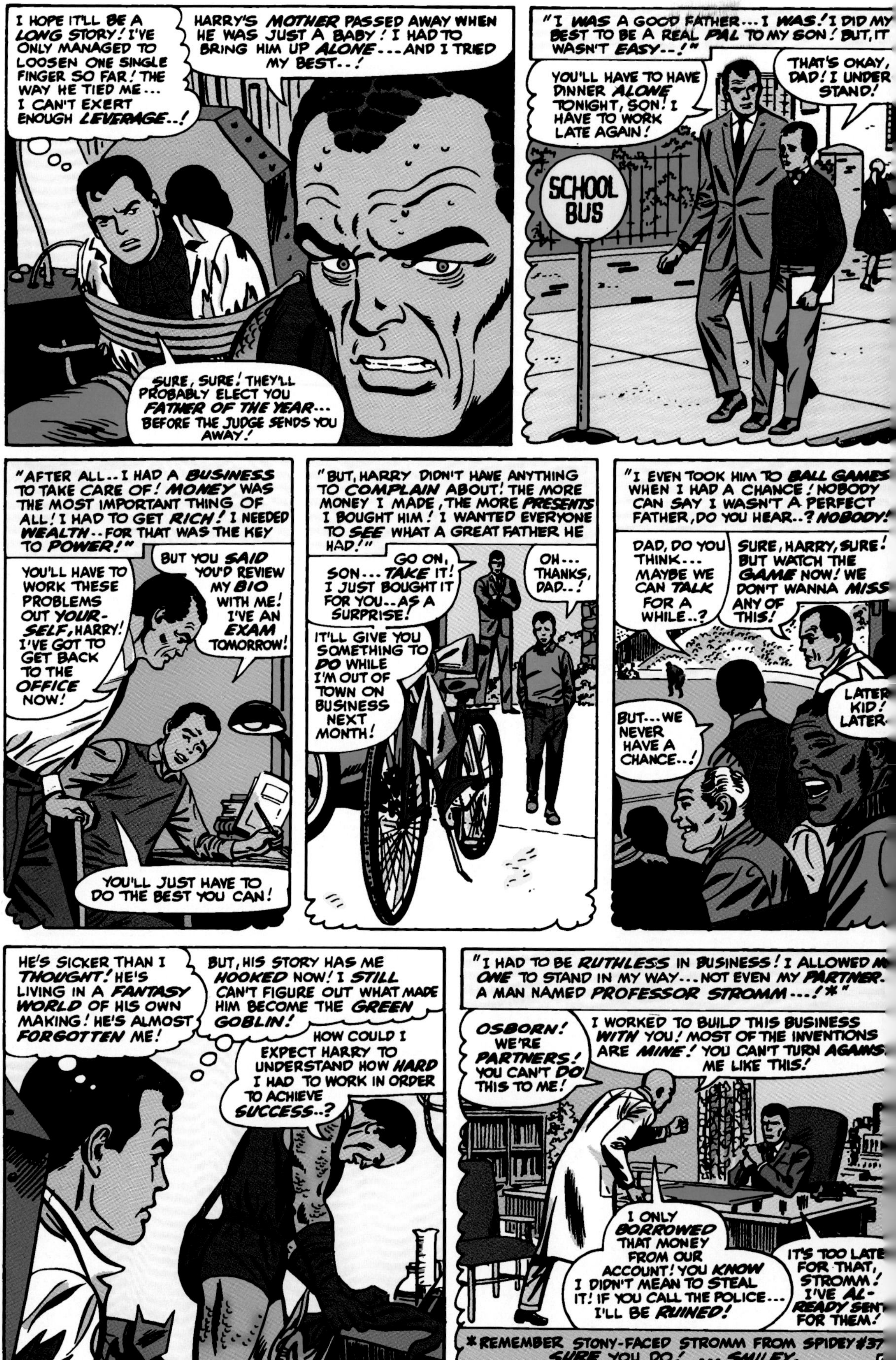
I HOPE IT'LL BE A LONG STORY! I'VE ONLY MANAGED TO LOOSEN ONE SINGLE FINGER SO FAR! THE WAY HE TIED ME... I CAN'T EXERT ENOUGH LEVERAGE..!
HARRY'S MOTHER PASSED AWAY WHEN HE WAS JUST A BABY! I HAD TO BRING HIM UP ALONE...AND I TRIED MY BEST..!
SURE, SURE! THEY'LL PROBABLY ELECT YOU FATHER OF THE YEAR... BEFORE THE JUDGE SENDS YOU AWAY!
"I WAS A GOOD FATHER...I WAS! I DID MY BEST TO BE A REAL PAL TO MY SON! BUT, IT WASN'T EASY--!"
YOU'LL HAVE TO HAVE DINNER ALONE TONIGHT, SON! I HAVE TO WORK LATE AGAIN!
THAT'S OKAY, DAD! I UNDER STAND!
SCHOOL BUS
"AFTER ALL..I HAD A BUSINESS TO TAKE CARE OF! MONEY WAS THE MOST IMPORTANT THING OF ALL! I HAD TO GET RICH! I NEEDED WEALTH..FOR THAT WAS THE KEY TO POWER!"
YOU'LL HAVE TO WORK THESE PROBLEMS OUT YOURSELF, HARRY! I'VE GOT TO GET BACK TO THE OFFICE NOW!
BUT YOU SAID YOU'D REVIEW MY BIO WITH ME! I'VE AN EXAM TOMORROW!
YOU'LL JUST HAVE TO DO THE BEST YOU CAN!
"BUT, HARRY DIDN'T HAVE ANYTHING TO COMPLAIN ABOUT! THE MORE MONEY I MADE, THE MORE PRESENTS I BOUGHT HIM! I WANTED EVERYONE TO SEE WHAT A GREAT FATHER HE HAD!"
GO ON, SON...TAKE IT! I JUST BOUGHT IT FOR YOU..AS A SURPRISE!
OH... THANKS, DAD..!
IT'LL GIVE YOU SOMETHING TO DO WHILE I'M OUT OF TOWN ON BUSINESS NEXT MONTH!
"I EVEN TOOK HIM TO BALL GAMES WHEN I HAD A CHANCE! NOBODY CAN SAY I WASN'T A PERFECT FATHER, DO YOU HEAR..? NOBODY!"
DAD, DO YOU THINK... MAYBE WE CAN TALK FOR A WHILE..?
SURE, HARRY, SURE! BUT WATCH THE GAME NOW! WE DON'T WANNA MISS ANY OF THIS!
BUT...WE NEVER HAVE A CHANCE..!
LATER KID! LATER.
HE'S SICKER THAN I THOUGHT! HE'S LIVING IN A FANTASY WORLD OF HIS OWN MAKING! HE'S ALMOST FORGOTTEN ME!
BUT, HIS STORY HAS ME HOOKED NOW! I STILL CAN'T FIGURE OUT WHAT MADE HIM BECOME THE GREEN GOBLIN!
HOW COULD I EXPECT HARRY TO UNDERSTAND HOW HARD I HAD TO WORK IN ORDER TO ACHIEVE SUCCESS..?
"I HAD TO BE RUTHLESS IN BUSINESS! I ALLOWED NO ONE TO STAND IN MY WAY...NOT EVEN MY PARTNER. A MAN NAMED PROFESSOR STROMM...!*"
OSBORN! WE'RE PARTNERS! YOU CAN'T DO THIS TO ME!
I WORKED TO BUILD THIS BUSINESS WITH YOU! MOST OF THE INVENTIONS ARE MINE! YOU CAN'T TURN AGAINS ME LIKE THIS!
I ONLY BORROWED THAT MONEY FROM OUR ACCOUNT! YOU KNOW I DIDN'T MEAN TO STEAL IT! IF YOU CALL THE POLICE... I'LL BE RUINED!
IT'S TOO LATE FOR THAT, STROMM! I'VE ALREADY SENT FOR THEM!
*REMEMBER STONY-FACED STROMM FROM SPIDEY #37 SURE YOU DO! ...SMILEY.

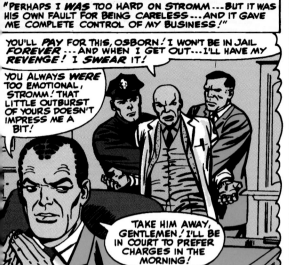

"PERHAPS I *WAS* TOO HARD ON STROMM... BUT IT WAS HIS OWN FAULT FOR BEING CARELESS... AND IT GAVE ME COMPLETE CONTROL OF MY BUSINESS!"

YOU'LL *PAY* FOR THIS, OSBORN! I WON'T BE IN JAIL *FOREVER*... AND WHEN I GET OUT... I'LL HAVE MY *REVENGE!* I *SWEAR* IT!

YOU ALWAYS *WERE* TOO EMOTIONAL, STROMM! THAT LITTLE OUTBURST OF YOURS DOESN'T IMPRESS ME A BIT!

TAKE HIM AWAY, GENTLEMEN! I'LL BE IN COURT TO PREFER CHARGES IN THE MORNING!

SO *THAT'S* WHY STROMM TRIED TO KILL YOU WITH THAT *ROBOT* OF HIS! AND THAT'S WHY YOU RESENTED *SPIDER-MAN'S* HELP!

WHAT A *JOKE! ME,* TRYING TO SAVE THE *GREEN GOBLIN!*

UH-OH! HE'S TOO *QUIET!* I'VE GOTTA GET HIM *TALKING* AGAIN!

I *STILL* DON'T GET IT, OSBORN! YOU BECAME WEALTHY... *SUCCESSFUL!* YOU ACHIEVED YOUR GOAL ---

SO, WHAT MADE YOU TURN TO *CRIME?* WHAT MADE YOU BECOME THE *GREEN GOBLIN?*

I'VE TOLD YOU *SO* MUCH... I MIGHT AS WELL TELL YOU THE *REST!* AFTER ALL, MY SECRET WILL DIE *WITH* YOU!

NOT IF *I* CAN HELP IT, MISTER!

THERE! THAT'S *ANOTHER* FINGER I MANAGED TO WORK LOOSE!

SO? WHAT HAPPENED? DID YOU WIN A GREEN COSTUME IN A *RAFFLE,* OR SOMETHING?

YOU'RE *MOCKING* ME, ARE YOU..?

"WELL, IT'S ALL RIGHT! YOU MAY *HAVE* YOUR LITTLE JOKE! IT'S THE *LAST* YOU'LL EVER ENJOY! AS FOR *ME,* I STILL REMEMBER THAT FATEFUL NIGHT... WHEN IT *HAPPENED --!*"

THESE NOTES OF STROMM'S... WHICH I FOUND IN HIS DESK... CONTAIN SOME NEW, STRANGE-LOOKING *FORMULAS!*

SINCE HE'S IN *PRISON* NOW, I'LL CHECK THEM OUT! IF THEY'RE *WORTH* ANYTHING, I'LL BE ABLE TO CASH IN ON THEM!

"AND THEN, *HARRY* CAME IN... BUT I COULDN'T BE BOTHERED WITH HIM AT A TIME LIKE THAT..."

DAD, HAVE YOU *FORGOTTEN?* IT'S *PARENTS' NIGHT* AT MY SCHOOL THIS EVENING! WE SHOULD *BE* THERE BY NOW!

FORGET IT, SON! I CAN'T MAKE IT NOW! YOU GO ON AHEAD... MAYBE I'LL GET THERE BEFORE IT'S OVER!

BUT, I THOUGHT..!

I SAID *FORGET IT!*

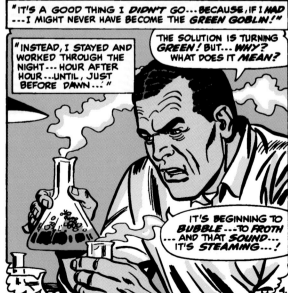

"IT'S A GOOD THING I *DIDN'T GO*... BECAUSE, IF I *HAD*... I MIGHT NEVER HAVE BECOME THE *GREEN GOBLIN!*"

"INSTEAD, I STAYED AND WORKED THROUGH THE NIGHT --- HOUR AFTER HOUR... UNTIL, JUST BEFORE DAWN...!"

THE SOLUTION IS TURNING *GREEN!* BUT... *WHY?* WHAT DOES IT *MEAN?*

IT'S BEGINNING TO *BUBBLE*... TO *FROTH* ... AND THAT *SOUND*... IT'S *STEAMING*...!

4.

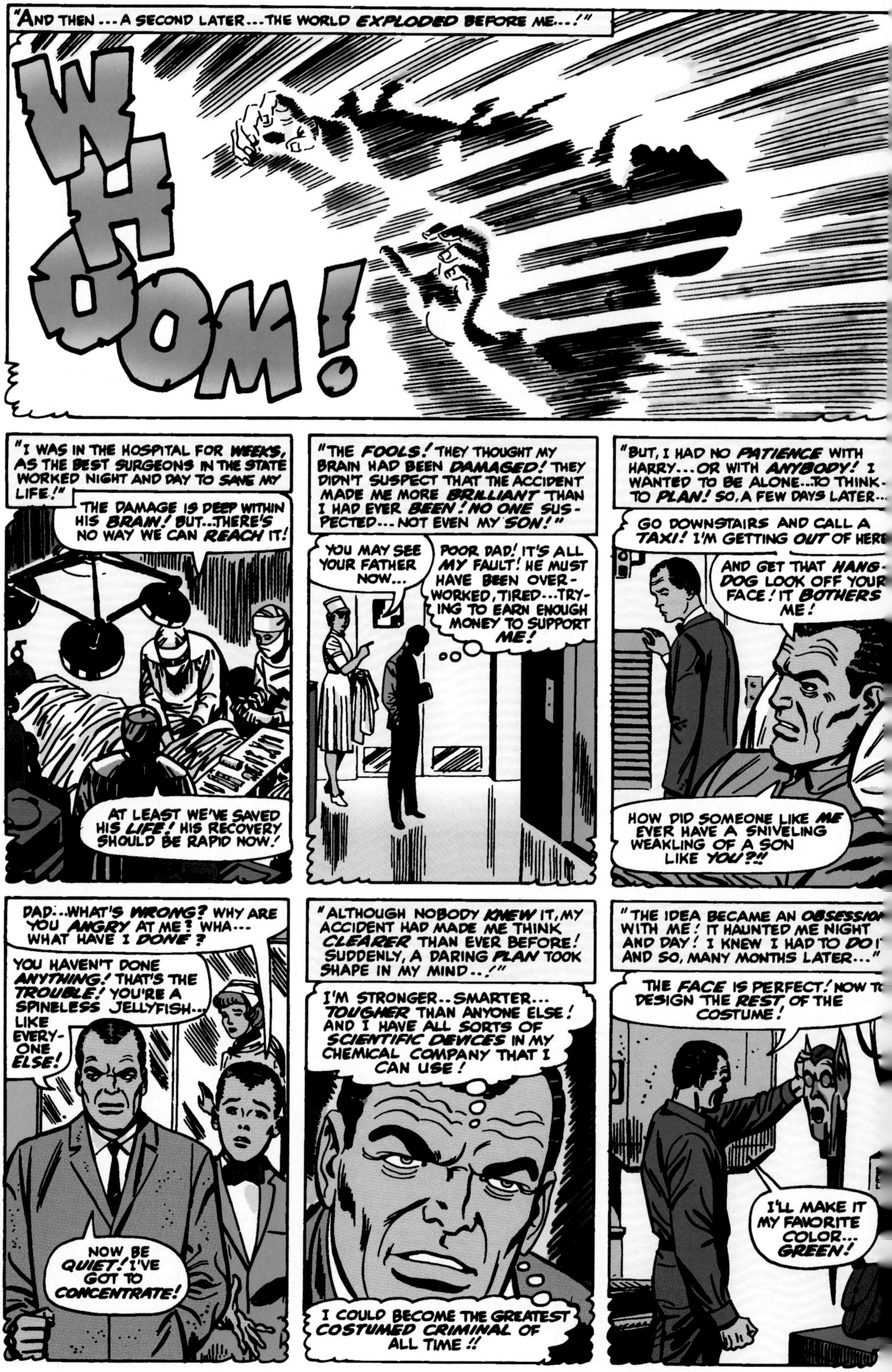
"AND THEN ... A SECOND LATER ... THE WORLD EXPLODED BEFORE ME...!"
WHOOM!
"I WAS IN THE HOSPITAL FOR WEEKS, AS THE BEST SURGEONS IN THE STATE WORKED NIGHT AND DAY TO SAVE MY LIFE!"
THE DAMAGE IS DEEP WITHIN HIS BRAIN! BUT...THERE'S NO WAY WE CAN REACH IT!
AT LEAST WE'VE SAVED HIS LIFE! HIS RECOVERY SHOULD BE RAPID NOW!
"THE FOOLS! THEY THOUGHT MY BRAIN HAD BEEN DAMAGED! THEY DIDN'T SUSPECT THAT THE ACCIDENT MADE ME MORE BRILLIANT THAN I HAD EVER BEEN! NO ONE SUSPECTED... NOT EVEN MY SON!"
YOU MAY SEE YOUR FATHER NOW...
POOR DAD! IT'S ALL MY FAULT! HE MUST HAVE BEEN OVER-WORKED, TIRED...TRYING TO EARN ENOUGH MONEY TO SUPPORT ME!
"BUT, I HAD NO PATIENCE WITH HARRY... OR WITH ANYBODY! I WANTED TO BE ALONE...TO THINK... TO PLAN! SO, A FEW DAYS LATER...
GO DOWNSTAIRS AND CALL A TAXI! I'M GETTING OUT OF HERE
AND GET THAT HANG-DOG LOOK OFF YOUR FACE! IT BOTHERS ME!
HOW DID SOMEONE LIKE ME EVER HAVE A SNIVELING WEAKLING OF A SON LIKE YOU?!!
DAD...WHAT'S WRONG? WHY ARE YOU ANGRY AT ME? WHA... WHAT HAVE I DONE?
YOU HAVEN'T DONE ANYTHING! THAT'S THE TROUBLE! YOU'RE A SPINELESS JELLYFISH... LIKE EVERYONE ELSE!
NOW BE QUIET! I'VE GOT TO CONCENTRATE!
"ALTHOUGH NOBODY KNEW IT, MY ACCIDENT HAD MADE ME THINK CLEARER THAN EVER BEFORE! SUDDENLY, A DARING PLAN TOOK SHAPE IN MY MIND...!"
I'M STRONGER...SMARTER... TOUGHER THAN ANYONE ELSE! AND I HAVE ALL SORTS OF SCIENTIFIC DEVICES IN MY CHEMICAL COMPANY THAT I CAN USE!
I COULD BECOME THE GREATEST COSTUMED CRIMINAL OF ALL TIME!!
"THE IDEA BECAME AN OBSESSION WITH ME! IT HAUNTED ME NIGHT AND DAY! I KNEW I HAD TO DO IT AND SO, MANY MONTHS LATER..."
THE FACE IS PERFECT! NOW TO DESIGN THE REST OF THE COSTUME!
I'LL MAKE IT MY FAVORITE COLOR... GREEN!

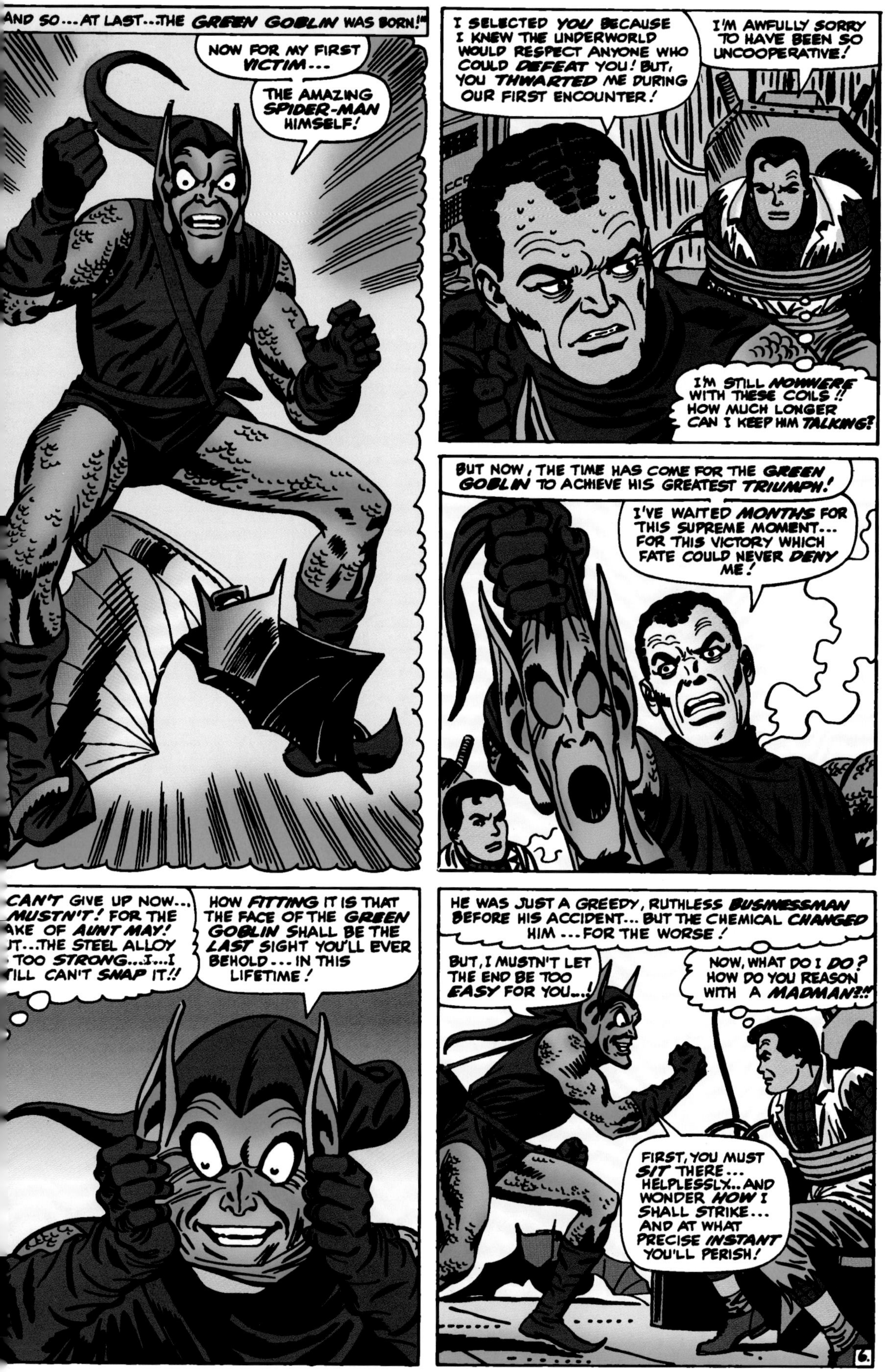
AND SO... AT LAST... THE GREEN GOBLIN WAS BORN!
NOW FOR MY FIRST VICTIM...
THE AMAZING SPIDER-MAN HIMSELF!
I SELECTED YOU BECAUSE I KNEW THE UNDERWORLD WOULD RESPECT ANYONE WHO COULD DEFEAT YOU! BUT, YOU THWARTED ME DURING OUR FIRST ENCOUNTER!
I'M AWFULLY SORRY TO HAVE BEEN SO UNCOOPERATIVE!
I'M STILL NOWHERE WITH THESE COILS!! HOW MUCH LONGER CAN I KEEP HIM TALKING?
BUT NOW, THE TIME HAS COME FOR THE GREEN GOBLIN TO ACHIEVE HIS GREATEST TRIUMPH!
I'VE WAITED MONTHS FOR THIS SUPREME MOMENT... FOR THIS VICTORY WHICH FATE COULD NEVER DENY ME!
CAN'T GIVE UP NOW... MUSTN'T! FOR THE AKE OF AUNT MAY! IT... THE STEEL ALLOY TOO STRONG... I... I TILL CAN'T SNAP IT!!
HOW FITTING IT IS THAT THE FACE OF THE GREEN GOBLIN SHALL BE THE LAST SIGHT YOU'LL EVER BEHOLD... IN THIS LIFETIME!
HE WAS JUST A GREEDY, RUTHLESS BUSINESSMAN BEFORE HIS ACCIDENT... BUT THE CHEMICAL CHANGED HIM... FOR THE WORSE!
BUT, I MUSTN'T LET THE END BE TOO EASY FOR YOU...!
NOW, WHAT DO I DO? HOW DO YOU REASON WITH A MADMAN?!!
FIRST, YOU MUST SIT THERE... HELPLESSLY... AND WONDER HOW I SHALL STRIKE... AND AT WHAT PRECISE INSTANT YOU'LL PERISH!
6.

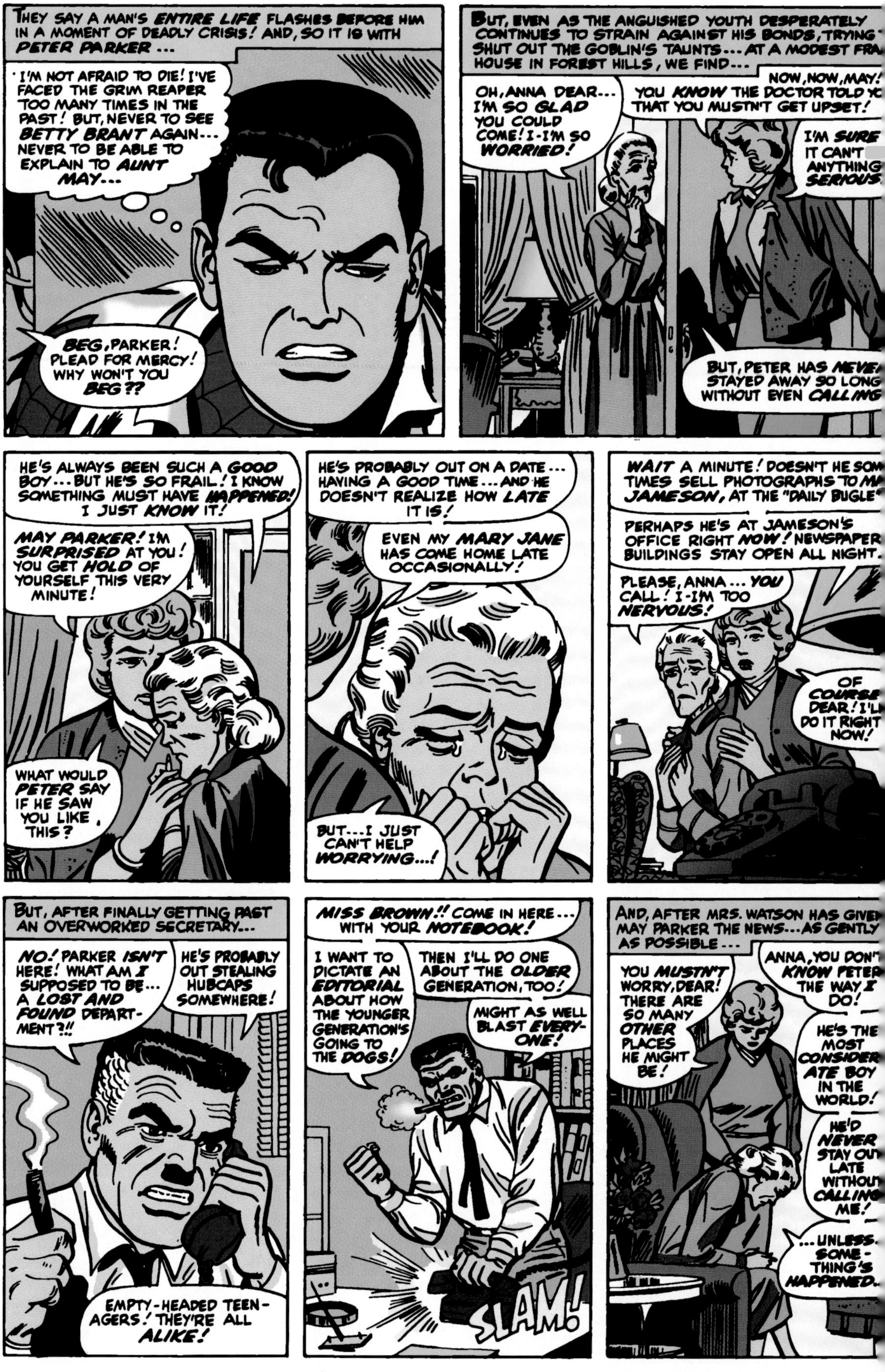
THEY SAY A MAN'S ENTIRE LIFE FLASHES BEFORE HIM IN A MOMENT OF DEADLY CRISIS! AND, SO IT IS WITH PETER PARKER...
I'M NOT AFRAID TO DIE! I'VE FACED THE GRIM REAPER TOO MANY TIMES IN THE PAST! BUT, NEVER TO SEE BETTY BRANT AGAIN... NEVER TO BE ABLE TO EXPLAIN TO AUNT MAY...
BEG, PARKER! PLEAD FOR MERCY! WHY WON'T YOU BEG??
BUT, EVEN AS THE ANGUISHED YOUTH DESPERATELY CONTINUES TO STRAIN AGAINST HIS BONDS, TRYING SHUT OUT THE GOBLIN'S TAUNTS... AT A MODEST FR HOUSE IN FOREST HILLS, WE FIND...
OH, ANNA DEAR... I'M SO GLAD YOU COULD COME! I-I'M SO WORRIED!
NOW, NOW, MAY! YOU KNOW THE DOCTOR TOLD YO THAT YOU MUSTN'T GET UPSET!
I'M SURE IT CAN'T ANYTHING SERIOUS
BUT, PETER HAS NEVE STAYED AWAY SO LONG WITHOUT EVEN CALLING
HE'S ALWAYS BEEN SUCH A GOOD BOY... BUT HE'S SO FRAIL! I KNOW SOMETHING MUST HAVE HAPPENED! I JUST KNOW IT!
MAY PARKER! I'M SURPRISED AT YOU! YOU GET HOLD OF YOURSELF THIS VERY MINUTE!
WHAT WOULD PETER SAY IF HE SAW YOU LIKE THIS?
HE'S PROBABLY OUT ON A DATE... HAVING A GOOD TIME... AND HE DOESN'T REALIZE HOW LATE IT IS!
EVEN MY MARY JANE HAS COME HOME LATE OCCASIONALLY!
BUT... I JUST CAN'T HELP WORRYING...!
WAIT A MINUTE! DOESN'T HE SOM TIMES SELL PHOTOGRAPHS TO M JAMESON, AT THE "DAILY BUGLE"
PERHAPS HE'S AT JAMESON'S OFFICE RIGHT NOW! NEWSPAPER BUILDINGS STAY OPEN ALL NIGHT.
PLEASE, ANNA... YOU CALL! I-I'M TOO NERVOUS!
OF COURSE DEAR! I'L DO IT RIGHT NOW!
BUT, AFTER FINALLY GETTING PAST AN OVERWORKED SECRETARY...
NO! PARKER ISN'T HERE! WHAT AM I SUPPOSED TO BE... A LOST AND FOUND DEPARTMENT?!!
HE'S PROBABLY OUT STEALING HUBCAPS SOMEWHERE!
EMPTY-HEADED TEEN-AGERS! THEY'RE ALL ALIKE!
MISS BROWN!! COME IN HERE... WITH YOUR NOTEBOOK!
I WANT TO DICTATE AN EDITORIAL ABOUT HOW THE YOUNGER GENERATION'S GOING TO THE DOGS!
THEN I'LL DO ONE ABOUT THE OLDER GENERATION, TOO!
MIGHT AS WELL BLAST EVERY-ONE!
SLAM!
AND, AFTER MRS. WATSON HAS GIVE MAY PARKER THE NEWS... AS GENTLY AS POSSIBLE...
YOU MUSTN'T WORRY, DEAR! THERE ARE SO MANY OTHER PLACES HE MIGHT BE!
ANNA, YOU DON'T KNOW PETER THE WAY I DO!
HE'S THE MOST CONSIDER-ATE BOY IN THE WORLD!
HE'D NEVER STAY OU LATE WITHOUT CALLING ME!
...UNLESS SOME-THING'S HAPPENED.

HE MIGHT BE IN **TROUBLE** SOMEWHERE! HE MIGHT **NEED** ME! IF ONLY I **KNEW**!

I'M GOING **OUT** FOR A MOMENT, MAY... BUT I'LL BE RIGHT **BACK**, HEAR? YOU JUST WAIT RIGHT THERE, DEAR... AND TRY NOT TO WORRY!

OH, PETER... PETER...

SHE'S GETTING **OVERWROUGHT**! SHE NEEDS A **SEDATIVE**! I'VE GOT TO CALL DR. BROMWELL!

MEANWHILE, AT A RAILROAD STATION IN THE MIDWEST, ANOTHER FEMALE WHO HAS PLAYED AN IMPORTANT ROLE IN THE LIFE OF PETER PARKER PAUSES BETWEEN TRAINS...

I **MUST** RETURN TO NEW YORK! I REALIZE NOW THAT A GIRL CAN NEVER RUN FROM A DECISION...

NO MATTER **HOW** PAINFUL IT MAY BE!

THIS IS **ART ROBERTS**, AT STATION **WLS** IN CHICAGO, WONDERING WHY NOTHING HAS BEEN HEARD OF **SPIDER-MAN** THESE PAST FEW DAYS...

SPIDER-MAN!! THE MASKED ADVENTURER WHOM PETER ADMIRES! HOW I HATE THE VERY SOUND OF HIS NAME!

HE REPRESENTS EVERYTHING I DREAD... **DANGER**... **UNCERTAINTY**... AND **FEAR**!

BUT, WHY DWELL ON SPIDER-MAN WHEN I HAVE A FAR **BIGGER** PROBLEM!?

IF I RETURN TO THE **DAILY BUGLE**, WILL MR. JAMESON GIVE ME MY OLD JOB BACK?

AND, IF HE DOES... WHAT WILL IT BE LIKE, SEEING **PETER PARKER** AND **NED LEEDS** AGAIN?

AND, WHAT WILL THEY SAY WHEN THEY SEE **ME**? WILL THERE STILL BE A PLACE IN THEIR LIVES FOR... **BETTY BRANT**?

THUS, THE SAD-EYED GIRL WALKS THROUGH THE STATION, IMMERSED IN HER OWN TROUBLED THOUGHTS... AND STRANGELY UNABLE TO ERASE THE HAUNTING IMAGE OF A COSTUMED FIGURE... A FIGURE WHO SEEMS TO SOMEHOW OVERSHADOW ALL ELSE AS HE SILENTLY SWINGS FROM MEMORY TO MEMORY....!

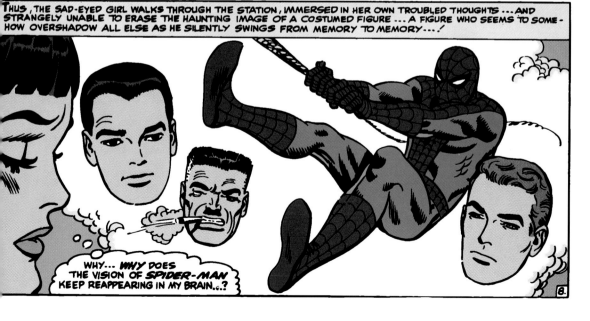

WHY... **WHY** DOES THE VISION OF **SPIDER-MAN** KEEP REAPPEARING IN MY BRAIN...?

8.

WHEN I THINK OF ALL THE TIMES I'VE *SEEN* SPIDER-MAN... SPOKEN TO HIM... AND YET, HE'S AN *ENIGMA!*

HE COULD BE *ANYBODY*... EVEN SOMEONE WHOM I *KNOW!*

BUT... I HOPE... AND *PRAY*... THAT HE *ISN'T!* I COULDN'T *STAND* IT IF HE WERE SOMEONE CLOSE TO ME... SOMEONE WHOM I *LOVE!*

ALL ABOARRRD!

PERHAPS, WHEN I RETURN TO NEW YORK... AND SEE *PETER* AGAIN... I'LL BE ABLE TO *FORGET* ABOUT SPIDER-MAN... FOREVER!

AS YOU PROBABLY GUESSED BY NOW, THE PAGES YOU'VE JUST READ ARE A TYPICAL MARVEL DEVICE FOR BRINGING NEW READERS UP TO DATE AS PAINLESSLY AS POSSIBLE! (WE JUST DIDN'T WANT YOU TO THINK YOU'D PICKED UP A ROMANCE BOOK BY MISTAKE!) BUT NOW, *FACE FRONT!* IT'LL BE *WEB-SPINNIN'* TIME BEFORE YOU KNOW IT...!

SO! YOU THINK YOU CAN ROB ME OF MY *SATISFACTION* BY SITTING THERE WITH YOUR EYES CLOSED!

WELL, IT WON'T *WORK!!*

THAT'S *IT,* GOBLIN! RANT AND RAVE AT ME... SAY *ANYTHING*... JUST SO LONG AS YOU KEEP *TALKING!*

IF ONLY I CAN KEEP *GOADING* HIM!

YOU'RE A *WASHOUT,* MAN! I BEAT YOU EVERY *TIME* WE FOUGHT BEFORE... AND I'LL FIND A WAY TO BEAT YOU *AGAIN!*

N... YO... LIE... DO YO... *HEAR*... YOU *LIE*... YOU *NEVE*... BEAT M...

I'LL *PROV*... IT TO YO...

I CAN PROJECT *MENTAL PICTURES* OF OUR PREVIOUS BATTLES BY MEANS OF THIS *RETRO-SCOPE* HELMET!

I'LL *SHOW* YOU THAT YOU NEVER BEAT ME! I WAS *ALWAYS* YOUR MASTER!! *ALWAYS!*

SURE! SURE! *ANYTHING* TO GIVE ME MORE *TIME!*

THERE! I'M SURE YOU REMEMBER *THOSE* THREE!

THE *ENFORCERS!* IT WAS T... FIRST TIME WE FOUGHT... YO... USED THEM TO *HELP* YOU!*

CLICK!

* SPIDEY # 14, NATCH! --STAN.

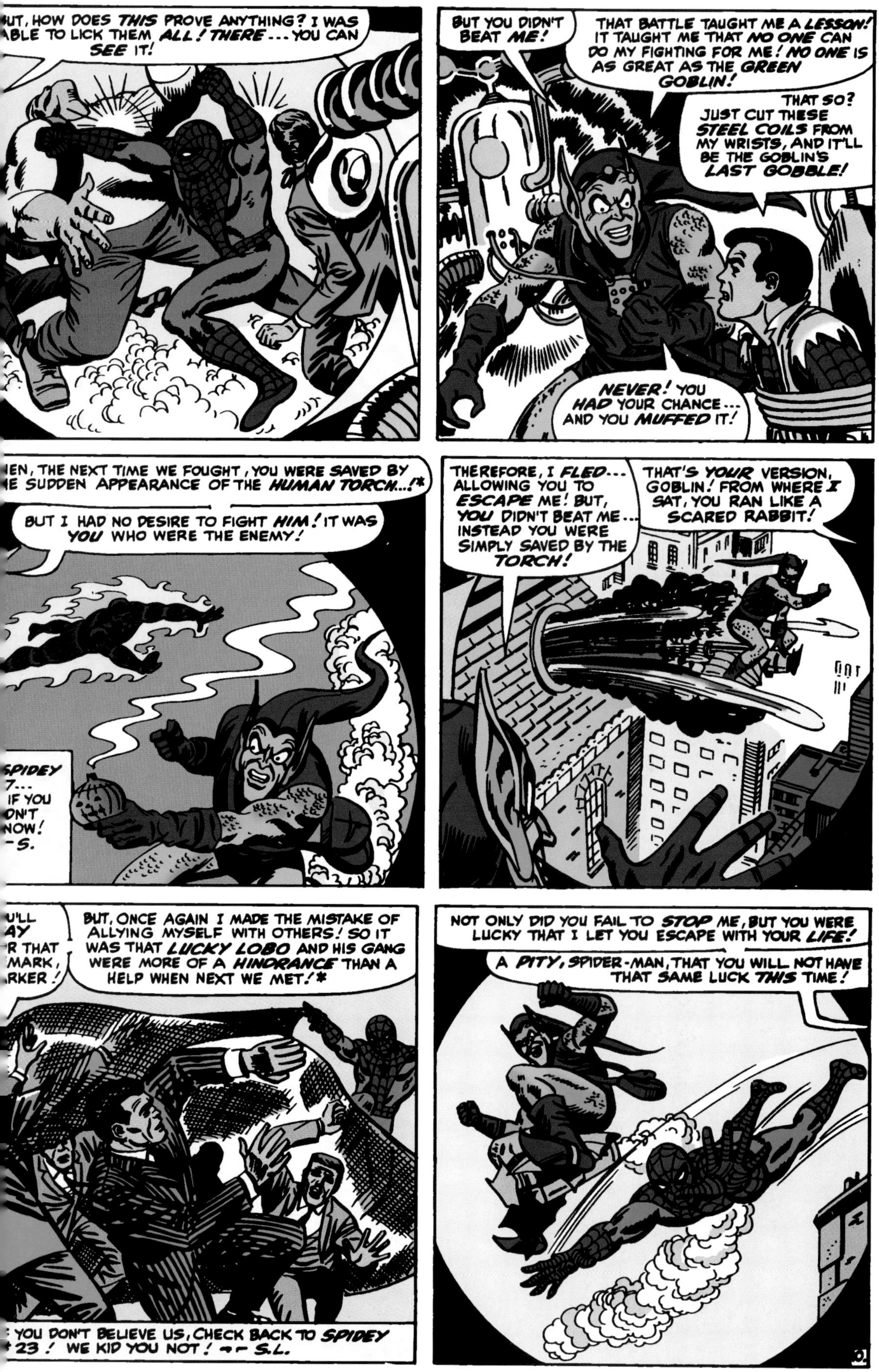

UT, HOW DOES THIS PROVE ANYTHING? I WAS ABLE TO LICK THEM ALL! THERE... YOU CAN SEE IT!
BUT YOU DIDN'T BEAT ME!
THAT BATTLE TAUGHT ME A LESSON! IT TAUGHT ME THAT NO ONE CAN DO MY FIGHTING FOR ME! NO ONE IS AS GREAT AS THE GREEN GOBLIN!
THAT SO? JUST CUT THESE STEEL COILS FROM MY WRISTS, AND IT'LL BE THE GOBLIN'S LAST GOBBLE!
NEVER! YOU HAD YOUR CHANCE... AND YOU MUFFED IT!
IEN, THE NEXT TIME WE FOUGHT, YOU WERE SAVED BY IE SUDDEN APPEARANCE OF THE HUMAN TORCH...!*
BUT I HAD NO DESIRE TO FIGHT HIM! IT WAS YOU WHO WERE THE ENEMY!
SPIDEY
7...
IF YOU
ON'T
NOW!
-S.
THEREFORE, I FLED... ALLOWING YOU TO ESCAPE ME! BUT, YOU DIDN'T BEAT ME... INSTEAD YOU WERE SIMPLY SAVED BY THE TORCH!
THAT'S YOUR VERSION, GOBLIN! FROM WHERE I SAT, YOU RAN LIKE A SCARED RABBIT!
U'LL
AY
R THAT
MARK,
RKER!
BUT, ONCE AGAIN I MADE THE MISTAKE OF ALLYING MYSELF WITH OTHERS! SO IT WAS THAT LUCKY LOBO AND HIS GANG WERE MORE OF A HINDRANCE THAN A HELP WHEN NEXT WE MET!*
YOU DON'T BELIEVE US, CHECK BACK TO SPIDEY 23! WE KID YOU NOT! -- S.L.
NOT ONLY DID YOU FAIL TO STOP ME, BUT YOU WERE LUCKY THAT I LET YOU ESCAPE WITH YOUR LIFE!
A PITY, SPIDER-MAN, THAT YOU WILL NOT HAVE THAT SAME LUCK THIS TIME!

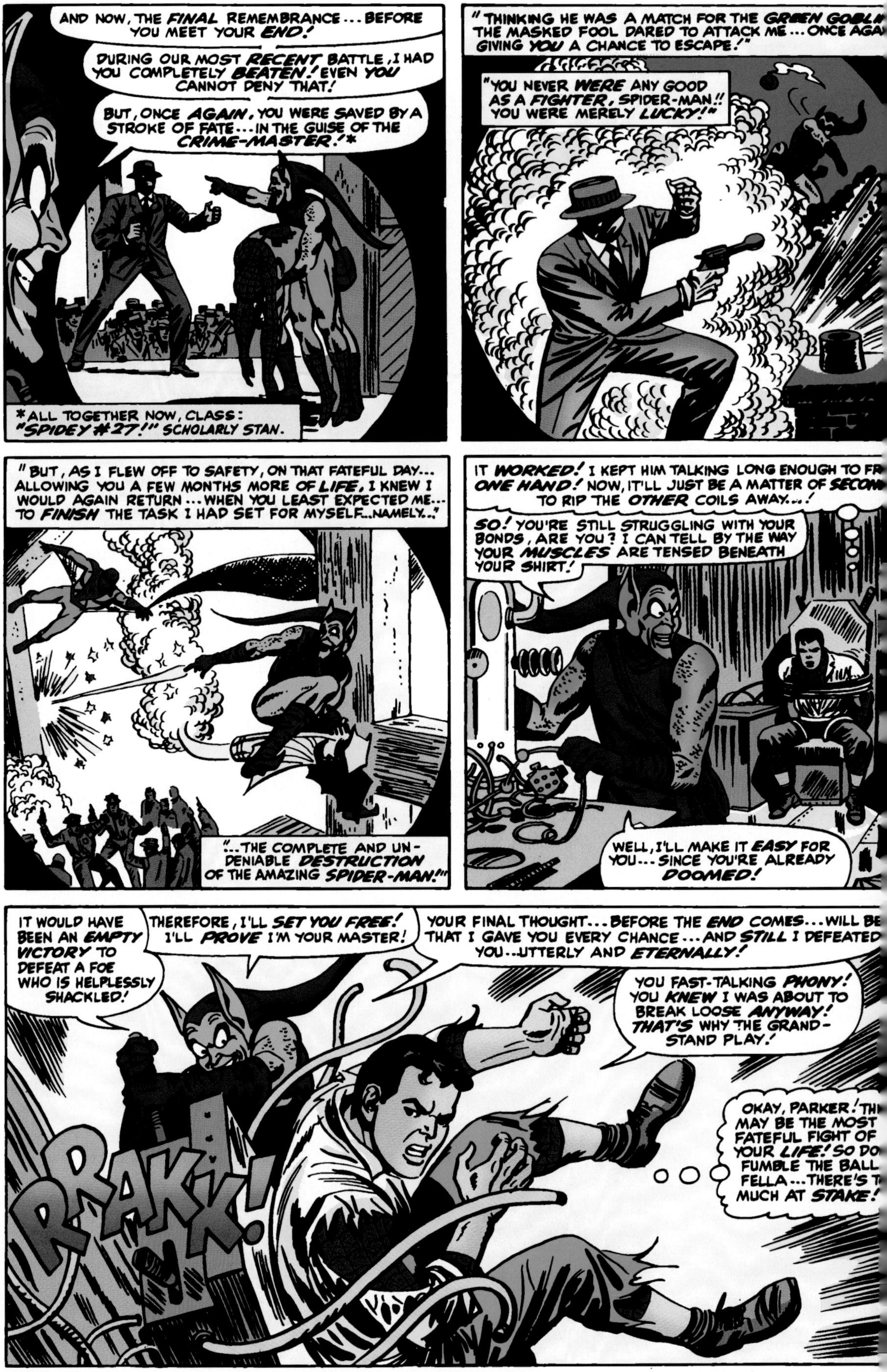
AND NOW, THE FINAL REMEMBRANCE... BEFORE YOU MEET YOUR END!
DURING OUR MOST RECENT BATTLE, I HAD YOU COMPLETELY BEATEN! EVEN YOU CANNOT DENY THAT!
BUT, ONCE AGAIN, YOU WERE SAVED BY A STROKE OF FATE... IN THE GUISE OF THE CRIME-MASTER!*
*ALL TOGETHER NOW, CLASS: "SPIDEY #27!" SCHOLARLY STAN.
"THINKING HE WAS A MATCH FOR THE GREEN GOBLI THE MASKED FOOL DARED TO ATTACK ME... ONCE AGA GIVING YOU A CHANCE TO ESCAPE!"
"YOU NEVER WERE ANY GOOD AS A FIGHTER, SPIDER-MAN!! YOU WERE MERELY LUCKY!"
"BUT, AS I FLEW OFF TO SAFETY, ON THAT FATEFUL DAY... ALLOWING YOU A FEW MONTHS MORE OF LIFE, I KNEW I WOULD AGAIN RETURN... WHEN YOU LEAST EXPECTED ME... TO FINISH THE TASK I HAD SET FOR MYSELF...NAMELY..."
"...THE COMPLETE AND UNDENIABLE DESTRUCTION OF THE AMAZING SPIDER-MAN!"
IT WORKED! I KEPT HIM TALKING LONG ENOUGH TO FR ONE HAND! NOW, IT'LL JUST BE A MATTER OF SECON TO RIP THE OTHER COILS AWAY...!
SO! YOU'RE STILL STRUGGLING WITH YOUR BONDS, ARE YOU? I CAN TELL BY THE WAY YOUR MUSCLES ARE TENSED BENEATH YOUR SHIRT!
WELL, I'LL MAKE IT EASY FOR YOU... SINCE YOU'RE ALREADY DOOMED!
IT WOULD HAVE BEEN AN EMPTY VICTORY TO DEFEAT A FOE WHO IS HELPLESSLY SHACKLED!
THEREFORE, I'LL SET YOU FREE! I'LL PROVE I'M YOUR MASTER!
YOUR FINAL THOUGHT... BEFORE THE END COMES... WILL BE THAT I GAVE YOU EVERY CHANCE... AND STILL I DEFEATED YOU...UTTERLY AND ETERNALLY!
YOU FAST-TALKING PHONY! YOU KNEW I WAS ABOUT TO BREAK LOOSE ANYWAY! THAT'S WHY THE GRAND-STAND PLAY!
OKAY, PARKER! TH MAY BE THE MOST FATEFUL FIGHT OF YOUR LIFE! SO DO FUMBLE THE BALL FELLA... THERE'S T MUCH AT STAKE!
RAKK!

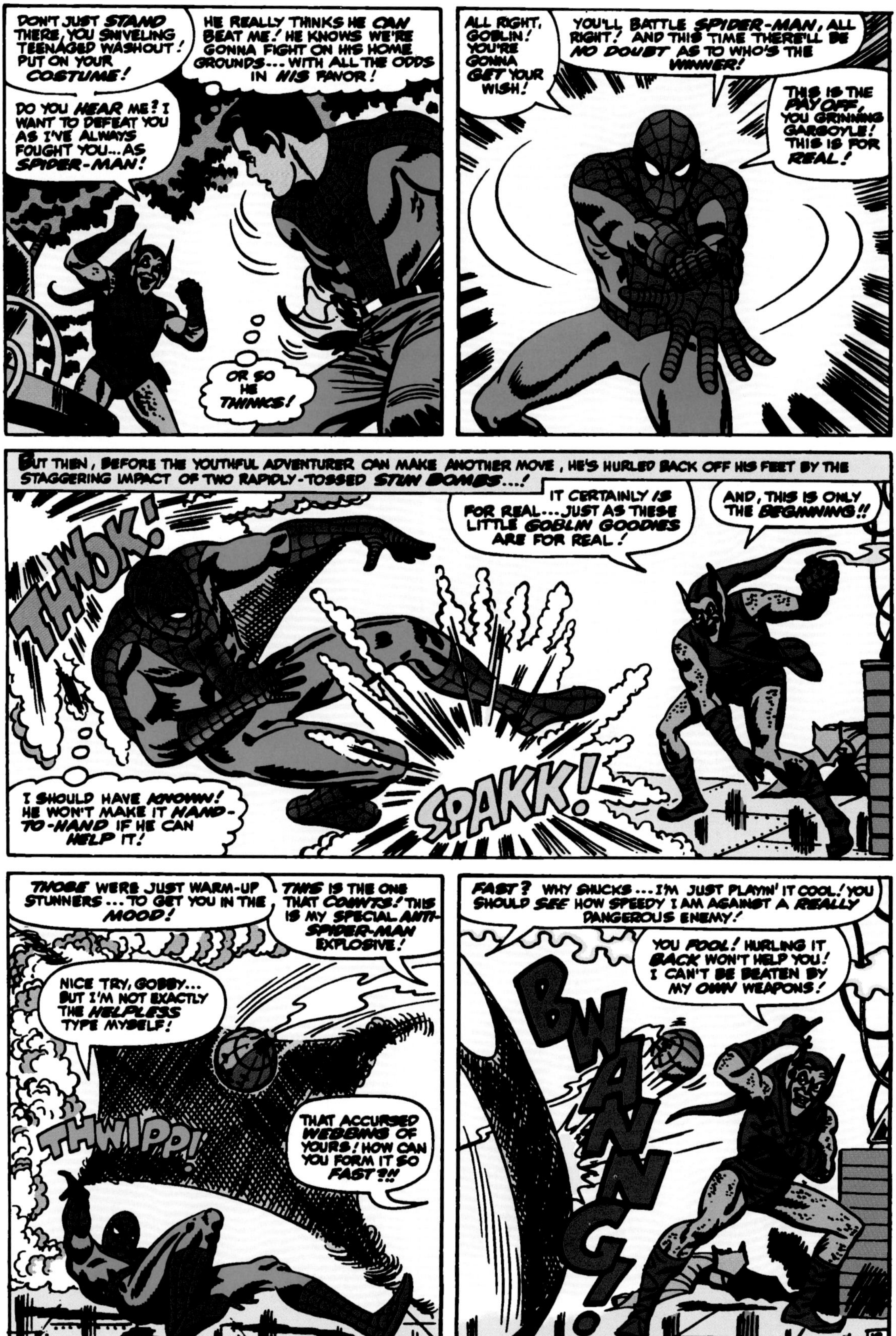
DON'T JUST STAND THERE, YOU SNIVELING TEENAGED WASHOUT! PUT ON YOUR COSTUME!
HE REALLY THINKS HE CAN BEAT ME! HE KNOWS WE'RE GONNA FIGHT ON HIS HOME GROUNDS... WITH ALL THE ODDS IN HIS FAVOR!
DO YOU HEAR ME? I WANT TO DEFEAT YOU AS I'VE ALWAYS FOUGHT YOU... AS SPIDER-MAN!
OR SO HE THINKS!
ALL RIGHT, GOBLIN! YOU'RE GONNA GET YOUR WISH!
YOU'LL BATTLE SPIDER-MAN, ALL RIGHT! AND THIS TIME THERE'LL BE NO DOUBT AS TO WHO'S THE WINNER!
THIS IS THE PAYOFF, YOU GRINNING GARGOYLE! THIS IS FOR REAL!
BUT THEN, BEFORE THE YOUTHFUL ADVENTURER CAN MAKE ANOTHER MOVE, HE'S HURLED BACK OFF HIS FEET BY THE STAGGERING IMPACT OF TWO RAPIDLY-TOSSED STUN BOMBS...!
THWOK!
IT CERTAINLY IS FOR REAL... JUST AS THESE LITTLE GOBLIN GOODIES ARE FOR REAL!
AND, THIS IS ONLY THE BEGINNING!!
I SHOULD HAVE KNOWN! HE WON'T MAKE IT HAND-TO-HAND IF HE CAN HELP IT!
SPAKK!
THOSE WERE JUST WARM-UP STUNNERS... TO GET YOU IN THE MOOD!
THIS IS THE ONE THAT COUNTS! THIS IS MY SPECIAL ANTI-SPIDER-MAN EXPLOSIVE!
NICE TRY, GOBBY... BUT I'M NOT EXACTLY THE HELPLESS TYPE MYSELF!
THWIPP!
THAT ACCURSED WEBBING OF YOURS! HOW CAN YOU FORM IT SO FAST?!!
FAST? WHY SHUCKS... I'M JUST PLAYIN' IT COOL! YOU SHOULD SEE HOW SPEEDY I AM AGAINST A REALLY DANGEROUS ENEMY!
YOU FOOL! HURLING IT BACK WON'T HELP YOU! I CAN'T BE BEATEN BY MY OWN WEAPONS!
BWANNG!
12

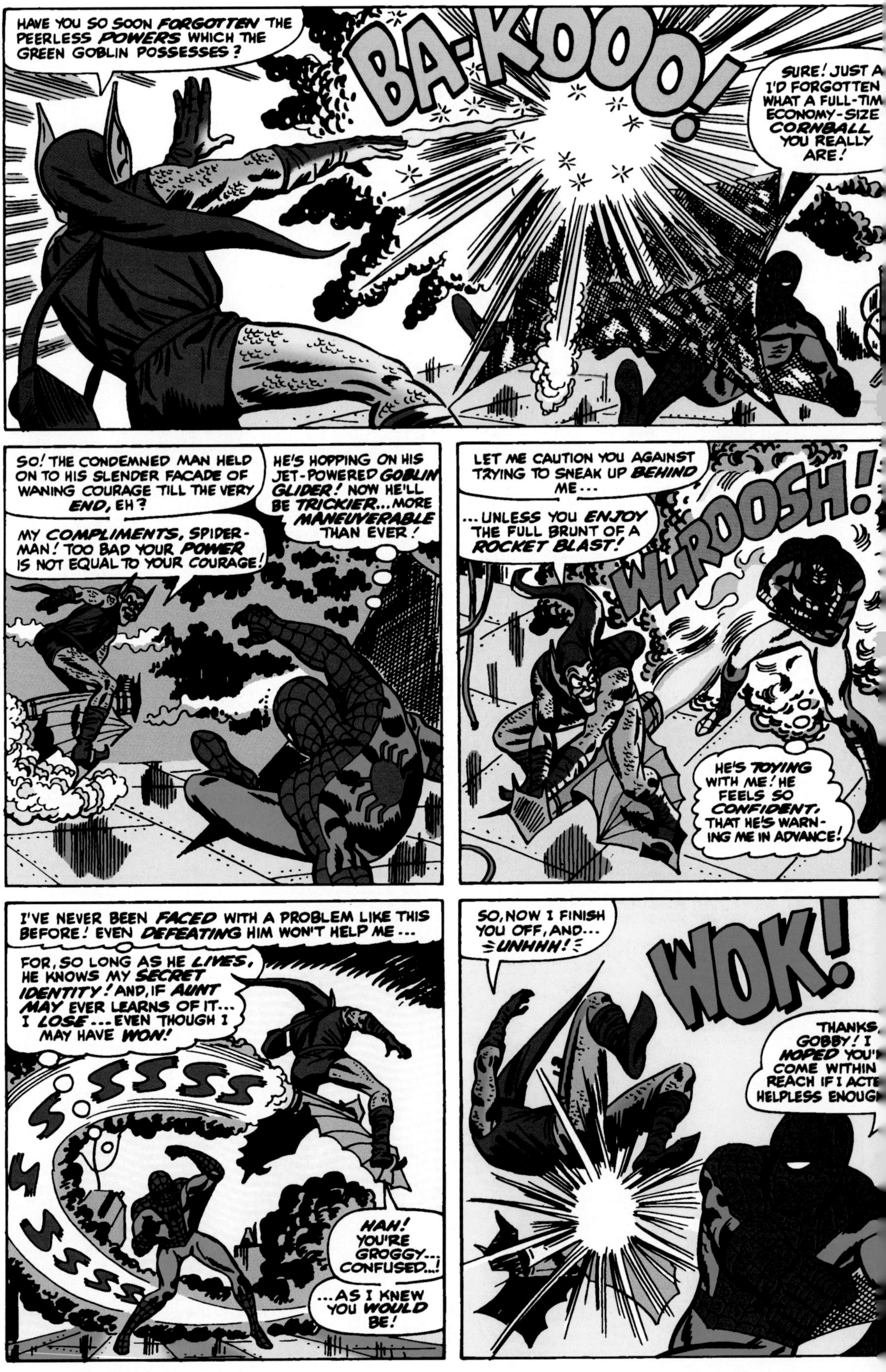
HAVE YOU SO SOON FORGOTTEN THE PEERLESS POWERS WHICH THE GREEN GOBLIN POSSESSES?
BA-KOOOO!
SURE! JUST A I'D FORGOTTEN WHAT A FULL-TIM ECONOMY-SIZE CORNBALL YOU REALLY ARE!
SO! THE CONDEMNED MAN HELD ON TO HIS SLENDER FACADE OF WANING COURAGE TILL THE VERY END, EH?
MY COMPLIMENTS, SPIDER-MAN! TOO BAD YOUR POWER IS NOT EQUAL TO YOUR COURAGE!
HE'S HOPPING ON HIS JET-POWERED GOBLIN GLIDER! NOW HE'LL BE TRICKIER...MORE MANEUVERABLE THAN EVER!
LET ME CAUTION YOU AGAINST TRYING TO SNEAK UP BEHIND ME...
...UNLESS YOU ENJOY THE FULL BRUNT OF A ROCKET BLAST!
WHROOSH!
HE'S TOYING WITH ME! HE FEELS SO CONFIDENT, THAT HE'S WARNING ME IN ADVANCE!
I'VE NEVER BEEN FACED WITH A PROBLEM LIKE THIS BEFORE! EVEN DEFEATING HIM WON'T HELP ME...
FOR, SO LONG AS HE LIVES, HE KNOWS MY SECRET IDENTITY! AND, IF AUNT MAY EVER LEARNS OF IT... I LOSE...EVEN THOUGH I MAY HAVE WON!
SSSSS
HAH! YOU'RE GROGGY... CONFUSED...!
...AS I KNEW YOU WOULD BE!
SO, NOW I FINISH YOU OFF, AND... UNHHH!
WOK!
THANKS GOBBY! I HOPED YOU' COME WITHIN REACH IF I ACTE HELPLESS ENOUG

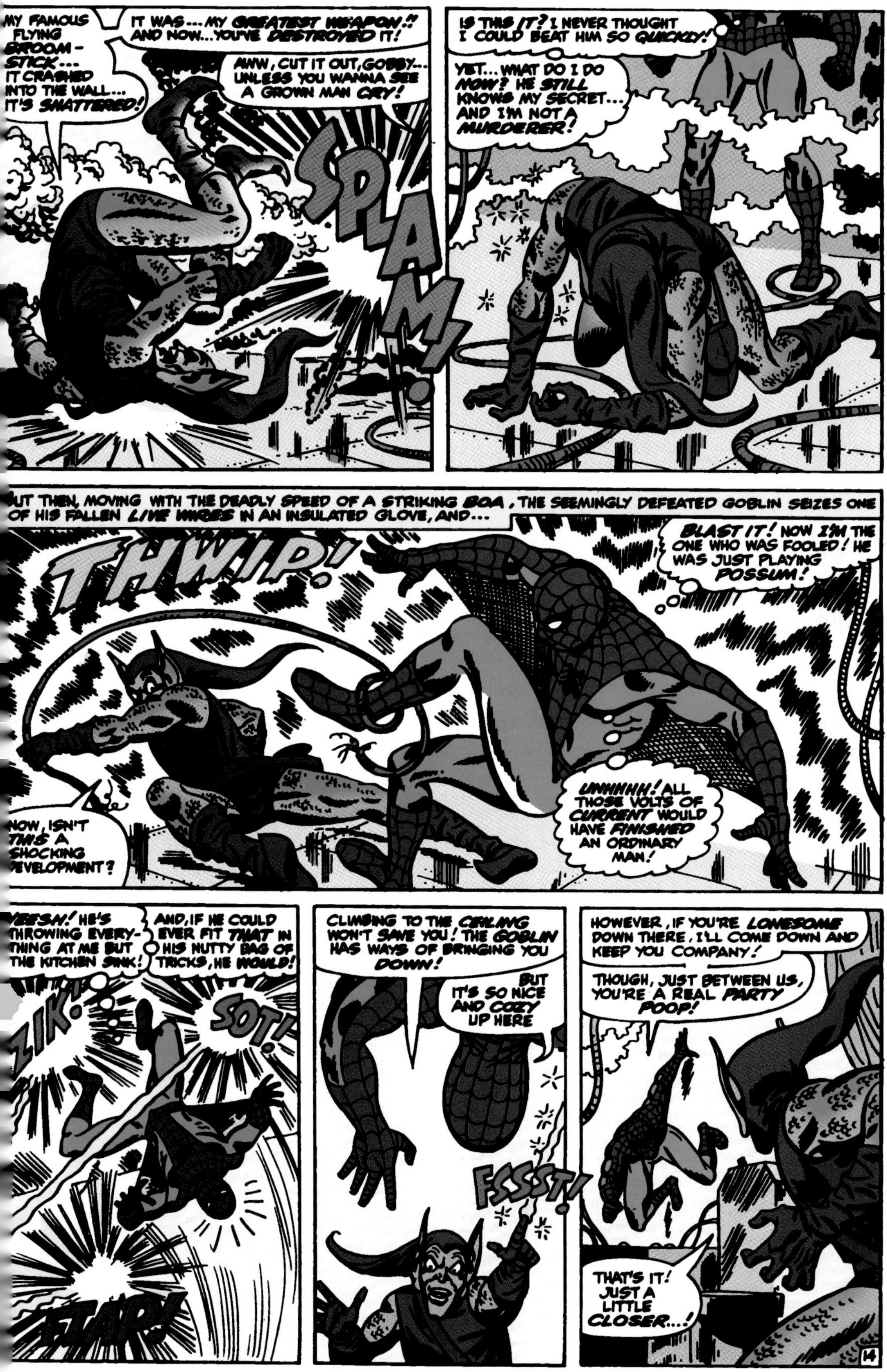
MY FAMOUS FLYING BROOM-STICK... IT CRASHED INTO THE WALL... IT'S SHATTERED!
IT WAS... MY GREATEST WEAPON!! AND NOW... YOU'VE DESTROYED IT!
AWW, CUT IT OUT, GOBBY... UNLESS YOU WANNA SEE A GROWN MAN CRY!
SPLAM!
IS THIS IT? I NEVER THOUGHT I COULD BEAT HIM SO QUICKLY!
YET... WHAT DO I DO NOW? HE STILL KNOWS MY SECRET... AND I'M NOT A MURDERER!
BUT THEN, MOVING WITH THE DEADLY SPEED OF A STRIKING BOA, THE SEEMINGLY DEFEATED GOBLIN SEIZES ONE OF HIS FALLEN LIVE WIRES IN AN INSULATED GLOVE, AND...
THWIP!
BLAST IT! NOW I'M THE ONE WHO WAS FOOLED! HE WAS JUST PLAYING POSSUM!
NOW, ISN'T THIS A SHOCKING DEVELOPMENT?
UNHHHH! ALL THOSE VOLTS OF CURRENT WOULD HAVE FINISHED AN ORDINARY MAN!
YEESH! HE'S THROWING EVERY-THING AT ME BUT THE KITCHEN SINK!
AND, IF HE COULD EVER FIT THAT IN HIS NUTTY BAG OF TRICKS, HE WOULD!
ZIK!
SOT!
FTAP!
CLIMBING TO THE CEILING WON'T SAVE YOU! THE GOBLIN HAS WAYS OF BRINGING YOU DOWN!
BUT IT'S SO NICE AND COZY UP HERE
FSSST!
HOWEVER, IF YOU'RE LONESOME DOWN THERE, I'LL COME DOWN AND KEEP YOU COMPANY!
THOUGH, JUST BETWEEN US, YOU'RE A REAL PARTY POOP!
THAT'S IT! JUST A LITTLE CLOSER...!
14

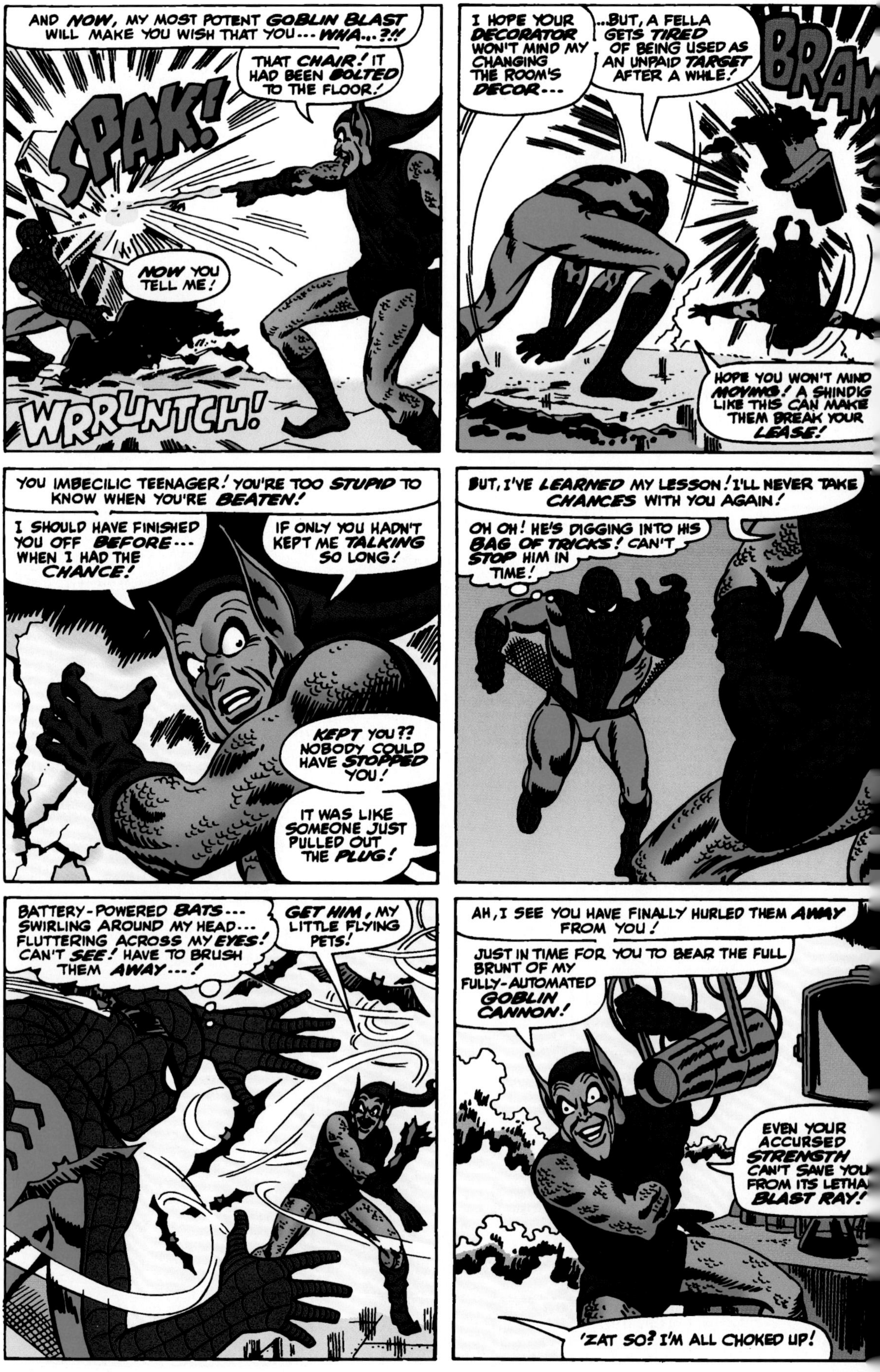
AND NOW, MY MOST POTENT GOBLIN BLAST WILL MAKE YOU WISH THAT YOU--- WHA...?!!
THAT CHAIR! IT HAD BEEN BOLTED TO THE FLOOR!
SPAK!
NOW YOU TELL ME!
WRRUNTCH!
I HOPE YOUR DECORATOR WON'T MIND MY CHANGING THE ROOM'S DECOR---
...BUT, A FELLA GETS TIRED OF BEING USED AS AN UNPAID TARGET AFTER A WHILE!
BRAM
HOPE YOU WON'T MIND MOVING! A SHINDIG LIKE THIS CAN MAKE THEM BREAK YOUR LEASE!
YOU IMBECILIC TEENAGER! YOU'RE TOO STUPID TO KNOW WHEN YOU'RE BEATEN!
I SHOULD HAVE FINISHED YOU OFF BEFORE--- WHEN I HAD THE CHANCE!
IF ONLY YOU HADN'T KEPT ME TALKING SO LONG!
KEPT YOU?? NOBODY COULD HAVE STOPPED YOU!
IT WAS LIKE SOMEONE JUST PULLED OUT THE PLUG!
BUT, I'VE LEARNED MY LESSON! I'LL NEVER TAKE CHANCES WITH YOU AGAIN!
OH OH! HE'S DIGGING INTO HIS BAG OF TRICKS! CAN'T STOP HIM IN TIME!
BATTERY-POWERED BATS--- SWIRLING AROUND MY HEAD--- FLUTTERING ACROSS MY EYES! CAN'T SEE! HAVE TO BRUSH THEM AWAY---!
GET HIM, MY LITTLE FLYING PETS!
AH, I SEE YOU HAVE FINALLY HURLED THEM AWAY FROM YOU!
JUST IN TIME FOR YOU TO BEAR THE FULL BRUNT OF MY FULLY-AUTOMATED GOBLIN CANNON!
EVEN YOUR ACCURSED STRENGTH CAN'T SAVE YOU FROM ITS LETHA BLAST RAY!
'ZAT SO? I'M ALL CHOKED UP!

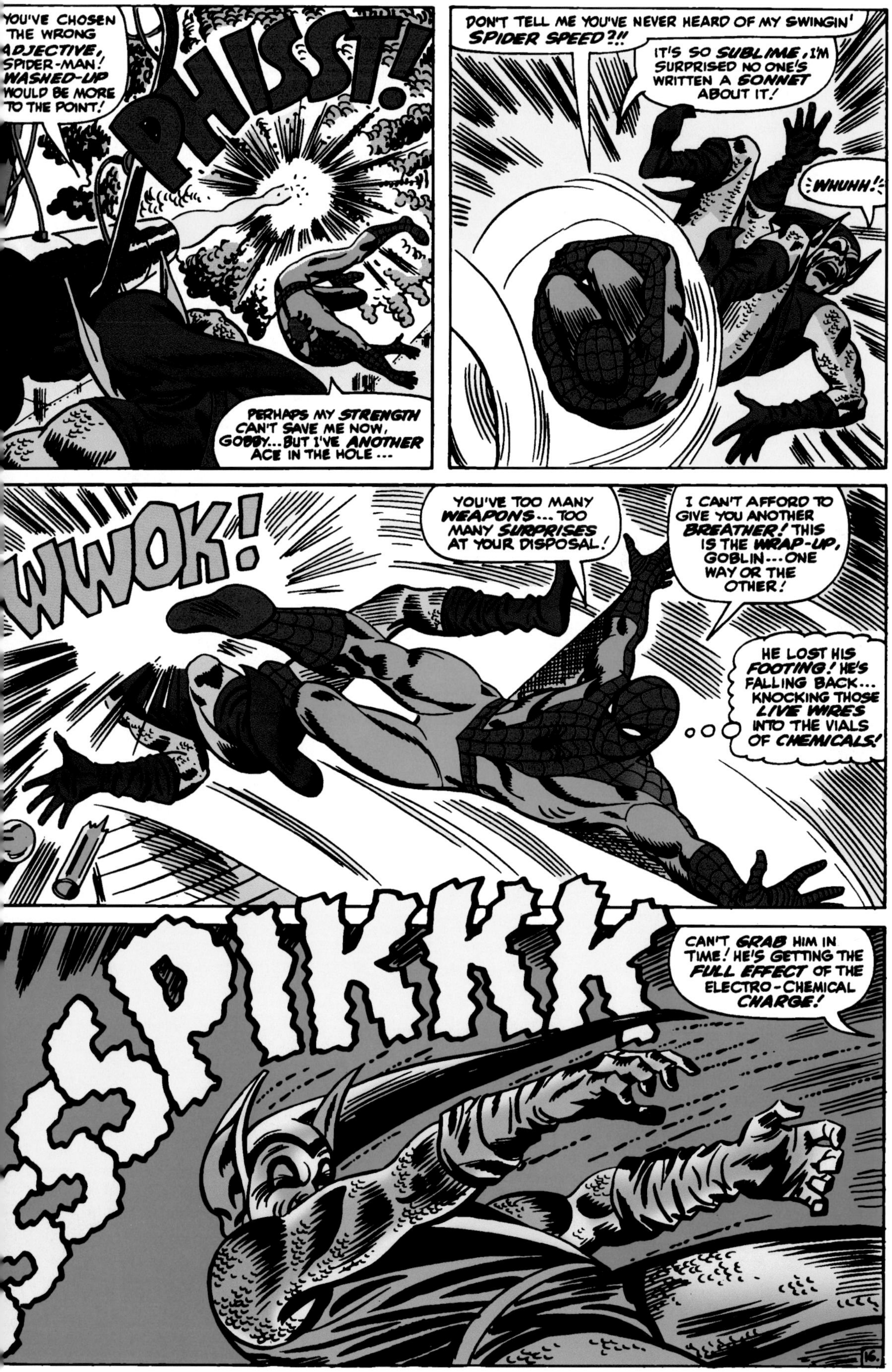

YOU'VE CHOSEN THE WRONG ADJECTIVE, SPIDER-MAN! WASHED-UP WOULD BE MORE TO THE POINT!
PHISST!
PERHAPS MY STRENGTH CAN'T SAVE ME NOW, GOBBY... BUT I'VE ANOTHER ACE IN THE HOLE...
DON'T TELL ME YOU'VE NEVER HEARD OF MY SWINGIN' SPIDER SPEED?!!
IT'S SO SUBLIME, I'M SURPRISED NO ONE'S WRITTEN A SONNET ABOUT IT!
WHUHH!
WWOK!
YOU'VE TOO MANY WEAPONS... TOO MANY SURPRISES AT YOUR DISPOSAL!
I CAN'T AFFORD TO GIVE YOU ANOTHER BREATHER! THIS IS THE WRAP-UP, GOBLIN... ONE WAY OR THE OTHER!
HE LOST HIS FOOTING! HE'S FALLING BACK... KNOCKING THOSE LIVE WIRES INTO THE VIALS OF CHEMICALS!
SSPIKKK
CAN'T GRAB HIM IN TIME! HE'S GETTING THE FULL EFFECT OF THE ELECTRO-CHEMICAL CHARGE!
16.

IT'S *OVER!* BUT HE ISN'T *MOVING!*

IS HE TRYING ANOTHER *TRICK?* NO...IT *CAN'T BE!* I *SAW* WHAT HAPPENED! *NOBODY* COULD FAKE SOMETHING LIKE *THAT!*

THERE'S ONLY *ONE* THING I HAVE TO FIND OUT...IS HE STILL *ALIVE?!*

I FEEL A *PULSE!* HE'S STILL *BREATHING!* THANK HEAVEN I DIDN'T *KILL* HIM!

BUT....IT'S THE ONE RESULT I *FEARED!* I'VE CONCLUSIVELY *DEFEATED* HIM... YET, HOW CAN I PREVENT HIM FROM BETRAYING MY *SECRET* AFTER I'VE TURNED HIM OVER TO THE *POLICE??*

HE'S STARTI... TO *SPEAK!* HE'S MUMBLING A NAME...

HARRY... MY SON... HARRY...!

YOU... *YOU'RE* NOT MY BOY! WHERE *IS* HARRY? WHO ARE *YOU?*

HE DOESN'T *RECOGNIZE* ME! HIS *MEMORY'S* GONE! OR....*IS* IT?

IT'S NOT HARD TO FAKE AMNESIA! THE GOBLIN IS CAPABLE OF *ANYTHING!*

AND YET...

HE COULDN'T FOOL MY *SPIDER SENSE!* IT WOULD *TINGLE* IF I WERE STILL IN ANY DANGER!

BUT I DON'T FEEL A *THING!* HE REALLY *DOESN'T* KNOW ME! HE DOESN'T EVEN REMEMBER OUR *FIGHT!* THE SUDDEN, SAVAGE IMPACT OF HIS *SMACK* HAS ACTUALLY AFFECTED HIS *MIND!*

THIS MEANS... THERE'S STILL *HOPE* FOR ME! AND... PERHAPS EVEN FOR *HIM!*

WHY AM I WEARING THIS STRANGE *COSTUME?* WHERE AM I? I...I MUST SEE MY *SON!* I HAVE TO *HELP* HIM WITH HIS *BIO...!*

IT'S *INCREDIBLE!* HE THINKS HARRY IS STILL IN *HIGH SCHOOL!* HIS MEMORY OF THE LAST FEW YEARS IS COMPLETELY *GONE!*

HE HAS *NO* KNOWLEDGE OF BEING THE *GREEN GOBLIN!*

ANYONE *IN* THERE? *OPEN UP!* THE PLACE IS *SMOKIN*... WE'RE GONNA *BREAK DOWN* THE DOOR!

THE *FIRE DEPARTMENT!* I'VE ONLY GOT *SECONDS* TO ACT!

PERHAPS I'VE NO *RIGHT* TO BE JUDGE AND JURY... BUT, WHY SHOULD HE BE PUNISHED FOR SOMETHING THAT HAPPENED WHEN HE WASN'T REALLY *HIMSELF*... SOMETHING HE CAN'T EVEN *REMEMBER* NOW?

AND THERE'S *HARRY* TO THINK OF! IT WOULD *BREAK* HIS HEART!

IF I CAN JUST CHANGE HIS *CLOTHES* FAST ENOUGH...!

STAND ASID... I'LL SHOOT T... LOCK OFF! IT'LL BE *FASTER!*

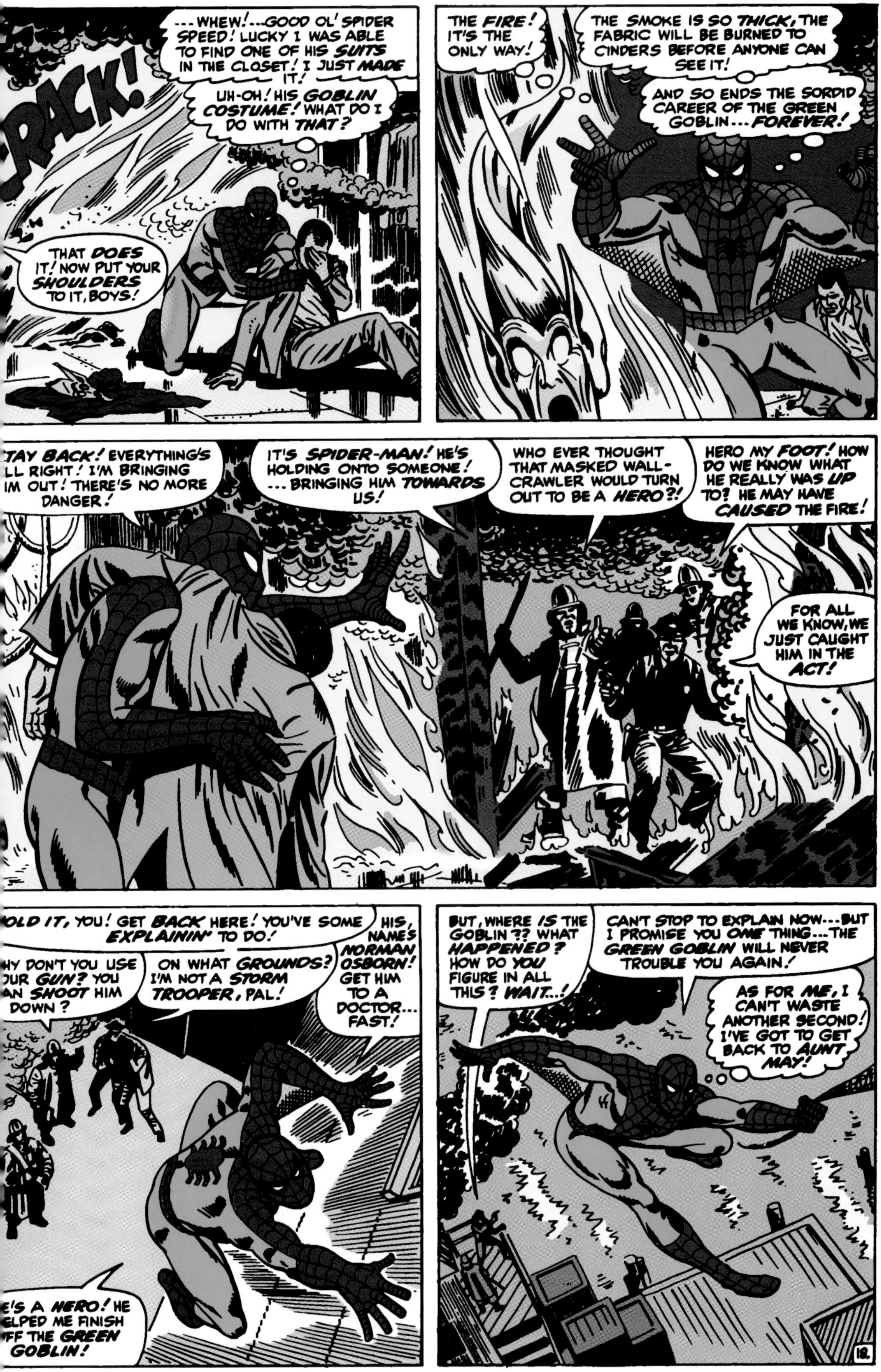
...WHEW!...GOOD OL' SPIDER SPEED! LUCKY I WAS ABLE TO FIND ONE OF HIS SUITS IN THE CLOSET! I JUST MADE IT!
UH-OH! HIS GOBLIN COSTUME! WHAT DO I DO WITH THAT?
CRACK!
THAT DOES IT! NOW PUT YOUR SHOULDERS TO IT, BOYS!
THE FIRE! IT'S THE ONLY WAY!
THE SMOKE IS SO THICK, THE FABRIC WILL BE BURNED TO CINDERS BEFORE ANYONE CAN SEE IT!
AND SO ENDS THE SORDID CAREER OF THE GREEN GOBLIN...FOREVER!
TAY BACK! EVERYTHING'S LL RIGHT! I'M BRINGING IM OUT! THERE'S NO MORE DANGER!
IT'S SPIDER-MAN! HE'S HOLDING ONTO SOMEONE! ...BRINGING HIM TOWARDS US!
WHO EVER THOUGHT THAT MASKED WALL-CRAWLER WOULD TURN OUT TO BE A HERO?!
HERO MY FOOT! HOW DO WE KNOW WHAT HE REALLY WAS UP TO? HE MAY HAVE CAUSED THE FIRE!
FOR ALL WE KNOW, WE JUST CAUGHT HIM IN THE ACT!
OLD IT, YOU! GET BACK HERE! YOU'VE SOME EXPLAININ' TO DO!
HY DON'T YOU USE OUR GUN? YOU AN SHOOT HIM DOWN?
ON WHAT GROUNDS? I'M NOT A STORM TROOPER, PAL!
HIS NAME'S NORMAN OSBORN! GET HIM TO A DOCTOR... FAST!
E'S A HERO! HE ELPED ME FINISH FF THE GREEN GOBLIN!
BUT, WHERE IS THE GOBLIN?? WHAT HAPPENED? HOW DO YOU FIGURE IN ALL THIS? WAIT...!
CAN'T STOP TO EXPLAIN NOW...BUT I PROMISE YOU ONE THING...THE GREEN GOBLIN WILL NEVER TROUBLE YOU AGAIN!
AS FOR ME, I CAN'T WASTE ANOTHER SECOND! I'VE GOT TO GET BACK TO AUNT MAY!
18.

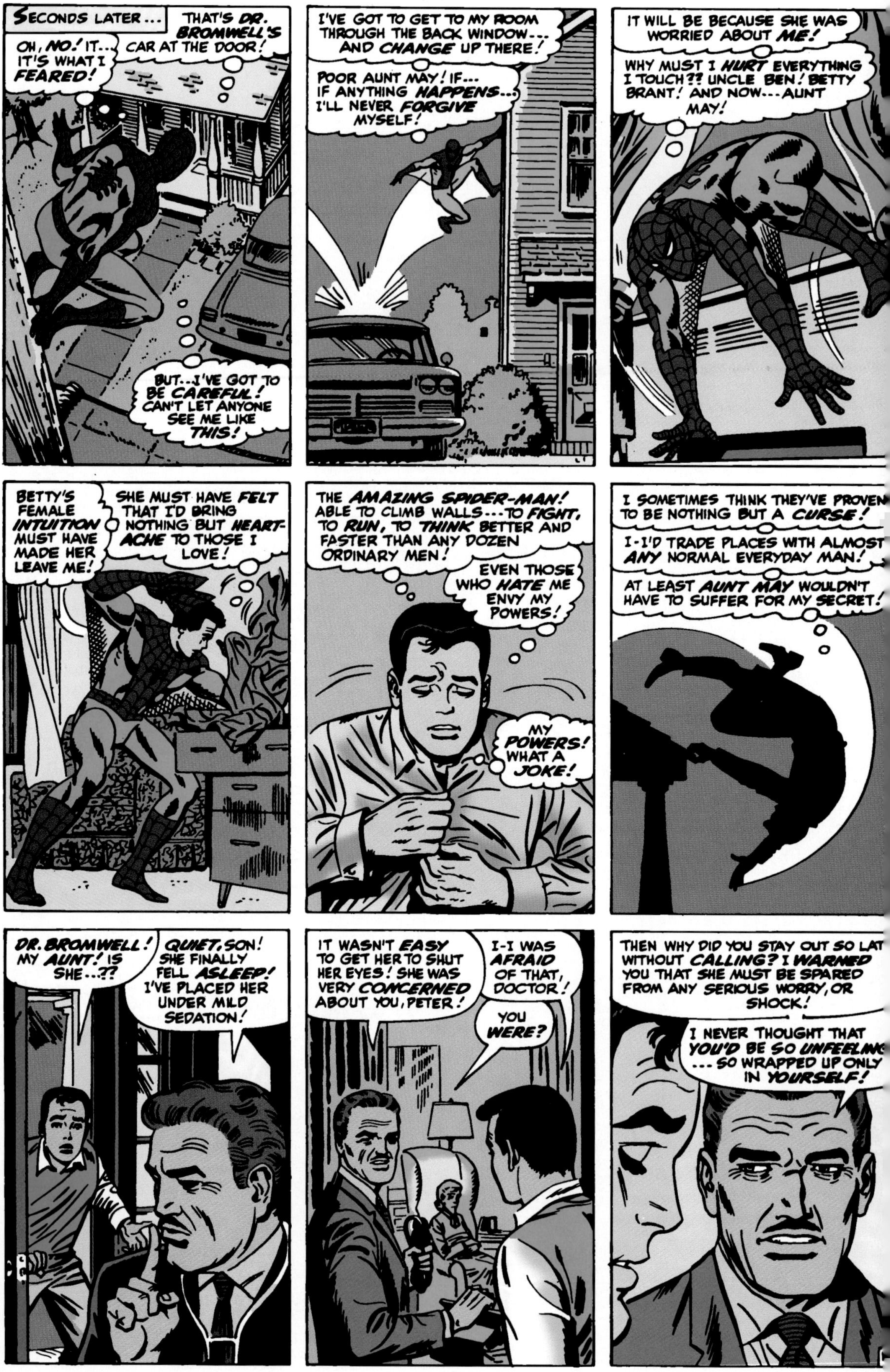
SECONDS LATER...
THAT'S DR. BROMWELL'S CAR AT THE DOOR!
OH, NO! IT... IT'S WHAT I FEARED!
BUT...I'VE GOT TO BE CAREFUL! CAN'T LET ANYONE SEE ME LIKE THIS!
I'VE GOT TO GET TO MY ROOM THROUGH THE BACK WINDOW... AND CHANGE UP THERE!
POOR AUNT MAY! IF... IF ANYTHING HAPPENS... I'LL NEVER FORGIVE MYSELF!
IT WILL BE BECAUSE SHE WAS WORRIED ABOUT ME!
WHY MUST I HURT EVERYTHING I TOUCH?? UNCLE BEN! BETTY BRANT! AND NOW... AUNT MAY!
BETTY'S FEMALE INTUITION MUST HAVE MADE HER LEAVE ME!
SHE MUST HAVE FELT THAT I'D BRING NOTHING BUT HEART-ACHE TO THOSE I LOVE!
THE AMAZING SPIDER-MAN! ABLE TO CLIMB WALLS... TO FIGHT, TO RUN, TO THINK BETTER AND FASTER THAN ANY DOZEN ORDINARY MEN!
EVEN THOSE WHO HATE ME ENVY MY POWERS!
MY POWERS! WHAT A JOKE!
I SOMETIMES THINK THEY'VE PROVEN TO BE NOTHING BUT A CURSE!
I-I'D TRADE PLACES WITH ALMOST ANY NORMAL EVERYDAY MAN!
AT LEAST AUNT MAY WOULDN'T HAVE TO SUFFER FOR MY SECRET!
DR. BROMWELL! MY AUNT! IS SHE...??
QUIET, SON! SHE FINALLY FELL ASLEEP! I'VE PLACED HER UNDER MILD SEDATION!
IT WASN'T EASY TO GET HER TO SHUT HER EYES! SHE WAS VERY CONCERNED ABOUT YOU, PETER!
I-I WAS AFRAID OF THAT, DOCTOR!
YOU WERE?
THEN WHY DID YOU STAY OUT SO LAT WITHOUT CALLING? I WARNED YOU THAT SHE MUST BE SPARED FROM ANY SERIOUS WORRY, OR SHOCK!
I NEVER THOUGHT THAT YOU'D BE SO UNFEELING ... SO WRAPPED UP ONLY IN YOURSELF!

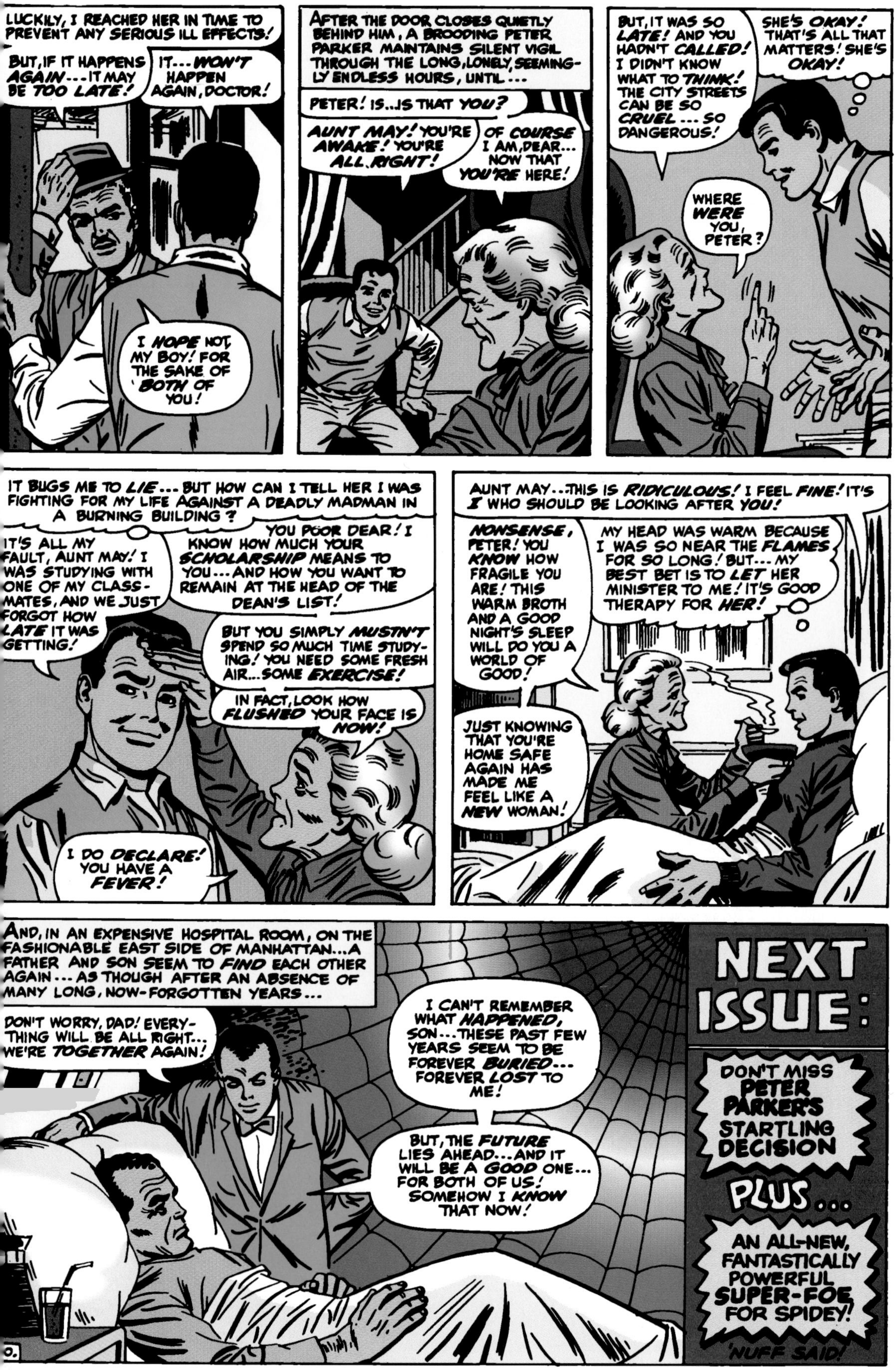

LUCKILY, I REACHED HER IN TIME TO PREVENT ANY SERIOUS ILL EFFECTS!
BUT, IF IT HAPPENS AGAIN... IT MAY BE TOO LATE!
IT... WON'T HAPPEN AGAIN, DOCTOR!
I HOPE NOT, MY BOY! FOR THE SAKE OF BOTH OF YOU!
AFTER THE DOOR CLOSES QUIETLY BEHIND HIM, A BROODING PETER PARKER MAINTAINS SILENT VIGIL THROUGH THE LONG, LONELY, SEEMINGLY ENDLESS HOURS, UNTIL...
PETER! IS.. IS THAT YOU?
AUNT MAY! YOU'RE AWAKE! YOU'RE ALL RIGHT!
OF COURSE I AM, DEAR... NOW THAT YOU'RE HERE!
BUT, IT WAS SO LATE! AND YOU HADN'T CALLED! I DIDN'T KNOW WHAT TO THINK! THE CITY STREETS CAN BE SO CRUEL... SO DANGEROUS!
SHE'S OKAY! THAT'S ALL THAT MATTERS! SHE'S OKAY!
WHERE WERE YOU, PETER?
IT BUGS ME TO LIE... BUT HOW CAN I TELL HER I WAS FIGHTING FOR MY LIFE AGAINST A DEADLY MADMAN IN A BURNING BUILDING?
IT'S ALL MY FAULT, AUNT MAY! I WAS STUDYING WITH ONE OF MY CLASSMATES, AND WE JUST FORGOT HOW LATE IT WAS GETTING!
YOU POOR DEAR! I KNOW HOW MUCH YOUR SCHOLARSHIP MEANS TO YOU... AND HOW YOU WANT TO REMAIN AT THE HEAD OF THE DEAN'S LIST!
BUT YOU SIMPLY MUSTN'T SPEND SO MUCH TIME STUDYING! YOU NEED SOME FRESH AIR... SOME EXERCISE!
IN FACT, LOOK HOW FLUSHED YOUR FACE IS NOW!
I DO DECLARE! YOU HAVE A FEVER!
AUNT MAY... THIS IS RIDICULOUS! I FEEL FINE! IT'S I WHO SHOULD BE LOOKING AFTER YOU!
NONSENSE, PETER! YOU KNOW HOW FRAGILE YOU ARE! THIS WARM BROTH AND A GOOD NIGHT'S SLEEP WILL DO YOU A WORLD OF GOOD!
MY HEAD WAS WARM BECAUSE I WAS SO NEAR THE FLAMES FOR SO LONG! BUT... MY BEST BET IS TO LET HER MINISTER TO ME! IT'S GOOD THERAPY FOR HER!
JUST KNOWING THAT YOU'RE HOME SAFE AGAIN HAS MADE ME FEEL LIKE A NEW WOMAN!
AND, IN AN EXPENSIVE HOSPITAL ROOM, ON THE FASHIONABLE EAST SIDE OF MANHATTAN... A FATHER AND SON SEEM TO FIND EACH OTHER AGAIN... AS THOUGH AFTER AN ABSENCE OF MANY LONG, NOW-FORGOTTEN YEARS...
DON'T WORRY, DAD! EVERYTHING WILL BE ALL RIGHT... WE'RE TOGETHER AGAIN!
I CAN'T REMEMBER WHAT HAPPENED, SON... THESE PAST FEW YEARS SEEM TO BE FOREVER BURIED... FOREVER LOST TO ME!
BUT, THE FUTURE LIES AHEAD... AND IT WILL BE A GOOD ONE... FOR BOTH OF US! SOMEHOW I KNOW THAT NOW!
NEXT ISSUE:
DON'T MISS PETER PARKER'S STARTLING DECISION
PLUS...
AN ALL-NEW, FANTASTICALLY POWERFUL SUPER-FOE FOR SPIDEY!
'NUFF SAID!

amazing spider-man #41

the AMAZING SPIDER-MAN
APPROVED BY THE COMICS CODE AUTHORITY
MARVEL COMICS GROUP
IND.
12¢ 41 OCT
"THE HORNS OF THE RHINO!"

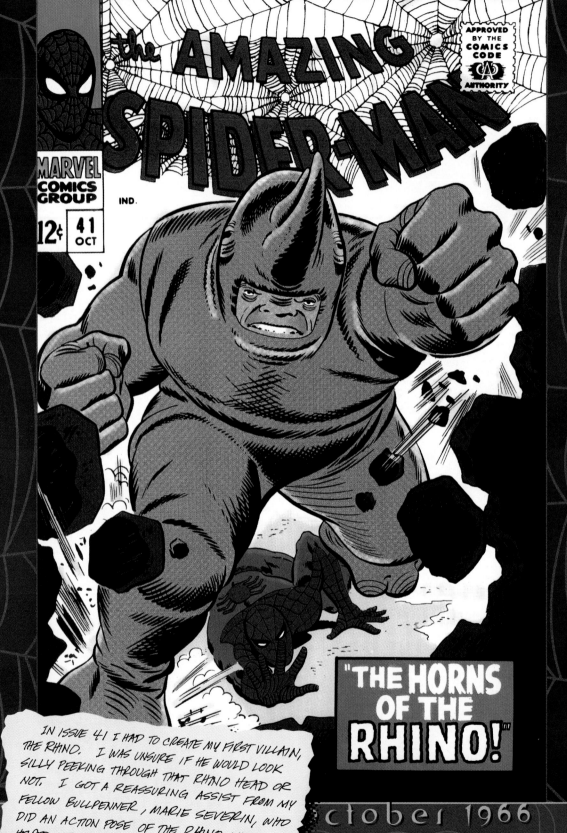

IN ISSUE 41 I HAD TO CREATE MY FIRST VILLAIN, THE RHINO. I WAS UNSURE IF HE WOULD LOOK SILLY PEEKING THROUGH THAT RHINO HEAD OR NOT. I GOT A REASSURING ASSIST FROM MY FELLOW BULLPENNER, MARIE SEVERIN, WHO DID AN ACTION POSE OF THE RHINO WHICH HELPED ME BELIEVE IN THE CHARACTER.

october 1966

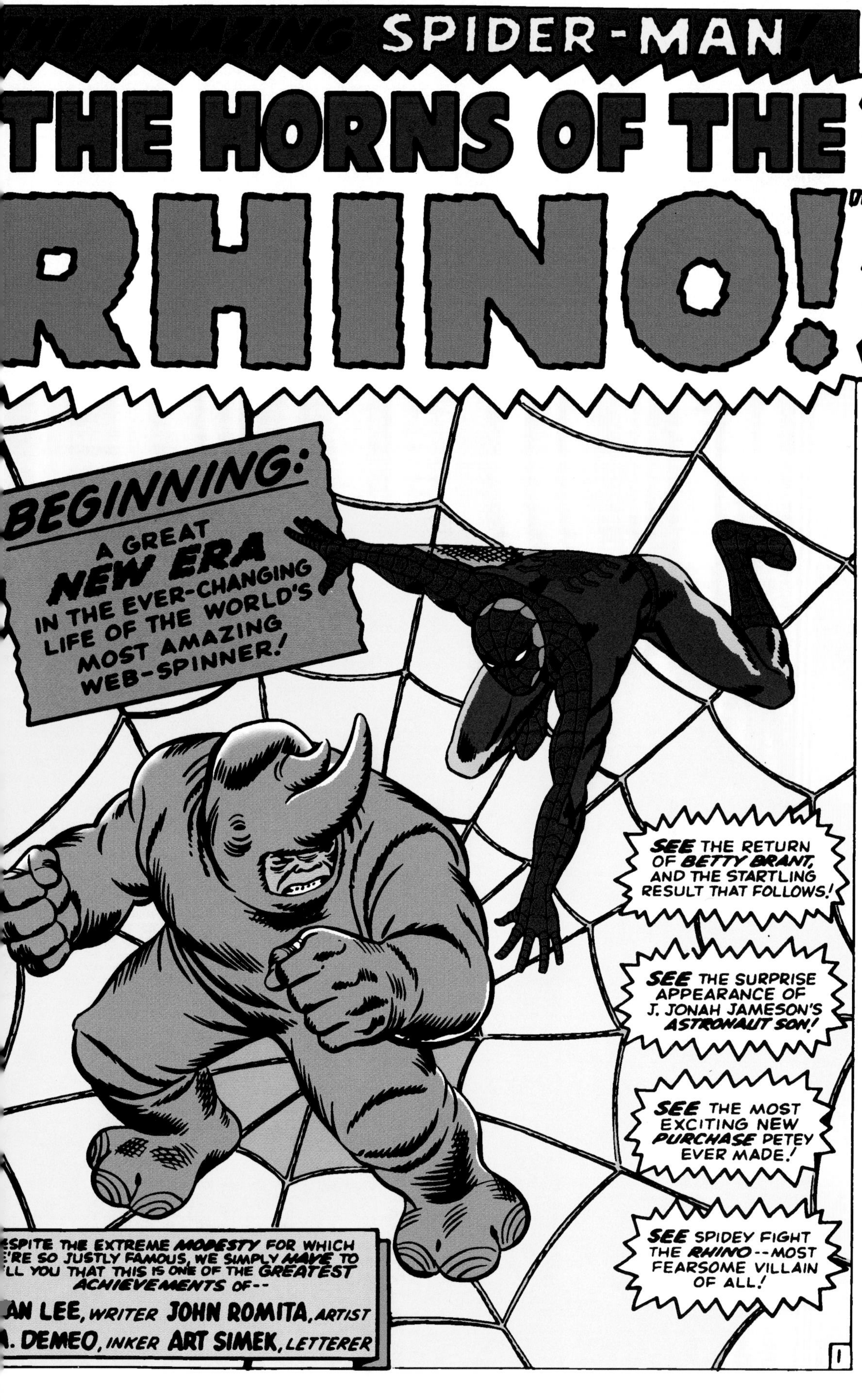

SPIDER-MAN
"THE HORNS OF THE RHINO!"
BEGINNING: A GREAT NEW ERA IN THE EVER-CHANGING LIFE OF THE WORLD'S MOST AMAZING WEB-SPINNER!
SEE THE RETURN OF BETTY BRANT, AND THE STARTLING RESULT THAT FOLLOWS!
SEE THE SURPRISE APPEARANCE OF J. JONAH JAMESON'S ASTRONAUT SON!
SEE THE MOST EXCITING NEW PURCHASE PETEY EVER MADE!
SEE SPIDEY FIGHT THE RHINO--MOST FEARSOME VILLAIN OF ALL!
ESPITE THE EXTREME MODESTY FOR WHICH 'RE SO JUSTLY FAMOUS, WE SIMPLY HAVE TO LL YOU THAT THIS IS ONE OF THE GREATEST ACHIEVEMENTS OF--
AN LEE, WRITER JOHN ROMITA, ARTIST
. DEMEO, INKER ART SIMEK, LETTERER
1

MOST SUPER HERO THRILLERS OPEN WITH CONTRIVED *ACTION*, IN ORDER TO HOOK YOU! BUT *WE* KNOW YOU'LL HANG AROUND--AND, TO *PROVE* OUR FAITH IN YOU, LET'S VISIT AUNT MAY...

I'M SO GLAD YOU DROPPED IN, ANNA!

SO AM *I*, MAY DEAR! THERE'S NOTHING LIKE HAVING SOME TEA AND A *TALK* WITH A GOOD FRIEND!

BESIDES, I'VE BEEN WANTING TO *ASK* YOU SOMETHING...

NOW THAT MY NIECE, MARY JANE, TOOK AN APARTMENT OF HER OWN, WHY DON'T YOU *SELL* THIS HOUSE AND MOVE IN WITH ME?

IT WOULD MEAN SUCH A *SAVING* FOR YOU--AND WE'D BE *COMPANY* FOR EACH OTHER!

ANNA MAY WATSON! IF YOU AREN'T THE *DEAREST* THING!

THEN, YOU'LL *DO* IT?

I'D *LOVE* TO, DEAR--BUT I JU COULDN'T! THERE'D BE NO ON TO LOOK AFTER POOR *PETER*

BUT, MAY--HE'S ALMOST *TWENTY*--HE'S GOING TO *COLLEGE!*

HE EVEN EARNS A LIVING BY SELLING *NEWS PHOTOS!*

BUT I'M THE ONLY RELATIVE HE *HAS!* THE DEAR BOY IS SO *DEPENDENT* UPON ME!

YOU KNOW HOW FRAIL, AND *FRAGILE* HE IS! IF I WEREN'T AROUND TO BE SURE HE EATS A BALANCED DIET, AND WEARS *"ARM* CLOTHES, I DON'T KNOW *WHAT* WOULD HAPPEN!

I SUPPOSE YOU KNOW BEST, DEAR! WELL, THANK YOU FOR THE TEA, MAY... I'M AFRAID I MUST RUN ALONG NOW!

IF PETER PARKER WERE *MY* NEPHEW, I'D TRY TO MAKE HIM MORE *INDEPENDENT!*

BUT HE'S PROBABLY THE TYPE THAT *LIKES* TO BE MOLLY-CODDLED!

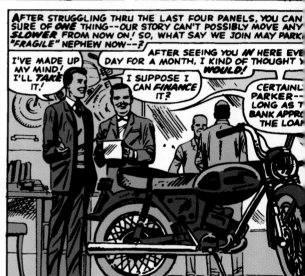

AFTER STRUGGLING THRU THE LAST FOUR PANELS, YOU CAN BE SURE OF *ONE* THING--OUR STORY CAN'T POSSIBLY MOVE ANY *SLOWER* FROM NOW ON! SO, WHAT SAY WE JOIN MAY PARK "FRAGILE" NEPHEW NOW--?

I'VE MADE UP MY MIND! I'LL *TAKE* IT!

AFTER SEEING YOU *IN* HERE EVE DAY FOR A MONTH, I KIND OF THOUGHT Y *WOULD!*

I SUPPOSE I CAN *FINANCE* IT?

CERTAINL PARKER-- LONG AS T BANK APPR THE LOAN

WE'LL NEED A *CREDIT REFERENCE*, OF COURSE!

OH, *THAT* WON'T BE ANY PROBLEM! I'VE BEEN SELLING PHOTOS TO *JONAH JAMESON* FOR YEARS! I'M SURE *HE'LL* VOUCH FOR ME!

WHY NOT CALL HIM *NOW*, WHILE I DRAW UP THE PAPERS?

SURE! I DON'T WANNA WASTE A *MINUTE!*

I WANT THOSE WHEELS SO BAD I CAN *TASTE* IT!

THUS, A FEW SECONDS LATER...

PARKER?? WHY IN BLAZES HAVEN'T YOU BROUGHT ME ANY *PHOTOS* THIS WEEK? IF YOU THINK--

WHAT?! YOU WANT TO BUY A *CYCLE*-- AND EXPECT *ME* TO RECOMMEND YOU FOR THE BANK LOAN?

YOU DIALED THE *WRONG* NUMBER, KID! TRY LOOKIN' UP *SANTA CLAUS!*

ANYTHING *WRONG,* DAD?

NAH! JUST SOME *PEST!*

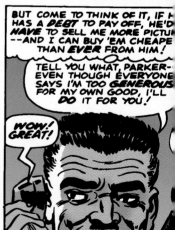

BUT COME TO THINK OF IT, IF H HAS A *DEBT* TO PAY OFF, HE'D *HAVE* TO SELL ME MORE PICTU --AND I CAN BUY 'EM CHEAPE THAN *EVER* FROM HIM!

TELL YOU WHAT, PARKER-- EVEN THOUGH EVERYONE SAYS I'M TOO *GENEROUS* FOR MY OWN GOOD, I'LL *DO* IT FOR YOU!

WOW! GREAT!

YEAH-- *CHORTLE-* GREAT!

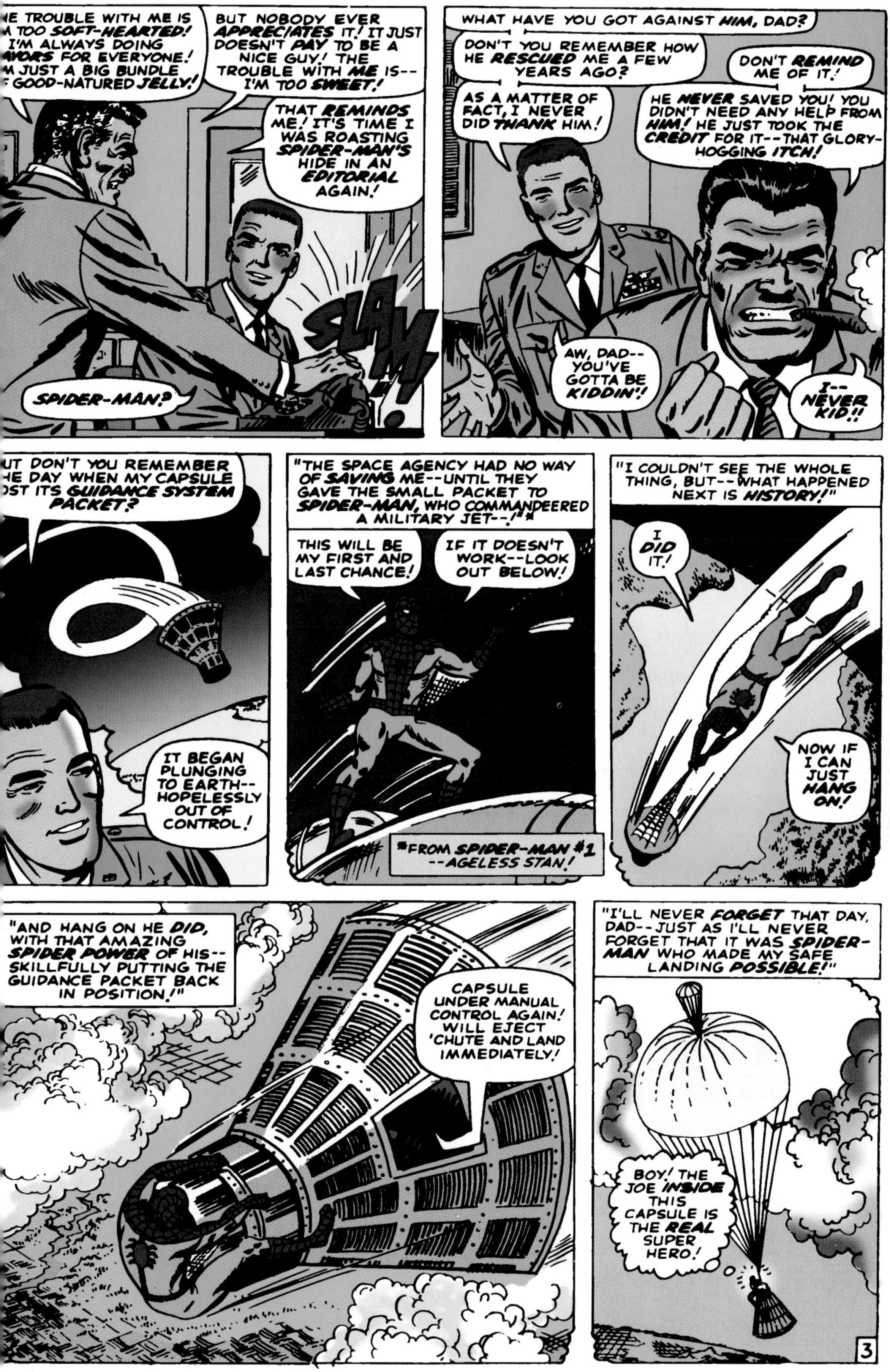
HE TROUBLE WITH ME IS M TOO SOFT-HEARTED! I'M ALWAYS DOING AVORS FOR EVERYONE! M JUST A BIG BUNDLE F GOOD-NATURED JELLY!
BUT NOBODY EVER APPRECIATES IT! IT JUST DOESN'T PAY TO BE A NICE GUY! THE TROUBLE WITH ME IS-- I'M TOO SWEET!
THAT REMINDS ME! IT'S TIME I WAS ROASTING SPIDER-MAN'S HIDE IN AN EDITORIAL AGAIN!
SLAM!
SPIDER-MAN?
WHAT HAVE YOU GOT AGAINST HIM, DAD?
DON'T YOU REMEMBER HOW HE RESCUED ME A FEW YEARS AGO?
AS A MATTER OF FACT, I NEVER DID THANK HIM!
DON'T REMIND ME OF IT!
HE NEVER SAVED YOU! YOU DIDN'T NEED ANY HELP FROM HIM! HE JUST TOOK THE CREDIT FOR IT--THAT GLORY-HOGGING ITCH!
AW, DAD-- YOU'VE GOTTA BE KIDDIN'!
I-- NEVER KID!!
UT DON'T YOU REMEMBER HE DAY WHEN MY CAPSULE OST ITS GUIDANCE SYSTEM PACKET?
IT BEGAN PLUNGING TO EARTH-- HOPELESSLY OUT OF CONTROL!
"THE SPACE AGENCY HAD NO WAY OF SAVING ME--UNTIL THEY GAVE THE SMALL PACKET TO SPIDER-MAN, WHO COMMANDEERED A MILITARY JET--!"*
THIS WILL BE MY FIRST AND LAST CHANCE!
IF IT DOESN'T WORK--LOOK OUT BELOW!
*FROM SPIDER-MAN #1 --AGELESS STAN!
"I COULDN'T SEE THE WHOLE THING, BUT--WHAT HAPPENED NEXT IS HISTORY!"
I DID IT!
NOW IF I CAN JUST HANG ON!
"AND HANG ON HE DID, WITH THAT AMAZING SPIDER POWER OF HIS--SKILLFULLY PUTTING THE GUIDANCE PACKET BACK IN POSITION!"
CAPSULE UNDER MANUAL CONTROL AGAIN! WILL EJECT 'CHUTE AND LAND IMMEDIATELY!
"I'LL NEVER FORGET THAT DAY, DAD--JUST AS I'LL NEVER FORGET THAT IT WAS SPIDER-MAN WHO MADE MY SAFE LANDING POSSIBLE!"
BOY! THE JOE INSIDE THIS CAPSULE IS THE REAL SUPER HERO!
3

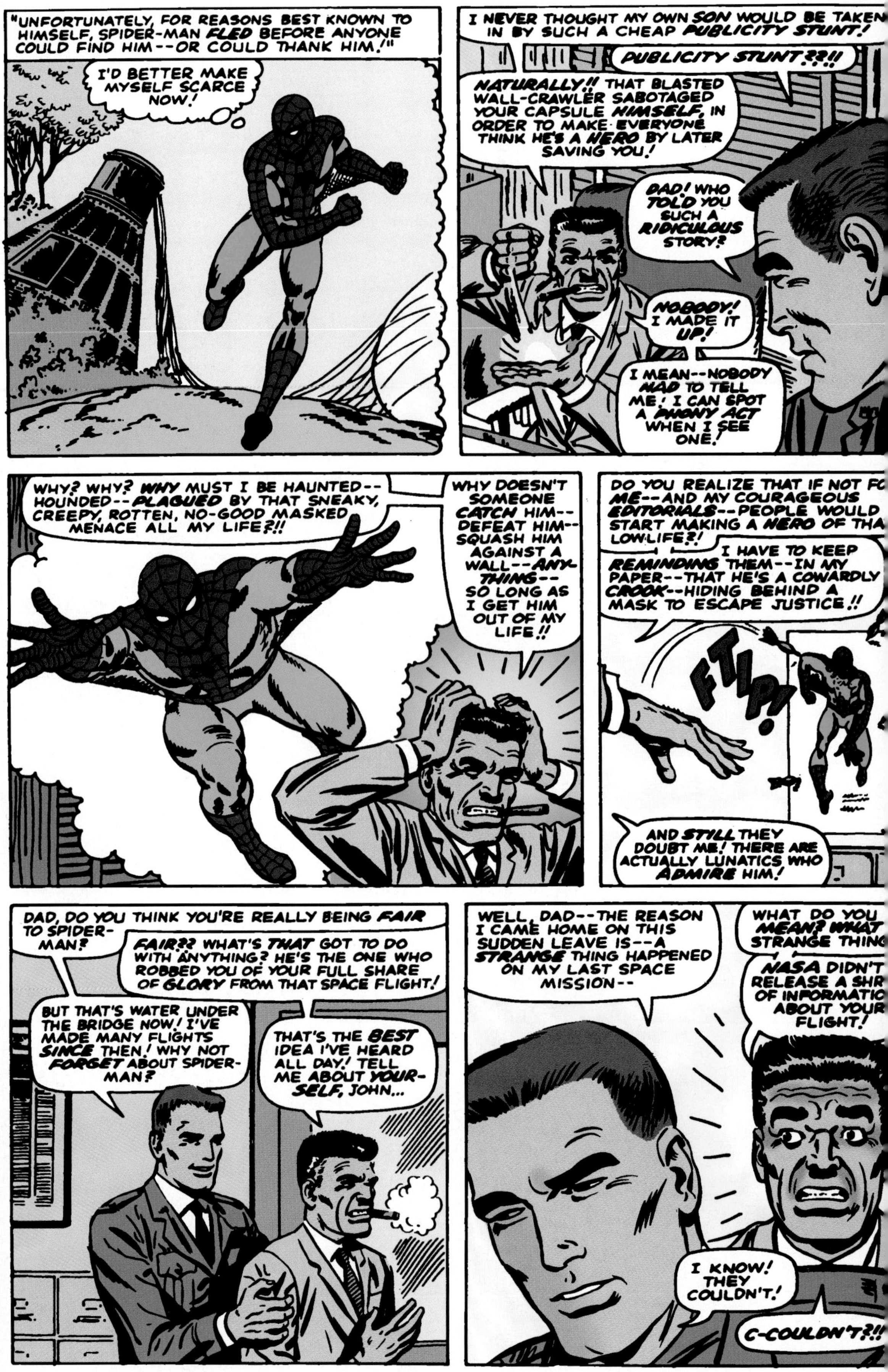
"UNFORTUNATELY, FOR REASONS BEST KNOWN TO HIMSELF, SPIDER-MAN FLED BEFORE ANYONE COULD FIND HIM--OR COULD THANK HIM!"
I'D BETTER MAKE MYSELF SCARCE NOW!
I NEVER THOUGHT MY OWN SON WOULD BE TAKEN IN BY SUCH A CHEAP PUBLICITY STUNT!
PUBLICITY STUNT??!!
NATURALLY!! THAT BLASTED WALL-CRAWLER SABOTAGED YOUR CAPSULE HIMSELF, IN ORDER TO MAKE EVERYONE THINK HE'S A HERO BY LATER SAVING YOU!
DAD! WHO TOLD YOU SUCH A RIDICULOUS STORY?
NOBODY! I MADE IT UP!
I MEAN--NOBODY HAD TO TELL ME! I CAN SPOT A PHONY ACT WHEN I SEE ONE!
WHY? WHY? WHY MUST I BE HAUNTED--HOUNDED--PLAGUED BY THAT SNEAKY, CREEPY, ROTTEN, NO-GOOD MASKED MENACE ALL MY LIFE?!!
WHY DOESN'T SOMEONE CATCH HIM--DEFEAT HIM--SQUASH HIM AGAINST A WALL--ANYTHING--SO LONG AS I GET HIM OUT OF MY LIFE!!
DO YOU REALIZE THAT IF NOT FO ME--AND MY COURAGEOUS EDITORIALS--PEOPLE WOULD START MAKING A HERO OF THA LOWLIFE?!
I HAVE TO KEEP REMINDING THEM--IN MY PAPER--THAT HE'S A COWARDLY CROOK--HIDING BEHIND A MASK TO ESCAPE JUSTICE!!
FTIP!
AND STILL THEY DOUBT ME! THERE ARE ACTUALLY LUNATICS WHO ADMIRE HIM!
DAD, DO YOU THINK YOU'RE REALLY BEING FAIR TO SPIDER-MAN?
FAIR?? WHAT'S THAT GOT TO DO WITH ANYTHING? HE'S THE ONE WHO ROBBED YOU OF YOUR FULL SHARE OF GLORY FROM THAT SPACE FLIGHT!
BUT THAT'S WATER UNDER THE BRIDGE NOW! I'VE MADE MANY FLIGHTS SINCE THEN! WHY NOT FORGET ABOUT SPIDER-MAN?
THAT'S THE BEST IDEA I'VE HEARD ALL DAY! TELL ME ABOUT YOURSELF, JOHN...
WELL, DAD--THE REASON I CAME HOME ON THIS SUDDEN LEAVE IS--A STRANGE THING HAPPENED ON MY LAST SPACE MISSION--
WHAT DO YOU MEAN? WHAT STRANGE THING
NASA DIDN'T RELEASE A SHR OF INFORMATIO ABOUT YOUR FLIGHT!
I KNOW! THEY COULDN'T!
C-COULDN'T?!!

EY HAD TO MAKE SURE THE
ACE SPORES WOULDN'T BE
HARMFUL TO EARTH, FIRST!

ACE
RES?
HAT
ACE
RES
!!

SINCE THE INFORMATION
HAS JUST BEEN
DECLASSIFIED, I CAN
TELL YOU NOW--!

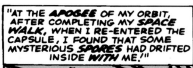

"AT THE APOGEE OF MY ORBIT,
AFTER COMPLETING MY SPACE
WALK, WHEN I RE-ENTERED THE
CAPSULE, I FOUND THAT SOME
MYSTERIOUS SPORES HAD DRIFTED
INSIDE WITH ME!"

"EVEN AFTER SPLASHDOWN,
THEY CLUNG TO MY SPACE
SUIT, THEN LATER TO MY BODY!"

THEY SEEM
HARMLESS
ENOUGH,
BUT--!

AS SUBJECTED TO INTENSIVE
TS FOR DAYS--AND EVERYTHING
EARED TO CHECK OUT A-OKAY!
SPORES THEMSELVES GREW
AKER AND WEAKER, AND FINALLY
FADED AWAY!"

CAN BE
LEASED
OW! THE
RES ARE
PLETELY
ONE!

BUT THEY MAY
HAVE HAD AN EFFECT
UPON HIM THAT WON'T
SHOW UP UNTIL
LATER!

HE MUST
BE KEPT UNDER
GUARD FOR
AT LEAST SIX
MONTHS!

CERTAIN NATIONS
WOULD GIVE ANY-
THING TO EXAMINE
HIM BEHIND THE
IRON CURTAIN!

"FROM THAT MOMENT ON, I'VE BEEN
UNDER CONTINUAL SURVEILLANCE!
ARMED AGENTS ACCOMPANY ME
EVERYWHERE!"

HOW LONG WILL
YOU FELLAS BE PLAYING NURSE-
MAID TO ME?

UNTIL WE CAN BE
ABSOLUTELY SURE
THOSE SPORES DIDN'T
AFFECT YOU IN ANY
WAY, COLONEL!

BECAUSE, IF
THEY DID,
YOU'D BE A
PRIZE CATCH
FOR ANY
HOSTILE
NATION ON
EARTH!

YOU SEE, DAD, THE SPACE AGENCY
MEDICS GAINED INVALUABLE
INFORMATION BY STUDYING THOSE
SPORES AND MY REACTIONS TO
THEM--INFORMATION THAT MAY
GIVE US THE BOOST WE NEED IN
THE SPACE RACE!

WHICH IS WHY THERE ARE
TWO AGENTS OUTSIDE THIS
DOOR RIGHT NOW--AND
ANOTHER TEAM READY TO
RELIEVE THEM EVERY
SIX HOURS!

, EVEN AS JONAH JAMESON IS STRUCK SPEECHLESS--FOR ONE OF THE FEW TIMES IN HIS LIFE--AN
ENT IS TRANSPIRING MANY MILES AWAY, AT OUR SOUTHERNMOST BORDER--AN EVENT WHICH IS DESTINED
SERIOUSLY AFFECT THE LIVES, AND THE SAFETY, OF OUR COLORFUL LITTLE CAST OF CHARACTERS--

AT LAST! AFTER ALL THE LONG
MONTHS OF WAITING--PREPARING--
COUNTING EVERY MINUTE AND
HOUR--IT'S FINALLY TIME--TIME
FOR THE RHINO TO STRIKE!!

HEY, SAM! WHAT IN THE NAME
OF CREATION DO YA CALL THAT?

I DUNNO!
BUT, WHAT-
EVER IT IS,
IT'S NOT
GETTING
PAST THIS
BORDER
CHECKPOINT
TILL WE
FIND OUT!

STOMP!

5

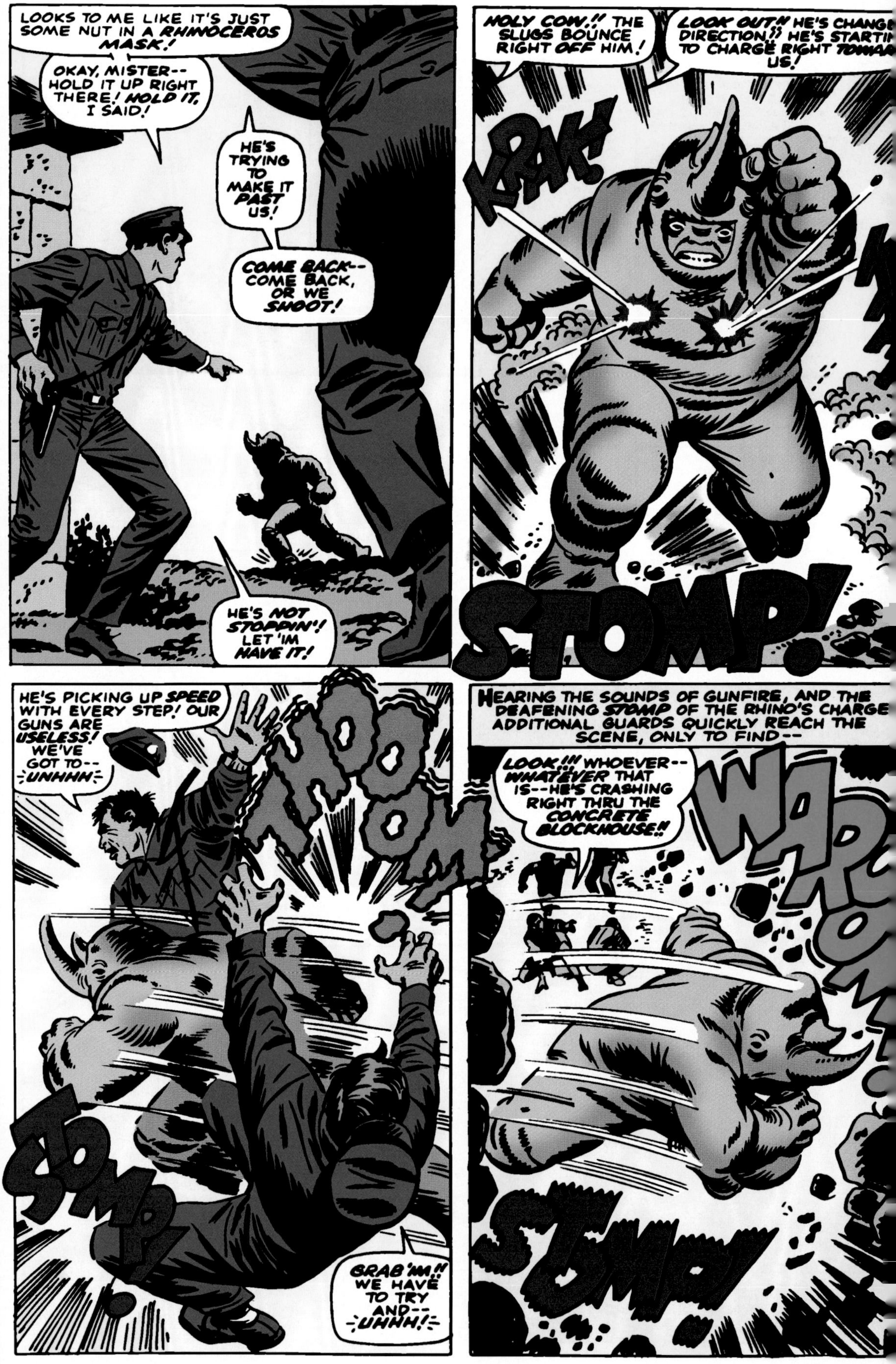

LOOKS TO ME LIKE IT'S JUST SOME NUT IN A RHINOCEROS MASK!
OKAY, MISTER-- HOLD IT UP RIGHT THERE! HOLD IT, I SAID!
HE'S TRYING TO MAKE IT PAST US!
COME BACK-- COME BACK, OR WE SHOOT!
HE'S NOT STOPPIN'! LET 'IM HAVE IT!
HOLY COW!! THE SLUGS BOUNCE RIGHT OFF HIM!
LOOK OUT!! HE'S CHANG DIRECTION!! HE'S STARTI TO CHARGE RIGHT TOWA US!
KRAK!
STOMP!
HE'S PICKING UP SPEED WITH EVERY STEP! OUR GUNS ARE USELESS! WE'VE GOT TO-- UNHHH!
WHOOOM
STOMP!
GRAB 'IM!! WE HAVE TO TRY AND-- UNHHH!
HEARING THE SOUNDS OF GUNFIRE, AND THE DEAFENING STOMP OF THE RHINO'S CHARGE, ADDITIONAL GUARDS QUICKLY REACH THE SCENE, ONLY TO FIND--
LOOK!!! WHOEVER-- WHATEVER THAT IS--HE'S CRASHING RIGHT THRU THE CONCRETE BLOCKHOUSE!!
STOMP!

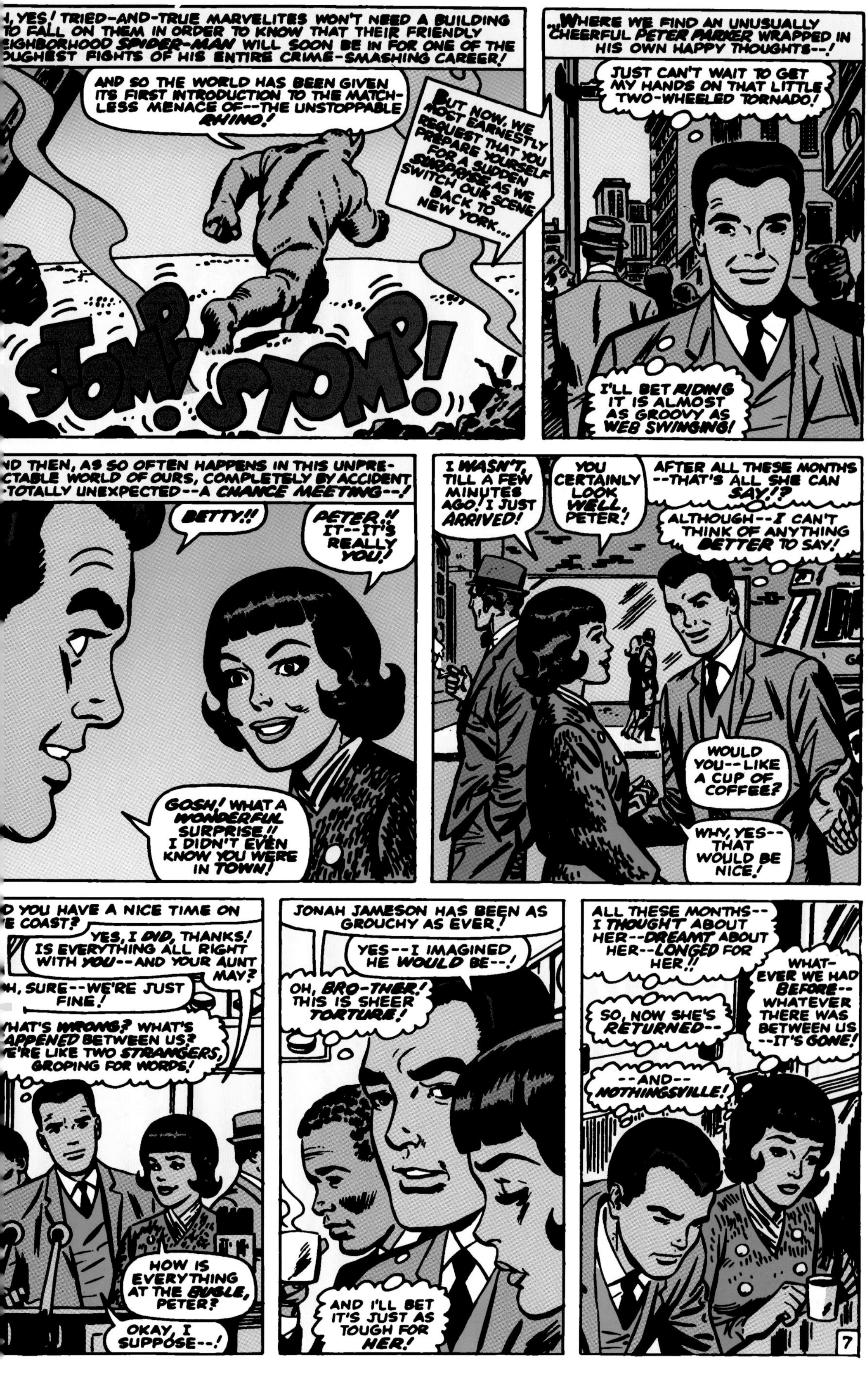
H, YES! TRIED-AND-TRUE MARVELITES WON'T NEED A BUILDING TO FALL ON THEM IN ORDER TO KNOW THAT THEIR FRIENDLY EIGHBORHOOD SPIDER-MAN WILL SOON BE IN FOR ONE OF THE OUGHEST FIGHTS OF HIS ENTIRE CRIME-SMASHING CAREER!
AND SO THE WORLD HAS BEEN GIVEN ITS FIRST INTRODUCTION TO THE MATCHLESS MENACE OF--THE UNSTOPPABLE RHINO!
BUT NOW, WE MOST EARNESTLY REQUEST THAT YOU PREPARE YOURSELF FOR A SUDDEN SURPRISE AS WE SWITCH OUR SCENE BACK TO NEW YORK...
STOMP! STOMP!
...WHERE WE FIND AN UNUSUALLY CHEERFUL PETER PARKER WRAPPED IN HIS OWN HAPPY THOUGHTS--!
JUST CAN'T WAIT TO GET MY HANDS ON THAT LITTLE TWO-WHEELED TORNADO!
I'LL BET RIDING IT IS ALMOST AS GROOVY AS WEB SWINGING!
ND THEN, AS SO OFTEN HAPPENS IN THIS UNPRE-CTABLE WORLD OF OURS, COMPLETELY BY ACCIDENT -TOTALLY UNEXPECTED--A CHANCE MEETING--!
BETTY!!
PETER!! IT--IT'S REALLY YOU!
GOSH! WHAT A WONDERFUL SURPRISE!! I DIDN'T EVEN KNOW YOU WERE IN TOWN!
I WASN'T, TILL A FEW MINUTES AGO! I JUST ARRIVED!
YOU CERTAINLY LOOK WELL, PETER!
AFTER ALL THESE MONTHS --THAT'S ALL SHE CAN SAY!?
ALTHOUGH--I CAN'T THINK OF ANYTHING BETTER TO SAY!
WOULD YOU--LIKE A CUP OF COFFEE?
WHY, YES-- THAT WOULD BE NICE!
D YOU HAVE A NICE TIME ON E COAST?
YES, I DID, THANKS! IS EVERYTHING ALL RIGHT WITH YOU--AND YOUR AUNT MAY?
H, SURE--WE'RE JUST FINE!
HAT'S WRONG? WHAT'S APPENED BETWEEN US? E'RE LIKE TWO STRANGERS, GROPING FOR WORDS!
HOW IS EVERYTHING AT THE BUGLE, PETER?
OKAY, I SUPPOSE--!
JONAH JAMESON HAS BEEN AS GROUCHY AS EVER!
YES--I IMAGINED HE WOULD BE--!
OH, BRO-THER! THIS IS SHEER TORTURE!
AND I'LL BET IT'S JUST AS TOUGH FOR HER!
ALL THESE MONTHS-- I THOUGHT ABOUT HER--DREAMT ABOUT HER--LONGED FOR HER!!
WHAT-EVER WE HAD BEFORE-- WHATEVER THERE WAS BETWEEN US --IT'S GONE!
SO, NOW SHE'S RETURNED--
--AND-- NOTHINGSVILLE!

NEXT I'LL BE ASKING HER IF SHE'S READ ANY *GOOD BOOKS* LATELY! IF ONLY--

HI, PETE! I *THOUGHT* I SAW YOU FROM THE WINDOW!

OH--HI, NED!

BETTY BRANT! AM I *DREAMING*--OR--?!!

NED LEEDS! I'D KNOW YOUR VOICE *ANYWHERE!*

BETTY! I CAN'T *TELL* YOU HOW GLAD I AM TO *SEE* YOU!

IT'S SO GOOD TO SEE *YOU* TOO, NED! I'VE THOUGHT ABOUT YOU SO OFTEN!

WE'VE SO MUCH TO *TALK* ABOUT-- I DON'T KNOW WHERE TO START!

I NEVER THOUGHT I'D BE SO *GLAD* TO SEE OL' NED!

LOOK, YOU TWO-- I JUST REMEMBERED-- I HAVE AN *APPOINTMENT!* I'M AFRAID I HAVE TO RUN OFF NOW!

OH, THAT'S TOO BAD, PETER!

WHO'S SHE KIDDIN' BETTY'S AS GLAD TO SEE ME GO AS I AM FOR THE CHANCE TO ESCAPE!

DON'T APOLOGIZE ON *MY* ACCOUNT, FELLA!

ONCE I THOUGHT I COULDN'T *LIVE* WITHOUT HER! NOW, SHE'S JUST ANOTHER GIRL NAMED BETTY!

BOY, HAVE *I* GROWN UP IN THESE PAST FEW MONTHS!

I'LL--EH--GIVE YOU A RING LATER ON SOMETIME, HEAR?

YES, PETER! YOU DO THAT!

THAT *SINKS* IT! SHE FEELS THE SAME WAY *I* DO! SHE DIDN'T EVEN BOTHER TO GIVE ME HER NEW ADDRESS!

SEE YOU AROUND, PETE!

I REALIZE *NOW*-- WE *NEVER* HAD ANYTHING IN COMMON! IT'S JUST THAT SHE WAS THE *FIRST* GIRL I EVER THOUGHT I LOVED! BUT, THESE MONTHS *AWAY* FROM HER--

SAY! WHAT'S *THAT?*

BULLETIN! THESE ARE THE FIRST NEWS PICTURES TO BE RELEASED FOR TELEVISION--

--OF THE NEW, INDESCRIBABLY DANGEROUS, AND SEEMINGLY *UNSTOPPABLE* MENACE WHO CALLS HIMSELF-- THE *RHINO!*

AFTER CRASHING THRO EVERY ROAD BLOCK, H APPEARS TO BE HEADED DIRECTLY TOWARDS *NEW YORK!*

THE *RHINO!* BOY, IF HE'S *HALF* AS TOUGH AS HE *LOOKS*--!!

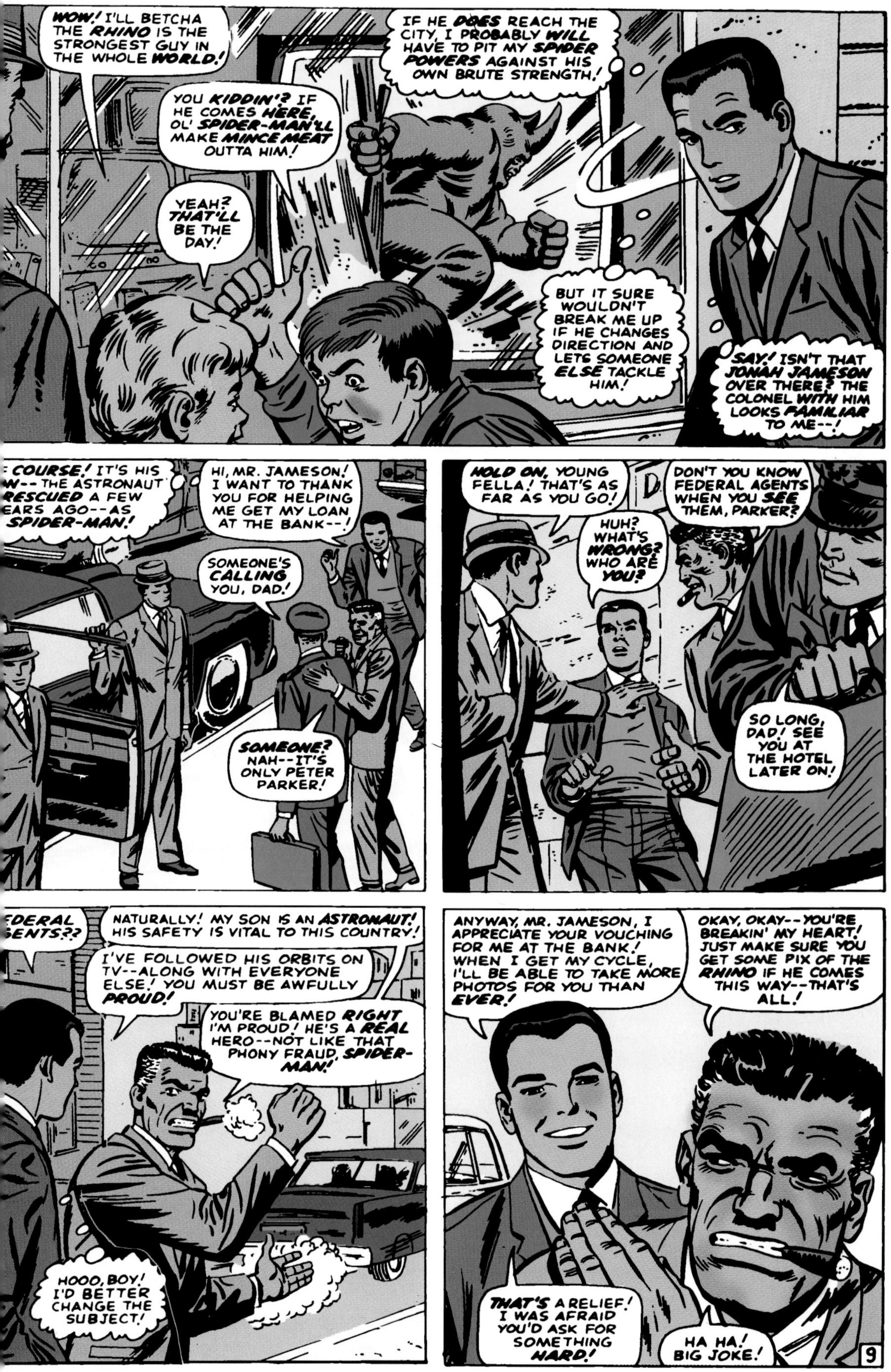

WOW! I'LL BETCHA THE RHINO IS THE STRONGEST GUY IN THE WHOLE WORLD!
YOU KIDDIN'? IF HE COMES HERE, OL' SPIDER-MAN'LL MAKE MINCE MEAT OUTTA HIM!
YEAH? THAT'LL BE THE DAY!
IF HE DOES REACH THE CITY, I PROBABLY WILL HAVE TO PIT MY SPIDER POWERS AGAINST HIS OWN BRUTE STRENGTH!
BUT IT SURE WOULDN'T BREAK ME UP IF HE CHANGES DIRECTION AND LETS SOMEONE ELSE TACKLE HIM!
SAY! ISN'T THAT JONAH JAMESON OVER THERE? THE COLONEL WITH HIM LOOKS FAMILIAR TO ME--!
COURSE! IT'S HIS
-- THE ASTRONAUT
RESCUED A FEW
EARS AGO--AS
SPIDER-MAN!
HI, MR. JAMESON! I WANT TO THANK YOU FOR HELPING ME GET MY LOAN AT THE BANK--!
SOMEONE'S CALLING YOU, DAD!
SOMEONE? NAH--IT'S ONLY PETER PARKER!
HOLD ON, YOUNG FELLA! THAT'S AS FAR AS YOU GO!
HUH? WHAT'S WRONG? WHO ARE YOU?
DON'T YOU KNOW FEDERAL AGENTS WHEN YOU SEE THEM, PARKER?
SO LONG, DAD! SEE YOU AT THE HOTEL LATER ON!
EDERAL
GENTS??
NATURALLY! MY SON IS AN ASTRONAUT! HIS SAFETY IS VITAL TO THIS COUNTRY!
I'VE FOLLOWED HIS ORBITS ON TV--ALONG WITH EVERYONE ELSE! YOU MUST BE AWFULLY PROUD!
YOU'RE BLAMED RIGHT I'M PROUD! HE'S A REAL HERO--NOT LIKE THAT PHONY FRAUD, SPIDER-MAN!
HOOO, BOY! I'D BETTER CHANGE THE SUBJECT!
ANYWAY, MR. JAMESON, I APPRECIATE YOUR VOUCHING FOR ME AT THE BANK! WHEN I GET MY CYCLE, I'LL BE ABLE TO TAKE MORE PHOTOS FOR YOU THAN EVER!
OKAY, OKAY--YOU'RE BREAKIN' MY HEART! JUST MAKE SURE YOU GET SOME PIX OF THE RHINO IF HE COMES THIS WAY--THAT'S ALL!
THAT'S A RELIEF! I WAS AFRAID YOU'D ASK FOR SOMETHING HARD!
HA HA! BIG JOKE!
9

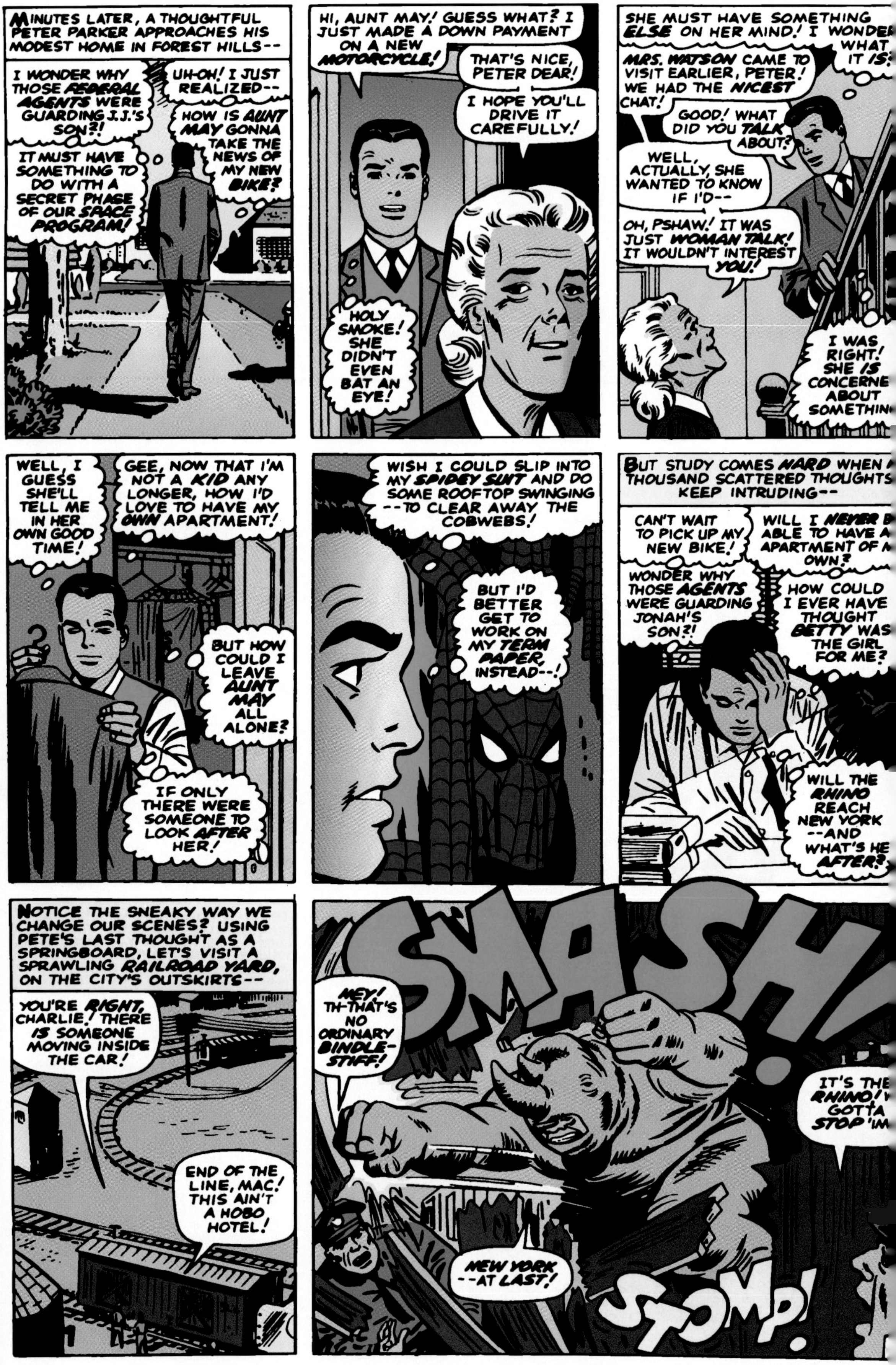
MINUTES LATER, A THOUGHTFUL PETER PARKER APPROACHES HIS MODEST HOME IN FOREST HILLS--
I WONDER WHY THOSE FEDERAL AGENTS WERE GUARDING J.J.'S SON?!
IT MUST HAVE SOMETHING TO DO WITH A SECRET PHASE OF OUR SPACE PROGRAM!
UH-OH! I JUST REALIZED--
HOW IS AUNT MAY GONNA TAKE THE NEWS OF MY NEW BIKE?
HI, AUNT MAY! GUESS WHAT? I JUST MADE A DOWN PAYMENT ON A NEW MOTORCYCLE!
THAT'S NICE, PETER DEAR!
I HOPE YOU'LL DRIVE IT CAREFULLY!
HOLY SMOKE! SHE DIDN'T EVEN BAT AN EYE!
SHE MUST HAVE SOMETHING ELSE ON HER MIND! I WONDER WHAT IT IS!
MRS. WATSON CAME TO VISIT EARLIER, PETER! WE HAD THE NICEST CHAT!
GOOD! WHAT DID YOU TALK ABOUT?
WELL, ACTUALLY, SHE WANTED TO KNOW IF I'D--
OH, PSHAW! IT WAS JUST WOMAN TALK! IT WOULDN'T INTEREST YOU!
I WAS RIGHT! SHE IS CONCERNED ABOUT SOMETHING
WELL, I GUESS SHE'LL TELL ME IN HER OWN GOOD TIME!
GEE, NOW THAT I'M NOT A KID ANY LONGER, HOW I'D LOVE TO HAVE MY OWN APARTMENT!
BUT HOW COULD I LEAVE AUNT MAY ALL ALONE?
IF ONLY THERE WERE SOMEONE TO LOOK AFTER HER!
WISH I COULD SLIP INTO MY SPIDEY SUIT AND DO SOME ROOFTOP SWINGING --TO CLEAR AWAY THE COBWEBS!
BUT I'D BETTER GET TO WORK ON MY TERM PAPER, INSTEAD--!
BUT STUDY COMES HARD WHEN A THOUSAND SCATTERED THOUGHTS KEEP INTRUDING--
CAN'T WAIT TO PICK UP MY NEW BIKE!
WILL I NEVER BE ABLE TO HAVE AN APARTMENT OF MY OWN?
WONDER WHY THOSE AGENTS WERE GUARDING JONAH'S SON?!
HOW COULD I EVER HAVE THOUGHT BETTY WAS THE GIRL FOR ME?
WILL THE RHINO REACH NEW YORK --AND WHAT'S HE AFTER?
NOTICE THE SNEAKY WAY WE CHANGE OUR SCENES? USING PETE'S LAST THOUGHT AS A SPRINGBOARD, LET'S VISIT A SPRAWLING RAILROAD YARD, ON THE CITY'S OUTSKIRTS--
YOU'RE RIGHT, CHARLIE! THERE IS SOMEONE MOVING INSIDE THE CAR!
END OF THE LINE, MAC! THIS AIN'T A HOBO HOTEL!
SMASH!
HEY! TH-THAT'S NO ORDINARY BINDLE-STIFF!
IT'S THE RHINO! W GOTTA STOP 'IM
NEW YORK --AT LAST!
STOMP!

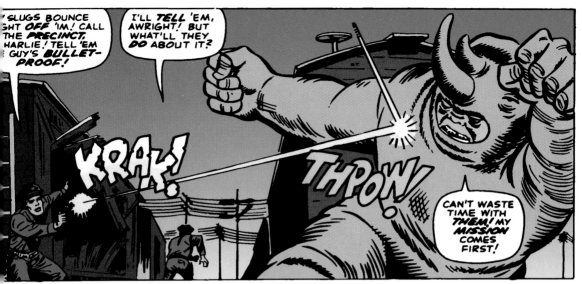

"SLUGS BOUNCE RIGHT OFF 'IM! CALL THE PRECINCT, CHARLIE! TELL 'EM THE GUY'S BULLET-PROOF!"

"I'LL TELL 'EM, AWRIGHT! BUT WHAT'LL THEY DO ABOUT IT?"

KRAK!

THPOW!

"CAN'T WASTE TIME WITH THEM! MY MISSION COMES FIRST!"

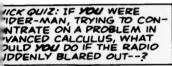

QUICK QUIZ: IF YOU WERE SPIDER-MAN, TRYING TO CONCENTRATE ON A PROBLEM IN ADVANCED CALCULUS, WHAT WOULD YOU DO IF THE RADIO SUDDENLY BLARED OUT--?

"BULLETIN! THE RAMPAGING RHINO HAS JUST BEEN SIGHTED ON NEW YORK'S WEST SIDE! ALL CITIZENS ARE URGED TO--"

"THE RHINO! NOBODY'S SAFE WHILE HE'S AT LARGE!"

WE SUSPECT YOU'D DO JUST WHAT PETER PARKER IS DOING--!

IF EVER IT WAS TIME FOR A FRIENDLY NEIGHBORHOOD SPIDER-MAN TO MAKE THE SCENE--

--THIS IS IT!

I DON'T KNOW WHAT THE RHINO'S AFTER...

...BUT IT MUST BE SOMETHING BIG TO BRING HIM HALF-WAY ACROSS THE COUNTRY!

AM I JUST CONVINCING MYSELF OF THAT BECAUSE I WANNA GO TO ACTION AGAIN?

WELL, WHAT'S THE DIFF-- SO LONG AS I STOP HIM!

MEANWHILE, AT LT. COL. JAMESON'S HOTEL SUITE--

KRAK! KRIK!

IT SOUNDED LIKE-- GUN-FIRE!

DAD! LISTEN! DID YOU HEAR THAT?

WE CAN'T STOP HIM! HE'S GONNA-- -UHHH!-

COLONEL JAMESON! LOOK OUT! IT'S THE-- -OOOHHH!-

STOMP!

GREAT CAESER'S GHOST! WHAT'S GOING ON OUT THERE?

TAKE COVER, DAD! THIS COULD BE SERIOUS!

11

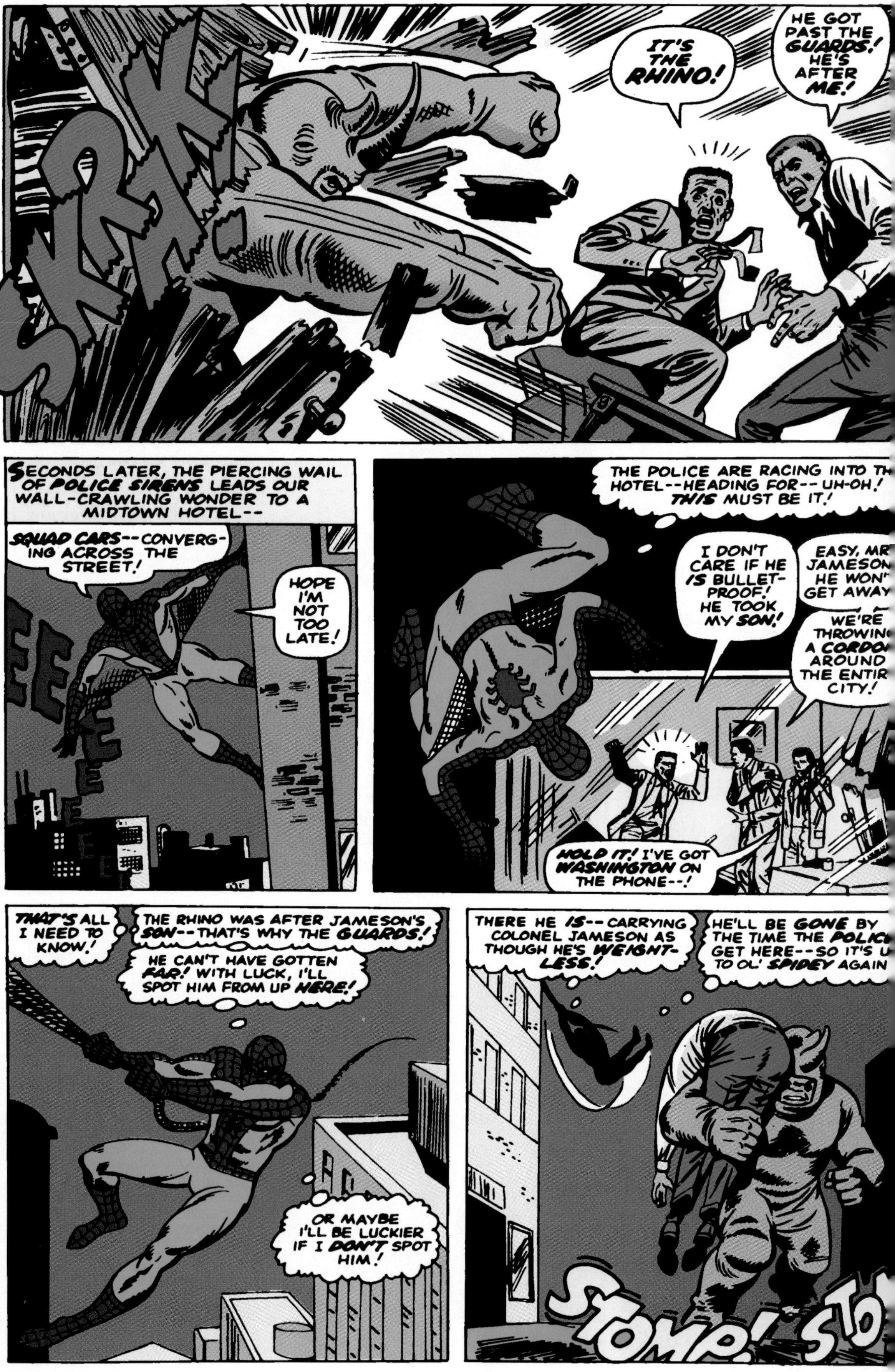
SPROK
IT'S THE RHINO!
HE GOT PAST THE GUARDS! HE'S AFTER ME!
SECONDS LATER, THE PIERCING WAIL OF POLICE SIRENS LEADS OUR WALL-CRAWLING WONDER TO A MIDTOWN HOTEL--
SQUAD CARS--CONVERGING ACROSS THE STREET!
HOPE I'M NOT TOO LATE!
EEEEE
THE POLICE ARE RACING INTO TH HOTEL--HEADING FOR--UH-OH! THIS MUST BE IT!
I DON'T CARE IF HE IS BULLET-PROOF! HE TOOK MY SON!
EASY, MR JAMESON HE WON' GET AWAY
WE'RE THROWIN A CORDO AROUND THE ENTIR CITY!
HOLD IT! I'VE GOT WASHINGTON ON THE PHONE--!
THAT'S ALL I NEED TO KNOW!
THE RHINO WAS AFTER JAMESON'S SON--THAT'S WHY THE GUARDS!
HE CAN'T HAVE GOTTEN FAR! WITH LUCK, I'LL SPOT HIM FROM UP HERE!
OR MAYBE I'LL BE LUCKIER IF I DON'T SPOT HIM!
THERE HE IS--CARRYING COLONEL JAMESON AS THOUGH HE'S WEIGHTLESS!
HE'LL BE GONE BY THE TIME THE POLIC GET HERE--SO IT'S U TO OL' SPIDEY AGAIN
STOMP! STO

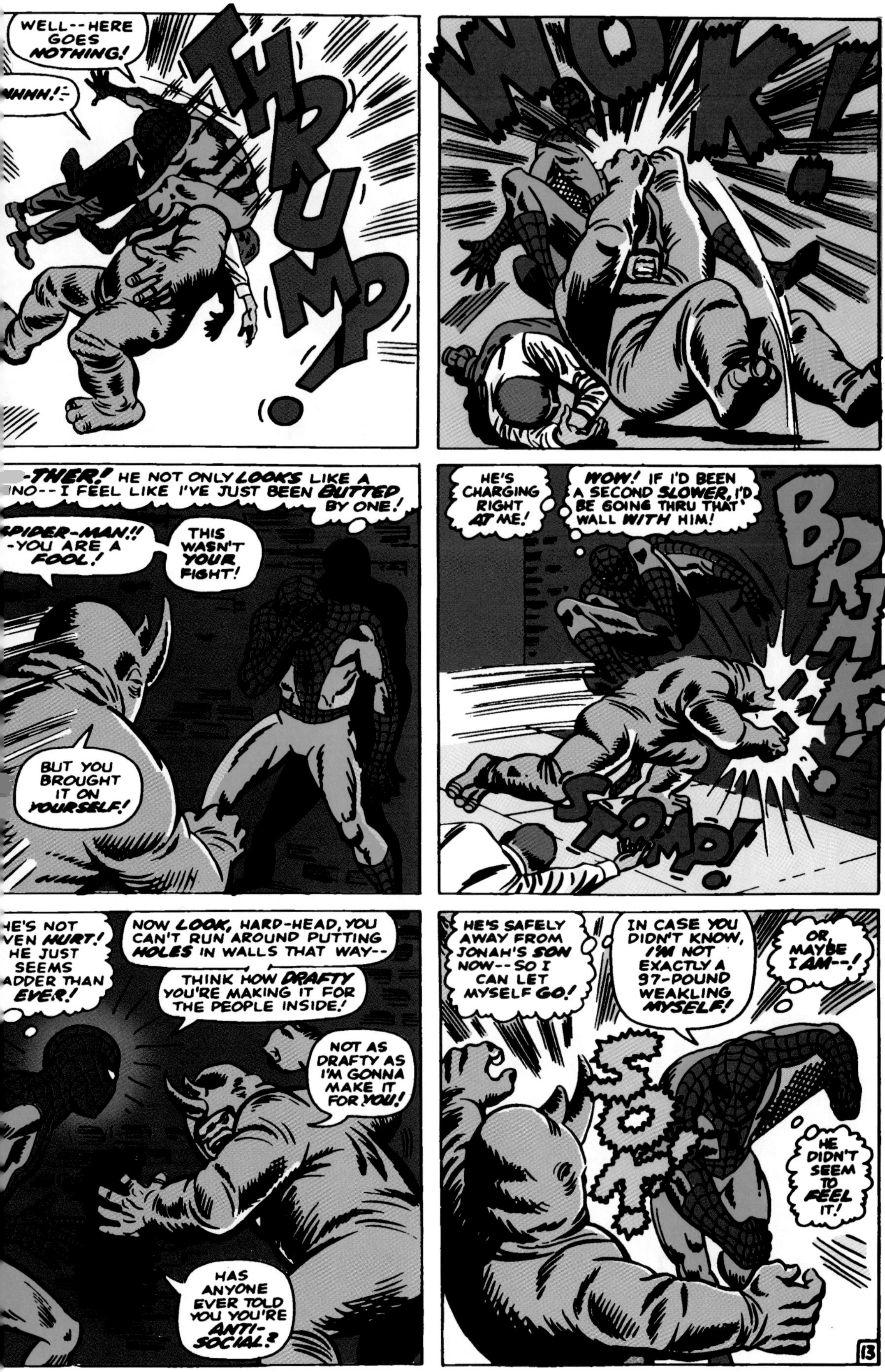

WELL--HERE GOES NOTHING!
NNNN!
THRUMP
WOK!
-THER! HE NOT ONLY LOOKS LIKE A
NO-- I FEEL LIKE I'VE JUST BEEN BUTTED BY ONE!
PIDER-MAN!! -YOU ARE A FOOL!
THIS WASN'T YOUR FIGHT!
BUT YOU BROUGHT IT ON YOURSELF!
HE'S CHARGING RIGHT AT ME!
WOW! IF I'D BEEN A SECOND SLOWER, I'D BE GOING THRU THAT WALL WITH HIM!
BRAK!
STOMP!
E'S NOT VEN HURT! HE JUST SEEMS ADDER THAN EVER!
NOW LOOK, HARD-HEAD, YOU CAN'T RUN AROUND PUTTING HOLES IN WALLS THAT WAY--
THINK HOW DRAFTY YOU'RE MAKING IT FOR THE PEOPLE INSIDE!
NOT AS DRAFTY AS I'M GONNA MAKE IT FOR YOU!
HAS ANYONE EVER TOLD YOU YOU'RE ANTI-SOCIAL?
HE'S SAFELY AWAY FROM JONAH'S SON NOW--SO I CAN LET MYSELF GO!
IN CASE YOU DIDN'T KNOW, I'M NOT EXACTLY A 97-POUND WEAKLING MYSELF!
OR, MAYBE I AM--!
SOK!
HE DIDN'T SEEM TO FEEL IT!
13

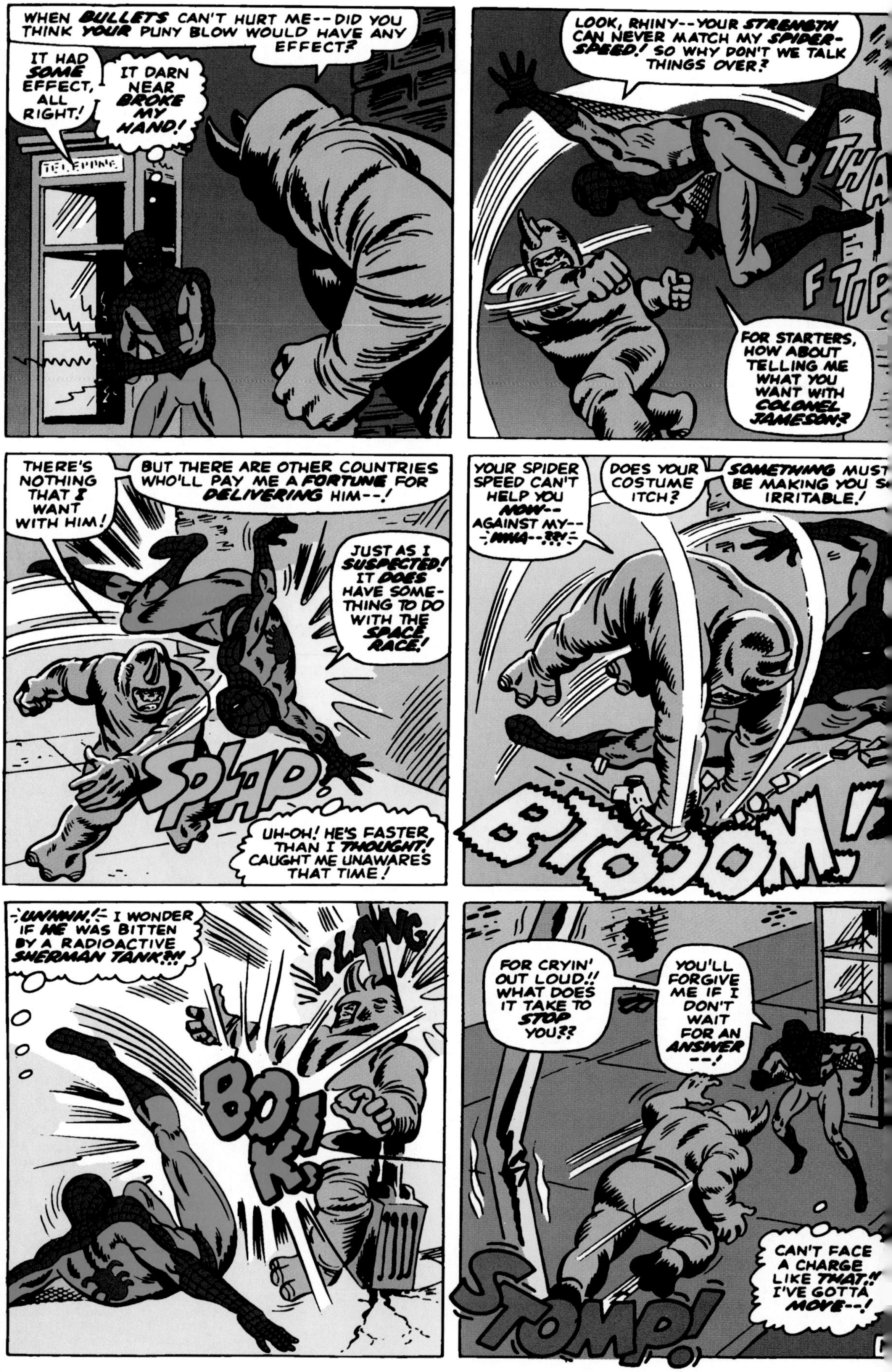
WHEN BULLETS CAN'T HURT ME--DID YOU THINK YOUR PUNY BLOW WOULD HAVE ANY EFFECT?
IT HAD SOME EFFECT, ALL RIGHT!
IT DARN NEAR BROKE MY HAND!
LOOK, RHINY--YOUR STRENGTH CAN NEVER MATCH MY SPIDER-SPEED! SO WHY DON'T WE TALK THINGS OVER?
FTIP
FOR STARTERS, HOW ABOUT TELLING ME WHAT YOU WANT WITH COLONEL JAMESON?
THERE'S NOTHING THAT I WANT WITH HIM!
BUT THERE ARE OTHER COUNTRIES WHO'LL PAY ME A FORTUNE FOR DELIVERING HIM--!
JUST AS I SUSPECTED! IT DOES HAVE SOMETHING TO DO WITH THE SPACE RACE!
SPHAP
UH-OH! HE'S FASTER THAN I THOUGHT! CAUGHT ME UNAWARES THAT TIME!
YOUR SPIDER SPEED CAN'T HELP YOU NOW--AGAINST MY-- WHA--??!
DOES YOUR COSTUME ITCH?
SOMETHING MUST BE MAKING YOU S IRRITABLE!
BTOOOM!
UNNNN! I WONDER IF HE WAS BITTEN BY A RADIOACTIVE SHERMAN TANK?!!
CLANG
BOK!
FOR CRYIN' OUT LOUD!! WHAT DOES IT TAKE TO STOP YOU??
YOU'LL FORGIVE ME IF I DON'T WAIT FOR AN ANSWER--!
CAN'T FACE A CHARGE LIKE THAT!! I'VE GOTTA MOVE--!
STOMP!

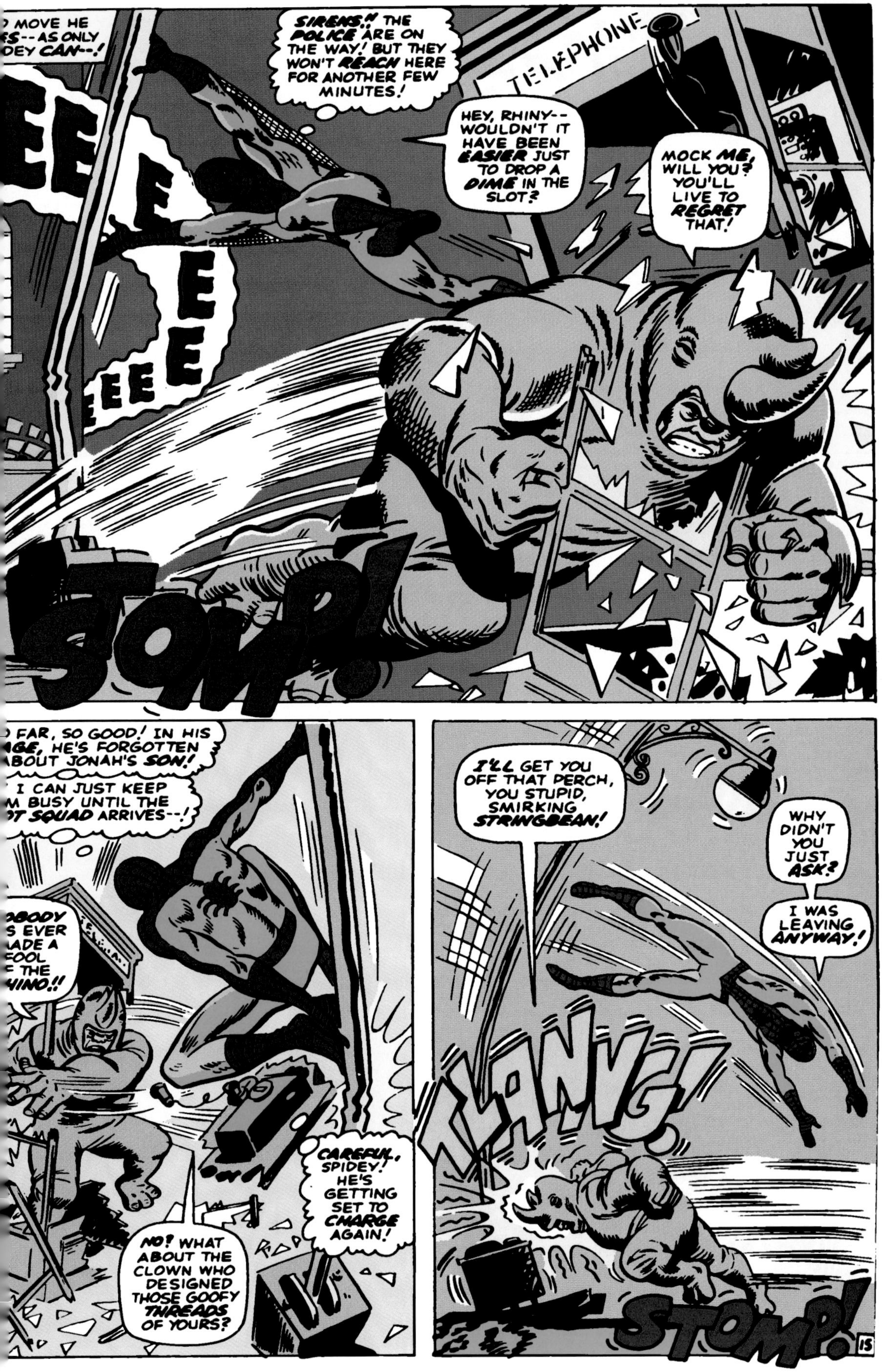

O MOVE HE
ES--AS ONLY
DEY CAN--!
SIRENS!! THE POLICE ARE ON THE WAY! BUT THEY WON'T REACH HERE FOR ANOTHER FEW MINUTES!
EEEEEEEE
TELEPHONE
HEY, RHINY-- WOULDN'T IT HAVE BEEN EASIER JUST TO DROP A DIME IN THE SLOT?
MOCK ME, WILL YOU? YOU'LL LIVE TO REGRET THAT!
STOMP!
O FAR, SO GOOD! IN HIS
AGE, HE'S FORGOTTEN
ABOUT JONAH'S SON!
I CAN JUST KEEP
M BUSY UNTIL THE
OT SQUAD ARRIVES--!
OBODY
S EVER
ADE A
FOOL
F THE
HINO.!!
NO? WHAT ABOUT THE CLOWN WHO DESIGNED THOSE GOOFY THREADS OF YOURS?
CAREFUL, SPIDEY! HE'S GETTING SET TO CHARGE AGAIN!
I'LL GET YOU OFF THAT PERCH, YOU STUPID, SMIRKING STRINGBEAN!
WHY DIDN'T YOU JUST ASK?
I WAS LEAVING ANYWAY!
KLANNG!
STOMP!
15

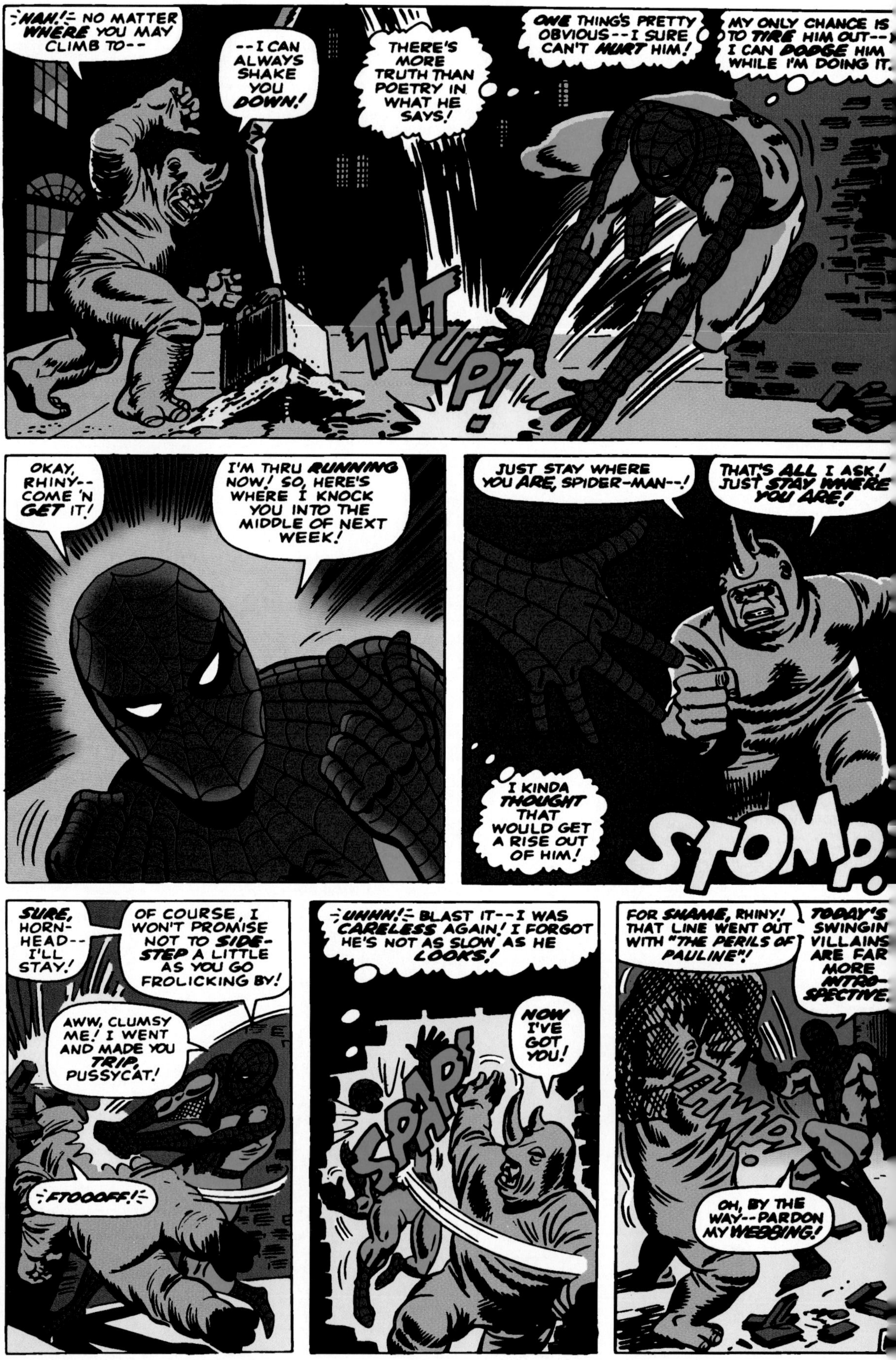

-NAH!- NO MATTER WHERE YOU MAY CLIMB TO--
--I CAN ALWAYS SHAKE YOU DOWN!
THERE'S MORE TRUTH THAN POETRY IN WHAT HE SAYS!
ONE THING'S PRETTY OBVIOUS--I SURE CAN'T HURT HIM!
MY ONLY CHANCE IS TO TIRE HIM OUT-- I CAN DODGE HIM WHILE I'M DOING IT.
THT UP!
OKAY, RHINY-- COME 'N GET IT!
I'M THRU RUNNING NOW! SO, HERE'S WHERE I KNOCK YOU INTO THE MIDDLE OF NEXT WEEK!
JUST STAY WHERE YOU ARE, SPIDER-MAN--!
THAT'S ALL I ASK! JUST STAY WHERE YOU ARE!
I KINDA THOUGHT THAT WOULD GET A RISE OUT OF HIM!
STOMP!
SURE, HORN-HEAD-- I'LL STAY!
OF COURSE, I WON'T PROMISE NOT TO SIDE-STEP A LITTLE AS YOU GO FROLICKING BY!
AWW, CLUMSY ME! I WENT AND MADE YOU TRIP, PUSSYCAT!
-FTOOOFF!-
-UNHH!- BLAST IT--I WAS CARELESS AGAIN! I FORGOT HE'S NOT AS SLOW AS HE LOOKS!
NOW I'VE GOT YOU!
SPAP!
FOR SHAME, RHINY! THAT LINE WENT OUT WITH "THE PERILS OF PAULINE"!
TODAY'S SWINGIN VILLAINS ARE FAR MORE INTRO-SPECTIVE.
THWIP
OH, BY THE WAY--PARDON MY WEBBING!

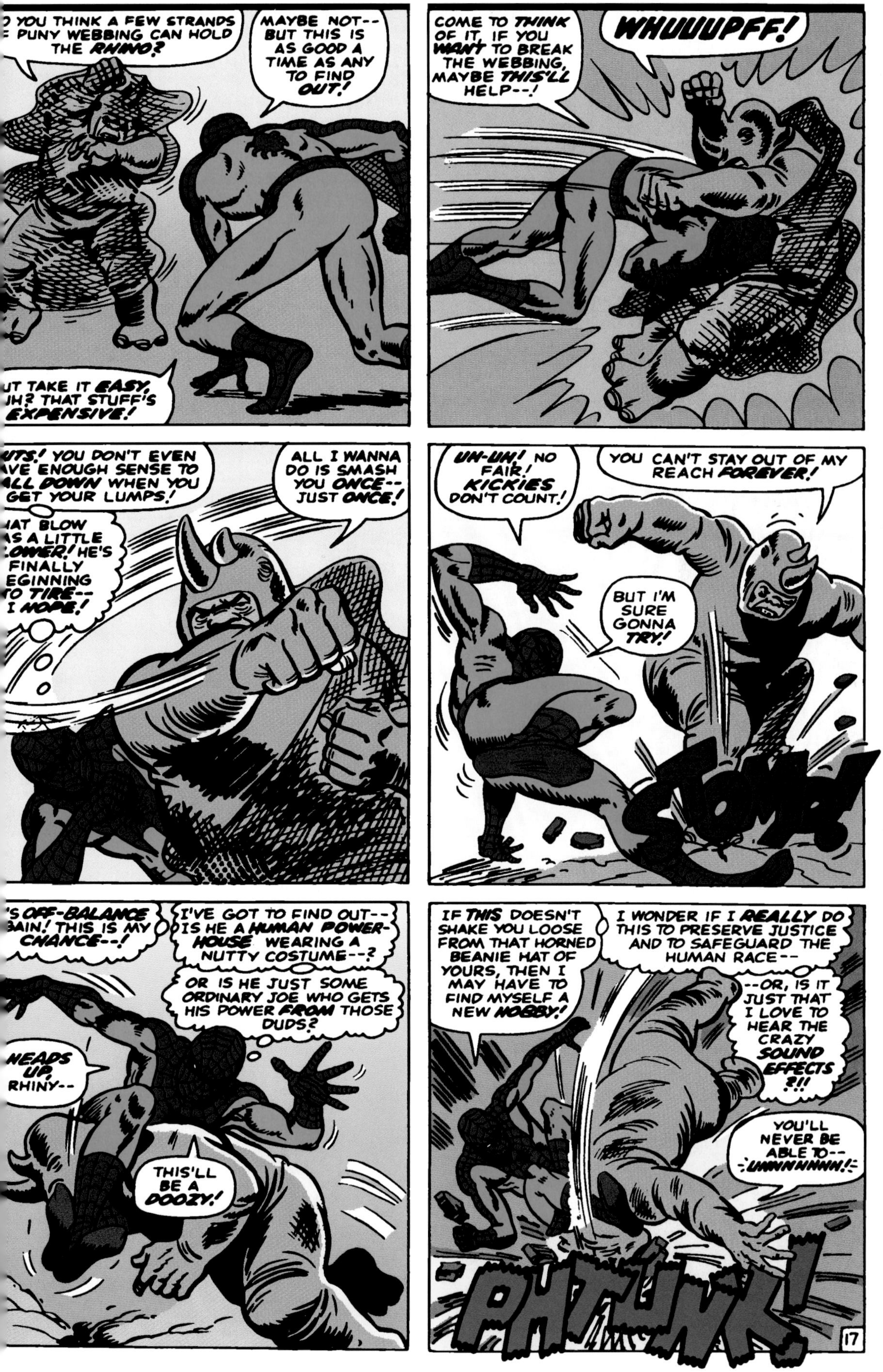
O YOU THINK A FEW STRANDS F PUNY WEBBING CAN HOLD THE RHINO?
MAYBE NOT-- BUT THIS IS AS GOOD A TIME AS ANY TO FIND OUT!
UT TAKE IT EASY, UH? THAT STUFF'S EXPENSIVE!
COME TO THINK OF IT, IF YOU WANT TO BREAK THE WEBBING, MAYBE THIS'LL HELP--!
WHUUUUPFF!
UTS! YOU DON'T EVEN AVE ENOUGH SENSE TO ALL DOWN WHEN YOU GET YOUR LUMPS!
ALL I WANNA DO IS SMASH YOU ONCE-- JUST ONCE!
AT BLOW AS A LITTLE OWER! HE'S FINALLY EGINNING TO TIRE-- I HOPE!
UH-UH! NO FAIR! KICKIES DON'T COUNT!
YOU CAN'T STAY OUT OF MY REACH FOREVER!
BUT I'M SURE GONNA TRY!
STOMP!
'S OFF-BALANCE AIN! THIS IS MY CHANCE--!
I'VE GOT TO FIND OUT-- IS HE A HUMAN POWER-HOUSE WEARING A NUTTY COSTUME--?
OR IS HE JUST SOME ORDINARY JOE WHO GETS HIS POWER FROM THOSE DUDS?
HEADS UP, RHINY--
THIS'LL BE A DOOZY!
IF THIS DOESN'T SHAKE YOU LOOSE FROM THAT HORNED BEANIE HAT OF YOURS, THEN I MAY HAVE TO FIND MYSELF A NEW HOBBY!
I WONDER IF I REALLY DO THIS TO PRESERVE JUSTICE AND TO SAFEGUARD THE HUMAN RACE--
--OR, IS IT JUST THAT I LOVE TO HEAR THE CRAZY SOUND EFFECTS?!!
YOU'LL NEVER BE ABLE TO-- UNNNNNNN!
PHTUNK!
17

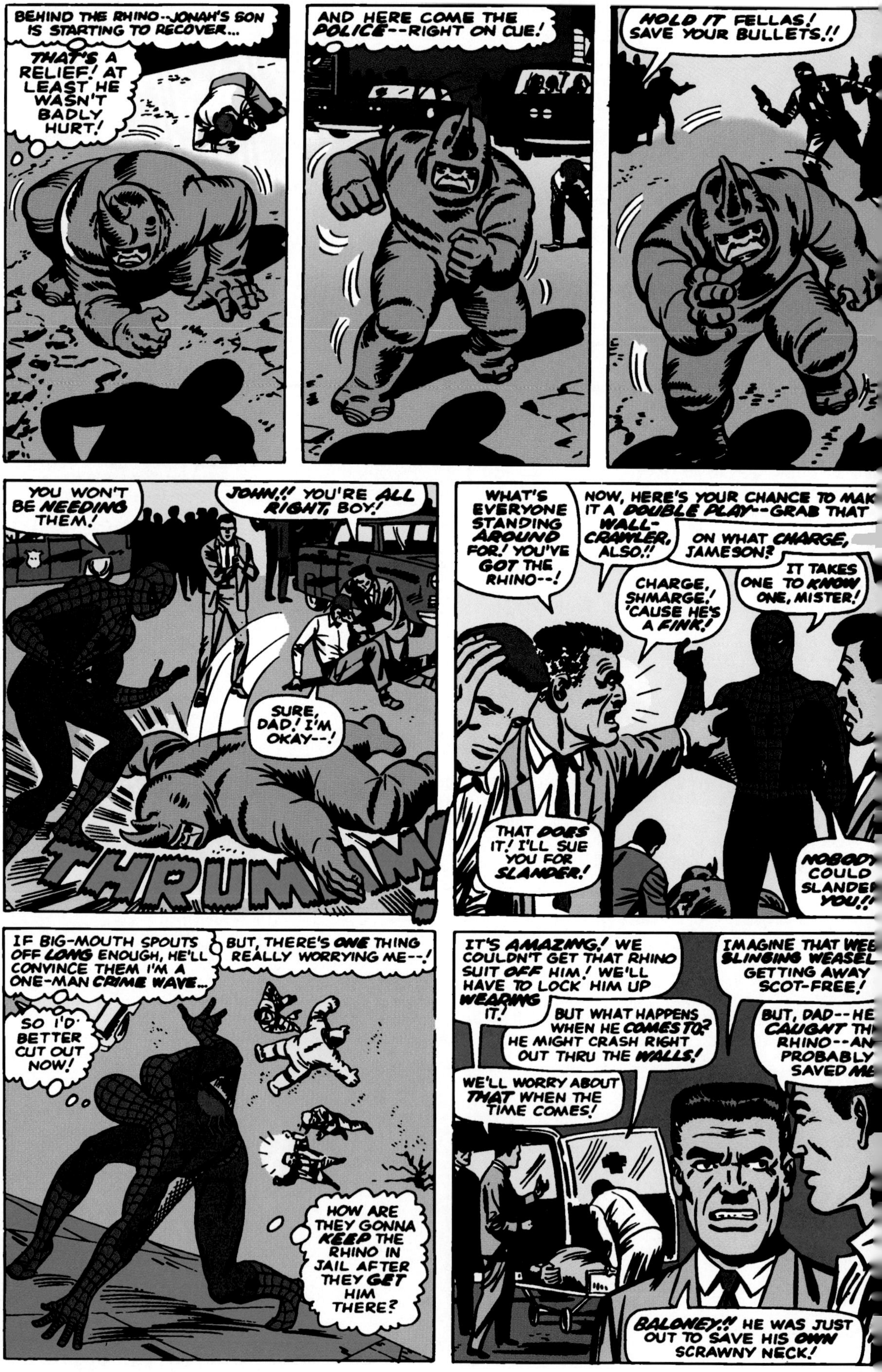

BEHIND THE RHINO--JONAH'S SON IS STARTING TO RECOVER...
THAT'S A RELIEF! AT LEAST HE WASN'T BADLY HURT!
AND HERE COME THE POLICE--RIGHT ON CUE!
HOLD IT FELLAS! SAVE YOUR BULLETS!!
YOU WON'T BE NEEDING THEM!
JOHN!! YOU'RE ALL RIGHT, BOY!
SURE, DAD! I'M OKAY--!
THRUMM!
WHAT'S EVERYONE STANDING AROUND FOR! YOU'VE GOT THE RHINO--!
NOW, HERE'S YOUR CHANCE TO MAK IT A DOUBLE PLAY--GRAB THAT WALL-CRAWLER, ALSO!!
ON WHAT CHARGE, JAMESON?
CHARGE, SHMARGE! 'CAUSE HE'S A FINK!
IT TAKES ONE TO KNOW ONE, MISTER!
THAT DOES IT! I'LL SUE YOU FOR SLANDER!
NOBODY COULD SLANDER YOU!!
IF BIG-MOUTH SPOUTS OFF LONG ENOUGH, HE'LL CONVINCE THEM I'M A ONE-MAN CRIME WAVE...
BUT, THERE'S ONE THING REALLY WORRYING ME--!
SO I'D BETTER CUT OUT NOW!
HOW ARE THEY GONNA KEEP THE RHINO IN JAIL AFTER THEY GET HIM THERE?
IT'S AMAZING! WE COULDN'T GET THAT RHINO SUIT OFF HIM! WE'LL HAVE TO LOCK HIM UP WEARING IT!
BUT WHAT HAPPENS WHEN HE COMES TO? HE MIGHT CRASH RIGHT OUT THRU THE WALLS!
WE'LL WORRY ABOUT THAT WHEN THE TIME COMES!
IMAGINE THAT WEB SLINGING WEASEL GETTING AWAY SCOT-FREE!
BUT, DAD--HE CAUGHT THE RHINO--AN PROBABLY SAVED ME
BALONEY!! HE WAS JUST OUT TO SAVE HIS OWN SCRAWNY NECK!

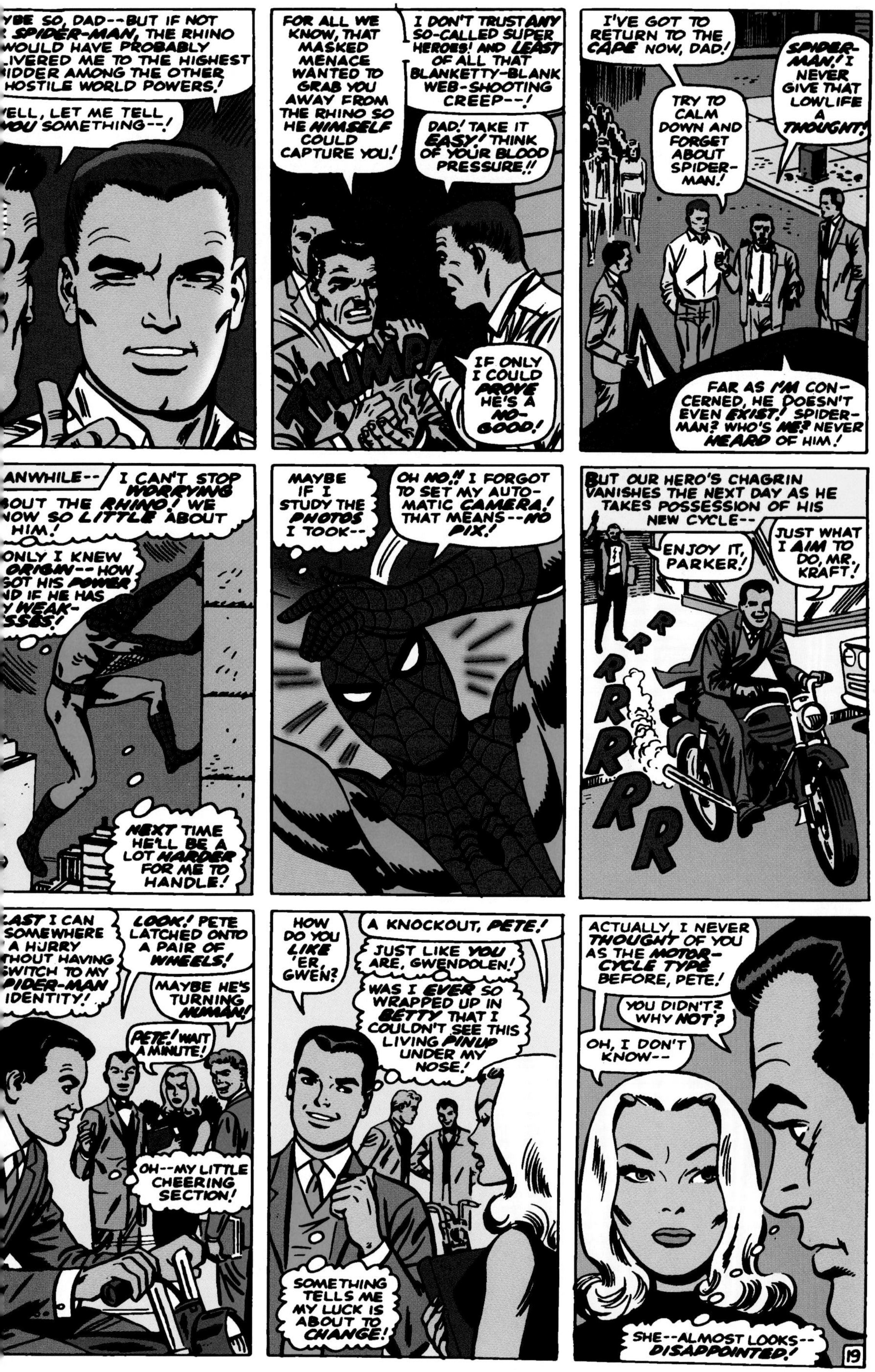

YBE SO, DAD--BUT IF NOT R SPIDER-MAN, THE RHINO WOULD HAVE PROBABLY LIVERED ME TO THE HIGHEST BIDDER AMONG THE OTHER HOSTILE WORLD POWERS!
WELL, LET ME TELL YOU SOMETHING--!
FOR ALL WE KNOW, THAT MASKED MENACE WANTED TO GRAB YOU AWAY FROM THE RHINO SO HE HIMSELF COULD CAPTURE YOU!
I DON'T TRUST ANY SO-CALLED SUPER HEROES! AND LEAST OF ALL THAT BLANKETTY-BLANK WEB-SHOOTING CREEP--!
DAD! TAKE IT EASY! THINK OF YOUR BLOOD PRESSURE!!
THUMP!
IF ONLY I COULD PROVE HE'S A NO-GOOD!
I'VE GOT TO RETURN TO THE CAPE NOW, DAD!
TRY TO CALM DOWN AND FORGET ABOUT SPIDER-MAN!
SPIDER-MAN! I NEVER GIVE THAT LOWLIFE A THOUGHT!
FAR AS I'M CONCERNED, HE DOESN'T EVEN EXIST! SPIDER-MAN? WHO'S HE? NEVER HEARD OF HIM!
ANWHILE--
I CAN'T STOP WORRYING BOUT THE RHINO! WE NOW SO LITTLE ABOUT HIM!
ONLY I KNEW ORIGIN-- HOW GOT HIS POWER ND IF HE HAS Y WEAK-SSES!
NEXT TIME HE'LL BE A LOT HARDER FOR ME TO HANDLE!
MAYBE IF I STUDY THE PHOTOS I TOOK--
OH NO!! I FORGOT TO SET MY AUTOMATIC CAMERA! THAT MEANS--NO PIX!
BUT OUR HERO'S CHAGRIN VANISHES THE NEXT DAY AS HE TAKES POSSESSION OF HIS NEW CYCLE--
ENJOY IT, PARKER!
JUST WHAT I AIM TO DO, MR. KRAFT!
RRRRRRR
EAST I CAN SOMEWHERE A HURRY THOUT HAVING SWITCH TO MY PIDER-MAN IDENTITY!
LOOK! PETE LATCHED ONTO A PAIR OF WHEELS!
MAYBE HE'S TURNING HUMAN!
PETE! WAIT A MINUTE!
OH--MY LITTLE CHEERING SECTION!
HOW DO YOU LIKE 'ER, GWEN?
A KNOCKOUT, PETE!
JUST LIKE YOU ARE, GWENDOLEN!
WAS I EVER SO WRAPPED UP IN BETTY THAT I COULDN'T SEE THIS LIVING PINUP UNDER MY NOSE!
SOMETHING TELLS ME MY LUCK IS ABOUT TO CHANGE!
ACTUALLY, I NEVER THOUGHT OF YOU AS THE MOTORCYCLE TYPE BEFORE, PETE!
YOU DIDN'T? WHY NOT?
OH, I DON'T KNOW--
SHE--ALMOST LOOKS--DISAPPOINTED!
19

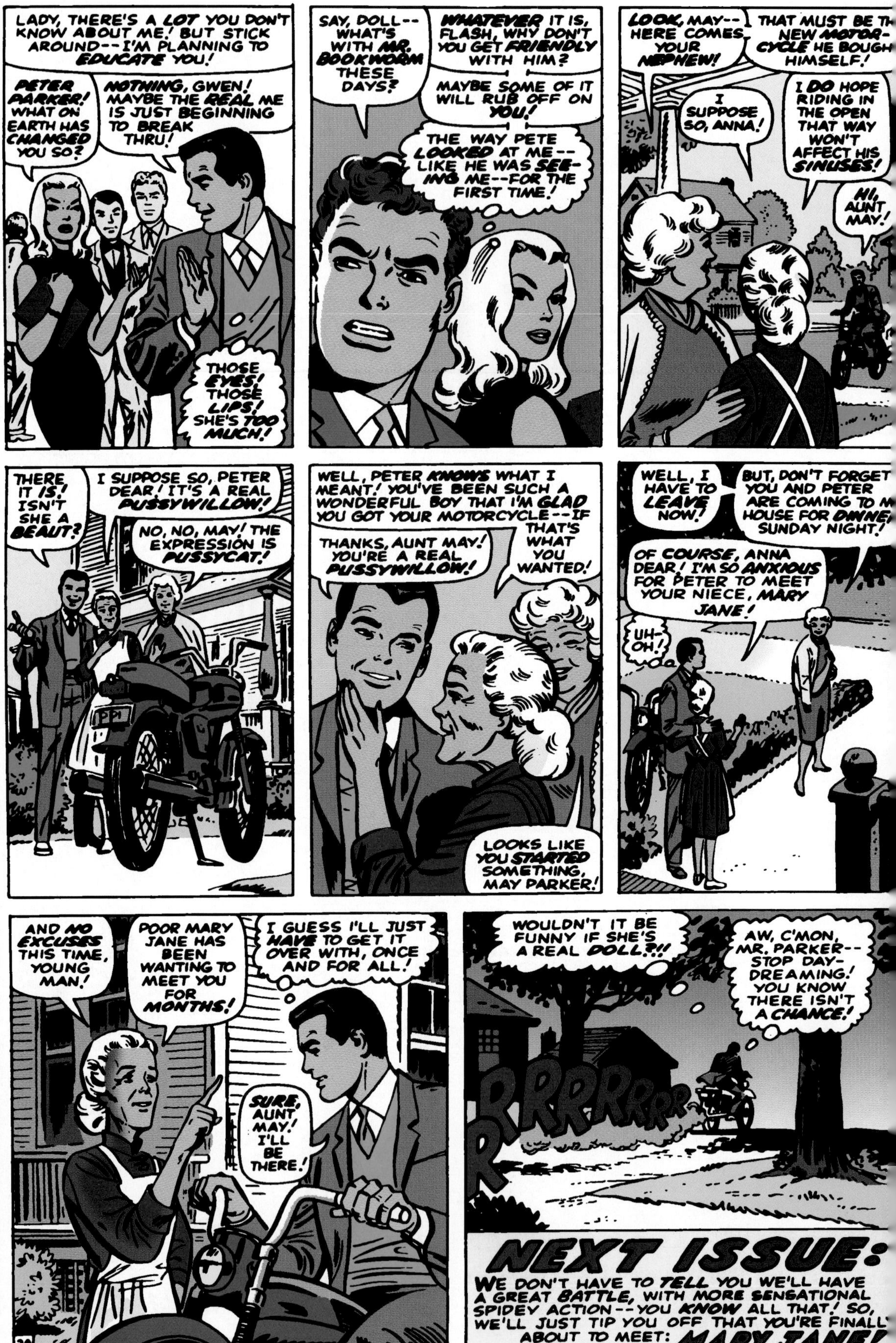
LADY, THERE'S A LOT YOU DON'T KNOW ABOUT ME! BUT STICK AROUND--I'M PLANNING TO EDUCATE YOU!
PETER PARKER! WHAT ON EARTH HAS CHANGED YOU SO?
NOTHING, GWEN! MAYBE THE REAL ME IS JUST BEGINNING TO BREAK THRU!
THOSE EYES! THOSE LIPS! SHE'S TOO MUCH!
SAY, DOLL-- WHAT'S WITH MR. BOOKWORM THESE DAYS?
WHATEVER IT IS, FLASH, WHY DON'T YOU GET FRIENDLY WITH HIM?
MAYBE SOME OF IT WILL RUB OFF ON YOU!
THE WAY PETE LOOKED AT ME-- LIKE HE WAS SEE-ING ME--FOR THE FIRST TIME!
LOOK, MAY-- HERE COMES YOUR NEPHEW!
THAT MUST BE TH NEW MOTOR-CYCLE HE BOUGH HIMSELF!
I SUPPOSE SO, ANNA!
I DO HOPE RIDING IN THE OPEN THAT WAY WON'T AFFECT HIS SINUSES!
HI, AUNT MAY!
THERE IT IS! ISN'T SHE A BEAUT?
I SUPPOSE SO, PETER DEAR! IT'S A REAL PUSSYWILLOW!
NO, NO, MAY! THE EXPRESSION IS PUSSYCAT!
PP1
WELL, PETER KNOWS WHAT I MEANT! YOU'VE BEEN SUCH A WONDERFUL BOY THAT I'M GLAD YOU GOT YOUR MOTORCYCLE--IF THAT'S WHAT YOU WANTED!
THANKS, AUNT MAY! YOU'RE A REAL PUSSYWILLOW!
LOOKS LIKE YOU STARTED SOMETHING, MAY PARKER!
WELL, I HAVE TO LEAVE NOW!
BUT, DON'T FORGET YOU AND PETER ARE COMING TO M HOUSE FOR DINNE SUNDAY NIGHT!
OF COURSE, ANNA DEAR! I'M SO ANXIOUS FOR PETER TO MEET YOUR NIECE, MARY JANE!
UH-OH!
AND NO EXCUSES THIS TIME, YOUNG MAN!
POOR MARY JANE HAS BEEN WANTING TO MEET YOU FOR MONTHS!
I GUESS I'LL JUST HAVE TO GET IT OVER WITH, ONCE AND FOR ALL!
SURE, AUNT MAY! I'LL BE THERE!
20
WOULDN'T IT BE FUNNY IF SHE'S A REAL DOLL?!!
AW, C'MON, MR. PARKER-- STOP DAY-DREAMING! YOU KNOW THERE ISN'T A CHANCE!
RRRRRRrrr
NEXT ISSUE:
WE DON'T HAVE TO TELL YOU WE'LL HAVE A GREAT BATTLE, WITH MORE SENSATIONAL SPIDEY ACTION--YOU KNOW ALL THAT! SO, WE'LL JUST TIP YOU OFF THAT YOU'RE FINALL ABOUT TO MEET: MARY JANE!

amazing spider-man #42

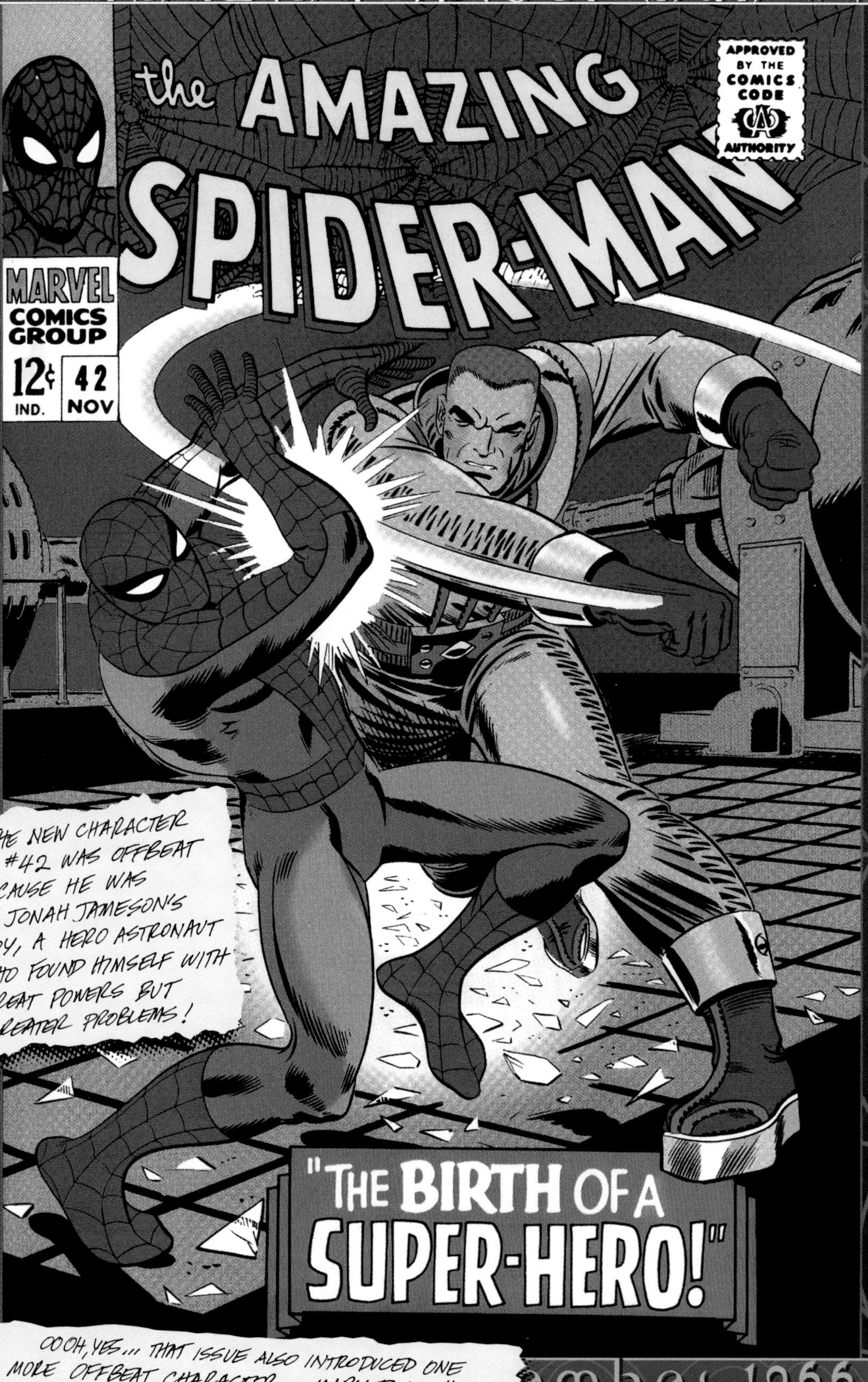
the AMAZING SPIDER-MAN
APPROVED BY THE COMICS CODE AUTHORITY
MARVEL COMICS GROUP
12¢ IND.
42 NOV
"THE BIRTH OF A SUPER-HERO!"

THE NEW CHARACTER IN #42 WAS OFFBEAT BECAUSE HE WAS J. JONAH JAMESON'S BOY, A HERO ASTRONAUT WHO FOUND HIMSELF WITH GREAT POWERS BUT GREATER PROBLEMS!

OOOH, YES... THAT ISSUE ALSO INTRODUCED ONE MORE OFFBEAT CHARACTER... MARY JANE WATSON! I BEGAN TO FEEL MORE AT HOME. I WAS A BIT PROUD OF THAT ONE.

ember 1966

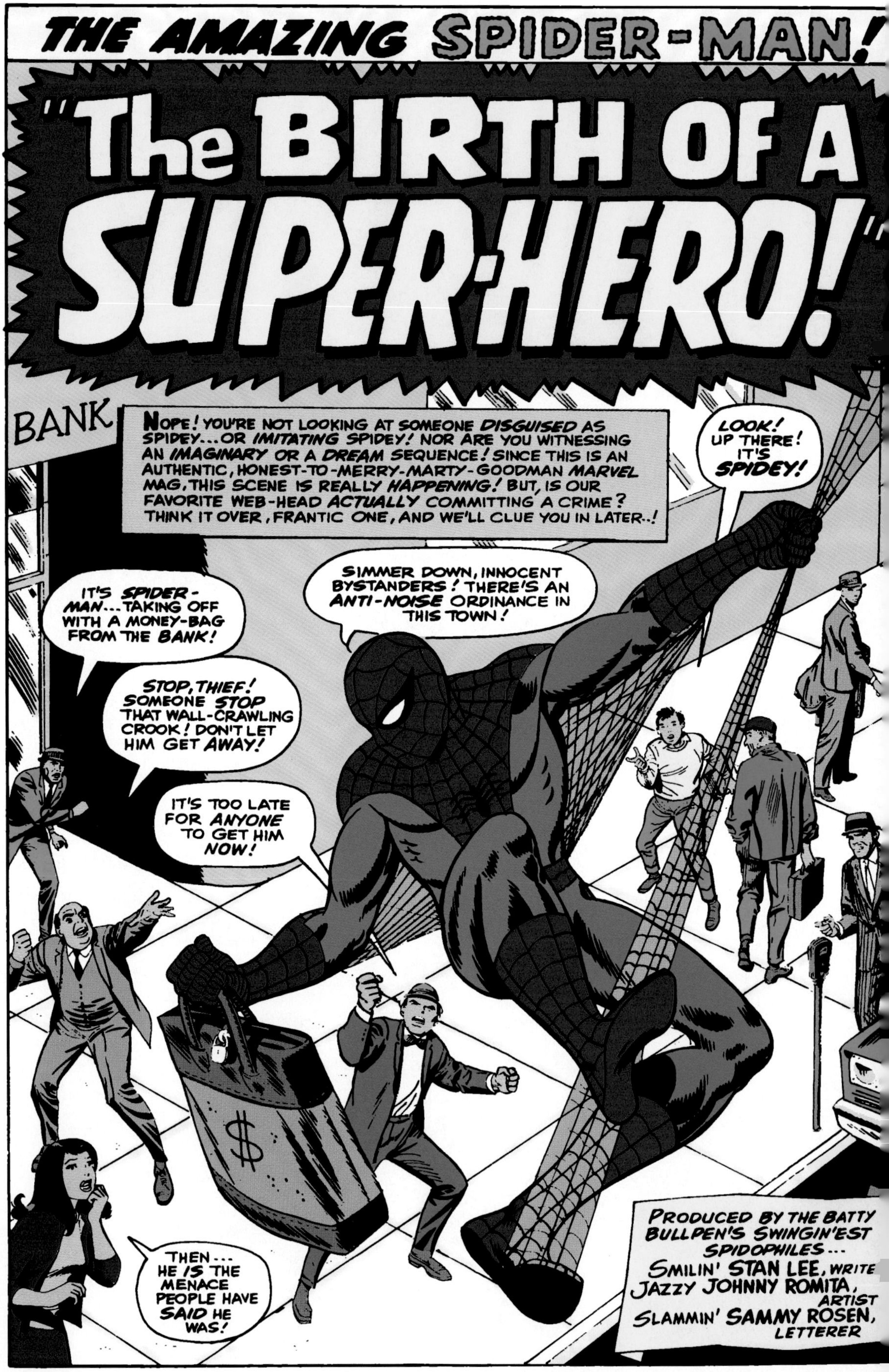
THE AMAZING SPIDER-MAN!
"The BIRTH OF A SUPER-HERO!"
BANK
NOPE! YOU'RE NOT LOOKING AT SOMEONE DISGUISED AS SPIDEY...OR IMITATING SPIDEY! NOR ARE YOU WITNESSING AN IMAGINARY OR A DREAM SEQUENCE! SINCE THIS IS AN AUTHENTIC, HONEST-TO-MERRY-MARTY-GOODMAN MARVEL MAG, THIS SCENE IS REALLY HAPPENING! BUT, IS OUR FAVORITE WEB-HEAD ACTUALLY COMMITTING A CRIME? THINK IT OVER, FRANTIC ONE, AND WE'LL CLUE YOU IN LATER..!
LOOK! UP THERE! IT'S SPIDEY!
SIMMER DOWN, INNOCENT BYSTANDERS! THERE'S AN ANTI-NOISE ORDINANCE IN THIS TOWN!
IT'S SPIDER-MAN...TAKING OFF WITH A MONEY-BAG FROM THE BANK!
STOP, THIEF! SOMEONE STOP THAT WALL-CRAWLING CROOK! DON'T LET HIM GET AWAY!
IT'S TOO LATE FOR ANYONE TO GET HIM NOW!
THEN... HE IS THE MENACE PEOPLE HAVE SAID HE WAS!
PRODUCED BY THE BATTY BULLPEN'S SWINGIN'EST SPIDOPHILES...
SMILIN' STAN LEE, WRITE
JAZZY JOHNNY ROMITA, ARTIST
SLAMMIN' SAMMY ROSEN, LETTERER

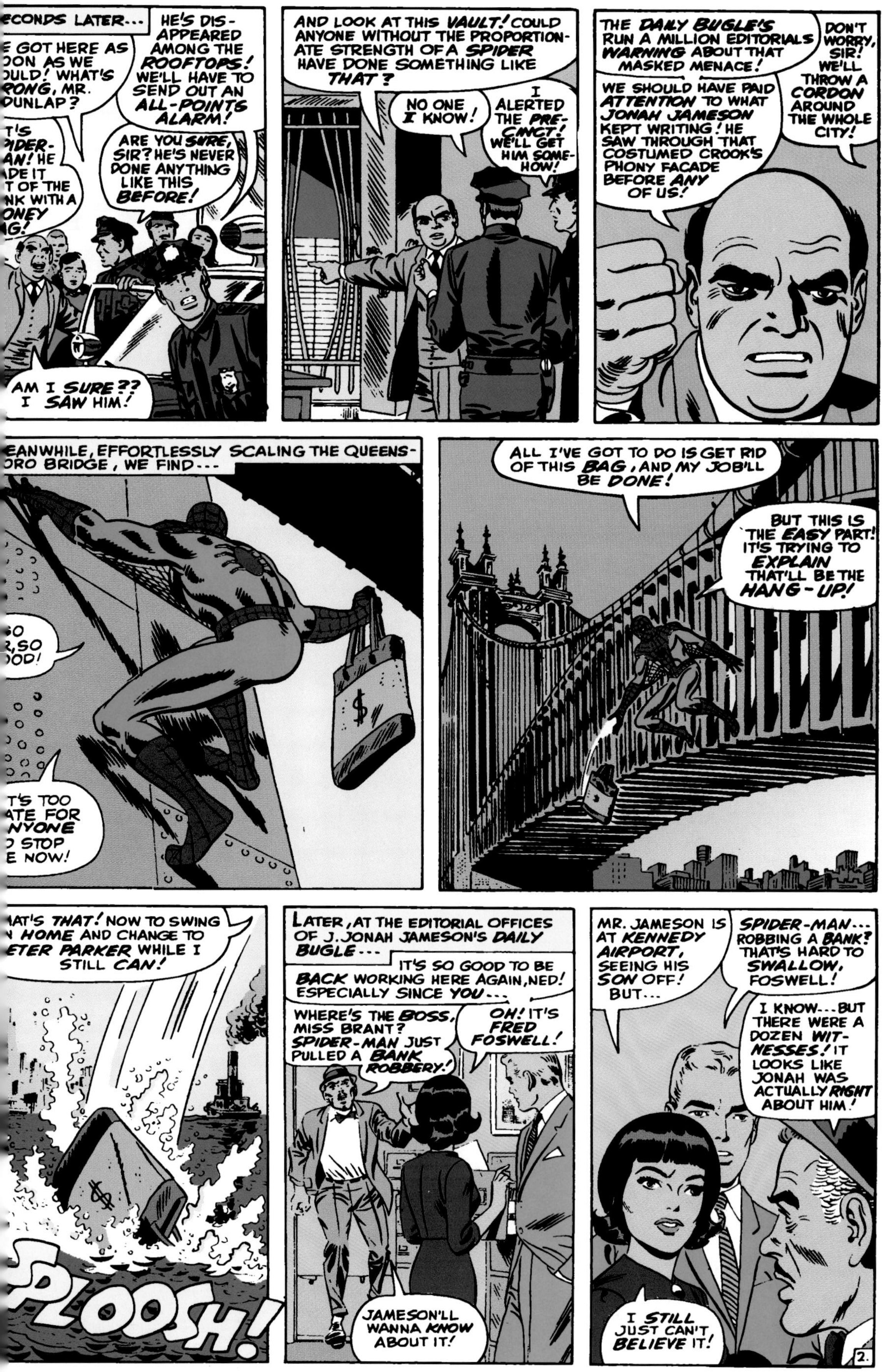

ECONDS LATER...
E GOT HERE AS OON AS WE OULD! WHAT'S RONG, MR. DUNLAP?
HE'S DIS-APPEARED AMONG THE ROOFTOPS! WE'LL HAVE TO SEND OUT AN ALL-POINTS ALARM!
T'S PIDER-AN! HE ADE IT T OF THE NK WITH A ONEY G!
ARE YOU SURE, SIR? HE'S NEVER DONE ANYTHING LIKE THIS BEFORE!
AM I SURE?? I SAW HIM!
AND LOOK AT THIS VAULT! COULD ANYONE WITHOUT THE PROPORTION-ATE STRENGTH OF A SPIDER HAVE DONE SOMETHING LIKE THAT?
NO ONE I KNOW!
I ALERTED THE PRE-CINCT! WE'LL GET HIM SOME-HOW!
THE DAILY BUGLE'S RUN A MILLION EDITORIALS WARNING ABOUT THAT MASKED MENACE!
WE SHOULD HAVE PAID ATTENTION TO WHAT JONAH JAMESON KEPT WRITING! HE SAW THROUGH THAT COSTUMED CROOK'S PHONY FACADE BEFORE ANY OF US!
DON'T WORRY, SIR! WE'LL THROW A CORDON AROUND THE WHOLE CITY!
EANWHILE, EFFORTLESSLY SCALING THE QUEENS-ORO BRIDGE, WE FIND---
O R, SO OOD!
T'S TOO ATE FOR NYONE O STOP E NOW!
ALL I'VE GOT TO DO IS GET RID OF THIS BAG, AND MY JOB'LL BE DONE!
BUT THIS IS THE EASY PART! IT'S TRYING TO EXPLAIN THAT'LL BE THE HANG-UP!
AT'S THAT! NOW TO SWING N HOME AND CHANGE TO ETER PARKER WHILE I STILL CAN!
PLOOSH!
LATER, AT THE EDITORIAL OFFICES OF J. JONAH JAMESON'S DAILY BUGLE---
IT'S SO GOOD TO BE BACK WORKING HERE AGAIN, NED! ESPECIALLY SINCE YOU---
WHERE'S THE BOSS, MISS BRANT? SPIDER-MAN JUST PULLED A BANK ROBBERY!
OH! IT'S FRED FOSWELL!
JAMESON'LL WANNA KNOW ABOUT IT!
MR. JAMESON IS AT KENNEDY AIRPORT, SEEING HIS SON OFF! BUT---
SPIDER-MAN--- ROBBING A BANK? THAT'S HARD TO SWALLOW, FOSWELL!
I KNOW---BUT THERE WERE A DOZEN WIT-NESSES! IT LOOKS LIKE JONAH WAS ACTUALLY RIGHT ABOUT HIM!
I STILL JUST CAN'T BELIEVE IT!
2.

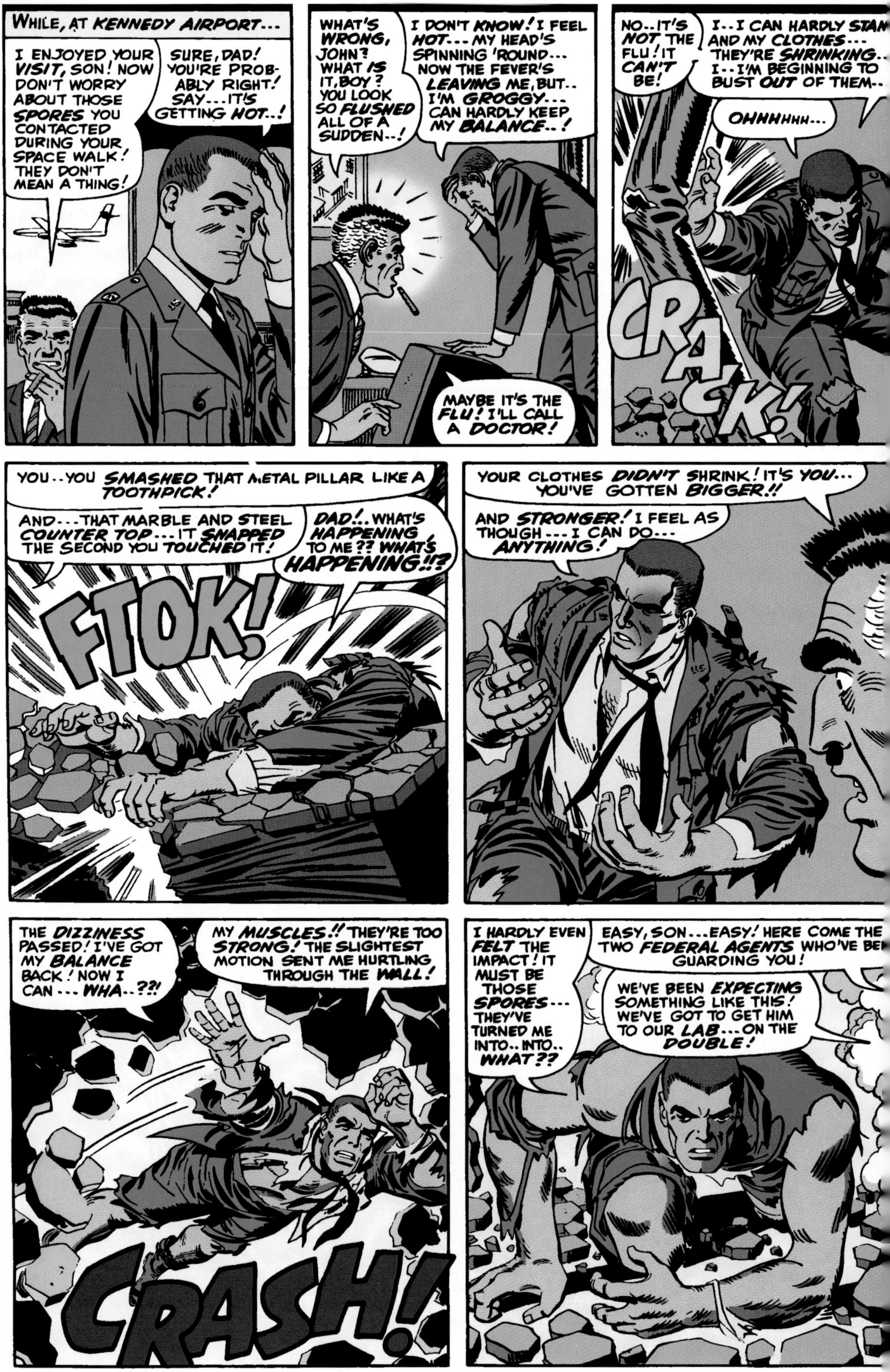
WHILE, AT KENNEDY AIRPORT...
I ENJOYED YOUR VISIT, SON! NOW DON'T WORRY ABOUT THOSE SPORES YOU CONTACTED DURING YOUR SPACE WALK! THEY DON'T MEAN A THING!
SURE, DAD! YOU'RE PROBABLY RIGHT! SAY...IT'S GETTING HOT..!
WHAT'S WRONG, JOHN? WHAT IS IT, BOY? YOU LOOK SO FLUSHED ALL OF A SUDDEN..!
I DON'T KNOW! I FEEL HOT... MY HEAD'S SPINNING 'ROUND... NOW THE FEVER'S LEAVING ME, BUT.. I'M GROGGY... CAN HARDLY KEEP MY BALANCE..!
MAYBE IT'S THE FLU! I'LL CALL A DOCTOR!
NO..IT'S NOT THE FLU! IT CAN'T BE!
I..I CAN HARDLY STAN
AND MY CLOTHES... THEY'RE SHRINKING.. I..I'M BEGINNING TO BUST OUT OF THEM..
OHHHHHH...
CRACK!
YOU..YOU SMASHED THAT METAL PILLAR LIKE A TOOTHPICK!
AND...THAT MARBLE AND STEEL COUNTER TOP... IT SNAPPED THE SECOND YOU TOUCHED IT!
DAD!..WHAT'S HAPPENING TO ME?? WHAT'S HAPPENING!!?
FTOK!
YOUR CLOTHES DIDN'T SHRINK! IT'S YOU... YOU'VE GOTTEN BIGGER!!
AND STRONGER! I FEEL AS THOUGH...I CAN DO... ANYTHING!
THE DIZZINESS PASSED! I'VE GOT MY BALANCE BACK! NOW I CAN...WHA..??!
MY MUSCLES!! THEY'RE TOO STRONG! THE SLIGHTEST MOTION SENT ME HURTLING THROUGH THE WALL!
CRASH!
I HARDLY EVEN FELT THE IMPACT! IT MUST BE THOSE SPORES... THEY'VE TURNED ME INTO..INTO.. WHAT??
EASY, SON...EASY! HERE COME THE TWO FEDERAL AGENTS WHO'VE BE GUARDING YOU!
WE'VE BEEN EXPECTING SOMETHING LIKE THIS! WE'VE GOT TO GET HIM TO OUR LAB...ON THE DOUBLE!

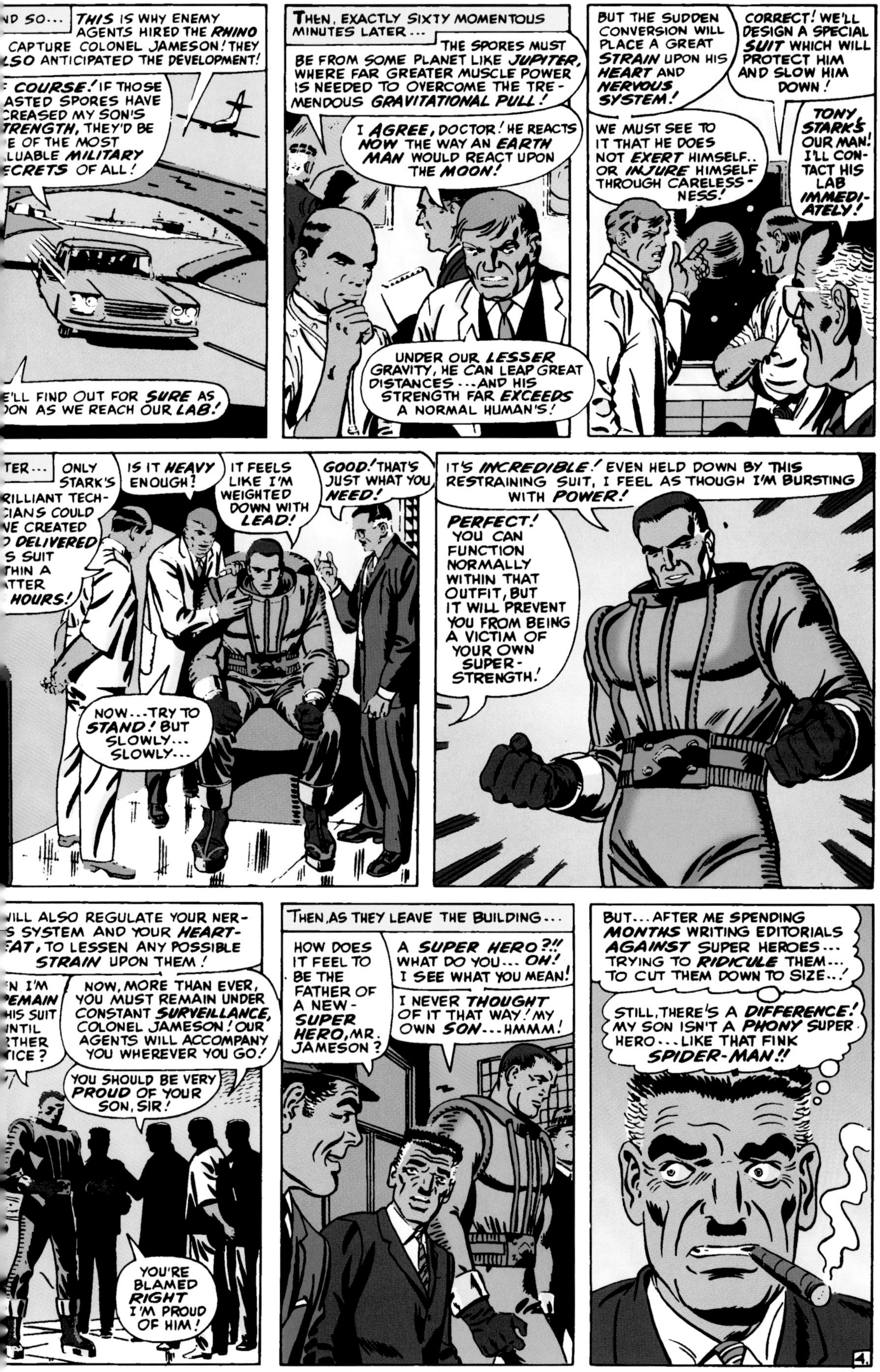
ND SO...
THIS IS WHY ENEMY AGENTS HIRED THE RHINO CAPTURE COLONEL JAMESON! THEY LSO ANTICIPATED THE DEVELOPMENT!
COURSE! IF THOSE ASTED SPORES HAVE CREASED MY SON'S TRENGTH, THEY'D BE E OF THE MOST LUABLE MILITARY ECRETS OF ALL!
E'LL FIND OUT FOR SURE AS OON AS WE REACH OUR LAB!
THEN, EXACTLY SIXTY MOMENTOUS MINUTES LATER...
THE SPORES MUST BE FROM SOME PLANET LIKE JUPITER, WHERE FAR GREATER MUSCLE POWER IS NEEDED TO OVERCOME THE TREMENDOUS GRAVITATIONAL PULL!
I AGREE, DOCTOR! HE REACTS NOW THE WAY AN EARTH MAN WOULD REACT UPON THE MOON!
UNDER OUR LESSER GRAVITY, HE CAN LEAP GREAT DISTANCES...AND HIS STRENGTH FAR EXCEEDS A NORMAL HUMAN'S!
BUT THE SUDDEN CONVERSION WILL PLACE A GREAT STRAIN UPON HIS HEART AND NERVOUS SYSTEM!
CORRECT! WE'LL DESIGN A SPECIAL SUIT WHICH WILL PROTECT HIM AND SLOW HIM DOWN!
WE MUST SEE TO IT THAT HE DOES NOT EXERT HIMSELF.. OR INJURE HIMSELF THROUGH CARELESSNESS!
TONY STARK'S OUR MAN! I'LL CONTACT HIS LAB IMMEDIATELY!
TER...
ONLY STARK'S RILLIANT TECHCIANS COULD VE CREATED D DELIVERED S SUIT THIN A TTER HOURS!
IS IT HEAVY ENOUGH?
IT FEELS LIKE I'M WEIGHTED DOWN WITH LEAD!
GOOD! THAT'S JUST WHAT YOU NEED!
NOW...TRY TO STAND! BUT SLOWLY... SLOWLY...
IT'S INCREDIBLE! EVEN HELD DOWN BY THIS RESTRAINING SUIT, I FEEL AS THOUGH I'M BURSTING WITH POWER!
PERFECT! YOU CAN FUNCTION NORMALLY WITHIN THAT OUTFIT, BUT IT WILL PREVENT YOU FROM BEING A VICTIM OF YOUR OWN SUPER-STRENGTH!
VILL ALSO REGULATE YOUR NERS SYSTEM AND YOUR HEART-AT, TO LESSEN ANY POSSIBLE STRAIN UPON THEM!
N I'M EMAIN HIS SUIT NTIL RTHER TICE?
NOW, MORE THAN EVER, YOU MUST REMAIN UNDER CONSTANT SURVEILLANCE, COLONEL JAMESON! OUR AGENTS WILL ACCOMPANY YOU WHEREVER YOU GO!
YOU SHOULD BE VERY PROUD OF YOUR SON, SIR!
YOU'RE BLAMED RIGHT I'M PROUD OF HIM!
THEN, AS THEY LEAVE THE BUILDING...
HOW DOES IT FEEL TO BE THE FATHER OF A NEW SUPER HERO, MR. JAMESON?
A SUPER HERO?!! WHAT DO YOU... OH! I SEE WHAT YOU MEAN!
I NEVER THOUGHT OF IT THAT WAY! MY OWN SON...HMMM!
BUT...AFTER ME SPENDING MONTHS WRITING EDITORIALS AGAINST SUPER HEROES... TRYING TO RIDICULE THEM... TO CUT THEM DOWN TO SIZE...!
STILL, THERE'S A DIFFERENCE! MY SON ISN'T A PHONY SUPER HERO...LIKE THAT FINK SPIDER-MAN!!
4.

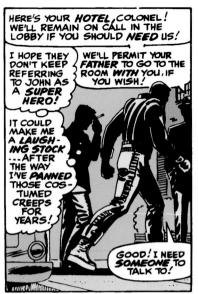

HERE'S YOUR *HOTEL*, COLONEL! WE'LL REMAIN ON CALL IN THE LOBBY IF YOU SHOULD *NEED* US!

I HOPE THEY DON'T KEEP REFERRING TO JOHN AS A *SUPER HERO!*

IT COULD MAKE ME A *LAUGHING STOCK*...AFTER THE WAY I'VE *PANNED* THOSE COSTUMED CREEPS FOR YEARS!

WE'LL PERMIT YOUR *FATHER* TO GO TO THE ROOM *WITH* YOU, IF YOU WISH!

GOOD! I NEED *SOMEONE* TO TALK TO!

THEN, UPON REACHING COLONEL JAMESON'S CLOSELY-GUARDED ROOM...

FOSWELL? THIS IS J.J.J.! WHAT'S GOING *ON* THERE WHILE I'M... *WHAT?!!*

SAY IT *AGAIN!!* ARE YOU *SURE??* YOU MEAN... THERE WERE *WITNESSES??* SO THERE *CAN'T* BE A MISTAKE THIS TIME!!

WHAT'S UP, DAD?

IT FINALLY *HAPPENED!* I'VE GOT THE PROOF I *NEED!* NOW THE WHOLE, CHICKEN-SCRATCHIN' WORLD WILL KNOW I WAS *RIGHT!*

THAT'S *SWELL*, DAD! GLAD TO *HEAR* IT!

BUT RIGHT ABOUT *WHAT??*

ABOUT *SPIDER-MAN!*

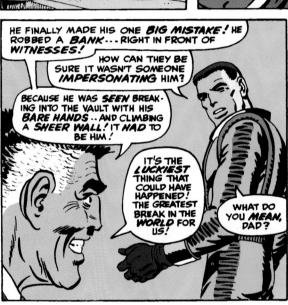

HE FINALLY MADE HIS ONE *BIG MISTAKE!* HE ROBBED A *BANK*...RIGHT IN FRONT OF *WITNESSES!*

HOW CAN THEY BE SURE IT WASN'T SOMEONE *IMPERSONATING* HIM?

BECAUSE HE WAS *SEEN* BREAKING INTO THE VAULT WITH HIS *BARE HANDS*..AND CLIMBING A *SHEER WALL!* IT *HAD* TO BE HIM!

IT'S THE *LUCKIEST* THING THAT COULD HAVE *HAPPENED!* THE GREATEST BREAK IN THE *WORLD* FOR US!

WHAT DO YOU *MEAN*, DAD?

DON'T YOU *SEE?* THAT WEB-HEAD HAS FOOLED *EVERYBODY* ALL THIS TIME!

I WAS THE ONLY ONE WHO SAW *THROUGH* HIM! BUT I WAS A LONE VOICE, CRYING IN THE WILDERNESS! NOBODY *BELIEVED* ME! THEY ALL *LAUGHED* AT ME!

NOW, NOT ONLY WILL THE WORLD KNOW I WAS *RIGHT*...BUT JUST THINK OF THE *TRIUMPH* IF MY OWN *SON* IS THE ONE TO *CATCH* THAT MISERABLE MASKED MADMAN!

YOU WANT *ME* TO GO AFTER HIM?

OF COURSE! THAT BANK ROBBERY PROVES I MUST HAVE BEEN *RIGHT* ABOUT *ALL* THE THINGS I ACCUSED HIM OF!

AND *NOW*...HE'S IN HIDING! WITH HIS SUPER-POWERS, IT MAY TAKE *YEARS* TO NAB HIM!

BUT *YOU'RE* EVEN STRONGER THAN *HE* IS! YOU'VE GOT TO SHOW THE WORLD WHAT A *REAL* SUPER HERO CAN DO! WHAT JONAH JAMESON'S *SON* CAN DO!

I NEVER LOOKED AT IT THAT WAY!

THINK WHAT IT WOULD MEAN TO *ME*...TO YOUR BUDDIES IN THE *SPACE PROGRAM*...TO ALL THE IMPRESSIONABLE *HERO WORSHIPPERS* EVERYWHERE!

YOU'VE GOT TO PROVE THAT *NO* CRUMMY *CROOK* CAN GET AWAY WITH ANYTHING...EVEN IF HE'S GOT SUPER POWERS!

GO GET 'IM, JOHNNY! SQUASH THAT WALL-CRAWLER LIKE A *BEDBUG!* YOU CAN *DO* IT!

OKAY DAD! YOU'RE *ON!*

THAT'S *MY* BOY!

WE SAW COLONEL JAMESON RUN *OUT* OF HERE...BEFORE WE COULD *STOP* HIM!

NOTHING TO BE *ALARMED* AT, MY GOOD MAN! HE'S OFF ON A MISSION OF *JUSTICE!*

WHAT *HAPPENED??* SPEAK *UP,* MAN!

BUT HE WAS *ORDERED* NOT TO GO OFF ALONE! IT'S *DANGEROUS!*

YOU *BET* IT IS.... TO *SPIDER-MAN!!*

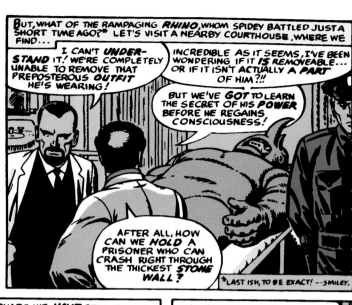

BUT, WHAT OF THE RAMPAGING *RHINO,* WHOM SPIDEY BATTLED JUST A *SHORT TIME AGO?* LET'S VISIT A NEARBY COURTHOUSE, WHERE WE FIND...

I CAN'T *UNDER-STAND* IT! WE'RE COMPLETELY UNABLE TO REMOVE THAT PREPOSTEROUS *OUTFIT* HE'S WEARING!

INCREDIBLE AS IT SEEMS, I'VE BEEN WONDERING IF IT *IS* REMOVEABLE... OR IF IT ISN'T ACTUALLY A *PART* OF HIM?!!

BUT WE'VE *GOT* TO LEARN THE SECRET OF HIS *POWER* BEFORE HE REGAINS CONSCIOUSNESS!

AFTER ALL, HOW CAN WE *HOLD* A PRISONER WHO CAN CRASH RIGHT THROUGH THE THICKEST *STONE WALL?*

*LAST ISH, TO BE EXACT! --SMILEY.

WHAT ABOUT *TRANQUILIZERS?* SURELY WE CAN RESTRAIN HIM *THAT* WAY!

NO DICE, DOCTOR! I'VE BROKEN THREE NEEDLES *ALREADY!*

NOTHING CAN PIERCE THAT *SKIN* OF HIS!

PERHAPS WE *HAVE* BEEN ON THE WRONG TRACK! IF THAT *ISN'T* A COSTUME...PERHAPS YOUR HIM IT REALLY *IS* SOME SORT OF SUPER-POWERFUL OUTER *HIDE*...

IT'S ALMOST *UN-THINKABLE!* AND YET, WHAT OTHER ANSWER CAN THERE *BE?*

IT'S FORTUNATE HE HASN'T *AWAKENED* YET! WE'D BETTER SUMMON SOME MORE *SPECIALISTS* BEFORE HE *DOES!* LET'S *GO!*

SLAM!

JUST WEARING A MACABRE *OUTFIT* ISN'T LIKELY TO GIVE HIM SUCH BRUTISH *POWER!*

AND, FURTHER DOWN THE HALL, AN ATTORNEY APPEARS BEFORE THE BENCH...

BUT YOUR HONOR-- I'VE SUCH A BUSY SCHEDULE...AND THERE ARE *OTHER* ATTORNEYS THE COURT MIGHT HAVE APPOINTED TO DEFEND THE *RHINO!*

I'M *AWARE* OF THAT, COUNSELOR! BUT, DUE TO THE *UNUSUAL* NATURE OF THE ACCUSED, I FELT SOMEONE WITH YOUR *EX-PERIENCE* IN BIZARRE CASES WAS NEEDED!

HOWEVER, *MR. NELSON,* IF YOU FEEL YOU *CANNOT* ACCEPT THE ASSIGNMENT, PERHAPS YOUR LAW PARTNER, *MATTHEW MURDOCK* IS AVAILABLE!

NO, YOUR HONOR! HE HAPPENS TO BE -- EH... *OUT OF TOWN,* AT THE MOMENT! *

*HE SURE *IS,* AS YOU'LL SEE IN *DAREDEVIL* #21, NOW ON SALE! ... PLUG-HAPPY STAN!

HOWEVER, I'VE RECONSIDERED THE MATTER...AND IF YOUR HONOR SO DESIRES, I SHALL ACCEPT THE DEFENSE OF THE PRISONER KNOWN AS *RHINO!*

EXCELLENT! AT THIS MOMENT YOUR CLIENT IS *UNCONSCIOUS* IN CELL-BLOCK B...WITH A TEAM OF POLICE PHYSICIANS IN ATTENDANCE!

I WOULD LIKE TO *CONSULT* WITH HIM AS SOON AS POSSIBLE!

6

HE'S CONSCIOUS!! LOOK OUT...!

NO CELL CAN HOLD THE RHINO!

BULLETS WON'T STOP 'IM! WHAT'LL WE DO?

SLAK!

I'M GETTING OUT... AND NOW!

BRAK!

STOMP!

STAND ASIDE! DON'T TRY TO STOP HIM! HELP IS ON THE WAY!

BTOOM!

HELP!? HAH! HOW CAN ANYTHING HALT THE RHINO'S CHARGE?!

DID YOU SEE IT?? THE WAY HE SMASHED THROUGH THAT BRICK WALL!!

NO MATTER! THEY'RE WAITING FOR HIM IN THE CORRIDOR... WITH THE ONE THING THAT MAY STOP HIM!

STOMP!

STOMP!

HERE HE COMES! LET 'IM HAVE IT... NOW!

STOMP!

AT THIS RANGE I CAN'T MISS!

SSSSS

HE'S SLOWING DOWN! LOOK... IT'S WORKING!!

THE ONE THING HIS RHINO HIDE COULDN'T PROTECT HIM FROM... A SPRAY TRANQUILIZER!

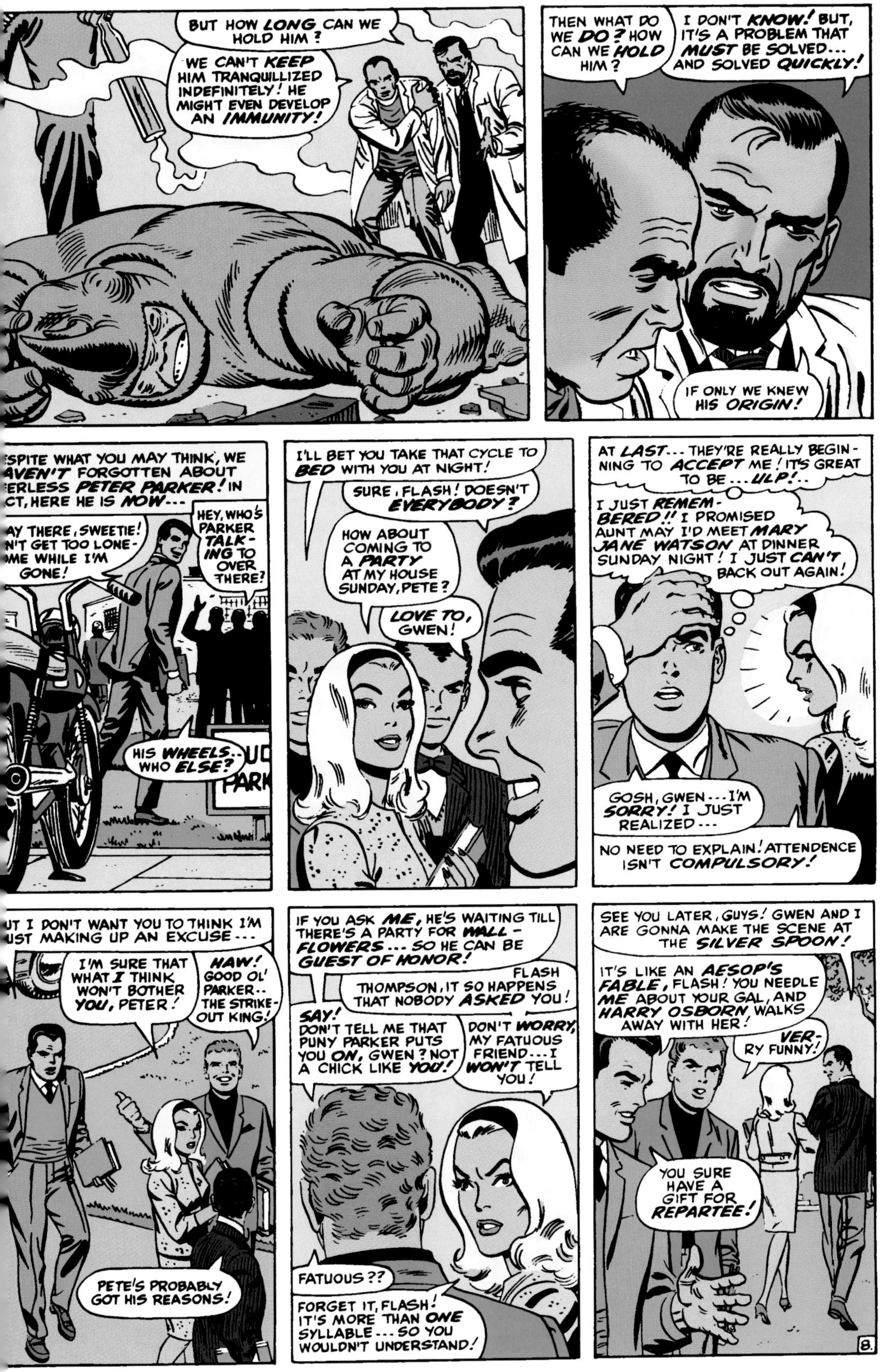
BUT HOW LONG CAN WE HOLD HIM?
WE CAN'T KEEP HIM TRANQUILLIZED INDEFINITELY! HE MIGHT EVEN DEVELOP AN IMMUNITY!
THEN WHAT DO WE DO? HOW CAN WE HOLD HIM?
I DON'T KNOW! BUT, IT'S A PROBLEM THAT MUST BE SOLVED... AND SOLVED QUICKLY!
IF ONLY WE KNEW HIS ORIGIN!
ESPITE WHAT YOU MAY THINK, WE AVEN'T FORGOTTEN ABOUT ERLESS PETER PARKER! IN CT, HERE HE IS NOW---
AY THERE, SWEETIE! N'T GET TOO LONE- ME WHILE I'M GONE!
HEY, WHO'S PARKER TALKING TO OVER THERE?
HIS WHEELS.. WHO ELSE?
I'LL BET YOU TAKE THAT CYCLE TO BED WITH YOU AT NIGHT!
SURE, FLASH! DOESN'T EVERYBODY?
HOW ABOUT COMING TO A PARTY AT MY HOUSE SUNDAY, PETE?
LOVE TO, GWEN!
AT LAST--- THEY'RE REALLY BEGIN-NING TO ACCEPT ME! IT'S GREAT TO BE... ULP!..
I JUST REMEMBERED!! I PROMISED AUNT MAY I'D MEET MARY JANE WATSON AT DINNER SUNDAY NIGHT! I JUST CAN'T BACK OUT AGAIN!
GOSH, GWEN--- I'M SORRY! I JUST REALIZED---
NO NEED TO EXPLAIN! ATTENDENCE ISN'T COMPULSORY!
UT I DON'T WANT YOU TO THINK I'M UST MAKING UP AN EXCUSE---
I'M SURE THAT WHAT I THINK WON'T BOTHER YOU, PETER!
HAW! GOOD OL' PARKER.. THE STRIKE-OUT KING!
PETE'S PROBABLY GOT HIS REASONS!
IF YOU ASK ME, HE'S WAITING TILL THERE'S A PARTY FOR WALL-FLOWERS... SO HE CAN BE GUEST OF HONOR!
FLASH THOMPSON, IT SO HAPPENS THAT NOBODY ASKED YOU!
SAY! DON'T TELL ME THAT PUNY PARKER PUTS YOU ON, GWEN? NOT A CHICK LIKE YOU!
DON'T WORRY, MY FATUOUS FRIEND--- I WON'T TELL YOU!
FATUOUS??
FORGET IT, FLASH! IT'S MORE THAN ONE SYLLABLE... SO YOU WOULDN'T UNDERSTAND!
SEE YOU LATER, GUYS! GWEN AND I ARE GONNA MAKE THE SCENE AT THE SILVER SPOON!
IT'S LIKE AN AESOP'S FABLE, FLASH! YOU NEEDLE ME ABOUT YOUR GAL, AND HARRY OSBORN WALKS AWAY WITH HER!
VER-RY FUNNY!
YOU SURE HAVE A GIFT FOR REPARTEE!

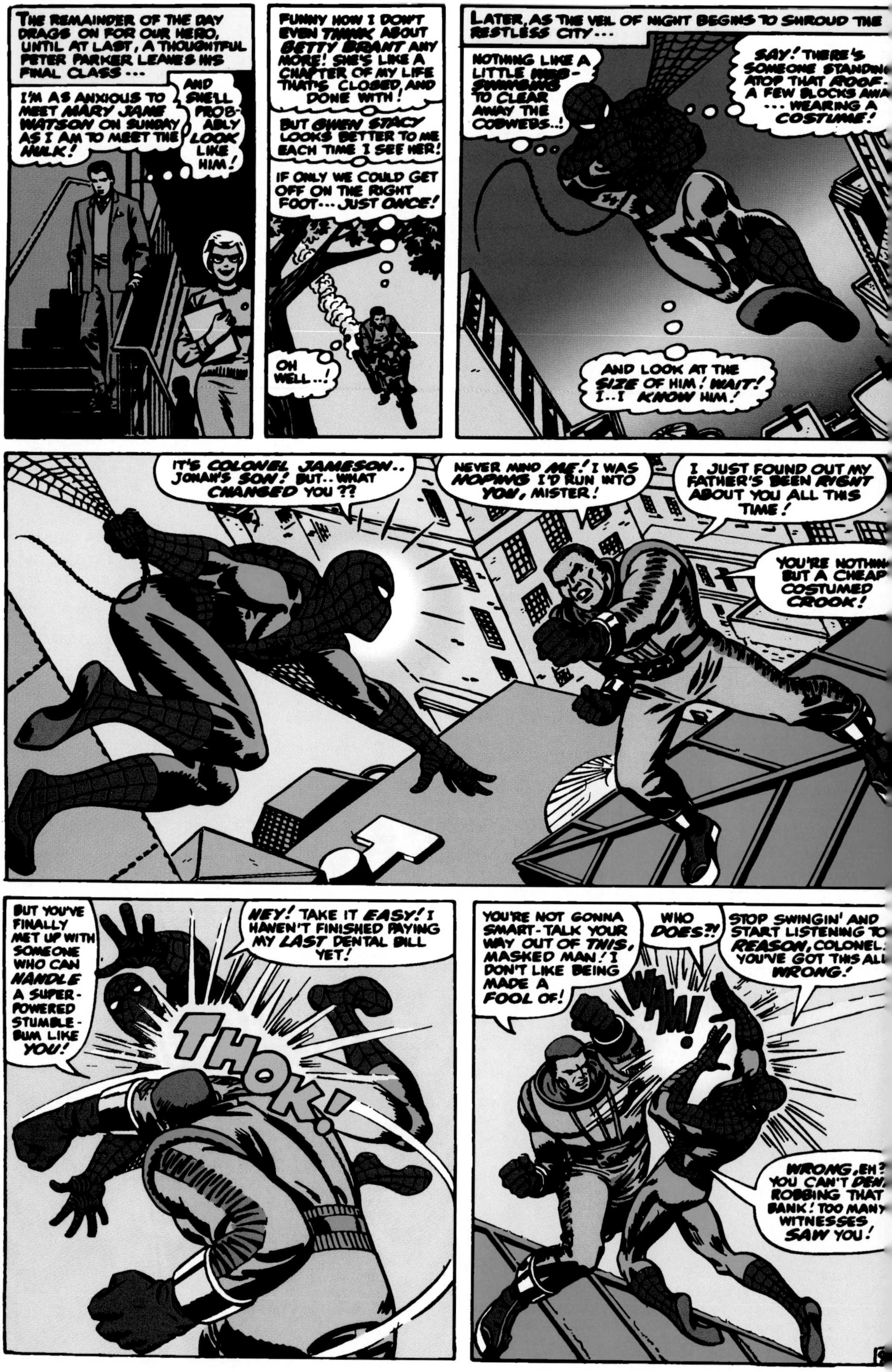
THE REMAINDER OF THE DAY DRAGS ON FOR OUR HERO, UNTIL AT LAST, A THOUGHTFUL PETER PARKER LEAVES HIS FINAL CLASS...
I'M AS ANXIOUS TO MEET MARY JANE WATSON ON SUNDAY AS I AM TO MEET THE HULK!
AND SHE'LL PROBABLY LOOK LIKE HIM!
FUNNY HOW I DON'T EVEN THINK ABOUT BETTY BRANT ANY MORE! SHE'S LIKE A CHAPTER OF MY LIFE THAT'S CLOSED AND DONE WITH!
BUT GWEN STACY LOOKS BETTER TO ME EACH TIME I SEE HER!
IF ONLY WE COULD GET OFF ON THE RIGHT FOOT... JUST ONCE!
OH WELL...!
LATER, AS THE VEIL OF NIGHT BEGINS TO SHROUD THE RESTLESS CITY...
NOTHING LIKE A LITTLE WEB-SWINGING TO CLEAR AWAY THE COBWEBS..!
SAY! THERE'S SOMEONE STANDING ATOP THAT ROOF A FEW BLOCKS AWAY... WEARING A COSTUME!
AND LOOK AT THE SIZE OF HIM! WAIT! I..I KNOW HIM!
IT'S COLONEL JAMESON.. JONAH'S SON! BUT.. WHAT CHANGED YOU??
NEVER MIND ME! I WAS HOPING I'D RUN INTO YOU, MISTER!
I JUST FOUND OUT MY FATHER'S BEEN RIGHT ABOUT YOU ALL THIS TIME!
YOU'RE NOTHING BUT A CHEAP COSTUMED CROOK!
BUT YOU'VE FINALLY MET UP WITH SOMEONE WHO CAN HANDLE A SUPER-POWERED STUMBLE-BUM LIKE YOU!
HEY! TAKE IT EASY! I HAVEN'T FINISHED PAYING MY LAST DENTAL BILL YET!
THOK!
YOU'RE NOT GONNA SMART-TALK YOUR WAY OUT OF THIS, MASKED MAN! I DON'T LIKE BEING MADE A FOOL OF!
WHO DOES?!
STOP SWINGIN' AND START LISTENING TO REASON, COLONEL! YOU'VE GOT THIS ALL WRONG!
WAM!
WRONG, EH? YOU CAN'T DENY ROBBING THAT BANK! TOO MANY WITNESSES SAW YOU!

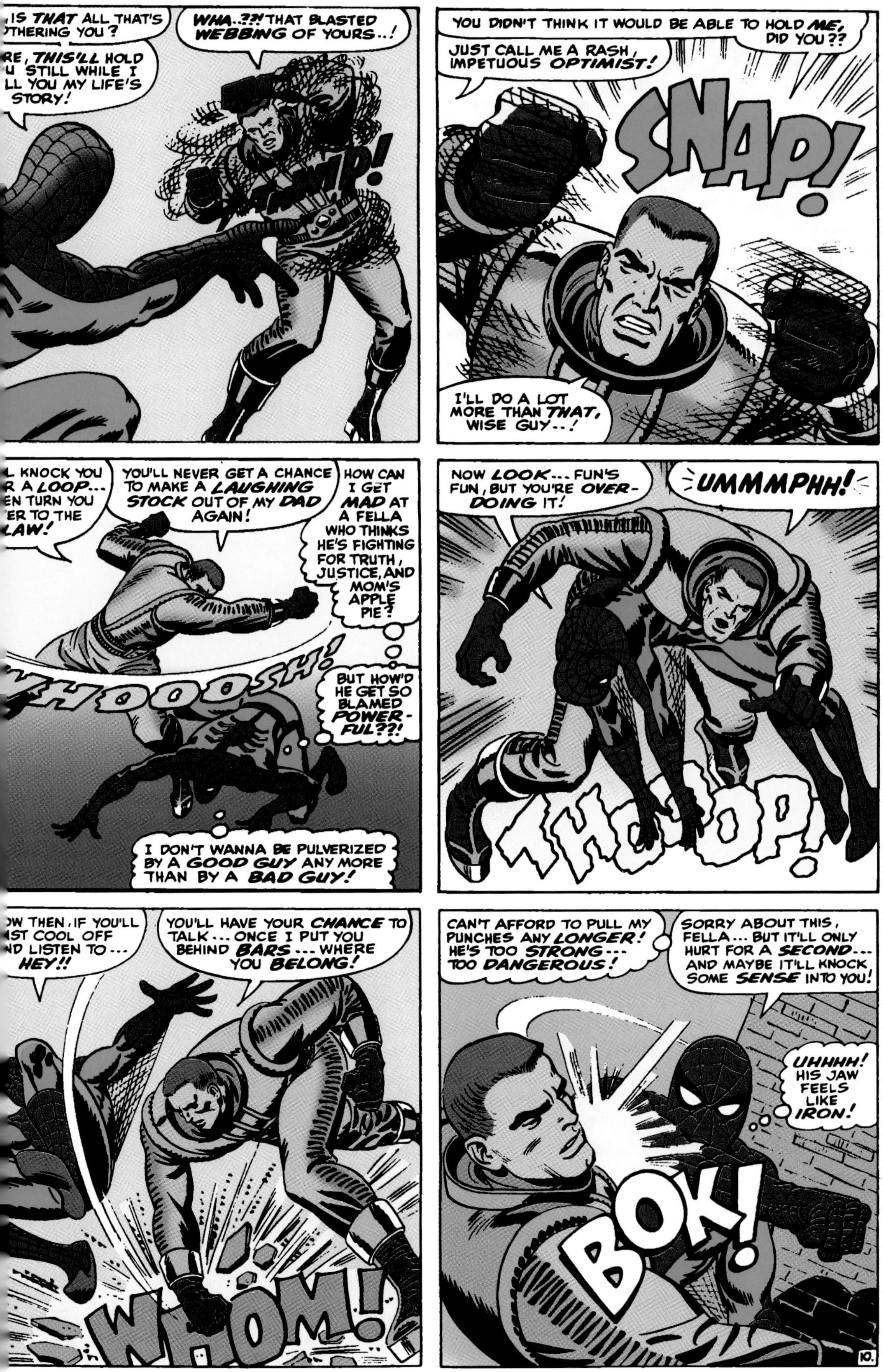

IS THAT ALL THAT'S OTHERING YOU?
RE, THIS'LL HOLD U STILL WHILE I LL YOU MY LIFE'S STORY!
WHA..?!? THAT BLASTED WEBBING OF YOURS..!
YOU DIDN'T THINK IT WOULD BE ABLE TO HOLD ME, DID YOU??
JUST CALL ME A RASH, IMPETUOUS OPTIMIST!
SNAP!
I'LL DO A LOT MORE THAN THAT, WISE GUY..!
L KNOCK YOU R A LOOP... EN TURN YOU ER TO THE LAW!
YOU'LL NEVER GET A CHANCE TO MAKE A LAUGHING STOCK OUT OF MY DAD AGAIN!
HOW CAN I GET MAD AT A FELLA WHO THINKS HE'S FIGHTING FOR TRUTH, JUSTICE, AND MOM'S APPLE PIE?
HOOOSH!
BUT HOW'D HE GET SO BLAMED POWER-FUL??!
I DON'T WANNA BE PULVERIZED BY A GOOD GUY ANY MORE THAN BY A BAD GUY!
NOW LOOK... FUN'S FUN, BUT YOU'RE OVER-DOING IT!
UMMMPHH!
OW THEN, IF YOU'LL ST COOL OFF ND LISTEN TO... HEY!!
YOU'LL HAVE YOUR CHANCE TO TALK... ONCE I PUT YOU BEHIND BARS... WHERE YOU BELONG!
CAN'T AFFORD TO PULL MY PUNCHES ANY LONGER! HE'S TOO STRONG--- TOO DANGEROUS!
SORRY ABOUT THIS, FELLA... BUT IT'LL ONLY HURT FOR A SECOND... AND MAYBE IT'LL KNOCK SOME SENSE INTO YOU!
UHHHH! HIS JAW FEELS LIKE IRON!
BOK!
10.

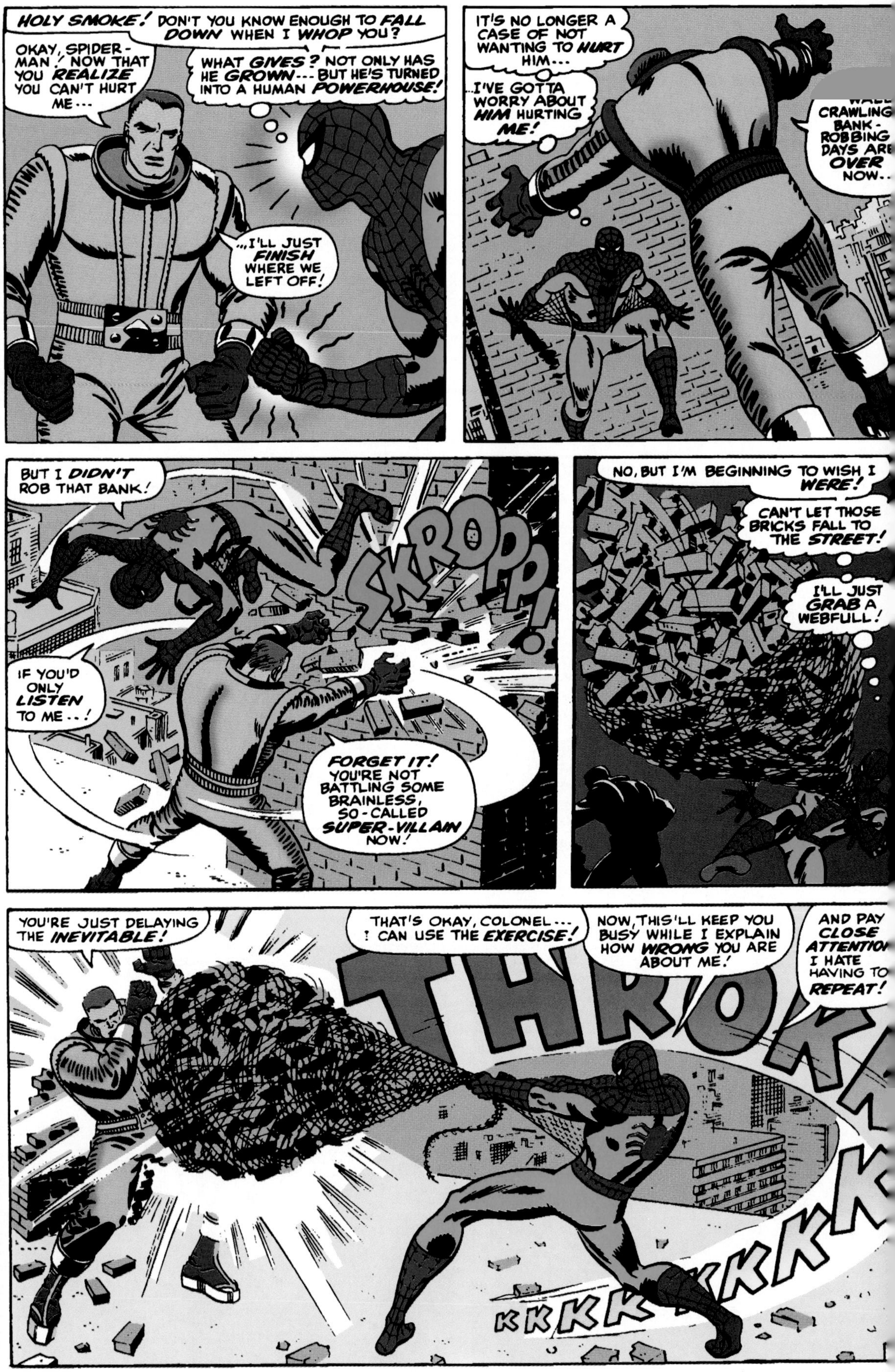
HOLY SMOKE! DON'T YOU KNOW ENOUGH TO FALL DOWN WHEN I WHOP YOU?
OKAY, SPIDER-MAN! NOW THAT YOU REALIZE YOU CAN'T HURT ME...
WHAT GIVES? NOT ONLY HAS HE GROWN--- BUT HE'S TURNED INTO A HUMAN POWERHOUSE!
...I'LL JUST FINISH WHERE WE LEFT OFF!
IT'S NO LONGER A CASE OF NOT WANTING TO HURT HIM...
I'VE GOTTA WORRY ABOUT HIM HURTING ME!
CRAWLING BANK-ROBBING DAYS ARE OVER NOW...
BUT I DIDN'T ROB THAT BANK!
SKROPP!
IF YOU'D ONLY LISTEN TO ME..!
FORGET IT! YOU'RE NOT BATTLING SOME BRAINLESS, SO-CALLED SUPER-VILLAIN NOW!
NO, BUT I'M BEGINNING TO WISH I WERE!
CAN'T LET THOSE BRICKS FALL TO THE STREET!
I'LL JUST GRAB A WEBFULL!
YOU'RE JUST DELAYING THE INEVITABLE!
THAT'S OKAY, COLONEL... I CAN USE THE EXERCISE!
NOW, THIS'LL KEEP YOU BUSY WHILE I EXPLAIN HOW WRONG YOU ARE ABOUT ME!
AND PAY CLOSE ATTENTION I HATE HAVING TO REPEAT!
THROK
KKKKKKKKK

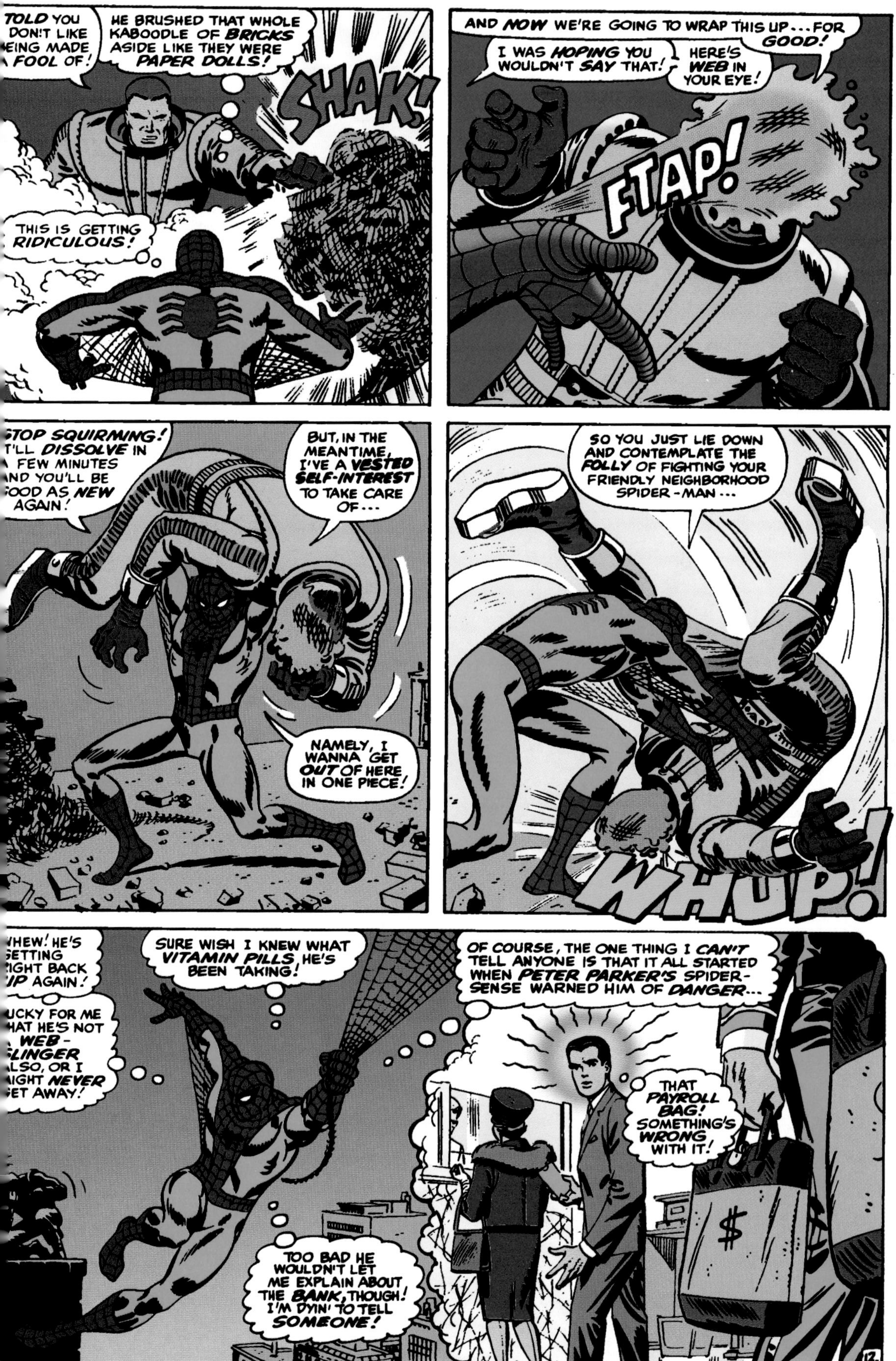

TOLD YOU DON!T LIKE EING MADE FOOL OF!
HE BRUSHED THAT WHOLE KABOODLE OF BRICKS ASIDE LIKE THEY WERE PAPER DOLLS!
SHAK!
THIS IS GETTING RIDICULOUS!
AND NOW WE'RE GOING TO WRAP THIS UP... FOR GOOD!
I WAS HOPING YOU WOULDN'T SAY THAT!
HERE'S WEB IN YOUR EYE!
FTAP!
STOP SQUIRMING! T'LL DISSOLVE IN FEW MINUTES ND YOU'LL BE OOD AS NEW AGAIN!
BUT, IN THE MEANTIME, I'VE A VESTED SELF-INTEREST TO TAKE CARE OF...
NAMELY, I WANNA GET OUT OF HERE IN ONE PIECE!
SO YOU JUST LIE DOWN AND CONTEMPLATE THE FOLLY OF FIGHTING YOUR FRIENDLY NEIGHBORHOOD SPIDER-MAN...
WHUP!
WHEW! HE'S GETTING IGHT BACK UP AGAIN!
UCKY FOR ME HAT HE'S NOT WEB-SLINGER ALSO, OR I IGHT NEVER ET AWAY!
SURE WISH I KNEW WHAT VITAMIN PILLS HE'S BEEN TAKING!
TOO BAD HE WOULDN'T LET ME EXPLAIN ABOUT THE BANK, THOUGH! I'M DYIN' TO TELL SOMEONE!
OF COURSE, THE ONE THING I CAN'T TELL ANYONE IS THAT IT ALL STARTED WHEN PETER PARKER'S SPIDER-SENSE WARNED HIM OF DANGER...
THAT PAYROLL BAG! SOMETHING'S WRONG WITH IT!
12.

GOOD THING I LEANED *CLOSE* TO IT! I COULDN'T MISTAKE THAT FAINT *TICKING* SOUND!

PAYROLL BAGS DON'T *USUALLY* CONTAIN *BOMBS*...AS FAR AS I KNOW!

I'VE GOTTA GET *BACK* THERE AGAIN... *FAST*.. AS SPIDER-MAN!

HE'S *LEAVING!* THAT MEANS HE'S ALREADY *PLANTED* THE PHONY MONEY BAG! NO TIME TO NAB HIM *NOW!*

SPIDER-MAN! HOLD IT! STOP, I SAY!

I CAN *GUESS* WHAT HIS *GAME* IS..!

AFTER THE BOMB GOES *OFF*... INSIDE THE VAULT.. HE CAN RETURN FOR *EASY* PICKIN'S!

WAIT! YOU CAN'T... HEY! WHAT THE ..?!!

SORRY, FRIEND! NO TIME TO EXPLAIN *NOW!*

FITT!

WHAT'S TO *EXPLAIN*?

ANYONE CAN SPOT A BANK ROBBERY!

HOLY COW! HE..HE'S BENDING THOSE *IRON* BARS WITH HIS *BARE* HANDS!

AW, IT'S NOTHING! ALL A FELLA *NEEDS* IS THE PROPORTIONATE STRENGTH OF A *SPIDER!*

SKREEEKK!

THERE'S THE BAG! NOW...IF ONLY I HAVE ENOUGH *TIME*..!

HE ROBBED THE *BANK!* DON'T LET HIM GET AWAY! *HELP!* STOP, THIEF! STOP, THIEF!

CAN'T STOP *NOW!* IT MAY *BLOW* AT ANY SECOND!

YOU WON'T *ESCAPE!* THERE'S NO PLACE YOU CAN HIDE! NO PLACE!

JONAH JAMESON WAS *RIGHT* ABOUT HIM! HE'S A *CROOK!*

FOR *ONCE* LUCK WAS *WITH* ME! I *MADE* IT!

IT CAN'T DO ANY *DAMAGE* NOW!

IT *EXPLODED* JUST AFTER IT HIT THE WATER! ANOTHER FEW SECONDS WOULD HAVE BEEN *TOO LATE!*

AND THEY'LL ALL KNOW I'M *INNOCENT* AS SOON AS THEY REALIZE NO MONEY'S *MISSING!*

BOY! WON'T JONAH BE SURPRISED!

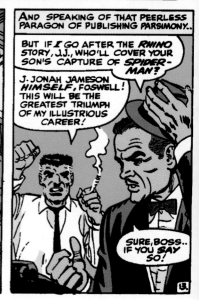

AND SPEAKING OF THAT PEERLESS PARAGON OF PUBLISHING PARSIMONY..

BUT IF *I* GO AFTER THE *RHINO* STORY, J.J., WHO'LL COVER YOUR SON'S CAPTURE OF *SPIDER-MAN?*

J. JONAH JAMESON *HIMSELF*, FOSWELL! THIS WILL BE THE GREATEST TRIUMPH OF MY ILLUSTRIOUS CAREER!

SURE, BOSS.. IF YOU *SAY* SO!

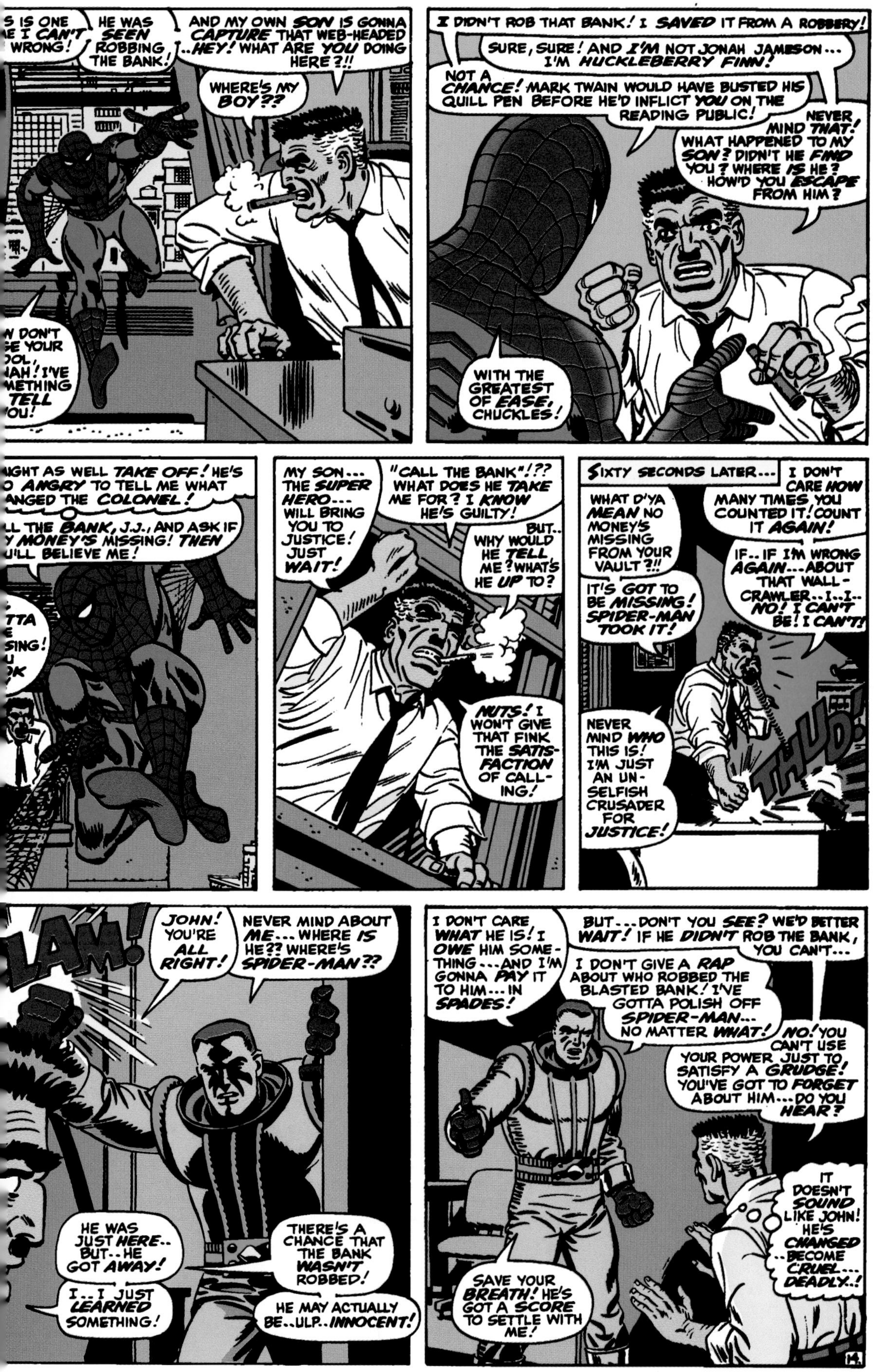
S IS ONE
E I CAN'T
WRONG!
HE WAS SEEN ROBBING THE BANK!
AND MY OWN SON IS GONNA CAPTURE THAT WEB-HEADED ..HEY! WHAT ARE YOU DOING HERE?!!
WHERE'S MY BOY??
N DON'T
E YOUR
OL,
AH! I'VE
METHING
TELL
OU!
I DIDN'T ROB THAT BANK! I SAVED IT FROM A ROBBERY!
SURE, SURE! AND I'M NOT JONAH JAMESON... I'M HUCKLEBERRY FINN!
NOT A CHANCE! MARK TWAIN WOULD HAVE BUSTED HIS QUILL PEN BEFORE HE'D INFLICT YOU ON THE READING PUBLIC!
NEVER MIND THAT! WHAT HAPPENED TO MY SON? DIDN'T HE FIND YOU? WHERE IS HE? HOW'D YOU ESCAPE FROM HIM?
WITH THE GREATEST OF EASE, CHUCKLES!
IGHT AS WELL TAKE OFF! HE'S
O ANGRY TO TELL ME WHAT
ANGED THE COLONEL!
LL THE BANK, J.J., AND ASK IF
Y MONEY'S MISSING! THEN
U'LL BELIEVE ME!
TTA
SING!
MY SON... THE SUPER HERO... WILL BRING YOU TO JUSTICE! JUST WAIT!
"CALL THE BANK"!?? WHAT DOES HE TAKE ME FOR? I KNOW HE'S GUILTY!
BUT.. WHY WOULD HE TELL ME? WHAT'S HE UP TO?
NUTS! I WON'T GIVE THAT FINK THE SATIS-FACTION OF CALL-ING!
SIXTY SECONDS LATER...
WHAT D'YA MEAN NO MONEY'S MISSING FROM YOUR VAULT?!!
I DON'T CARE HOW MANY TIMES YOU COUNTED IT! COUNT IT AGAIN!
IT'S GOT TO BE MISSING! SPIDER-MAN TOOK IT!
IF.. IF I'M WRONG AGAIN... ABOUT THAT WALL-CRAWLER.. I.. I.. NO! I CAN'T BE! I CAN'T!
NEVER MIND WHO THIS IS! I'M JUST AN UN-SELFISH CRUSADER FOR JUSTICE!
THUD!
LAM!
JOHN! YOU'RE ALL RIGHT!
NEVER MIND ABOUT ME... WHERE IS HE?? WHERE'S SPIDER-MAN??
HE WAS JUST HERE.. BUT.. HE GOT AWAY!
I.. I JUST LEARNED SOMETHING!
THERE'S A CHANCE THAT THE BANK WASN'T ROBBED!
HE MAY ACTUALLY BE.. ULP.. INNOCENT!
I DON'T CARE WHAT HE IS! I OWE HIM SOME-THING... AND I'M GONNA PAY IT TO HIM... IN SPADES!
BUT... DON'T YOU SEE? WE'D BETTER WAIT! IF HE DIDN'T ROB THE BANK, YOU CAN'T...
I DON'T GIVE A RAP ABOUT WHO ROBBED THE BLASTED BANK! I'VE GOTTA POLISH OFF SPIDER-MAN... NO MATTER WHAT!
NO! YOU CAN'T USE YOUR POWER JUST TO SATISFY A GRUDGE! YOU'VE GOT TO FORGET ABOUT HIM... DO YOU HEAR?
IT DOESN'T SOUND LIKE JOHN! HE'S CHANGED ...BECOME CRUEL... DEADLY..!
SAVE YOUR BREATH! HE'S GOT A SCORE TO SETTLE WITH ME!
14

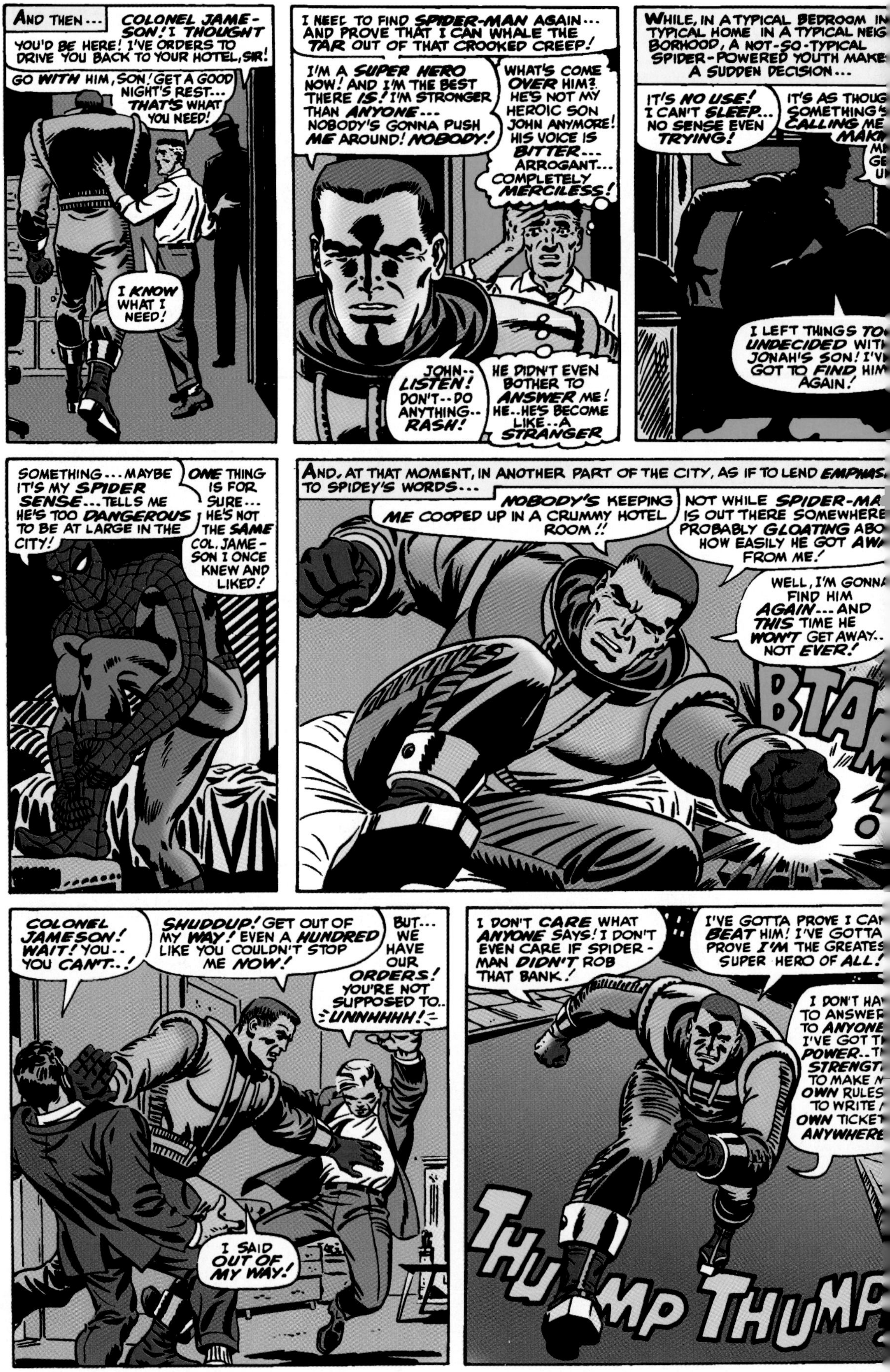

AND THEN...
COLONEL JAMESON! I THOUGHT YOU'D BE HERE! I'VE ORDERS TO DRIVE YOU BACK TO YOUR HOTEL, SIR!
GO WITH HIM, SON! GET A GOOD NIGHT'S REST... THAT'S WHAT YOU NEED!
I KNOW WHAT I NEED!
I NEED TO FIND SPIDER-MAN AGAIN... AND PROVE THAT I CAN WHALE THE TAR OUT OF THAT CROOKED CREEP!
I'M A SUPER HERO NOW! AND I'M THE BEST THERE IS! I'M STRONGER THAN ANYONE... NOBODY'S GONNA PUSH ME AROUND! NOBODY!
WHAT'S COME OVER HIM? HE'S NOT MY HEROIC SON JOHN ANYMORE! HIS VOICE IS BITTER... ARROGANT... COMPLETELY MERCILESS!
JOHN.. LISTEN! DON'T--DO ANYTHING.. RASH!
HE DIDN'T EVEN BOTHER TO ANSWER ME! HE..HE'S BECOME LIKE..A STRANGER
WHILE, IN A TYPICAL BEDROOM IN TYPICAL HOME IN A TYPICAL NEIG BORHOOD, A NOT-SO-TYPICAL SPIDER-POWERED YOUTH MAKES A SUDDEN DECISION...
IT'S NO USE! I CAN'T SLEEP... NO SENSE EVEN TRYING!
IT'S AS THOUG SOMETHING'S CALLING ME MAKI
I LEFT THINGS TOO UNDECIDED WITH JONAH'S SON! I'VE GOT TO FIND HIM AGAIN!
SOMETHING... MAYBE IT'S MY SPIDER SENSE... TELLS ME HE'S TOO DANGEROUS TO BE AT LARGE IN THE CITY!
ONE THING IS FOR SURE... HE'S NOT THE SAME COL. JAMESON I ONCE KNEW AND LIKED!
AND, AT THAT MOMENT, IN ANOTHER PART OF THE CITY, AS IF TO LEND EMPHAS TO SPIDEY'S WORDS...
NOBODY'S KEEPING ME COOPED UP IN A CRUMMY HOTEL ROOM!!
NOT WHILE SPIDER-MA IS OUT THERE SOMEWHERE PROBABLY GLOATING ABO HOW EASILY HE GOT AWA FROM ME!
WELL, I'M GONNA FIND HIM AGAIN... AND THIS TIME HE WON'T GET AWAY.. NOT EVER!
BTA
COLONEL JAMESON! WAIT! YOU.. YOU CAN'T..!
SHUDDUP! GET OUT OF MY WAY! EVEN A HUNDRED LIKE YOU COULDN'T STOP ME NOW!
BUT... WE HAVE OUR ORDERS! YOU'RE NOT SUPPOSED TO.. UNNHHHH!
I SAID OUT OF MY WAY!
I DON'T CARE WHAT ANYONE SAYS! I DON'T EVEN CARE IF SPIDER-MAN DIDN'T ROB THAT BANK!
I'VE GOTTA PROVE I CA BEAT HIM! I'VE GOTTA PROVE I'M THE GREATES SUPER HERO OF ALL!
I DON'T HA TO ANSWER TO ANYONE I'VE GOT T POWER.. T STRENGT TO MAKE M OWN RULES TO WRITE OWN TICKET ANYWHERE
THUMP THUMP

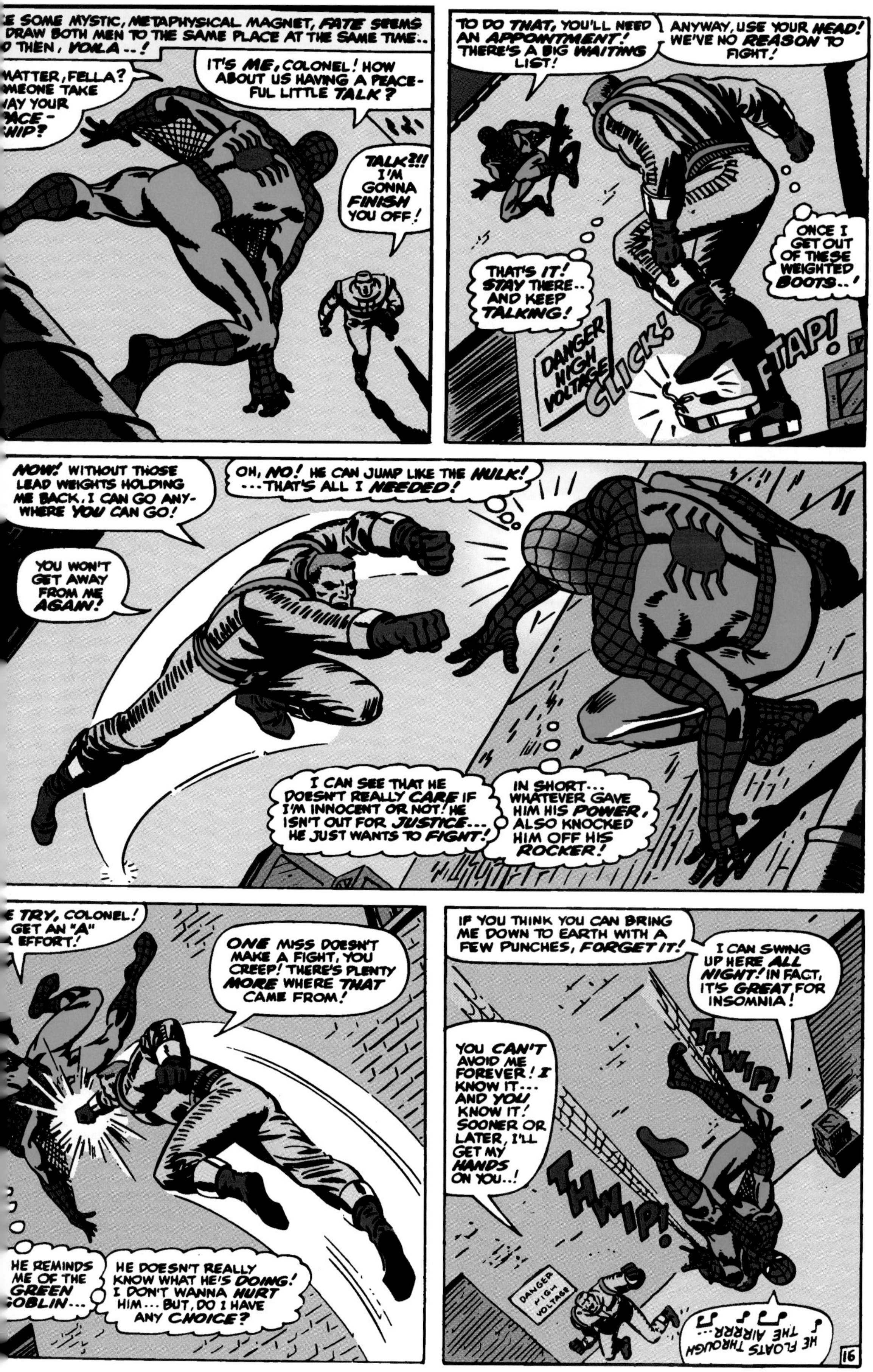
E SOME MYSTIC, METAPHYSICAL MAGNET, FATE SEEMS DRAW BOTH MEN TO THE SAME PLACE AT THE SAME TIME.. O THEN, VOILA..!
MATTER, FELLA? MEONE TAKE AY YOUR ACE- HIP?
IT'S ME, COLONEL! HOW ABOUT US HAVING A PEACE-FUL LITTLE TALK?
TALK?!! I'M GONNA FINISH YOU OFF!
TO DO THAT, YOU'LL NEED AN APPOINTMENT! THERE'S A BIG WAITING LIST!
ANYWAY, USE YOUR HEAD! WE'VE NO REASON TO FIGHT!
THAT'S IT! STAY THERE.. AND KEEP TALKING!
ONCE I GET OUT OF THESE WEIGHTED BOOTS..!
DANGER HIGH VOLTAGE
CLICK!
TAP!
NOW! WITHOUT THOSE LEAD WEIGHTS HOLDING ME BACK, I CAN GO ANYWHERE YOU CAN GO!
OH, NO! HE CAN JUMP LIKE THE HULK! ---THAT'S ALL I NEEDED!
YOU WON'T GET AWAY FROM ME AGAIN!
I CAN SEE THAT HE DOESN'T REALLY CARE IF I'M INNOCENT OR NOT! HE ISN'T OUT FOR JUSTICE... HE JUST WANTS TO FIGHT!
IN SHORT... WHATEVER GAVE HIM HIS POWER, ALSO KNOCKED HIM OFF HIS ROCKER!
E TRY, COLONEL! GET AN "A" EFFORT!
ONE MISS DOESN'T MAKE A FIGHT, YOU CREEP! THERE'S PLENTY MORE WHERE THAT CAME FROM!
HE REMINDS ME OF THE GREEN GOBLIN...
HE DOESN'T REALLY KNOW WHAT HE'S DOING! I DON'T WANNA HURT HIM... BUT, DO I HAVE ANY CHOICE?
IF YOU THINK YOU CAN BRING ME DOWN TO EARTH WITH A FEW PUNCHES, FORGET IT!
I CAN SWING UP HERE ALL NIGHT! IN FACT, IT'S GREAT FOR INSOMNIA!
THWIP!
YOU CAN'T AVOID ME FOREVER! I KNOW IT... AND YOU KNOW IT! SOONER OR LATER, I'LL GET MY HANDS ON YOU...!
THWIP!
DANGER HIGH VOLTAGE
HE FLOATS THROUGH THE AIRRR...
16

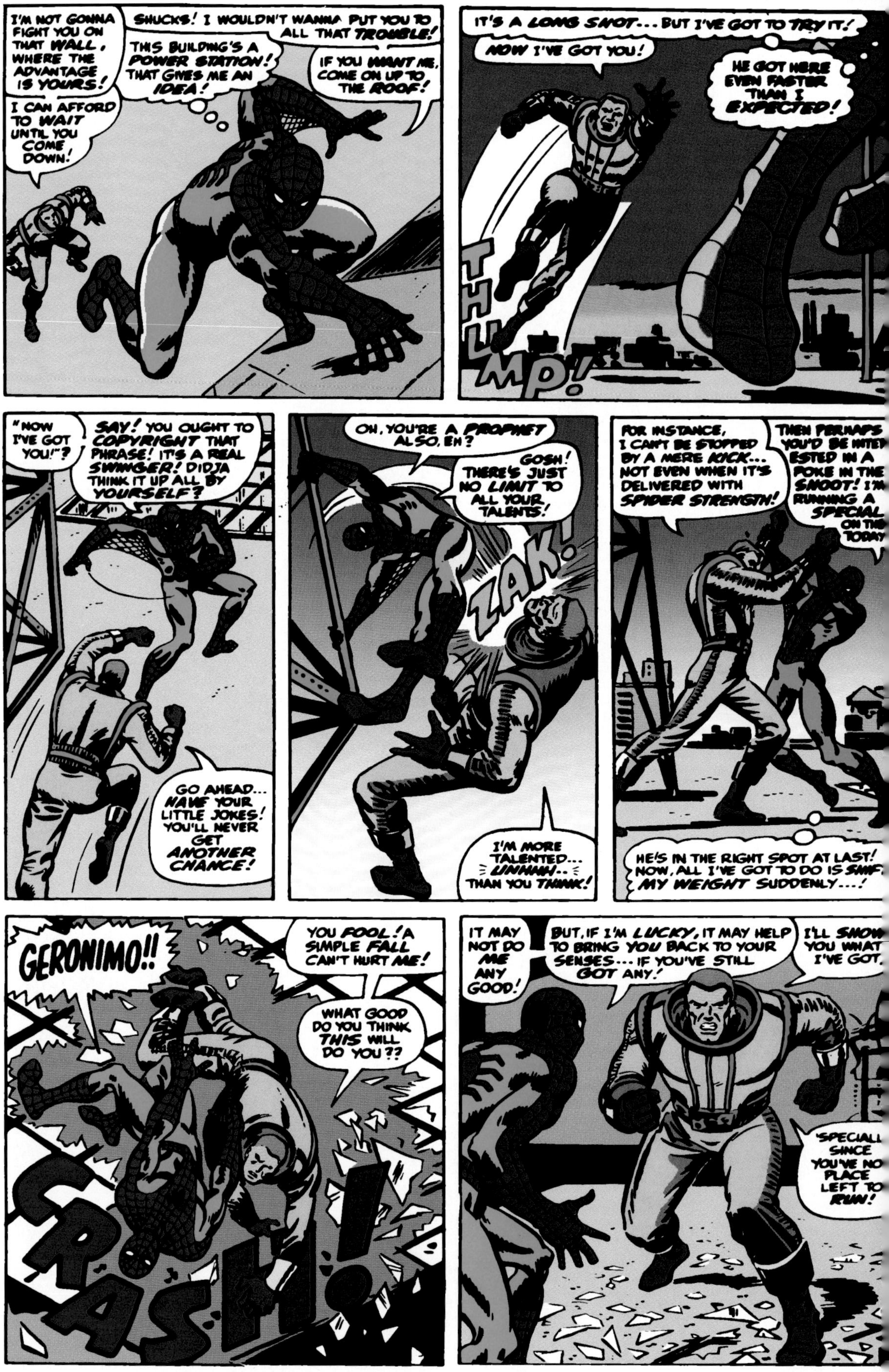

I'M NOT GONNA FIGHT YOU ON THAT WALL, WHERE THE ADVANTAGE IS YOURS!
I CAN AFFORD TO WAIT UNTIL YOU COME DOWN!
SHUCKS! I WOULDN'T WANNA PUT YOU TO ALL THAT TROUBLE!
THIS BUILDING'S A POWER STATION! THAT GIVES ME AN IDEA!
IF YOU WANT ME, COME ON UP TO THE ROOF!
IT'S A LONG SHOT... BUT I'VE GOT TO TRY IT!
NOW I'VE GOT YOU!
HE GOT HERE EVEN FASTER THAN I EXPECTED!
THLUMP!
"NOW I'VE GOT YOU!"?
SAY! YOU OUGHT TO COPYRIGHT THAT PHRASE! IT'S A REAL SWINGER! DIDJA THINK IT UP ALL BY YOURSELF?
GO AHEAD... HAVE YOUR LITTLE JOKES! YOU'LL NEVER GET ANOTHER CHANCE!
OH, YOU'RE A PROPHET ALSO, EH?
GOSH! THERE'S JUST NO LIMIT TO ALL YOUR TALENTS!
ZAK!
I'M MORE TALENTED... UNHHH.. THAN YOU THINK!
FOR INSTANCE, I CAN'T BE STOPPED BY A MERE KICK... NOT EVEN WHEN IT'S DELIVERED WITH SPIDER STRENGTH!
THEN PERHAPS YOU'D BE INTER ESTED IN A POKE IN THE SNOOT! I'M RUNNING A SPECIAL ON THEM TODAY
HE'S IN THE RIGHT SPOT AT LAST! NOW, ALL I'VE GOT TO DO IS SHIFT MY WEIGHT SUDDENLY...!
GERONIMO!!
YOU FOOL! A SIMPLE FALL CAN'T HURT ME!
WHAT GOOD DO YOU THINK THIS WILL DO YOU??
CRASH!
IT MAY NOT DO ME ANY GOOD!
BUT, IF I'M LUCKY, IT MAY HELP TO BRING YOU BACK TO YOUR SENSES... IF YOU'VE STILL GOT ANY!
I'LL SHOW YOU WHAT I'VE GOT,
'SPECIALLY SINCE YOU'VE NO PLACE LEFT TO RUN!

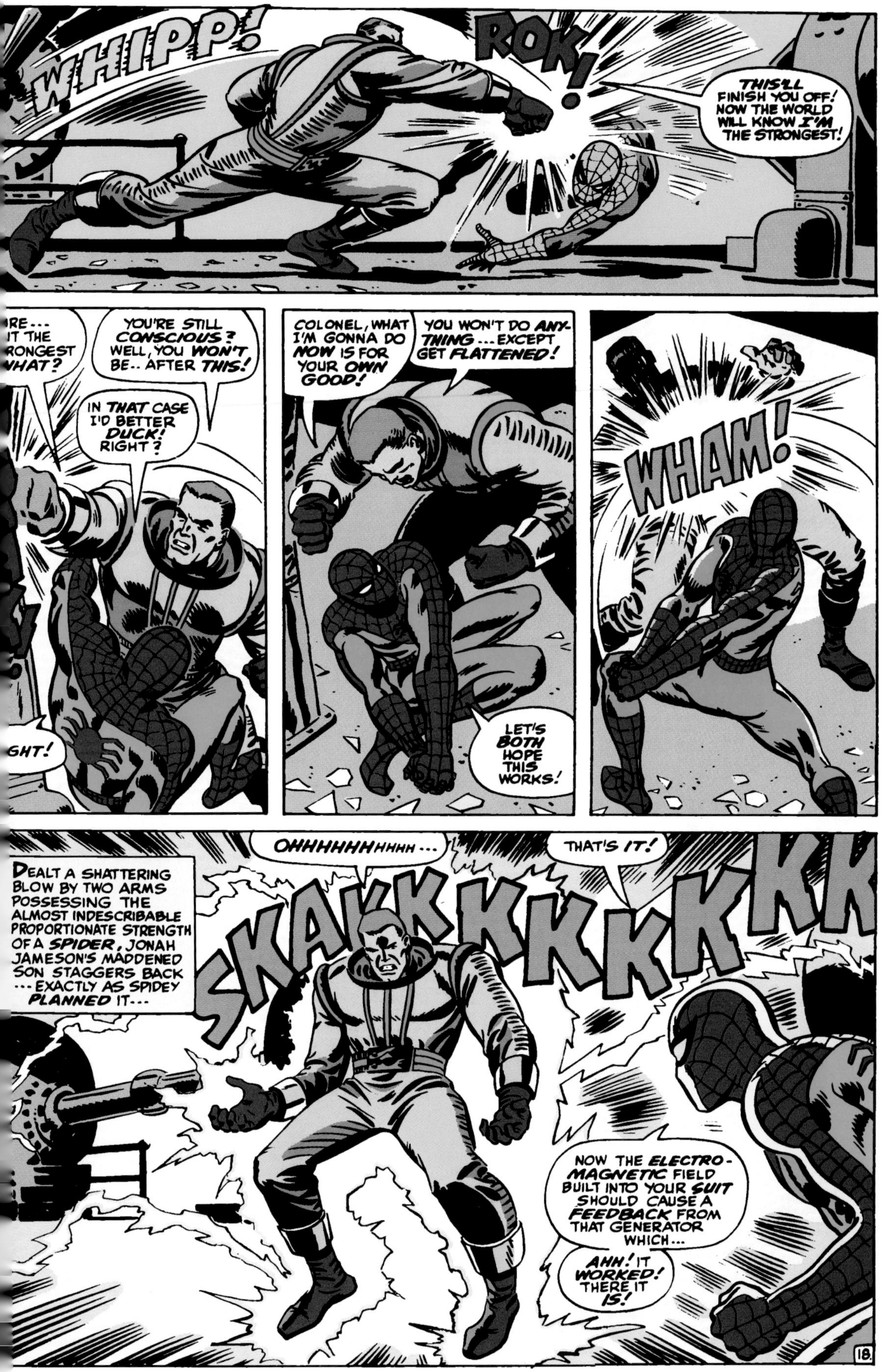
WHIPP!
ROK!
THIS'LL FINISH YOU OFF! NOW THE WORLD WILL KNOW I'M THE STRONGEST!
YOU'RE STILL CONSCIOUS? WELL, YOU WON'T BE.. AFTER THIS!
IN THAT CASE I'D BETTER DUCK! RIGHT?
COLONEL, WHAT I'M GONNA DO NOW IS FOR YOUR OWN GOOD!
YOU WON'T DO ANY-THING ... EXCEPT GET FLATTENED!
LET'S BOTH HOPE THIS WORKS!
WHAM!
DEALT A SHATTERING BLOW BY TWO ARMS POSSESSING THE ALMOST INDESCRIBABLE PROPORTIONATE STRENGTH OF A SPIDER, JONAH JAMESON'S MADDENED SON STAGGERS BACK ... EXACTLY AS SPIDEY PLANNED IT...
OHHHHHHHHHHH...
THAT'S IT!
SKAKKKKKKKK
NOW THE ELECTRO-MAGNETIC FIELD BUILT INTO YOUR SUIT SHOULD CAUSE A FEEDBACK FROM THAT GENERATOR WHICH...
AHH! IT WORKED! THERE IT IS!

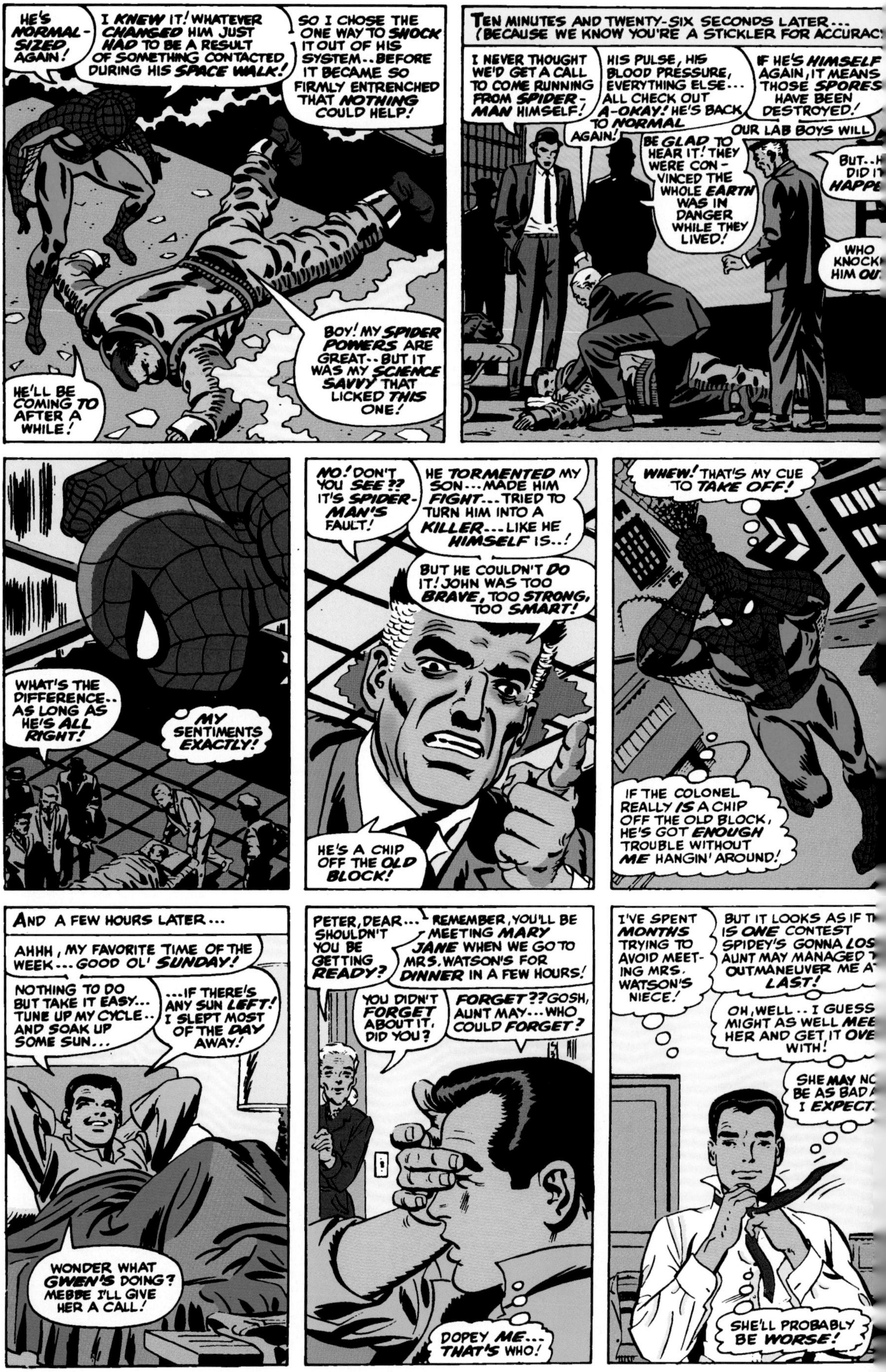
HE'S NORMAL-SIZED AGAIN!
I KNEW IT! WHATEVER CHANGED HIM JUST HAD TO BE A RESULT OF SOMETHING CONTACTED DURING HIS SPACE WALK!
SO I CHOSE THE ONE WAY TO SHOCK IT OUT OF HIS SYSTEM--BEFORE IT BECAME SO FIRMLY ENTRENCHED THAT NOTHING COULD HELP!
HE'LL BE COMING TO AFTER A WHILE!
BOY! MY SPIDER POWERS ARE GREAT--BUT IT WAS MY SCIENCE SAVVY THAT LICKED THIS ONE!
TEN MINUTES AND TWENTY-SIX SECONDS LATER... (BECAUSE WE KNOW YOU'RE A STICKLER FOR ACCURAC
I NEVER THOUGHT WE'D GET A CALL TO COME RUNNING FROM SPIDER-MAN HIMSELF!
HIS PULSE, HIS BLOOD PRESSURE, EVERYTHING ELSE... ALL CHECK OUT A-OKAY! HE'S BACK TO NORMAL AGAIN!
IF HE'S HIMSELF AGAIN, IT MEANS THOSE SPORES HAVE BEEN DESTROYED!
OUR LAB BOYS WILL BE GLAD TO HEAR IT! THEY WERE CONVINCED THE WHOLE EARTH WAS IN DANGER WHILE THEY LIVED!
BUT..H DID IT HAPPE
WHO KNOCK HIM OU
WHAT'S THE DIFFERENCE.. AS LONG AS HE'S ALL RIGHT!
MY SENTIMENTS EXACTLY!
NO! DON'T YOU SEE?? IT'S SPIDER-MAN'S FAULT!
HE TORMENTED MY SON...MADE HIM FIGHT...TRIED TO TURN HIM INTO A KILLER...LIKE HE HIMSELF IS..!
BUT HE COULDN'T DO IT! JOHN WAS TOO BRAVE, TOO STRONG, TOO SMART!
HE'S A CHIP OFF THE OLD BLOCK!
WHEW! THAT'S MY CUE TO TAKE OFF!
IF THE COLONEL REALLY IS A CHIP OFF THE OLD BLOCK, HE'S GOT ENOUGH TROUBLE WITHOUT ME HANGIN' AROUND!
AND A FEW HOURS LATER...
AHHH, MY FAVORITE TIME OF THE WEEK...GOOD OL' SUNDAY!
NOTHING TO DO BUT TAKE IT EASY... TUNE UP MY CYCLE.. AND SOAK UP SOME SUN...
...IF THERE'S ANY SUN LEFT! I SLEPT MOST OF THE DAY AWAY!
WONDER WHAT GWEN'S DOING? MEBBE I'LL GIVE HER A CALL!
PETER, DEAR... SHOULDN'T YOU BE GETTING READY?
REMEMBER, YOU'LL BE MEETING MARY JANE WHEN WE GO TO MRS. WATSON'S FOR DINNER IN A FEW HOURS!
YOU DIDN'T FORGET ABOUT IT, DID YOU?
FORGET?? GOSH, AUNT MAY...WHO COULD FORGET?
DOPEY ME... THAT'S WHO!
I'VE SPENT MONTHS TRYING TO AVOID MEETING MRS. WATSON'S NIECE!
BUT IT LOOKS AS IF T IS ONE CONTEST SPIDEY'S GONNA LOS AUNT MAY MANAGED T OUTMANEUVER ME A LAST!
OH, WELL.. I GUESS MIGHT AS WELL MEE HER AND GET IT OVE WITH!
SHE MAY NO BE AS BAD A I EXPECT.
SHE'LL PROBABLY BE WORSE!

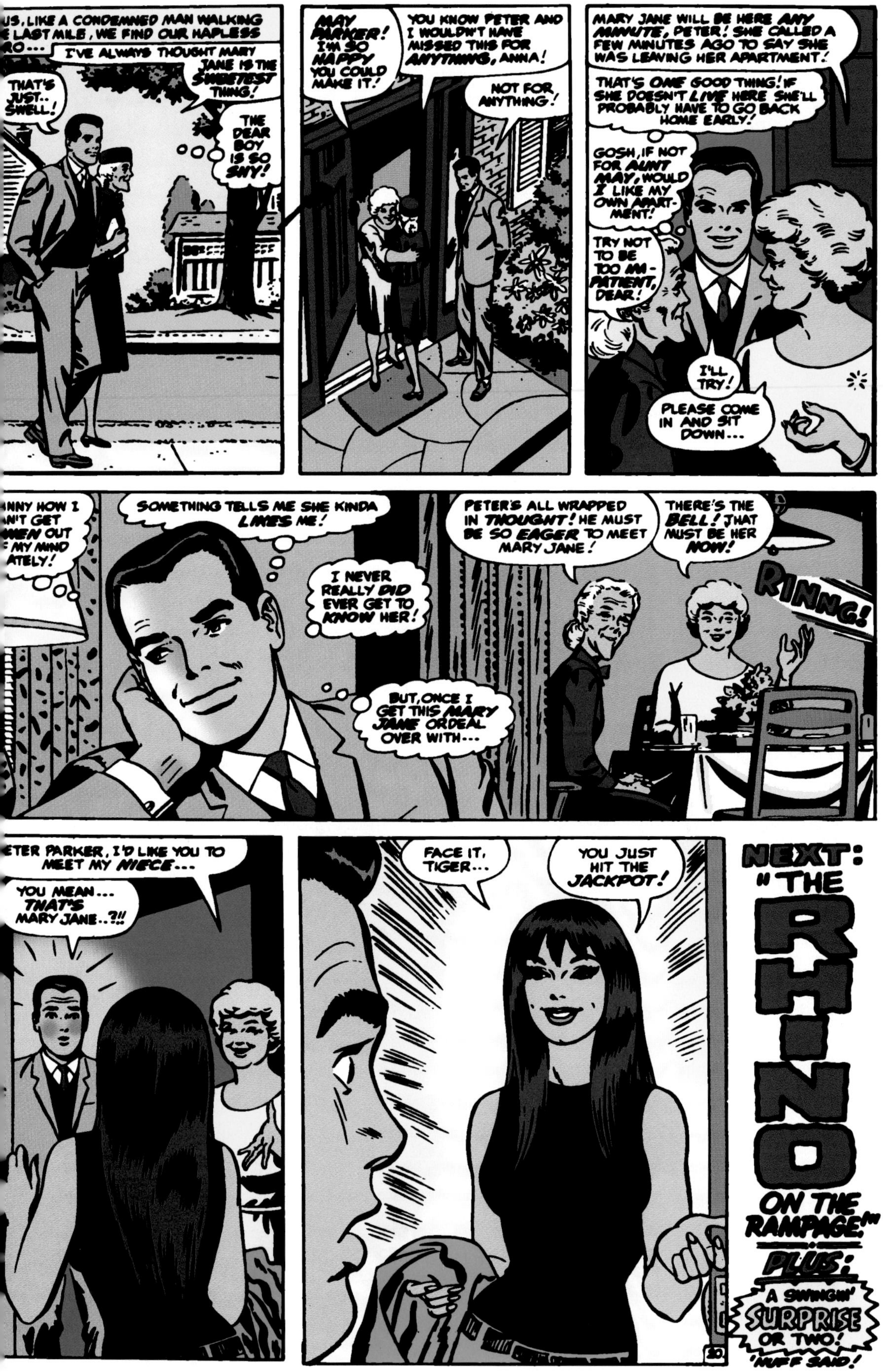
US, LIKE A CONDEMNED MAN WALKING E LAST MILE, WE FIND OUR HAPLESS RO...
I'VE ALWAYS THOUGHT MARY JANE IS THE SWEETEST THING!
THAT'S JUST.. SWELL!
THE DEAR BOY IS SO SHY!
MAY PARKER! I'M SO HAPPY YOU COULD MAKE IT!
YOU KNOW PETER AND I WOULDN'T HAVE MISSED THIS FOR ANYTHING, ANNA!
NOT FOR ANYTHING!
MARY JANE WILL BE HERE ANY MINUTE, PETER! SHE CALLED A FEW MINUTES AGO TO SAY SHE WAS LEAVING HER APARTMENT!
THAT'S ONE GOOD THING! IF SHE DOESN'T LIVE HERE SHE'LL PROBABLY HAVE TO GO BACK HOME EARLY!
GOSH, IF NOT FOR AUNT MAY, WOULD I LIKE MY OWN APARTMENT!
TRY NOT TO BE TOO IM-PATIENT, DEAR!
I'LL TRY!
PLEASE COME IN AND SIT DOWN...
NNY HOW I N'T GET EN OUT MY MIND ATELY!
SOMETHING TELLS ME SHE KINDA LIKES ME!
I NEVER REALLY DID EVER GET TO KNOW HER!
BUT, ONCE I GET THIS MARY JANE ORDEAL OVER WITH...
PETER'S ALL WRAPPED IN THOUGHT! HE MUST BE SO EAGER TO MEET MARY JANE!
THERE'S THE BELL! THAT MUST BE HER NOW!
RINNG!
ETER PARKER, I'D LIKE YOU TO MEET MY NIECE...
YOU MEAN... THAT'S MARY JANE..?!!
FACE IT, TIGER...
YOU JUST HIT THE JACKPOT!
20
NEXT: "THE RHINO ON THE RAMPAGE!"
PLUS: A SWINGIN' SURPRISE OR TWO!
'NUFF SAID!

amazing spider-man #50

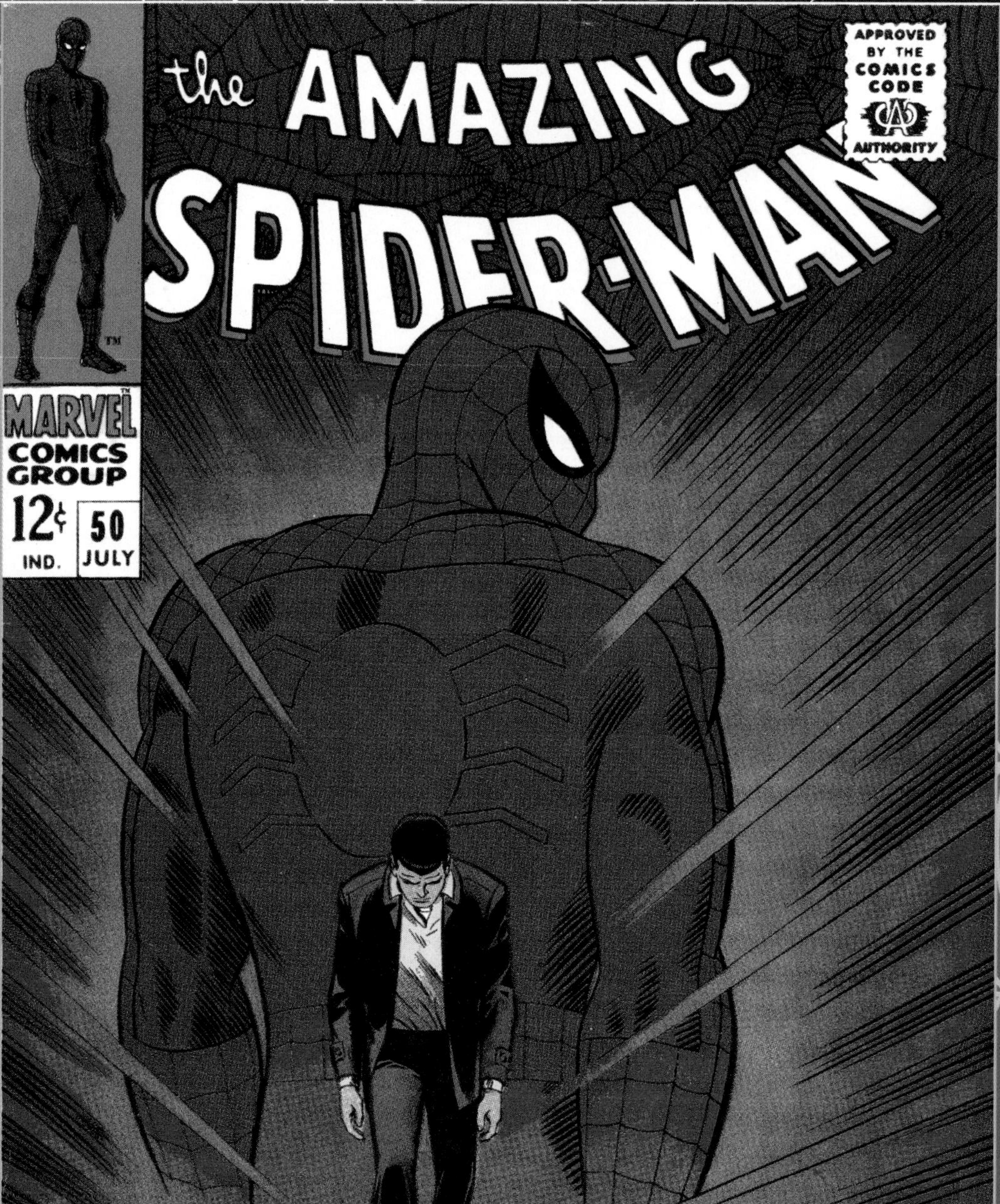
the AMAZING SPIDER-MAN
APPROVED BY THE COMICS CODE AUTHORITY
MARVEL COMICS GROUP
12¢ IND.
50 JULY
"SPIDER-MAN NO MORE!"

BY ISSUE 50, DESPITE DEADLINE PRESSURES, I WAS HAVING FUN. THE KINGPIN WAS PLANNED TO BE AS DIFFERENT FROM OTHER CRIME BOSSES AS I COULD THINK UP AND QUICKLY BECAME MY FAVORITE VILLAIN.

july 1967

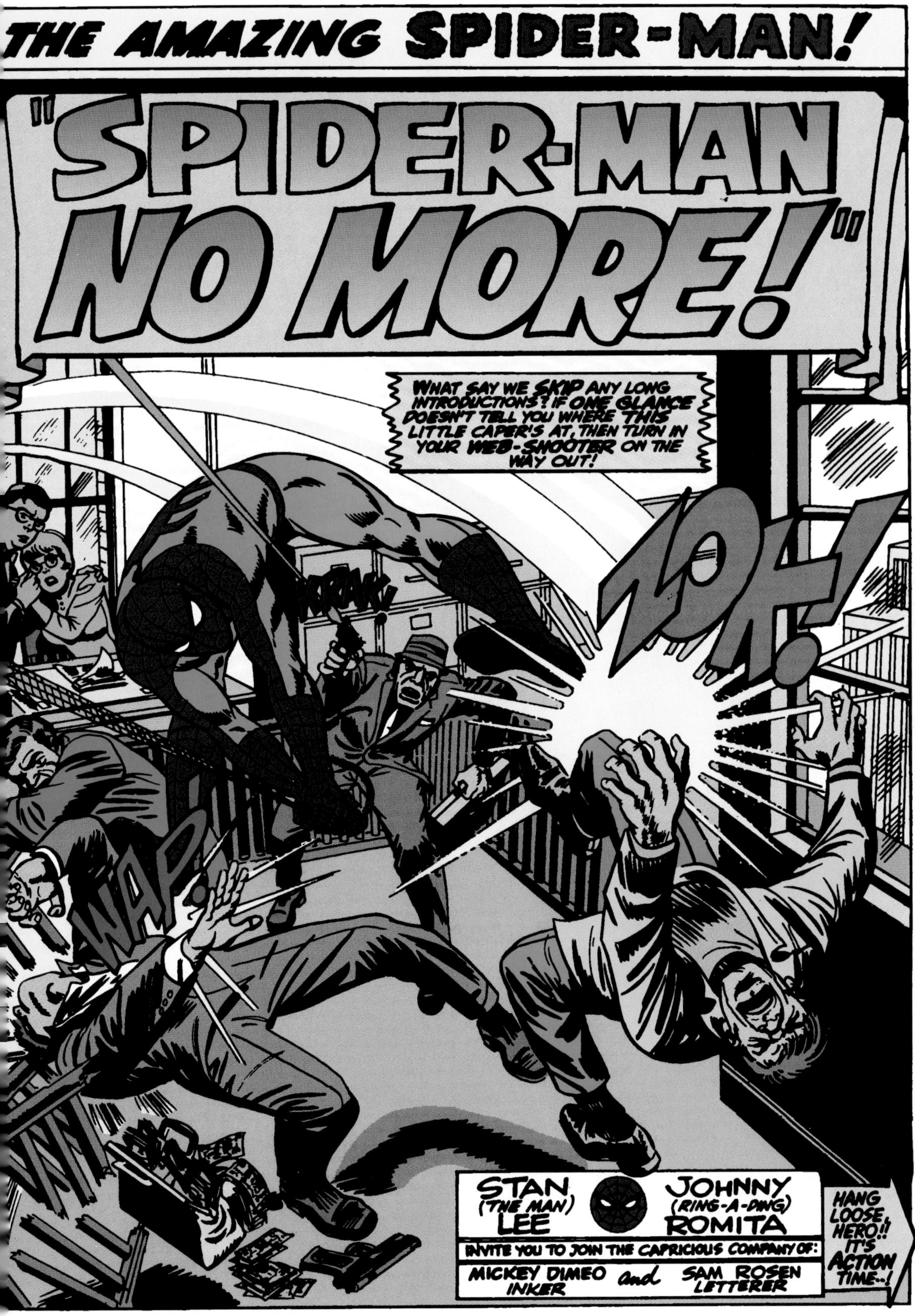
THE AMAZING SPIDER-MAN!
"SPIDER-MAN NO MORE!"
WHAT SAY WE SKIP ANY LONG INTRODUCTIONS? IF ONE GLANCE DOESN'T TELL YOU WHERE THIS LITTLE CAPER'S AT, THEN TURN IN YOUR WEB-SHOOTER ON THE WAY OUT!
KRAK!
ZOK!
WAP!
STAN (THE MAN) LEE
JOHNNY (RING-A-DING) ROMITA
INVITE YOU TO JOIN THE CAPRICIOUS COMPANY OF:
MICKEY DIMEO INKER and SAM ROSEN LETTERER
HANG LOOSE, HERO!! IT'S ACTION TIME..!

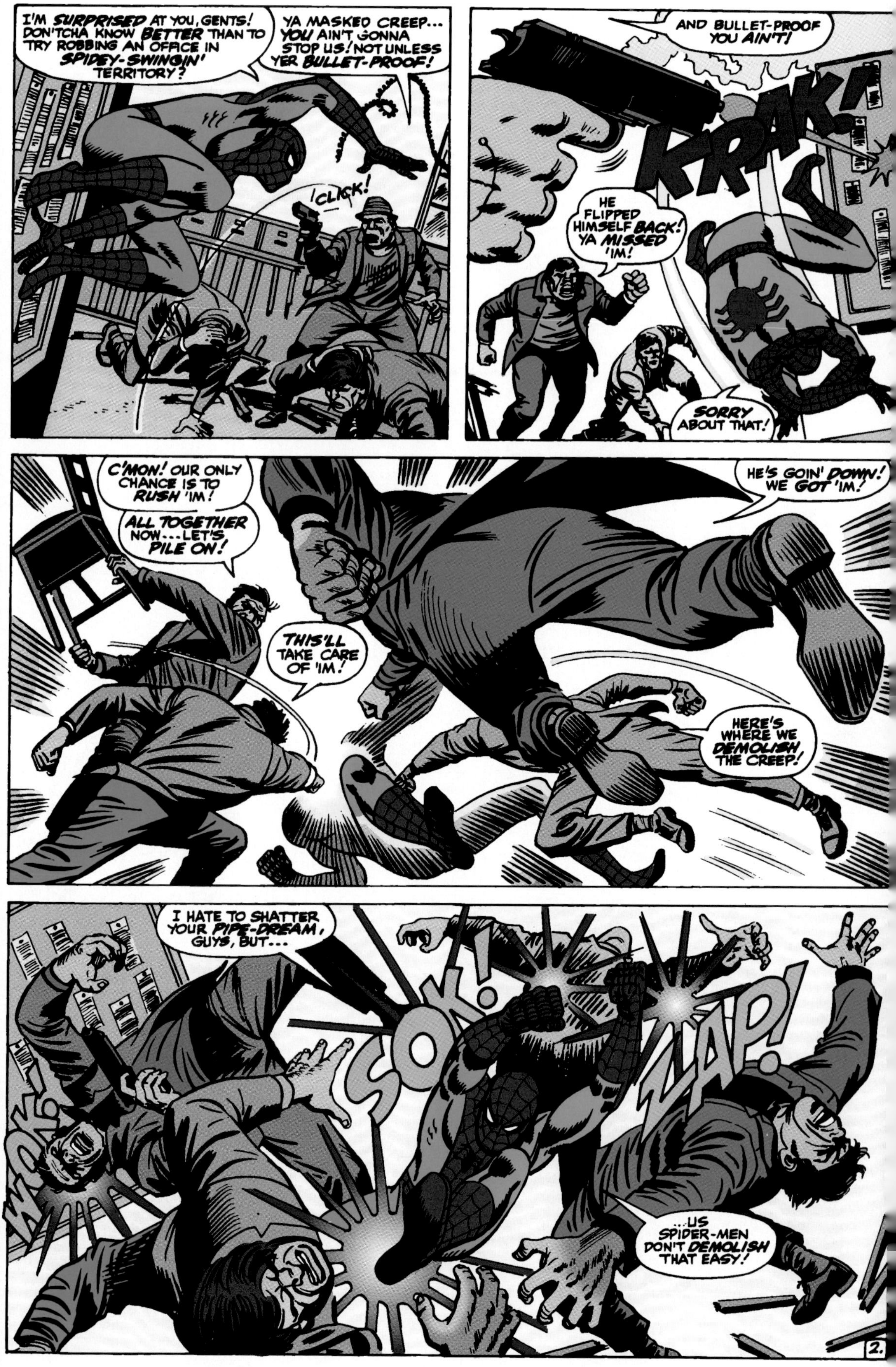
I'M SURPRISED AT YOU, GENTS! DON'TCHA KNOW BETTER THAN TO TRY ROBBING AN OFFICE IN SPIDEY-SWINGIN' TERRITORY?
YA MASKED CREEP... YOU AIN'T GONNA STOP US! NOT UNLESS YER BULLET-PROOF!
CLICK!
AND BULLET-PROOF YOU AIN'T!
K-RAK!
HE FLIPPED HIMSELF BACK! YA MISSED 'IM!
SORRY ABOUT THAT!
C'MON! OUR ONLY CHANCE IS TO RUSH 'IM!
ALL TOGETHER NOW... LET'S PILE ON!
HE'S GOIN' DOWN! WE GOT 'IM!
THIS'LL TAKE CARE OF 'IM!
HERE'S WHERE WE DEMOLISH THE CREEP!
I HATE TO SHATTER YOUR PIPE-DREAM, GUYS, BUT...
SOK!
ZAP!
...US SPIDER-MEN DON'T DEMOLISH THAT EASY!

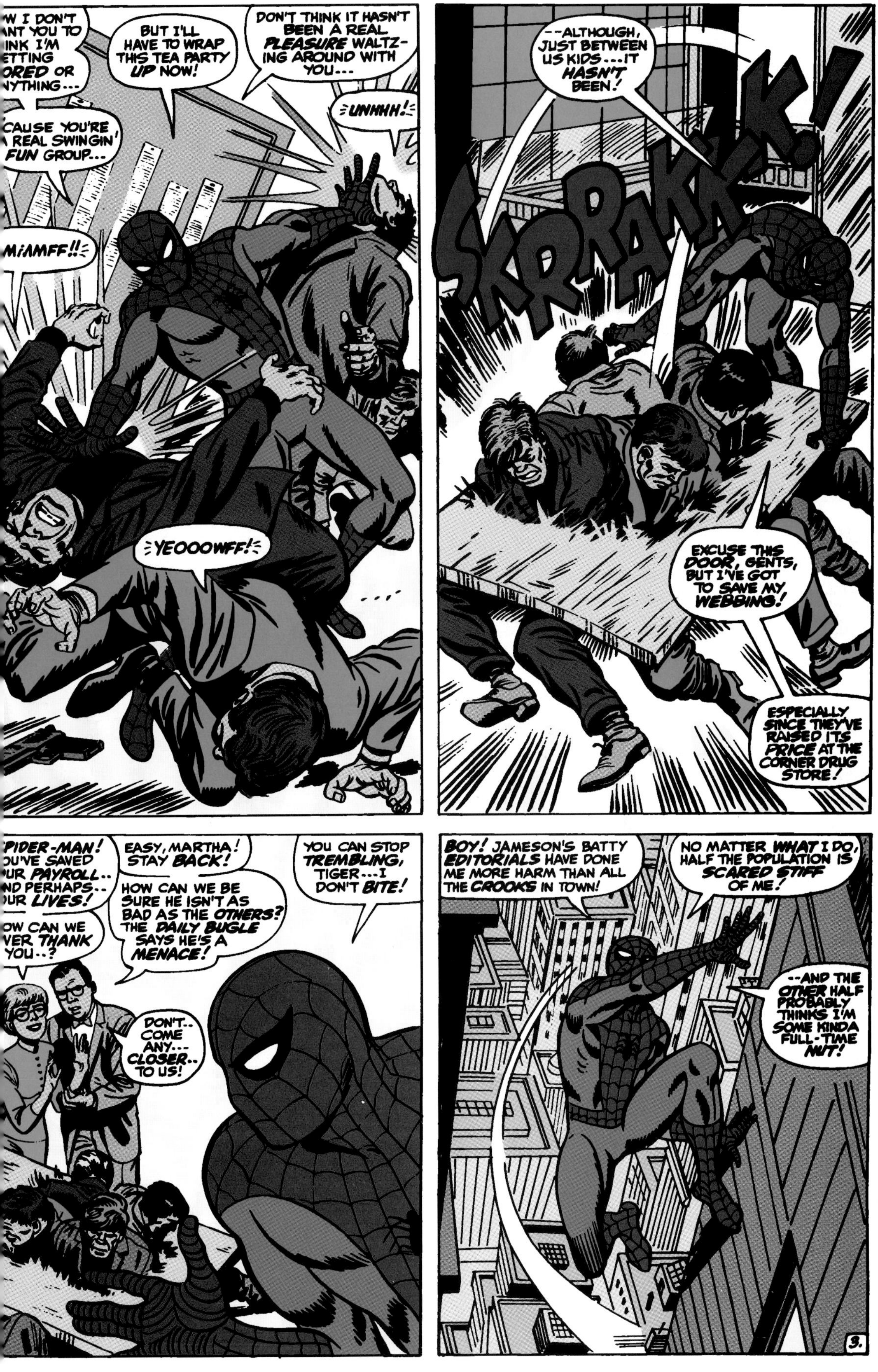

W I DON'T
NT YOU TO
INK I'M
ETTING
ORED OR
NYTHING...
BUT I'LL HAVE TO WRAP THIS TEA PARTY UP NOW!
DON'T THINK IT HASN'T BEEN A REAL PLEASURE WALTZ-ING AROUND WITH YOU...
CAUSE YOU'RE
REAL SWINGIN'
FUN GROUP...
UNHHH!
MIAMFF!!
YEOOOWFF!
--ALTHOUGH, JUST BETWEEN US KIDS...IT HASN'T BEEN!
SKRRAKKK!
EXCUSE THIS DOOR, GENTS, BUT I'VE GOT TO SAVE MY WEBBING!
ESPECIALLY SINCE THEY'VE RAISED ITS PRICE AT THE CORNER DRUG STORE!
PIDER-MAN!
OU'VE SAVED
UR PAYROLL..
ND PERHAPS..
UR LIVES!
OW CAN WE
VER THANK
YOU..?
EASY, MARTHA! STAY BACK!
HOW CAN WE BE SURE HE ISN'T AS BAD AS THE OTHERS? THE DAILY BUGLE SAYS HE'S A MENACE!
YOU CAN STOP TREMBLING, TIGER...I DON'T BITE!
DON'T.. COME ANY... CLOSER.. TO US!
BOY! JAMESON'S BATTY EDITORIALS HAVE DONE ME MORE HARM THAN ALL THE CROOKS IN TOWN!
NO MATTER WHAT I DO, HALF THE POPULATION IS SCARED STIFF OF ME!
--AND THE OTHER HALF PROBABLY THINKS I'M SOME KINDA FULL-TIME NUT!
3.

WELL, WHO *CARES* WHAT PEOPLE THINK, ANYWAY?

THAT'S JUST THE *TROUBLE*-- I *CARE!*

EVERYONE *FLIPS* OVER THE *FF*...

CAPTAIN AMERICA TURNS 'EM ON...

THEY THINK *DAREDEVIL'S* THE COOLEST..

BUT, JUST MENTION *SPIDER-MAN*...AND *FREEZE-VILLE!*

I'LL NEVER UNDER-STAND HOW IT *HAPPENED!*

I DON'T STEAL CANDY FROM BABIES, OR TIE TIN CANS ON PUPPY DOGS!

THE *PUBLIC!* THE MORE I *HELP* THEM--- THE MORE THEY *HATE* ME!

IT'S A *JAMESO* FAULT! HE'S THE *PUBL* CONVIN* ME, GENG KHAN WAS *PIKER.*

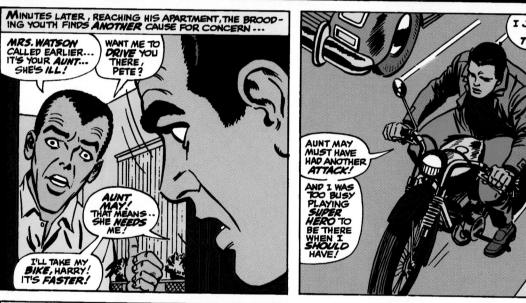

MINUTES LATER, REACHING HIS APARTMENT, THE BROODING YOUTH FINDS *ANOTHER* CAUSE FOR CONCERN...

MRS. WATSON CALLED EARLIER... IT'S YOUR *AUNT*... SHE'S ILL!

WANT ME TO *DRIVE* YOU THERE, PETE?

AUNT MAY! THAT MEANS.. SHE *NEEDS* ME!

I'LL TAKE MY *BIKE*, HARRY! IT'S *FASTER!*

I JUST PRAY I'M NOT... *TOO LATE!*

AUNT MAY MUST HAVE HAD ANOTHER *ATTACK!*

AND I WAS TOO *BUSY* PLAYING *SUPER HERO* TO BE THERE WHEN I *SHOULD* HAVE!

MRS. WATSON! I GOT HERE AS FAST AS I *COULD!* WHAT *HAPPENED??*

IT'S ALL RIGHT, PETER! SHE'S *RESTING* NOW! LUCKILY, THE *DOCTOR* WAS JUST PASSING BY! IF NOT FOR *THAT!..*

WHERE IS SHE? CAN I *SEE* HER?

SHE KEPT *CALLING* FOR YOU...WONDERING WHERE YOU *WERE!* SHE WAS SO *WORRIED!*

BUT THEN, DR. BROMWELL MANAGED TO GIVE HER A *SEDATIVE!*

IF I HAD BEEN AT *HOME*... LIKE ANY *OTHER* NORMAL GUY... THEY COULD HAVE REACHED ME *FAST!*

BUT *NO*...I WAS OUT.. FLEXING MY MUSCLES... TRYING TO HELP THE VERY PEOPLE WHO *FEAR* ME!

WE'D BETTER LET HER *SLEEP*, PETER! I'LL TELL HER YOU WERE HERE!

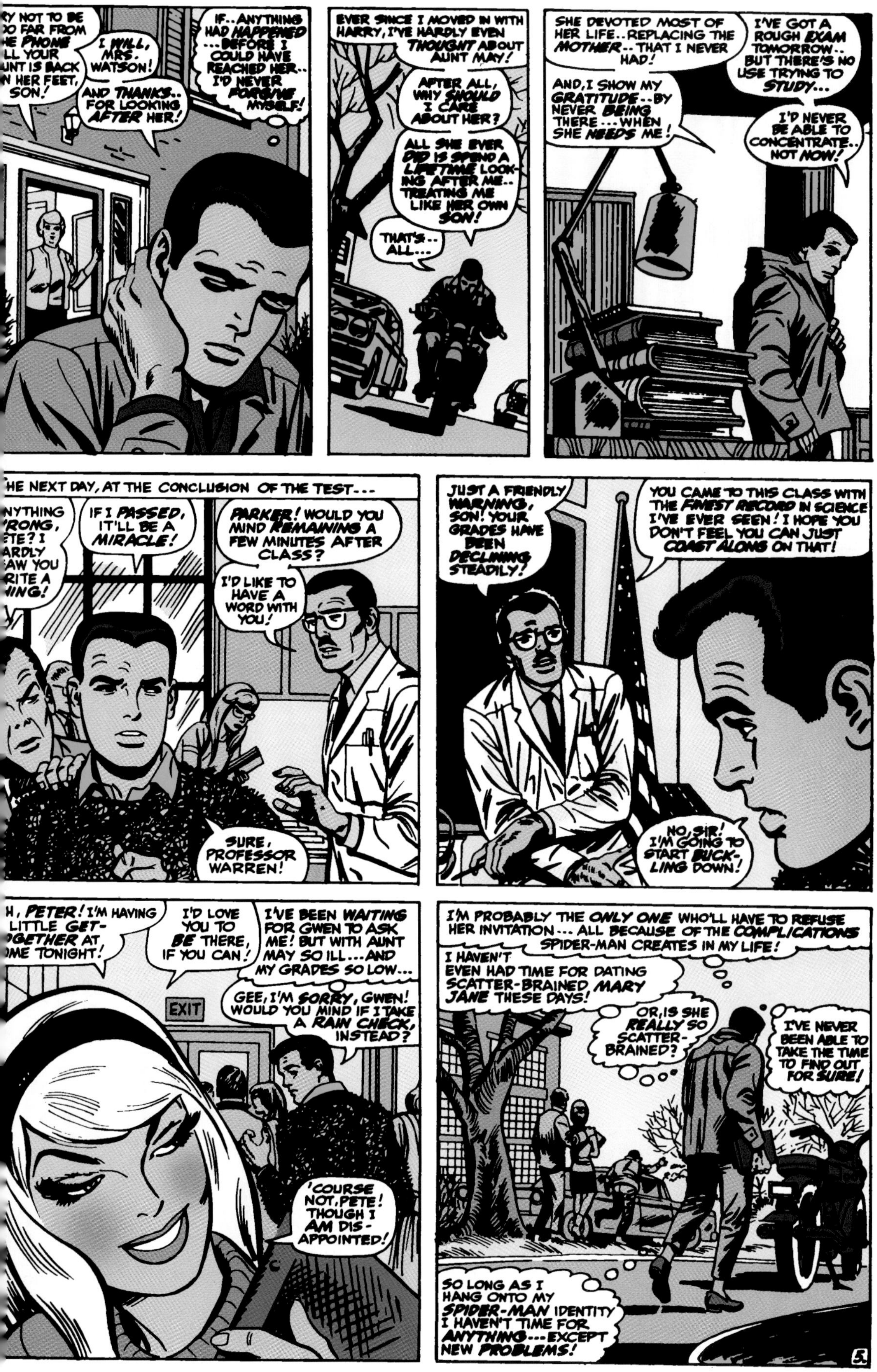

RY NOT TO BE OO FAR FROM HE PHONE LL YOUR UNT IS BACK N HER FEET, SON!
I WILL, MRS. WATSON!
AND THANKS.. FOR LOOKING AFTER HER!
IF.. ANYTHING HAD HAPPENED ...BEFORE I COULD HAVE REACHED HER.. I'D NEVER FORGIVE MYSELF!
EVER SINCE I MOVED IN WITH HARRY, I'VE HARDLY EVEN THOUGHT ABOUT AUNT MAY!
AFTER ALL, WHY SHOULD I CARE ABOUT HER?
ALL SHE EVER DID IS SPEND A LIFETIME LOOKING AFTER ME.. TREATING ME LIKE HER OWN SON!
THAT'S.. ALL...
SHE DEVOTED MOST OF HER LIFE..REPLACING THE MOTHER.. THAT I NEVER HAD!
AND, I SHOW MY GRATITUDE..BY NEVER BEING THERE... WHEN SHE NEEDS ME!
I'VE GOT A ROUGH EXAM TOMORROW.. BUT THERE'S NO USE TRYING TO STUDY...
I'D NEVER BE ABLE TO CONCENTRATE.. NOT NOW!
HE NEXT DAY, AT THE CONCLUSION OF THE TEST---
NYTHING RONG, ETE? I ARDLY AW YOU RITE A ING!
IF I PASSED, IT'LL BE A MIRACLE!
PARKER! WOULD YOU MIND REMAINING A FEW MINUTES AFTER CLASS?
I'D LIKE TO HAVE A WORD WITH YOU!
SURE, PROFESSOR WARREN!
JUST A FRIENDLY WARNING, SON! YOUR GRADES HAVE BEEN DECLINING STEADILY!
YOU CAME TO THIS CLASS WITH THE FINEST RECORD IN SCIENCE I'VE EVER SEEN! I HOPE YOU DON'T FEEL YOU CAN JUST COAST ALONG ON THAT!
NO, SIR! I'M GOING TO START BUCKLING DOWN!
H, PETER! I'M HAVING LITTLE GET-OGETHER AT OME TONIGHT!
I'D LOVE YOU TO BE THERE, IF YOU CAN!
I'VE BEEN WAITING FOR GWEN TO ASK ME! BUT WITH AUNT MAY SO ILL... AND MY GRADES SO LOW...
EXIT
GEE, I'M SORRY, GWEN! WOULD YOU MIND IF I TAKE A RAIN CHECK, INSTEAD?
'COURSE NOT, PETE! THOUGH I AM DISAPPOINTED!
I'M PROBABLY THE ONLY ONE WHO'LL HAVE TO REFUSE HER INVITATION... ALL BECAUSE OF THE COMPLICATIONS SPIDER-MAN CREATES IN MY LIFE!
I HAVEN'T EVEN HAD TIME FOR DATING SCATTER-BRAINED MARY JANE THESE DAYS!
OR, IS SHE REALLY SO SCATTER-BRAINED?
I'VE NEVER BEEN ABLE TO TAKE THE TIME TO FIND OUT FOR SURE!
SO LONG AS I HANG ONTO MY SPIDER-MAN IDENTITY I HAVEN'T TIME FOR ANYTHING... EXCEPT NEW PROBLEMS!
5.

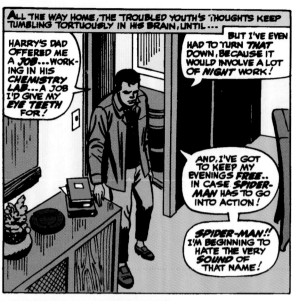

ALL THE WAY HOME, THE TROUBLED YOUTH'S THOUGHTS KEEP TUMBLING TORTUOUSLY IN HIS BRAIN, UNTIL...

HARRY'S DAD OFFERED ME A JOB...WORKING IN HIS CHEMISTRY LAB...A JOB I'D GIVE MY EYE TEETH FOR!

BUT I'VE EVEN HAD TO TURN THAT DOWN, BECAUSE IT WOULD INVOLVE A LOT OF NIGHT WORK!

AND, I'VE GOT TO KEEP MY EVENINGS FREE...IN CASE SPIDER-MAN HAS TO GO INTO ACTION!

SPIDER-MAN!! I'M BEGINNING TO HATE THE VERY SOUND OF THAT NAME!

BUT, HATE IT OR NOT, NO SOONER DOES HE TURN ON THE T.V., THAN THAT SOBRIQUET CONTINUES TO HAUNT THE BROODING ADVENTURER...

MAYBE IF I HEAR THE NEWS FOR A WHILE, I'LL--OH NO!

...AND MY NEWSPAPER CHALLENGES ANYONE TO PROVE THAT SPIDER-MAN ISN'T A PUBLIC ENEMY!

IT'S JAMESON AGAIN...USING THE SHOW HE SPONSORS TO STIR UP THE PEOPLE AGAINST ME!

SOME MISGUIDED FOOLS CALL HIM A SUPER HERO! BUT, WHY DOES HE OPERATE OUTSIDE THE LAW? WHY DOES HE CLOAK HIS IDENTITY BEHIND THAT UGLY FRIGHT MASK?!!

LET ME TELL YOU WHY...

BECAUSE HE'S REALLY AN EGOMANIAC...A NEUROTIC TROUBLE-MAKER, FLAUNTING HIS POWER BEFORE THE ORDINARY CITIZENS WHOM HE DESPISES!

FOR ALL WE KNOW, HE HIMSELF PROVOKES THE CRIMINALS WHOM HE LATER SEEMS TO DEFEAT!

DO WE WANT OUR YOUNGSTERS TO MAKE AN IDOL OF A MENTALLY-DISTURBED MENACE??

I SAY NO!! WE MUST FIND HIM... UNMASK HIM...AND THEN...DESTROY HIM!!

AS PUBLISHER OF THE DAILY BUGLE, I OFFER ONE THOUSAND DOLLARS FOR THE CAPTURE AND CONVICTION OF THAT WEB-SLINGING, WALL-CRAWLING MOCKERY OF A MAN...

A THOUSAND DOLLARS REWARD... JUST FOR ME?!

HE..HATES ME..FAR MORE THAN I THOUGHT..!

AGNAVOX

THE TIME HAS COME TO RID OURSELVES OF THAT FALSE FACED FREAK WHO HIDES BY DAY AND TRIES TO TAKE THE LAW INTO HIS OWN HANDS UNDER COVER OF NIGHT!

THE TERRIBLE THING IS... HE MEANS IT! HE ACTUALLY BELIEVES WHAT HE SAYS! HE SINCERELY THINKS I AM A THREAT TO SOCIETY!

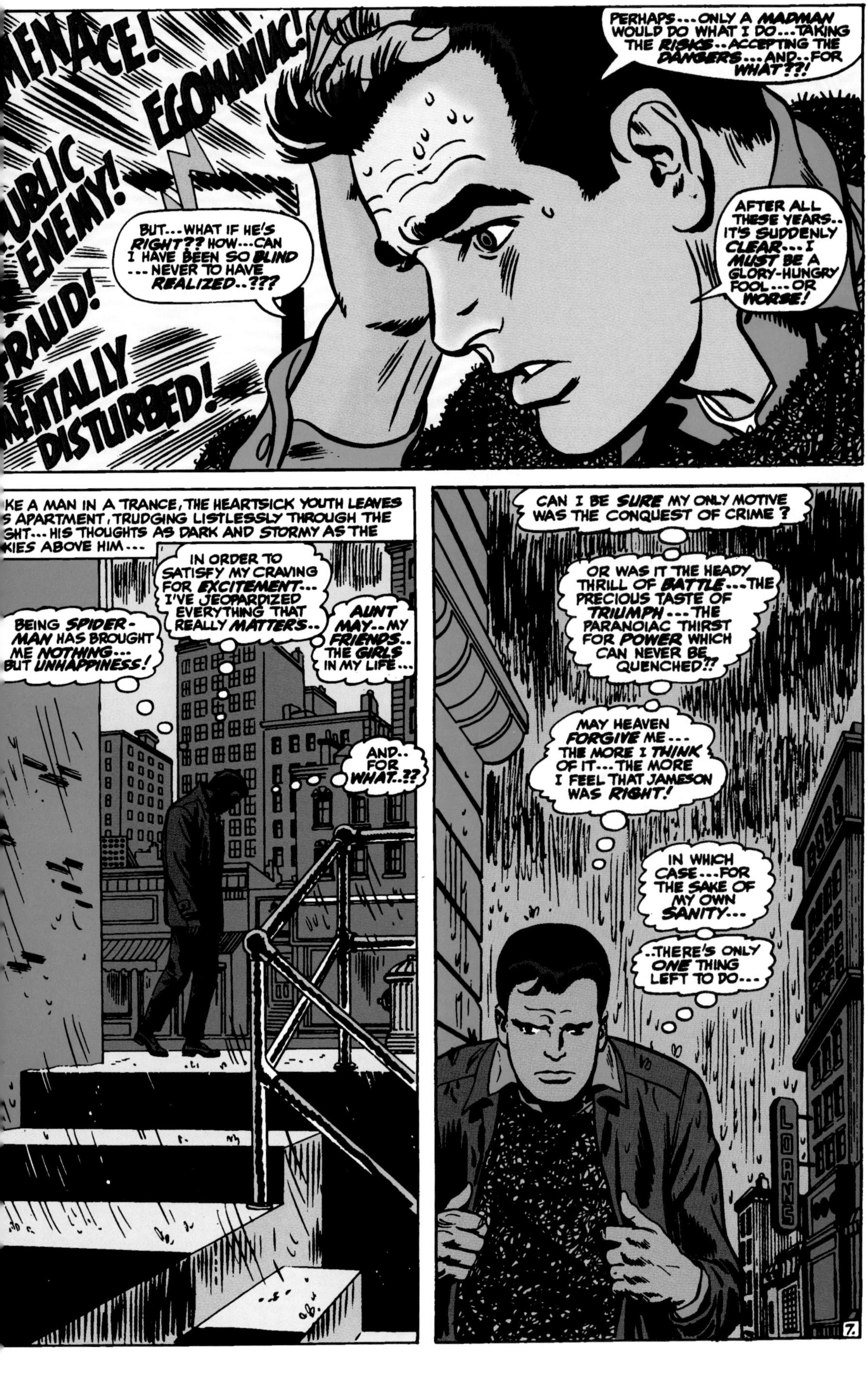
MENACE!
UBLIC ENEMY!
EGOMANIAC!
FRAUD!
ENTALLY DISTURBED!
PERHAPS... ONLY A MADMAN WOULD DO WHAT I DO... TAKING THE RISKS.. ACCEPTING THE DANGERS... AND.. FOR WHAT??!
BUT... WHAT IF HE'S RIGHT?? HOW... CAN I HAVE BEEN SO BLIND ... NEVER TO HAVE REALIZED..???
AFTER ALL THESE YEARS.. IT'S SUDDENLY CLEAR... I MUST BE A GLORY-HUNGRY FOOL... OR WORSE!
KE A MAN IN A TRANCE, THE HEARTSICK YOUTH LEAVES S APARTMENT, TRUDGING LISTLESSLY THROUGH THE GHT... HIS THOUGHTS AS DARK AND STORMY AS THE KIES ABOVE HIM...
BEING SPIDER-MAN HAS BROUGHT ME NOTHING... BUT UNHAPPINESS!
IN ORDER TO SATISFY MY CRAVING FOR EXCITEMENT... I'VE JEOPARDIZED EVERYTHING THAT REALLY MATTERS..
AUNT MAY.. MY FRIENDS.. THE GIRLS IN MY LIFE...
AND.. FOR WHAT..??
CAN I BE SURE MY ONLY MOTIVE WAS THE CONQUEST OF CRIME?
OR WAS IT THE HEADY THRILL OF BATTLE... THE PRECIOUS TASTE OF TRIUMPH... THE PARANOIAC THIRST FOR POWER WHICH CAN NEVER BE QUENCHED??
MAY HEAVEN FORGIVE ME... THE MORE I THINK OF IT... THE MORE I FEEL THAT JAMESON WAS RIGHT!
IN WHICH CASE... FOR THE SAKE OF MY OWN SANITY...
..THERE'S ONLY ONE THING LEFT TO DO...
LOANS
7.

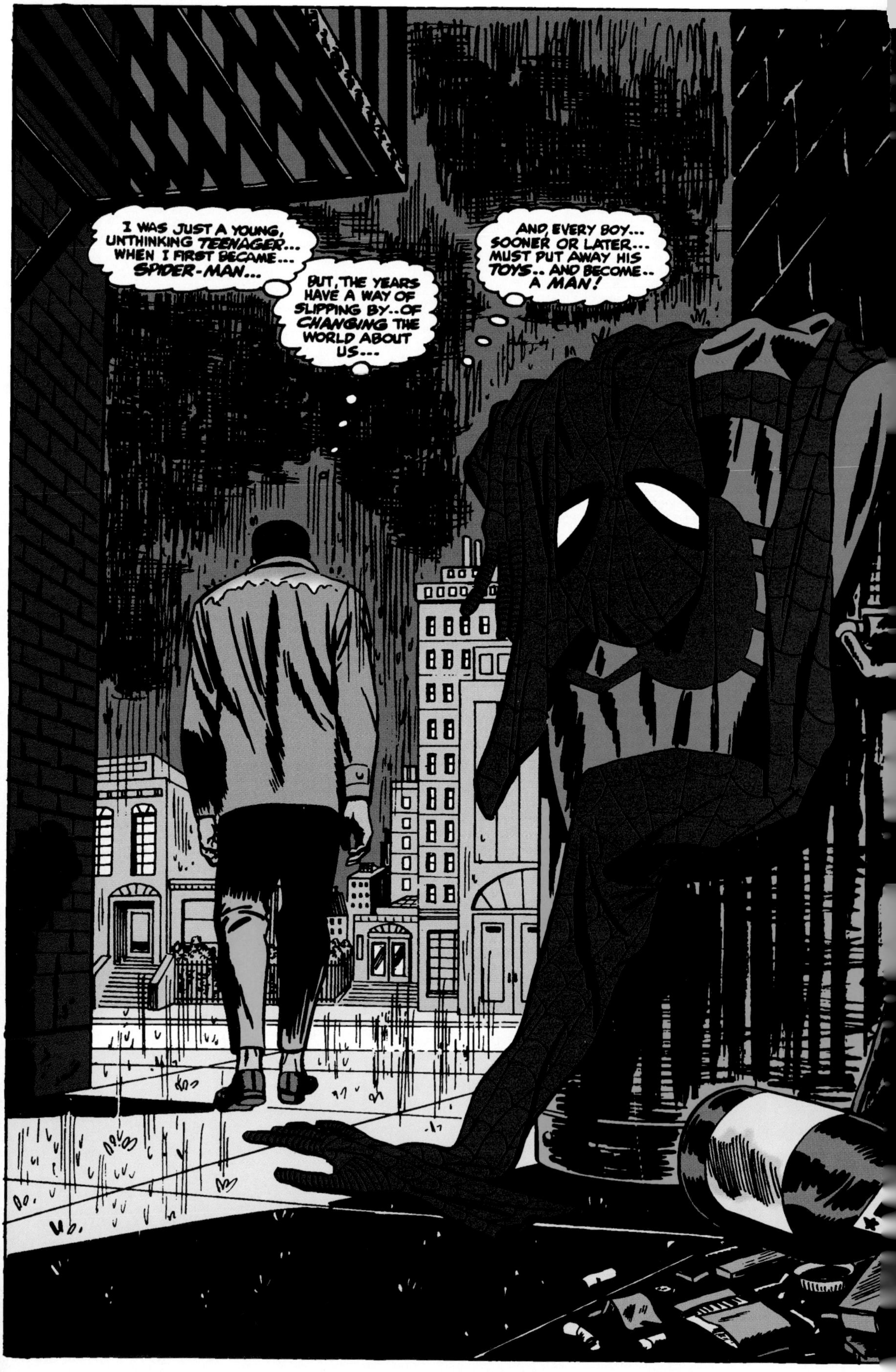
I WAS JUST A YOUNG, UNTHINKING TEENAGER... WHEN I FIRST BECAME... SPIDER-MAN...
BUT, THE YEARS HAVE A WAY OF SLIPPING BY.. OF CHANGING THE WORLD ABOUT US...
AND, EVERY BOY... SOONER OR LATER... MUST PUT AWAY HIS TOYS.. AND BECOME.. A MAN!

...DESPITE WHAT YOU MAY THINK...OUR TALE IS NOT ENDED! FOR, THE VERY NEXT MORNING...

...LD IT! ...OP!

WAIT! THAT'S MR. JAMESON'S PRIVATE OFFICE!

MAINTAIN YOUR COOL, LADY!

WHEN HE SEES WHAT I'VE GOT HERE, HE'LL GIVE YA A MEDAL!

HEY, JAMESON... OPEN UP! THIS IS YOUR LUCKY DAY, MISTER!

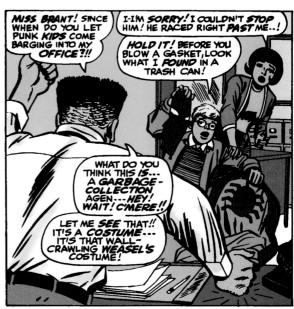

MISS BRANT! SINCE WHEN DO YOU LET PUNK KIDS COME BARGING INTO MY OFFICE?!!

I-I'M SORRY! I COULDN'T STOP HIM! HE RACED RIGHT PAST ME...!

HOLD IT! BEFORE YOU BLOW A GASKET, LOOK WHAT I FOUND IN A TRASH CAN!

WHAT DO YOU THINK THIS IS... A GARBAGE-COLLECTION AGEN...HEY! WAIT! C'MERE!!

LET ME SEE THAT!! IT'S A COSTUME... IT'S THAT WALL-CRAWLING WEASEL'S COSTUME!

...L BE HANGED IF ...ISN'T! IT LOOKS ...KE THE REAL ...CCOY!

AND, IF YOU FOUND IT IN A TRASH CAN... IT CAN ONLY MEAN.. ONE THING..!!

DON'T JUST STAND THERE, MISS BRANT! GET ME THE CITY DESK..AND I MEAN NOW!

YEAH! YEAH! YOU HEARD ME RIGHT! I'M HOLDING IT NOW!!

PUT OUT AN EXTRA! SPLASH IT ACROSS THE FRONT PAGE!!

YOU RATE A REWARD, KID! GRAB A FREE COPY OF THE BUGLE ON THE WAY OUT!

THAT'S A REWARD?

...LAS, WE WILL NEVER KNOW WHETHER OUR DISILLUSIONED ...UNGSTER EVER TOOK HIS FREE COPY OR NOT, FOR WE ...OW LEAP AHEAD TO THE NEXT MORNING...

...W ABOUT ...AT? THEY ...UND HIS ...OSTUME IN A ...ASH CAN!!

THAT WEB-SLINGIN' WONDER WOULDN'T EVER QUIT! SOMEONE MUST HAVE BEATEN HIM!

...N'T ...T IT! ...YBE ...'S ...ST ...AG!

I'LL BELIEVE IT WHEN I SEE IT!

JAMESON WILL PRINT ANYTHING TO SELL HIS PAPER!

SPECIAL EDITION

EXTRA DAILY BUGLE

IS SPIDER-MAN THRU?

EVERY COPY I PRINTED SOLD OUT! THIS IS THE SCOOP OF A LIFETIME!

AFTER ALL THESE YEARS, I FINALLY GOT SOME GOOD OUT OF THAT MASKED MISANTHROPE! EVERYTHING'S COMING UP ROSES!

BUT, IF SOMETHING HAPPENED TO SPIDER-MAN, WHY DIDN'T THE POLICE MAKE THE ANNOUNCEMENT?

WE DON'T KNOW ANY MORE ABOUT IT THAN YOU!

BUT WE'RE STARTING AN INVESTIGATION NOW!

IS IT TRUE, MOM? IS IT TRUE?

LET'S HOPE NOT, JOEY! 9.

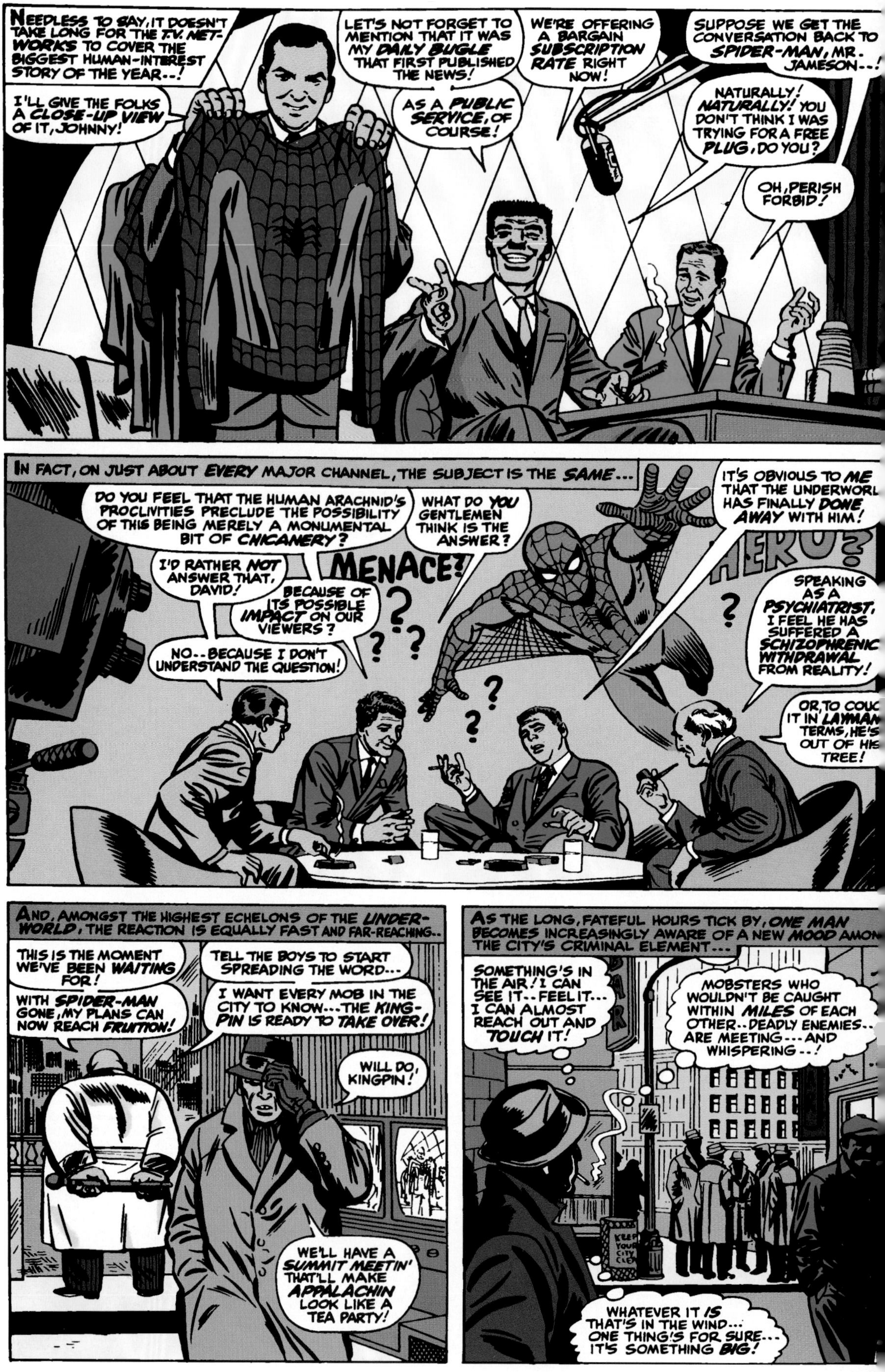
NEEDLESS TO SAY, IT DOESN'T TAKE LONG FOR THE T.V. NETWORKS TO COVER THE BIGGEST HUMAN-INTEREST STORY OF THE YEAR--!
I'LL GIVE THE FOLKS A CLOSE-UP VIEW OF IT, JOHNNY!
LET'S NOT FORGET TO MENTION THAT IT WAS MY DAILY BUGLE THAT FIRST PUBLISHED THE NEWS!
AS A PUBLIC SERVICE, OF COURSE!
WE'RE OFFERING A BARGAIN SUBSCRIPTION RATE RIGHT NOW!
SUPPOSE WE GET THE CONVERSATION BACK TO SPIDER-MAN, MR. JAMESON--!
NATURALLY! NATURALLY! YOU DON'T THINK I WAS TRYING FOR A FREE PLUG, DO YOU?
OH, PERISH FORBID!
IN FACT, ON JUST ABOUT EVERY MAJOR CHANNEL, THE SUBJECT IS THE SAME...
DO YOU FEEL THAT THE HUMAN ARACHNID'S PROCLIVITIES PRECLUDE THE POSSIBILITY OF THIS BEING MERELY A MONUMENTAL BIT OF CHICANERY?
I'D RATHER NOT ANSWER THAT, DAVID!
BECAUSE OF ITS POSSIBLE IMPACT ON OUR VIEWERS?
NO--BECAUSE I DON'T UNDERSTAND THE QUESTION!
WHAT DO YOU GENTLEMEN THINK IS THE ANSWER?
MENACE?
HERO?
IT'S OBVIOUS TO ME THAT THE UNDERWORL HAS FINALLY DONE AWAY WITH HIM!
SPEAKING AS A PSYCHIATRIST, I FEEL HE HAS SUFFERED A SCHIZOPHRENIC WITHDRAWAL FROM REALITY!
OR, TO COUC IT IN LAYMAN TERMS, HE'S OUT OF HIS TREE!
AND, AMONGST THE HIGHEST ECHELONS OF THE UNDERWORLD, THE REACTION IS EQUALLY FAST AND FAR-REACHING..
THIS IS THE MOMENT WE'VE BEEN WAITING FOR!
WITH SPIDER-MAN GONE, MY PLANS CAN NOW REACH FRUITION!
TELL THE BOYS TO START SPREADING THE WORD...
I WANT EVERY MOB IN THE CITY TO KNOW...THE KINGPIN IS READY TO TAKE OVER!
WILL DO, KINGPIN!
WE'LL HAVE A SUMMIT MEETIN' THAT'LL MAKE APPALACHIN LOOK LIKE A TEA PARTY!
AS THE LONG, FATEFUL HOURS TICK BY, ONE MAN BECOMES INCREASINGLY AWARE OF A NEW MOOD AMON THE CITY'S CRIMINAL ELEMENT...
SOMETHING'S IN THE AIR! I CAN SEE IT--FEEL IT... I CAN ALMOST REACH OUT AND TOUCH IT!
MOBSTERS WHO WOULDN'T BE CAUGHT WITHIN MILES OF EACH OTHER--DEADLY ENEMIES--ARE MEETING---AND WHISPERING--!
WHATEVER IT IS THAT'S IN THE WIND... ONE THING'S FOR SURE... IT'S SOMETHING BIG!

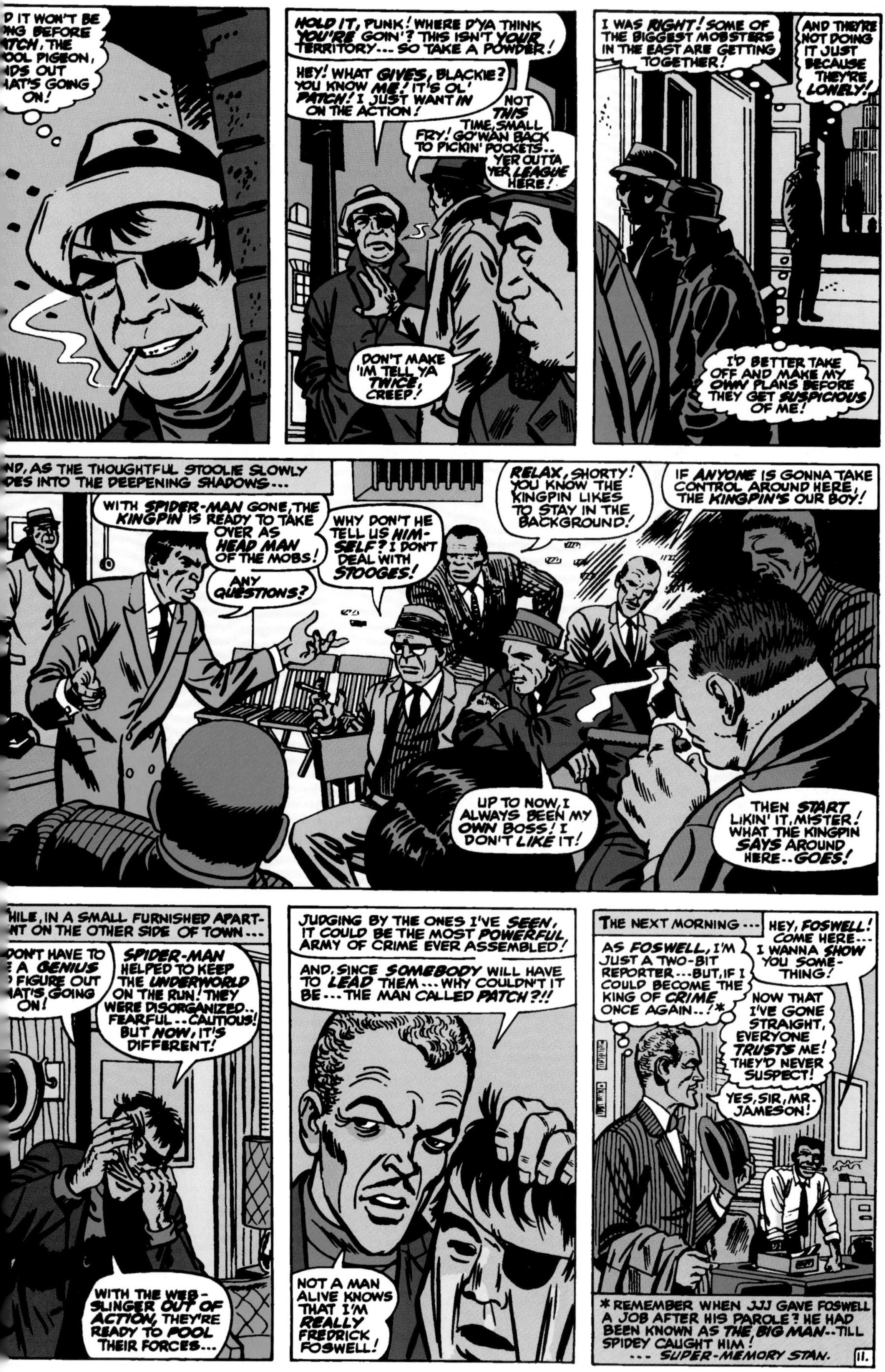

D IT WON'T BE
NG BEFORE
ATCH, THE
OOL PIGEON,
NDS OUT
HAT'S GOING
ON!
HOLD IT, PUNK! WHERE D'YA THINK YOU'RE GOIN'? THIS ISN'T YOUR TERRITORY... SO TAKE A POWDER!
HEY! WHAT GIVES, BLACKIE? YOU KNOW ME! IT'S OL' PATCH! I JUST WANT IN ON THE ACTION!
NOT THIS TIME, SMALL FRY! GO'WAN BACK TO PICKIN' POCKETS.. YER OUTTA YER LEAGUE HERE!
DON'T MAKE 'IM TELL YA TWICE, CREEP!
I WAS RIGHT! SOME OF THE BIGGEST MOBSTERS IN THE EAST ARE GETTING TOGETHER!
AND THEY'RE NOT DOING IT JUST BECAUSE THEY'RE LONELY!
I'D BETTER TAKE OFF AND MAKE MY OWN PLANS BEFORE THEY GET SUSPICIOUS OF ME!
ND, AS THE THOUGHTFUL STOOLIE SLOWLY
DES INTO THE DEEPENING SHADOWS...
WITH SPIDER-MAN GONE, THE KINGPIN IS READY TO TAKE OVER AS HEAD MAN OF THE MOBS!
ANY QUESTIONS?
WHY DON'T HE TELL US HIM-SELF? I DON'T DEAL WITH STOOGES!
RELAX, SHORTY! YOU KNOW THE KINGPIN LIKES TO STAY IN THE BACKGROUND!
IF ANYONE IS GONNA TAKE CONTROL AROUND HERE, THE KINGPIN'S OUR BOY!
UP TO NOW, I ALWAYS BEEN MY OWN BOSS! I DON'T LIKE IT!
THEN START LIKIN' IT, MISTER! WHAT THE KINGPIN SAYS AROUND HERE.. GOES!
HILE, IN A SMALL FURNISHED APART-
NT ON THE OTHER SIDE OF TOWN...
DON'T HAVE TO
E A GENIUS
O FIGURE OUT
HAT'S GOING
ON!
SPIDER-MAN HELPED TO KEEP THE UNDERWORLD ON THE RUN! THEY WERE DISORGANIZED.. FEARFUL... CAUTIOUS! BUT NOW, IT'S DIFFERENT!
WITH THE WEB-SLINGER OUT OF ACTION, THEY'RE READY TO POOL THEIR FORCES...
JUDGING BY THE ONES I'VE SEEN, IT COULD BE THE MOST POWERFUL ARMY OF CRIME EVER ASSEMBLED!
AND, SINCE SOMEBODY WILL HAVE TO LEAD THEM... WHY COULDN'T IT BE... THE MAN CALLED PATCH?!!
NOT A MAN ALIVE KNOWS THAT I'M REALLY FREDRICK FOSWELL!
THE NEXT MORNING...
HEY, FOSWELL! COME HERE... I WANNA SHOW YOU SOME-THING!
AS FOSWELL, I'M JUST A TWO-BIT REPORTER... BUT, IF I COULD BECOME THE KING OF CRIME ONCE AGAIN..!*
NOW THAT I'VE GONE STRAIGHT, EVERYONE TRUSTS ME! THEY'D NEVER SUSPECT!
YES, SIR, MR. JAMESON!
*REMEMBER WHEN JJJ GAVE FOSWELL A JOB AFTER HIS PAROLE? HE HAD BEEN KNOWN AS THE BIG MAN--TILL SPIDEY CAUGHT HIM! ... SUPER-MEMORY STAN.
11.

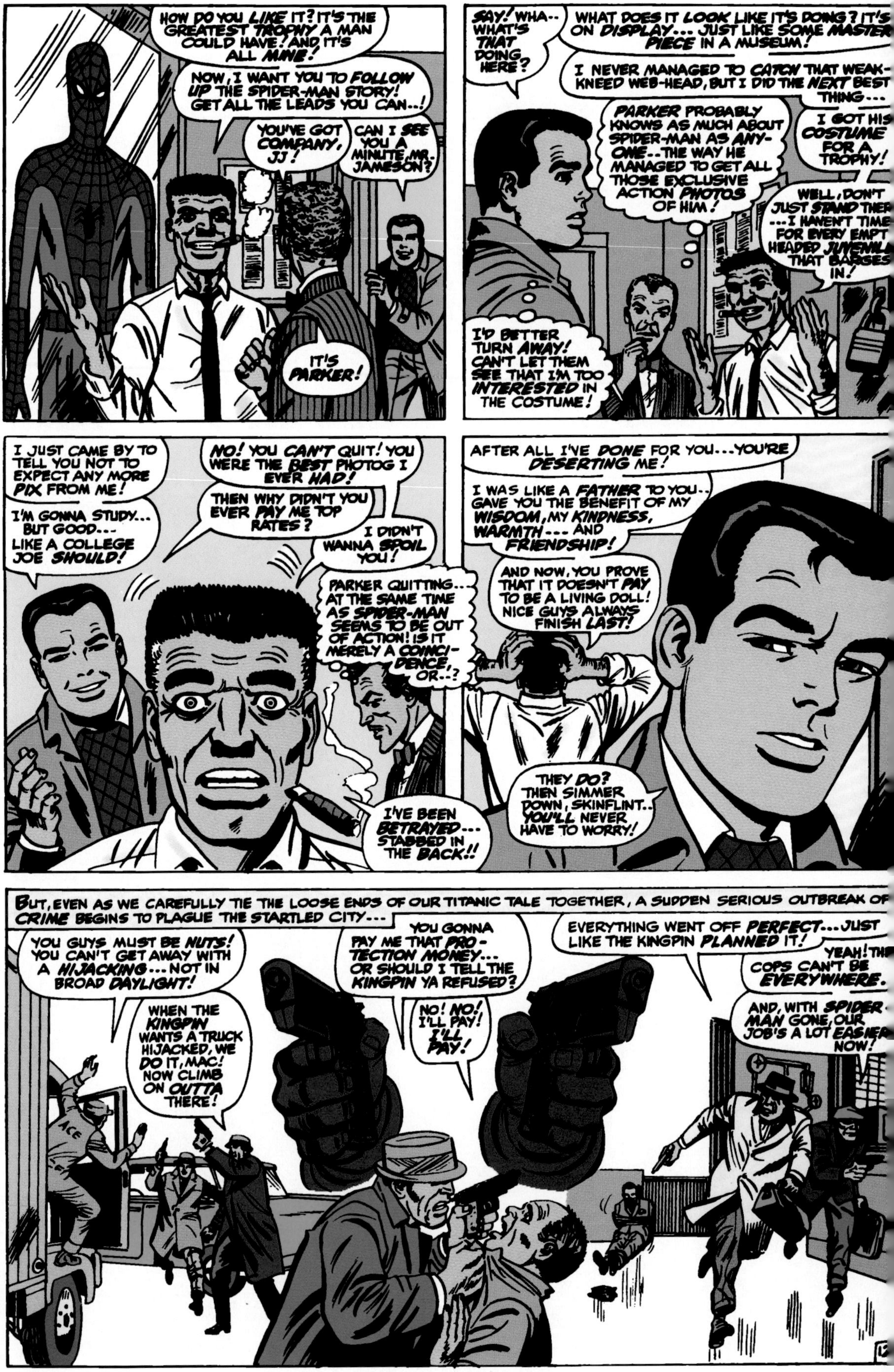

HOW DO YOU LIKE IT? IT'S THE GREATEST TROPHY A MAN COULD HAVE! AND IT'S ALL MINE!
NOW, I WANT YOU TO FOLLOW UP THE SPIDER-MAN STORY! GET ALL THE LEADS YOU CAN..!
YOU'VE GOT COMPANY, JJ!
CAN I SEE YOU A MINUTE, MR. JAMESON?
IT'S PARKER!
SAY! WHA-- WHAT'S THAT DOING HERE?
WHAT DOES IT LOOK LIKE IT'S DOING? IT'S ON DISPLAY... JUST LIKE SOME MASTER PIECE IN A MUSEUM!
I NEVER MANAGED TO CATCH THAT WEAK-KNEED WEB-HEAD, BUT I DID THE NEXT BEST THING...
I GOT HIS COSTUME FOR A TROPHY!
PARKER PROBABLY KNOWS AS MUCH ABOUT SPIDER-MAN AS ANY-ONE..THE WAY HE MANAGED TO GET ALL THOSE EXCLUSIVE ACTION PHOTOS OF HIM!
I'D BETTER TURN AWAY! CAN'T LET THEM SEE THAT I'M TOO INTERESTED IN THE COSTUME!
I JUST CAME BY TO TELL YOU NOT TO EXPECT ANY MORE PIX FROM ME!
I'M GONNA STUDY... BUT GOOD... LIKE A COLLEGE JOE SHOULD!
NO! YOU CAN'T QUIT! YOU WERE THE BEST PHOTOG I EVER HAD!
THEN WHY DIDN'T YOU EVER PAY ME TOP RATES?
I DIDN'T WANNA SPOIL YOU!
PARKER QUITTING... AT THE SAME TIME AS SPIDER-MAN SEEMS TO BE OUT OF ACTION! IS IT MERELY A COINCI-DENCE, OR..?
I'VE BEEN BETRAYED... STABBED IN THE BACK!!
AFTER ALL I'VE DONE FOR YOU...YOU'RE DESERTING ME!
I WAS LIKE A FATHER TO YOU.. GAVE YOU THE BENEFIT OF MY WISDOM, MY KINDNESS, WARMTH... AND FRIENDSHIP!
AND NOW, YOU PROVE THAT IT DOESN'T PAY TO BE A LIVING DOLL! NICE GUYS ALWAYS FINISH LAST!
THEY DO? THEN SIMMER DOWN, SKINFLINT.. YOU'LL NEVER HAVE TO WORRY!
BUT, EVEN AS WE CAREFULLY TIE THE LOOSE ENDS OF OUR TITANIC TALE TOGETHER, A SUDDEN SERIOUS OUTBREAK OF CRIME BEGINS TO PLAGUE THE STARTLED CITY...
YOU GUYS MUST BE NUTS! YOU CAN'T GET AWAY WITH A HIJACKING... NOT IN BROAD DAYLIGHT!
WHEN THE KINGPIN WANTS A TRUCK HIJACKED, WE DO IT, MAC! NOW CLIMB ON OUTTA THERE!
ACE
YOU GONNA PAY ME THAT PRO-TECTION MONEY... OR SHOULD I TELL THE KINGPIN YA REFUSED?
NO! NO! I'LL PAY! I'LL PAY!
EVERYTHING WENT OFF PERFECT... JUST LIKE THE KINGPIN PLANNED IT!
YEAH! THE COPS CAN'T BE EVERYWHERE.
AND, WITH SPIDER-MAN GONE, OUR JOB'S A LOT EASIER NOW!

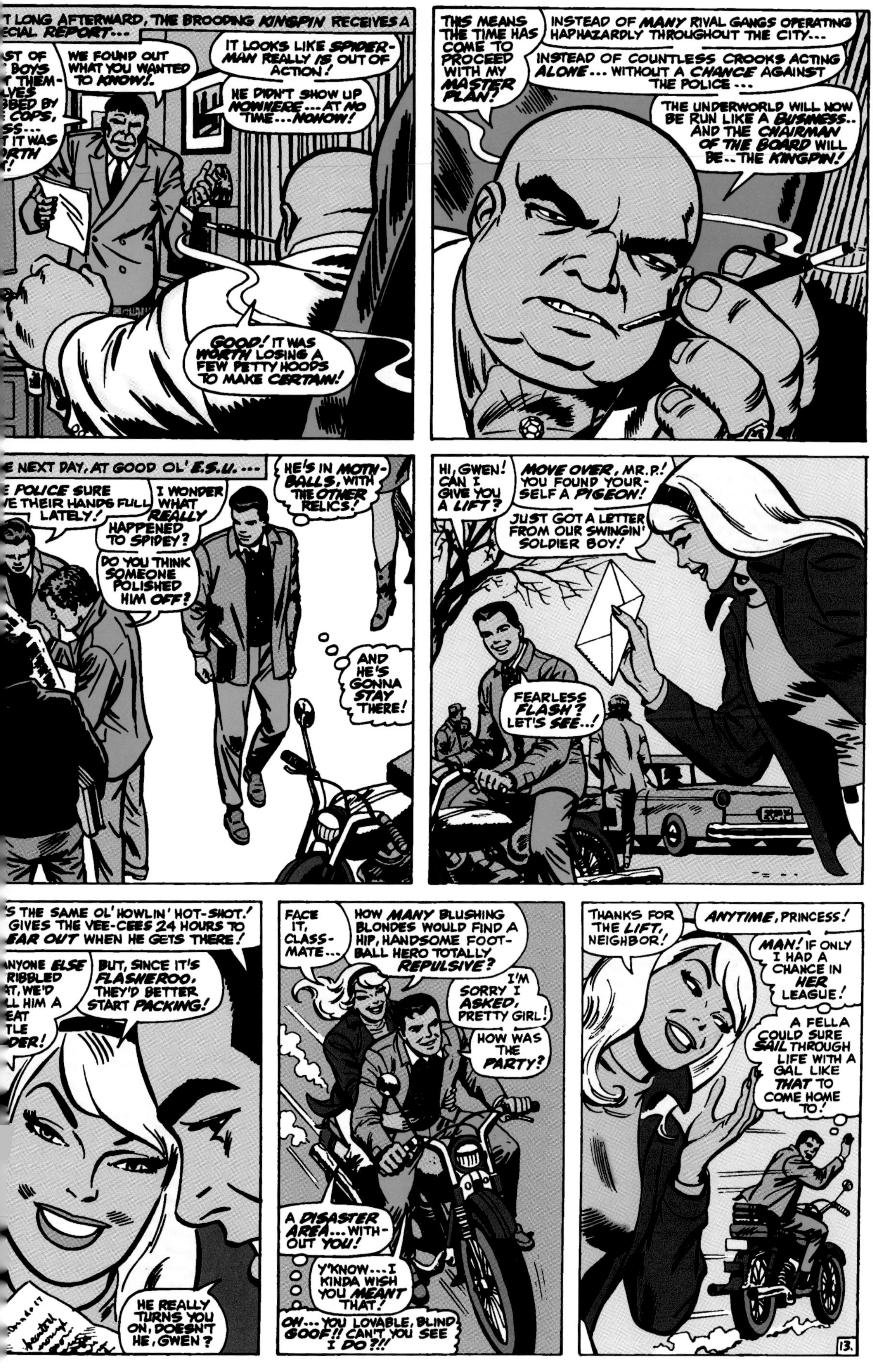

T LONG AFTERWARD, THE BROODING KINGPIN RECEIVES A ECIAL REPORT...
ST OF BOYS T THEM- LVES BBED BY E COPS, SS... T IT WAS ORTH !
WE FOUND OUT WHAT YOU WANTED TO KNOW!.
IT LOOKS LIKE SPIDER-MAN REALLY IS OUT OF ACTION!
HE DIDN'T SHOW UP NOWHERE... AT NO TIME... NOHOW!
GOOD! IT WAS WORTH LOSING A FEW PETTY HOODS TO MAKE CERTAIN!
THIS MEANS THE TIME HAS COME TO PROCEED WITH MY MASTER PLAN!
INSTEAD OF MANY RIVAL GANGS OPERATING HAPHAZARDLY THROUGHOUT THE CITY...
INSTEAD OF COUNTLESS CROOKS ACTING ALONE... WITHOUT A CHANCE AGAINST THE POLICE...
THE UNDERWORLD WILL NOW BE RUN LIKE A BUSINESS.. AND THE CHAIRMAN OF THE BOARD WILL BE.. THE KINGPIN!
E NEXT DAY, AT GOOD OL' E.S.U. ...
E POLICE SURE VE THEIR HANDS FULL LATELY!
I WONDER WHAT REALLY HAPPENED TO SPIDEY?
DO YOU THINK SOMEONE POLISHED HIM OFF?
HE'S IN MOTH-BALLS, WITH THE OTHER RELICS!
AND HE'S GONNA STAY THERE!
HI, GWEN! CAN I GIVE YOU A LIFT?
MOVE OVER, MR. P.! YOU FOUND YOUR-SELF A PIGEON!
JUST GOT A LETTER FROM OUR SWINGIN' SOLDIER BOY!
FEARLESS FLASH? LET'S SEE..!
'S THE SAME OL' HOWLIN' HOT-SHOT! GIVES THE VEE-CEES 24 HOURS TO EAR OUT WHEN HE GETS THERE!
NYONE ELSE RIBBLED T, WE'D LL HIM A EAT TLE DER!
BUT, SINCE IT'S FLASHEROO, THEY'D BETTER START PACKING!
HE REALLY TURNS YOU ON, DOESN'T HE, GWEN?
FACE IT, CLASS-MATE...
HOW MANY BLUSHING BLONDES WOULD FIND A HIP, HANDSOME FOOT-BALL HERO TOTALLY REPULSIVE?
I'M SORRY I ASKED, PRETTY GIRL!
HOW WAS THE PARTY?
A DISASTER AREA... WITH-OUT YOU!
Y'KNOW... I KINDA WISH YOU MEANT THAT!
OH... YOU LOVABLE, BLIND GOOF!! CAN'T YOU SEE I DO?!!
THANKS FOR THE LIFT, NEIGHBOR!
ANYTIME, PRINCESS!
MAN! IF ONLY I HAD A CHANCE IN HER LEAGUE!
A FELLA COULD SURE SAIL THROUGH LIFE WITH A GAL LIKE THAT TO COME HOME TO!
13.

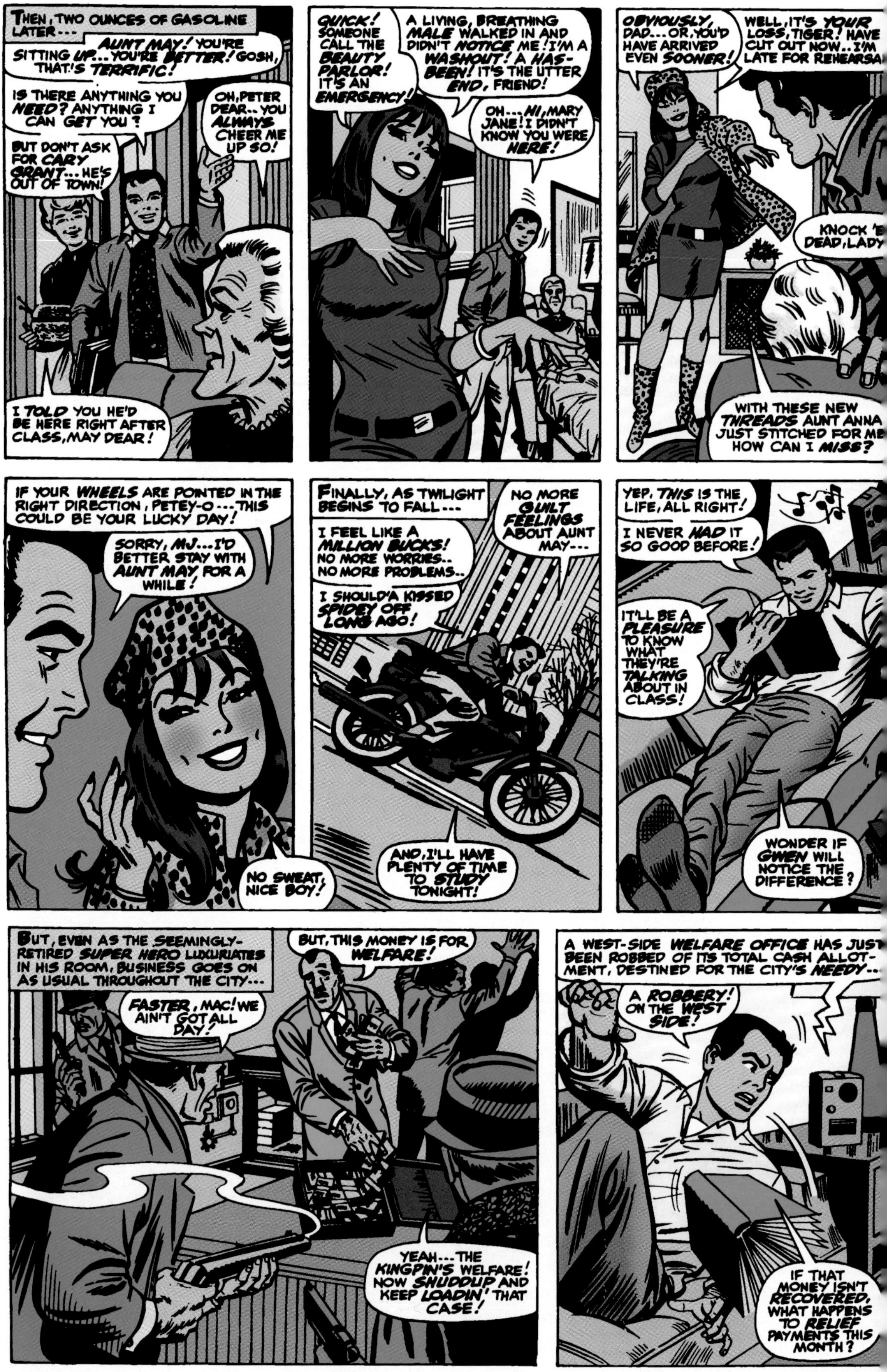
THEN, TWO OUNCES OF GASOLINE LATER...
AUNT MAY! YOU'RE SITTING UP... YOU'RE BETTER! GOSH, THAT'S TERRIFIC!
IS THERE ANYTHING YOU NEED? ANYTHING I CAN GET YOU?
BUT DON'T ASK FOR CARY GRANT... HE'S OUT OF TOWN!
OH, PETER DEAR.. YOU ALWAYS CHEER ME UP SO!
I TOLD YOU HE'D BE HERE RIGHT AFTER CLASS, MAY DEAR!
QUICK! SOMEONE CALL THE BEAUTY PARLOR! IT'S AN EMERGENCY!
A LIVING, BREATHING MALE WALKED IN AND DIDN'T NOTICE ME! I'M A WASHOUT! A HAS-BEEN! IT'S THE UTTER END, FRIEND!
OH... HI, MARY JANE! I DIDN'T KNOW YOU WERE HERE!
OBVIOUSLY, DAD... OR, YOU'D HAVE ARRIVED EVEN SOONER!
WELL, IT'S YOUR LOSS, TIGER! HAVE CUT OUT NOW.. I'M LATE FOR REHEARSA
KNOCK 'E DEAD, LADY
WITH THESE NEW THREADS AUNT ANNA JUST STITCHED FOR ME HOW CAN I MISS?
IF YOUR WHEELS ARE POINTED IN THE RIGHT DIRECTION, PETEY-O --- THIS COULD BE YOUR LUCKY DAY!
SORRY, MJ...I'D BETTER STAY WITH AUNT MAY FOR A WHILE!
NO SWEAT, NICE BOY!
FINALLY, AS TWILIGHT BEGINS TO FALL---
I FEEL LIKE A MILLION BUCKS! NO MORE WORRIES.. NO MORE PROBLEMS..
NO MORE GUILT FEELINGS ABOUT AUNT MAY---
I SHOULD'A KISSED SPIDEY OFF LONG AGO!
AND, I'LL HAVE PLENTY OF TIME TO STUDY TONIGHT!
YEP, THIS IS THE LIFE, ALL RIGHT!
I NEVER HAD IT SO GOOD BEFORE!
IT'LL BE A PLEASURE TO KNOW WHAT THEY'RE TALKING ABOUT IN CLASS!
WONDER IF GWEN WILL NOTICE THE DIFFERENCE?
BUT, EVEN AS THE SEEMINGLY-RETIRED SUPER HERO LUXURIATES IN HIS ROOM, BUSINESS GOES ON AS USUAL THROUGHOUT THE CITY---
FASTER, MAC! WE AIN'T GOT ALL DAY!
BUT, THIS MONEY IS FOR WELFARE!
YEAH--- THE KINGPIN'S WELFARE! NOW SHUDDUP AND KEEP LOADIN' THAT CASE!
A WEST-SIDE WELFARE OFFICE HAS JUST BEEN ROBBED OF ITS TOTAL CASH ALLOT-MENT, DESTINED FOR THE CITY'S NEEDY--
A ROBBERY! ON THE WEST SIDE!
IF THAT MONEY ISN'T RECOVERED, WHAT HAPPENS TO RELIEF PAYMENTS THIS MONTH?

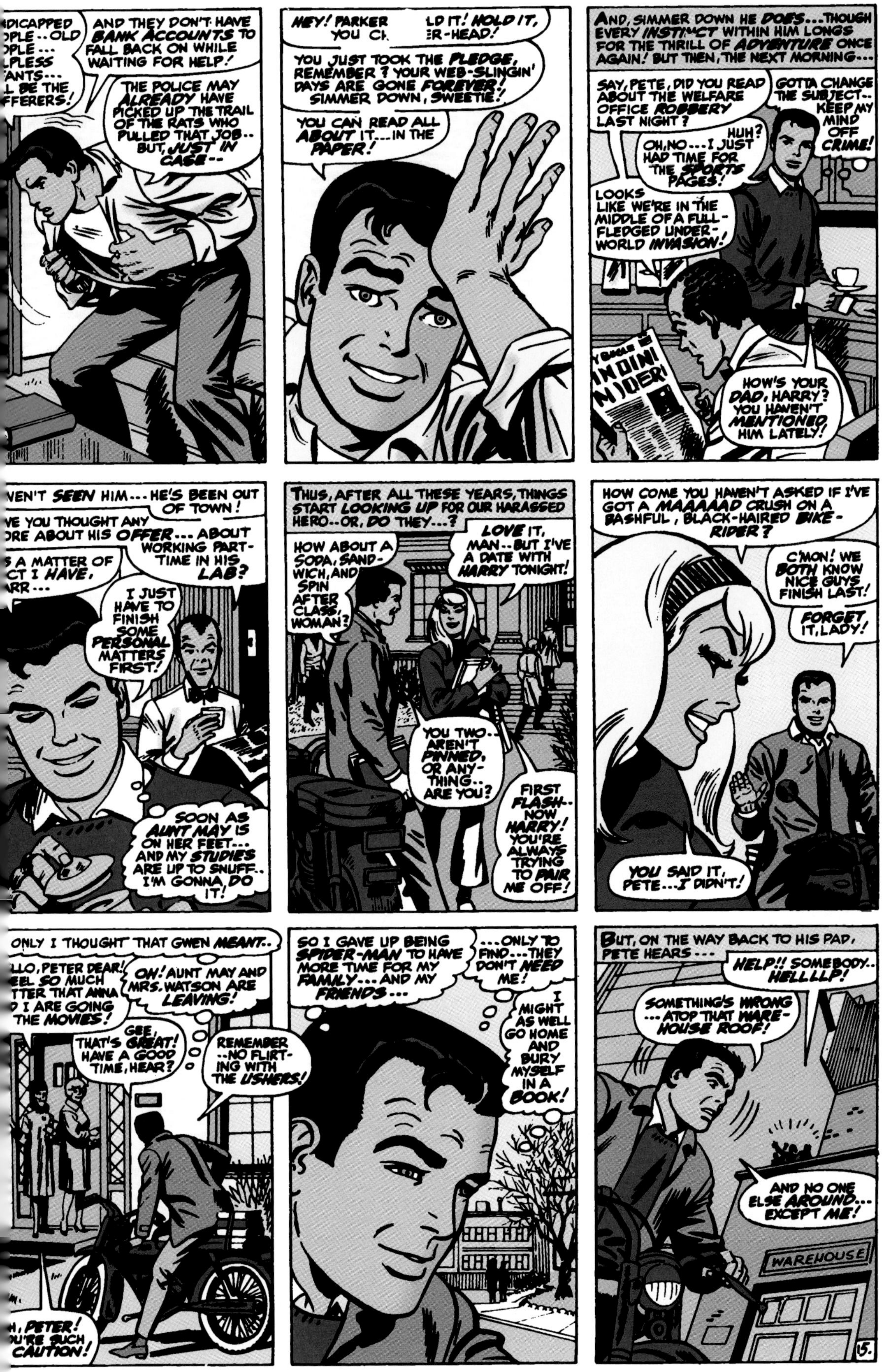
NDICAPPED OPLE--OLD OPLE... LPLESS FANTS... L BE THE FFERERS!
AND THEY DON'T HAVE BANK ACCOUNTS TO FALL BACK ON WHILE WAITING FOR HELP!
THE POLICE MAY ALREADY HAVE PICKED UP THE TRAIL OF THE RATS WHO PULLED THAT JOB.. BUT, JUST IN CASE--
HEY! PARKER LD IT! HOLD IT, YOU CH ER-HEAD!
YOU JUST TOOK THE PLEDGE, REMEMBER? YOUR WEB-SLINGIN' DAYS ARE GONE FOREVER! SIMMER DOWN, SWEETIE!
YOU CAN READ ALL ABOUT IT... IN THE PAPER!
AND, SIMMER DOWN HE DOES... THOUGH EVERY INSTINCT WITHIN HIM LONGS FOR THE THRILL OF ADVENTURE ONCE AGAIN! BUT THEN, THE NEXT MORNING...
SAY, PETE, DID YOU READ ABOUT THE WELFARE OFFICE ROBBERY LAST NIGHT?
HUH?
GOTTA CHANGE THE SUBJECT-- KEEP MY MIND OFF CRIME!
OH, NO... I JUST HAD TIME FOR THE SPORTS PAGES!
LOOKS LIKE WE'RE IN THE MIDDLE OF A FULL-FLEDGED UNDER-WORLD INVASION!
HOW'S YOUR DAD, HARRY? YOU HAVEN'T MENTIONED HIM LATELY!
VEN'T SEEN HIM... HE'S BEEN OUT OF TOWN!
VE YOU THOUGHT ANY ORE ABOUT HIS OFFER... ABOUT WORKING PART-TIME IN HIS LAB?
S A MATTER OF CT I HAVE, ARR...
I JUST HAVE TO FINISH SOME PERSONAL MATTERS FIRST!
SOON AS AUNT MAY IS ON HER FEET... AND MY STUDIES ARE UP TO SNUFF.. I'M GONNA DO IT!
THUS, AFTER ALL THESE YEARS, THINGS START LOOKING UP FOR OUR HARASSED HERO..OR, DO THEY...?
HOW ABOUT A SODA, SAND-WICH, AND SPIN AFTER CLASS, WOMAN?
LOVE IT, MAN.. BUT I'VE A DATE WITH HARRY TONIGHT!
YOU TWO.. AREN'T PINNED, OR ANY-THING.. ARE YOU?
FIRST FLASH.. NOW HARRY! YOU'RE ALWAYS TRYING TO PAIR ME OFF!
HOW COME YOU HAVEN'T ASKED IF I'VE GOT A MAAAAAD CRUSH ON A BASHFUL, BLACK-HAIRED BIKE-RIDER?
C'MON! WE BOTH KNOW NICE GUYS FINISH LAST!
FORGET IT, LADY!
YOU SAID IT, PETE... I DIDN'T!
ONLY I THOUGHT THAT GWEN MEANT..
ELLO, PETER DEAR! EEL SO MUCH TTER THAT ANNA D I ARE GOING THE MOVIES!
OH! AUNT MAY AND MRS. WATSON ARE LEAVING!
GEE, THAT'S GREAT! HAVE A GOOD TIME, HEAR?
REMEMBER --NO FLIRT-ING WITH THE USHERS!
H, PETER! OU'RE SUCH CAUTION!
SO I GAVE UP BEING SPIDER-MAN TO HAVE MORE TIME FOR MY FAMILY... AND MY FRIENDS...
...ONLY TO FIND...THEY DON'T NEED ME!
I MIGHT AS WELL GO HOME AND BURY MYSELF IN A BOOK!
BUT, ON THE WAY BACK TO HIS PAD, PETE HEARS...
HELP!! SOMEBODY.. HELLLLP!
SOMETHING'S WRONG --ATOP THAT WARE-HOUSE ROOF!
AND NO ONE ELSE AROUND... EXCEPT ME!
WAREHOUSE
15.

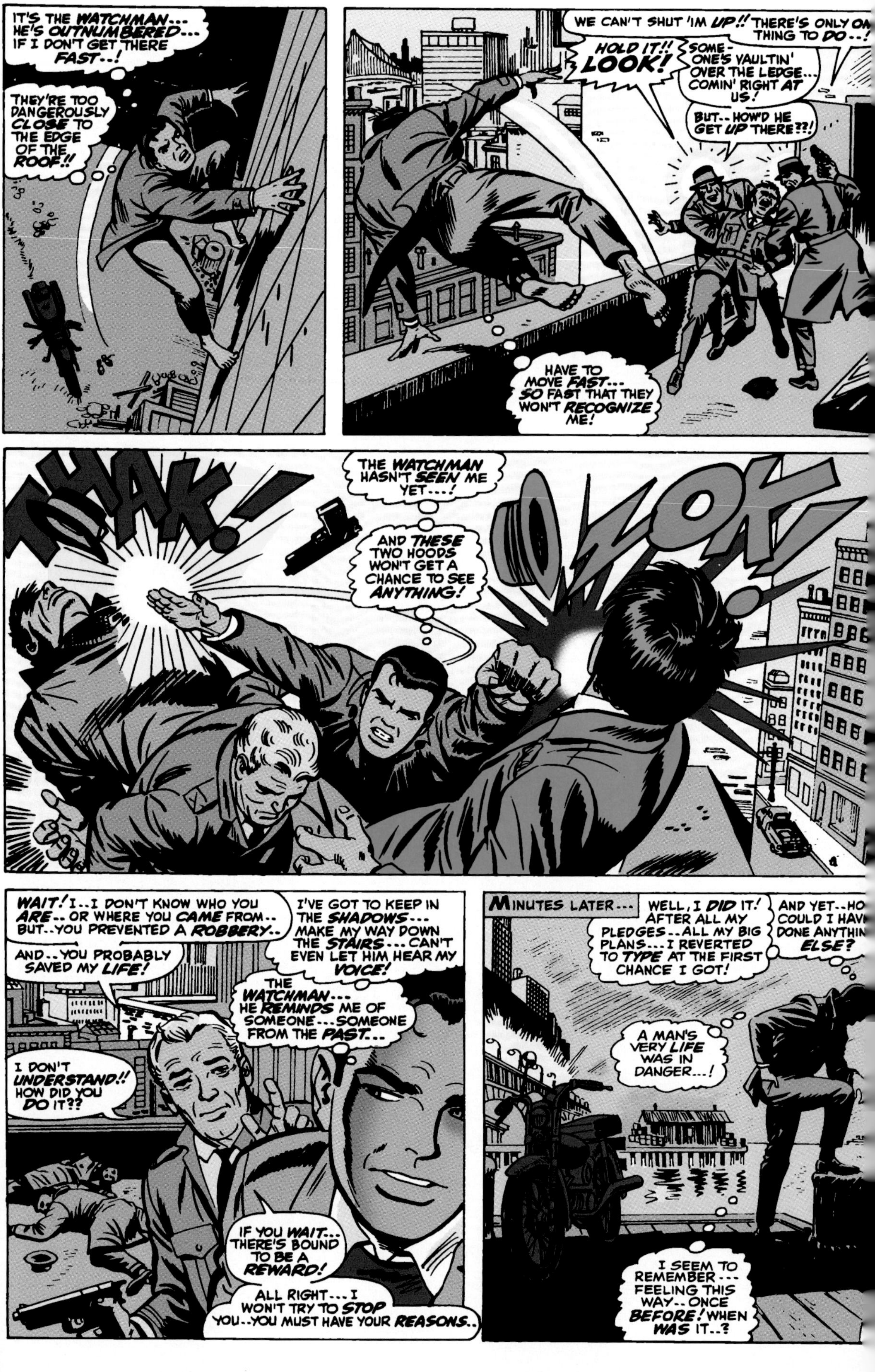
IT'S THE WATCHMAN... HE'S OUTNUMBERED... IF I DON'T GET THERE FAST..!
THEY'RE TOO DANGEROUSLY CLOSE TO THE EDGE OF THE ROOF!!
WE CAN'T SHUT 'IM UP!! THERE'S ONLY ONE THING TO DO..!
HOLD IT!! LOOK!
SOME-ONE'S VAULTIN' OVER THE LEDGE... COMIN' RIGHT AT US!
BUT.. HOW'D HE GET UP THERE??!
HAVE TO MOVE FAST... SO FAST THAT THEY WON'T RECOGNIZE ME!
THAK!!
THE WATCHMAN HASN'T SEEN ME YET...!
AND THESE TWO HOODS WON'T GET A CHANCE TO SEE ANYTHING!
ZOK!
WAIT! I..I DON'T KNOW WHO YOU ARE.. OR WHERE YOU CAME FROM.. BUT..YOU PREVENTED A ROBBERY..
AND..YOU PROBABLY SAVED MY LIFE!
I'VE GOT TO KEEP IN THE SHADOWS... MAKE MY WAY DOWN THE STAIRS... CAN'T EVEN LET HIM HEAR MY VOICE!
THE WATCHMAN... HE REMINDS ME OF SOMEONE... SOMEONE FROM THE PAST...
I DON'T UNDERSTAND!! HOW DID YOU DO IT??
IF YOU WAIT... THERE'S BOUND TO BE A REWARD!
ALL RIGHT... I WON'T TRY TO STOP YOU..YOU MUST HAVE YOUR REASONS..
MINUTES LATER...
WELL, I DID IT! AFTER ALL MY PLEDGES..ALL MY BIG PLANS... I REVERTED TO TYPE AT THE FIRST CHANCE I GOT!
AND YET..HOW COULD I HAVE DONE ANYTHING ELSE?
A MAN'S VERY LIFE WAS IN DANGER...!
I SEEM TO REMEMBER... FEELING THIS WAY.. ONCE BEFORE! WHEN WAS IT..?

OF COURSE! NOW I KNOW!! THAT'S WHY THE WATCHMAN SEEMED SO FAMILIAR...

UNCLE BEN!! HE REMINDED ME OF MY UNCLE BEN!!

HOW COULD I HAVE FORGOTTEN?? IT SEEMS LIKE ONLY YESTERDAY NOW...

AUNT MAY... AND UNCLE BEN... THE ONLY FAMILY THAT I EVER KNEW..!

THEY WERE THE GREATEST FOLKS THAT ANYONE COULD HAVE... KIND, LOVING, GENEROUS...

I'LL NEVER FORGET UNCLE BEN SAVING FOR MONTHS TO BUY ME MY FIRST MICROSCOPE...

THEN, WHEN I HAD THE LAB ACCIDENT WHICH GAVE ME MY SPIDER-MAN POWERS, I JUST BECAME A COSTUMED ADVENTURER FOR KICKS... AND THE MONEY I THOUGHT IT WOULD BRING!

I HOPED I'D BE ABLE TO PAY UNCLE BEN BACK AT LEAST A FRACTION OF WHAT I OWED HIM...!

AND WHEN IT CAME TO CHASING CRIMINALS, I WAS MORE THAN WILLING TO "LET GEORGE DO IT!"

EVEN WHEN I WAS YELLED AT OR NOT EVEN TRYING TO STOP A FLEEING BURGLAR, I SHRUGGED IT OFF! AFTER ALL, IT WASN'T ANY OF MY BUSINESS...

OR, SO I THOUGHT...

...UNTIL I LEARNED THAT THE BURGLAR HAD ACTUALLY COMMITTED A MURDER... AND HIS VICTIM HAD BEEN...

UNCLE BEN!!

THAT WAS THE TURNING POINT...

THAT'S WHEN I BECAME SPIDER-MAN --FOR REAL!!

17.

ONE OF THE FIRST VICTORIES IN MY CRIME-BUSTING CAREER CAME A SHORT TIME LATER, WHEN I CORNERED AN ARMED ROBBER..

EVEN WITH HIS GUN, HE WAS NO MATCH FOR MY SPIDER-POWERS...AND I DUSTED HIM OFF FAST AND EASY....!

BUT, A MINUTE LATER, I GOT THE NEXT GREAT SURPRISE OF MY LIFE...

IT'S HIM!! HE'S THE ONE...WHO KILLED..UNCLE BEN!!

AND, THEN, I WAS SUDDENLY HIT BY THE SHOCKING REALIZATION WHICH HAS HAUNTED ME..FROM THAT MOMENT ON---

I HAD A CHANCE TO STOP HIM...WHEN HE RAN PAST ME THAT DAY...AND I DIDN'T!

BUT, IF ONLY I HAD DONE SO...

UNCLE BEN WOULD BE ALIVE TODAY!

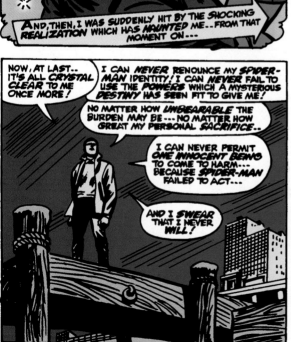

NOW, AT LAST.. IT'S ALL CRYSTAL CLEAR TO ME ONCE MORE!

I CAN NEVER RENOUNCE MY SPIDER-MAN IDENTITY! I CAN NEVER FAIL TO USE THE POWERS WHICH A MYSTERIOUS DESTINY HAS SEEN FIT TO GIVE ME!

NO MATTER HOW UNBEARABLE THE BURDEN MAY BE --- NO MATTER HOW GREAT MY PERSONAL SACRIFICE..

I CAN NEVER PERMIT ONE INNOCENT BEING TO COME TO HARM...BECAUSE SPIDER-MAN FAILED TO ACT...

AND I SWEAR THAT I NEVER WILL!

WHILE, AT THE PALATIAL HEADQUARTERS OF THE COLD-BLOODED KINGPIN, WE FIND---

EVER HEAR OF THE BIG MAN, MISTER?

YOU'RE LOOKING AT HIM!

I RAN THE RACKETS IN T[HIS] TOWN---BEFORE SPIDER-MAN PU[T] ME ON ICE!

BUT THE WEB-SLINGER'S GONE NOW, SO I'M AIM-ING TO RUN THINGS AGAIN!

I REMEMBER YOU, FOSWELL! I THOUGHT YOU H[AD] GONE STRAIGHT[!]

SO DID I! BUT I CAN'T STAND BY AND WATCH SOMEONE ELSE PICK UP WHERE I LEFT OFF!

IF ANYONE'S GONNA ORGANIZE THE MOBS--- IT'S GOTTA BE ME!

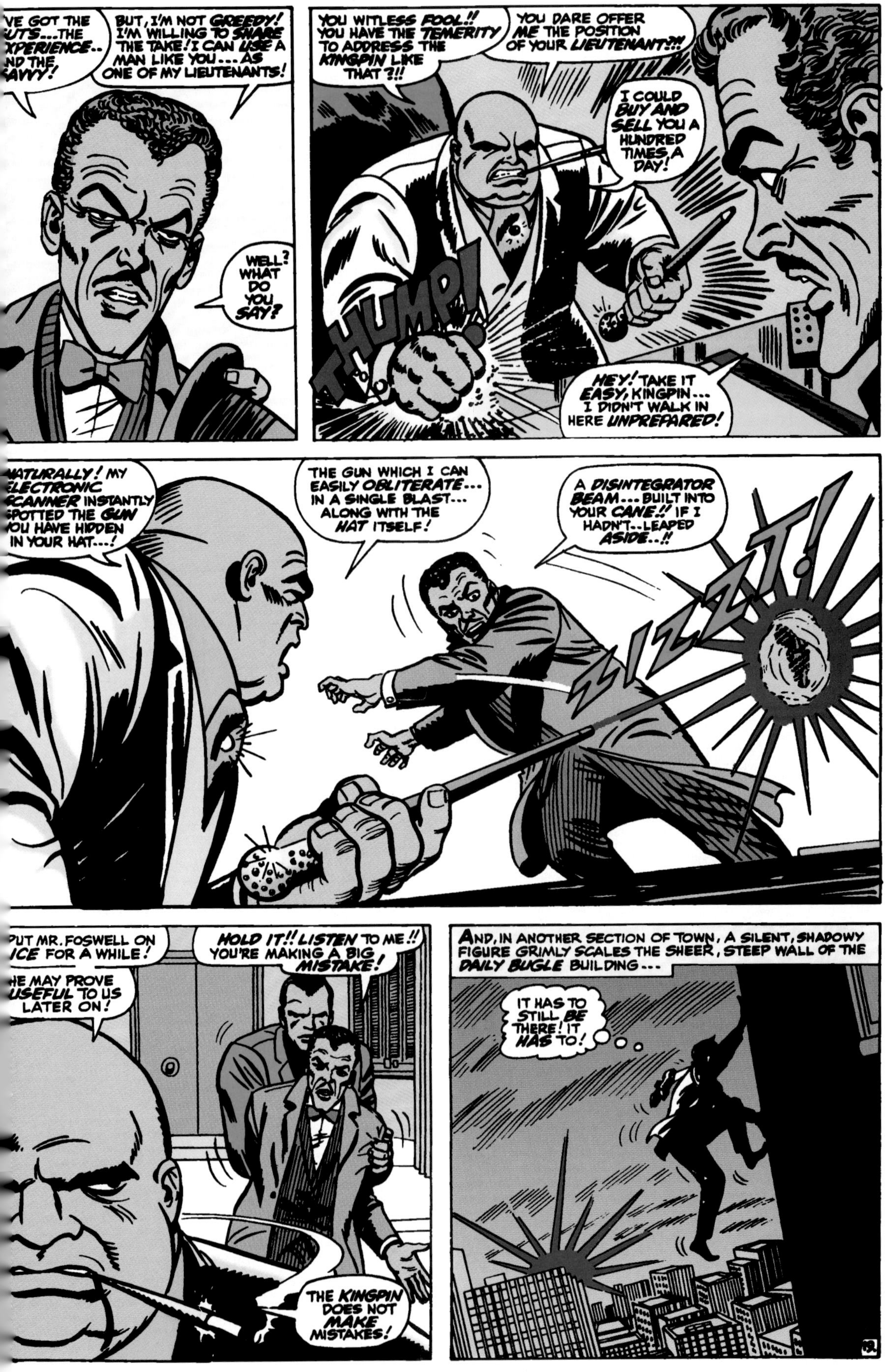

'VE GOT THE GUTS...THE EXPERIENCE.. AND THE SAVVY!
BUT, I'M NOT GREEDY! I'M WILLING TO SHARE THE TAKE! I CAN USE A MAN LIKE YOU... AS ONE OF MY LIEUTENANTS!
WELL? WHAT DO YOU SAY?
YOU WITLESS FOOL!! YOU HAVE THE TEMERITY TO ADDRESS THE KINGPIN LIKE THAT?!!
YOU DARE OFFER ME THE POSITION OF YOUR LIEUTENANT?!!
I COULD BUY AND SELL YOU A HUNDRED TIMES A DAY!
THUMP!
HEY! TAKE IT EASY, KINGPIN... I DIDN'T WALK IN HERE UNPREPARED!
NATURALLY! MY ELECTRONIC SCANNER INSTANTLY SPOTTED THE GUN YOU HAVE HIDDEN IN YOUR HAT...!
THE GUN WHICH I CAN EASILY OBLITERATE... IN A SINGLE BLAST... ALONG WITH THE HAT ITSELF!
A DISINTEGRATOR BEAM... BUILT INTO YOUR CANE!! IF I HADN'T..LEAPED ASIDE..!!
ZIZZZT!
PUT MR. FOSWELL ON ICE FOR A WHILE!
HE MAY PROVE USEFUL TO US LATER ON!
HOLD IT!! LISTEN TO ME!! YOU'RE MAKING A BIG MISTAKE!
THE KINGPIN DOES NOT MAKE MISTAKES!
AND, IN ANOTHER SECTION OF TOWN, A SILENT, SHADOWY FIGURE GRIMLY SCALES THE SHEER, STEEP WALL OF THE DAILY BUGLE BUILDING...
IT HAS TO STILL BE THERE! IT HAS TO!
19

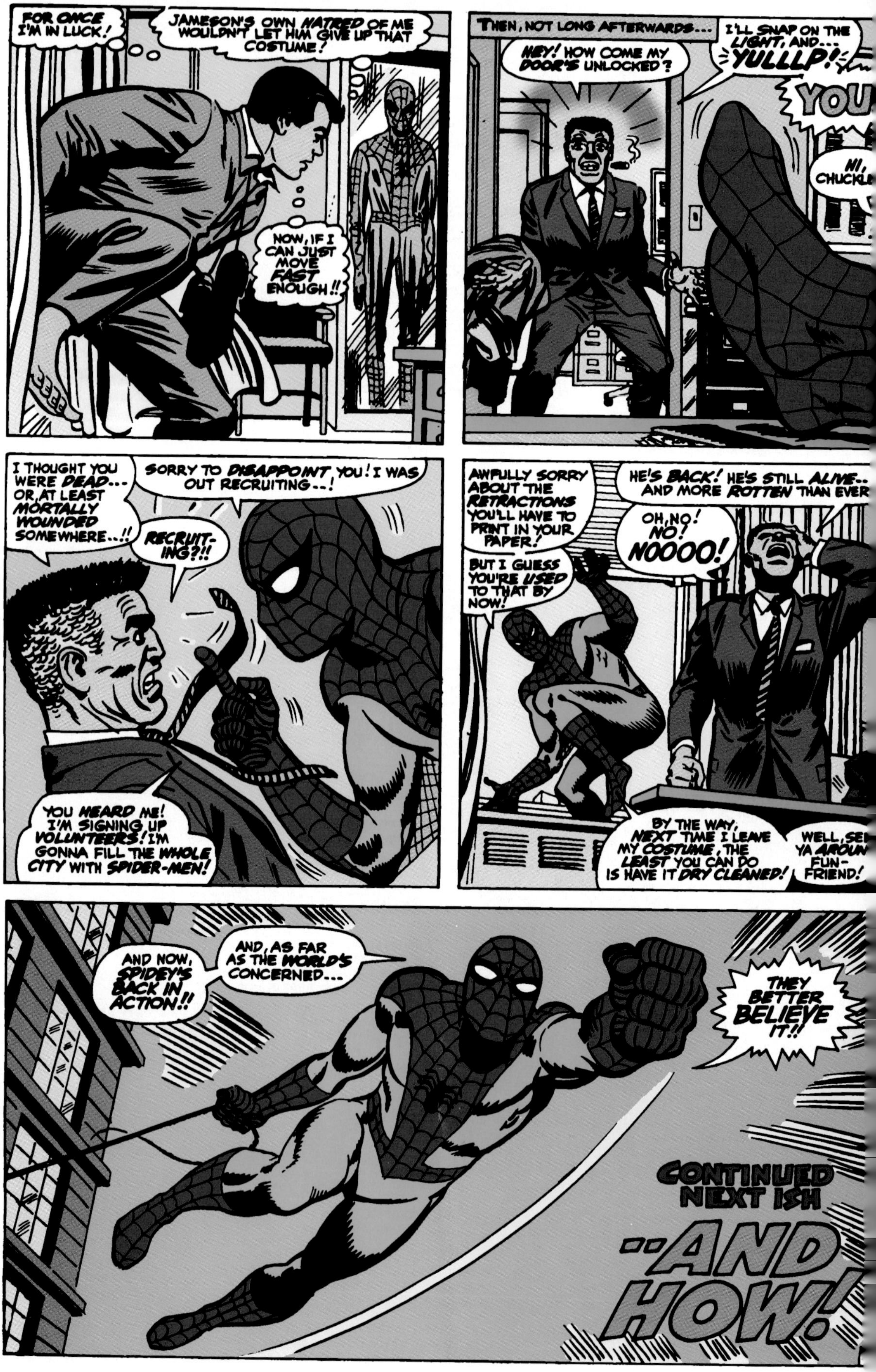
FOR ONCE I'M IN LUCK!
JAMESON'S OWN HATRED OF ME WOULDN'T LET HIM GIVE UP THAT COSTUME!
NOW, IF I CAN JUST MOVE FAST ENOUGH!!
THEN, NOT LONG AFTERWARDS...
HEY! HOW COME MY DOOR'S UNLOCKED?
I'LL SNAP ON THE LIGHT, AND... YULLLP!
YOU
HI, CHUCKL
I THOUGHT YOU WERE DEAD... OR, AT LEAST MORTALLY WOUNDED SOMEWHERE...!!
SORRY TO DISAPPOINT YOU! I WAS OUT RECRUITING..!
RECRUIT-ING?!!
YOU HEARD ME! I'M SIGNING UP VOLUNTEERS! I'M GONNA FILL THE WHOLE CITY WITH SPIDER-MEN!
AWFULLY SORRY ABOUT THE RETRACTIONS YOU'LL HAVE TO PRINT IN YOUR PAPER!
BUT I GUESS YOU'RE USED TO THAT BY NOW!
HE'S BACK! HE'S STILL ALIVE.. AND MORE ROTTEN THAN EVER
OH, NO! NO! NOOOO!
BY THE WAY, NEXT TIME I LEAVE MY COSTUME, THE LEAST YOU CAN DO IS HAVE IT DRY CLEANED!
WELL, SE
YA AROUN
FUN-FRIEND!
AND NOW, SPIDEY'S BACK IN ACTION!!
AND, AS FAR AS THE WORLD'S CONCERNED...
THEY BETTER BELIEVE IT!!
CONTINUED NEXT ISH
--AND HOW!

amazing spider-man #68

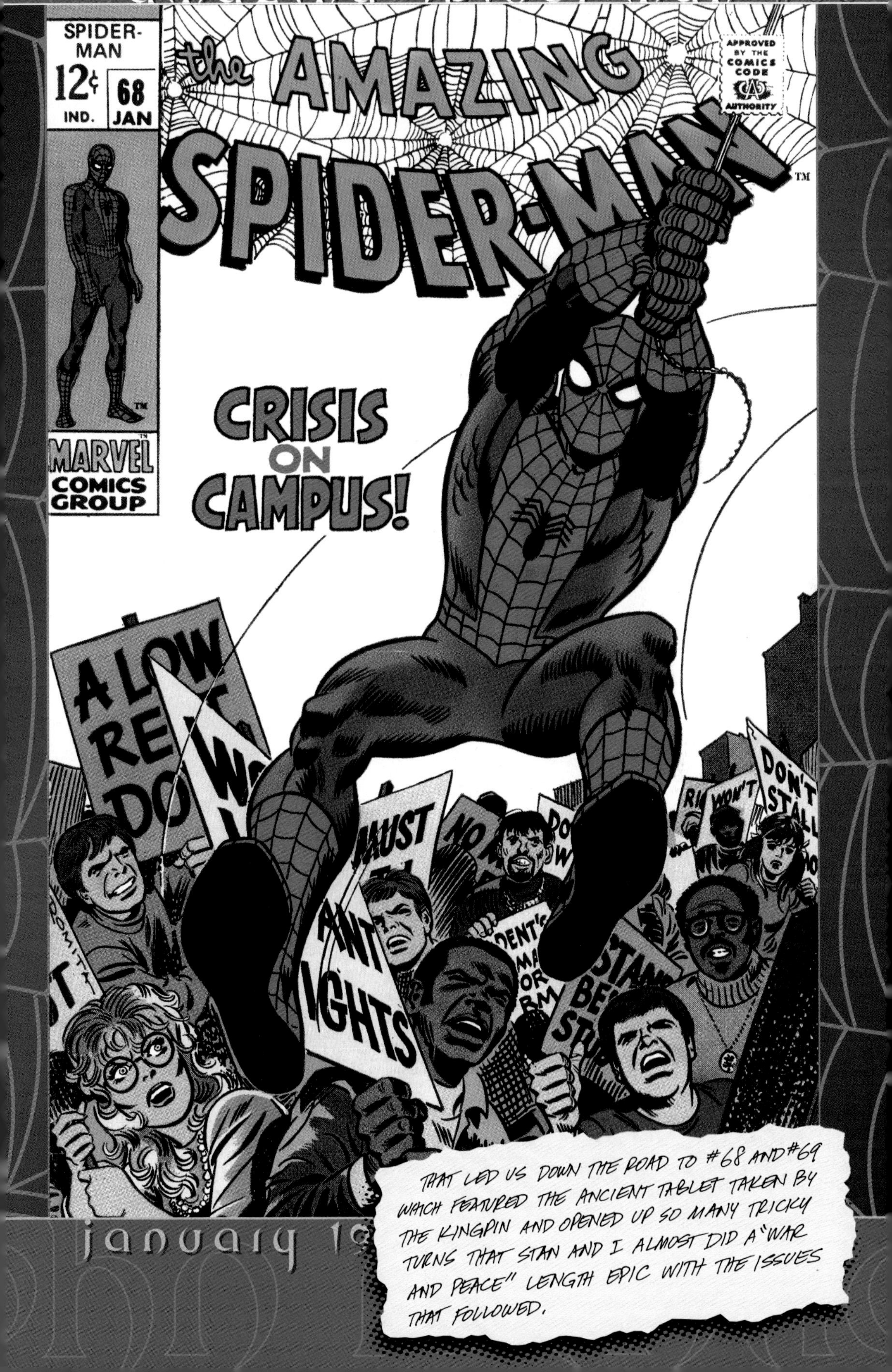
SPIDER-MAN
12¢
68
IND.
JAN
the AMAZING SPIDER-MAN
APPROVED BY THE COMICS CODE AUTHORITY
CRISIS ON CAMPUS!
MARVEL COMICS GROUP

january 19

THAT LED US DOWN THE ROAD TO #68 AND #69 WHICH FEATURED THE ANCIENT TABLET TAKEN BY THE KINGPIN AND OPENED UP SO MANY TRICKY TURNS THAT STAN AND I ALMOST DID A "WAR AND PEACE" LENGTH EPIC WITH THE ISSUES THAT FOLLOWED.

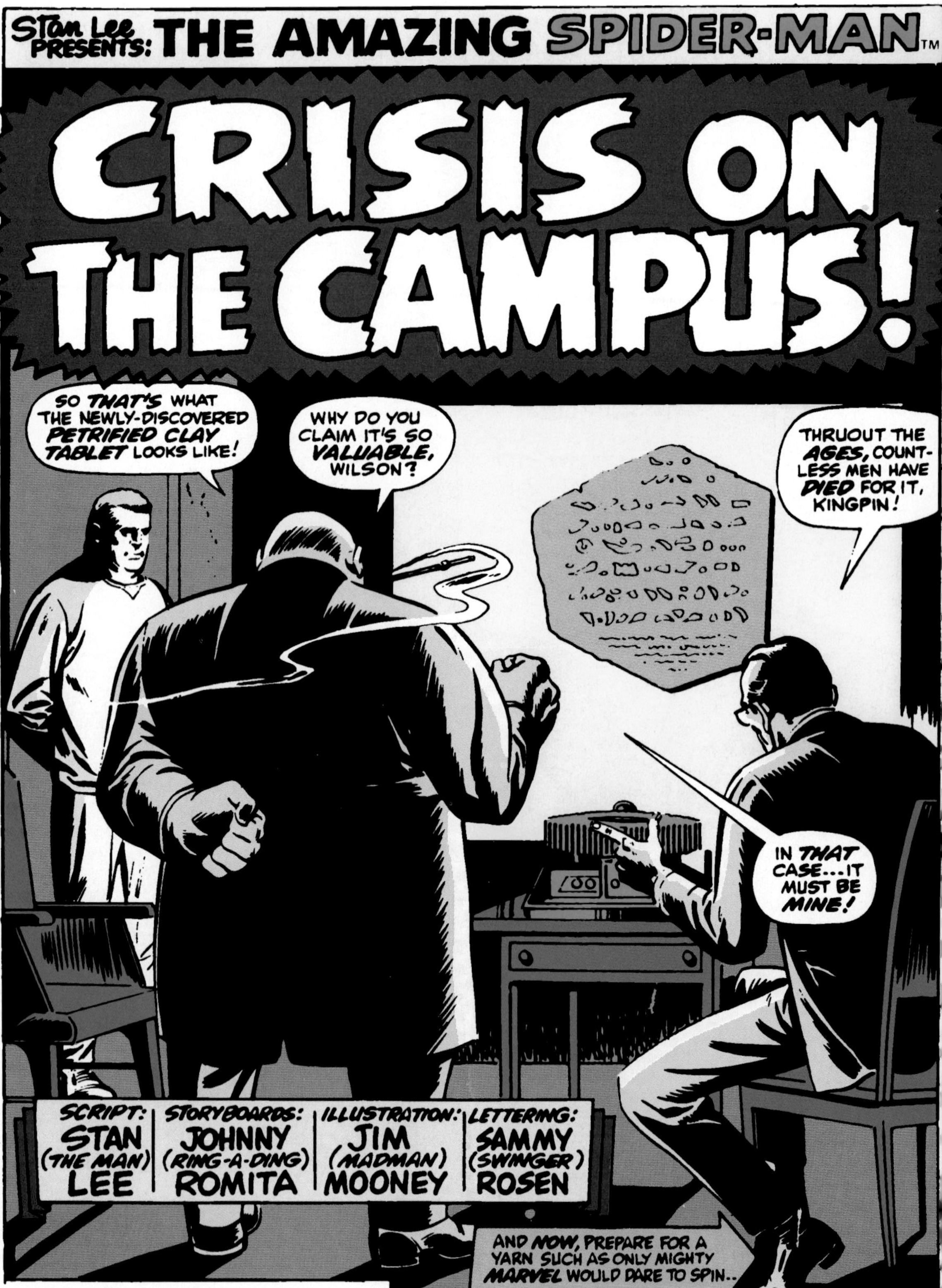
STAN LEE PRESENTS: THE AMAZING SPIDER-MAN™
CRISIS ON THE CAMPUS!
SO THAT'S WHAT THE NEWLY-DISCOVERED PETRIFIED CLAY TABLET LOOKS LIKE!
WHY DO YOU CLAIM IT'S SO VALUABLE, WILSON?
THRUOUT THE AGES, COUNTLESS MEN HAVE DIED FOR IT, KINGPIN!
IN THAT CASE...IT MUST BE MINE!
SCRIPT: STAN (THE MAN) LEE
STORYBOARDS: JOHNNY (RING-A-DING) ROMITA
ILLUSTRATION: JIM (MADMAN) MOONEY
LETTERING: SAMMY (SWINGER) ROSEN
AND NOW, PREPARE FOR A YARN SUCH AS ONLY MIGHTY MARVEL WOULD DARE TO SPIN..

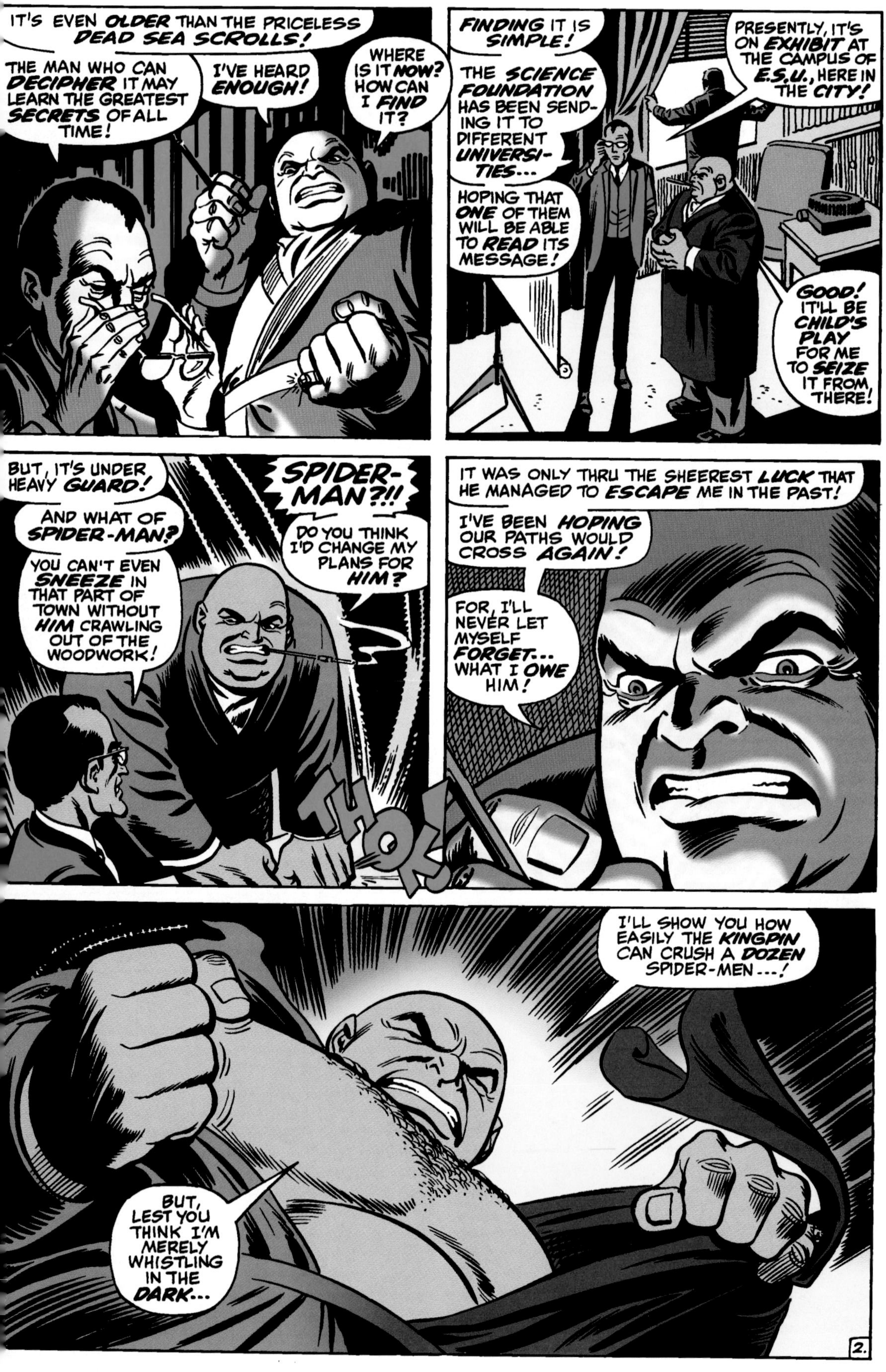
IT'S EVEN OLDER THAN THE PRICELESS DEAD SEA SCROLLS!
THE MAN WHO CAN DECIPHER IT MAY LEARN THE GREATEST SECRETS OF ALL TIME!
I'VE HEARD ENOUGH!
WHERE IS IT NOW? HOW CAN I FIND IT?
FINDING IT IS SIMPLE!
THE SCIENCE FOUNDATION HAS BEEN SENDING IT TO DIFFERENT UNIVERSITIES...
HOPING THAT ONE OF THEM WILL BE ABLE TO READ ITS MESSAGE!
PRESENTLY, IT'S ON EXHIBIT AT THE CAMPUS OF E.S.U., HERE IN THE CITY!
GOOD! IT'LL BE CHILD'S PLAY FOR ME TO SEIZE IT FROM THERE!
BUT, IT'S UNDER HEAVY GUARD!
AND WHAT OF SPIDER-MAN?
YOU CAN'T EVEN SNEEZE IN THAT PART OF TOWN WITHOUT HIM CRAWLING OUT OF THE WOODWORK!
SPIDER-MAN?!!
DO YOU THINK I'D CHANGE MY PLANS FOR HIM?
THOK
IT WAS ONLY THRU THE SHEEREST LUCK THAT HE MANAGED TO ESCAPE ME IN THE PAST!
I'VE BEEN HOPING OUR PATHS WOULD CROSS AGAIN!
FOR, I'LL NEVER LET MYSELF FORGET... WHAT I OWE HIM!
BUT, LEST YOU THINK I'M MERELY WHISTLING IN THE DARK...
I'LL SHOW YOU HOW EASILY THE KINGPIN CAN CRUSH A DOZEN SPIDER-MEN...!
2.

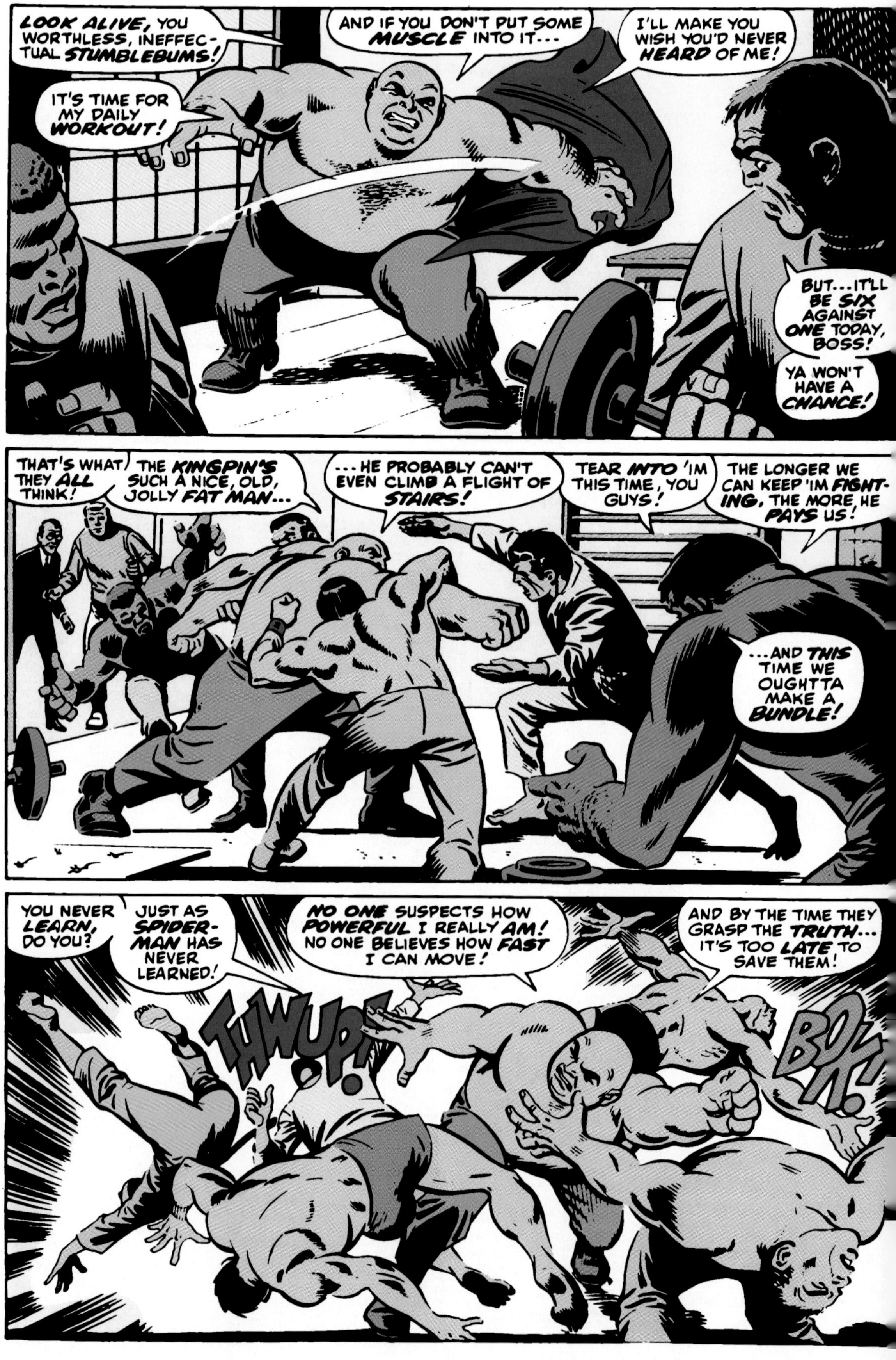
LOOK ALIVE, YOU WORTHLESS, INEFFECTUAL STUMBLEBUMS!
IT'S TIME FOR MY DAILY WORKOUT!
AND IF YOU DON'T PUT SOME MUSCLE INTO IT...
I'LL MAKE YOU WISH YOU'D NEVER HEARD OF ME!
BUT...IT'LL BE SIX AGAINST ONE TODAY, BOSS!
YA WON'T HAVE A CHANCE!
THAT'S WHAT THEY ALL THINK!
THE KINGPIN'S SUCH A NICE, OLD, JOLLY FAT MAN...
...HE PROBABLY CAN'T EVEN CLIMB A FLIGHT OF STAIRS!
TEAR INTO 'IM THIS TIME, YOU GUYS!
THE LONGER WE CAN KEEP 'IM FIGHTING, THE MORE HE PAYS US!
...AND THIS TIME WE OUGHTTA MAKE A BUNDLE!
YOU NEVER LEARN, DO YOU?
JUST AS SPIDER-MAN HAS NEVER LEARNED!
NO ONE SUSPECTS HOW POWERFUL I REALLY AM! NO ONE BELIEVES HOW FAST I CAN MOVE!
AND BY THE TIME THEY GRASP THE TRUTH... IT'S TOO LATE TO SAVE THEM!

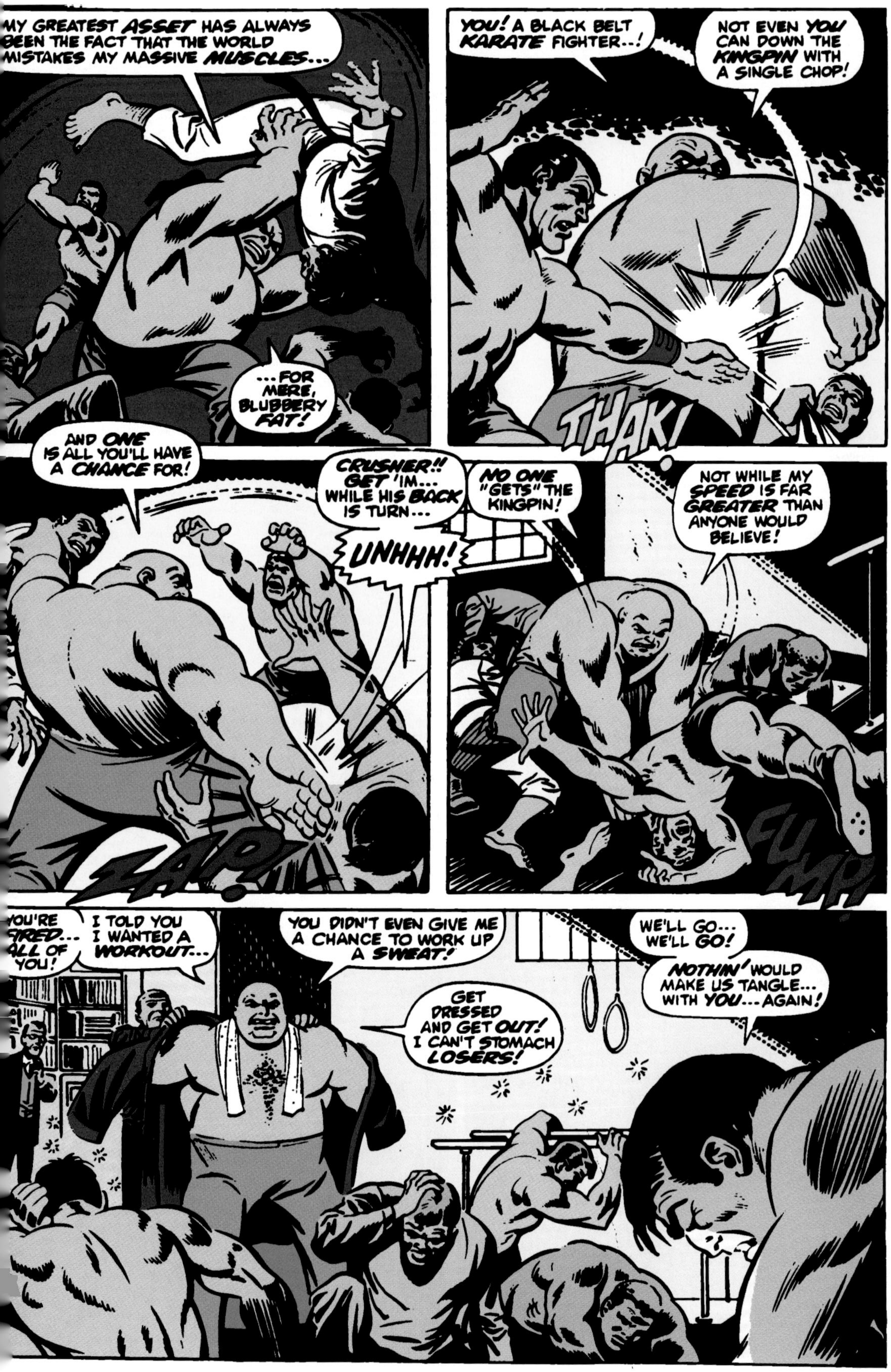
MY GREATEST ASSET HAS ALWAYS BEEN THE FACT THAT THE WORLD MISTAKES MY MASSIVE MUSCLES...
...FOR MERE, BLUBBERY FAT!
YOU! A BLACK BELT KARATE FIGHTER..!
NOT EVEN YOU CAN DOWN THE KINGPIN WITH A SINGLE CHOP!
THAK!
AND ONE IS ALL YOU'LL HAVE A CHANCE FOR!
CRUSHER!! GET 'IM... WHILE HIS BACK IS TURN...
UNHHH!
ZAP!
NO ONE "GETS" THE KINGPIN!
NOT WHILE MY SPEED IS FAR GREATER THAN ANYONE WOULD BELIEVE!
FUMP!
YOU'RE FIRED... ALL OF YOU!
I TOLD YOU I WANTED A WORKOUT...
YOU DIDN'T EVEN GIVE ME A CHANCE TO WORK UP A SWEAT!
GET DRESSED AND GET OUT! I CAN'T STOMACH LOSERS!
WE'LL GO... WE'LL GO!
NOTHIN' WOULD MAKE US TANGLE... WITH YOU... AGAIN!

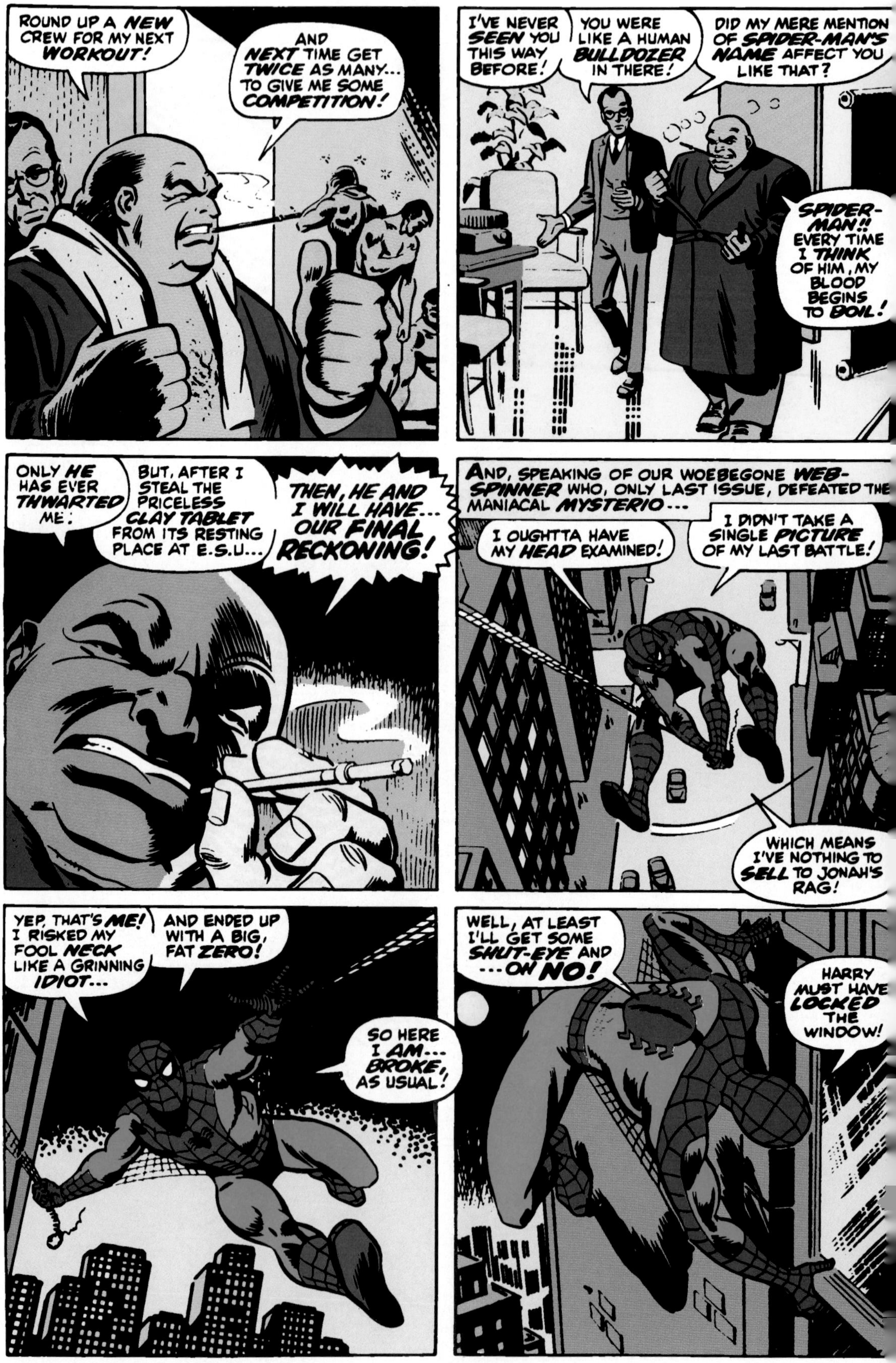
ROUND UP A NEW CREW FOR MY NEXT WORKOUT!
AND NEXT TIME GET TWICE AS MANY... TO GIVE ME SOME COMPETITION!
I'VE NEVER SEEN YOU THIS WAY BEFORE!
YOU WERE LIKE A HUMAN BULLDOZER IN THERE!
DID MY MERE MENTION OF SPIDER-MAN'S NAME AFFECT YOU LIKE THAT?
SPIDER-MAN!! EVERY TIME I THINK OF HIM, MY BLOOD BEGINS TO BOIL!
ONLY HE HAS EVER THWARTED ME.
BUT, AFTER I STEAL THE PRICELESS CLAY TABLET FROM ITS RESTING PLACE AT E.S.U...
THEN, HE AND I WILL HAVE... OUR FINAL RECKONING!
AND, SPEAKING OF OUR WOEBEGONE WEB-SPINNER WHO, ONLY LAST ISSUE, DEFEATED THE MANIACAL MYSTERIO...
I OUGHTTA HAVE MY HEAD EXAMINED!
I DIDN'T TAKE A SINGLE PICTURE OF MY LAST BATTLE!
WHICH MEANS I'VE NOTHING TO SELL TO JONAH'S RAG!
YEP, THAT'S ME! I RISKED MY FOOL NECK LIKE A GRINNING IDIOT...
AND ENDED UP WITH A BIG, FAT ZERO!
SO HERE I AM... BROKE, AS USUAL!
WELL, AT LEAST I'LL GET SOME SHUT-EYE AND ...OH NO!
HARRY MUST HAVE LOCKED THE WINDOW!

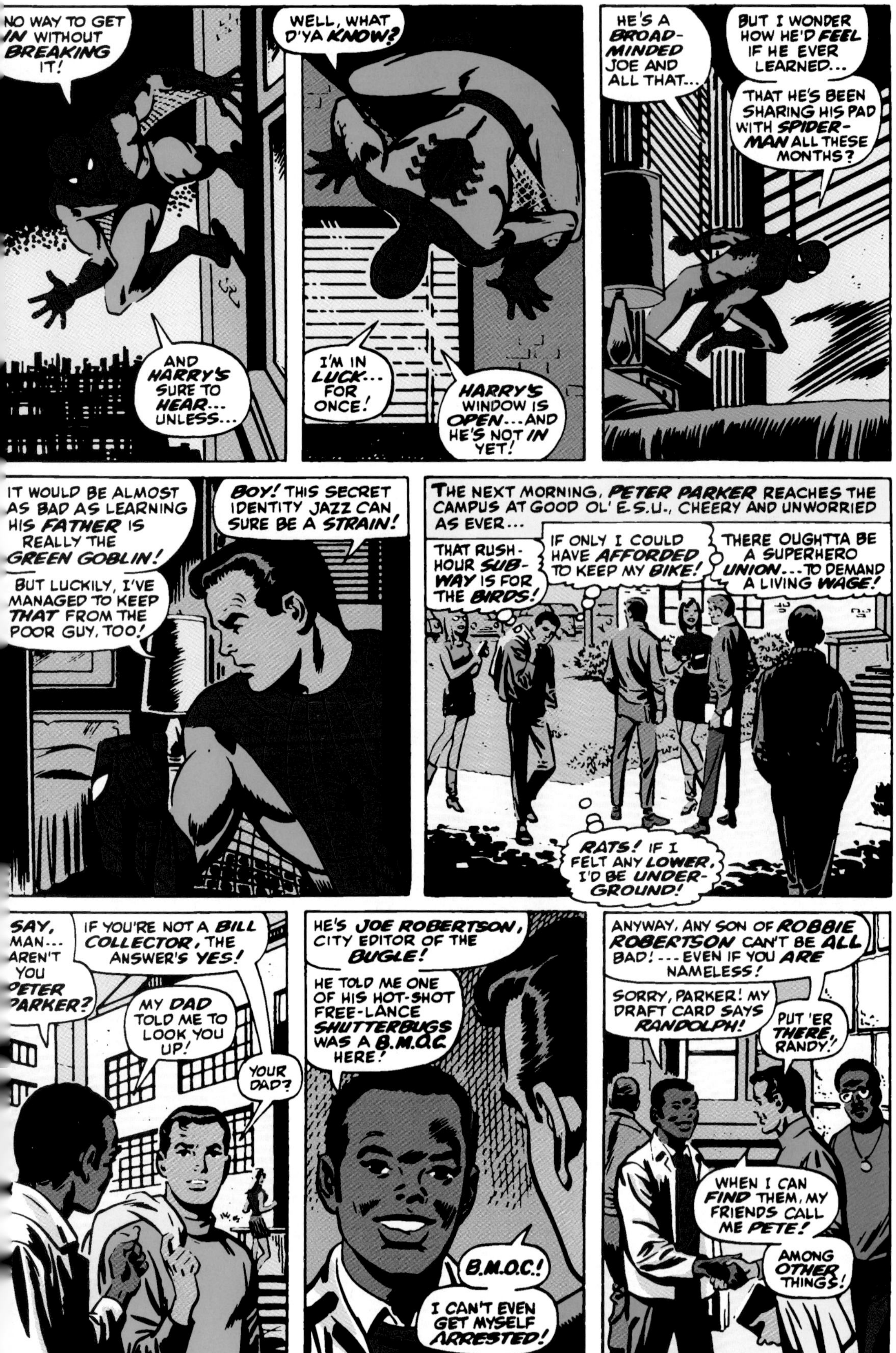
NO WAY TO GET IN WITHOUT BREAKING IT!
AND HARRY'S SURE TO HEAR... UNLESS...
WELL, WHAT D'YA KNOW?
I'M IN LUCK... FOR ONCE!
HARRY'S WINDOW IS OPEN... AND HE'S NOT IN YET!
HE'S A BROAD-MINDED JOE AND ALL THAT...
BUT I WONDER HOW HE'D FEEL IF HE EVER LEARNED...
THAT HE'S BEEN SHARING HIS PAD WITH SPIDER-MAN ALL THESE MONTHS?
IT WOULD BE ALMOST AS BAD AS LEARNING HIS FATHER IS REALLY THE GREEN GOBLIN!
BUT LUCKILY, I'VE MANAGED TO KEEP THAT FROM THE POOR GUY, TOO!
BOY! THIS SECRET IDENTITY JAZZ CAN SURE BE A STRAIN!
THE NEXT MORNING, PETER PARKER REACHES THE CAMPUS AT GOOD OL' E.S.U., CHEERY AND UNWORRIED AS EVER...
THAT RUSH-HOUR SUBWAY IS FOR THE BIRDS!
IF ONLY I COULD HAVE AFFORDED TO KEEP MY BIKE!
THERE OUGHTTA BE A SUPERHERO UNION... TO DEMAND A LIVING WAGE!
RATS! IF I FELT ANY LOWER, I'D BE UNDER-GROUND!
SAY, MAN... AREN'T YOU PETER PARKER?
IF YOU'RE NOT A BILL COLLECTOR, THE ANSWER'S YES!
MY DAD TOLD ME TO LOOK YOU UP!
YOUR DAD?
HE'S JOE ROBERTSON, CITY EDITOR OF THE BUGLE!
HE TOLD ME ONE OF HIS HOT-SHOT FREE-LANCE SHUTTERBUGS WAS A B.M.O.C. HERE!
B.M.O.C.!
I CAN'T EVEN GET MYSELF ARRESTED!
ANYWAY, ANY SON OF ROBBIE ROBERTSON CAN'T BE ALL BAD! --- EVEN IF YOU ARE NAMELESS!
SORRY, PARKER! MY DRAFT CARD SAYS RANDOLPH!
PUT 'ER THERE, RANDY!
WHEN I CAN FIND THEM, MY FRIENDS CALL ME PETE!
AMONG OTHER THINGS!

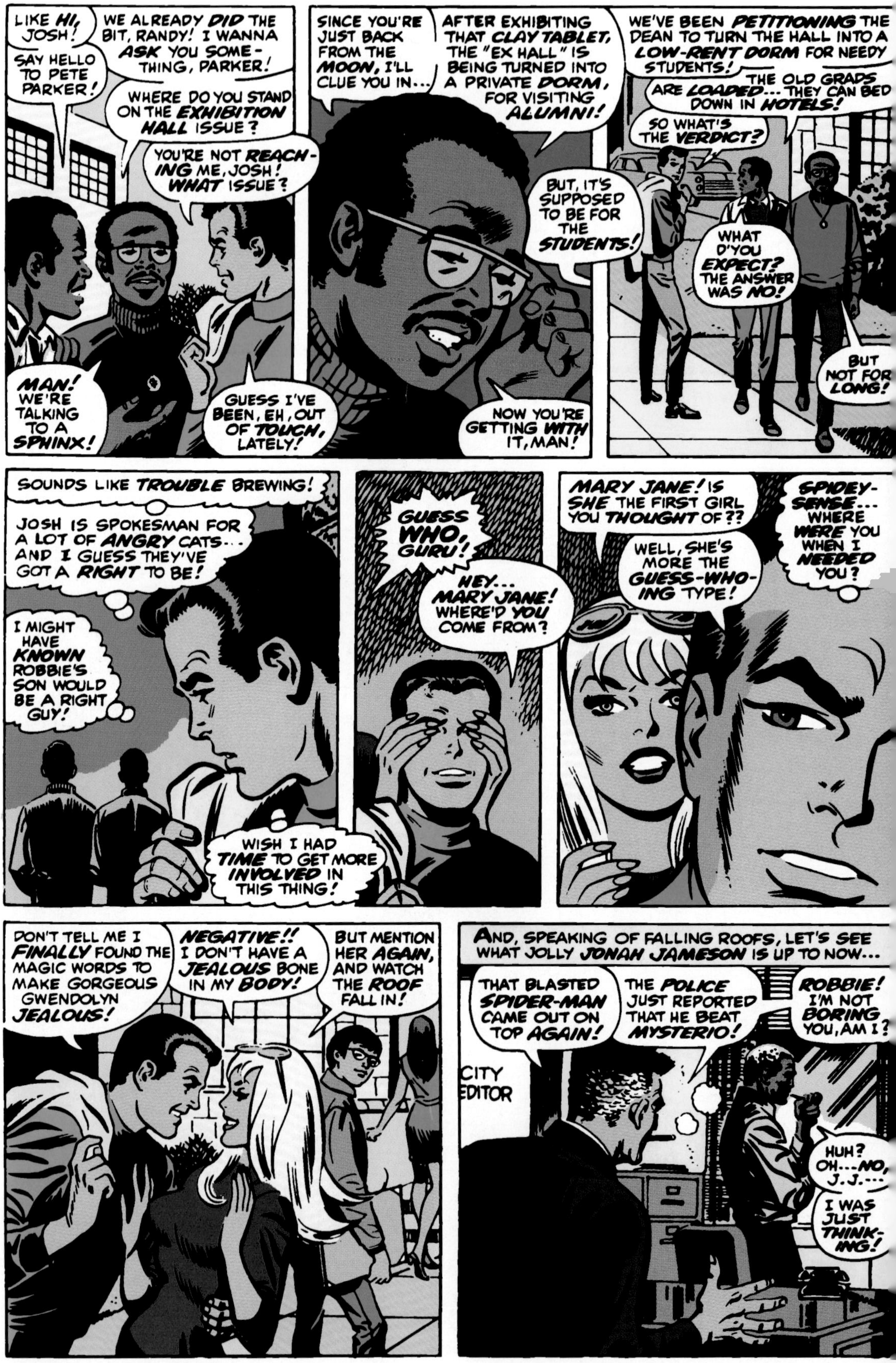
LIKE HI, JOSH!
SAY HELLO TO PETE PARKER!
WE ALREADY DID THE BIT, RANDY! I WANNA ASK YOU SOME-THING, PARKER!
WHERE DO YOU STAND ON THE EXHIBITION HALL ISSUE?
YOU'RE NOT REACH-ING ME, JOSH! WHAT ISSUE?
MAN! WE'RE TALKING TO A SPHINX!
GUESS I'VE BEEN, EH, OUT OF TOUCH, LATELY!
SINCE YOU'RE JUST BACK FROM THE MOON, I'LL CLUE YOU IN...
AFTER EXHIBITING THAT CLAY TABLET, THE "EX HALL" IS BEING TURNED INTO A PRIVATE DORM, FOR VISITING ALUMNI!
BUT, IT'S SUPPOSED TO BE FOR THE STUDENTS!
NOW YOU'RE GETTING WITH IT, MAN!
WE'VE BEEN PETITIONING THE DEAN TO TURN THE HALL INTO A LOW-RENT DORM FOR NEEDY STUDENTS!
THE OLD GRADS ARE LOADED... THEY CAN BED DOWN IN HOTELS!
SO WHAT'S THE VERDICT?
WHAT D'YOU EXPECT? THE ANSWER WAS NO!
BUT NOT FOR LONG!
SOUNDS LIKE TROUBLE BREWING!
JOSH IS SPOKESMAN FOR A LOT OF ANGRY CATS... AND I GUESS THEY'VE GOT A RIGHT TO BE!
I MIGHT HAVE KNOWN ROBBIE'S SON WOULD BE A RIGHT GUY!
WISH I HAD TIME TO GET MORE INVOLVED IN THIS THING!
GUESS WHO, GURU!
HEY... MARY JANE! WHERE'D YOU COME FROM?
MARY JANE! IS SHE THE FIRST GIRL YOU THOUGHT OF??
WELL, SHE'S MORE THE GUESS-WHO-ING TYPE!
SPIDEY-SENSE... WHERE WERE YOU WHEN I NEEDED YOU?
DON'T TELL ME I FINALLY FOUND THE MAGIC WORDS TO MAKE GORGEOUS GWENDOLYN JEALOUS!
NEGATIVE!! I DON'T HAVE A JEALOUS BONE IN MY BODY!
BUT MENTION HER AGAIN, AND WATCH THE ROOF FALL IN!
AND, SPEAKING OF FALLING ROOFS, LET'S SEE WHAT JOLLY JONAH JAMESON IS UP TO NOW...
THAT BLASTED SPIDER-MAN CAME OUT ON TOP AGAIN!
THE POLICE JUST REPORTED THAT HE BEAT MYSTERIO!
ROBBIE! I'M NOT BORING YOU, AM I?
CITY EDITOR
HUH? OH... NO, J.J....
I WAS JUST THINK-ING!

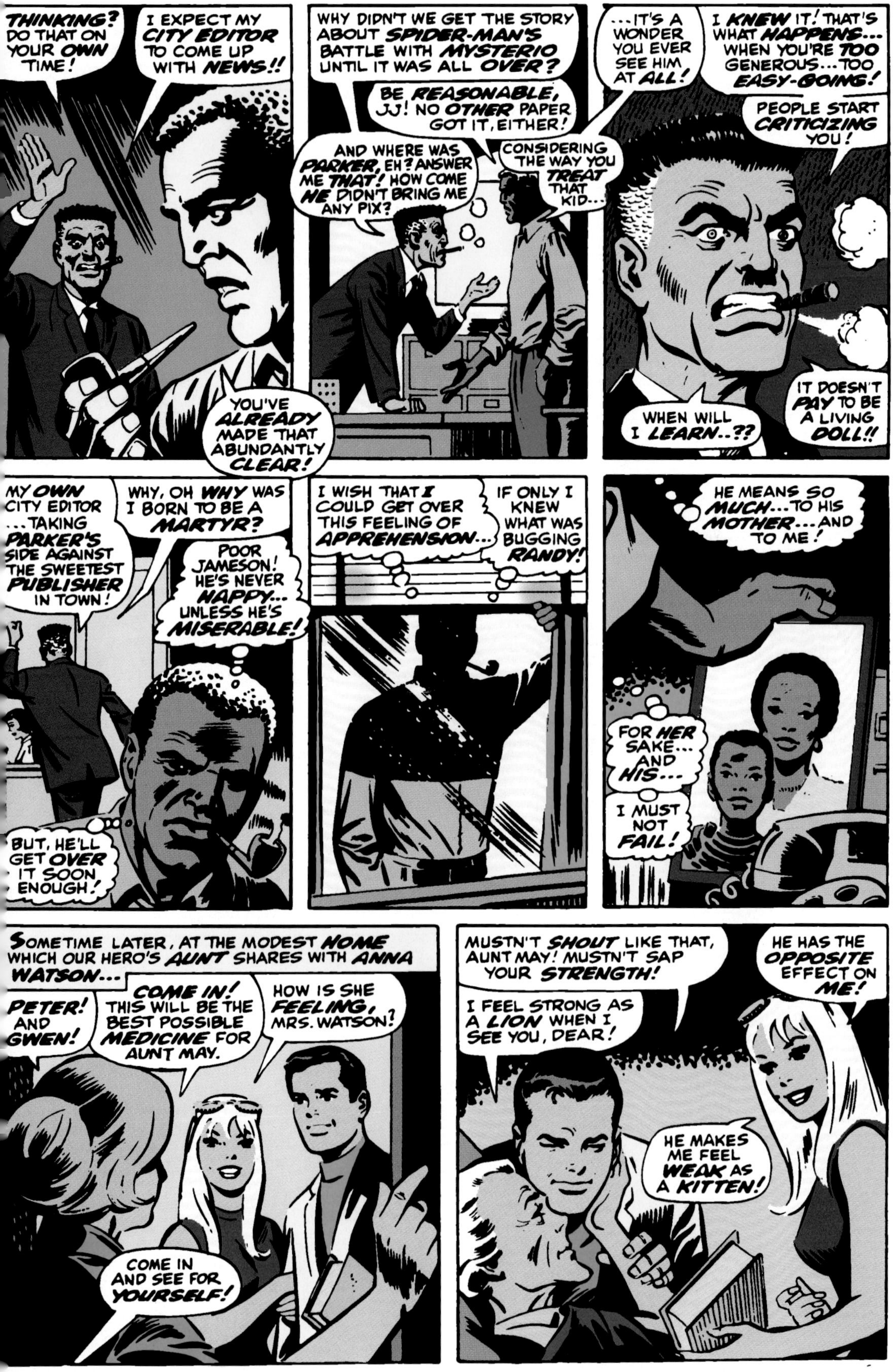
THINKING? DO THAT ON YOUR OWN TIME!
I EXPECT MY CITY EDITOR TO COME UP WITH NEWS!!
YOU'VE ALREADY MADE THAT ABUNDANTLY CLEAR!
WHY DIDN'T WE GET THE STORY ABOUT SPIDER-MAN'S BATTLE WITH MYSTERIO UNTIL IT WAS ALL OVER?
BE REASONABLE, JJ! NO OTHER PAPER GOT IT, EITHER!
AND WHERE WAS PARKER, EH? ANSWER ME THAT! HOW COME HE DIDN'T BRING ME ANY PIX?
CONSIDERING THE WAY YOU TREAT THAT KID...
...IT'S A WONDER YOU EVER SEE HIM AT ALL!
I KNEW IT! THAT'S WHAT HAPPENS... WHEN YOU'RE TOO GENEROUS... TOO EASY-GOING!
PEOPLE START CRITICIZING YOU!
WHEN WILL I LEARN..??
IT DOESN'T PAY TO BE A LIVING DOLL!!
MY OWN CITY EDITOR ...TAKING PARKER'S SIDE AGAINST THE SWEETEST PUBLISHER IN TOWN!
WHY, OH WHY WAS I BORN TO BE A MARTYR?
POOR JAMESON! HE'S NEVER HAPPY... UNLESS HE'S MISERABLE!
BUT, HE'LL GET OVER IT SOON ENOUGH!
I WISH THAT I COULD GET OVER THIS FEELING OF APPREHENSION...
IF ONLY I KNEW WHAT WAS BUGGING RANDY!
HE MEANS SO MUCH... TO HIS MOTHER... AND TO ME!
FOR HER SAKE... AND HIS...
I MUST NOT FAIL!
SOMETIME LATER, AT THE MODEST HOME WHICH OUR HERO'S AUNT SHARES WITH ANNA WATSON...
PETER! AND GWEN!
COME IN! THIS WILL BE THE BEST POSSIBLE MEDICINE FOR AUNT MAY.
HOW IS SHE FEELING, MRS. WATSON?
COME IN AND SEE FOR YOURSELF!
MUSTN'T SHOUT LIKE THAT, AUNT MAY! MUSTN'T SAP YOUR STRENGTH!
I FEEL STRONG AS A LION WHEN I SEE YOU, DEAR!
HE HAS THE OPPOSITE EFFECT ON ME!
HE MAKES ME FEEL WEAK AS A KITTEN!

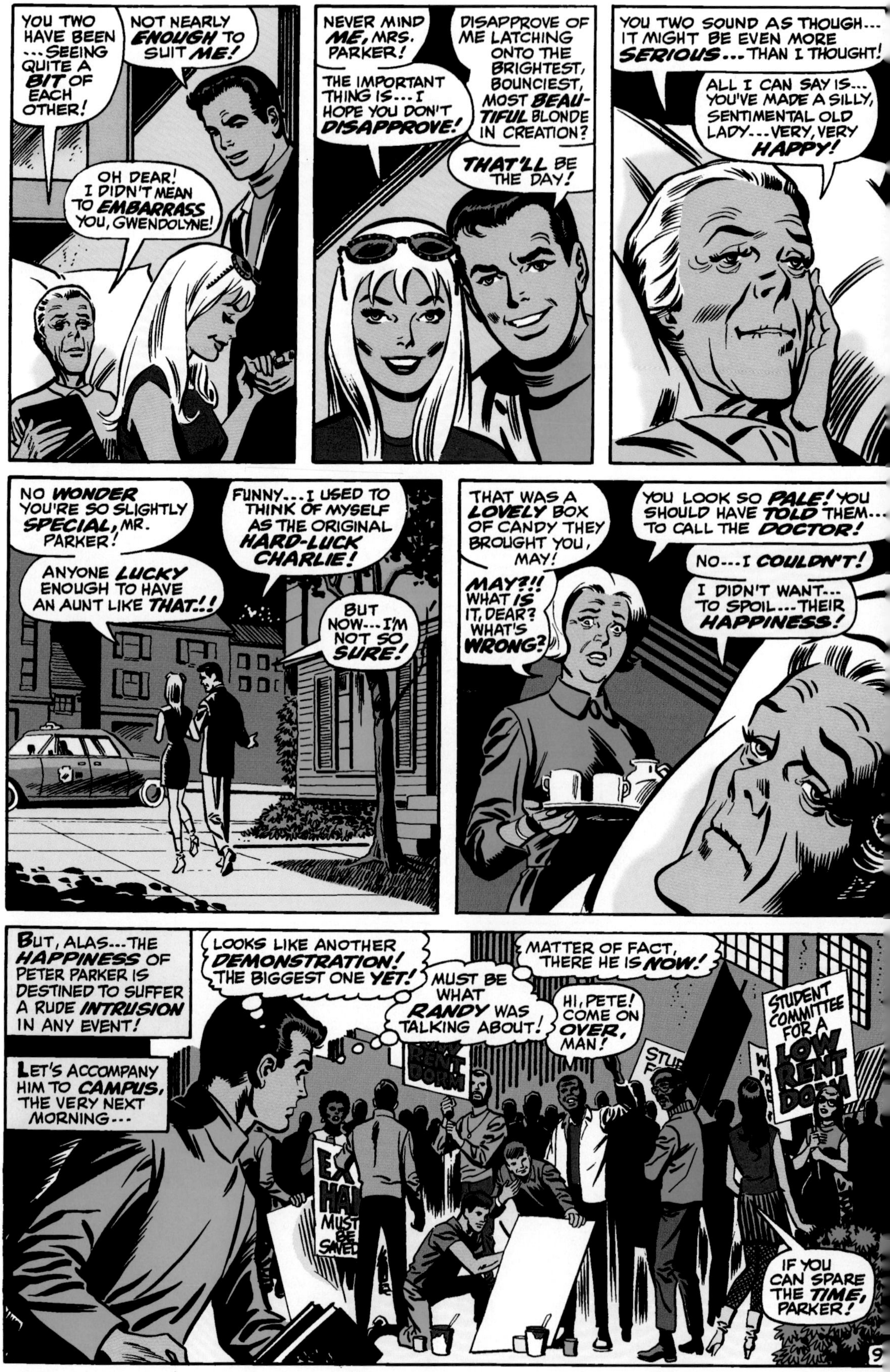

YOU TWO HAVE BEEN ...SEEING QUITE A BIT OF EACH OTHER!
NOT NEARLY ENOUGH TO SUIT ME!
OH DEAR! I DIDN'T MEAN TO EMBARRASS YOU, GWENDOLYNE!
NEVER MIND ME, MRS. PARKER!
THE IMPORTANT THING IS... I HOPE YOU DON'T DISAPPROVE!
DISAPPROVE OF ME LATCHING ONTO THE BRIGHTEST, BOUNCIEST, MOST BEAUTIFUL BLONDE IN CREATION?
THAT'LL BE THE DAY!
YOU TWO SOUND AS THOUGH... IT MIGHT BE EVEN MORE SERIOUS... THAN I THOUGHT!
ALL I CAN SAY IS... YOU'VE MADE A SILLY, SENTIMENTAL OLD LADY... VERY, VERY HAPPY!
NO WONDER YOU'RE SO SLIGHTLY SPECIAL, MR. PARKER!
ANYONE LUCKY ENOUGH TO HAVE AN AUNT LIKE THAT!!
FUNNY... I USED TO THINK OF MYSELF AS THE ORIGINAL HARD-LUCK CHARLIE!
BUT NOW... I'M NOT SO SURE!
THAT WAS A LOVELY BOX OF CANDY THEY BROUGHT YOU, MAY!
MAY?!! WHAT IS IT, DEAR? WHAT'S WRONG?
YOU LOOK SO PALE! YOU SHOULD HAVE TOLD THEM... TO CALL THE DOCTOR!
NO... I COULDN'T!
I DIDN'T WANT... TO SPOIL... THEIR HAPPINESS!
BUT, ALAS... THE HAPPINESS OF PETER PARKER IS DESTINED TO SUFFER A RUDE INTRUSION IN ANY EVENT!
LET'S ACCOMPANY HIM TO CAMPUS, THE VERY NEXT MORNING...
LOOKS LIKE ANOTHER DEMONSTRATION! THE BIGGEST ONE YET!
MUST BE WHAT RANDY WAS TALKING ABOUT!
MATTER OF FACT, THERE HE IS NOW!
HI, PETE! COME ON OVER, MAN!
STUDENT COMMITTEE FOR A LOW RENT DORM
RENT DORM
MUST BE SAVED
IF YOU CAN SPARE THE TIME, PARKER!

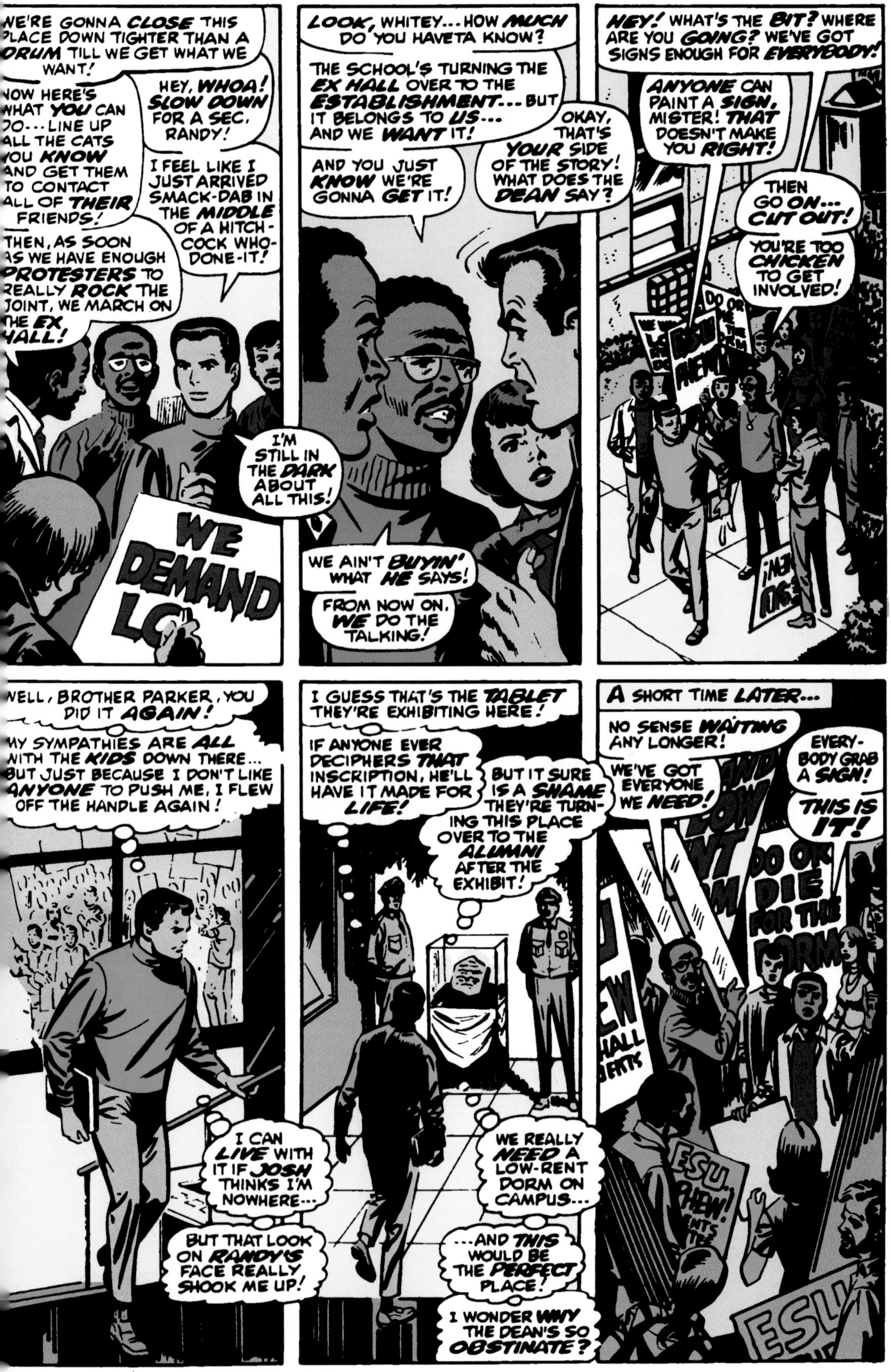

WE'RE GONNA CLOSE THIS PLACE DOWN TIGHTER THAN A DRUM TILL WE GET WHAT WE WANT!
NOW HERE'S WHAT YOU CAN DO--- LINE UP ALL THE CATS YOU KNOW AND GET THEM TO CONTACT ALL OF THEIR FRIENDS!
HEY, WHOA! SLOW DOWN FOR A SEC, RANDY!
I FEEL LIKE I JUST ARRIVED SMACK-DAB IN THE MIDDLE OF A HITCH-COCK WHO-DONE-IT!
THEN, AS SOON AS WE HAVE ENOUGH PROTESTERS TO REALLY ROCK THE JOINT, WE MARCH ON THE EX HALL!
I'M STILL IN THE DARK ABOUT ALL THIS!
WE DEMAND LO
LOOK, WHITEY... HOW MUCH DO YOU HAVETA KNOW?
THE SCHOOL'S TURNING THE EX HALL OVER TO THE ESTABLISHMENT... BUT IT BELONGS TO US... AND WE WANT IT!
AND YOU JUST KNOW WE'RE GONNA GET IT!
OKAY, THAT'S YOUR SIDE OF THE STORY! WHAT DOES THE DEAN SAY?
WE AIN'T BUYIN' WHAT HE SAYS!
FROM NOW ON, WE DO THE TALKING!
HEY! WHAT'S THE BIT? WHERE ARE YOU GOING? WE'VE GOT SIGNS ENOUGH FOR EVERYBODY!
ANYONE CAN PAINT A SIGN, MISTER! THAT DOESN'T MAKE YOU RIGHT!
THEN GO ON... CUT OUT!
YOU'RE TOO CHICKEN TO GET INVOLVED!
WELL, BROTHER PARKER, YOU DID IT AGAIN!
MY SYMPATHIES ARE ALL WITH THE KIDS DOWN THERE... BUT JUST BECAUSE I DON'T LIKE ANYONE TO PUSH ME, I FLEW OFF THE HANDLE AGAIN!
I CAN LIVE WITH IT IF JOSH THINKS I'M NOWHERE...
BUT THAT LOOK ON RANDY'S FACE REALLY SHOOK ME UP!
I GUESS THAT'S THE TABLET THEY'RE EXHIBITING HERE!
IF ANYONE EVER DECIPHERS THAT INSCRIPTION, HE'LL HAVE IT MADE FOR LIFE!
BUT IT SURE IS A SHAME THEY'RE TURNING THIS PLACE OVER TO THE ALUMNI AFTER THE EXHIBIT!
WE REALLY NEED A LOW-RENT DORM ON CAMPUS...
...AND THIS WOULD BE THE PERFECT PLACE!
I WONDER WHY THE DEAN'S SO OBSTINATE?
A SHORT TIME LATER...
NO SENSE WAITING ANY LONGER!
WE'VE GOT EVERYONE WE NEED!
EVERY-BODY GRAB A SIGN!
THIS IS IT!
DO OR DIE FOR THE DORM

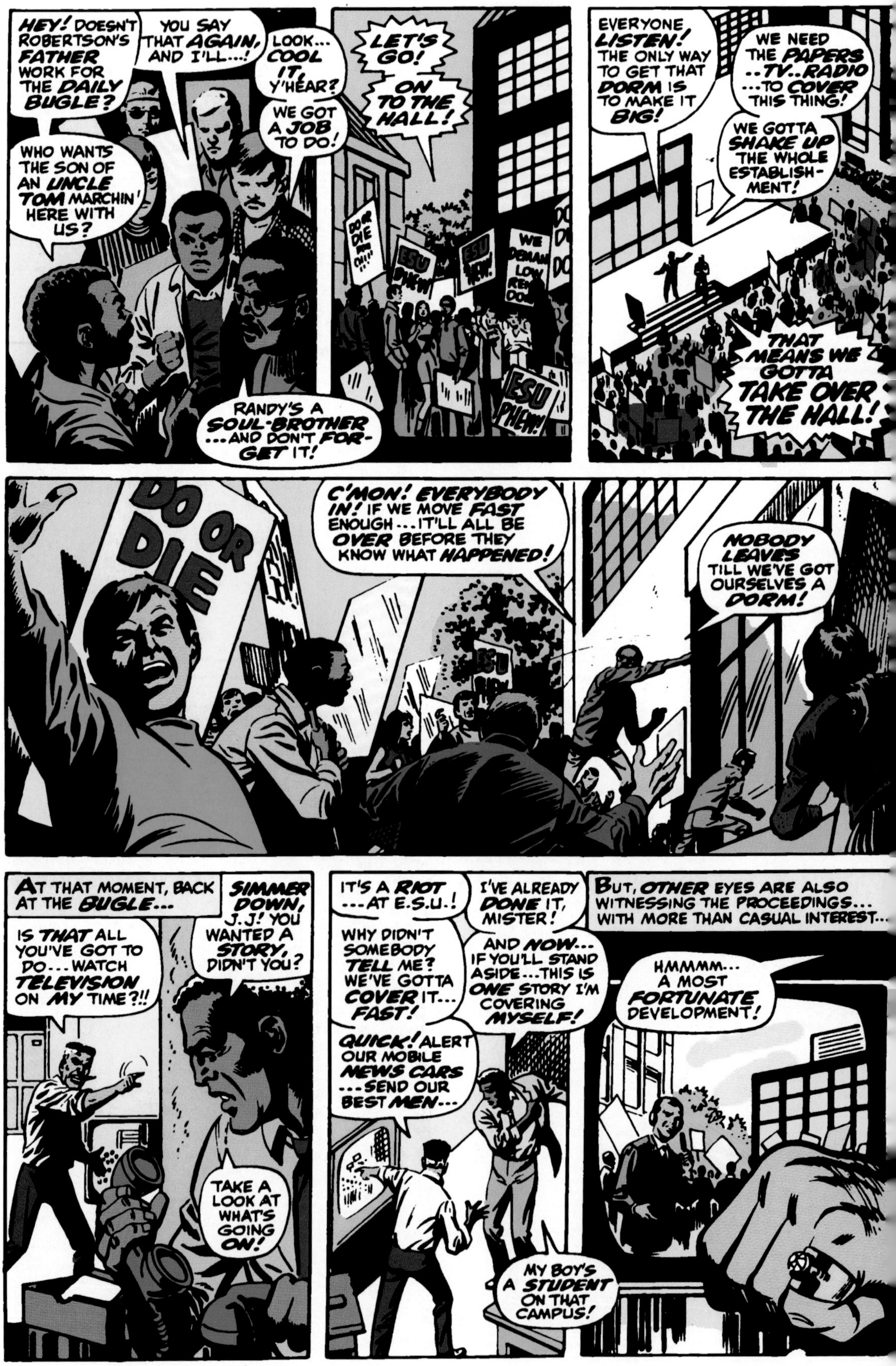
HEY! DOESN'T ROBERTSON'S FATHER WORK FOR THE DAILY BUGLE?
YOU SAY THAT AGAIN, AND I'LL...!
LOOK... COOL IT, Y'HEAR?
WE GOT A JOB TO DO!
WHO WANTS THE SON OF AN UNCLE TOM MARCHIN' HERE WITH US?
RANDY'S A SOUL-BROTHER ...AND DON'T FOR-GET IT!
LET'S GO!
ON TO THE HALL!
DO OR DIE
ESU PHEW!
WE DEMAND LOW RENT DORMS
EVERYONE LISTEN! THE ONLY WAY TO GET THAT DORM IS TO MAKE IT BIG!
WE NEED THE PAPERS --TV..RADIO ...TO COVER THIS THING!
WE GOTTA SHAKE UP THE WHOLE ESTABLISH-MENT!
THAT MEANS WE GOTTA TAKE OVER THE HALL!
DO OR DIE
C'MON! EVERYBODY IN! IF WE MOVE FAST ENOUGH...IT'LL ALL BE OVER BEFORE THEY KNOW WHAT HAPPENED!
NOBODY LEAVES TILL WE'VE GOT OURSELVES A DORM!
AT THAT MOMENT, BACK AT THE BUGLE...
IS THAT ALL YOU'VE GOT TO DO...WATCH TELEVISION ON MY TIME?!!
SIMMER DOWN, J.J! YOU WANTED A STORY, DIDN'T YOU?
TAKE A LOOK AT WHAT'S GOING ON!
IT'S A RIOT ...AT E.S.U.!
WHY DIDN'T SOMEBODY TELL ME? WE'VE GOTTA COVER IT... FAST!
QUICK! ALERT OUR MOBILE NEWS CARS ...SEND OUR BEST MEN...
I'VE ALREADY DONE IT, MISTER!
AND NOW... IF YOU'LL STAND ASIDE...THIS IS ONE STORY I'M COVERING MYSELF!
MY BOY'S A STUDENT ON THAT CAMPUS!
BUT, OTHER EYES ARE ALSO WITNESSING THE PROCEEDINGS... WITH MORE THAN CASUAL INTEREST...
HMMMM... A MOST FORTUNATE DEVELOPMENT!

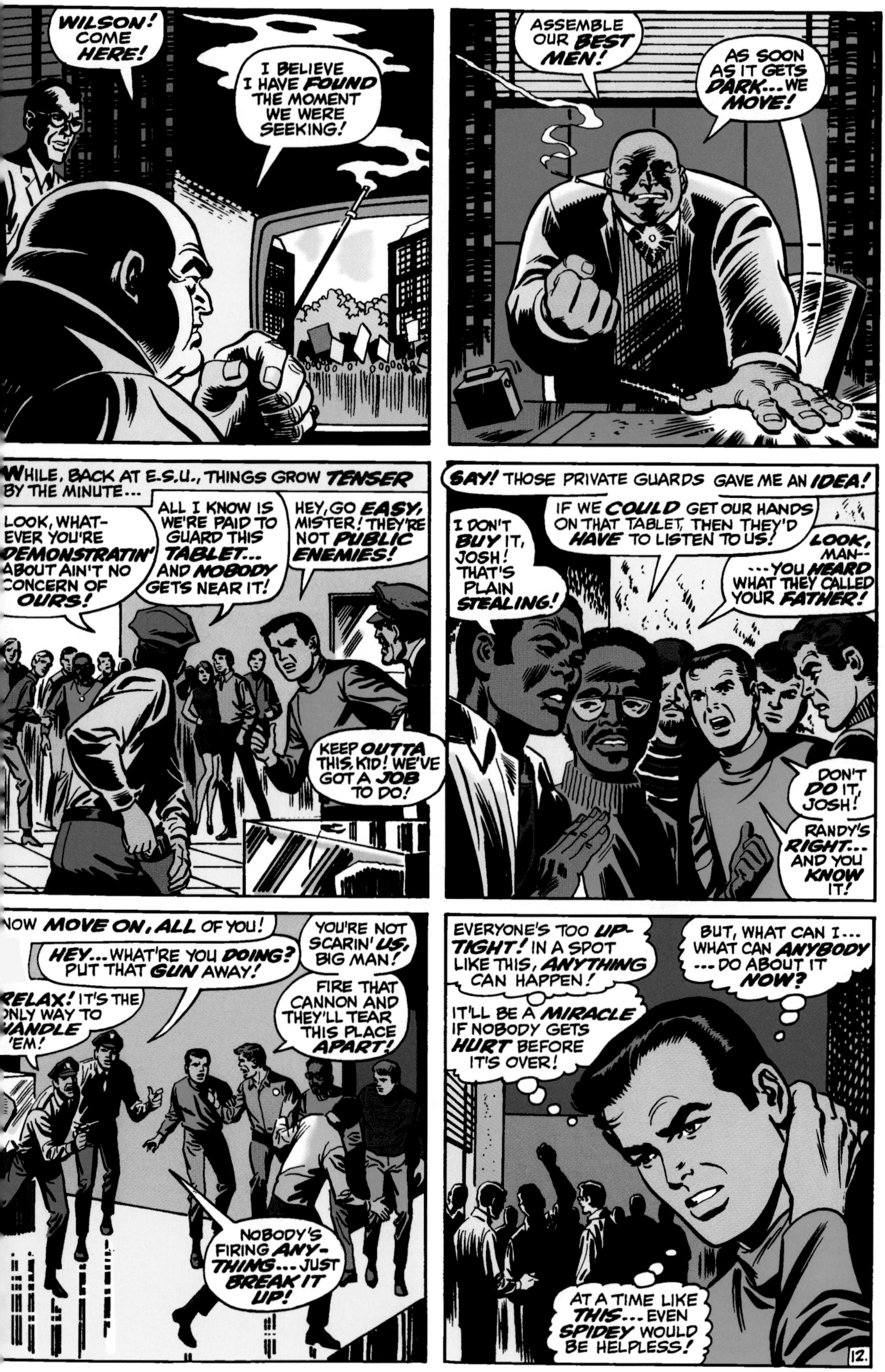
WILSON! COME HERE!
I BELIEVE I HAVE FOUND THE MOMENT WE WERE SEEKING!
ASSEMBLE OUR BEST MEN!
AS SOON AS IT GETS DARK... WE MOVE!
WHILE, BACK AT E.S.U., THINGS GROW TENSER BY THE MINUTE...
LOOK, WHAT-EVER YOU'RE DEMONSTRATIN' ABOUT AIN'T NO CONCERN OF OURS!
ALL I KNOW IS WE'RE PAID TO GUARD THIS TABLET... AND NOBODY GETS NEAR IT!
HEY, GO EASY, MISTER! THEY'RE NOT PUBLIC ENEMIES!
KEEP OUTTA THIS, KID! WE'VE GOT A JOB TO DO!
SAY! THOSE PRIVATE GUARDS GAVE ME AN IDEA!
IF WE COULD GET OUR HANDS ON THAT TABLET, THEN THEY'D HAVE TO LISTEN TO US!
I DON'T BUY IT, JOSH! THAT'S PLAIN STEALING!
LOOK, MAN-- ...YOU HEARD WHAT THEY CALLED YOUR FATHER!
DON'T DO IT, JOSH!
RANDY'S RIGHT... AND YOU KNOW IT!
NOW MOVE ON, ALL OF YOU!
HEY... WHAT'RE YOU DOING? PUT THAT GUN AWAY!
YOU'RE NOT SCARIN' US, BIG MAN!
RELAX! IT'S THE ONLY WAY TO HANDLE 'EM!
FIRE THAT CANNON AND THEY'LL TEAR THIS PLACE APART!
NOBODY'S FIRING ANY-THING... JUST BREAK IT UP!
EVERYONE'S TOO UP-TIGHT! IN A SPOT LIKE THIS, ANYTHING CAN HAPPEN!
IT'LL BE A MIRACLE IF NOBODY GETS HURT BEFORE IT'S OVER!
BUT, WHAT CAN I... WHAT CAN ANYBODY ...DO ABOUT IT NOW?
AT A TIME LIKE THIS... EVEN SPIDEY WOULD BE HELPLESS!
12.

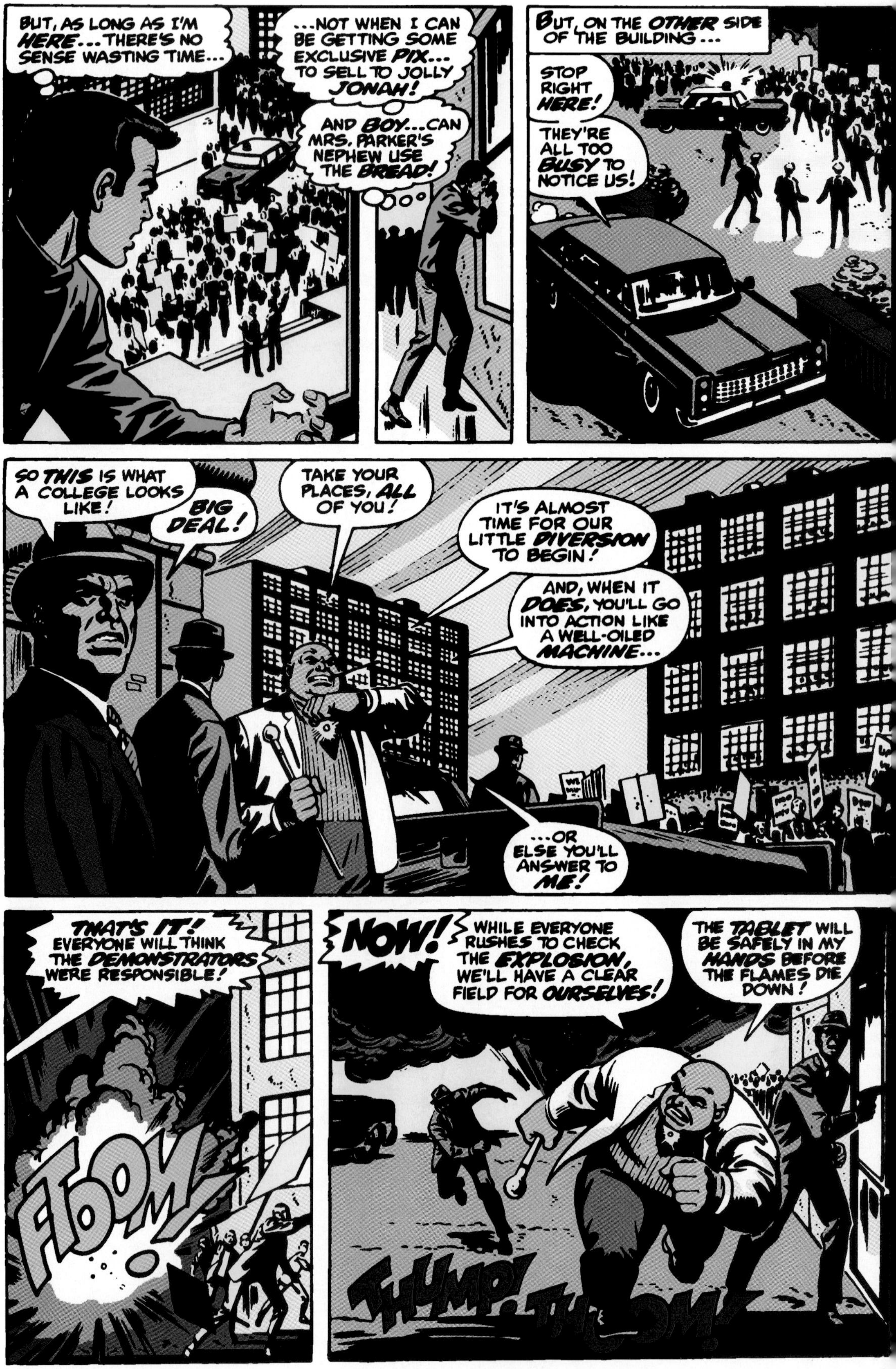

BUT, AS LONG AS I'M HERE... THERE'S NO SENSE WASTING TIME...
...NOT WHEN I CAN BE GETTING SOME EXCLUSIVE PIX... TO SELL TO JOLLY JONAH!
AND BOY...CAN MRS. PARKER'S NEPHEW USE THE BREAD!
BUT, ON THE OTHER SIDE OF THE BUILDING...
STOP RIGHT HERE!
THEY'RE ALL TOO BUSY TO NOTICE US!
SO THIS IS WHAT A COLLEGE LOOKS LIKE!
BIG DEAL!
TAKE YOUR PLACES, ALL OF YOU!
IT'S ALMOST TIME FOR OUR LITTLE DIVERSION TO BEGIN!
AND, WHEN IT DOES, YOU'LL GO INTO ACTION LIKE A WELL-OILED MACHINE...
...OR ELSE YOU'LL ANSWER TO ME!
THAT'S IT! EVERYONE WILL THINK THE DEMONSTRATORS WERE RESPONSIBLE!
FTOOM
NOW!
WHILE EVERYONE RUSHES TO CHECK THE EXPLOSION, WE'LL HAVE A CLEAR FIELD FOR OURSELVES!
THE TABLET WILL BE SAFELY IN MY HANDS BEFORE THE FLAMES DIE DOWN!
THUMP! THOOM!

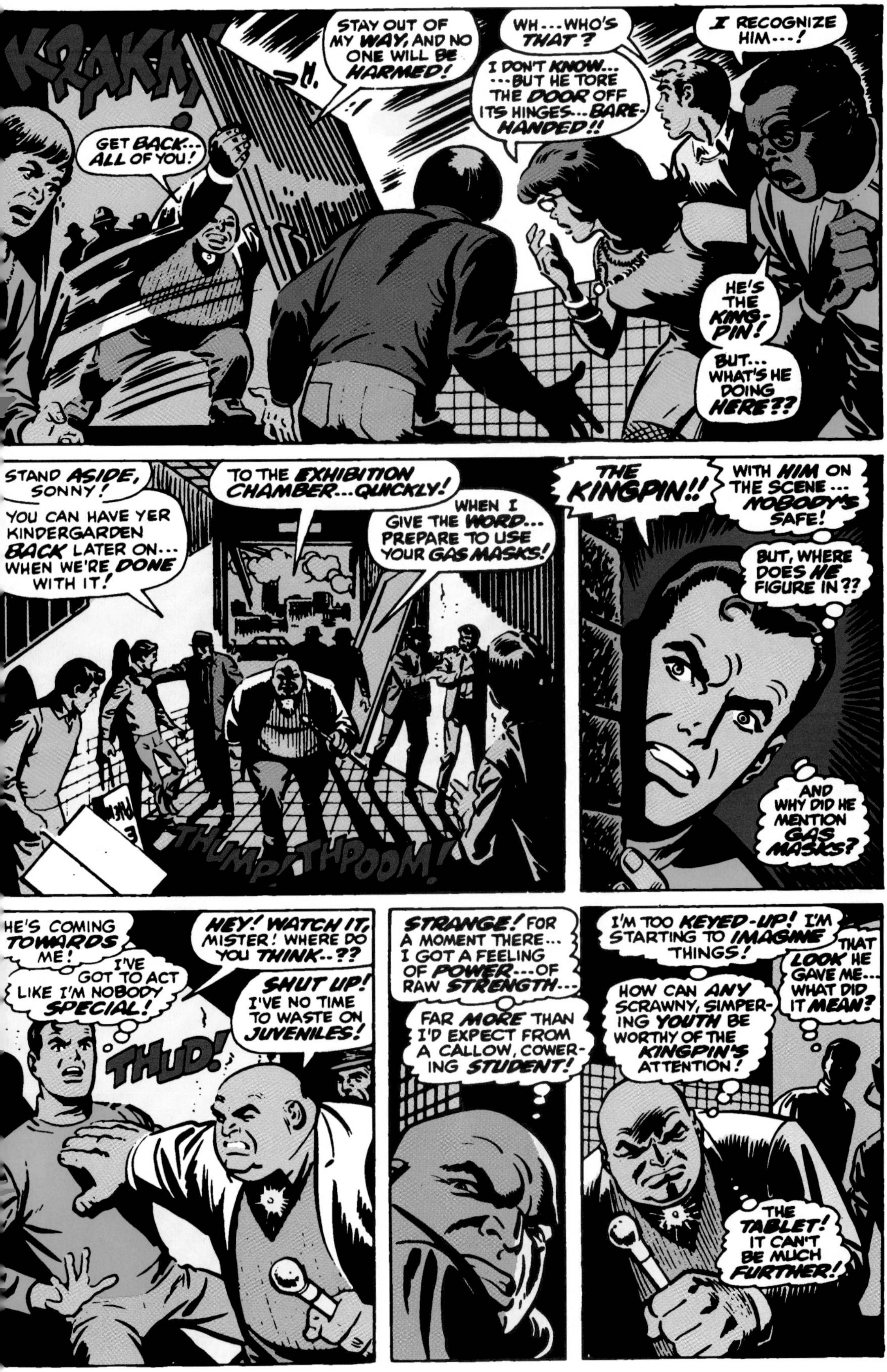
KRAKK!
STAY OUT OF MY WAY, AND NO ONE WILL BE HARMED!
GET BACK... ALL OF YOU!
WH...WHO'S THAT?
I DON'T KNOW... ...BUT HE TORE THE DOOR OFF ITS HINGES... BARE-HANDED!!
I RECOGNIZE HIM...!
HE'S THE KING-PIN!
BUT... WHAT'S HE DOING HERE??
STAND ASIDE, SONNY!
YOU CAN HAVE YER KINDERGARDEN BACK LATER ON... WHEN WE'RE DONE WITH IT!
TO THE EXHIBITION CHAMBER...QUICKLY!
WHEN I GIVE THE WORD... PREPARE TO USE YOUR GAS MASKS!
THUMP! THPOOM!
THE KINGPIN!!
WITH HIM ON THE SCENE... NOBODY'S SAFE!
BUT, WHERE DOES HE FIGURE IN??
AND WHY DID HE MENTION GAS MASKS?
HE'S COMING TOWARDS ME!
I'VE GOT TO ACT LIKE I'M NOBODY SPECIAL!
HEY! WATCH IT, MISTER! WHERE DO YOU THINK--??
SHUT UP! I'VE NO TIME TO WASTE ON JUVENILES!
THUD!
STRANGE! FOR A MOMENT THERE... I GOT A FEELING OF POWER...OF RAW STRENGTH...
FAR MORE THAN I'D EXPECT FROM A CALLOW, COWER-ING STUDENT!
I'M TOO KEYED-UP! I'M STARTING TO IMAGINE THINGS!
THAT LOOK HE GAVE ME... WHAT DID IT MEAN?
HOW CAN ANY SCRAWNY, SIMPER-ING YOUTH BE WORTHY OF THE KINGPIN'S ATTENTION!
THE TABLET! IT CAN'T BE MUCH FURTHER!

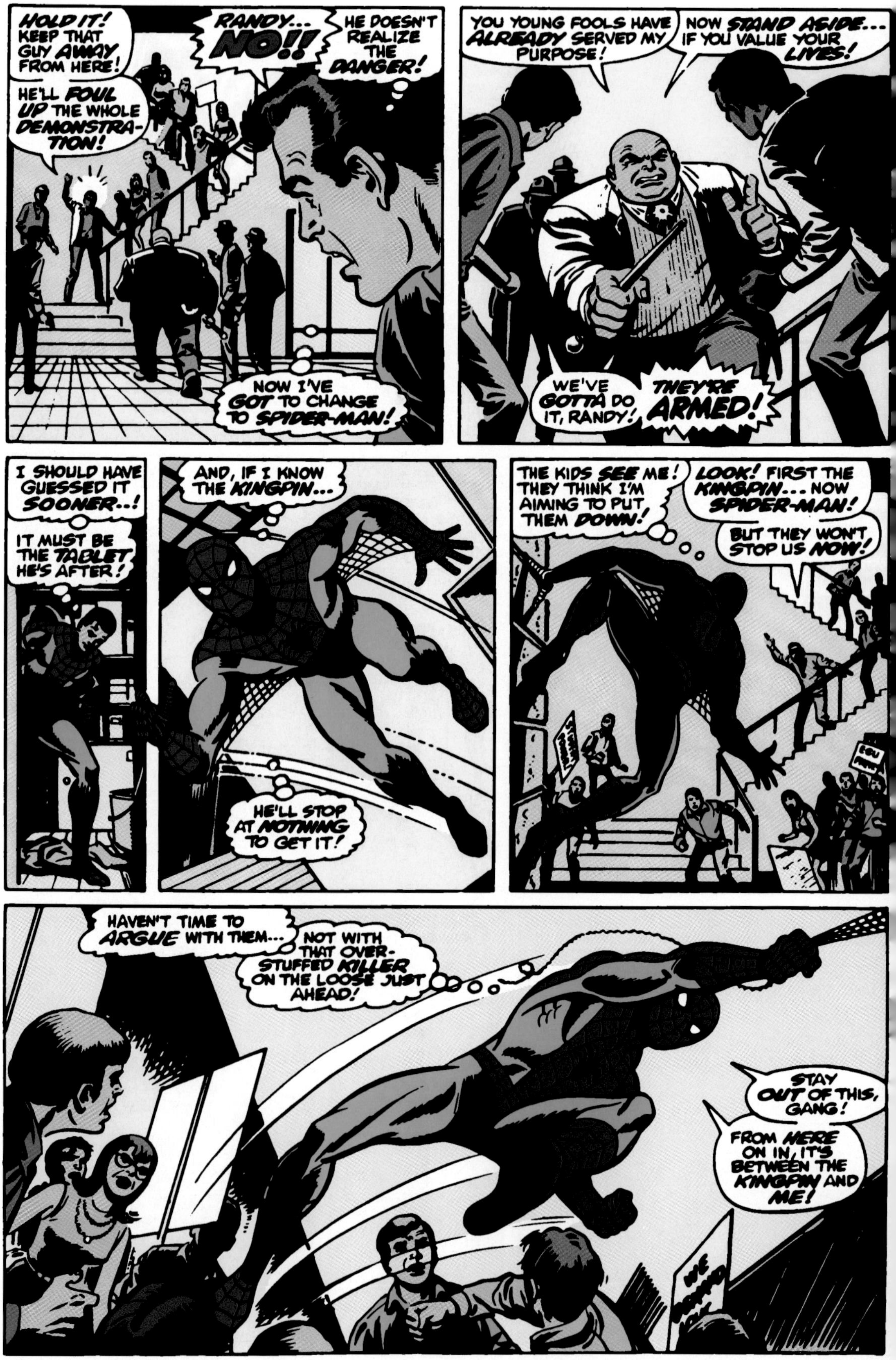
HOLD IT! KEEP THAT GUY AWAY FROM HERE!
HE'LL FOUL UP THE WHOLE DEMONSTRATION!
RANDY... NO!!
HE DOESN'T REALIZE THE DANGER!
NOW I'VE GOT TO CHANGE TO SPIDER-MAN!
YOU YOUNG FOOLS HAVE ALREADY SERVED MY PURPOSE!
NOW STAND ASIDE... IF YOU VALUE YOUR LIVES!
WE'VE GOTTA DO IT, RANDY!
THEY'RE ARMED!
I SHOULD HAVE GUESSED IT SOONER..!
IT MUST BE THE TABLET HE'S AFTER!
AND, IF I KNOW THE KINGPIN...
HE'LL STOP AT NOTHING TO GET IT!
THE KIDS SEE ME! THEY THINK I'M AIMING TO PUT THEM DOWN!
LOOK! FIRST THE KINGPIN... NOW SPIDER-MAN!
BUT THEY WON'T STOP US NOW!
HAVEN'T TIME TO ARGUE WITH THEM...
NOT WITH THAT OVER-STUFFED KILLER ON THE LOOSE JUST AHEAD!
STAY OUT OF THIS, GANG!
FROM HERE ON IN, IT'S BETWEEN THE KINGPIN AND ME!

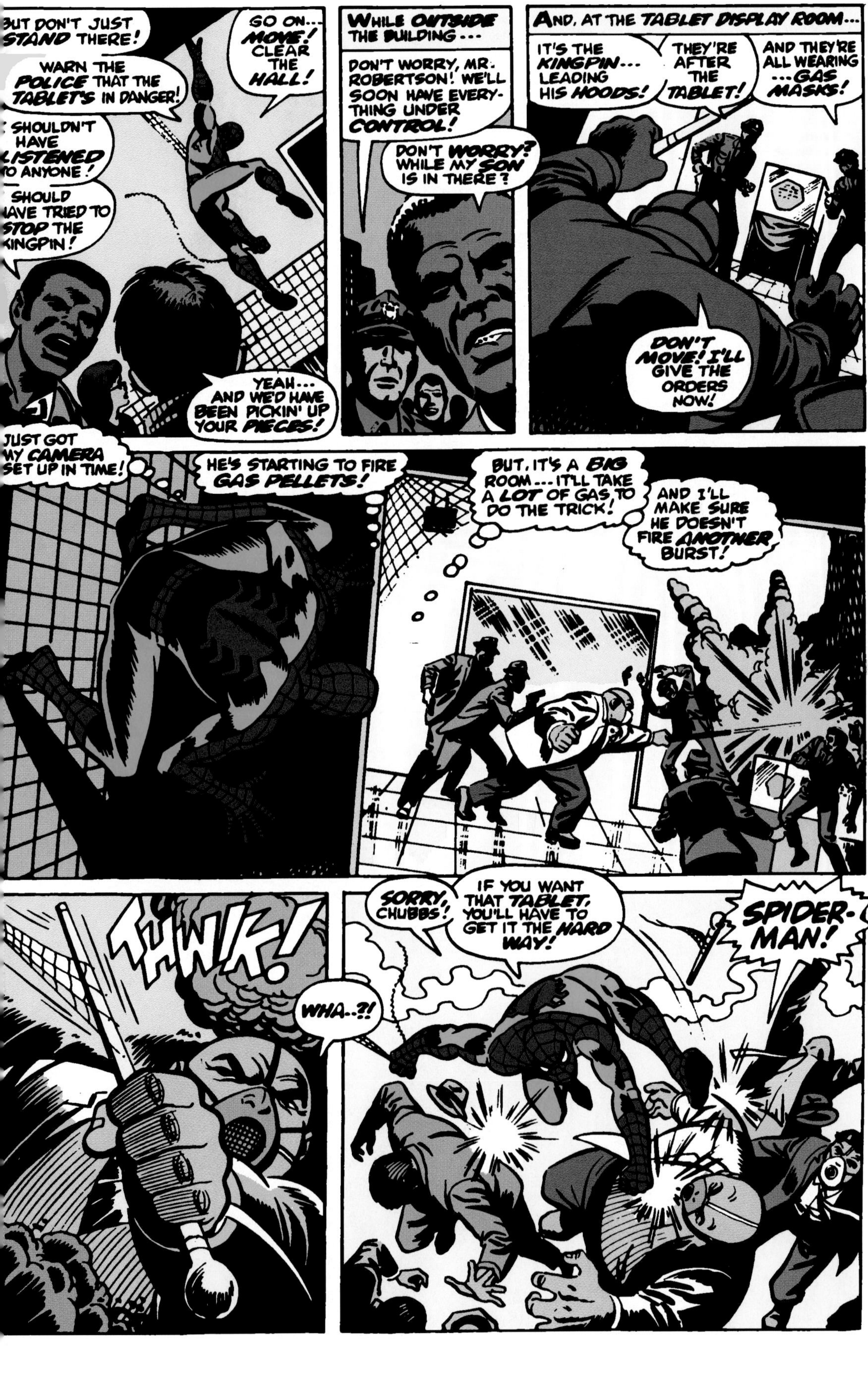

BUT DON'T JUST STAND THERE!
WARN THE POLICE THAT THE TABLET'S IN DANGER!
GO ON... MOVE! CLEAR THE HALL!
I SHOULDN'T HAVE LISTENED TO ANYONE!
I SHOULD HAVE TRIED TO STOP THE KINGPIN!
YEAH... AND WE'D HAVE BEEN PICKIN' UP YOUR PIECES!
WHILE OUTSIDE THE BUILDING...
DON'T WORRY, MR. ROBERTSON! WE'LL SOON HAVE EVERYTHING UNDER CONTROL!
DON'T WORRY? WHILE MY SON IS IN THERE?
AND, AT THE TABLET DISPLAY ROOM...
IT'S THE KINGPIN... LEADING HIS HOODS!
THEY'RE AFTER THE TABLET!
AND THEY'RE ALL WEARING ...GAS MASKS!
DON'T MOVE! I'LL GIVE THE ORDERS NOW!
JUST GOT MY CAMERA SET UP IN TIME!
HE'S STARTING TO FIRE GAS PELLETS!
BUT, IT'S A BIG ROOM... IT'LL TAKE A LOT OF GAS TO DO THE TRICK!
AND I'LL MAKE SURE HE DOESN'T FIRE ANOTHER BURST!
THWIK!
WHA..?!
SORRY, CHUBBS!
IF YOU WANT THAT TABLET, YOU'LL HAVE TO GET IT THE HARD WAY!
SPIDER-MAN!

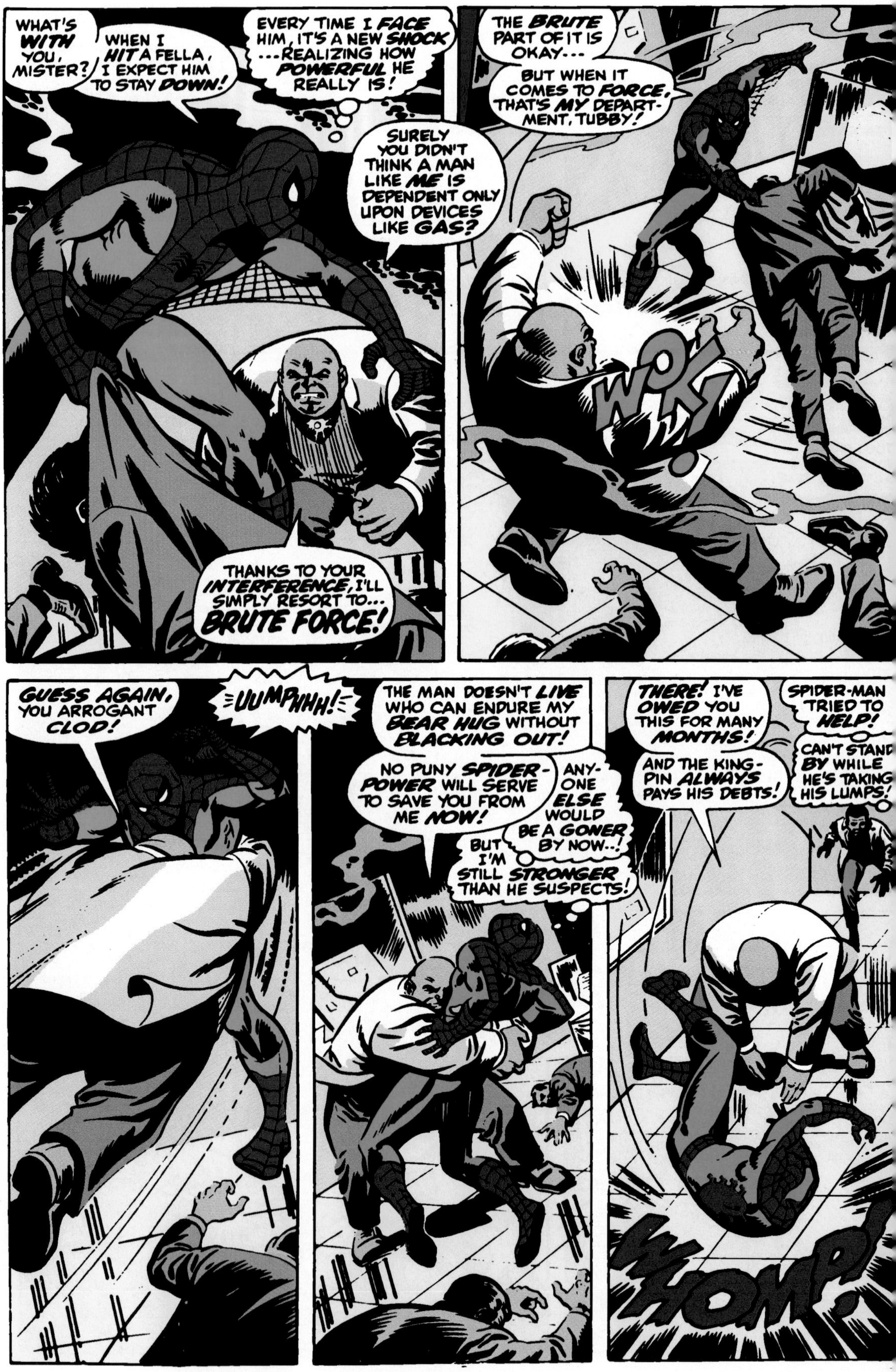

WHAT'S WITH YOU, MISTER?
WHEN I HIT A FELLA, I EXPECT HIM TO STAY DOWN!
EVERY TIME I FACE HIM, IT'S A NEW SHOCK ---REALIZING HOW POWERFUL HE REALLY IS!
SURELY YOU DIDN'T THINK A MAN LIKE ME IS DEPENDENT ONLY UPON DEVICES LIKE GAS?
THANKS TO YOUR INTERFERENCE, I'LL SIMPLY RESORT TO... BRUTE FORCE!
THE BRUTE PART OF IT IS OKAY---
BUT WHEN IT COMES TO FORCE, THAT'S MY DEPART-MENT, TUBBY!
WOK!
GUESS AGAIN, YOU ARROGANT CLOD!
UUMPHHH!
THE MAN DOESN'T LIVE WHO CAN ENDURE MY BEAR HUG WITHOUT BLACKING OUT!
NO PUNY SPIDER-POWER WILL SERVE TO SAVE YOU FROM ME NOW!
ANY-ONE ELSE WOULD BE A GONER BY NOW..!
BUT I'M STILL STRONGER THAN HE SUSPECTS!
THERE! I'VE OWED YOU THIS FOR MANY MONTHS!
AND THE KING-PIN ALWAYS PAYS HIS DEBTS!
SPIDER-MAN TRIED TO HELP!
CAN'T STAND BY WHILE HE'S TAKING HIS LUMPS!
WHOMP!

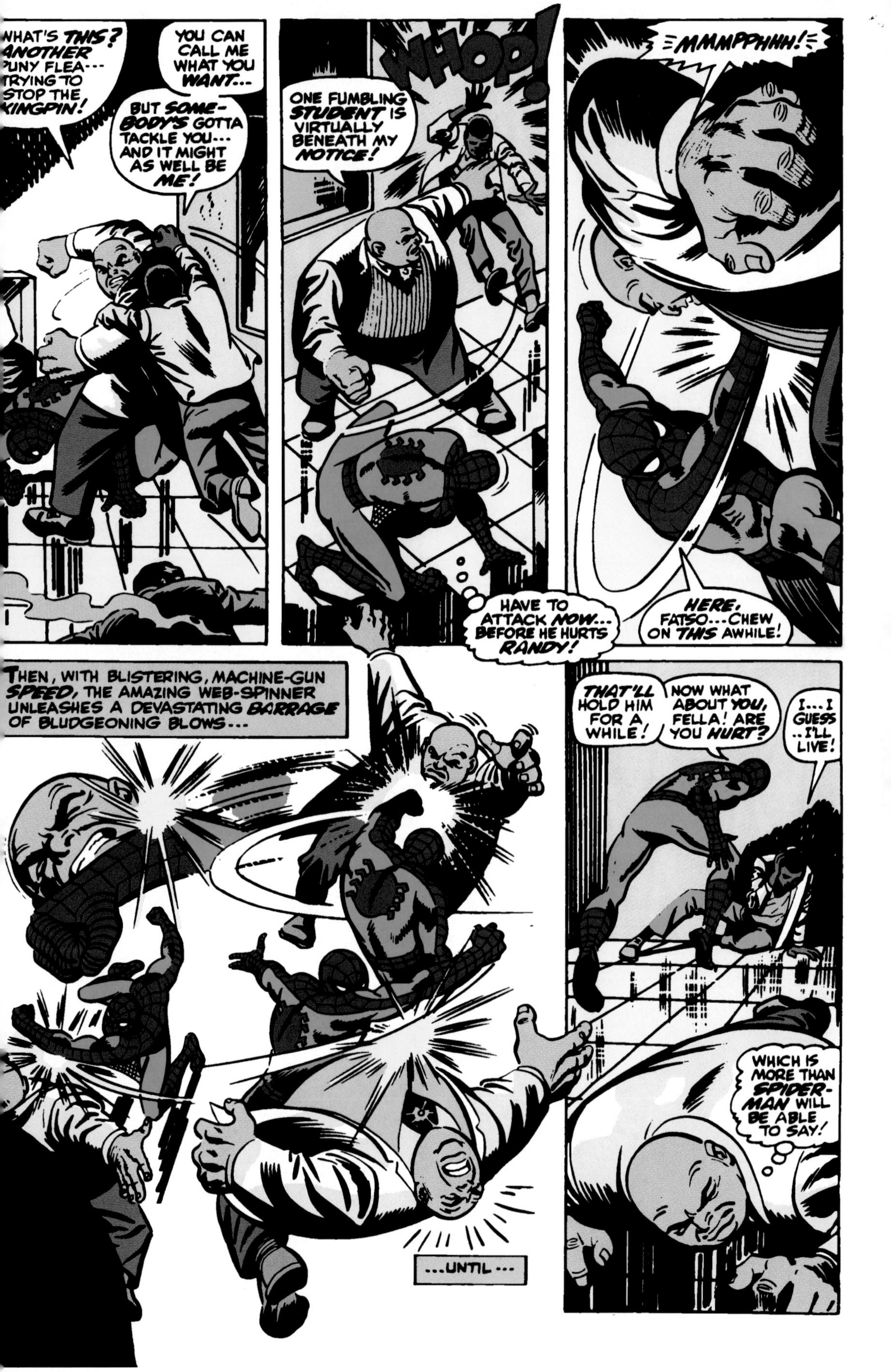
WHAT'S THIS? ANOTHER PUNY FLEA--- TRYING TO STOP THE KINGPIN!
YOU CAN CALL ME WHAT YOU WANT...
BUT SOME-BODY'S GOTTA TACKLE YOU--- AND IT MIGHT AS WELL BE ME!
WHOP!
ONE FUMBLING STUDENT IS VIRTUALLY BENEATH MY NOTICE!
HAVE TO ATTACK NOW... BEFORE HE HURTS RANDY!
MMMPPHHH!
HERE, FATSO---CHEW ON THIS AWHILE!
THEN, WITH BLISTERING, MACHINE-GUN SPEED, THE AMAZING WEB-SPINNER UNLEASHES A DEVASTATING BARRAGE OF BLUDGEONING BLOWS---
...UNTIL...
THAT'LL HOLD HIM FOR A WHILE!
NOW WHAT ABOUT YOU, FELLA! ARE YOU HURT?
I...I GUESS ..I'LL LIVE!
WHICH IS MORE THAN SPIDER-MAN WILL BE ABLE TO SAY!

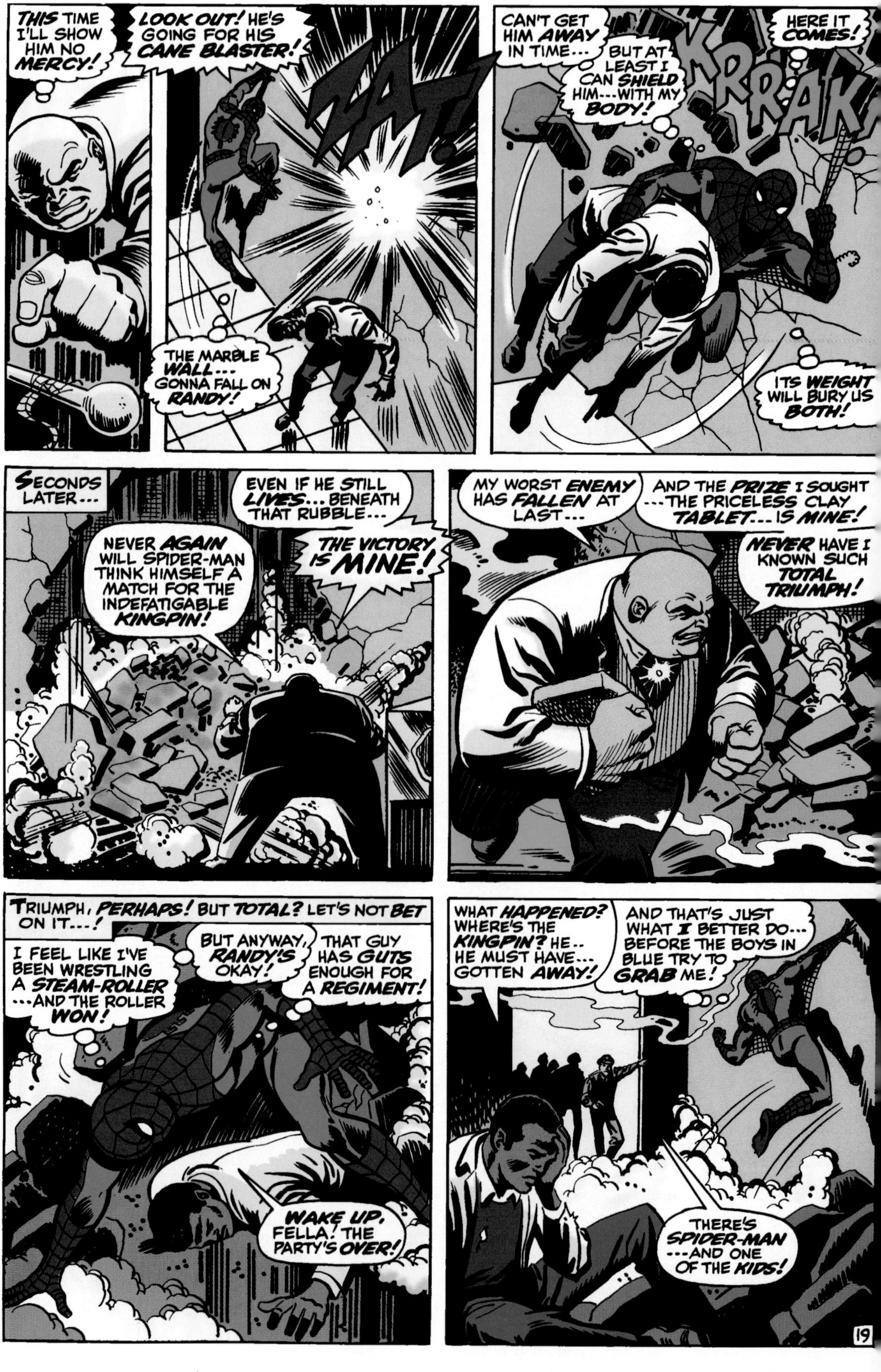
THIS TIME I'LL SHOW HIM NO MERCY!
LOOK OUT! HE'S GOING FOR HIS CANE BLASTER!
ZAT!
THE MARBLE WALL... GONNA FALL ON RANDY!
CAN'T GET HIM AWAY IN TIME...
BUT AT LEAST I CAN SHIELD HIM---WITH MY BODY!
HERE IT COMES!
KRRAK!
ITS WEIGHT WILL BURY US BOTH!
SECONDS LATER...
EVEN IF HE STILL LIVES... BENEATH THAT RUBBLE...
NEVER AGAIN WILL SPIDER-MAN THINK HIMSELF A MATCH FOR THE INDEFATIGABLE KINGPIN!
THE VICTORY IS MINE!
MY WORST ENEMY HAS FALLEN AT LAST...
AND THE PRIZE I SOUGHT ---THE PRICELESS CLAY TABLET... IS MINE!
NEVER HAVE I KNOWN SUCH TOTAL TRIUMPH!
TRIUMPH, PERHAPS! BUT TOTAL? LET'S NOT BET ON IT...!
I FEEL LIKE I'VE BEEN WRESTLING A STEAM-ROLLER ---AND THE ROLLER WON!
BUT ANYWAY, RANDY'S OKAY!
THAT GUY HAS GUTS ENOUGH FOR A REGIMENT!
WAKE UP, FELLA! THE PARTY'S OVER!
WHAT HAPPENED? WHERE'S THE KINGPIN? HE.. HE MUST HAVE... GOTTEN AWAY!
AND THAT'S JUST WHAT I BETTER DO... BEFORE THE BOYS IN BLUE TRY TO GRAB ME!
THERE'S SPIDER-MAN ---AND ONE OF THE KIDS!
19

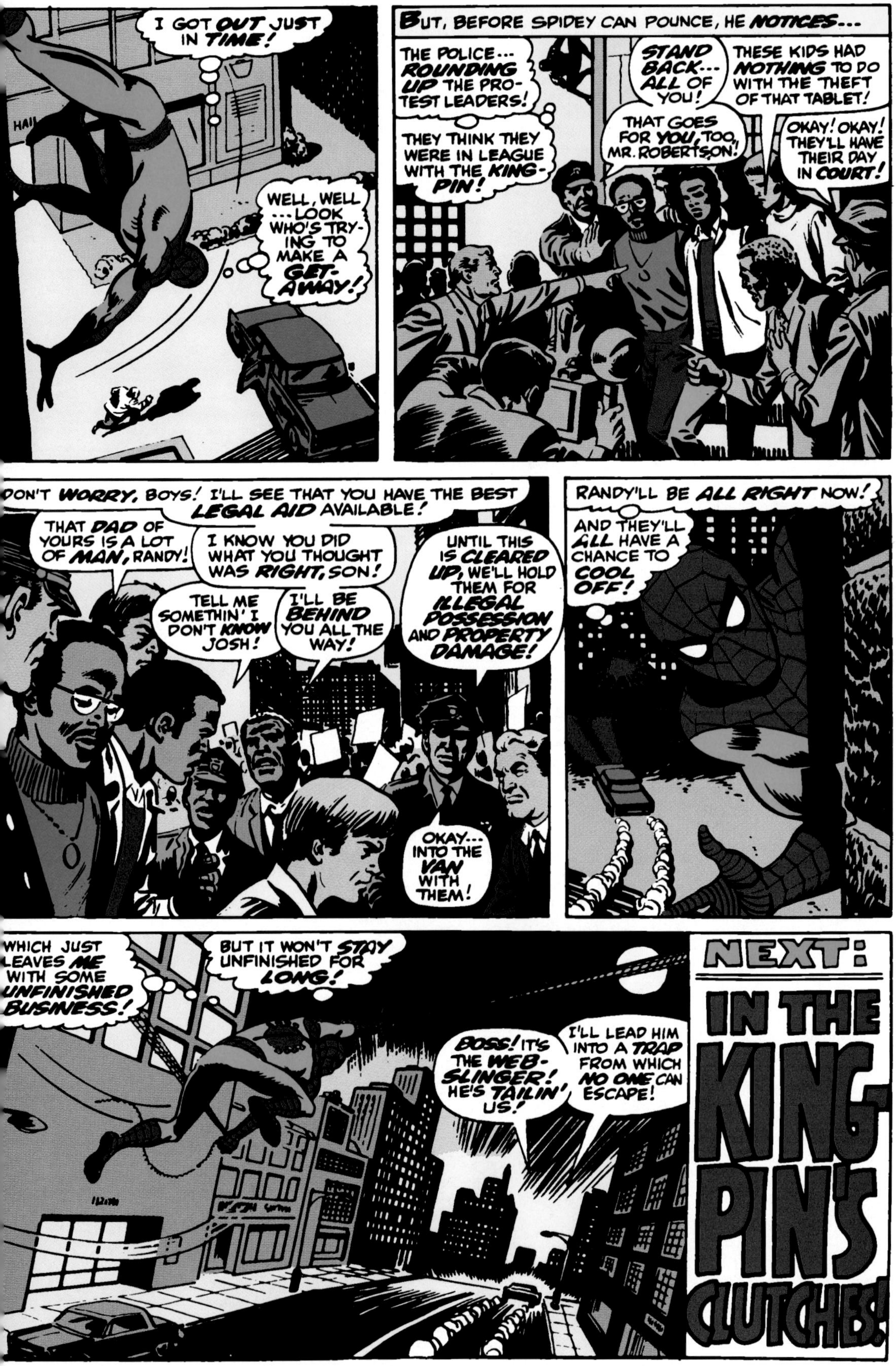
I GOT OUT JUST IN TIME!
WELL, WELL ...LOOK WHO'S TRYING TO MAKE A GET-AWAY!
BUT, BEFORE SPIDEY CAN POUNCE, HE NOTICES...
THE POLICE... ROUNDING UP THE PROTEST LEADERS!
THEY THINK THEY WERE IN LEAGUE WITH THE KING-PIN!
STAND BACK... ALL OF YOU!
THESE KIDS HAD NOTHING TO DO WITH THE THEFT OF THAT TABLET!
THAT GOES FOR YOU, TOO, MR. ROBERTSON!
OKAY! OKAY! THEY'LL HAVE THEIR DAY IN COURT!
DON'T WORRY, BOYS! I'LL SEE THAT YOU HAVE THE BEST LEGAL AID AVAILABLE!
THAT DAD OF YOURS IS A LOT OF MAN, RANDY!
I KNOW YOU DID WHAT YOU THOUGHT WAS RIGHT, SON!
TELL ME SOMETHIN' I DON'T KNOW JOSH!
I'LL BE BEHIND YOU ALL THE WAY!
UNTIL THIS IS CLEARED UP, WE'LL HOLD THEM FOR ILLEGAL POSSESSION AND PROPERTY DAMAGE!
OKAY... INTO THE VAN WITH THEM!
RANDY'LL BE ALL RIGHT NOW!
AND THEY'LL ALL HAVE A CHANCE TO COOL OFF!
WHICH JUST LEAVES ME WITH SOME UNFINISHED BUSINESS!
BUT IT WON'T STAY UNFINISHED FOR LONG!
BOSS! IT'S THE WEB-SLINGER! HE'S TAILIN' US!
I'LL LEAD HIM INTO A TRAP FROM WHICH NO ONE CAN ESCAPE!
NEXT:
IN THE KING-PIN'S CLUTCHES!

amazing spider-man #69

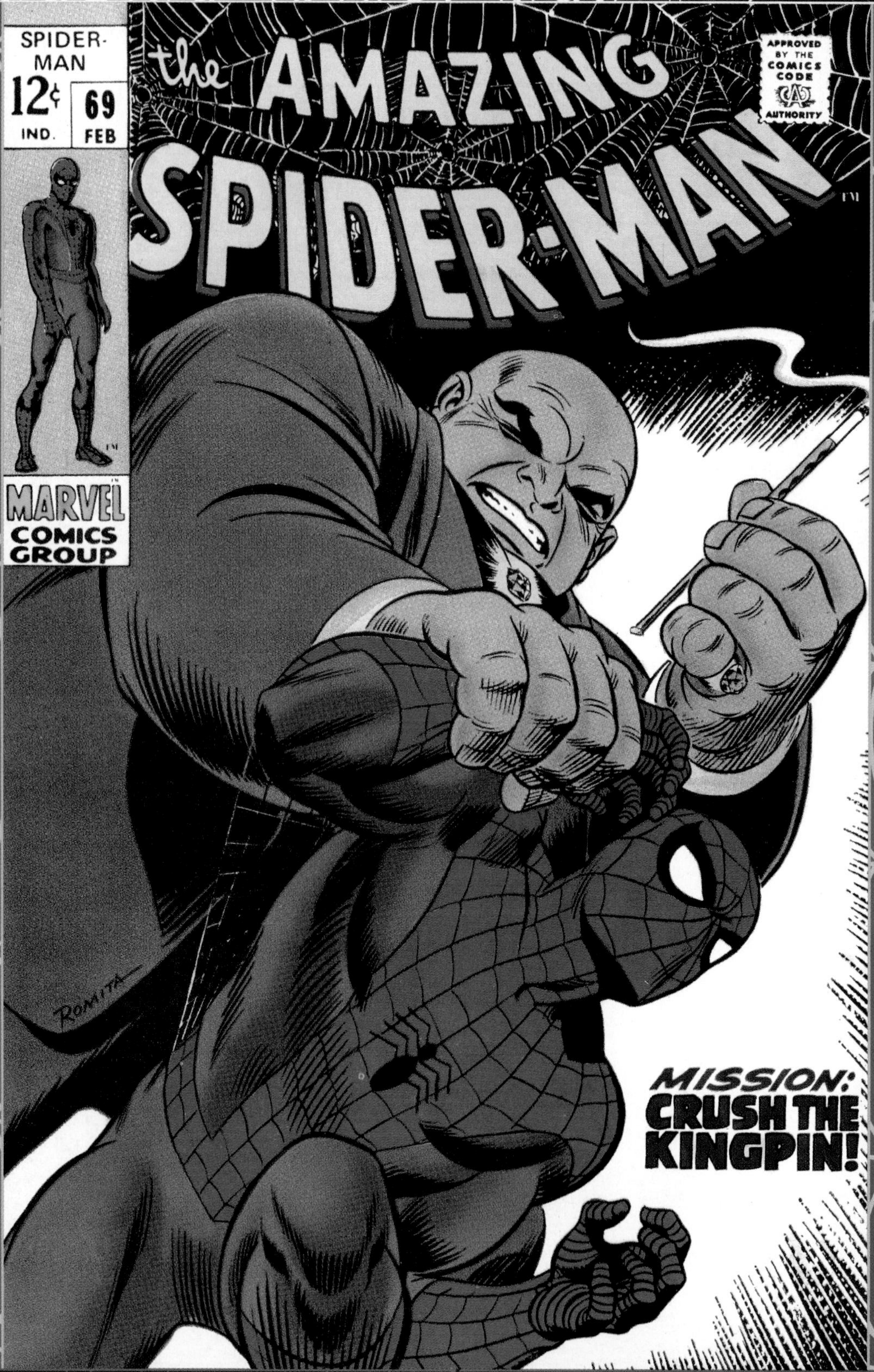

february 1969

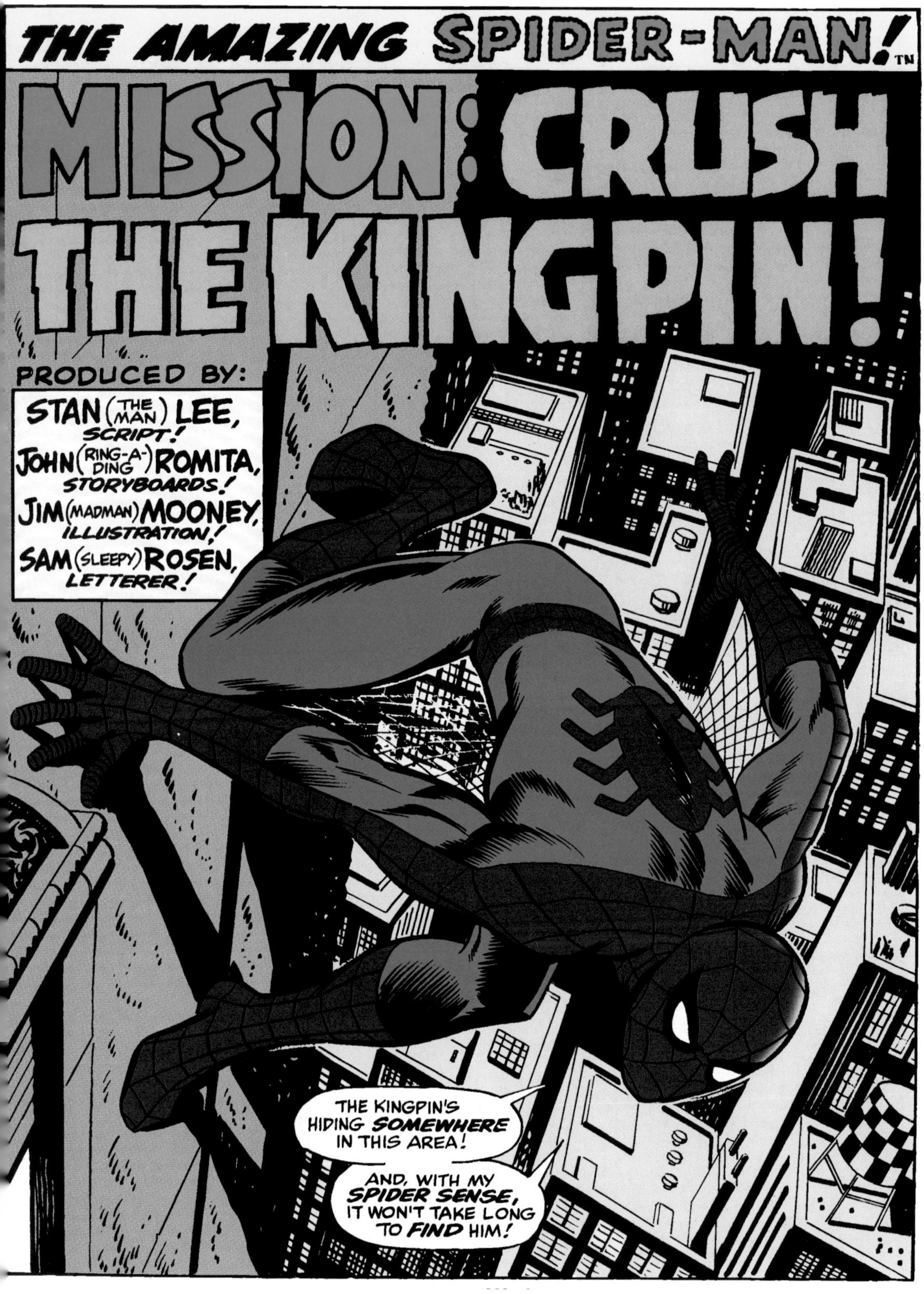

THE AMAZING SPIDER-MAN!™
MISSION: CRUSH THE KINGPIN!
PRODUCED BY:
STAN (THE MAN) LEE, SCRIPT!
JOHN (RING-A-DING) ROMITA, STORYBOARDS!
JIM (MADMAN) MOONEY, ILLUSTRATION!
SAM (SLEEPY) ROSEN, LETTERER!
THE KINGPIN'S HIDING SOMEWHERE IN THIS AREA!
AND, WITH MY SPIDER SENSE, IT WON'T TAKE LONG TO FIND HIM!

I CAN'T LET HIM GET AWAY WITH STEALING THAT PRICELESS TABLET FROM THE CAMPUS' EXHIBITION HALL!

...ESPECIALLY SINCE MR. ROBERTSON'S SON, RANDY, AND THE OTHER PROTEST LEADERS...

...ARE BEING BOOKED ON CHARGES OF AIDING THE KINGPIN IN HIS THEFT!

NOT TO MENTION THE FACT THAT THE TABLET IS SO PRICELESS, THAT FATSO CAN SELL IT TO ANY NATION HE CHOOSES!*

UH-OH! SPIDER-SENSE IS STARTING TO TINGLE!

I'M GETTING CLOSE!

*HOW'S THAT FOR A SNEAKY WAY TO SUMMARIZE OUR LAST ISH? ---SUBTLE STAN.

AND, JUST A FEW FATEFUL YARDS AWAY, WE FIND...

YOU DID IT, KINGPIN! IT WAS A STROKE OF GENIUS FOR YOU TO USE THE STUDENT PROTEST DEMONSTRATION AS A COVER FOR STEALING THE TABLET!

BUT WHAT ABOUT SPIDER-MAN, BOSS?

COULD YOU EXPECT ANY LESS...FROM ME?

YEAH! THE BLASTED WEB-SPINNER IS STILL ON OUR TRAIL!

FORGET SPIDER-MAN! LOOK AT THE PRIZE I'VE WON!

THIS ANCIENT CLAY TABLET IS OLDER THAN THE DEAD SEA SCROLLS!

WHOEVER DECIPHERS IT WILL LEARN THE GREATEST SECRETS OF ALL TIME!

AND IT'S MINE! MINE!

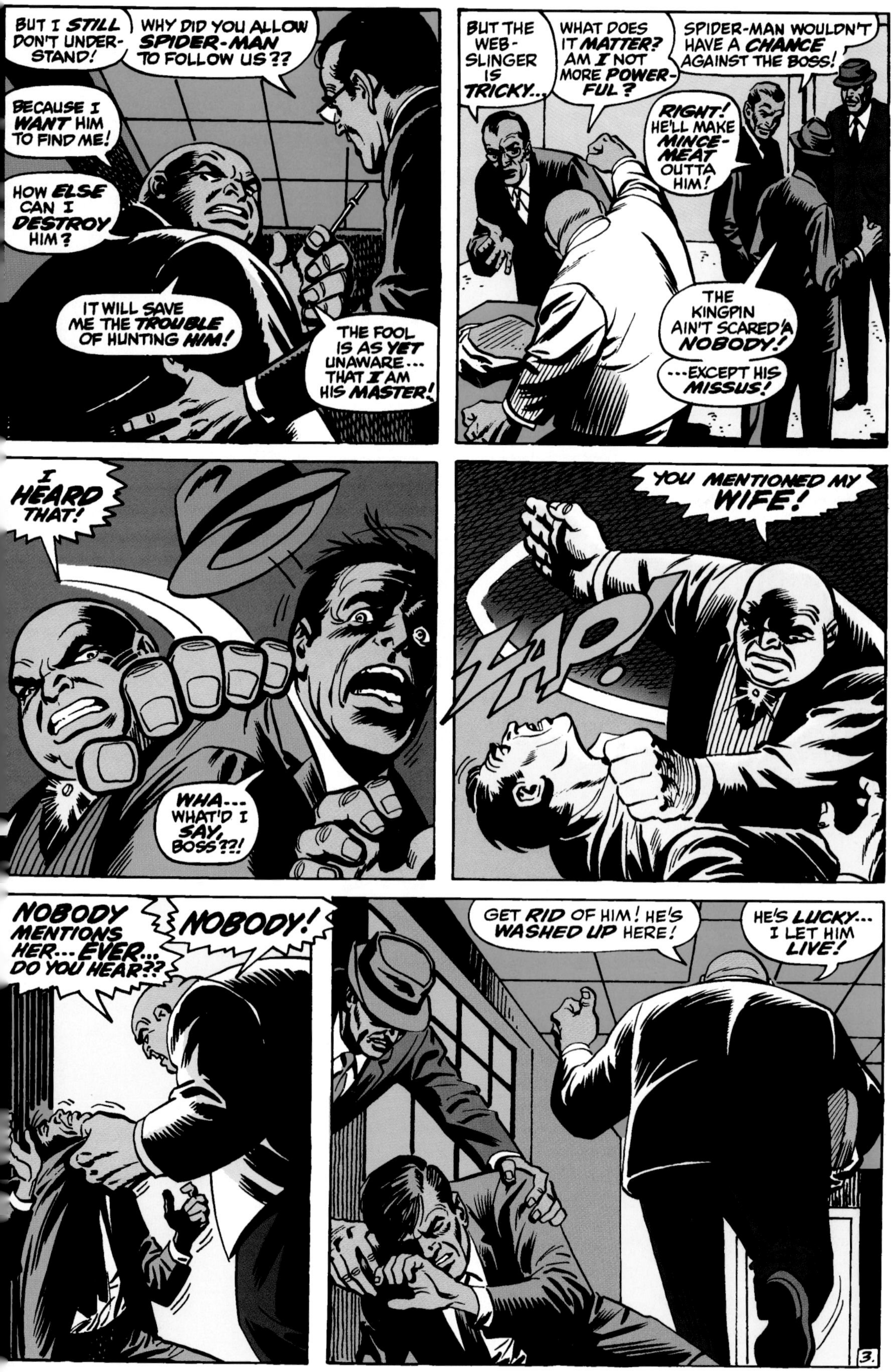
BUT I STILL DON'T UNDER-STAND!
WHY DID YOU ALLOW SPIDER-MAN TO FOLLOW US??
BECAUSE I WANT HIM TO FIND ME!
HOW ELSE CAN I DESTROY HIM?
IT WILL SAVE ME THE TROUBLE OF HUNTING HIM!
THE FOOL IS AS YET UNAWARE... THAT I AM HIS MASTER!
BUT THE WEB-SLINGER IS TRICKY...
WHAT DOES IT MATTER? AM I NOT MORE POWER-FUL?
SPIDER-MAN WOULDN'T HAVE A CHANCE AGAINST THE BOSS!
RIGHT! HE'LL MAKE MINCE-MEAT OUTTA HIM!
THE KINGPIN AIN'T SCARED'A NOBODY!
...EXCEPT HIS MISSUS!
I HEARD THAT!
WHA... WHAT'D I SAY, BOSS??!
YOU MENTIONED MY WIFE!
SLAP!
NOBODY MENTIONS HER... EVER... DO YOU HEAR??
NOBODY!
GET RID OF HIM! HE'S WASHED UP HERE!
HE'S LUCKY... I LET HIM LIVE!
3.

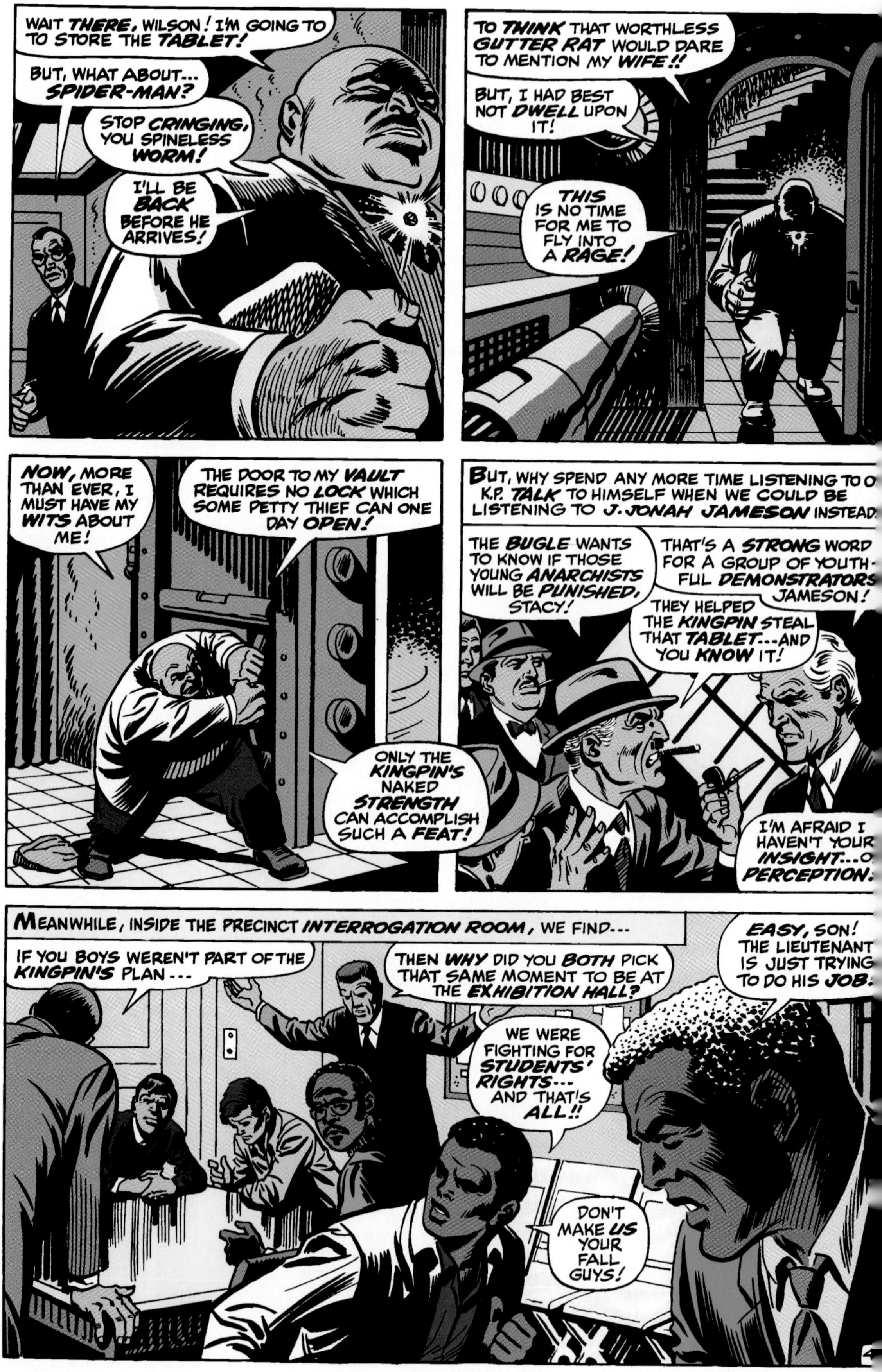
WAIT THERE, WILSON! I'M GOING TO TO STORE THE TABLET!
BUT, WHAT ABOUT... SPIDER-MAN?
STOP CRINGING, YOU SPINELESS WORM!
I'LL BE BACK BEFORE HE ARRIVES!
TO THINK THAT WORTHLESS GUTTER RAT WOULD DARE TO MENTION MY WIFE!!
BUT, I HAD BEST NOT DWELL UPON IT!
THIS IS NO TIME FOR ME TO FLY INTO A RAGE!
NOW, MORE THAN EVER, I MUST HAVE MY WITS ABOUT ME!
THE DOOR TO MY VAULT REQUIRES NO LOCK WHICH SOME PETTY THIEF CAN ONE DAY OPEN!
ONLY THE KINGPIN'S NAKED STRENGTH CAN ACCOMPLISH SUCH A FEAT!
BUT, WHY SPEND ANY MORE TIME LISTENING TO O K.P. TALK TO HIMSELF WHEN WE COULD BE LISTENING TO J. JONAH JAMESON INSTEAD
THE BUGLE WANTS TO KNOW IF THOSE YOUNG ANARCHISTS WILL BE PUNISHED, STACY!
THAT'S A STRONG WORD FOR A GROUP OF YOUTH-FUL DEMONSTRATORS JAMESON!
THEY HELPED THE KINGPIN STEAL THAT TABLET---AND YOU KNOW IT!
I'M AFRAID I HAVEN'T YOUR INSIGHT...O PERCEPTION
MEANWHILE, INSIDE THE PRECINCT INTERROGATION ROOM, WE FIND---
IF YOU BOYS WEREN'T PART OF THE KINGPIN'S PLAN ---
THEN WHY DID YOU BOTH PICK THAT SAME MOMENT TO BE AT THE EXHIBITION HALL?
EASY, SON! THE LIEUTENANT IS JUST TRYING TO DO HIS JOB
WE WERE FIGHTING FOR STUDENTS' RIGHTS... AND THAT'S ALL!!
DON'T MAKE US YOUR FALL GUYS!

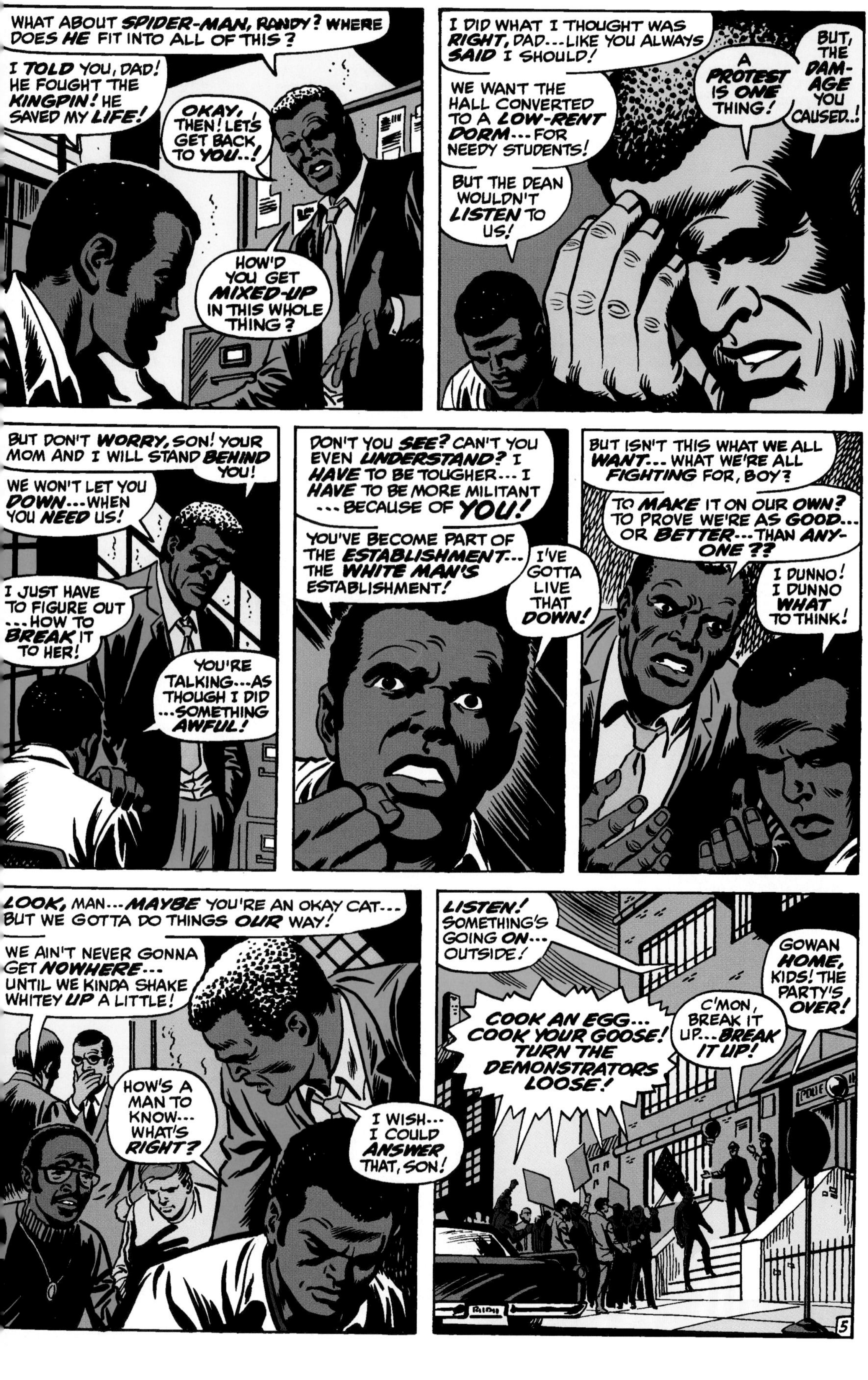
WHAT ABOUT SPIDER-MAN, RANDY? WHERE DOES HE FIT INTO ALL OF THIS?
I TOLD YOU, DAD! HE FOUGHT THE KINGPIN! HE SAVED MY LIFE!
OKAY, THEN! LET'S GET BACK TO YOU..!
HOW'D YOU GET MIXED-UP IN THIS WHOLE THING?
I DID WHAT I THOUGHT WAS RIGHT, DAD...LIKE YOU ALWAYS SAID I SHOULD!
WE WANT THE HALL CONVERTED TO A LOW-RENT DORM... FOR NEEDY STUDENTS!
BUT THE DEAN WOULDN'T LISTEN TO US!
A PROTEST IS ONE THING!
BUT, THE DAMAGE YOU CAUSED..!
BUT DON'T WORRY, SON! YOUR MOM AND I WILL STAND BEHIND YOU!
WE WON'T LET YOU DOWN...WHEN YOU NEED US!
I JUST HAVE TO FIGURE OUT...HOW TO BREAK IT TO HER!
YOU'RE TALKING...AS THOUGH I DID...SOMETHING AWFUL!
DON'T YOU SEE? CAN'T YOU EVEN UNDERSTAND? I HAVE TO BE TOUGHER... I HAVE TO BE MORE MILITANT ...BECAUSE OF YOU!
YOU'VE BECOME PART OF THE ESTABLISHMENT... THE WHITE MAN'S ESTABLISHMENT!
I'VE GOTTA LIVE THAT DOWN!
BUT ISN'T THIS WHAT WE ALL WANT... WHAT WE'RE ALL FIGHTING FOR, BOY?
TO MAKE IT ON OUR OWN? TO PROVE WE'RE AS GOOD... OR BETTER...THAN ANYONE??
I DUNNO! I DUNNO WHAT TO THINK!
LOOK, MAN...MAYBE YOU'RE AN OKAY CAT... BUT WE GOTTA DO THINGS OUR WAY!
WE AIN'T NEVER GONNA GET NOWHERE... UNTIL WE KINDA SHAKE WHITEY UP A LITTLE!
HOW'S A MAN TO KNOW... WHAT'S RIGHT?
I WISH... I COULD ANSWER THAT, SON!
LISTEN! SOMETHING'S GOING ON... OUTSIDE!
COOK AN EGG... COOK YOUR GOOSE! TURN THE DEMONSTRATORS LOOSE!
C'MON, BREAK IT UP...BREAK IT UP!
GOWAN HOME, KIDS! THE PARTY'S OVER!
5

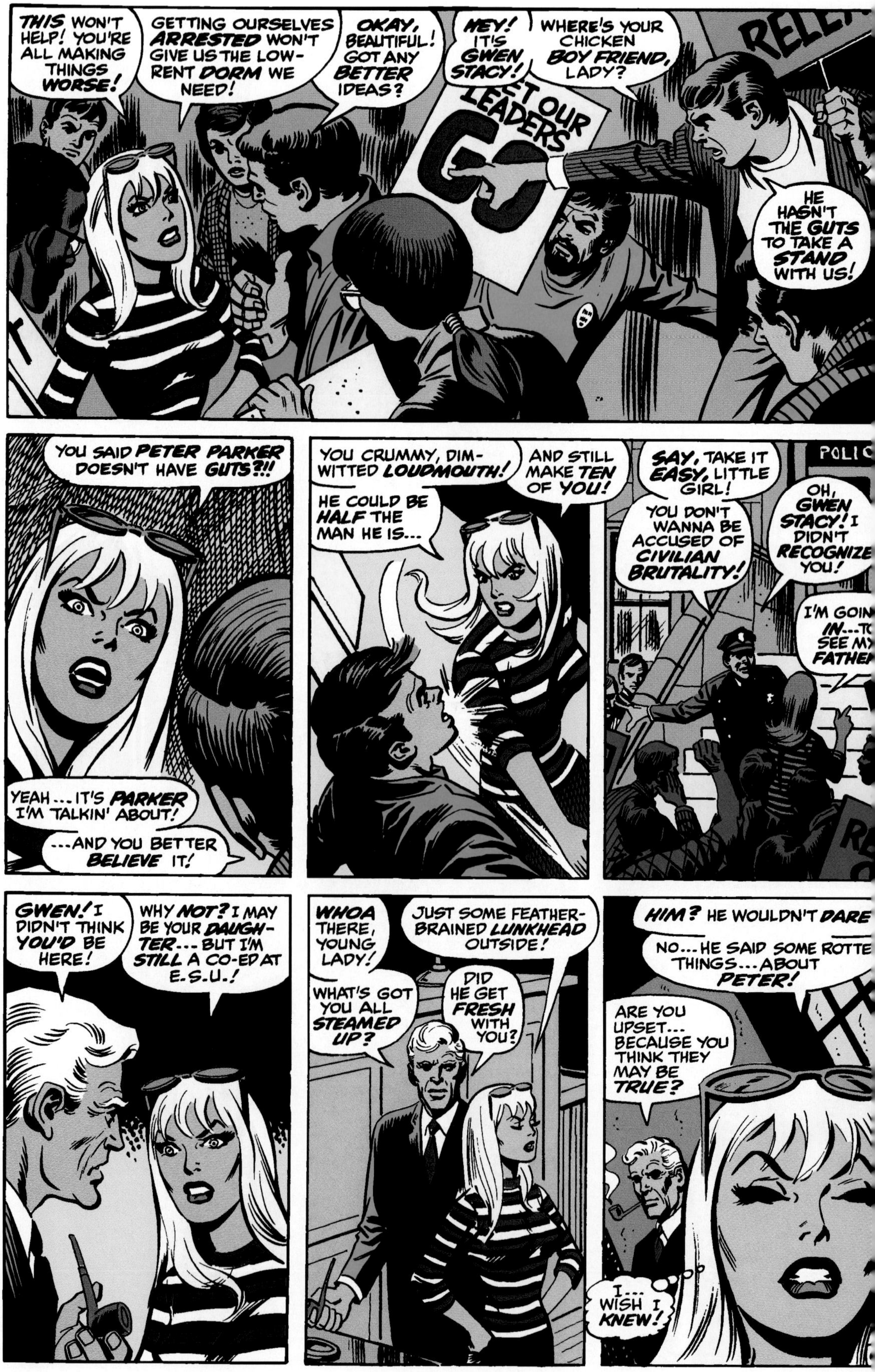

THIS WON'T HELP! YOU'RE ALL MAKING THINGS WORSE!
GETTING OURSELVES ARRESTED WON'T GIVE US THE LOW-RENT DORM WE NEED!
OKAY, BEAUTIFUL! GOT ANY BETTER IDEAS?
HEY! IT'S GWEN STACY!
WHERE'S YOUR CHICKEN BOY FRIEND, LADY?
HE HASN'T THE GUTS TO TAKE A STAND WITH US!
LEADERS GO
YOU SAID PETER PARKER DOESN'T HAVE GUTS?!!
YEAH... IT'S PARKER I'M TALKIN' ABOUT!
...AND YOU BETTER BELIEVE IT!
YOU CRUMMY, DIM-WITTED LOUDMOUTH!
HE COULD BE HALF THE MAN HE IS...
AND STILL MAKE TEN OF YOU!
SAY, TAKE IT EASY, LITTLE GIRL!
YOU DON'T WANNA BE ACCUSED OF CIVILIAN BRUTALITY!
OH, GWEN STACY! I DIDN'T RECOGNIZE YOU!
GWEN! I DIDN'T THINK YOU'D BE HERE!
WHY NOT? I MAY BE YOUR DAUGHTER... BUT I'M STILL A CO-ED AT E.S.U.!
WHOA THERE, YOUNG LADY!
WHAT'S GOT YOU ALL STEAMED UP?
JUST SOME FEATHER-BRAINED LUNKHEAD OUTSIDE!
DID HE GET FRESH WITH YOU?
ARE YOU UPSET... BECAUSE YOU THINK THEY MAY BE TRUE?
I... WISH I KNEW!

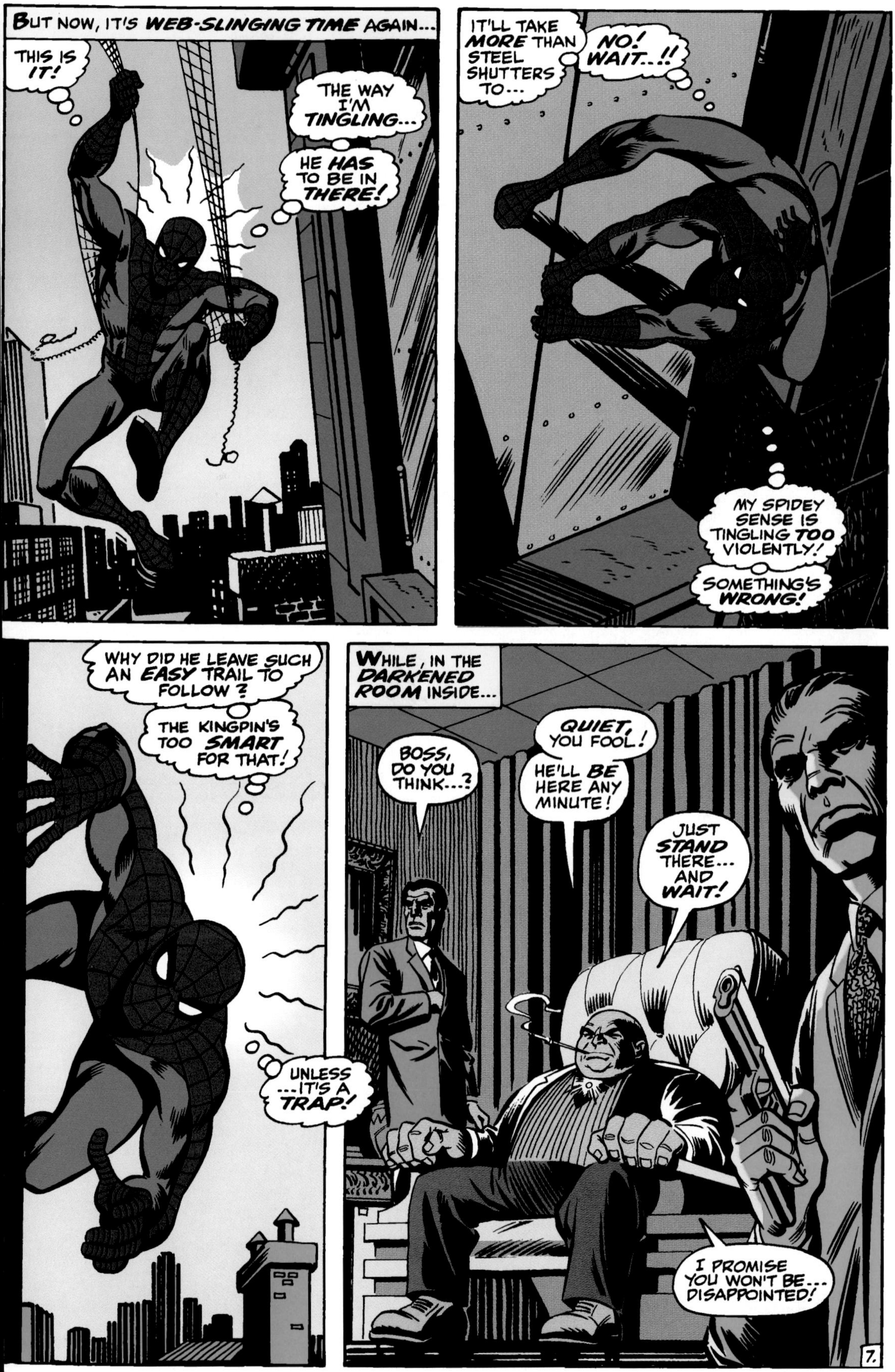
BUT NOW, IT'S WEB-SLINGING TIME AGAIN...
THIS IS IT!
THE WAY I'M TINGLING...
HE HAS TO BE IN THERE!
IT'LL TAKE MORE THAN STEEL SHUTTERS TO...
NO! WAIT..!!
MY SPIDEY SENSE IS TINGLING TOO VIOLENTLY!
SOMETHING'S WRONG!
WHY DID HE LEAVE SUCH AN EASY TRAIL TO FOLLOW?
THE KINGPIN'S TOO SMART FOR THAT!
UNLESS ...IT'S A TRAP!
WHILE, IN THE DARKENED ROOM INSIDE...
BOSS, DO YOU THINK...?
QUIET, YOU FOOL!
HE'LL BE HERE ANY MINUTE!
JUST STAND THERE... AND WAIT!
I PROMISE YOU WON'T BE... DISAPPOINTED!
7.

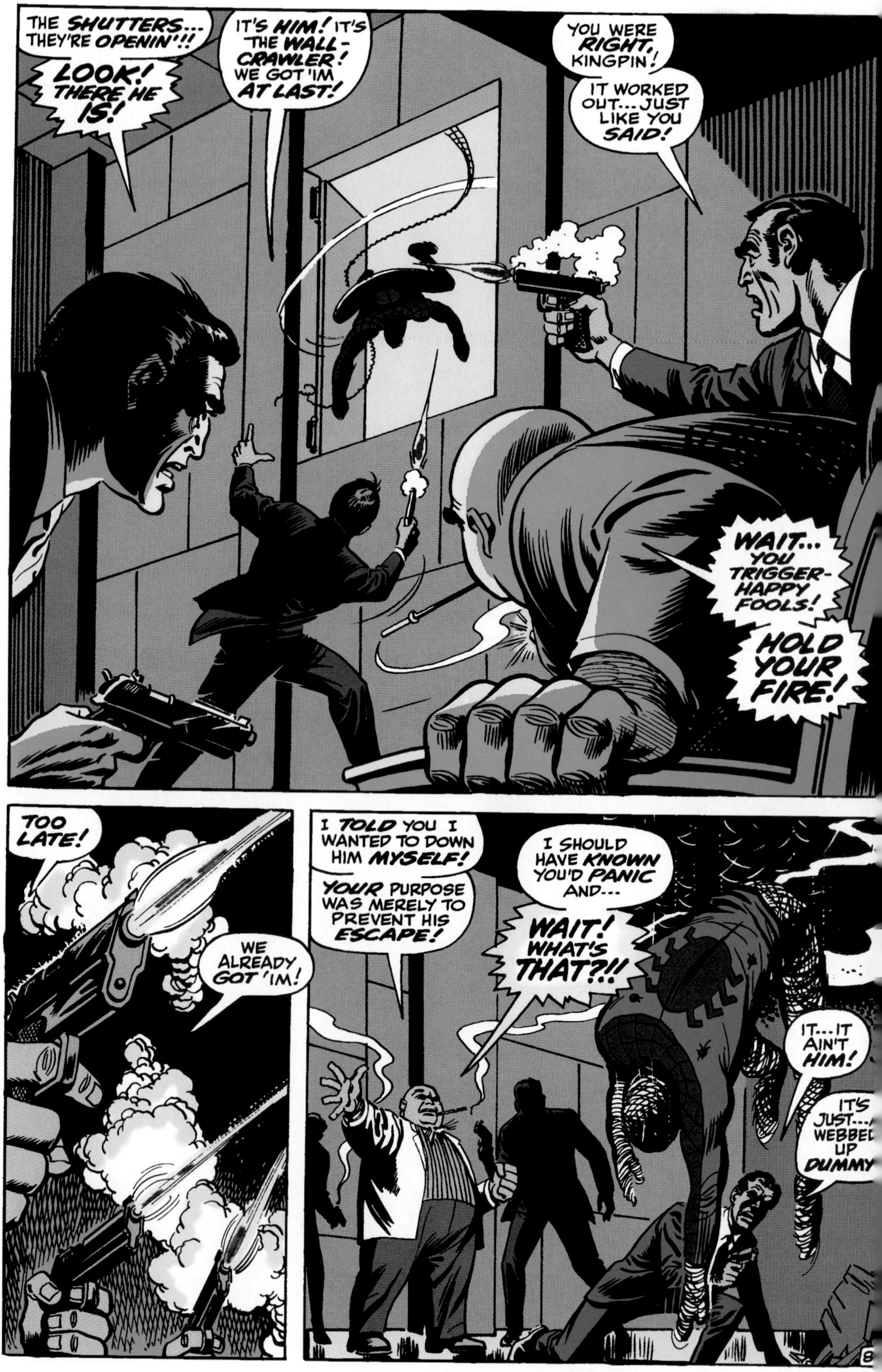

THE SHUTTERS... THEY'RE OPENIN'!!
LOOK! THERE HE IS!
IT'S HIM! IT'S THE WALL-CRAWLER! WE GOT 'IM AT LAST!
YOU WERE RIGHT, KINGPIN!
IT WORKED OUT... JUST LIKE YOU SAID!
WAIT... YOU TRIGGER-HAPPY FOOLS!
HOLD YOUR FIRE!
TOO LATE!
WE ALREADY GOT 'IM!
I TOLD YOU I WANTED TO DOWN HIM MYSELF!
YOUR PURPOSE WAS MERELY TO PREVENT HIS ESCAPE!
I SHOULD HAVE KNOWN YOU'D PANIC AND---
WAIT! WHAT'S THAT?!!
IT... IT AIN'T HIM!
IT'S JUST... WEBBED UP DUMMY

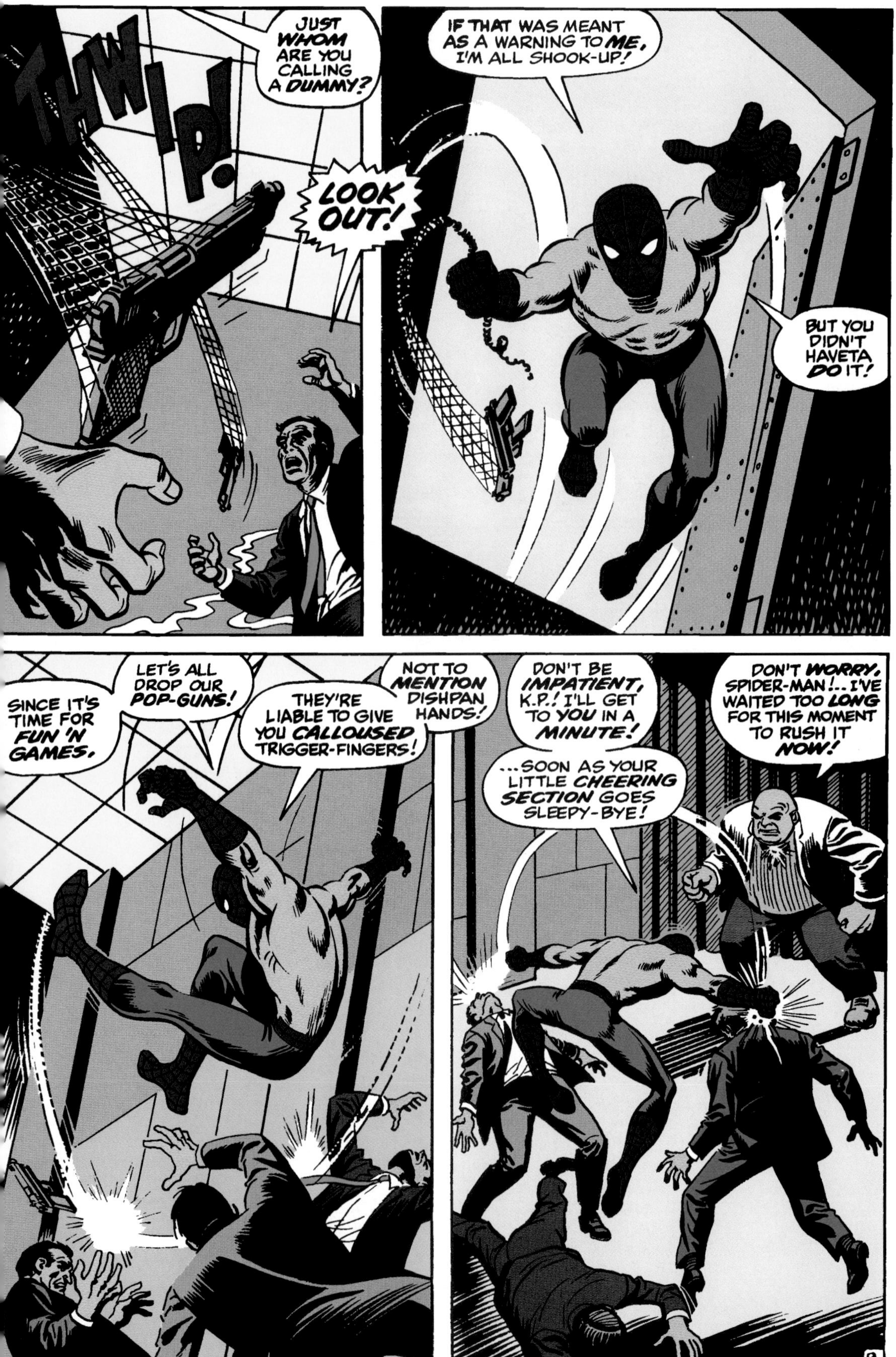
THWIP!
JUST WHOM ARE YOU CALLING A DUMMY?
LOOK OUT!
IF THAT WAS MEANT AS A WARNING TO ME, I'M ALL SHOOK-UP!
BUT YOU DIDN'T HAVETA DO IT!
SINCE IT'S TIME FOR FUN 'N GAMES,
LET'S ALL DROP OUR POP-GUNS!
THEY'RE LIABLE TO GIVE YOU CALLOUSED TRIGGER-FINGERS!
NOT TO MENTION DISHPAN HANDS!
DON'T BE IMPATIENT, K.P.! I'LL GET TO YOU IN A MINUTE!
...SOON AS YOUR LITTLE CHEERING SECTION GOES SLEEPY-BYE!
DON'T WORRY, SPIDER-MAN!...I'VE WAITED TOO LONG FOR THIS MOMENT TO RUSH IT NOW!
9.

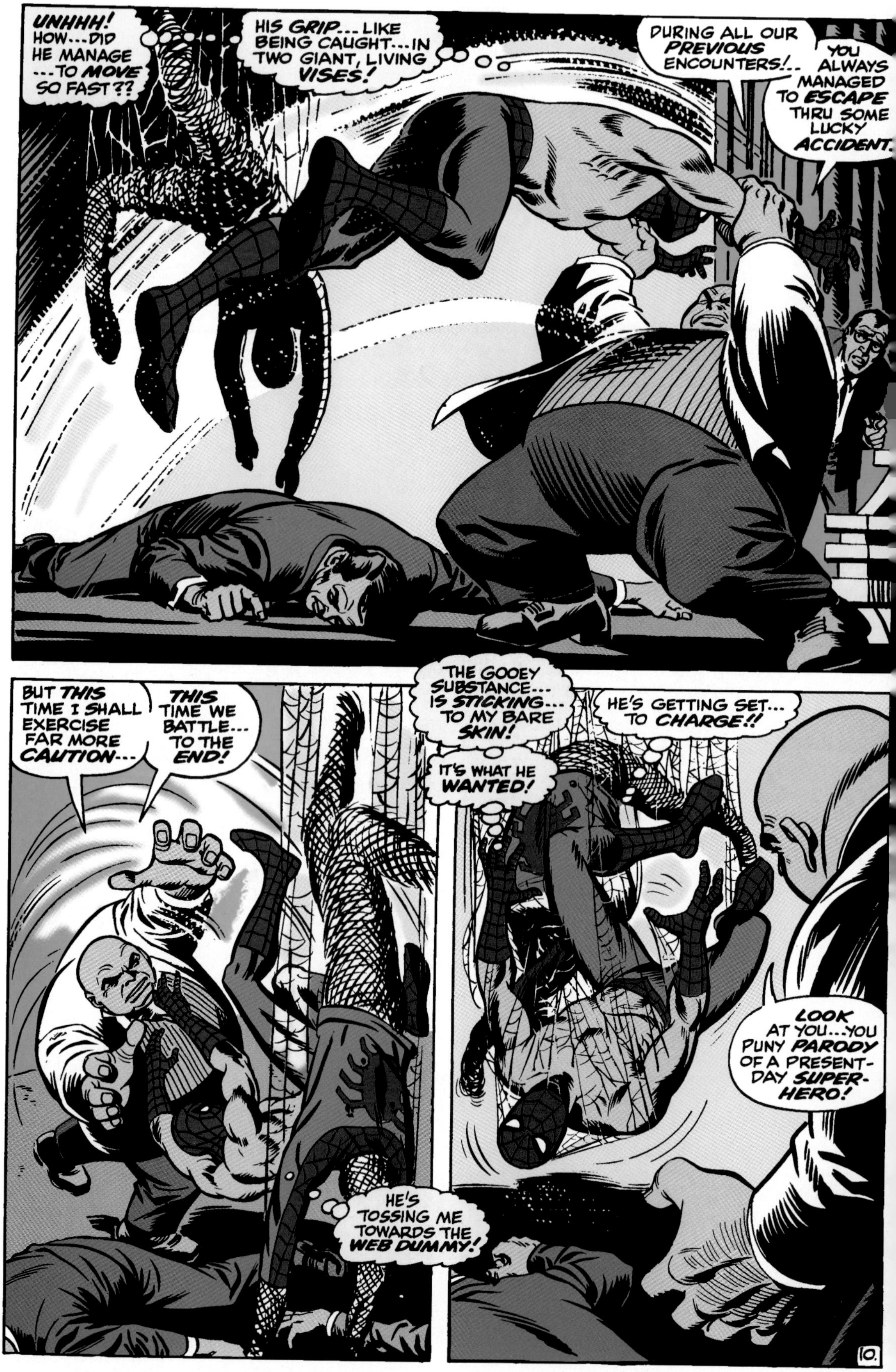

UNHHH! HOW...DID HE MANAGE ...TO MOVE SO FAST??
HIS GRIP... LIKE BEING CAUGHT...IN TWO GIANT, LIVING VISES!
DURING ALL OUR PREVIOUS ENCOUNTERS!..
YOU ALWAYS MANAGED TO ESCAPE THRU SOME LUCKY ACCIDENT.
BUT THIS TIME I SHALL EXERCISE FAR MORE CAUTION...
THIS TIME WE BATTLE... TO THE END!
HE'S TOSSING ME TOWARDS THE WEB DUMMY!
THE GOOEY SUBSTANCE... IS STICKING... TO MY BARE SKIN!
IT'S WHAT HE WANTED!
HE'S GETTING SET... TO CHARGE!!
LOOK AT YOU...YOU PUNY PARODY OF A PRESENT-DAY SUPER-HERO!
10.

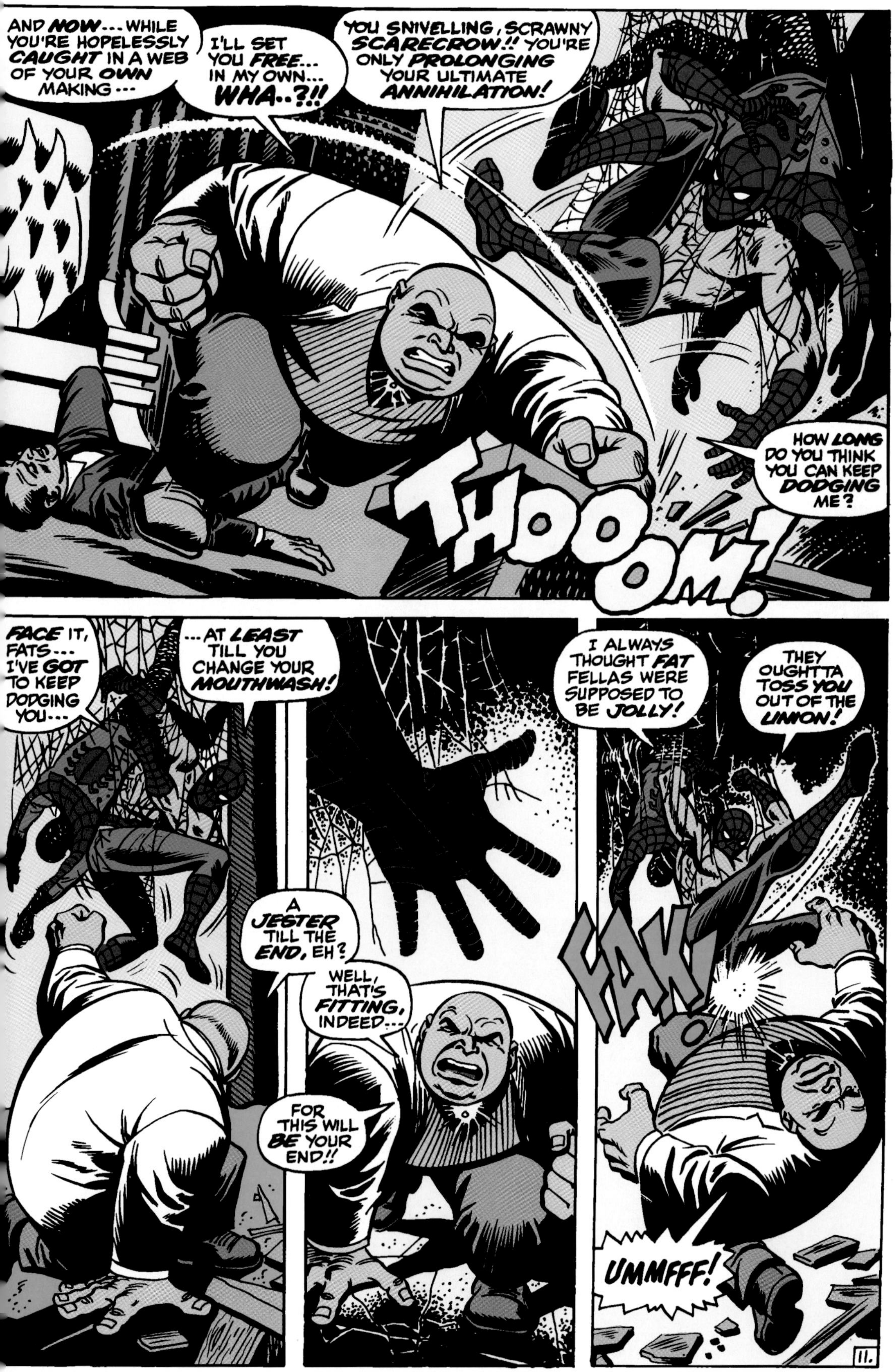
AND NOW... WHILE YOU'RE HOPELESSLY CAUGHT IN A WEB OF YOUR OWN MAKING...
I'LL SET YOU FREE... IN MY OWN... WHA..?!!
YOU SNIVELLING, SCRAWNY SCARECROW!! YOU'RE ONLY PROLONGING YOUR ULTIMATE ANNIHILATION!
HOW LONG DO YOU THINK YOU CAN KEEP DODGING ME?
THOOOM!
FACE IT, FATS... I'VE GOT TO KEEP DODGING YOU...
...AT LEAST TILL YOU CHANGE YOUR MOUTHWASH!
A JESTER TILL THE END, EH?
WELL, THAT'S FITTING, INDEED...
FOR THIS WILL BE YOUR END!!
I ALWAYS THOUGHT FAT FELLAS WERE SUPPOSED TO BE JOLLY!
THEY OUGHTTA TOSS YOU OUT OF THE UNION!
FAK!
UMMFFF!

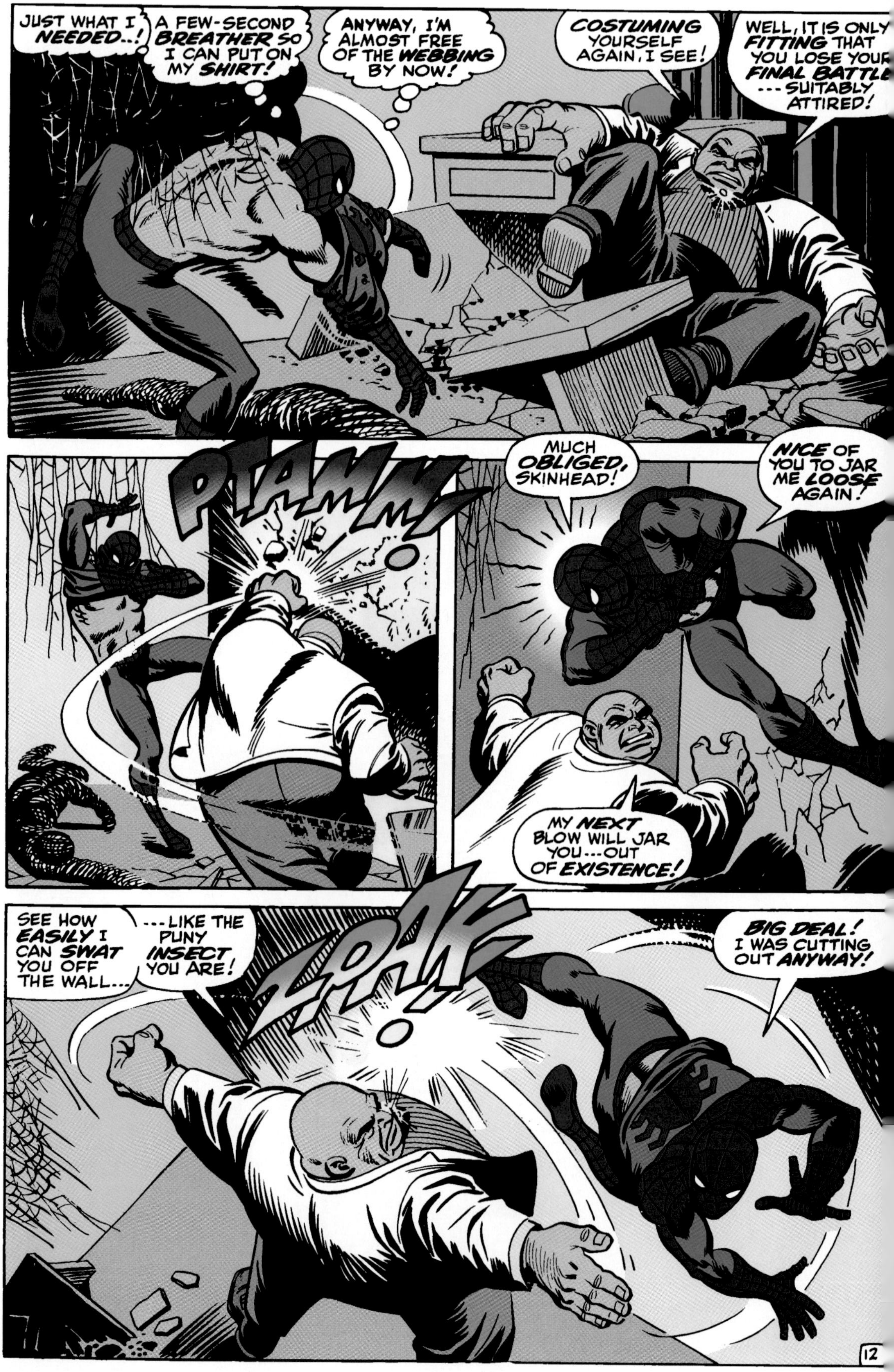
JUST WHAT I NEEDED..!
A FEW-SECOND BREATHER SO I CAN PUT ON MY SHIRT!
ANYWAY, I'M ALMOST FREE OF THE WEBBING BY NOW!
COSTUMING YOURSELF AGAIN, I SEE!
WELL, IT IS ONLY FITTING THAT YOU LOSE YOUR FINAL BATTLE --- SUITABLY ATTIRED!
PTAMM!
MUCH OBLIGED, SKINHEAD!
NICE OF YOU TO JAR ME LOOSE AGAIN!
MY NEXT BLOW WILL JAR YOU---OUT OF EXISTENCE!
SEE HOW EASILY I CAN SWAT YOU OFF THE WALL...
---LIKE THE PUNY INSECT YOU ARE!
ZPAK!
BIG DEAL! I WAS CUTTING OUT ANYWAY!
12

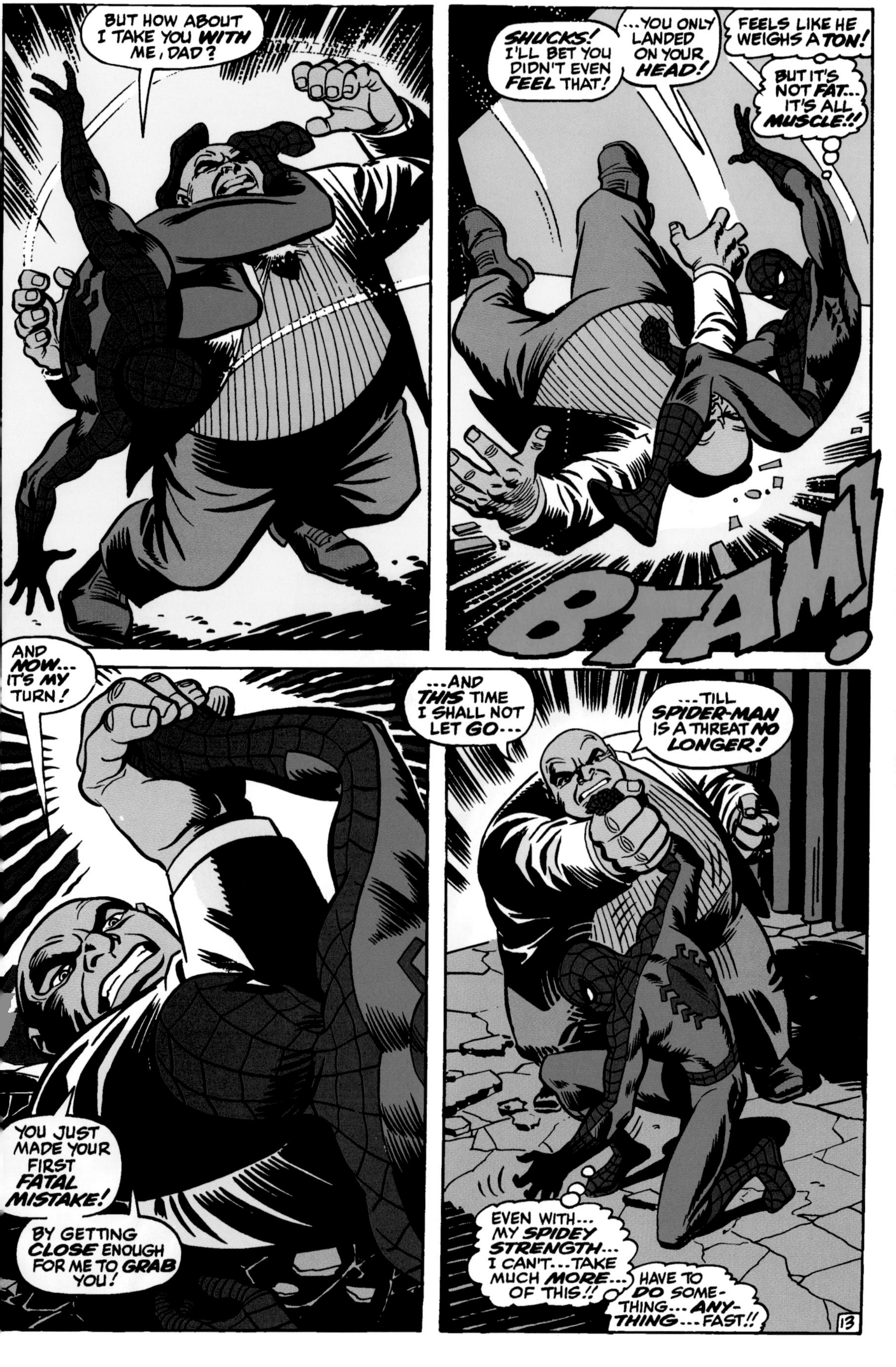
BUT HOW ABOUT I TAKE YOU WITH ME, DAD?
SHUCKS! I'LL BET YOU DIDN'T EVEN FEEL THAT!
...YOU ONLY LANDED ON YOUR HEAD!
FEELS LIKE HE WEIGHS A TON!
BUT IT'S NOT FAT... IT'S ALL MUSCLE!!
BTAM!
AND NOW... IT'S MY TURN!
YOU JUST MADE YOUR FIRST FATAL MISTAKE!
BY GETTING CLOSE ENOUGH FOR ME TO GRAB YOU!
...AND THIS TIME I SHALL NOT LET GO...
...TILL SPIDER-MAN IS A THREAT NO LONGER!
EVEN WITH... MY SPIDEY STRENGTH... I CAN'T... TAKE MUCH MORE... OF THIS!!
HAVE TO DO SOME-THING... ANY-THING... FAST!!
13

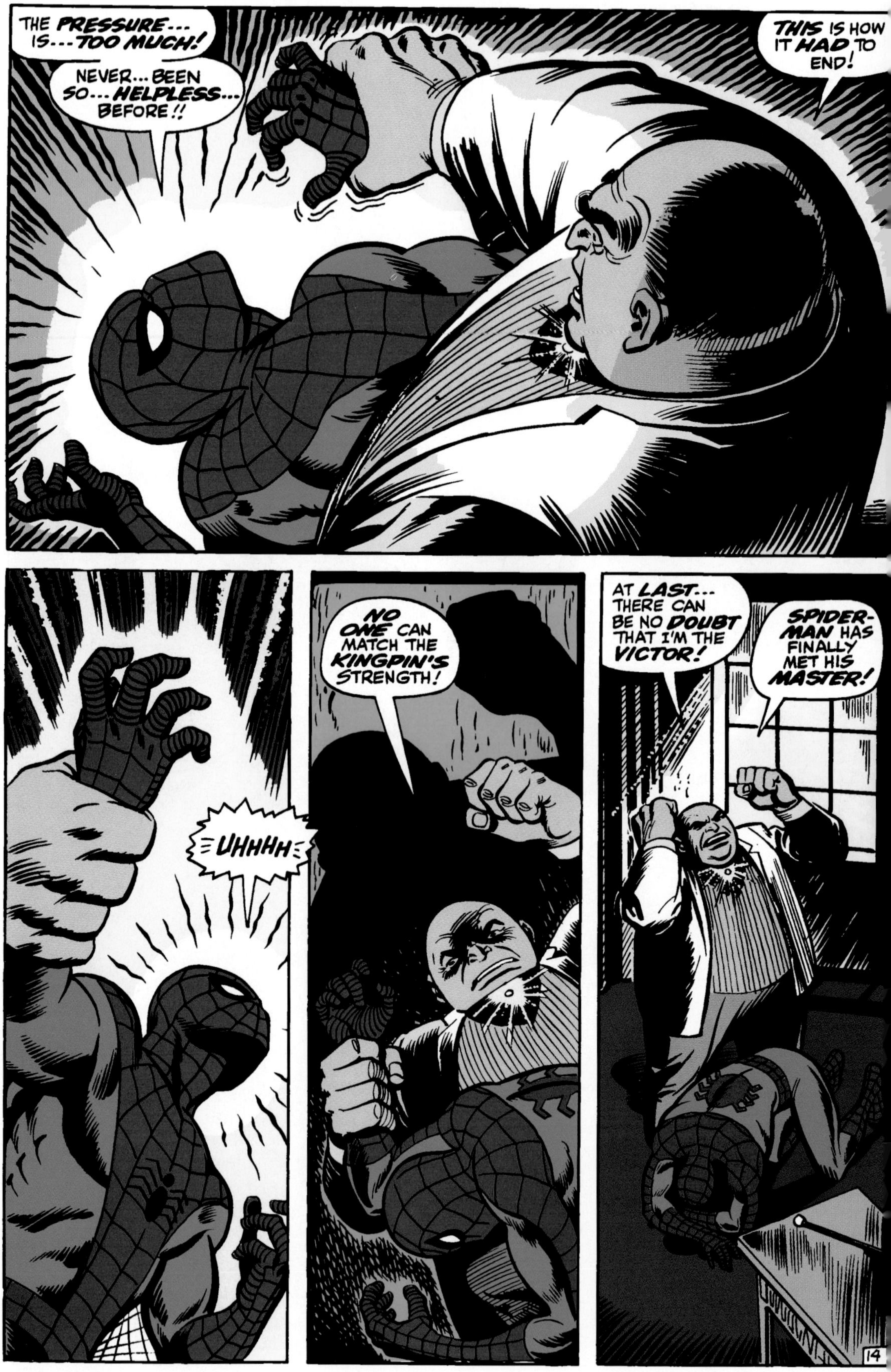
THE PRESSURE... IS... TOO MUCH!
NEVER... BEEN SO... HELPLESS... BEFORE!!
THIS IS HOW IT HAD TO END!
UHHHH
NO ONE CAN MATCH THE KINGPIN'S STRENGTH!
AT LAST... THERE CAN BE NO DOUBT THAT I'M THE VICTOR!
SPIDER-MAN HAS FINALLY MET HIS MASTER!
14

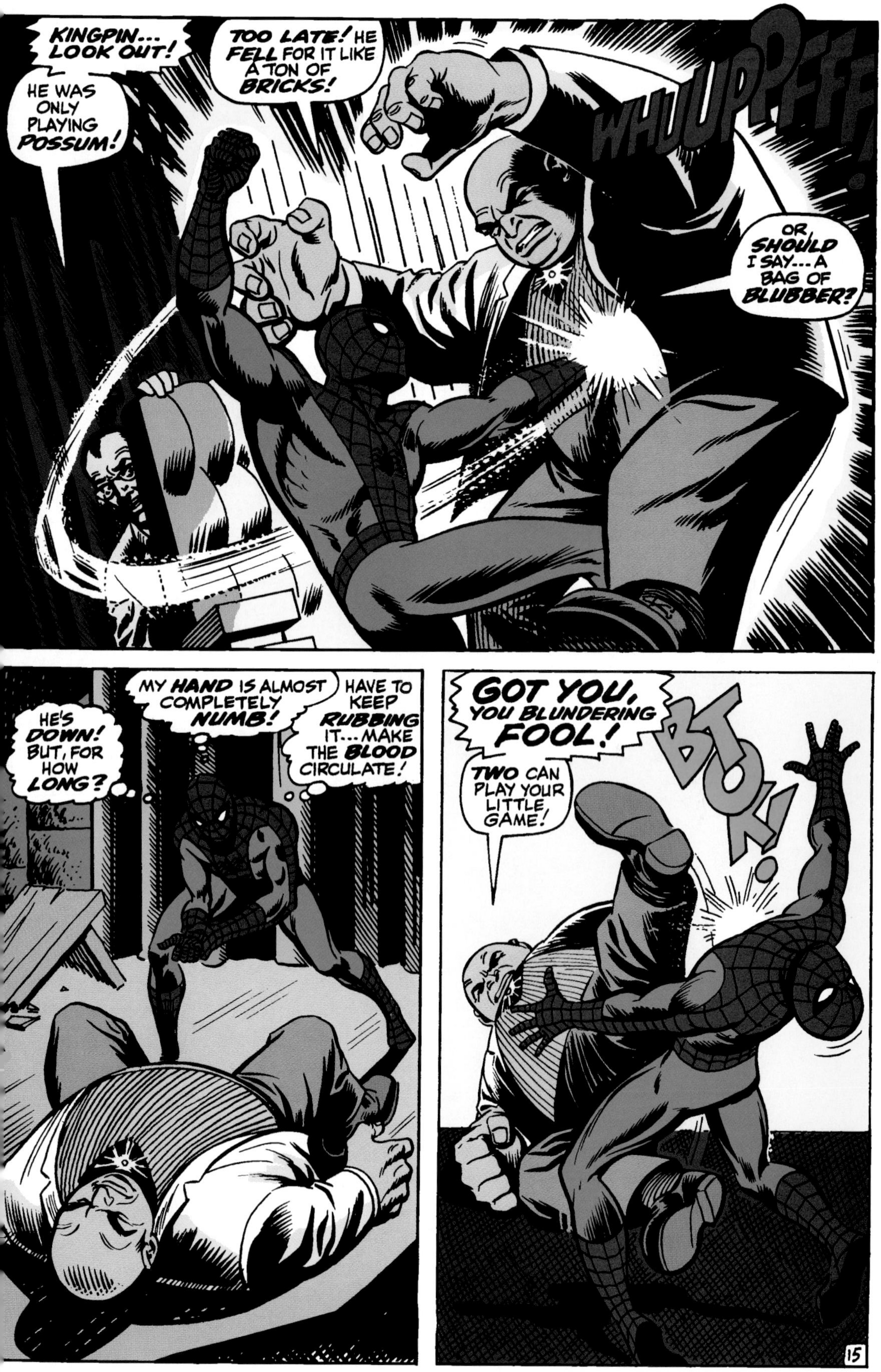
KINGPIN... LOOK OUT!
HE WAS ONLY PLAYING POSSUM!
TOO LATE! HE FELL FOR IT LIKE A TON OF BRICKS!
WHUUPPFFF!
OR, SHOULD I SAY... A BAG OF BLUBBER?
HE'S DOWN! BUT, FOR HOW LONG?
MY HAND IS ALMOST COMPLETELY NUMB!
HAVE TO KEEP RUBBING IT... MAKE THE BLOOD CIRCULATE!
GOT YOU, YOU BLUNDERING FOOL!
TWO CAN PLAY YOUR LITTLE GAME!
BTOK!

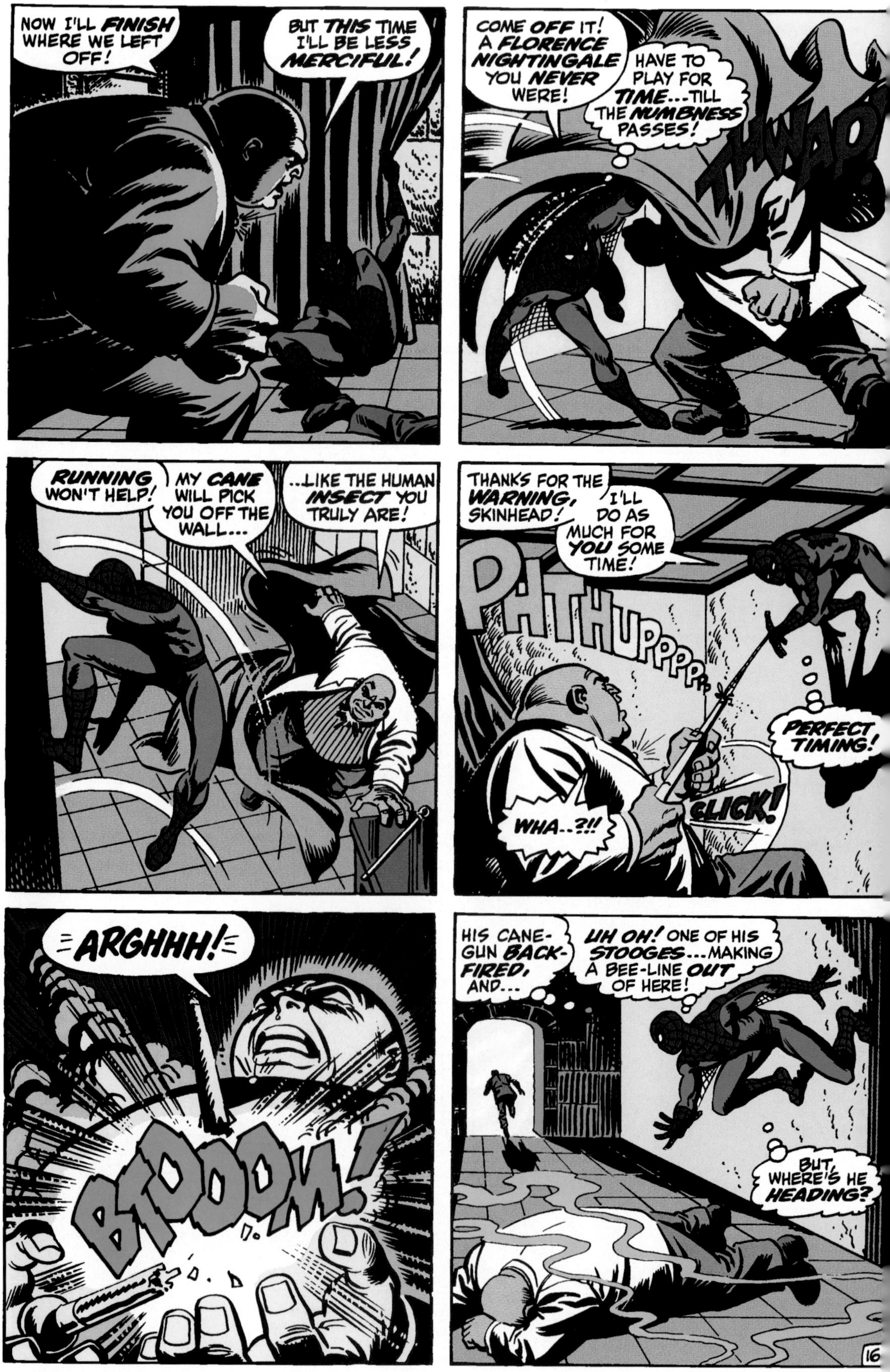
NOW I'LL FINISH WHERE WE LEFT OFF!
BUT THIS TIME I'LL BE LESS MERCIFUL!
COME OFF IT! A FLORENCE NIGHTINGALE YOU NEVER WERE!
HAVE TO PLAY FOR TIME...TILL THE NUMBNESS PASSES!
THWAP!
RUNNING WON'T HELP!
MY CANE WILL PICK YOU OFF THE WALL...
...LIKE THE HUMAN INSECT YOU TRULY ARE!
THANKS FOR THE WARNING, SKINHEAD!
I'LL DO AS MUCH FOR YOU SOME TIME!
PTHUPPPP
PERFECT TIMING!
CLICK!
WHA..?!!
ARGHHH!
BTOOM!
HIS CANE-GUN BACK-FIRED, AND...
UH OH! ONE OF HIS STOOGES...MAKING A BEE-LINE OUT OF HERE!
BUT, WHERE'S HE HEADING?
16

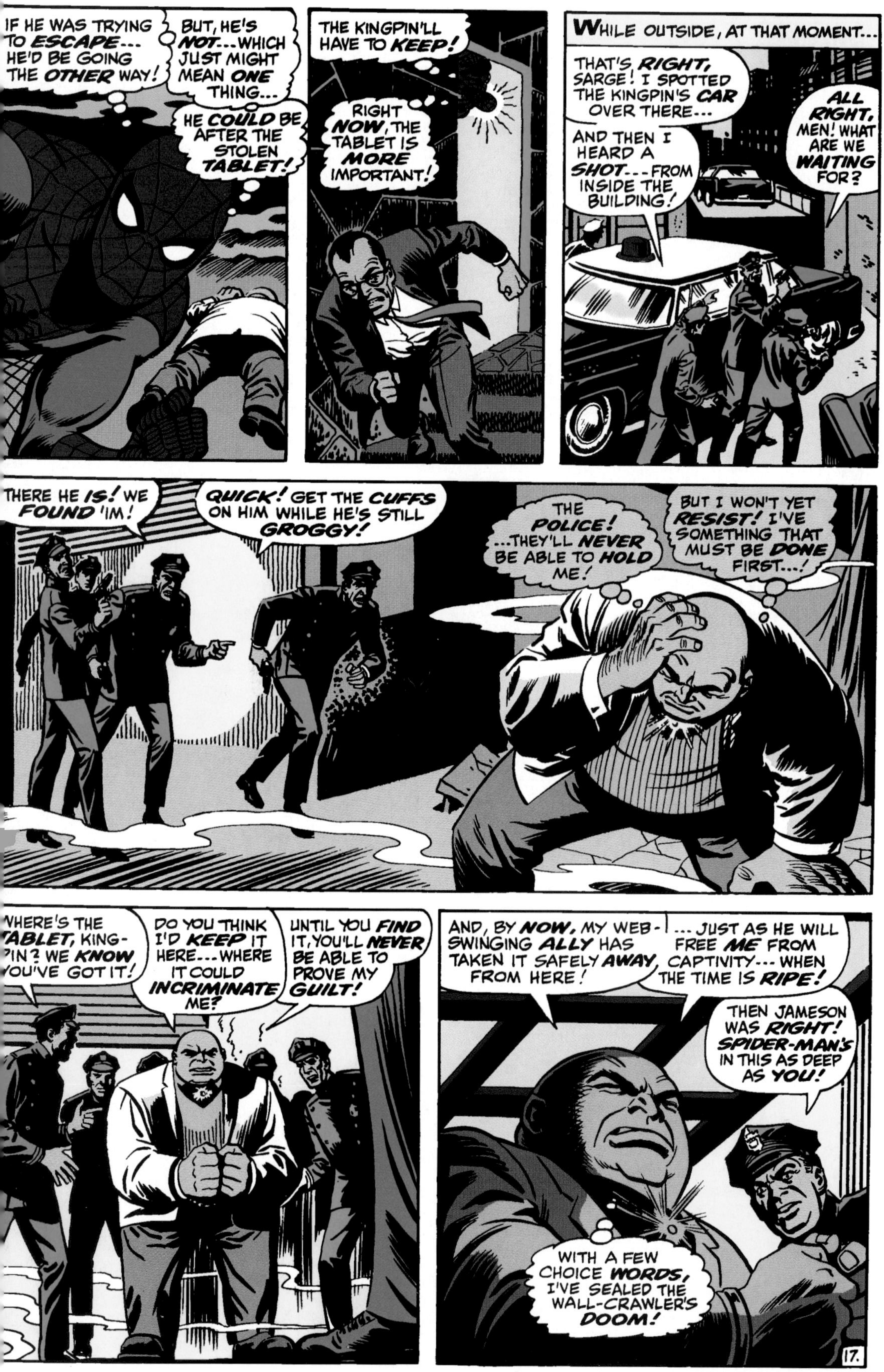
IF HE WAS TRYING TO ESCAPE... HE'D BE GOING THE OTHER WAY!
BUT, HE'S NOT... WHICH JUST MIGHT MEAN ONE THING...
HE COULD BE AFTER THE STOLEN TABLET!
THE KINGPIN'LL HAVE TO KEEP!
RIGHT NOW, THE TABLET IS MORE IMPORTANT!
WHILE OUTSIDE, AT THAT MOMENT...
THAT'S RIGHT, SARGE! I SPOTTED THE KINGPIN'S CAR OVER THERE...
AND THEN I HEARD A SHOT--- FROM INSIDE THE BUILDING!
ALL RIGHT, MEN! WHAT ARE WE WAITING FOR?
THERE HE IS! WE FOUND 'IM!
QUICK! GET THE CUFFS ON HIM WHILE HE'S STILL GROGGY!
THE POLICE! ...THEY'LL NEVER BE ABLE TO HOLD ME!
BUT I WON'T YET RESIST! I'VE SOMETHING THAT MUST BE DONE FIRST...!
WHERE'S THE TABLET, KING-PIN? WE KNOW YOU'VE GOT IT!
DO YOU THINK I'D KEEP IT HERE... WHERE IT COULD INCRIMINATE ME?
UNTIL YOU FIND IT, YOU'LL NEVER BE ABLE TO PROVE MY GUILT!
AND, BY NOW, MY WEB-SWINGING ALLY HAS TAKEN IT SAFELY AWAY FROM HERE!
...JUST AS HE WILL FREE ME FROM CAPTIVITY--- WHEN THE TIME IS RIPE!
THEN JAMESON WAS RIGHT! SPIDER-MAN'S IN THIS AS DEEP AS YOU!
WITH A FEW CHOICE WORDS, I'VE SEALED THE WALL-CRAWLER'S DOOM!
17.

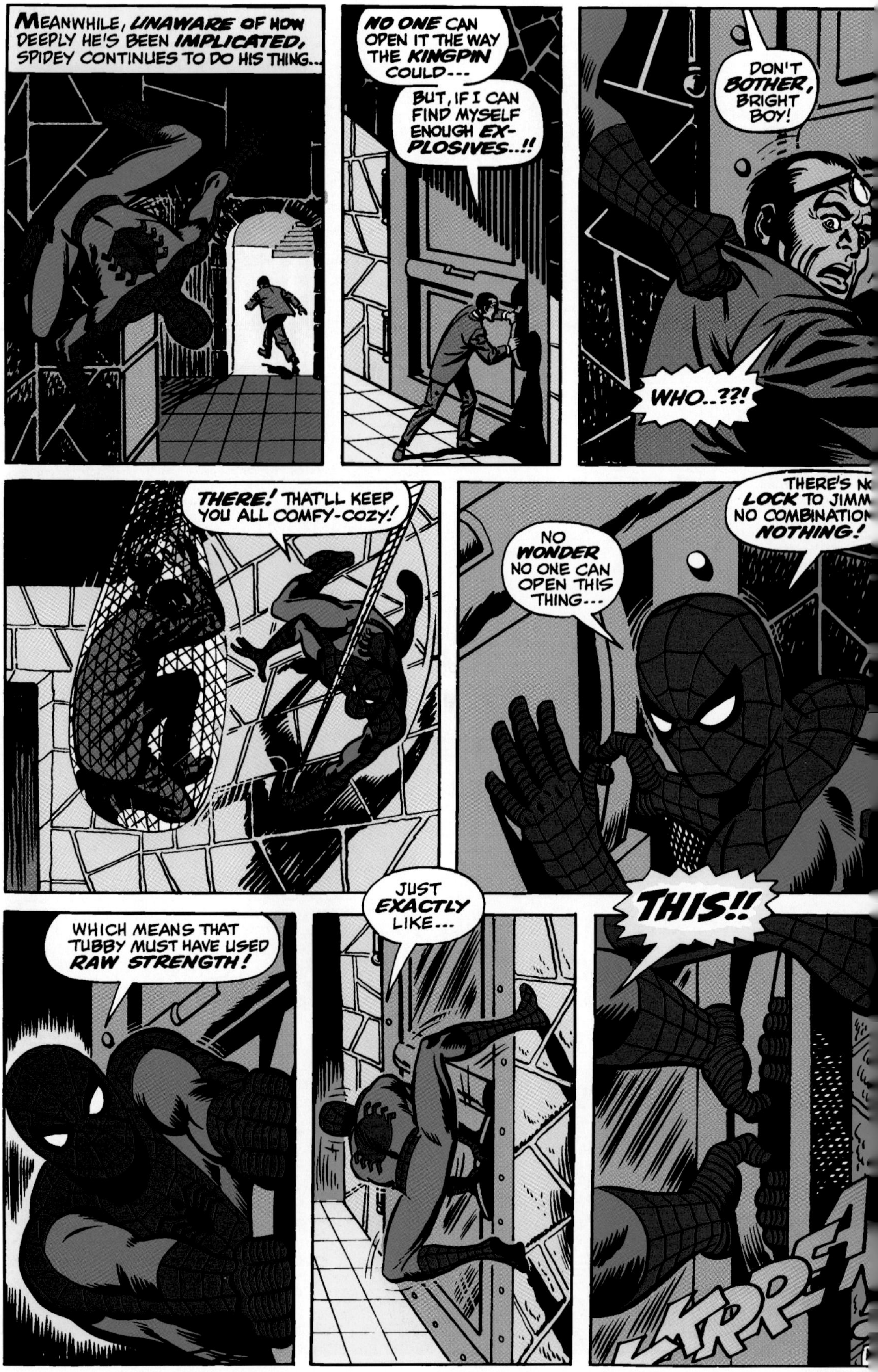
MEANWHILE, UNAWARE OF HOW DEEPLY HE'S BEEN IMPLICATED, SPIDEY CONTINUES TO DO HIS THING...
NO ONE CAN OPEN IT THE WAY THE KINGPIN COULD---
BUT, IF I CAN FIND MYSELF ENOUGH EX-PLOSIVES..!!
DON'T BOTHER, BRIGHT BOY!
WHO..??!
THERE! THAT'LL KEEP YOU ALL COMFY-COZY!
THERE'S NO LOCK TO JIMM NO COMBINATION NOTHING!
NO WONDER NO ONE CAN OPEN THIS THING---
WHICH MEANS THAT TUBBY MUST HAVE USED RAW STRENGTH!
JUST EXACTLY LIKE...
THIS!!

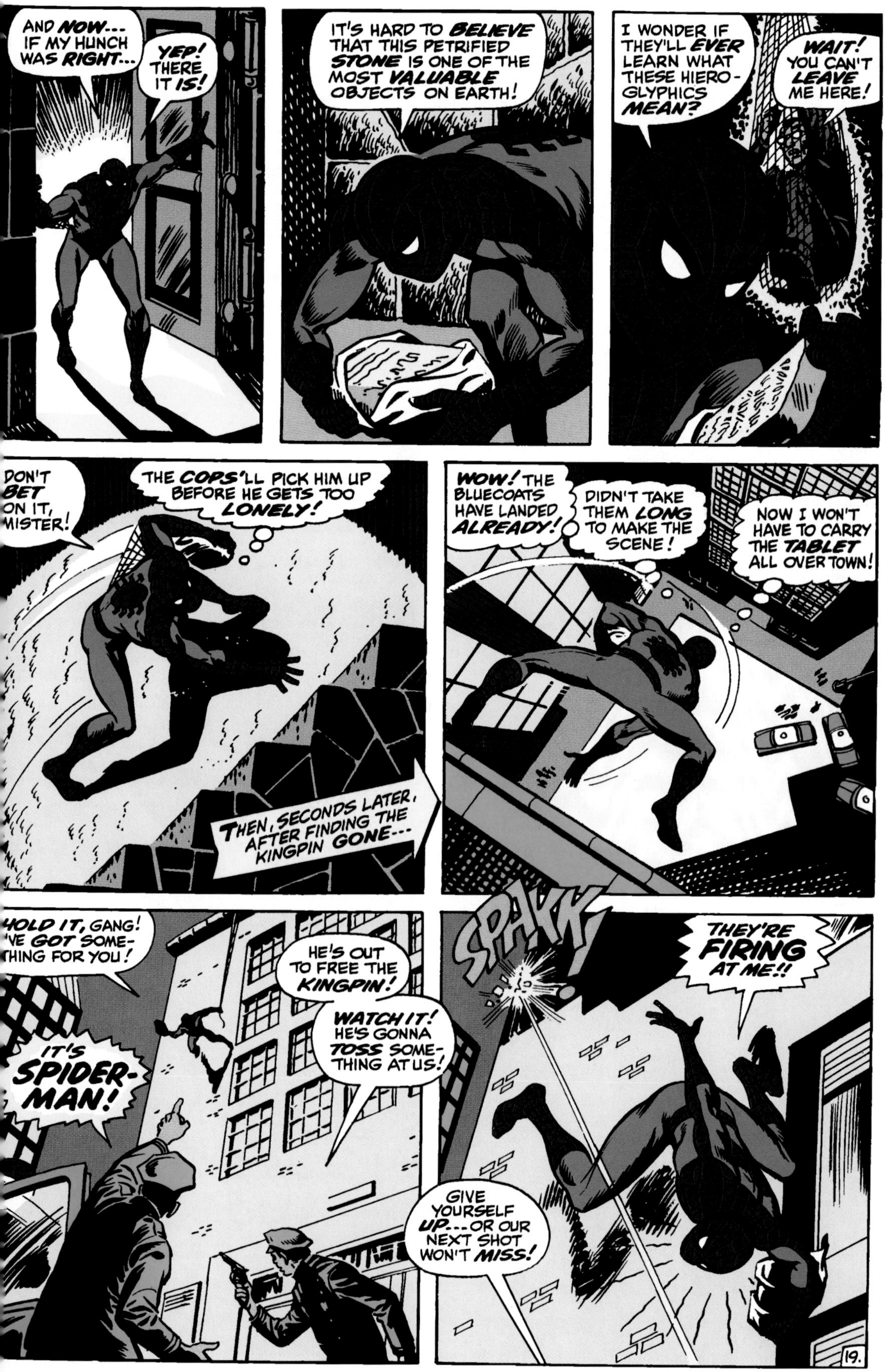

AND NOW... IF MY HUNCH WAS RIGHT...
YEP! THERE IT IS!
IT'S HARD TO BELIEVE THAT THIS PETRIFIED STONE IS ONE OF THE MOST VALUABLE OBJECTS ON EARTH!
I WONDER IF THEY'LL EVER LEARN WHAT THESE HIERO-GLYPHICS MEAN?
WAIT! YOU CAN'T LEAVE ME HERE!
DON'T BET ON IT, MISTER!
THE COPS'LL PICK HIM UP BEFORE HE GETS TOO LONELY!
THEN, SECONDS LATER, AFTER FINDING THE KINGPIN GONE---
WOW! THE BLUECOATS HAVE LANDED ALREADY!
DIDN'T TAKE THEM LONG TO MAKE THE SCENE!
NOW I WON'T HAVE TO CARRY THE TABLET ALL OVER TOWN!
HOLD IT, GANG! VE GOT SOME-THING FOR YOU!
IT'S SPIDER-MAN!
HE'S OUT TO FREE THE KINGPIN!
WATCH IT! HE'S GONNA TOSS SOME-THING AT US!
SPAKK
THEY'RE FIRING AT ME!!
GIVE YOURSELF UP...OR OUR NEXT SHOT WON'T MISS!

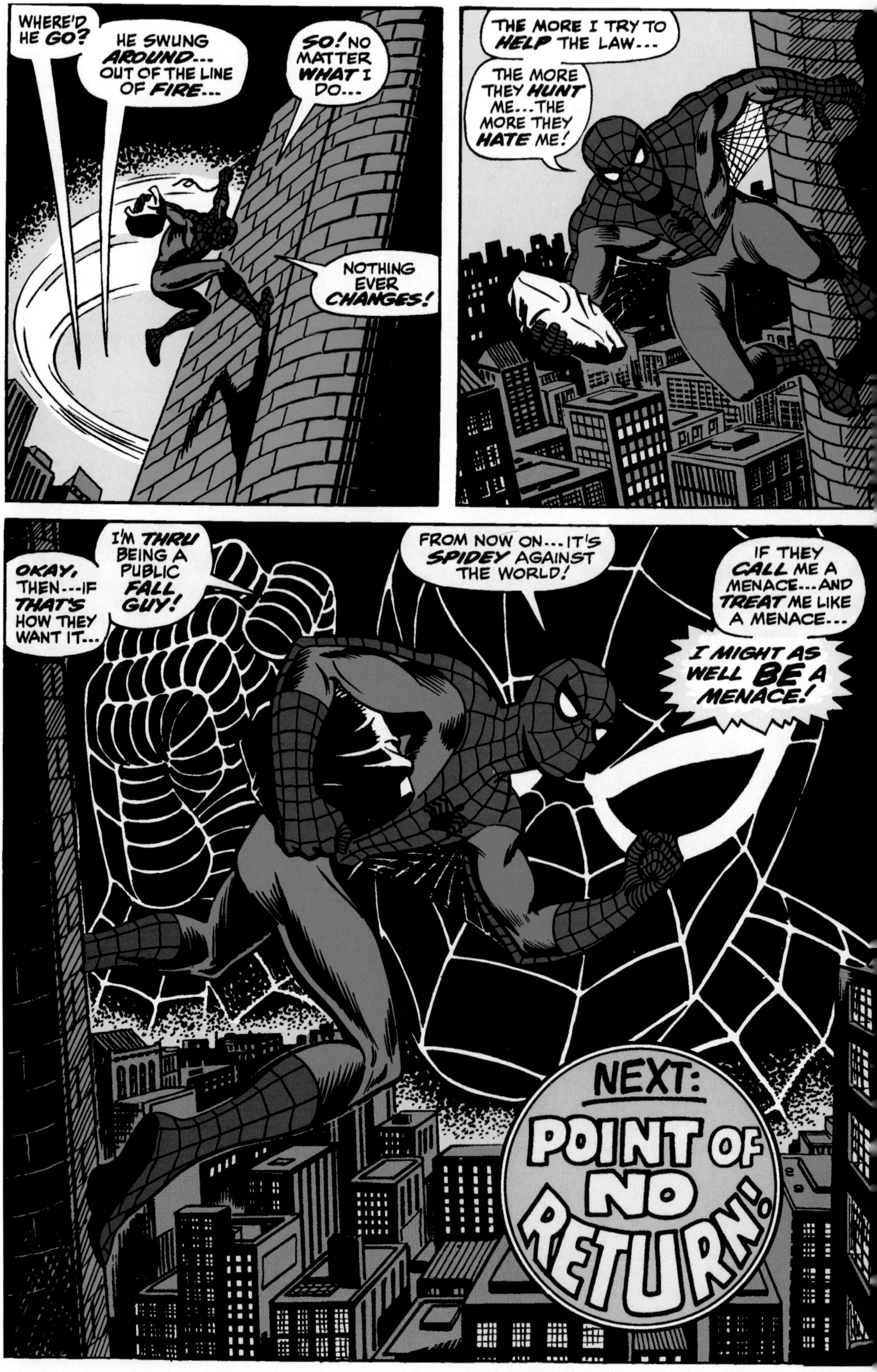
WHERE'D HE GO?
HE SWUNG AROUND... OUT OF THE LINE OF FIRE...
SO! NO MATTER WHAT I DO...
NOTHING EVER CHANGES!
THE MORE I TRY TO HELP THE LAW...
THE MORE THEY HUNT ME... THE MORE THEY HATE ME!
OKAY, THEN---IF THAT'S HOW THEY WANT IT...
I'M THRU BEING A PUBLIC FALL GUY!
FROM NOW ON... IT'S SPIDEY AGAINST THE WORLD!
IF THEY CALL ME A MENACE... AND TREAT ME LIKE A MENACE...
I MIGHT AS WELL BE A MENACE!
NEXT: POINT OF NO RETURN!

amazing spider-man #108

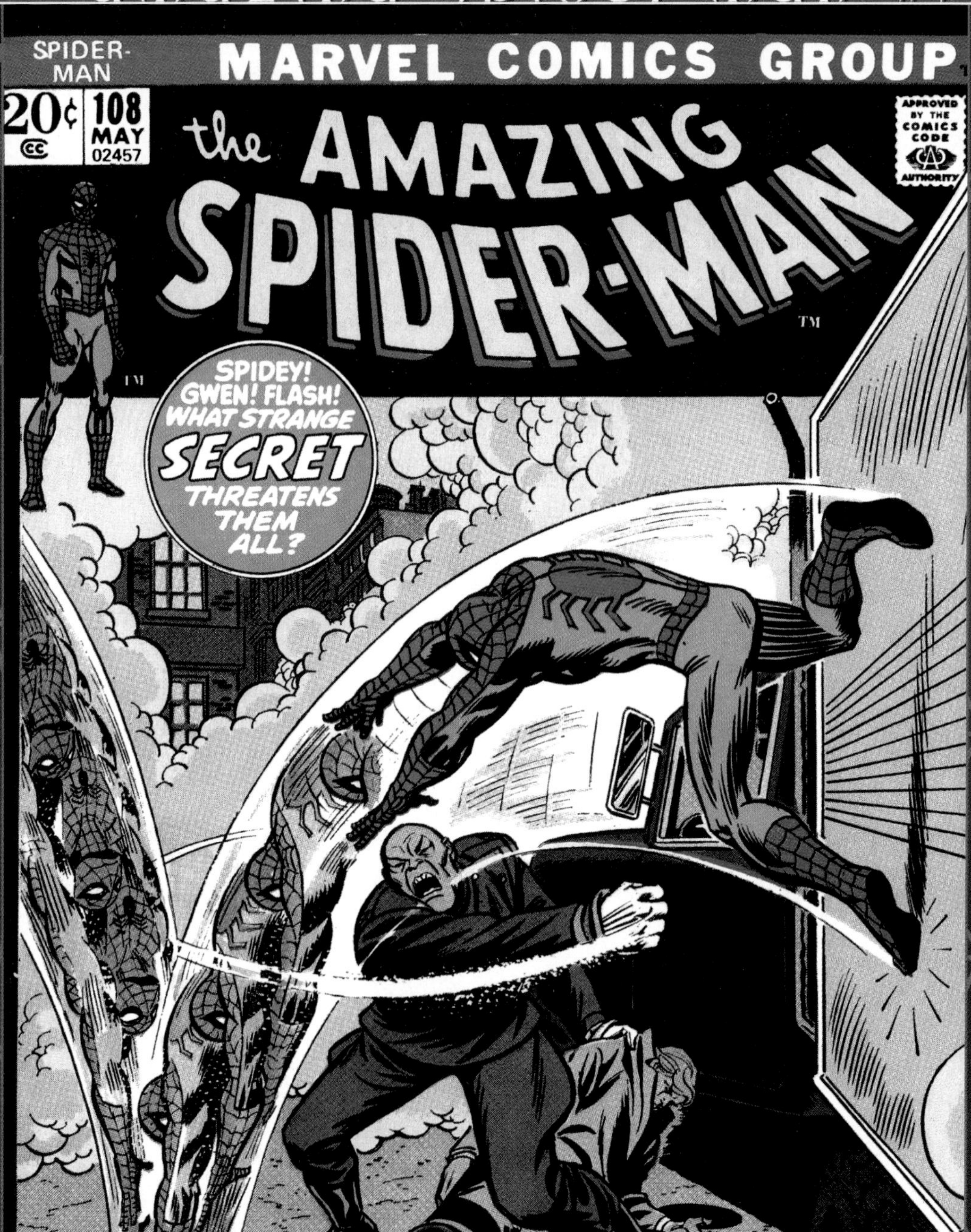
SPIDER-MAN
MARVEL COMICS GROUP
20¢ CC
108 MAY 02457
APPROVED BY THE COMICS CODE AUTHORITY
the AMAZING SPIDER-MAN
TM
SPIDEY! GWEN! FLASH! WHAT STRANGE SECRET THREATENS THEM ALL?
ROMITA
NEW! UNEXPECTED!
MARKED FOR

may 1972

THE VIETNAM STORY LINE OF #108-109 HAS BEEN KNOWN AS MY FAVORITE SEQUENCE OF ALL MY SPIDER-MAN STORIES. THIS GAVE ME SO MANY CHANCES TO ENJOY THE ART CHORES. MY IDOL WAS MILTON CANIFF, WHOSE "TERRY AND THE PIRATES" OF MY YOUTH GUIDED ME ON EVERY PAGE IN THESE TWO STORIES.

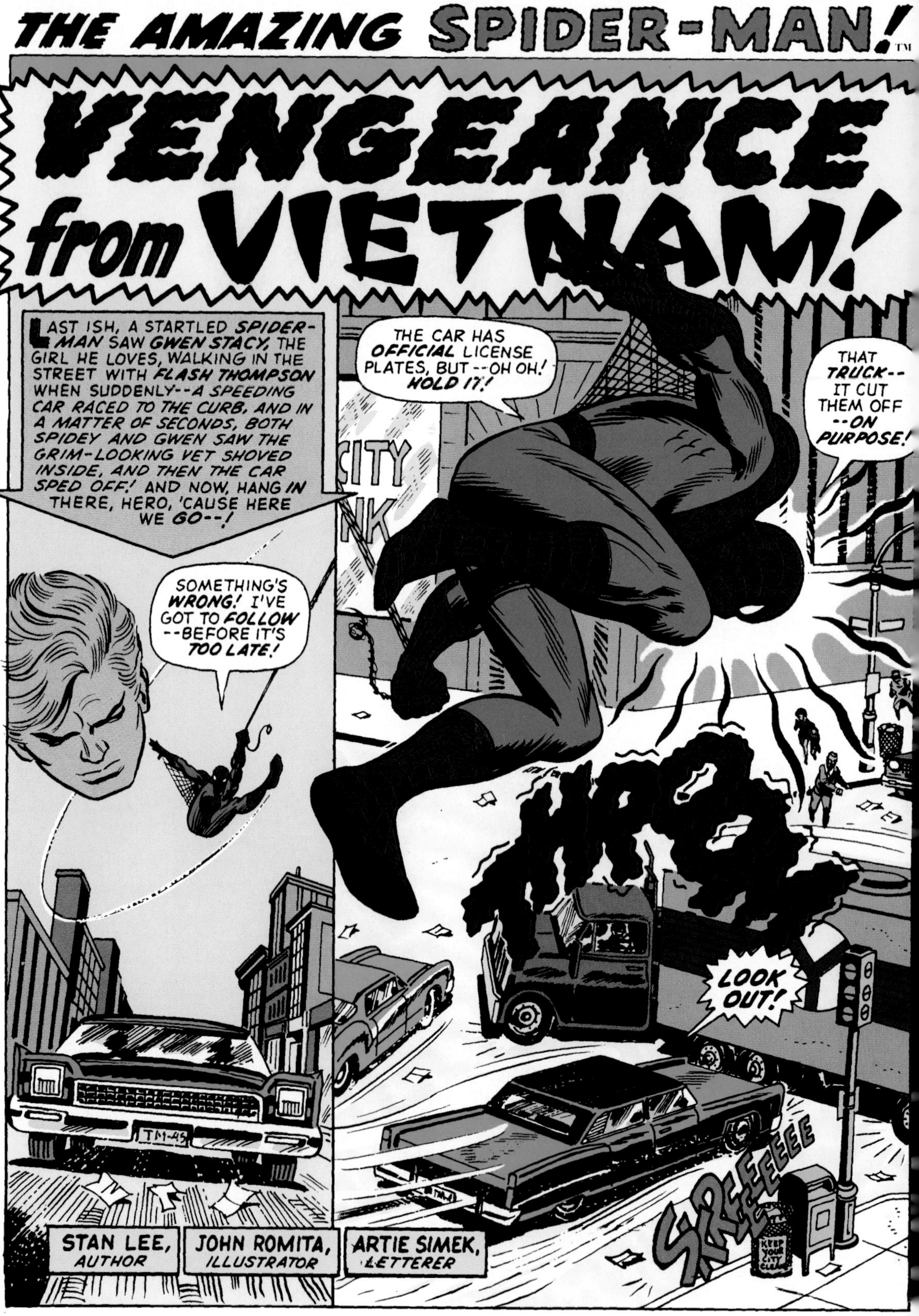
THE AMAZING SPIDER-MAN!™
VENGEANCE from VIETNAM!
LAST ISH, A STARTLED SPIDER-MAN SAW GWEN STACY, THE GIRL HE LOVES, WALKING IN THE STREET WITH FLASH THOMPSON WHEN SUDDENLY--A SPEEDING CAR RACED TO THE CURB, AND IN A MATTER OF SECONDS, BOTH SPIDEY AND GWEN SAW THE GRIM-LOOKING VET SHOVED INSIDE, AND THEN THE CAR SPED OFF! AND NOW, HANG IN THERE, HERO, 'CAUSE HERE WE GO--!
SOMETHING'S WRONG! I'VE GOT TO FOLLOW --BEFORE IT'S TOO LATE!
TM-45
STAN LEE, AUTHOR
JOHN ROMITA, ILLUSTRATOR
ARTIE SIMEK, LETTERER
THE CAR HAS OFFICIAL LICENSE PLATES, BUT --OH OH! HOLD IT!
THAT TRUCK-- IT CUT THEM OFF --ON PURPOSE!
CITY
NK
THOK
LOOK OUT!
SKREEEEEE
KEEP YOUR CITY CLEAN

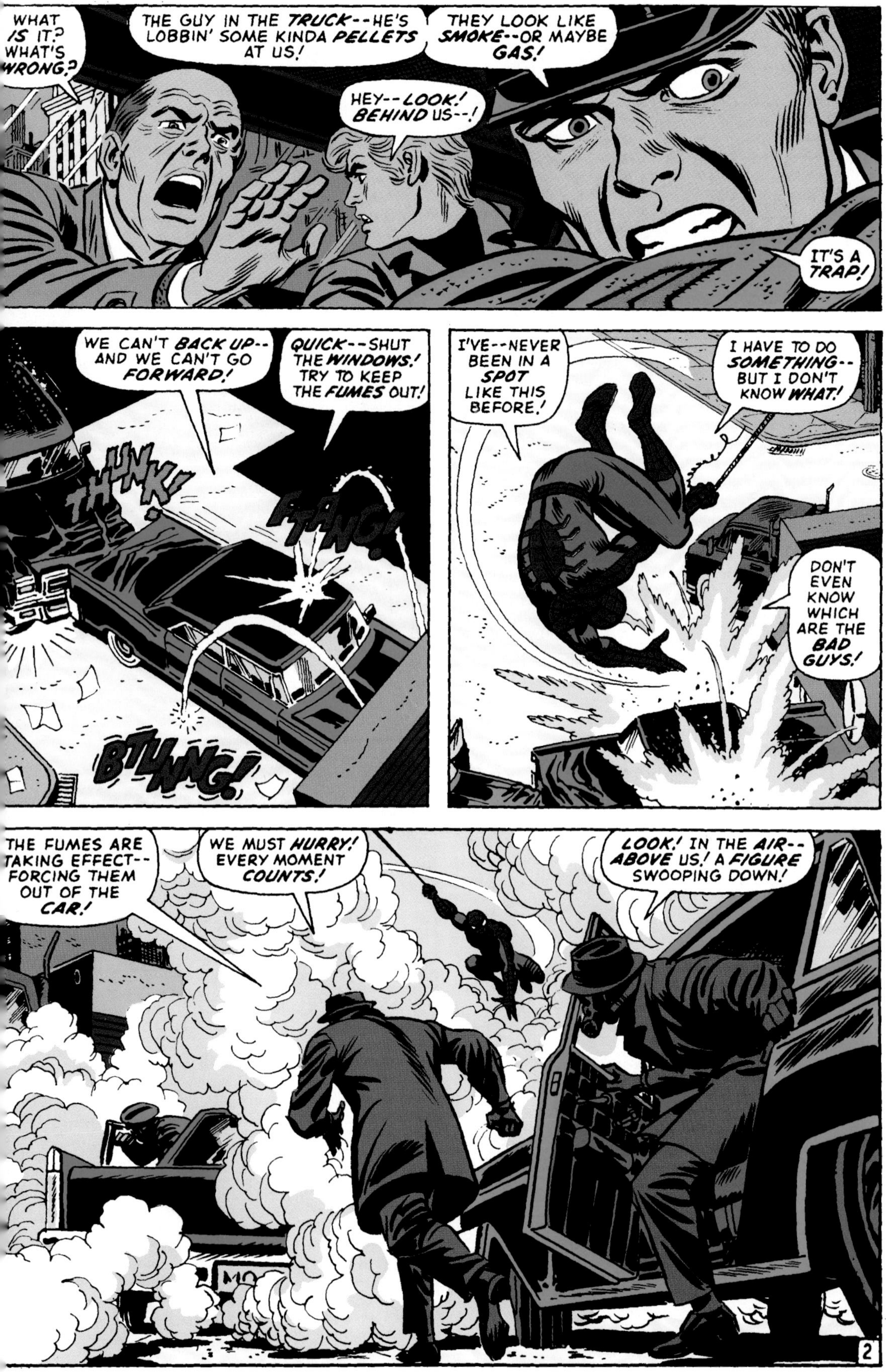
WHAT IS IT? WHAT'S WRONG?
THE GUY IN THE TRUCK--HE'S LOBBIN' SOME KINDA PELLETS AT US!
THEY LOOK LIKE SMOKE--OR MAYBE GAS!
HEY--LOOK! BEHIND US--!
IT'S A TRAP!
WE CAN'T BACK UP--AND WE CAN'T GO FORWARD!
QUICK--SHUT THE WINDOWS! TRY TO KEEP THE FUMES OUT!
THUNK!
PTANG!
BTUNNG!
I'VE--NEVER BEEN IN A SPOT LIKE THIS BEFORE!
I HAVE TO DO SOMETHING--BUT I DON'T KNOW WHAT!
DON'T EVEN KNOW WHICH ARE THE BAD GUYS!
THE FUMES ARE TAKING EFFECT--FORCING THEM OUT OF THE CAR!
WE MUST HURRY! EVERY MOMENT COUNTS!
LOOK! IN THE AIR--ABOVE US! A FIGURE SWOOPING DOWN!
2

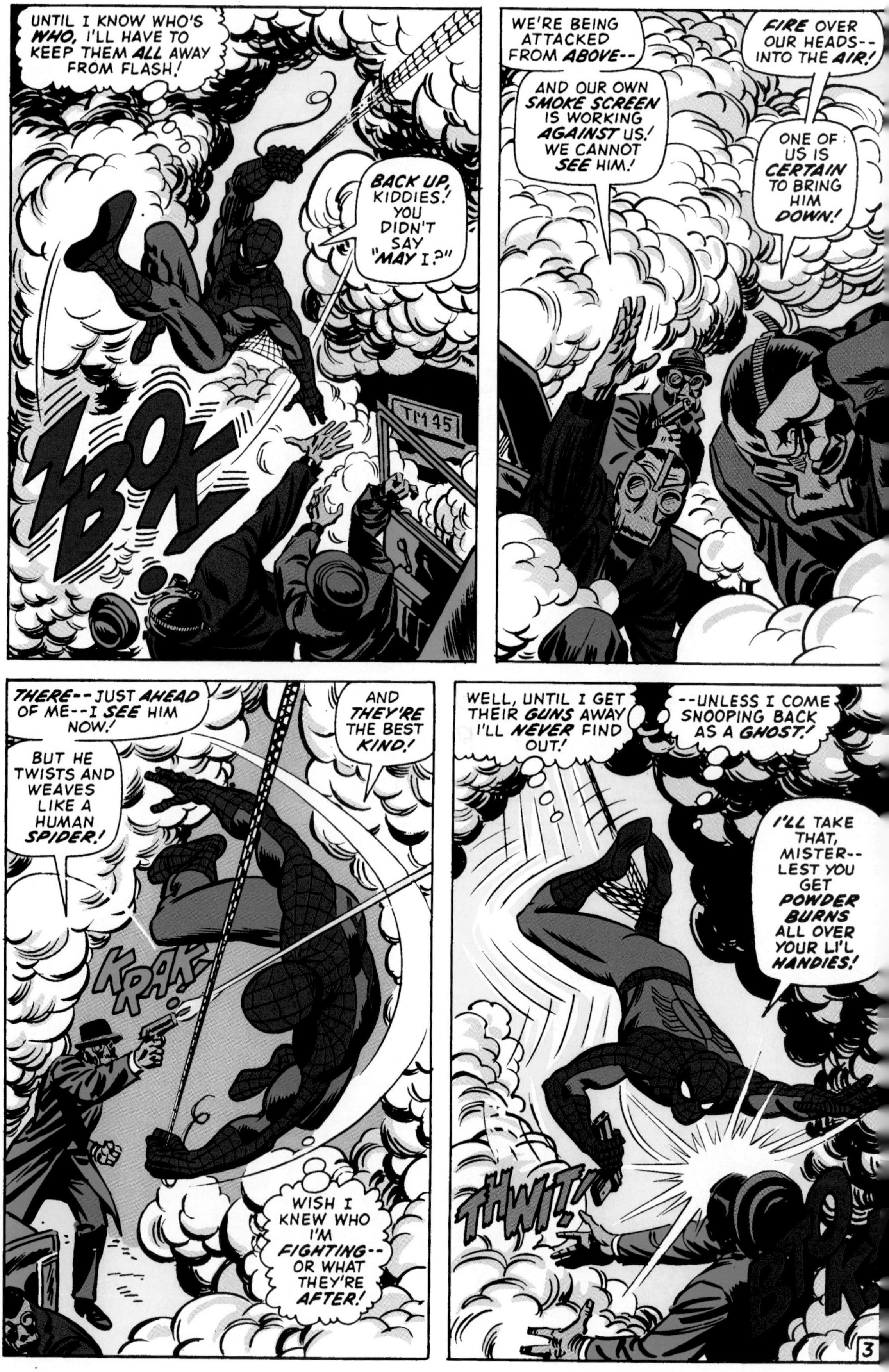
UNTIL I KNOW WHO'S WHO, I'LL HAVE TO KEEP THEM ALL AWAY FROM FLASH!
BACK UP, KIDDIES! YOU DIDN'T SAY "MAY I?"
ZBOK!
TM 45
WE'RE BEING ATTACKED FROM ABOVE--
AND OUR OWN SMOKE SCREEN IS WORKING AGAINST US! WE CANNOT SEE HIM!
FIRE OVER OUR HEADS--INTO THE AIR!
ONE OF US IS CERTAIN TO BRING HIM DOWN!
THERE--JUST AHEAD OF ME--I SEE HIM NOW!
BUT HE TWISTS AND WEAVES LIKE A HUMAN SPIDER!
AND THEY'RE THE BEST KIND!
KRAK!
WISH I KNEW WHO I'M FIGHTING--OR WHAT THEY'RE AFTER!
WELL, UNTIL I GET THEIR GUNS AWAY I'LL NEVER FIND OUT!
--UNLESS I COME SNOOPING BACK AS A GHOST!
I'LL TAKE THAT, MISTER--LEST YOU GET POWDER BURNS ALL OVER YOUR LI'L HANDIES!
THWIT!
3

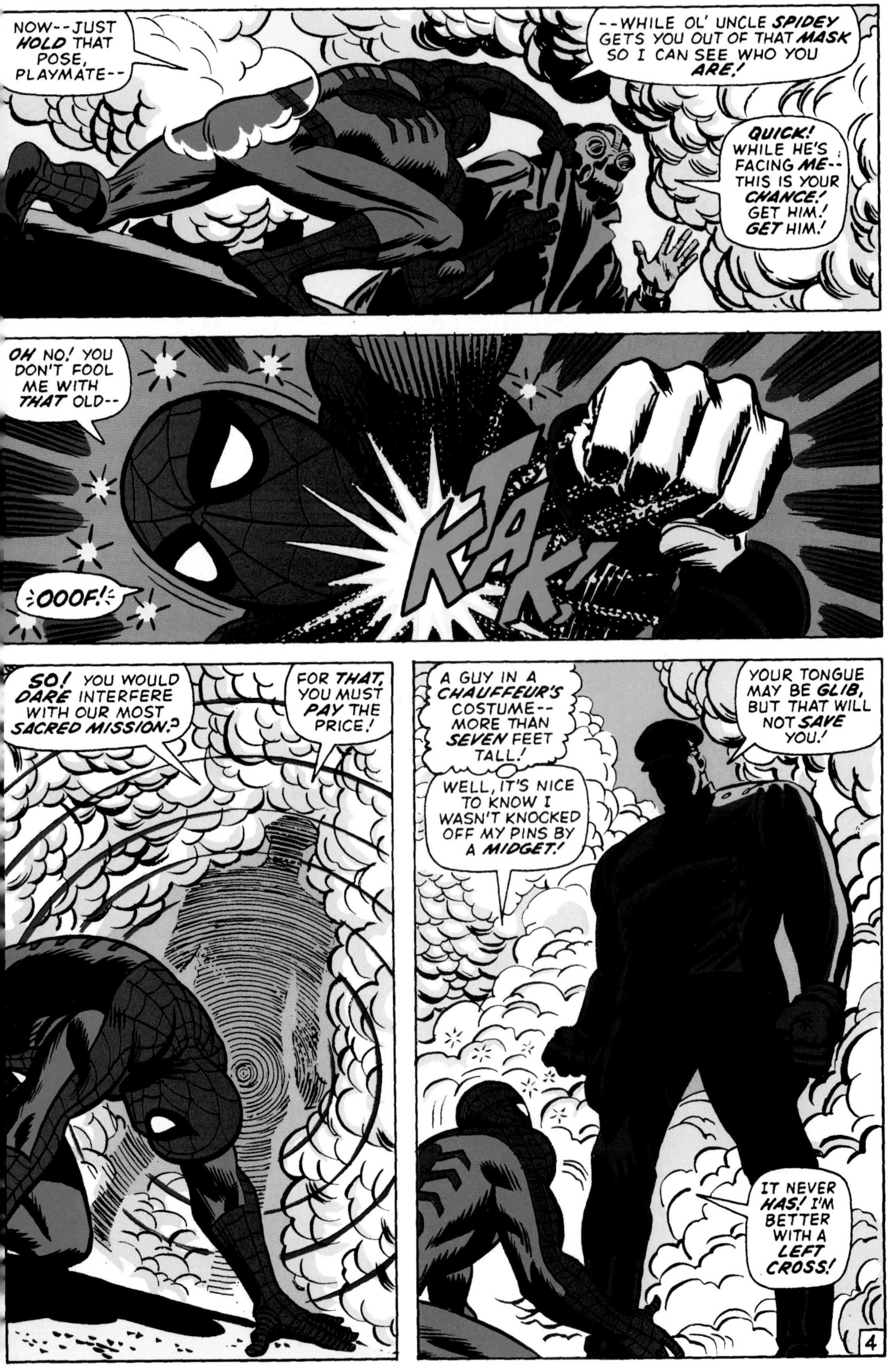
NOW--JUST HOLD THAT POSE, PLAYMATE--
--WHILE OL' UNCLE SPIDEY GETS YOU OUT OF THAT MASK SO I CAN SEE WHO YOU ARE!
QUICK! WHILE HE'S FACING ME--THIS IS YOUR CHANCE! GET HIM! GET HIM!
OH NO! YOU DON'T FOOL ME WITH THAT OLD--
OOOF!
TAKK!
SO! YOU WOULD DARE INTERFERE WITH OUR MOST SACRED MISSION?
FOR THAT, YOU MUST PAY THE PRICE!
A GUY IN A CHAUFFEUR'S COSTUME--MORE THAN SEVEN FEET TALL!
WELL, IT'S NICE TO KNOW I WASN'T KNOCKED OFF MY PINS BY A MIDGET!
YOUR TONGUE MAY BE GLIB, BUT THAT WILL NOT SAVE YOU!
IT NEVER HAS! I'M BETTER WITH A LEFT CROSS!
4

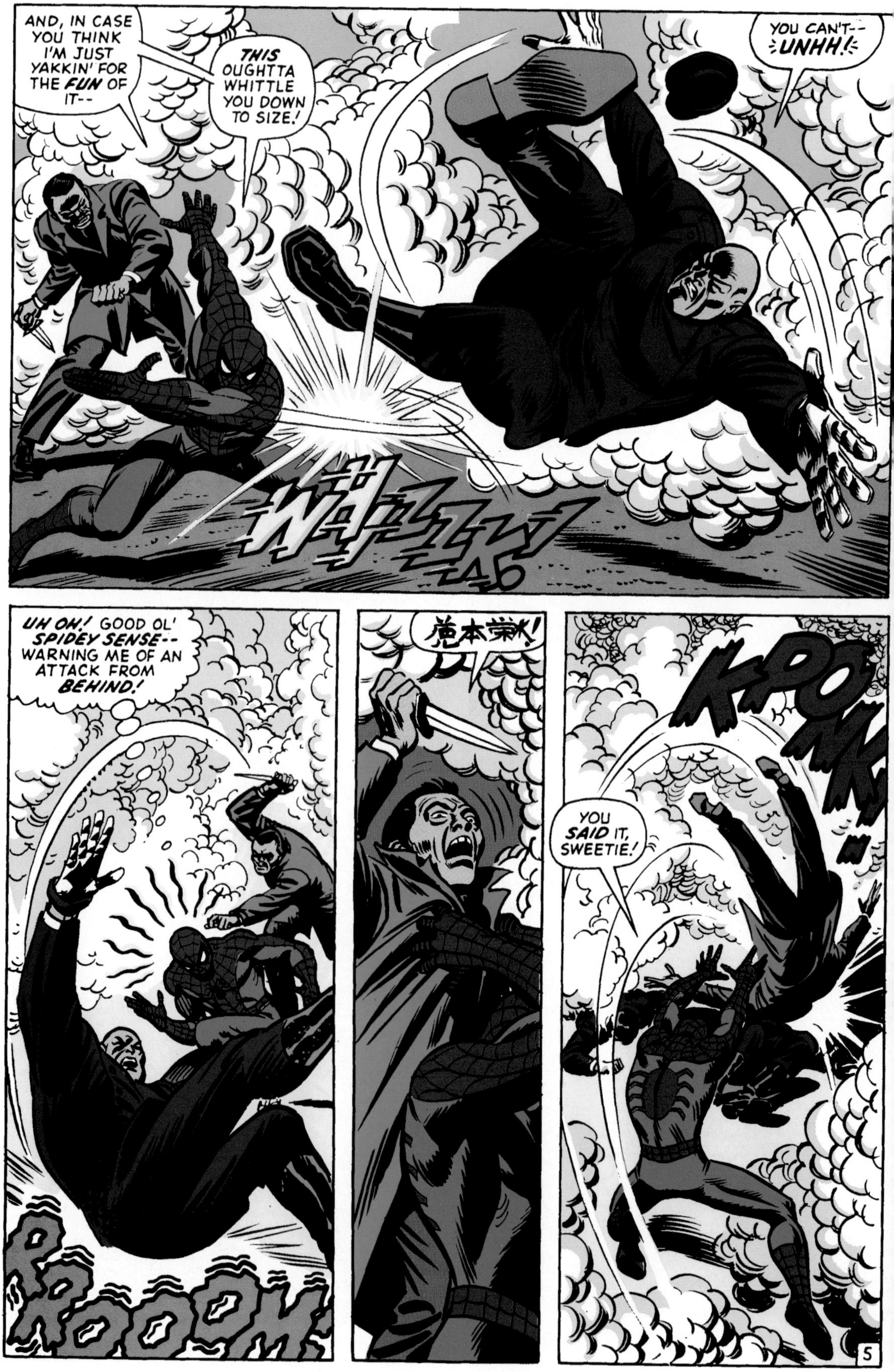
AND, IN CASE YOU THINK I'M JUST YAKKIN' FOR THE FUN OF IT--
THIS OUGHTTA WHITTLE YOU DOWN TO SIZE!
YOU CAN'T-- UNHH!
UH OH! GOOD OL' SPIDEY SENSE-- WARNING ME OF AN ATTACK FROM BEHIND!
KPONK!!
YOU SAID IT, SWEETIE!
5

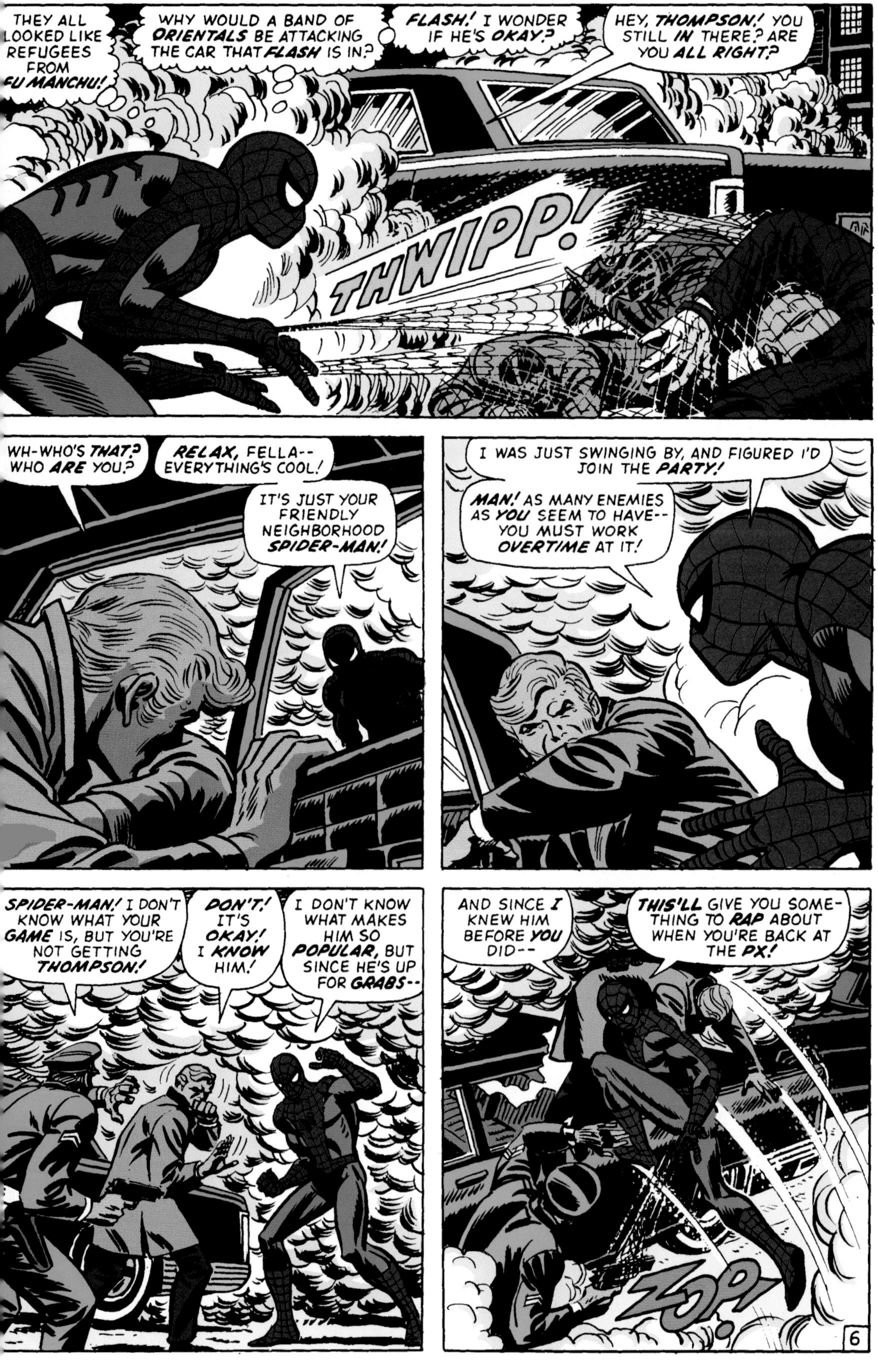
THEY ALL LOOKED LIKE REFUGEES FROM FU MANCHU!
WHY WOULD A BAND OF ORIENTALS BE ATTACKING THE CAR THAT FLASH IS IN?
FLASH! I WONDER IF HE'S OKAY?
HEY, THOMPSON! YOU STILL IN THERE? ARE YOU ALL RIGHT?
THWIPP!
WH-WHO'S THAT? WHO ARE YOU?
RELAX, FELLA-- EVERYTHING'S COOL!
IT'S JUST YOUR FRIENDLY NEIGHBORHOOD SPIDER-MAN!
I WAS JUST SWINGING BY, AND FIGURED I'D JOIN THE PARTY!
MAN! AS MANY ENEMIES AS YOU SEEM TO HAVE-- YOU MUST WORK OVERTIME AT IT!
SPIDER-MAN! I DON'T KNOW WHAT YOUR GAME IS, BUT YOU'RE NOT GETTING THOMPSON!
DON'T! IT'S OKAY! I KNOW HIM!
I DON'T KNOW WHAT MAKES HIM SO POPULAR, BUT SINCE HE'S UP FOR GRABS--
AND SINCE I KNEW HIM BEFORE YOU DID--
THIS'LL GIVE YOU SOMETHING TO RAP ABOUT WHEN YOU'RE BACK AT THE PX!
ZOP!

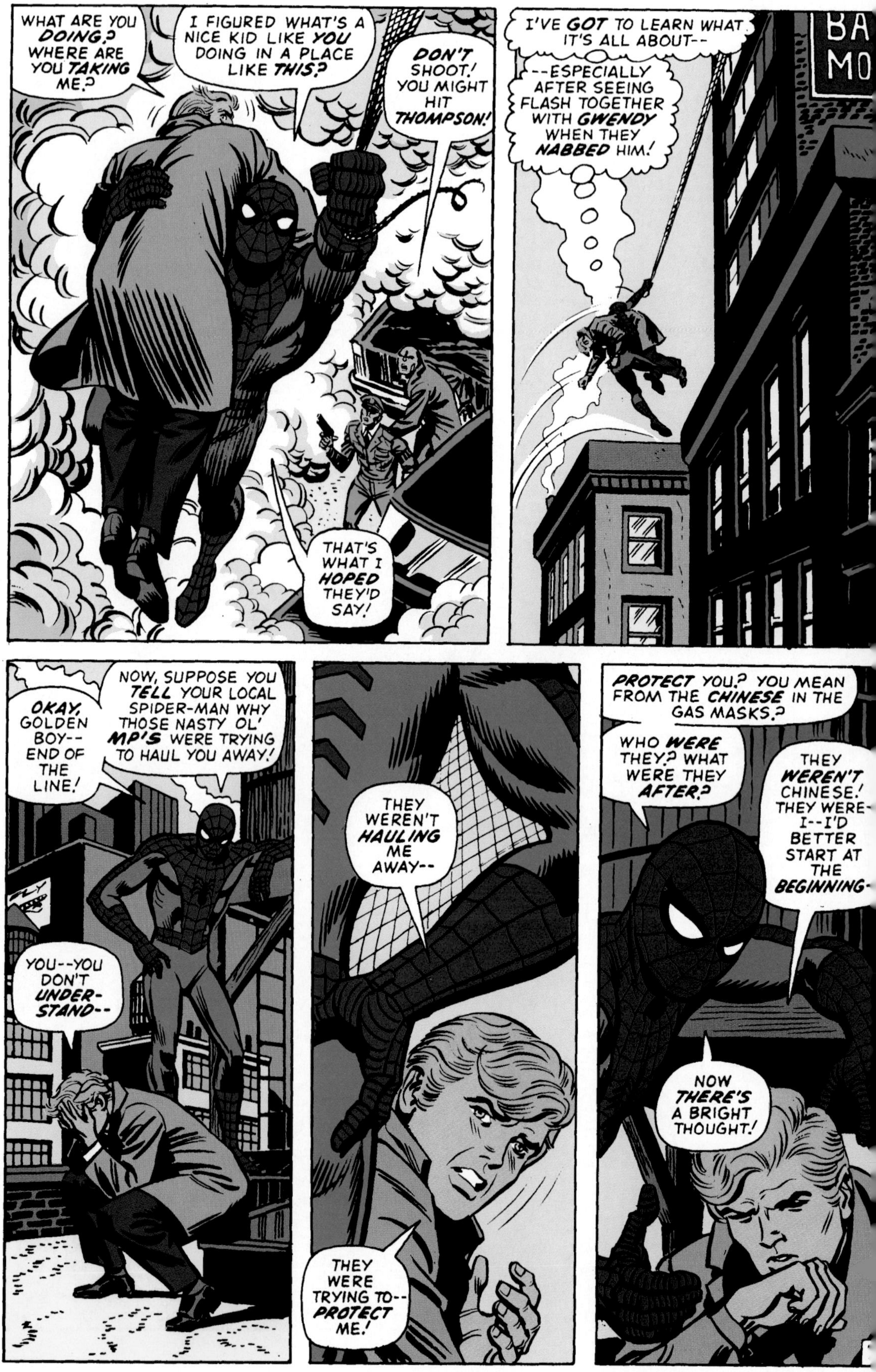
WHAT ARE YOU DOING? WHERE ARE YOU TAKING ME?
I FIGURED WHAT'S A NICE KID LIKE YOU DOING IN A PLACE LIKE THIS?
DON'T SHOOT! YOU MIGHT HIT THOMPSON!
THAT'S WHAT I HOPED THEY'D SAY!
I'VE GOT TO LEARN WHAT IT'S ALL ABOUT--
--ESPECIALLY AFTER SEEING FLASH TOGETHER WITH GWENDY WHEN THEY NABBED HIM!
OKAY, GOLDEN BOY-- END OF THE LINE!
NOW, SUPPOSE YOU TELL YOUR LOCAL SPIDER-MAN WHY THOSE NASTY OL' MP'S WERE TRYING TO HAUL YOU AWAY!
YOU--YOU DON'T UNDER-STAND--
THEY WEREN'T HAULING ME AWAY--
THEY WERE TRYING TO-- PROTECT ME!
PROTECT YOU? YOU MEAN FROM THE CHINESE IN THE GAS MASKS?
WHO WERE THEY? WHAT WERE THEY AFTER?
THEY WEREN'T CHINESE! THEY WERE-- I--I'D BETTER START AT THE BEGINNING--
NOW THERE'S A BRIGHT THOUGHT!

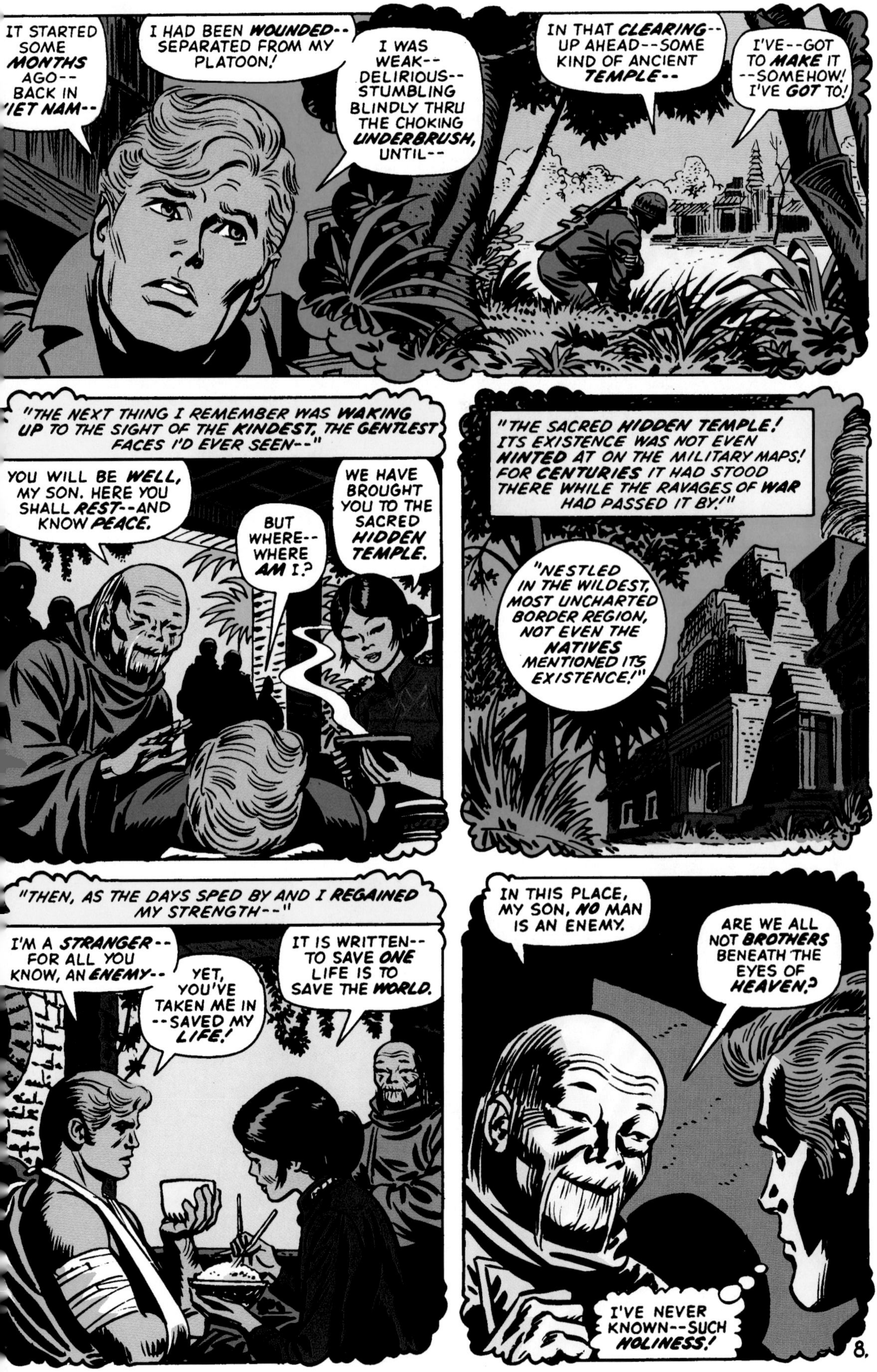
IT STARTED SOME MONTHS AGO-- BACK IN VIET NAM--
I HAD BEEN WOUNDED-- SEPARATED FROM MY PLATOON!
I WAS WEAK-- DELIRIOUS-- STUMBLING BLINDLY THRU THE CHOKING UNDERBRUSH, UNTIL--
IN THAT CLEARING-- UP AHEAD--SOME KIND OF ANCIENT TEMPLE--
I'VE--GOT TO MAKE IT --SOMEHOW! I'VE GOT TO!
"THE NEXT THING I REMEMBER WAS WAKING UP TO THE SIGHT OF THE KINDEST, THE GENTLEST FACES I'D EVER SEEN--"
YOU WILL BE WELL, MY SON. HERE YOU SHALL REST--AND KNOW PEACE.
BUT WHERE-- WHERE AM I?
WE HAVE BROUGHT YOU TO THE SACRED HIDDEN TEMPLE.
"THE SACRED HIDDEN TEMPLE! ITS EXISTENCE WAS NOT EVEN HINTED AT ON THE MILITARY MAPS! FOR CENTURIES IT HAD STOOD THERE WHILE THE RAVAGES OF WAR HAD PASSED IT BY!"
"NESTLED IN THE WILDEST, MOST UNCHARTED BORDER REGION, NOT EVEN THE NATIVES MENTIONED ITS EXISTENCE!"
"THEN, AS THE DAYS SPED BY AND I REGAINED MY STRENGTH--"
I'M A STRANGER-- FOR ALL YOU KNOW, AN ENEMY--
YET, YOU'VE TAKEN ME IN --SAVED MY LIFE!
IT IS WRITTEN-- TO SAVE ONE LIFE IS TO SAVE THE WORLD.
IN THIS PLACE, MY SON, NO MAN IS AN ENEMY.
ARE WE ALL NOT BROTHERS BENEATH THE EYES OF HEAVEN?
I'VE NEVER KNOWN--SUCH HOLINESS!

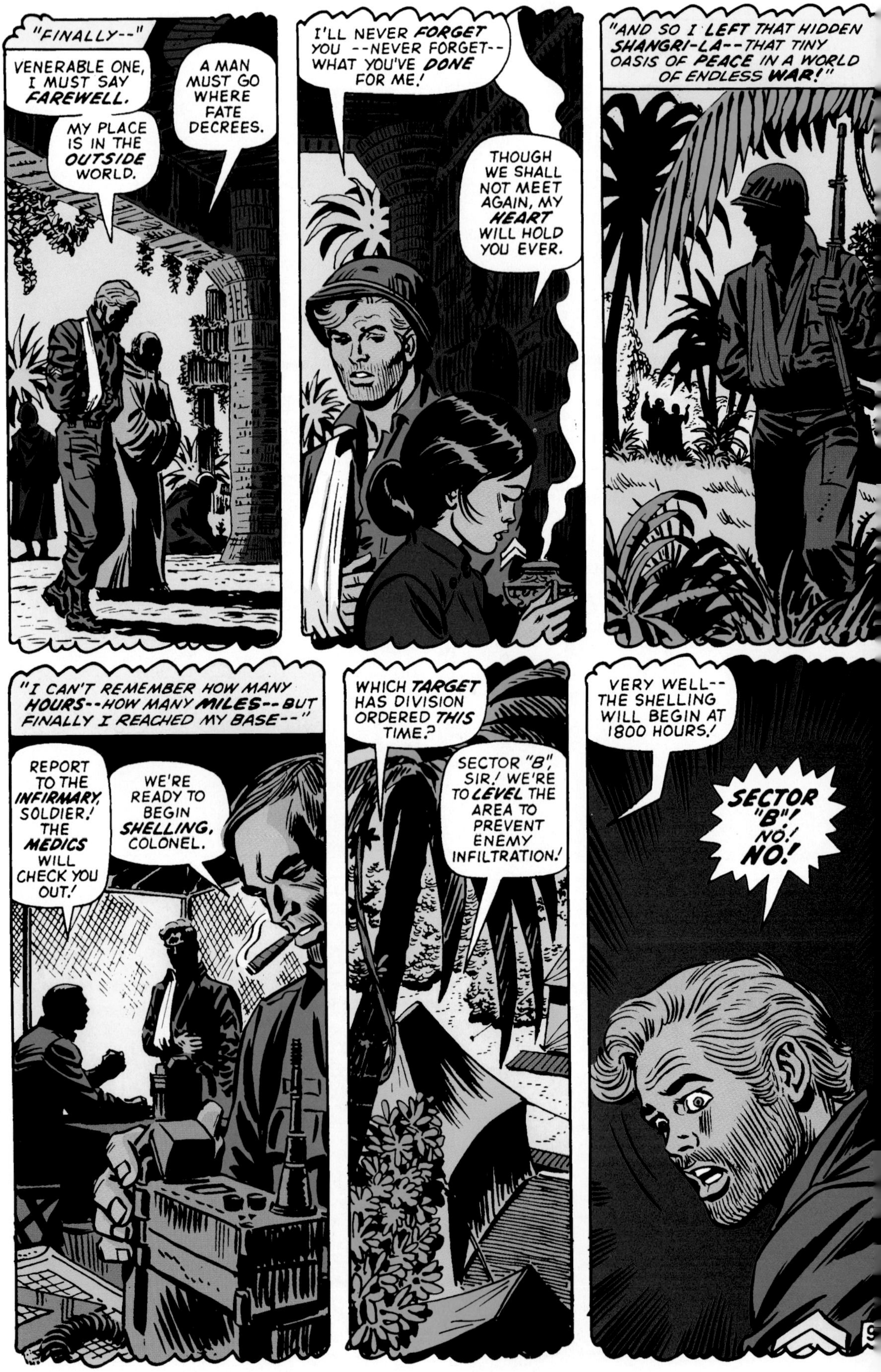
"FINALLY--"
VENERABLE ONE, I MUST SAY FAREWELL.
MY PLACE IS IN THE OUTSIDE WORLD.
A MAN MUST GO WHERE FATE DECREES.
I'LL NEVER FORGET YOU --NEVER FORGET-- WHAT YOU'VE DONE FOR ME!
THOUGH WE SHALL NOT MEET AGAIN, MY HEART WILL HOLD YOU EVER.
"AND SO I LEFT THAT HIDDEN SHANGRI-LA--THAT TINY OASIS OF PEACE IN A WORLD OF ENDLESS WAR!"
"I CAN'T REMEMBER HOW MANY HOURS--HOW MANY MILES--BUT FINALLY I REACHED MY BASE--"
REPORT TO THE INFIRMARY, SOLDIER! THE MEDICS WILL CHECK YOU OUT!
WE'RE READY TO BEGIN SHELLING, COLONEL.
WHICH TARGET HAS DIVISION ORDERED THIS TIME?
SECTOR "B", SIR! WE'RE TO LEVEL THE AREA TO PREVENT ENEMY INFILTRATION!
VERY WELL-- THE SHELLING WILL BEGIN AT 1800 HOURS!
SECTOR "B"! NO! NO!

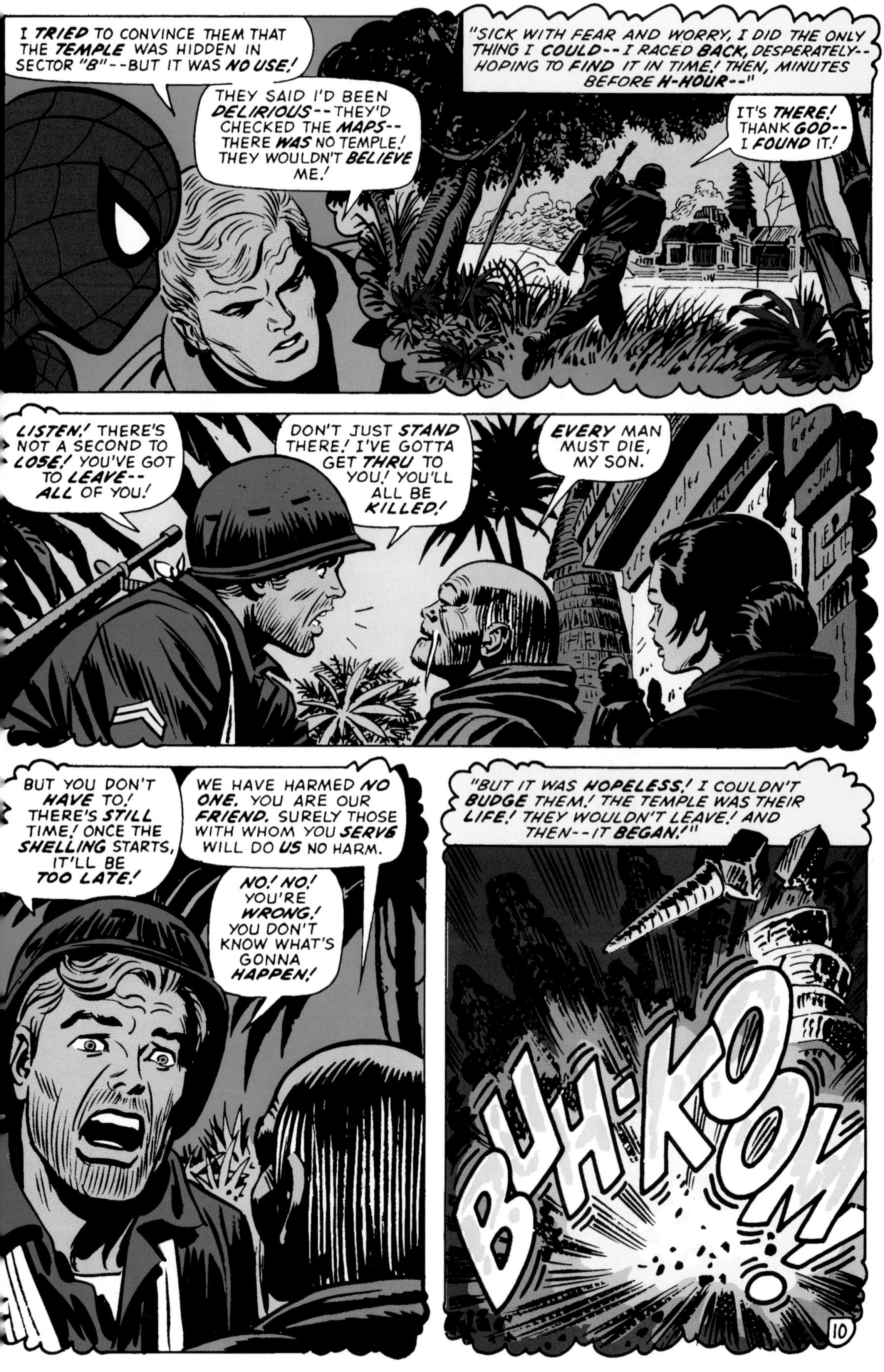
I TRIED TO CONVINCE THEM THAT THE TEMPLE WAS HIDDEN IN SECTOR "B"--BUT IT WAS NO USE!
THEY SAID I'D BEEN DELIRIOUS--THEY'D CHECKED THE MAPS--THERE WAS NO TEMPLE! THEY WOULDN'T BELIEVE ME!
"SICK WITH FEAR AND WORRY, I DID THE ONLY THING I COULD--I RACED BACK, DESPERATELY--HOPING TO FIND IT IN TIME! THEN, MINUTES BEFORE H-HOUR--"
IT'S THERE! THANK GOD--I FOUND IT!
LISTEN! THERE'S NOT A SECOND TO LOSE! YOU'VE GOT TO LEAVE--ALL OF YOU!
DON'T JUST STAND THERE! I'VE GOTTA GET THRU TO YOU! YOU'LL ALL BE KILLED!
EVERY MAN MUST DIE, MY SON.
BUT YOU DON'T HAVE TO! THERE'S STILL TIME! ONCE THE SHELLING STARTS, IT'LL BE TOO LATE!
WE HAVE HARMED NO ONE. YOU ARE OUR FRIEND. SURELY THOSE WITH WHOM YOU SERVE WILL DO US NO HARM.
NO! NO! YOU'RE WRONG! YOU DON'T KNOW WHAT'S GONNA HAPPEN!
"BUT IT WAS HOPELESS! I COULDN'T BUDGE THEM! THE TEMPLE WAS THEIR LIFE! THEY WOULDN'T LEAVE! AND THEN--IT BEGAN!"
BUH-KOOM!
10

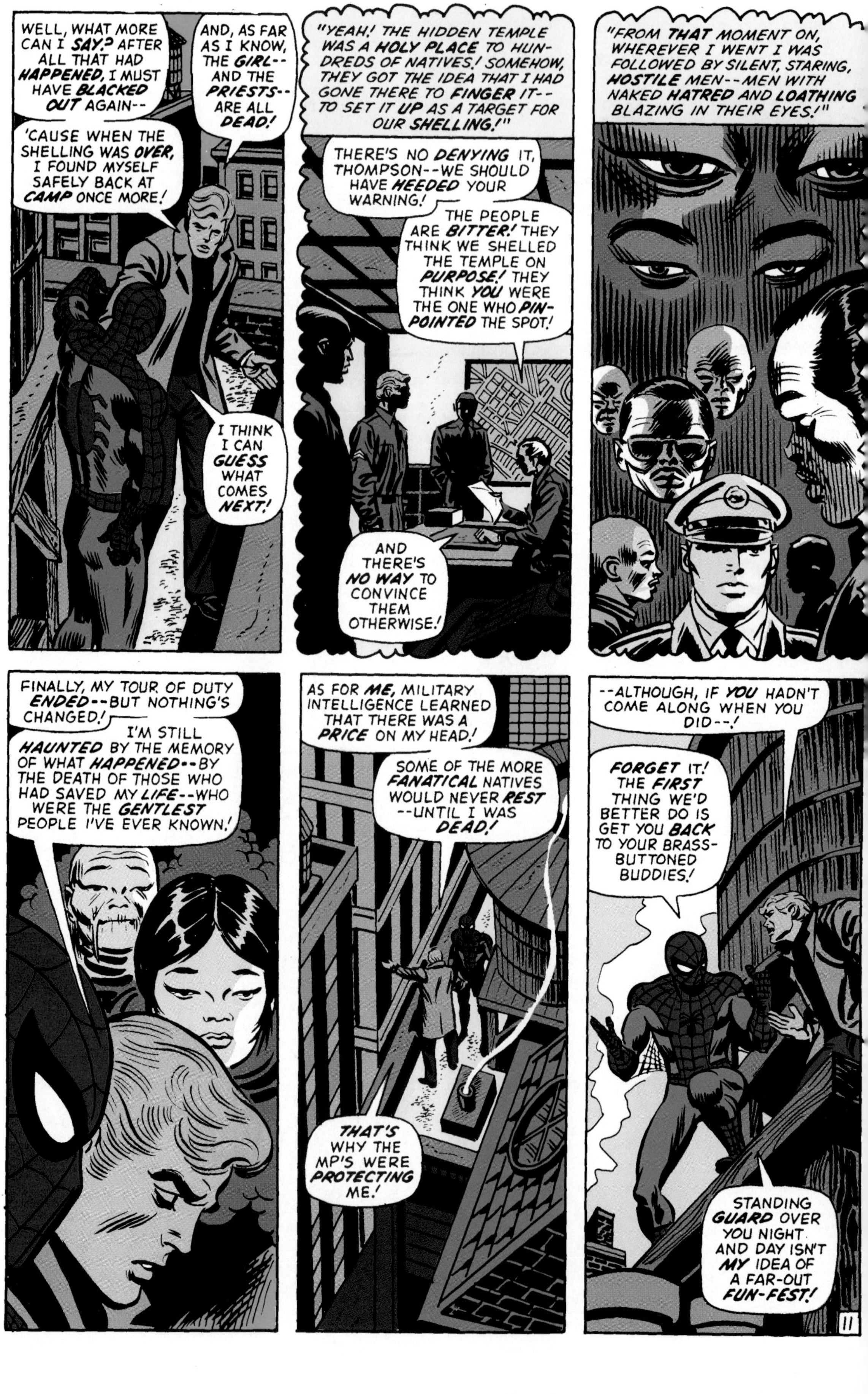
WELL, WHAT MORE CAN I SAY? AFTER ALL THAT HAD HAPPENED, I MUST HAVE BLACKED OUT AGAIN--
AND, AS FAR AS I KNOW, THE GIRL--AND THE PRIESTS--ARE ALL DEAD!
'CAUSE WHEN THE SHELLING WAS OVER, I FOUND MYSELF SAFELY BACK AT CAMP ONCE MORE!
I THINK I CAN GUESS WHAT COMES NEXT!
"YEAH! THE HIDDEN TEMPLE WAS A HOLY PLACE TO HUNDREDS OF NATIVES! SOMEHOW, THEY GOT THE IDEA THAT I HAD GONE THERE TO FINGER IT--TO SET IT UP AS A TARGET FOR OUR SHELLING!"
THERE'S NO DENYING IT, THOMPSON--WE SHOULD HAVE HEEDED YOUR WARNING!
THE PEOPLE ARE BITTER! THEY THINK WE SHELLED THE TEMPLE ON PURPOSE! THEY THINK YOU WERE THE ONE WHO PIN-POINTED THE SPOT!
AND THERE'S NO WAY TO CONVINCE THEM OTHERWISE!
"FROM THAT MOMENT ON, WHEREVER I WENT I WAS FOLLOWED BY SILENT, STARING, HOSTILE MEN--MEN WITH NAKED HATRED AND LOATHING BLAZING IN THEIR EYES!"
FINALLY, MY TOUR OF DUTY ENDED--BUT NOTHING'S CHANGED!
I'M STILL HAUNTED BY THE MEMORY OF WHAT HAPPENED--BY THE DEATH OF THOSE WHO HAD SAVED MY LIFE--WHO WERE THE GENTLEST PEOPLE I'VE EVER KNOWN!
AS FOR ME, MILITARY INTELLIGENCE LEARNED THAT THERE WAS A PRICE ON MY HEAD!
SOME OF THE MORE FANATICAL NATIVES WOULD NEVER REST --UNTIL I WAS DEAD!
THAT'S WHY THE MP'S WERE PROTECTING ME!
--ALTHOUGH, IF YOU HADN'T COME ALONG WHEN YOU DID--!
FORGET IT! THE FIRST THING WE'D BETTER DO IS GET YOU BACK TO YOUR BRASS-BUTTONED BUDDIES!
STANDING GUARD OVER YOU NIGHT AND DAY ISN'T MY IDEA OF A FAR-OUT FUN-FEST!
11

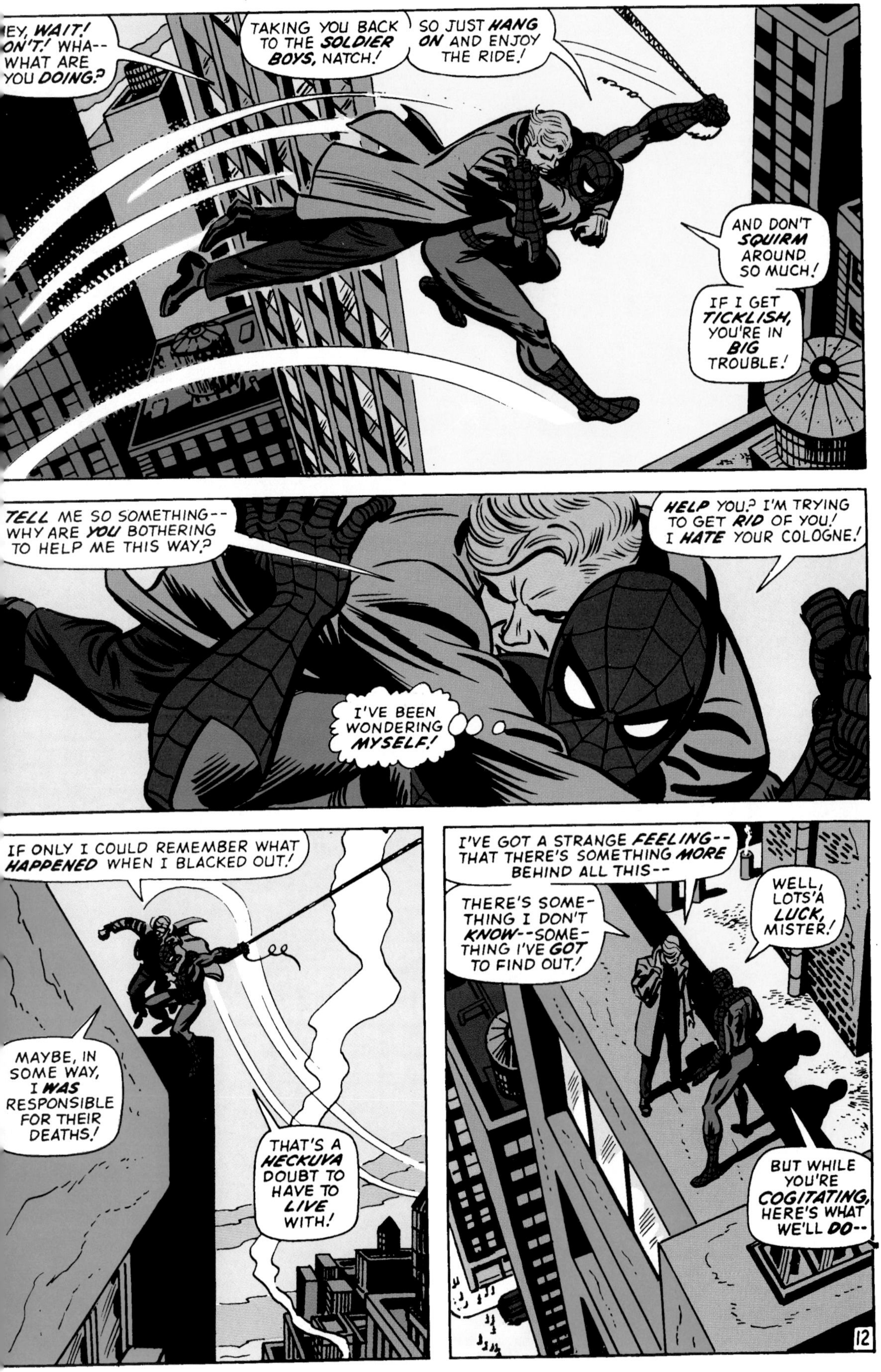
EY, WAIT! ON'T! WHA-- WHAT ARE YOU DOING?
TAKING YOU BACK TO THE SOLDIER BOYS, NATCH!
SO JUST HANG ON AND ENJOY THE RIDE!
AND DON'T SQUIRM AROUND SO MUCH!
IF I GET TICKLISH, YOU'RE IN BIG TROUBLE!
TELL ME SO SOMETHING-- WHY ARE YOU BOTHERING TO HELP ME THIS WAY?
HELP YOU? I'M TRYING TO GET RID OF YOU! I HATE YOUR COLOGNE!
I'VE BEEN WONDERING MYSELF!
IF ONLY I COULD REMEMBER WHAT HAPPENED WHEN I BLACKED OUT!
MAYBE, IN SOME WAY, I WAS RESPONSIBLE FOR THEIR DEATHS!
THAT'S A HECKUVA DOUBT TO HAVE TO LIVE WITH!
I'VE GOT A STRANGE FEELING-- THAT THERE'S SOMETHING MORE BEHIND ALL THIS--
THERE'S SOMETHING I DON'T KNOW--SOMETHING I'VE GOT TO FIND OUT!
WELL, LOTS'A LUCK, MISTER!
BUT WHILE YOU'RE COGITATING, HERE'S WHAT WE'LL DO--
12

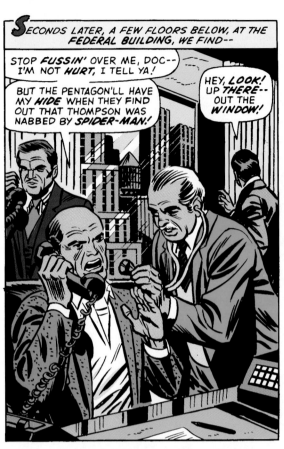

SECONDS LATER, A FEW FLOORS BELOW, AT THE *FEDERAL BUILDING*, WE FIND--

STOP *FUSSIN'* OVER ME, DOC-- I'M NOT *HURT*, I TELL YA!

BUT THE PENTAGON'LL HAVE MY *HIDE* WHEN THEY FIND OUT THAT THOMPSON WAS NABBED BY *SPIDER-MAN!*

HEY, *LOOK!* UP *THERE*-- OUT THE *WINDOW!*

IT'S HIM!!

DON'T JUST *STAND* THERE! OPEN THE WINDOW AND LET 'IM *IN!*

IT'S *SPIDER-MAN!* HE WAS TRYING TO *KILL* HIM!

NO! YOU'VE GOT IT ALL *WRONG!* HE WAS TRYING TO *HELP* ME!

THE *WEB-SWINGER*-- BOTHERING TO *HELP* YOU? BUT *WHY?* I DON'T GET IT!

SIT HIM IN THE CHAIR! I'D BETTER GIVE HIM A FAST *CHECK-UP!*

I FIRST RAN INTO SPIDER-MAN *YEARS* AGO-- WHEN I WAS STILL IN *HIGH SCHOOL!* IN FACT, I EVEN FORMED A SPIDEY *FAN CLUB!*

I NEVER HAD A CLUE TO WHO HE REALLY *WAS*--BUT I ALWAYS FIGURED HE WAS THE *GREATEST!*

I DUNNO-- MAYBE *THAT'S* WHY HE SIDED WITH ME NOW! MAYBE HE *REMEMBERS!*

WELL, I'D RATHER HAVE HIM *WITH* ME THAN *AGAINST* ME --*THAT'S* FOR SURE!

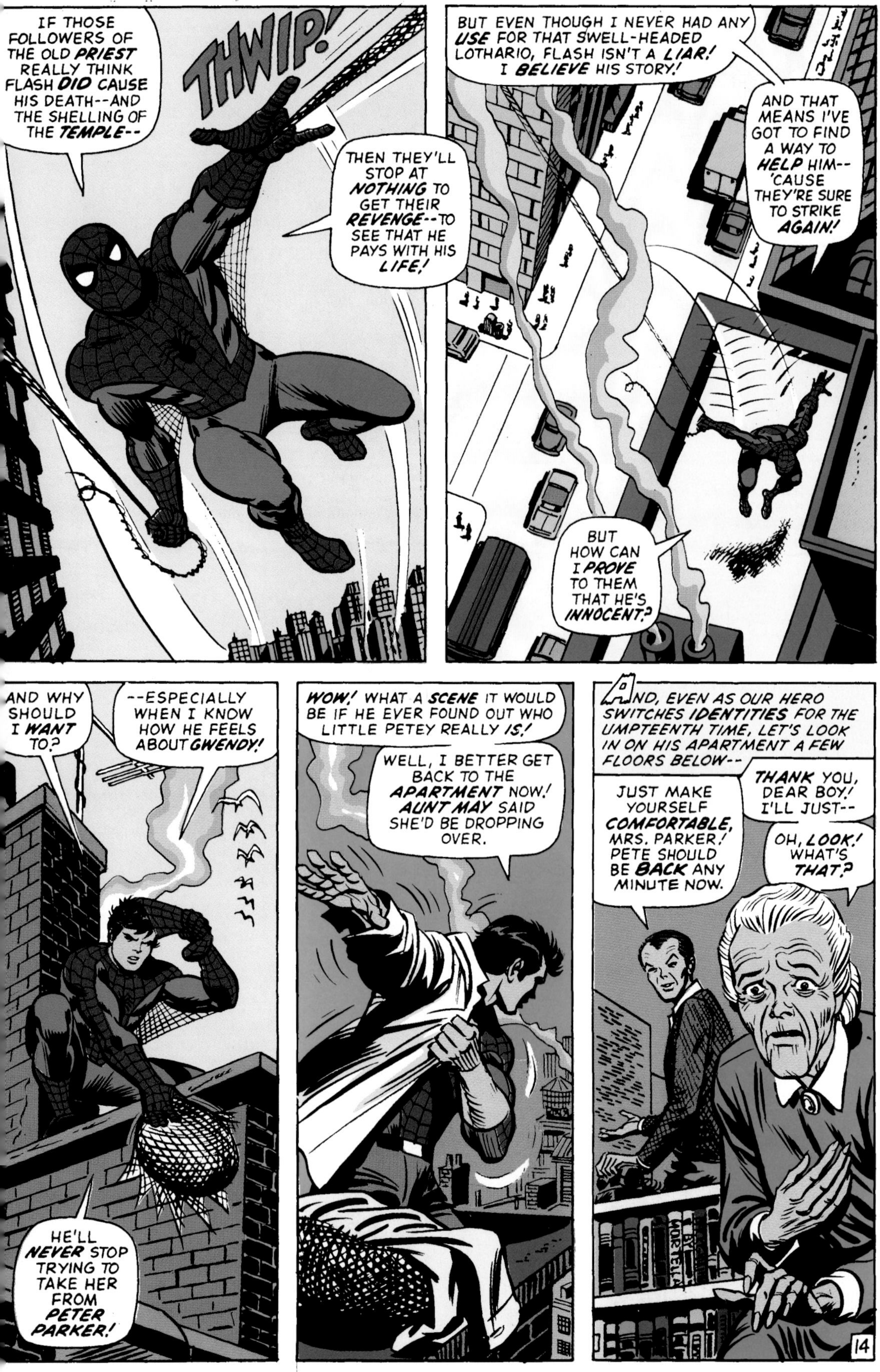
IF THOSE FOLLOWERS OF THE OLD PRIEST REALLY THINK FLASH DID CAUSE HIS DEATH--AND THE SHELLING OF THE TEMPLE--
THWIP!
THEN THEY'LL STOP AT NOTHING TO GET THEIR REVENGE--TO SEE THAT HE PAYS WITH HIS LIFE!
BUT EVEN THOUGH I NEVER HAD ANY USE FOR THAT SWELL-HEADED LOTHARIO, FLASH ISN'T A LIAR! I BELIEVE HIS STORY!
AND THAT MEANS I'VE GOT TO FIND A WAY TO HELP HIM--'CAUSE THEY'RE SURE TO STRIKE AGAIN!
BUT HOW CAN I PROVE TO THEM THAT HE'S INNOCENT?
AND WHY SHOULD I WANT TO?
--ESPECIALLY WHEN I KNOW HOW HE FEELS ABOUT GWENDY!
HE'LL NEVER STOP TRYING TO TAKE HER FROM PETER PARKER!
WOW! WHAT A SCENE IT WOULD BE IF HE EVER FOUND OUT WHO LITTLE PETEY REALLY IS!
WELL, I BETTER GET BACK TO THE APARTMENT NOW! AUNT MAY SAID SHE'D BE DROPPING OVER.
AND, EVEN AS OUR HERO SWITCHES IDENTITIES FOR THE UMPTEENTH TIME, LET'S LOOK IN ON HIS APARTMENT A FEW FLOORS BELOW--
JUST MAKE YOURSELF COMFORTABLE, MRS. PARKER! PETE SHOULD BE BACK ANY MINUTE NOW.
THANK YOU, DEAR BOY! I'LL JUST--
OH, LOOK! WHAT'S THAT?
14

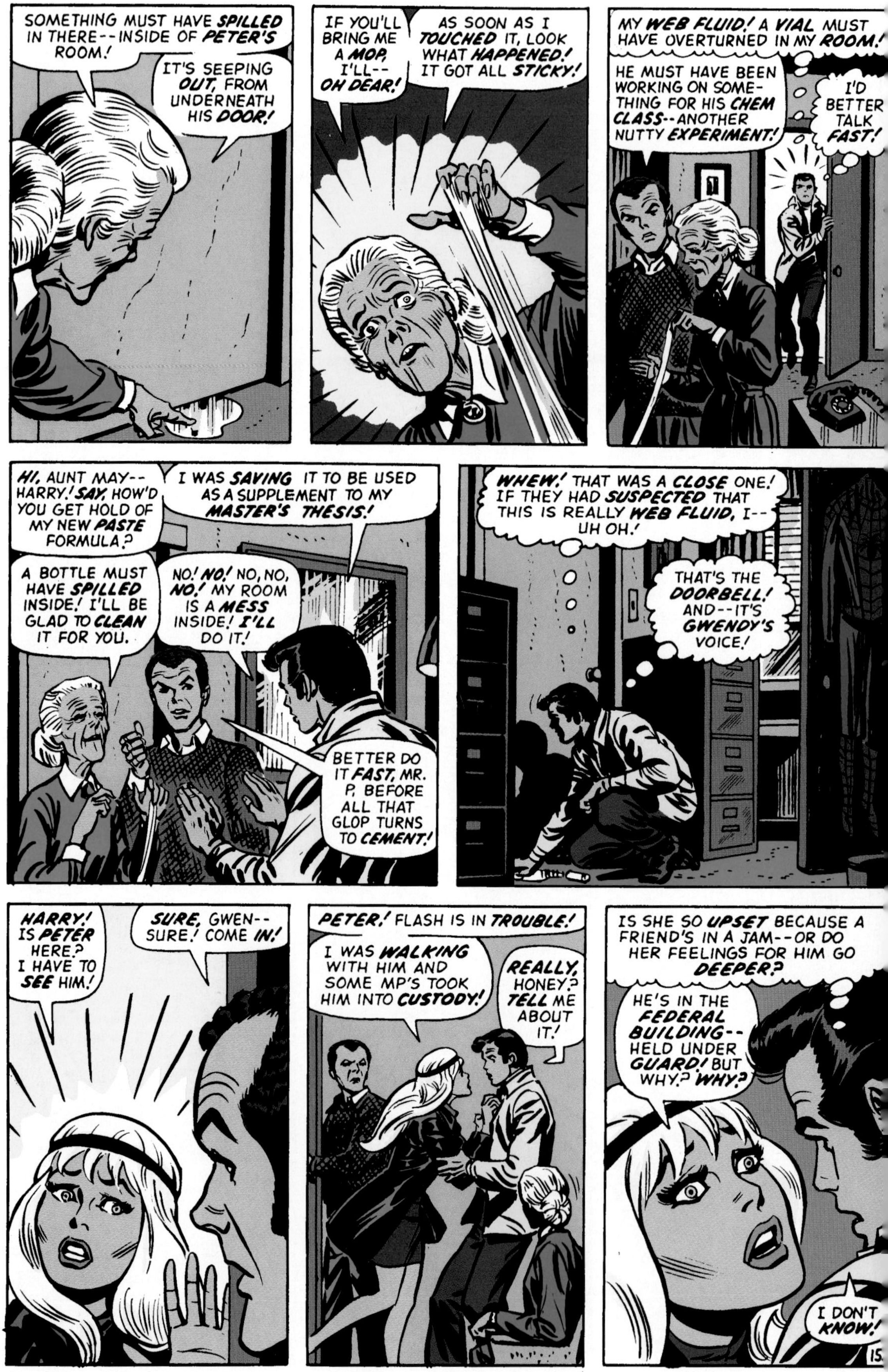
SOMETHING MUST HAVE SPILLED IN THERE--INSIDE OF PETER'S ROOM!
IT'S SEEPING OUT, FROM UNDERNEATH HIS DOOR!
IF YOU'LL BRING ME A MOP, I'LL-- OH DEAR!
AS SOON AS I TOUCHED IT, LOOK WHAT HAPPENED! IT GOT ALL STICKY!
MY WEB FLUID! A VIAL MUST HAVE OVERTURNED IN MY ROOM!
HE MUST HAVE BEEN WORKING ON SOMETHING FOR HIS CHEM CLASS--ANOTHER NUTTY EXPERIMENT!
I'D BETTER TALK FAST!
HI, AUNT MAY-- HARRY! SAY, HOW'D YOU GET HOLD OF MY NEW PASTE FORMULA?
I WAS SAVING IT TO BE USED AS A SUPPLEMENT TO MY MASTER'S THESIS!
A BOTTLE MUST HAVE SPILLED INSIDE! I'LL BE GLAD TO CLEAN IT FOR YOU.
NO! NO! NO, NO, NO! MY ROOM IS A MESS INSIDE! I'LL DO IT!
BETTER DO IT FAST, MR. P, BEFORE ALL THAT GLOP TURNS TO CEMENT!
WHEW! THAT WAS A CLOSE ONE! IF THEY HAD SUSPECTED THAT THIS IS REALLY WEB FLUID, I-- UH OH!
THAT'S THE DOORBELL! AND--IT'S GWENDY'S VOICE!
HARRY! IS PETER HERE? I HAVE TO SEE HIM!
SURE, GWEN-- SURE! COME IN!
PETER! FLASH IS IN TROUBLE!
I WAS WALKING WITH HIM AND SOME MP'S TOOK HIM INTO CUSTODY!
REALLY, HONEY? TELL ME ABOUT IT!
IS SHE SO UPSET BECAUSE A FRIEND'S IN A JAM--OR DO HER FEELINGS FOR HIM GO DEEPER?
HE'S IN THE FEDERAL BUILDING--HELD UNDER GUARD! BUT WHY? WHY?
I DON'T KNOW!
15

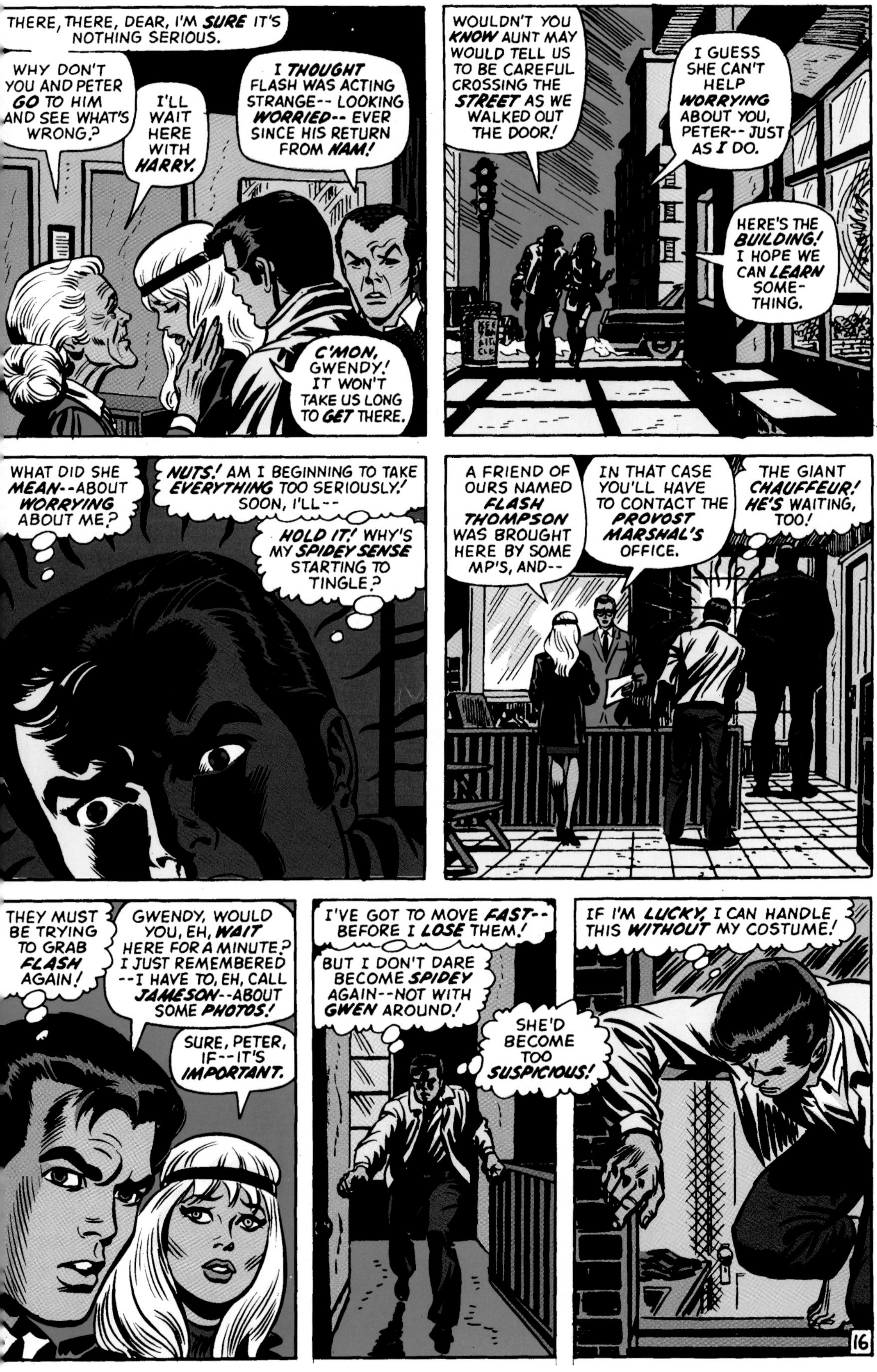
THERE, THERE, DEAR, I'M SURE IT'S NOTHING SERIOUS.
WHY DON'T YOU AND PETER GO TO HIM AND SEE WHAT'S WRONG?
I'LL WAIT HERE WITH HARRY.
I THOUGHT FLASH WAS ACTING STRANGE-- LOOKING WORRIED-- EVER SINCE HIS RETURN FROM NAM!
C'MON, GWENDY! IT WON'T TAKE US LONG TO GET THERE.
WOULDN'T YOU KNOW AUNT MAY WOULD TELL US TO BE CAREFUL CROSSING THE STREET AS WE WALKED OUT THE DOOR!
I GUESS SHE CAN'T HELP WORRYING ABOUT YOU, PETER-- JUST AS I DO.
HERE'S THE BUILDING! I HOPE WE CAN LEARN SOME-THING.
WHAT DID SHE MEAN--ABOUT WORRYING ABOUT ME?
NUTS! AM I BEGINNING TO TAKE EVERYTHING TOO SERIOUSLY! SOON, I'LL--
HOLD IT! WHY'S MY SPIDEY SENSE STARTING TO TINGLE?
A FRIEND OF OURS NAMED FLASH THOMPSON WAS BROUGHT HERE BY SOME MP'S, AND--
IN THAT CASE YOU'LL HAVE TO CONTACT THE PROVOST MARSHAL'S OFFICE.
THE GIANT CHAUFFEUR! HE'S WAITING, TOO!
THEY MUST BE TRYING TO GRAB FLASH AGAIN!
GWENDY, WOULD YOU, EH, WAIT HERE FOR A MINUTE? I JUST REMEMBERED --I HAVE TO, EH, CALL JAMESON--ABOUT SOME PHOTOS!
SURE, PETER, IF--IT'S IMPORTANT.
I'VE GOT TO MOVE FAST-- BEFORE I LOSE THEM!
BUT I DON'T DARE BECOME SPIDEY AGAIN--NOT WITH GWEN AROUND!
SHE'D BECOME TOO SUSPICIOUS!
IF I'M LUCKY, I CAN HANDLE THIS WITHOUT MY COSTUME!
16

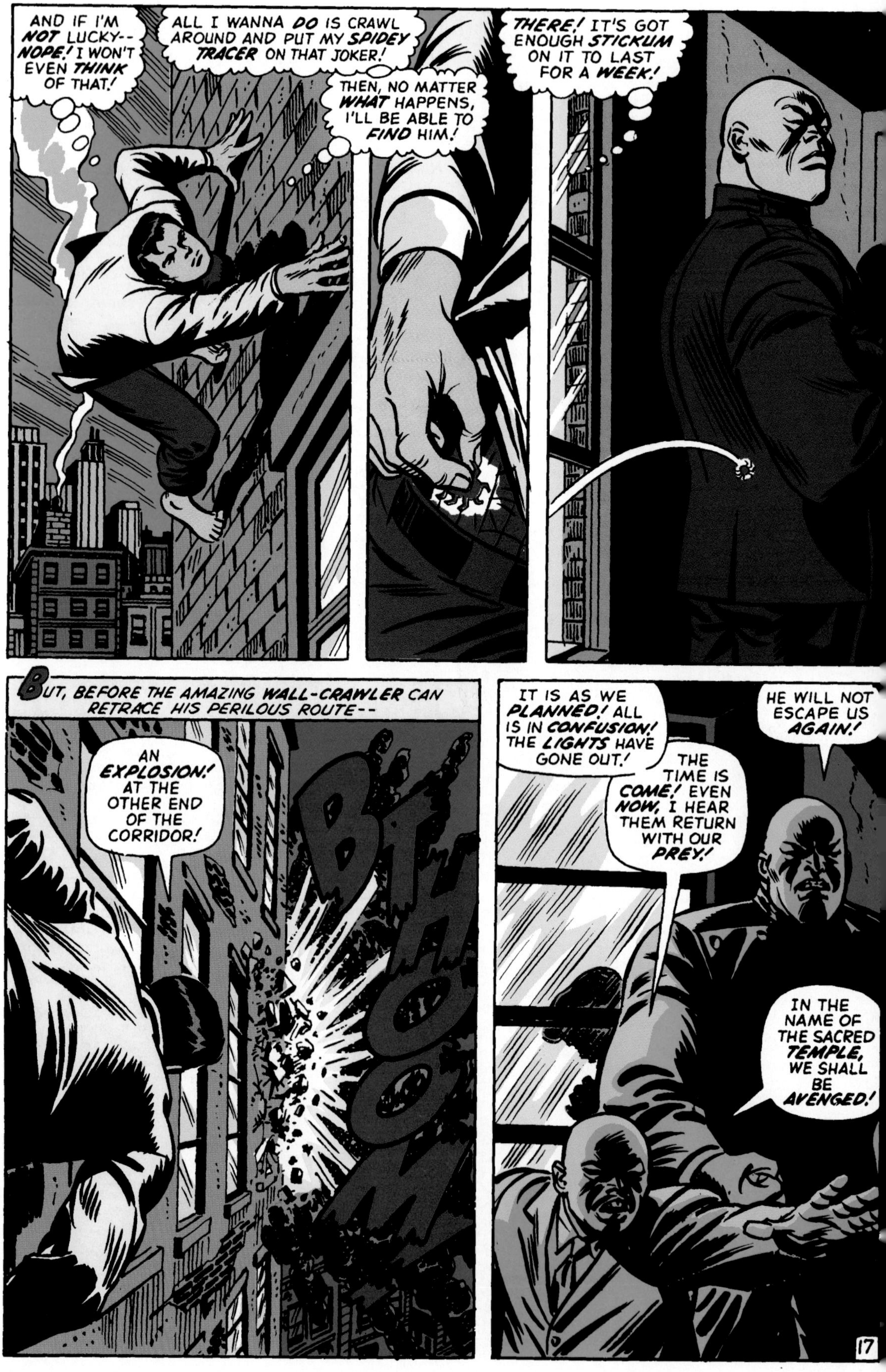
AND IF I'M NOT LUCKY-- NOPE! I WON'T EVEN THINK OF THAT!
ALL I WANNA DO IS CRAWL AROUND AND PUT MY SPIDEY TRACER ON THAT JOKER!
THEN, NO MATTER WHAT HAPPENS, I'LL BE ABLE TO FIND HIM!
THERE! IT'S GOT ENOUGH STICKUM ON IT TO LAST FOR A WEEK!
BUT, BEFORE THE AMAZING WALL-CRAWLER CAN RETRACE HIS PERILOUS ROUTE--
AN EXPLOSION! AT THE OTHER END OF THE CORRIDOR!
IT IS AS WE PLANNED! ALL IS IN CONFUSION! THE LIGHTS HAVE GONE OUT!
HE WILL NOT ESCAPE US AGAIN!
THE TIME IS COME! EVEN NOW, I HEAR THEM RETURN WITH OUR PREY!
IN THE NAME OF THE SACRED TEMPLE, WE SHALL BE AVENGED!

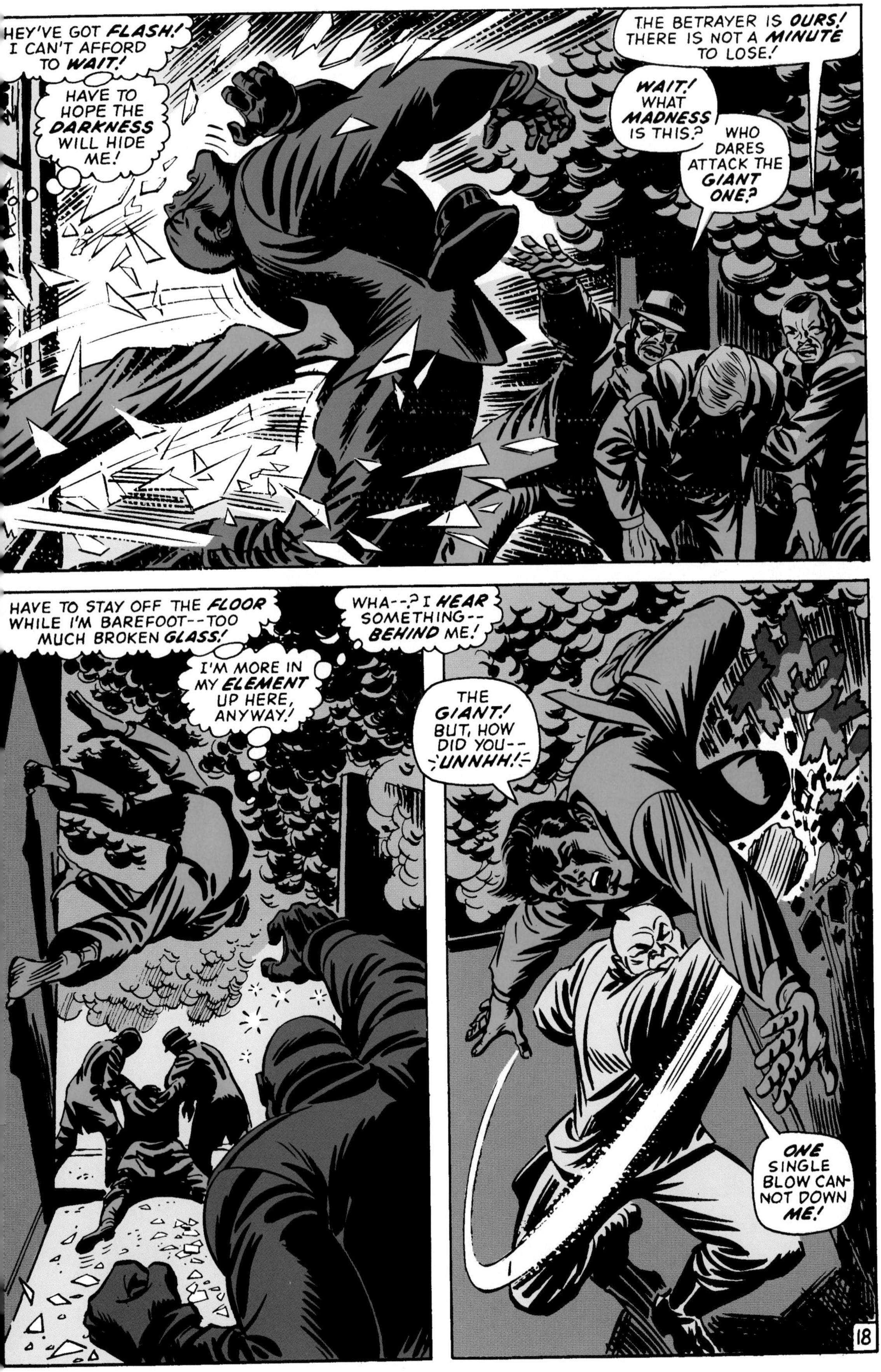
HEY'VE GOT FLASH! I CAN'T AFFORD TO WAIT!
HAVE TO HOPE THE DARKNESS WILL HIDE ME!
THE BETRAYER IS OURS! THERE IS NOT A MINUTE TO LOSE!
WAIT! WHAT MADNESS IS THIS?
WHO DARES ATTACK THE GIANT ONE?
HAVE TO STAY OFF THE FLOOR WHILE I'M BAREFOOT--TOO MUCH BROKEN GLASS!
I'M MORE IN MY ELEMENT UP HERE, ANYWAY!
WHA--? I HEAR SOMETHING--BEHIND ME!
THE GIANT! BUT, HOW DID YOU--UNNHH!
ONE SINGLE BLOW CAN-NOT DOWN ME!

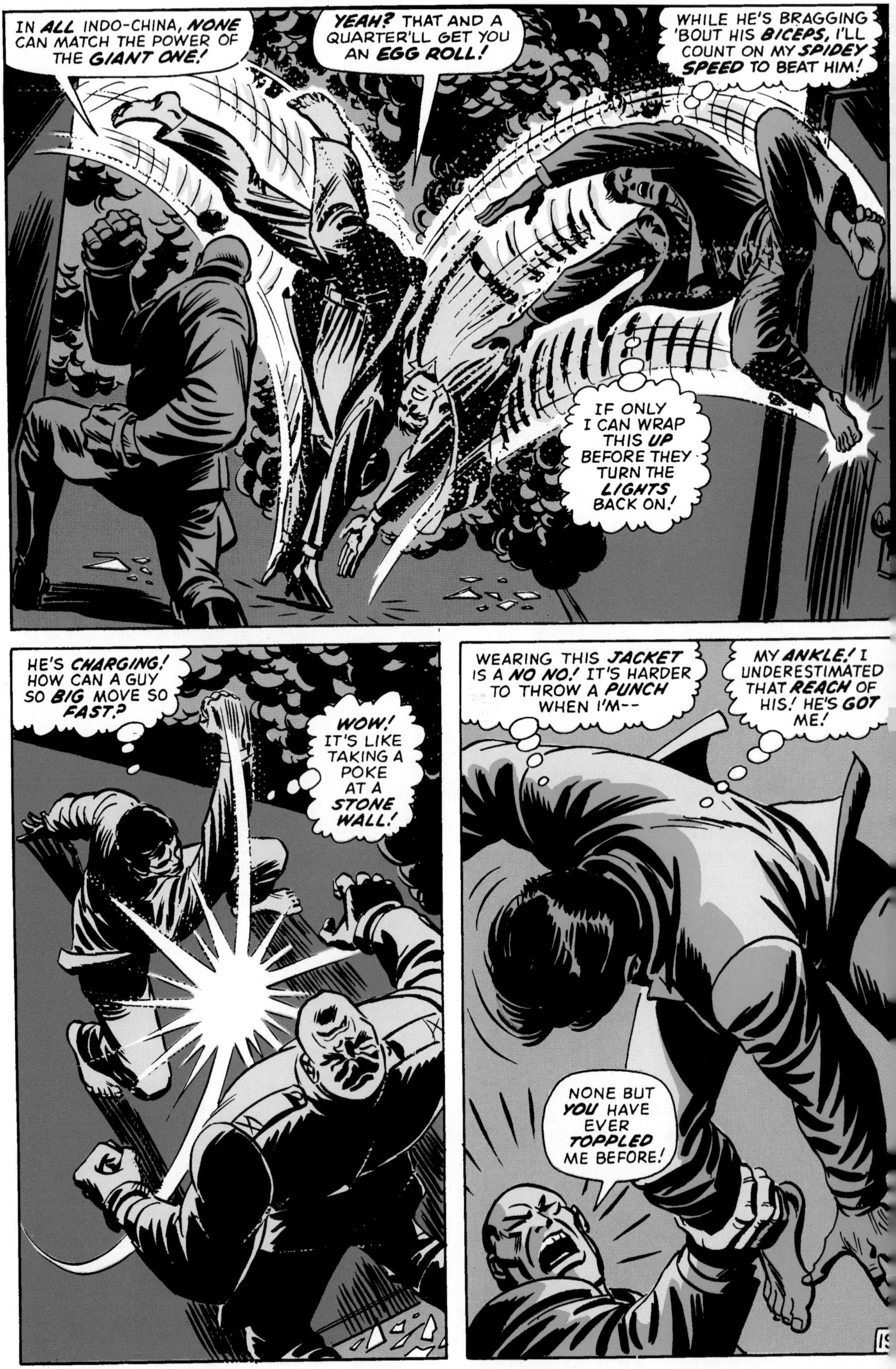
IN ALL INDO-CHINA, NONE CAN MATCH THE POWER OF THE GIANT ONE!
YEAH? THAT AND A QUARTER'LL GET YOU AN EGG ROLL!
WHILE HE'S BRAGGING 'BOUT HIS BICEPS, I'LL COUNT ON MY SPIDEY SPEED TO BEAT HIM!
IF ONLY I CAN WRAP THIS UP BEFORE THEY TURN THE LIGHTS BACK ON!
HE'S CHARGING! HOW CAN A GUY SO BIG MOVE SO FAST?
WOW! IT'S LIKE TAKING A POKE AT A STONE WALL!
WEARING THIS JACKET IS A NO NO! IT'S HARDER TO THROW A PUNCH WHEN I'M--
MY ANKLE! I UNDERESTIMATED THAT REACH OF HIS! HE'S GOT ME!
NONE BUT YOU HAVE EVER TOPPLED ME BEFORE!

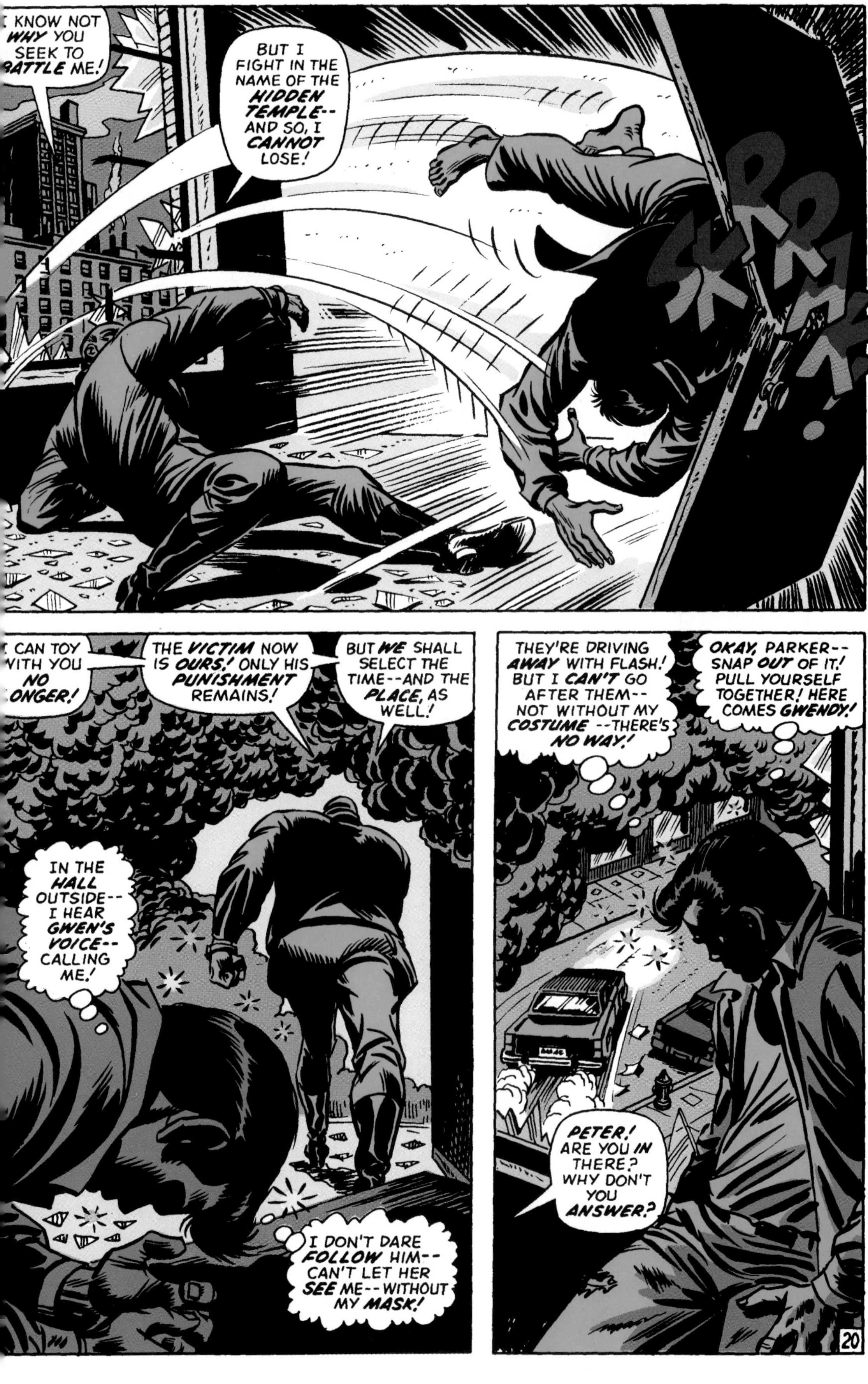
I KNOW NOT WHY YOU SEEK TO BATTLE ME!
BUT I FIGHT IN THE NAME OF THE HIDDEN TEMPLE-- AND SO, I CANNOT LOSE!
SKRRAKK!
I CAN TOY WITH YOU NO LONGER!
THE VICTIM NOW IS OURS! ONLY HIS PUNISHMENT REMAINS!
BUT WE SHALL SELECT THE TIME--AND THE PLACE, AS WELL!
IN THE HALL OUTSIDE-- I HEAR GWEN'S VOICE-- CALLING ME!
I DON'T DARE FOLLOW HIM-- CAN'T LET HER SEE ME--WITHOUT MY MASK!
THEY'RE DRIVING AWAY WITH FLASH! BUT I CAN'T GO AFTER THEM-- NOT WITHOUT MY COSTUME --THERE'S NO WAY!
OKAY, PARKER-- SNAP OUT OF IT! PULL YOURSELF TOGETHER! HERE COMES GWENDY!
PETER! ARE YOU IN THERE? WHY DON'T YOU ANSWER?
20

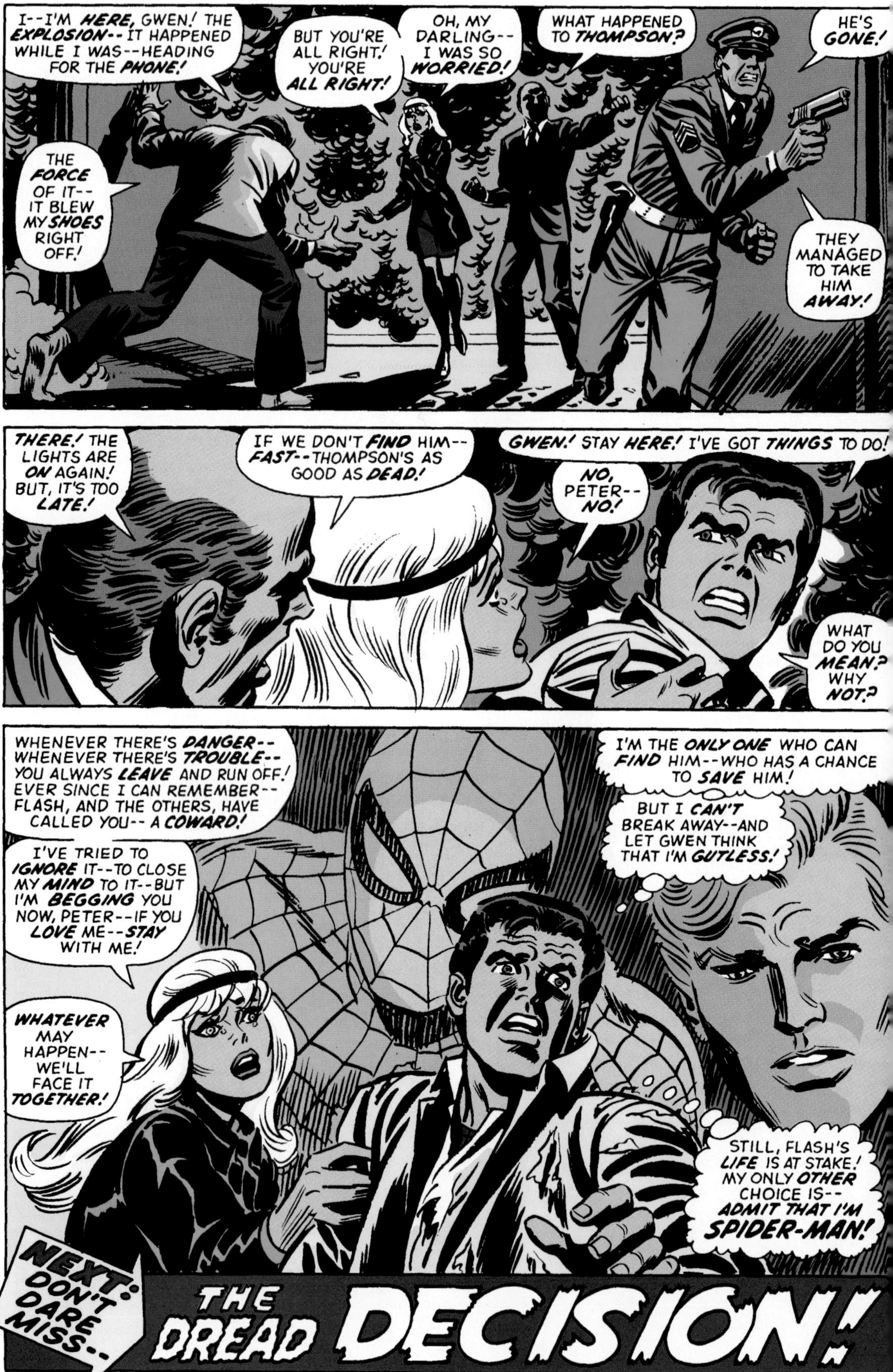
I--I'M HERE, GWEN! THE EXPLOSION-- IT HAPPENED WHILE I WAS--HEADING FOR THE PHONE!
THE FORCE OF IT-- IT BLEW MY SHOES RIGHT OFF!
BUT YOU'RE ALL RIGHT! YOU'RE ALL RIGHT!
OH, MY DARLING-- I WAS SO WORRIED!
WHAT HAPPENED TO THOMPSON?
HE'S GONE!
THEY MANAGED TO TAKE HIM AWAY!
THERE! THE LIGHTS ARE ON AGAIN! BUT, IT'S TOO LATE!
IF WE DON'T FIND HIM-- FAST--THOMPSON'S AS GOOD AS DEAD!
GWEN! STAY HERE! I'VE GOT THINGS TO DO!
NO, PETER-- NO!
WHAT DO YOU MEAN? WHY NOT?
WHENEVER THERE'S DANGER-- WHENEVER THERE'S TROUBLE-- YOU ALWAYS LEAVE AND RUN OFF! EVER SINCE I CAN REMEMBER-- FLASH, AND THE OTHERS, HAVE CALLED YOU-- A COWARD!
I'VE TRIED TO IGNORE IT--TO CLOSE MY MIND TO IT--BUT I'M BEGGING YOU NOW, PETER--IF YOU LOVE ME--STAY WITH ME!
WHATEVER MAY HAPPEN-- WE'LL FACE IT TOGETHER!
I'M THE ONLY ONE WHO CAN FIND HIM--WHO HAS A CHANCE TO SAVE HIM!
BUT I CAN'T BREAK AWAY--AND LET GWEN THINK THAT I'M GUTLESS!
STILL, FLASH'S LIFE IS AT STAKE! MY ONLY OTHER CHOICE IS-- ADMIT THAT I'M SPIDER-MAN!
NEXT: DON'T DARE MISS..
THE DREAD DECISION!

amazing spider-man #109

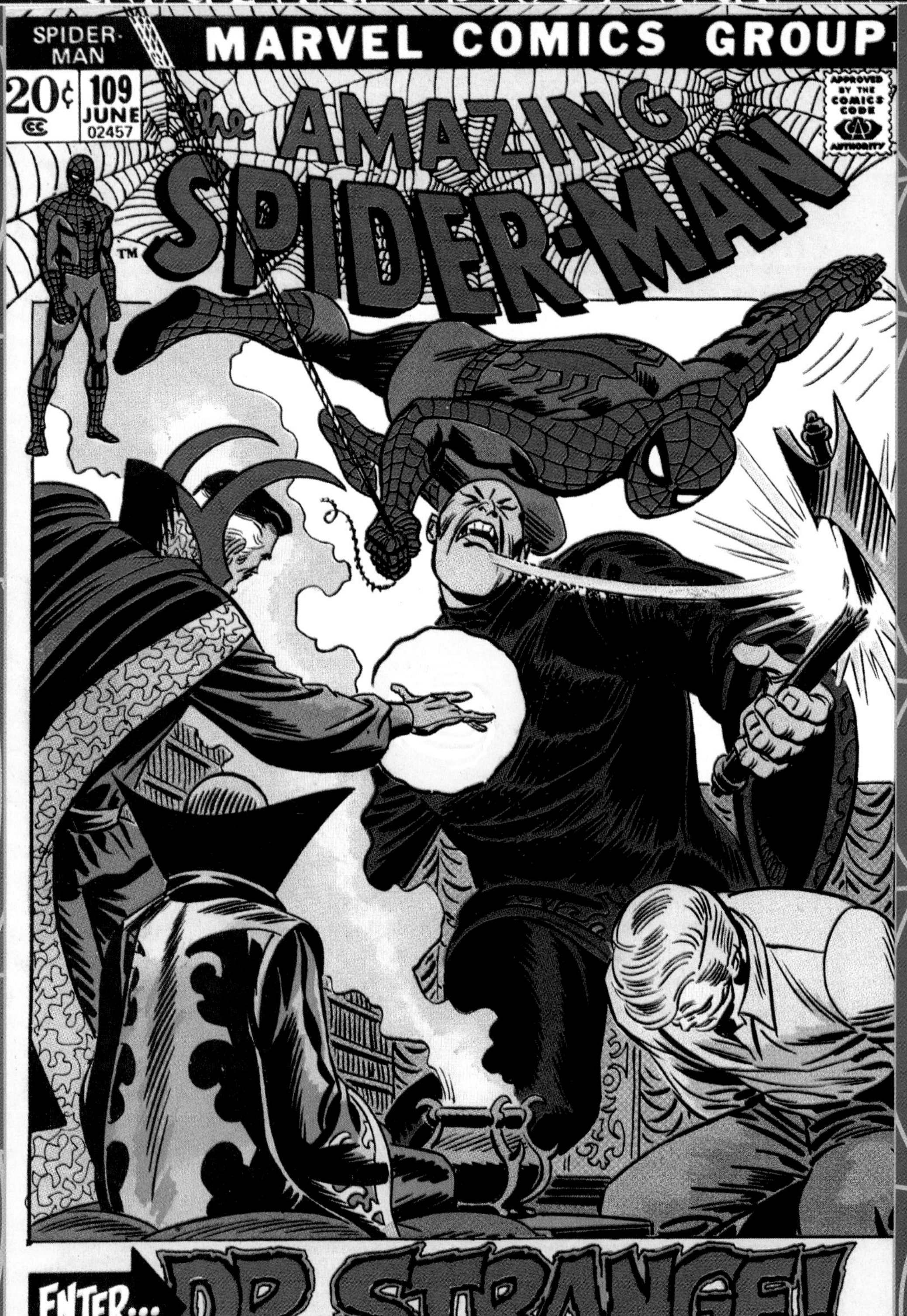
SPIDER-MAN
MARVEL COMICS GROUP
20¢
109
JUNE
02457
APPROVED BY THE COMICS CODE AUTHORITY
the AMAZING SPIDER-MAN
ENTER...
DR. STRANGE!

june 1972

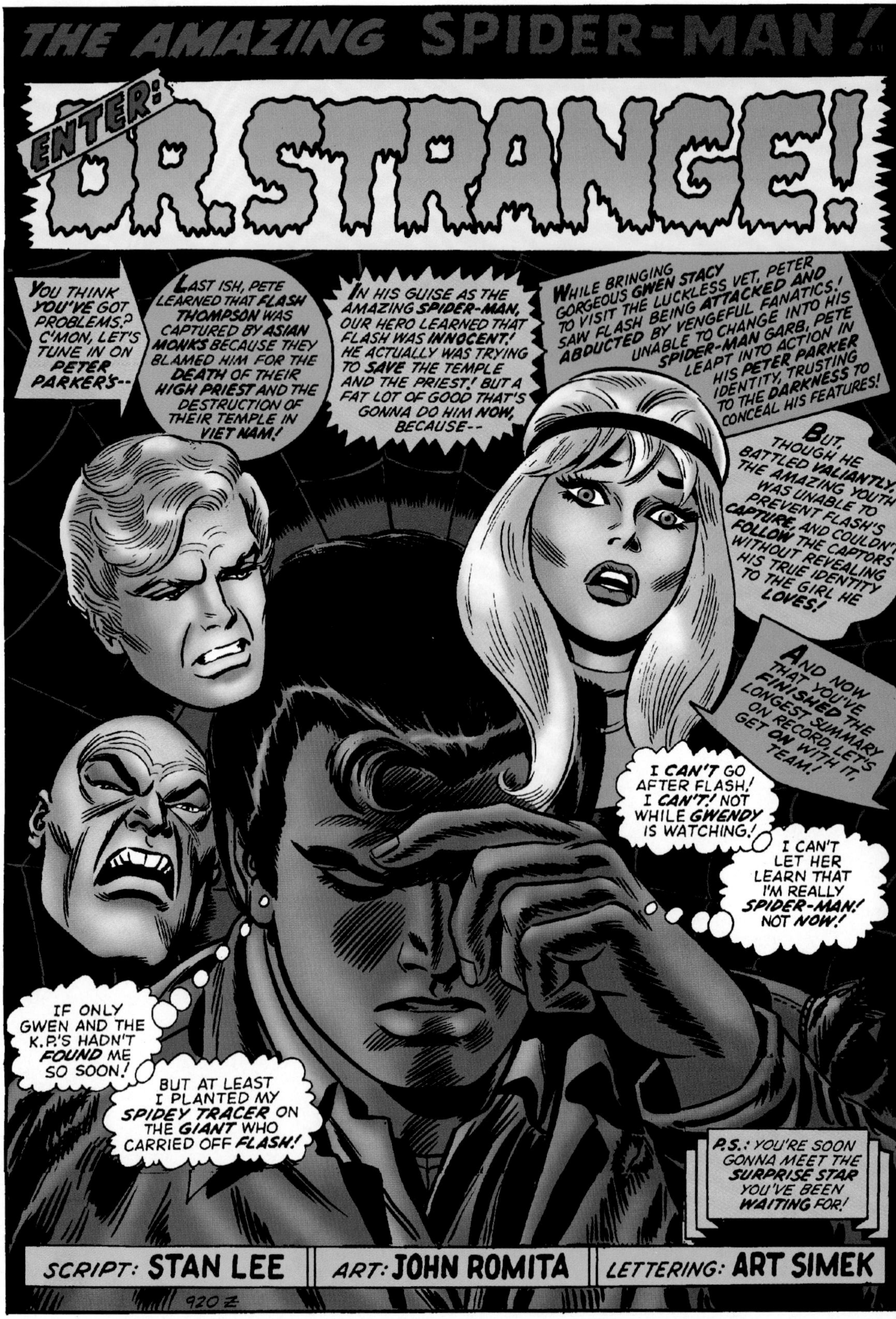

THE AMAZING SPIDER-MAN!
ENTER: DR. STRANGE!
YOU THINK YOU'VE GOT PROBLEMS? C'MON, LET'S TUNE IN ON PETER PARKER'S--
LAST ISH, PETE LEARNED THAT FLASH THOMPSON WAS CAPTURED BY ASIAN MONKS BECAUSE THEY BLAMED HIM FOR THE DEATH OF THEIR HIGH PRIEST AND THE DESTRUCTION OF THEIR TEMPLE IN VIET NAM!
IN HIS GUISE AS THE AMAZING SPIDER-MAN, OUR HERO LEARNED THAT FLASH WAS INNOCENT! HE ACTUALLY WAS TRYING TO SAVE THE TEMPLE AND THE PRIEST! BUT A FAT LOT OF GOOD THAT'S GONNA DO HIM NOW, BECAUSE--
WHILE BRINGING GORGEOUS GWEN STACY TO VISIT THE LUCKLESS VET, PETER SAW FLASH BEING ATTACKED AND ABDUCTED BY VENGEFUL FANATICS! UNABLE TO CHANGE INTO HIS SPIDER-MAN GARB, PETE LEAPT INTO ACTION IN HIS PETER PARKER IDENTITY, TRUSTING TO THE DARKNESS TO CONCEAL HIS FEATURES!
BUT, THOUGH HE BATTLED VALIANTLY, THE AMAZING YOUTH WAS UNABLE TO PREVENT FLASH'S CAPTURE, AND COULDN'T FOLLOW THE CAPTORS WITHOUT REVEALING HIS TRUE IDENTITY TO THE GIRL HE LOVES!
AND NOW THAT YOU'VE FINISHED THE LONGEST SUMMARY ON RECORD, LET'S GET ON WITH IT, TEAM!
I CAN'T GO AFTER FLASH! I CAN'T! NOT WHILE GWENDY IS WATCHING!
I CAN'T LET HER LEARN THAT I'M REALLY SPIDER-MAN! NOT NOW!
IF ONLY GWEN AND THE K.P.'S HADN'T FOUND ME SO SOON!
BUT AT LEAST I PLANTED MY SPIDEY TRACER ON THE GIANT WHO CARRIED OFF FLASH!
P.S.: YOU'RE SOON GONNA MEET THE SURPRISE STAR YOU'VE BEEN WAITING FOR!
SCRIPT: STAN LEE
ART: JOHN ROMITA
LETTERING: ART SIMEK
920 Z

WOW! THE GUY WHO CUT OUT WITH **THOMPSON** MUST'A BEEN A LIVIN' **GIANT!**

I'M GLAD YOU DIDN'T RUN **OFF** THIS TIME, PETER!

IN THE **PAST,** EVERYONE CALLED YOU **GUTLESS** BECAUSE YOU ALWAYS DUCKED **OUT** WHENEVER THERE WAS **TROUBLE!**

GET **EVERY** AVAILABLE MAN ON THE **STREET!**

I WANT HIM **FOUND,** DO YOU HEAR? I WANT THOMPSON **FOUND!**

IT'S NOT TO BE **BELIEVED!**

SPIDEY CAN'T TAKE OFF TO SAVE **FLASH** WITHOUT HER THINKING THAT **PARKER'S** CHICKEN.

THESE YOUR **SHOES,** SON? FOUND 'EM IN THE **HALL!**

I HAVE TO THINK **FAST!** I TOOK THEM **OFF** SO I COULD CLIMB THE **WALLS** WITH MY **SPIDEY** POWER!

OH YEAH, **SURE!** THE EXPLOSION MUST HAVE BLOWN THEM OFF WHEN IT **CAUGHT** ME!

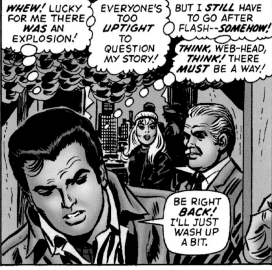

WHEW! LUCKY FOR ME THERE **WAS** AN EXPLOSION!

EVERYONE'S TOO **UPTIGHT** TO QUESTION MY STORY!

BUT I **STILL** HAVE TO GO AFTER FLASH--**SOMEHOW!**

THINK, WEB-HEAD, **THINK!** THERE **MUST** BE A WAY!

BE RIGHT **BACK!** I'LL JUST WASH UP A BIT.

OKAY! AT LEAST I'M **ALONE** NOW!

BUT EVERY SECOND I **WASTE** IS PUTTING POOR **FLASH** IN EVEN GREATER **DANGER!**

I NEED SOME **EXCUSE--** AN EXCUSE TO GO **AFTER** HIM!

WAS

OH, **BROTHER!** I FORGOT MY **COLLAR** WAS OPEN--WITH THE TOP OF MY **SPIDEY SHIRT** PEEKING THRU!

IF ANYONE HAD **SPOTTED** IT-- I COULD HAVE KISSED MY **COVER** GOODBYE!

HEY, **WAIT** A MINUTE! THIS GIVES ME AN **IDEA!**

I'VE GOT MY **COSTUME--** AND MY **CIVVIES** WITH ME!

SO, IF MY **LUCK** JUST HOLDS OUT--

2

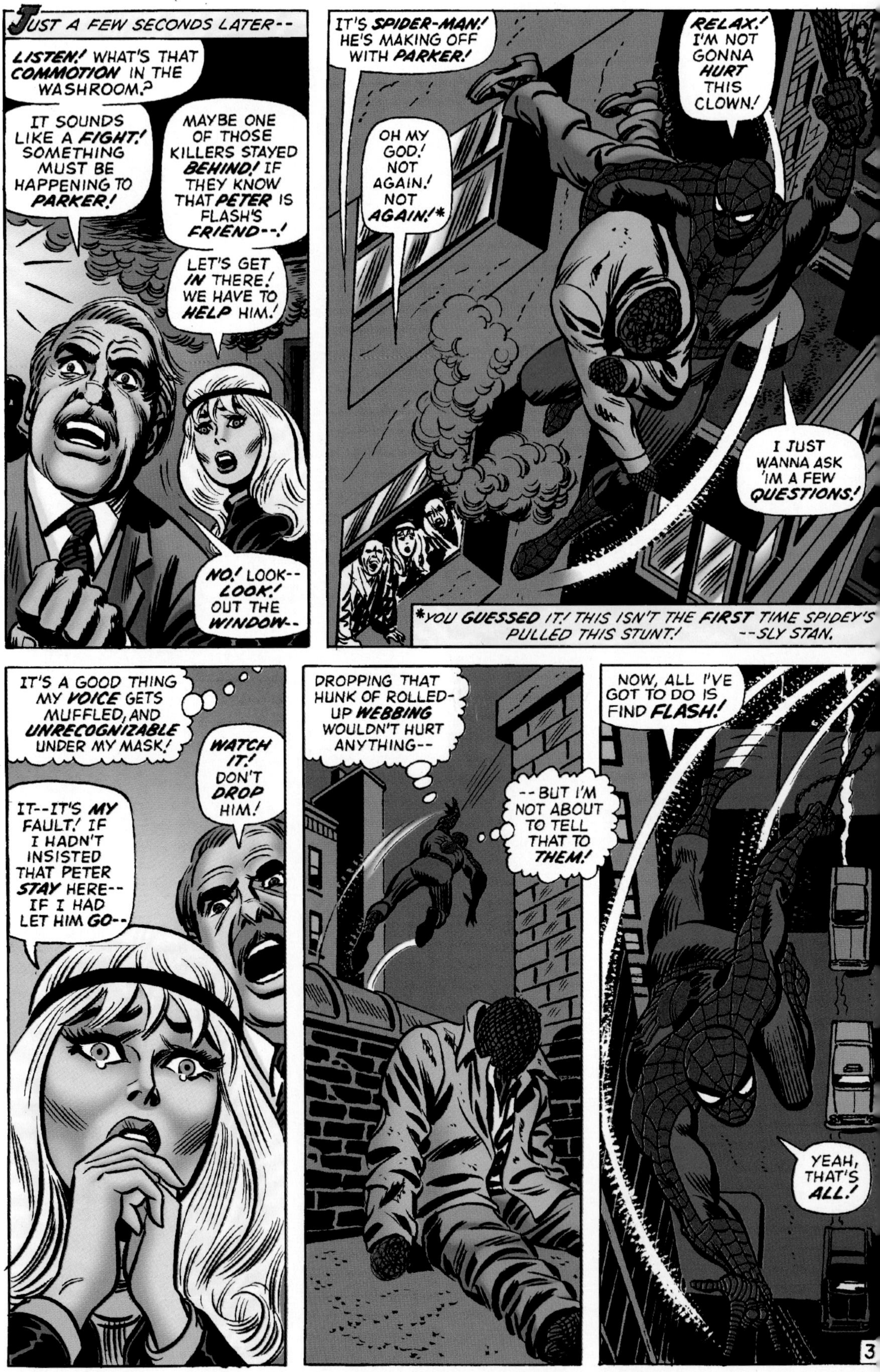
JUST A FEW SECONDS LATER--
LISTEN! WHAT'S THAT COMMOTION IN THE WASHROOM?
IT SOUNDS LIKE A FIGHT! SOMETHING MUST BE HAPPENING TO PARKER!
MAYBE ONE OF THOSE KILLERS STAYED BEHIND! IF THEY KNOW THAT PETER IS FLASH'S FRIEND--!
LET'S GET IN THERE! WE HAVE TO HELP HIM!
NO! LOOK--LOOK! OUT THE WINDOW--
IT'S SPIDER-MAN! HE'S MAKING OFF WITH PARKER!
OH MY GOD! NOT AGAIN! NOT AGAIN!*
RELAX! I'M NOT GONNA HURT THIS CLOWN!
I JUST WANNA ASK 'IM A FEW QUESTIONS!
*YOU GUESSED IT! THIS ISN'T THE FIRST TIME SPIDEY'S PULLED THIS STUNT! --SLY STAN.
IT'S A GOOD THING MY VOICE GETS MUFFLED, AND UNRECOGNIZABLE UNDER MY MASK!
WATCH IT! DON'T DROP HIM!
IT--IT'S MY FAULT! IF I HADN'T INSISTED THAT PETER STAY HERE-- IF I HAD LET HIM GO--
DROPPING THAT HUNK OF ROLLED-UP WEBBING WOULDN'T HURT ANYTHING--
--BUT I'M NOT ABOUT TO TELL THAT TO THEM!
NOW, ALL I'VE GOT TO DO IS FIND FLASH!
YEAH, THAT'S ALL!

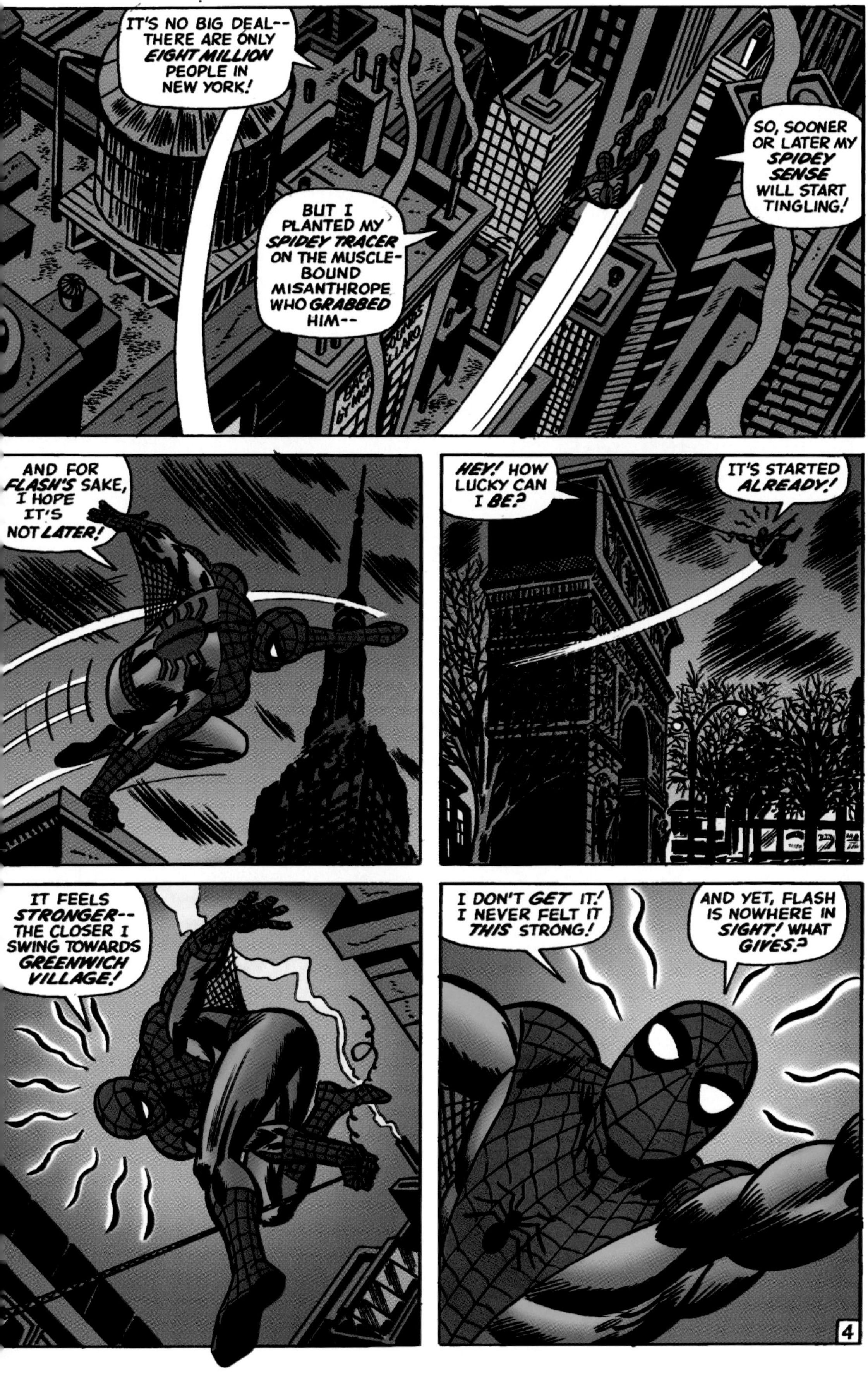
IT'S NO BIG DEAL-- THERE ARE ONLY EIGHT MILLION PEOPLE IN NEW YORK!
BUT I PLANTED MY SPIDEY TRACER ON THE MUSCLE-BOUND MISANTHROPE WHO GRABBED HIM--
SO, SOONER OR LATER MY SPIDEY SENSE WILL START TINGLING!
AND FOR FLASH'S SAKE, I HOPE IT'S NOT LATER!
HEY! HOW LUCKY CAN I BE?
IT'S STARTED ALREADY!
IT FEELS STRONGER-- THE CLOSER I SWING TOWARDS GREENWICH VILLAGE!
I DON'T GET IT! I NEVER FELT IT THIS STRONG!
AND YET, FLASH IS NOWHERE IN SIGHT! WHAT GIVES?

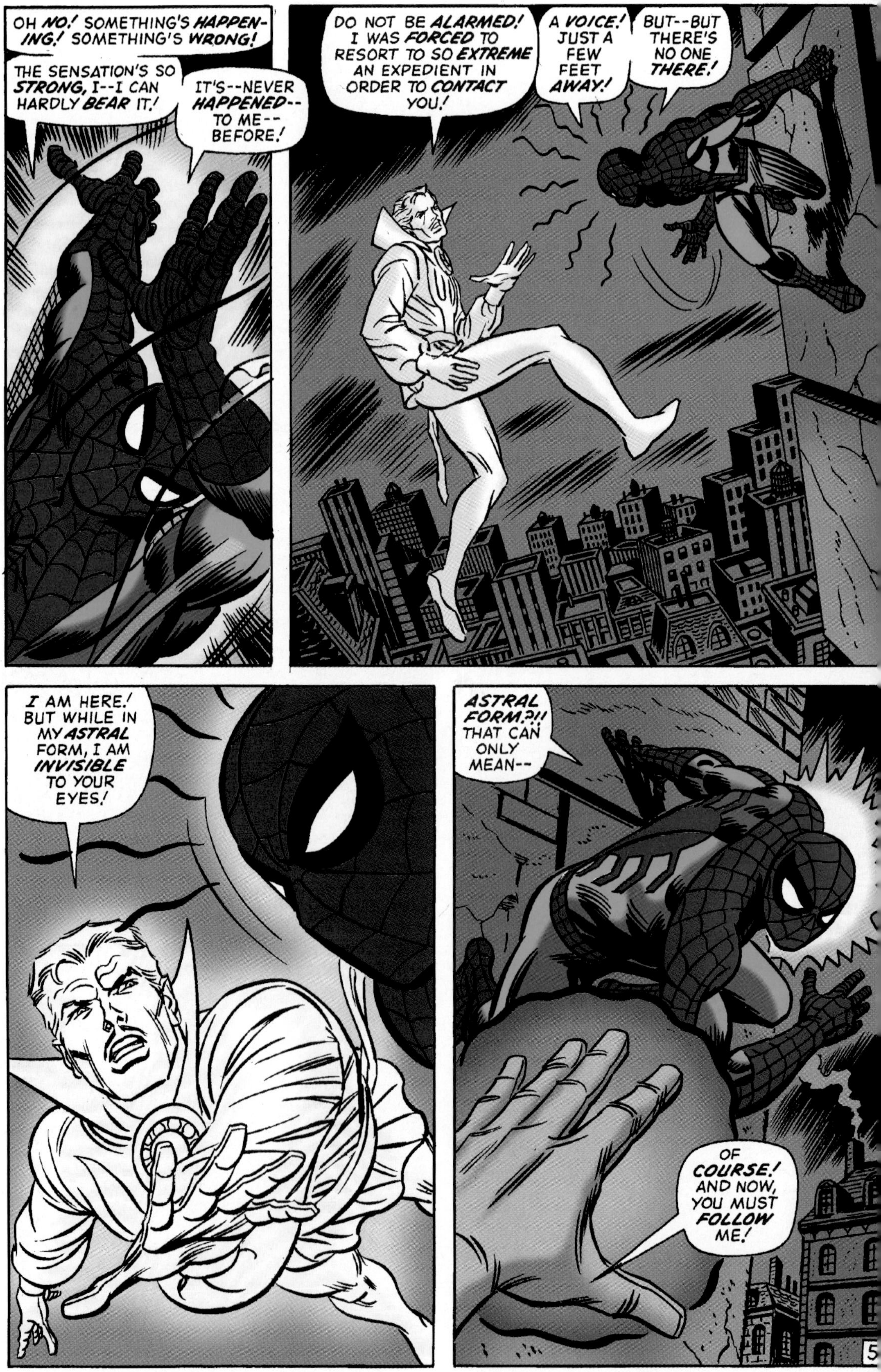

OH NO! SOMETHING'S HAPPENING! SOMETHING'S WRONG!
THE SENSATION'S SO STRONG, I--I CAN HARDLY BEAR IT!
IT'S--NEVER HAPPENED--TO ME--BEFORE!
DO NOT BE ALARMED! I WAS FORCED TO RESORT TO SO EXTREME AN EXPEDIENT IN ORDER TO CONTACT YOU!
A VOICE! JUST A FEW FEET AWAY!
BUT--BUT THERE'S NO ONE THERE!
I AM HERE! BUT WHILE IN MY ASTRAL FORM, I AM INVISIBLE TO YOUR EYES!
ASTRAL FORM?!! THAT CAN ONLY MEAN--
OF COURSE! AND NOW, YOU MUST FOLLOW ME!
5

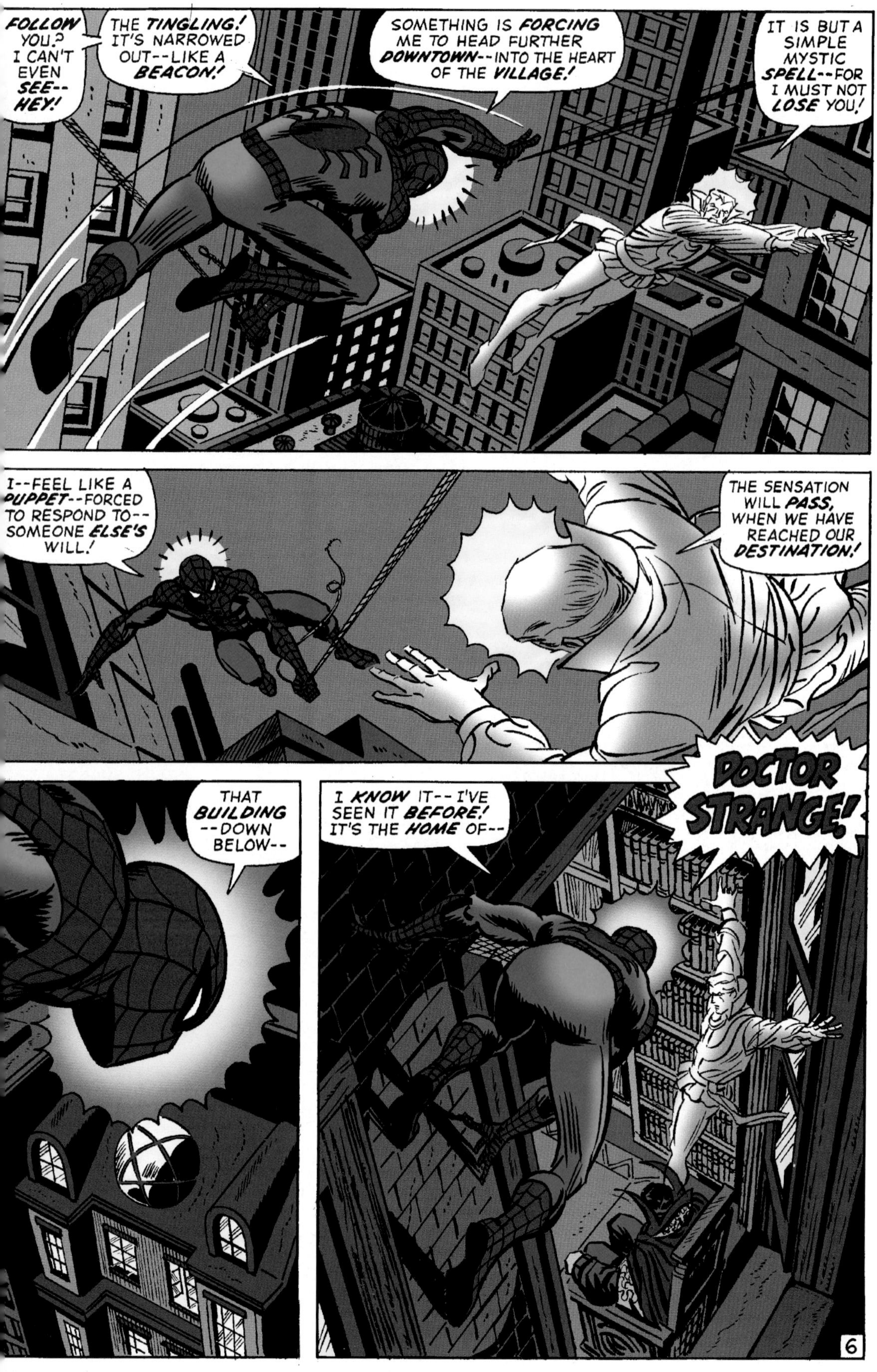
FOLLOW YOU? I CAN'T EVEN SEE-- HEY!
THE TINGLING! IT'S NARROWED OUT--LIKE A BEACON!
SOMETHING IS FORCING ME TO HEAD FURTHER DOWNTOWN--INTO THE HEART OF THE VILLAGE!
IT IS BUT A SIMPLE MYSTIC SPELL--FOR I MUST NOT LOSE YOU!
I--FEEL LIKE A PUPPET--FORCED TO RESPOND TO--SOMEONE ELSE'S WILL!
THE SENSATION WILL PASS, WHEN WE HAVE REACHED OUR DESTINATION!
THAT BUILDING --DOWN BELOW--
I KNOW IT-- I'VE SEEN IT BEFORE! IT'S THE HOME OF--
DOCTOR STRANGE!

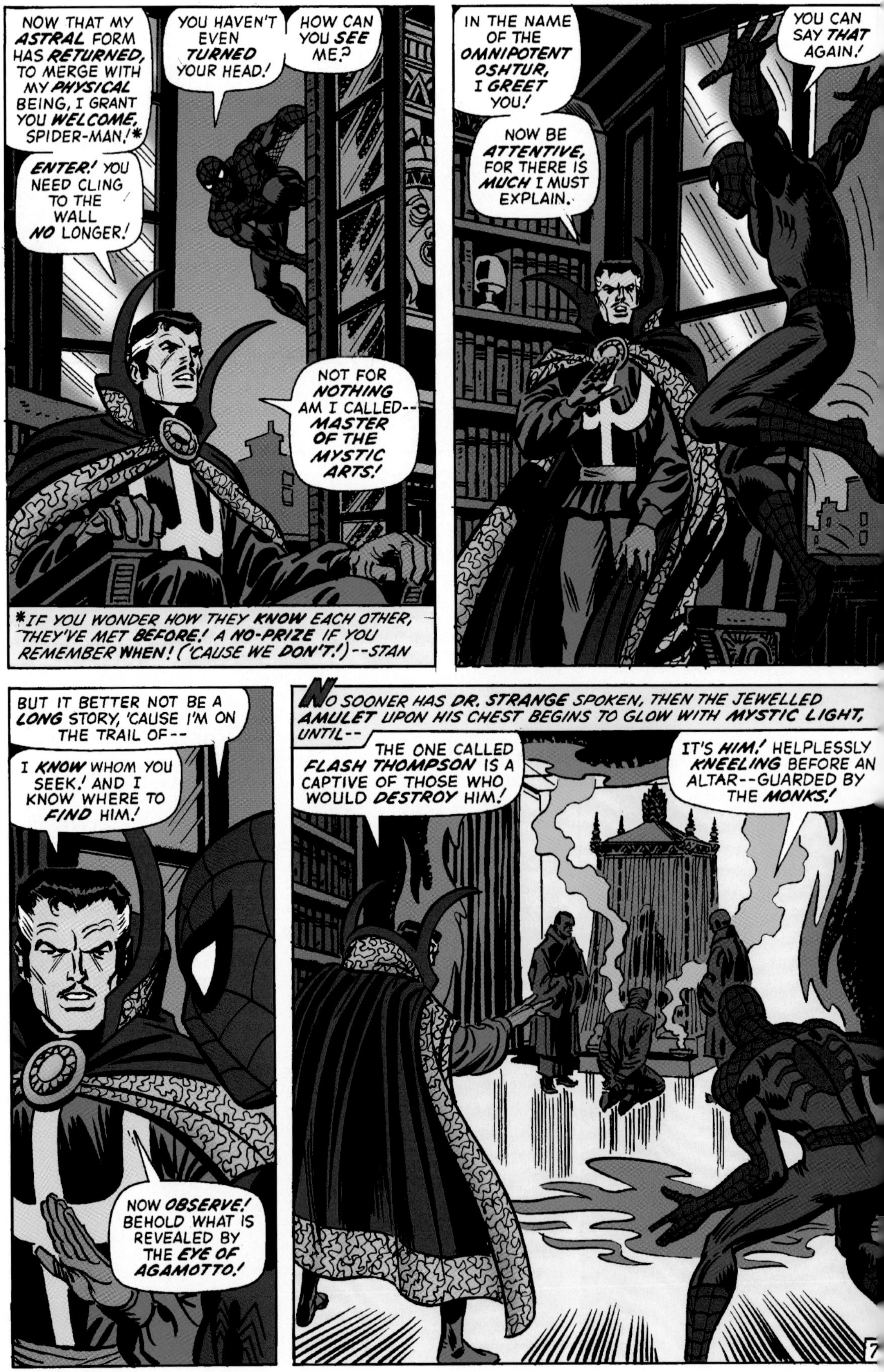
NOW THAT MY ASTRAL FORM HAS RETURNED, TO MERGE WITH MY PHYSICAL BEING, I GRANT YOU WELCOME, SPIDER-MAN!*
ENTER! YOU NEED CLING TO THE WALL NO LONGER!
YOU HAVEN'T EVEN TURNED YOUR HEAD!
HOW CAN YOU SEE ME?
NOT FOR NOTHING AM I CALLED--MASTER OF THE MYSTIC ARTS!
*IF YOU WONDER HOW THEY KNOW EACH OTHER, THEY'VE MET BEFORE! A NO-PRIZE IF YOU REMEMBER WHEN! ('CAUSE WE DON'T!) --STAN
IN THE NAME OF THE OMNIPOTENT OSHTUR, I GREET YOU!
NOW BE ATTENTIVE, FOR THERE IS MUCH I MUST EXPLAIN.
YOU CAN SAY THAT AGAIN!
BUT IT BETTER NOT BE A LONG STORY, 'CAUSE I'M ON THE TRAIL OF--
I KNOW WHOM YOU SEEK! AND I KNOW WHERE TO FIND HIM!
NOW OBSERVE! BEHOLD WHAT IS REVEALED BY THE EYE OF AGAMOTTO!
NO SOONER HAS DR. STRANGE SPOKEN, THEN THE JEWELLED AMULET UPON HIS CHEST BEGINS TO GLOW WITH MYSTIC LIGHT, UNTIL--
THE ONE CALLED FLASH THOMPSON IS A CAPTIVE OF THOSE WHO WOULD DESTROY HIM!
IT'S HIM! HELPLESSLY KNEELING BEFORE AN ALTAR--GUARDED BY THE MONKS!
7

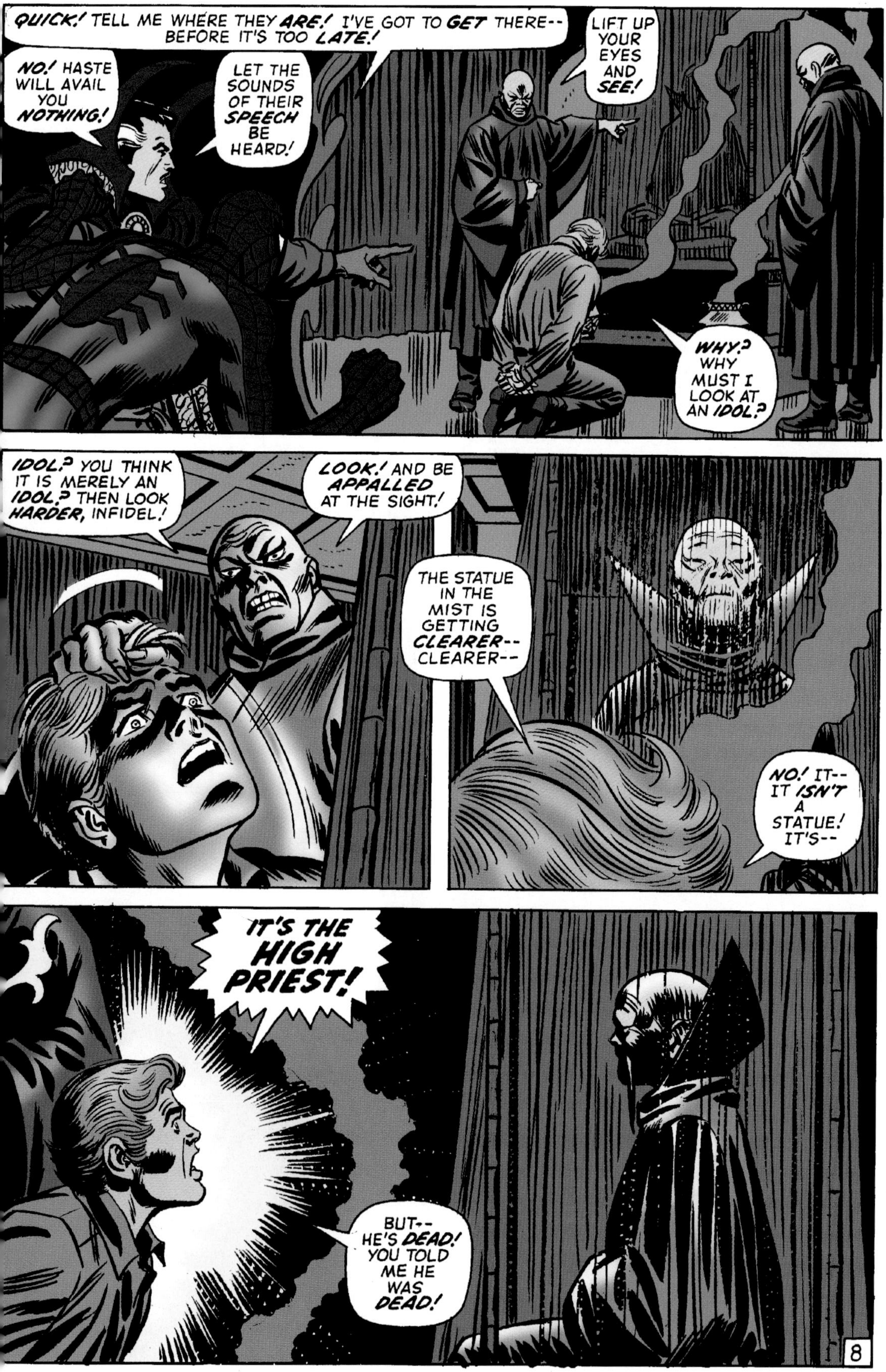
QUICK! TELL ME WHERE THEY ARE! I'VE GOT TO GET THERE-- BEFORE IT'S TOO LATE!
NO! HASTE WILL AVAIL YOU NOTHING!
LET THE SOUNDS OF THEIR SPEECH BE HEARD!
LIFT UP YOUR EYES AND SEE!
WHY? WHY MUST I LOOK AT AN IDOL?
IDOL? YOU THINK IT IS MERELY AN IDOL? THEN LOOK HARDER, INFIDEL!
LOOK! AND BE APPALLED AT THE SIGHT!
THE STATUE IN THE MIST IS GETTING CLEARER-- CLEARER--
NO! IT-- IT ISN'T A STATUE! IT'S--
IT'S THE HIGH PRIEST!
BUT-- HE'S DEAD! YOU TOLD ME HE WAS DEAD!
8

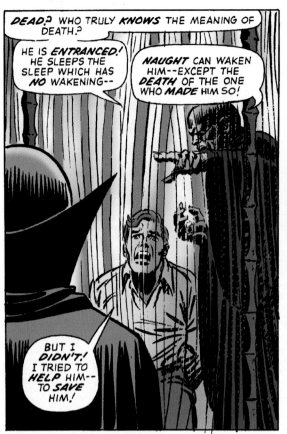

DEAD? WHO TRULY *KNOWS* THE MEANING OF DEATH?

HE IS *ENTRANCED!* HE SLEEPS THE SLEEP WHICH HAS *NO* WAKENING--

NAUGHT CAN WAKEN HIM--EXCEPT THE *DEATH* OF THE ONE WHO *MADE* HIM SO!

BUT I *DIDN'T!* I TRIED TO *HELP* HIM-- TO *SAVE* HIM!

SILENCE! IT HAS BEEN *DECREED!*

YOU HAVE CAPTURED HIS *SPIRIT* BY YOUR *MURDEROUS* ACT! ONLY YOUR *DEATH* CAN *RELEASE* IT!

WHEN THE *HOLY HOUR* DRAWS NEAR, YOU WILL BE *SACRIFICED* AT THE ALTAR OF THE *MOST HIGH!* WHEN THE *LIFE* HAS LEFT *YOUR* BODY, IT WILL ENTER *HIS!*

THEN WILL HE *LIVE* AGAIN?

WHO NOW *INTRUDES?*

IT IS I--*SHA SHAN*-- HUMBLE *DAUGHTER* OF HIM WHO IS ONCE AND DEPARTED.!

YES, *I*--WHO HAVE LOST *FATHER* AND SAGE--EVEN AS YE HAVE LOST A *PRIEST* MOST EXALTED.!

GENTLE ONE, *ENTER!*

SHA SHAN! THE GIRL WHO *BEFRIENDED* ME!

YOU KNOW I HAD *NOTHING* TO DO WITH THE *SHELLING!* I CAME TO YOUR *VILLAGE* TO *WARN* YOU--TO HELP YOU *ESCAPE!*

TELL THEM, SHA SHAN! YOU MUST MAKE THEM *BELIEVE!*

IT IS NOT FOR *ME* TO DISPUTE THE WORDS OF THOSE WHO SERVE MY *FATHER!*

9

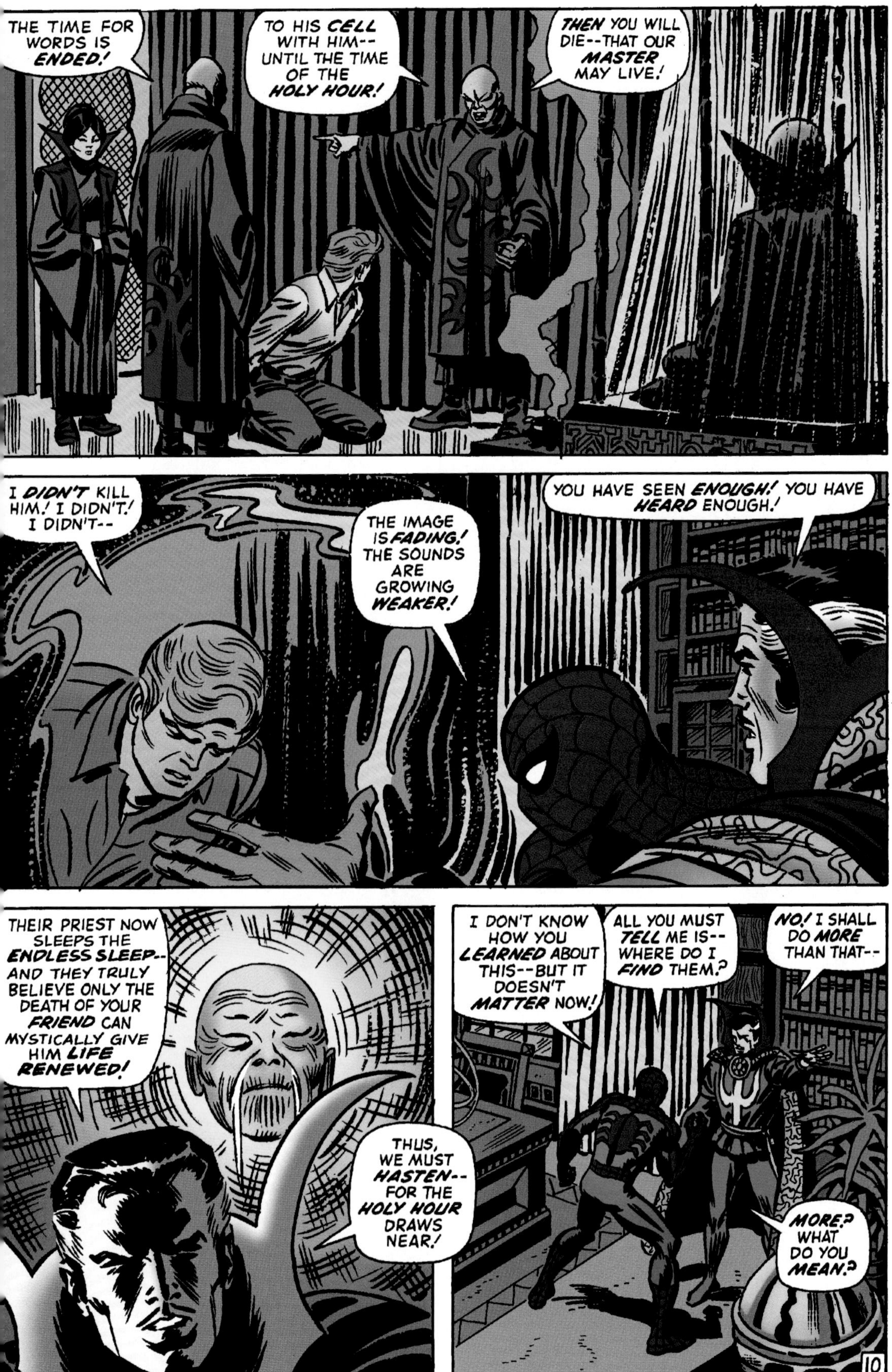
THE TIME FOR WORDS IS ENDED!
TO HIS CELL WITH HIM-- UNTIL THE TIME OF THE HOLY HOUR!
THEN YOU WILL DIE--THAT OUR MASTER MAY LIVE!
I DIDN'T KILL HIM! I DIDN'T! I DIDN'T--
THE IMAGE IS FADING! THE SOUNDS ARE GROWING WEAKER!
YOU HAVE SEEN ENOUGH! YOU HAVE HEARD ENOUGH!
THEIR PRIEST NOW SLEEPS THE ENDLESS SLEEP-- AND THEY TRULY BELIEVE ONLY THE DEATH OF YOUR FRIEND CAN MYSTICALLY GIVE HIM LIFE RENEWED!
THUS, WE MUST HASTEN-- FOR THE HOLY HOUR DRAWS NEAR!
I DON'T KNOW HOW YOU LEARNED ABOUT THIS--BUT IT DOESN'T MATTER NOW!
ALL YOU MUST TELL ME IS-- WHERE DO I FIND THEM?
NO! I SHALL DO MORE THAN THAT--
MORE? WHAT DO YOU MEAN?
10

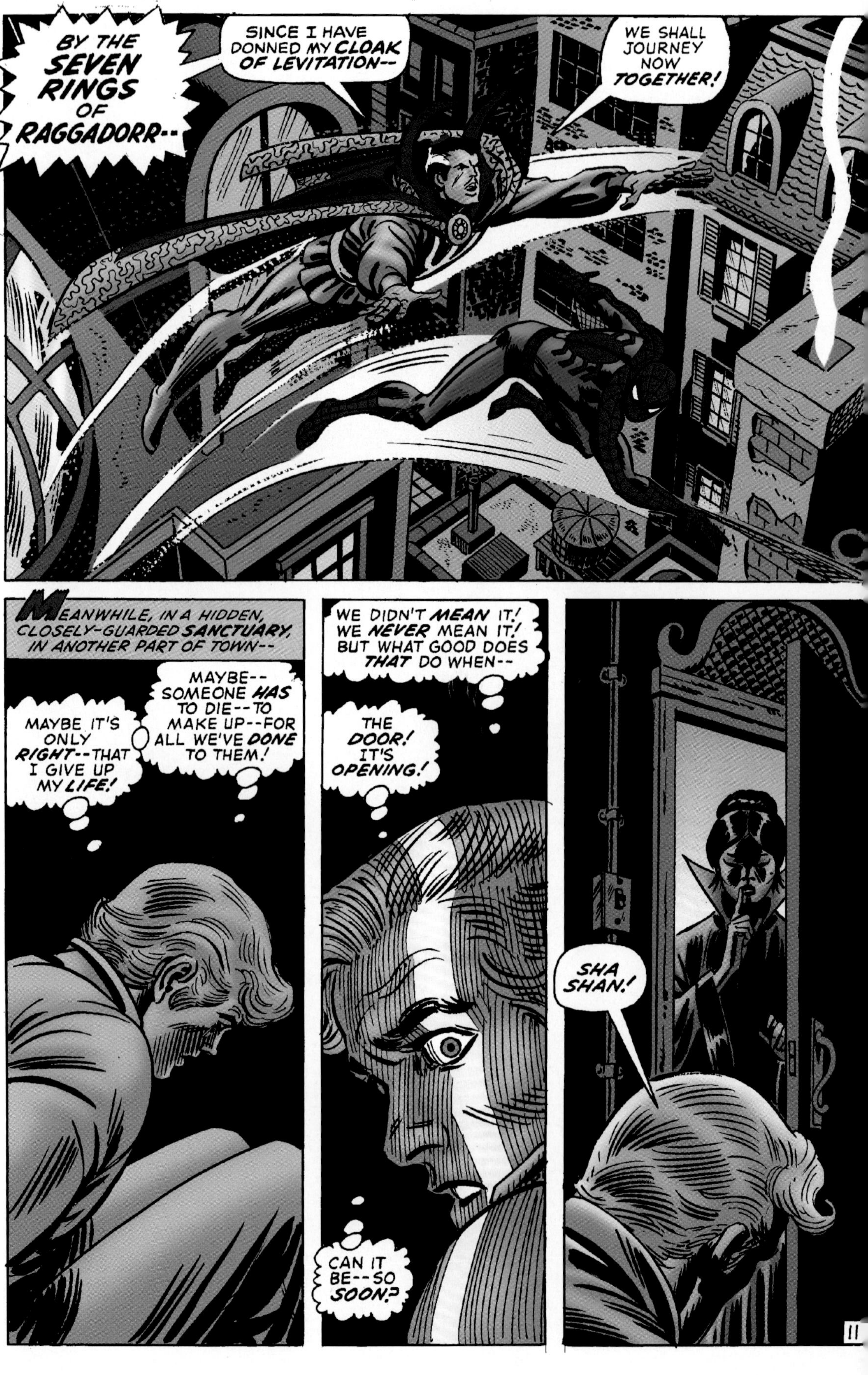
BY THE SEVEN RINGS OF RAGGADORR--
SINCE I HAVE DONNED MY CLOAK OF LEVITATION--
WE SHALL JOURNEY NOW TOGETHER!
MEANWHILE, IN A HIDDEN, CLOSELY-GUARDED SANCTUARY, IN ANOTHER PART OF TOWN--
MAYBE IT'S ONLY RIGHT--THAT I GIVE UP MY LIFE!
MAYBE-- SOMEONE HAS TO DIE--TO MAKE UP--FOR ALL WE'VE DONE TO THEM!
WE DIDN'T MEAN IT! WE NEVER MEAN IT! BUT WHAT GOOD DOES THAT DO WHEN--
THE DOOR! IT'S OPENING!
CAN IT BE--SO SOON?
SHA SHAN!

YOU MUST BE *SILENT!* THEY MUST NOT *FIND* ME HERE! NOW HEED THE *WORDS* I SPEAK--

YOU-- YOU'VE COME TO *HELP* ME!

IS IT NOT *FITTING?* AM I NOT MY FATHER'S *CHILD?*

THEN *WHY?* WHY DIDN'T YOU SPEAK IN MY *BEHALF?*

SO *STRONGLY* DO THEY THIRST FOR *VENGEANCE*-- THEY WOULD NOT *BELIEVE!*

BUT SHA SHAN *REMEMBERS!*

YOU CAME TO THE TEMPLE, TO *WARN* US OF THE SHELLING!

YOU WOULD NOT SEEK *SAFETY* FOR YOURSELF, THOUGH WE PAID YOU NO *HEED!*

AND SO, YOU *TOO* WERE FELLED BY FALLING BOMBS!

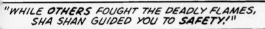

"WHILE *OTHERS* FOUGHT THE DEADLY FLAMES, SHA SHAN GUIDED YOU TO *SAFETY!*"

HOLD IT, SERGEANT! THAT'S ONE OF OUR MEN!

WHAT'S HE *DOIN'* HERE?

WHAT'S THE *DIFFERENCE?* LET'S *GET* 'IM!

"MY HEART *REJOICED* THAT YOU HAD BEEN *FOUND!* BUT, WHEN I RETURNED TO THE TEMPLE RUINS--"

THEY *GRIEVE*-- FOR MY *FATHER!*

HE HAS BEEN *TAKEN* FROM US!

THIS LOSS MUST BE *AVENGED,* MY BROTHER!

12.

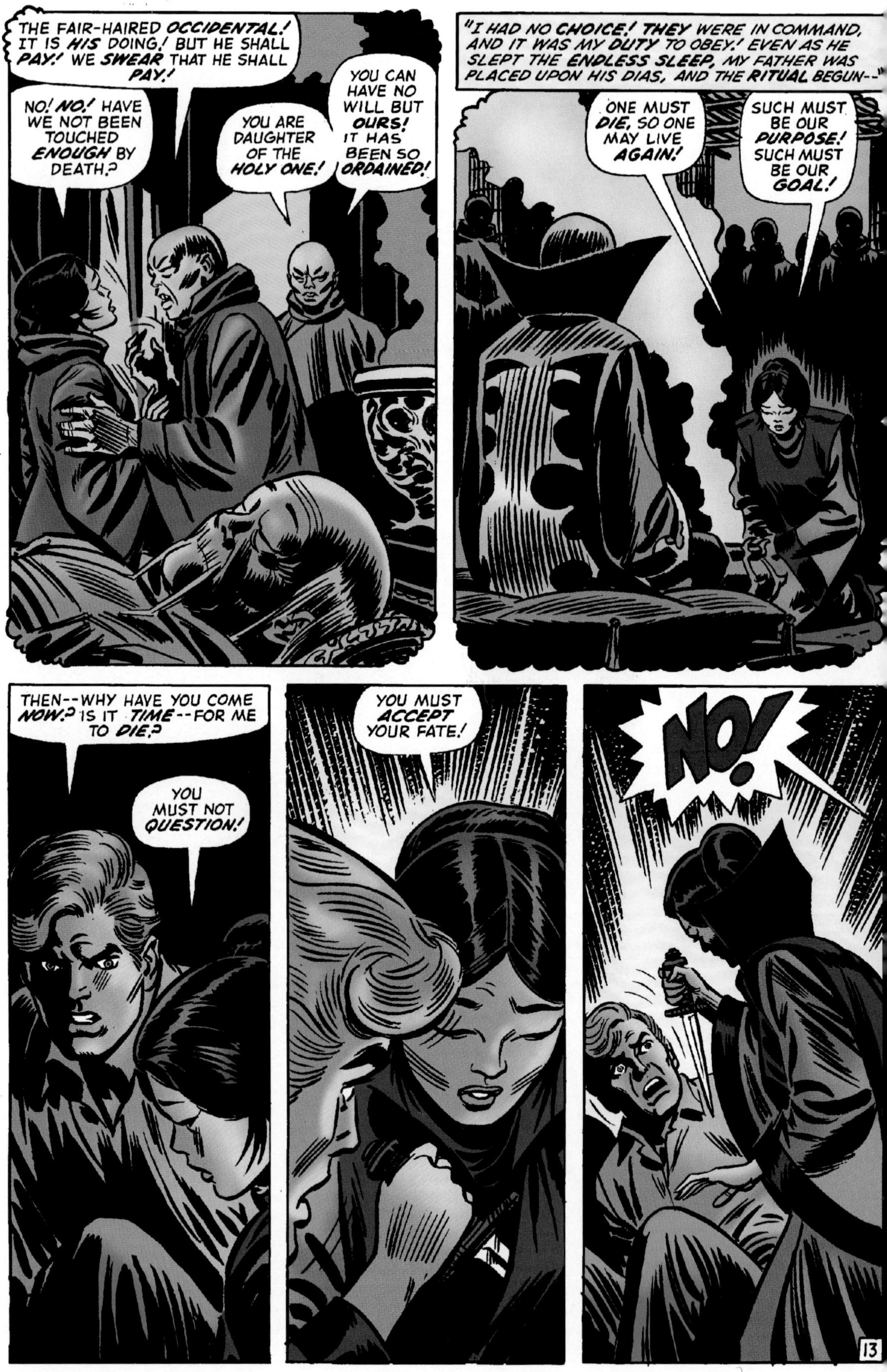
THE FAIR-HAIRED OCCIDENTAL! IT IS HIS DOING! BUT HE SHALL PAY! WE SWEAR THAT HE SHALL PAY!
NO! NO! HAVE WE NOT BEEN TOUCHED ENOUGH BY DEATH?
YOU ARE DAUGHTER OF THE HOLY ONE!
YOU CAN HAVE NO WILL BUT OURS! IT HAS BEEN SO ORDAINED!
"I HAD NO CHOICE! THEY WERE IN COMMAND, AND IT WAS MY DUTY TO OBEY! EVEN AS HE SLEPT THE ENDLESS SLEEP, MY FATHER WAS PLACED UPON HIS DIAS, AND THE RITUAL BEGUN--"
ONE MUST DIE, SO ONE MAY LIVE AGAIN!
SUCH MUST BE OUR PURPOSE! SUCH MUST BE OUR GOAL!
THEN--WHY HAVE YOU COME NOW? IS IT TIME--FOR ME TO DIE?
YOU MUST NOT QUESTION!
YOU MUST ACCEPT YOUR FATE!
NO!
13

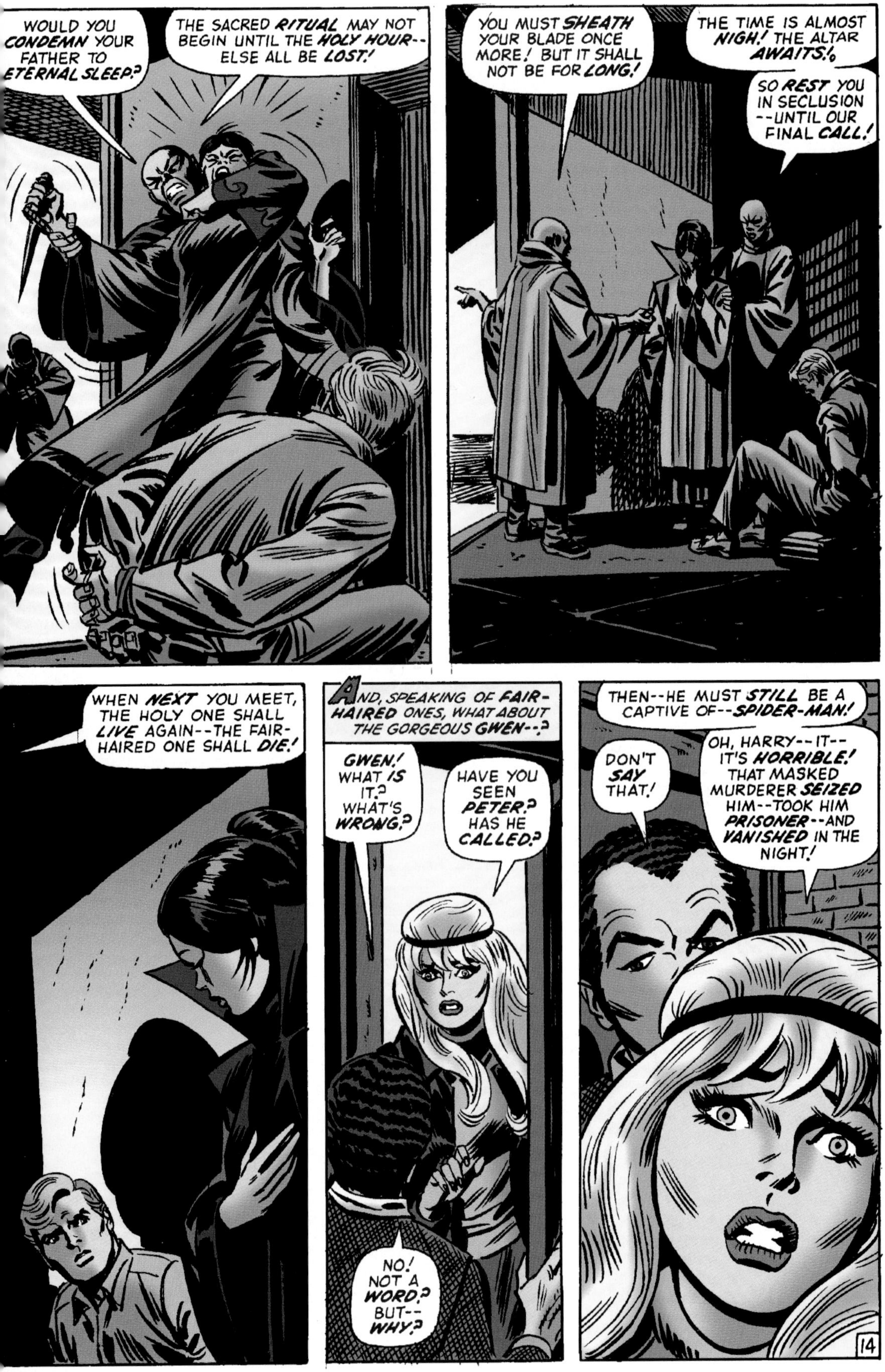
WOULD YOU CONDEMN YOUR FATHER TO ETERNAL SLEEP?
THE SACRED RITUAL MAY NOT BEGIN UNTIL THE HOLY HOUR--ELSE ALL BE LOST!
YOU MUST SHEATH YOUR BLADE ONCE MORE! BUT IT SHALL NOT BE FOR LONG!
THE TIME IS ALMOST NIGH! THE ALTAR AWAITS!
SO REST YOU IN SECLUSION --UNTIL OUR FINAL CALL!
WHEN NEXT YOU MEET, THE HOLY ONE SHALL LIVE AGAIN--THE FAIR-HAIRED ONE SHALL DIE!
AND, SPEAKING OF FAIR-HAIRED ONES, WHAT ABOUT THE GORGEOUS GWEN--?
GWEN! WHAT IS IT? WHAT'S WRONG?
HAVE YOU SEEN PETER? HAS HE CALLED?
NO! NOT A WORD? BUT--WHY?
THEN--HE MUST STILL BE A CAPTIVE OF--SPIDER-MAN!
DON'T SAY THAT!
OH, HARRY--IT--IT'S HORRIBLE! THAT MASKED MURDERER SEIZED HIM--TOOK HIM PRISONER--AND VANISHED IN THE NIGHT!
14

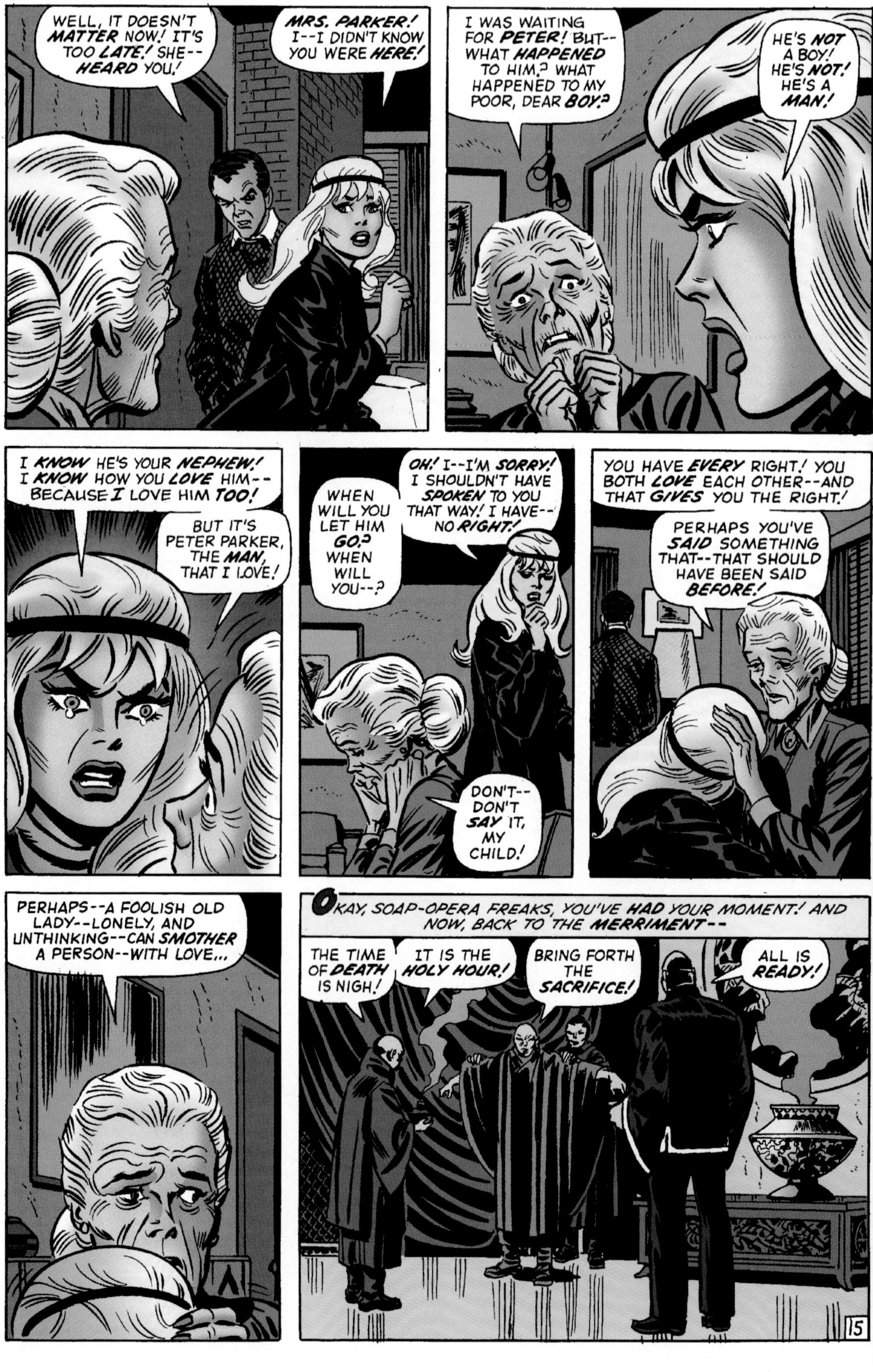

WELL, IT DOESN'T MATTER NOW! IT'S TOO LATE! SHE--HEARD YOU!
MRS. PARKER! I--I DIDN'T KNOW YOU WERE HERE!
I WAS WAITING FOR PETER! BUT--WHAT HAPPENED TO HIM? WHAT HAPPENED TO MY POOR, DEAR BOY?
HE'S NOT A BOY! HE'S NOT! HE'S A MAN!
I KNOW HE'S YOUR NEPHEW! I KNOW HOW YOU LOVE HIM--BECAUSE I LOVE HIM TOO!
BUT IT'S PETER PARKER, THE MAN, THAT I LOVE!
WHEN WILL YOU LET HIM GO? WHEN WILL YOU--?
OH! I--I'M SORRY! I SHOULDN'T HAVE SPOKEN TO YOU THAT WAY! I HAVE--NO RIGHT!
DON'T--DON'T SAY IT, MY CHILD!
YOU HAVE EVERY RIGHT! YOU BOTH LOVE EACH OTHER--AND THAT GIVES YOU THE RIGHT!
PERHAPS YOU'VE SAID SOMETHING THAT--THAT SHOULD HAVE BEEN SAID BEFORE!
PERHAPS--A FOOLISH OLD LADY--LONELY, AND UNTHINKING--CAN SMOTHER A PERSON--WITH LOVE...
OKAY, SOAP-OPERA FREAKS, YOU'VE HAD YOUR MOMENT! AND NOW, BACK TO THE MERRIMENT--
THE TIME OF DEATH IS NIGH!
IT IS THE HOLY HOUR!
BRING FORTH THE SACRIFICE!
ALL IS READY!

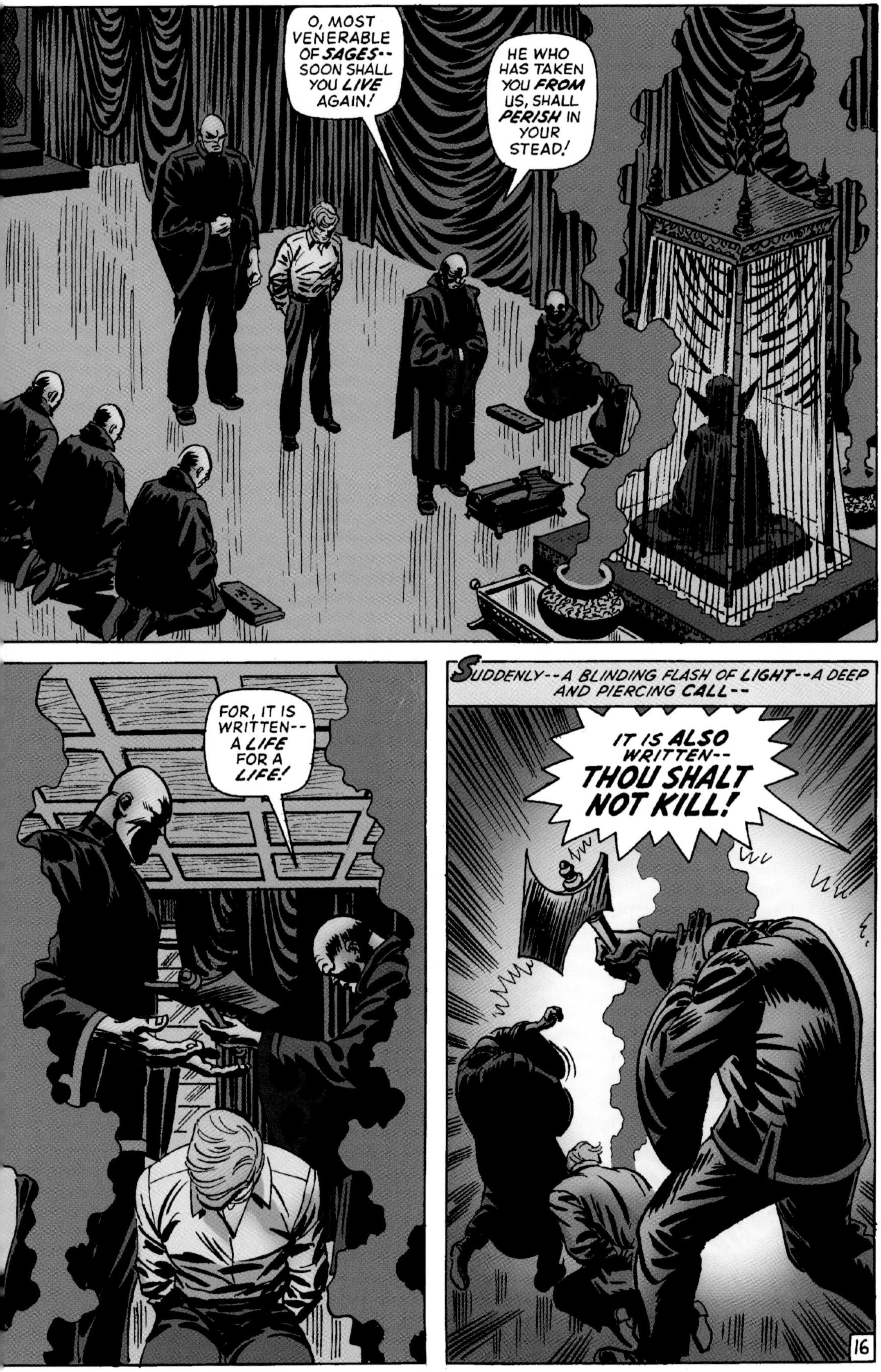

O, MOST VENERABLE OF SAGES-- SOON SHALL YOU LIVE AGAIN!
HE WHO HAS TAKEN YOU FROM US, SHALL PERISH IN YOUR STEAD!
FOR, IT IS WRITTEN-- A LIFE FOR A LIFE!
SUDDENLY--A BLINDING FLASH OF LIGHT--A DEEP AND PIERCING CALL--
IT IS ALSO WRITTEN-- THOU SHALT NOT KILL!
16

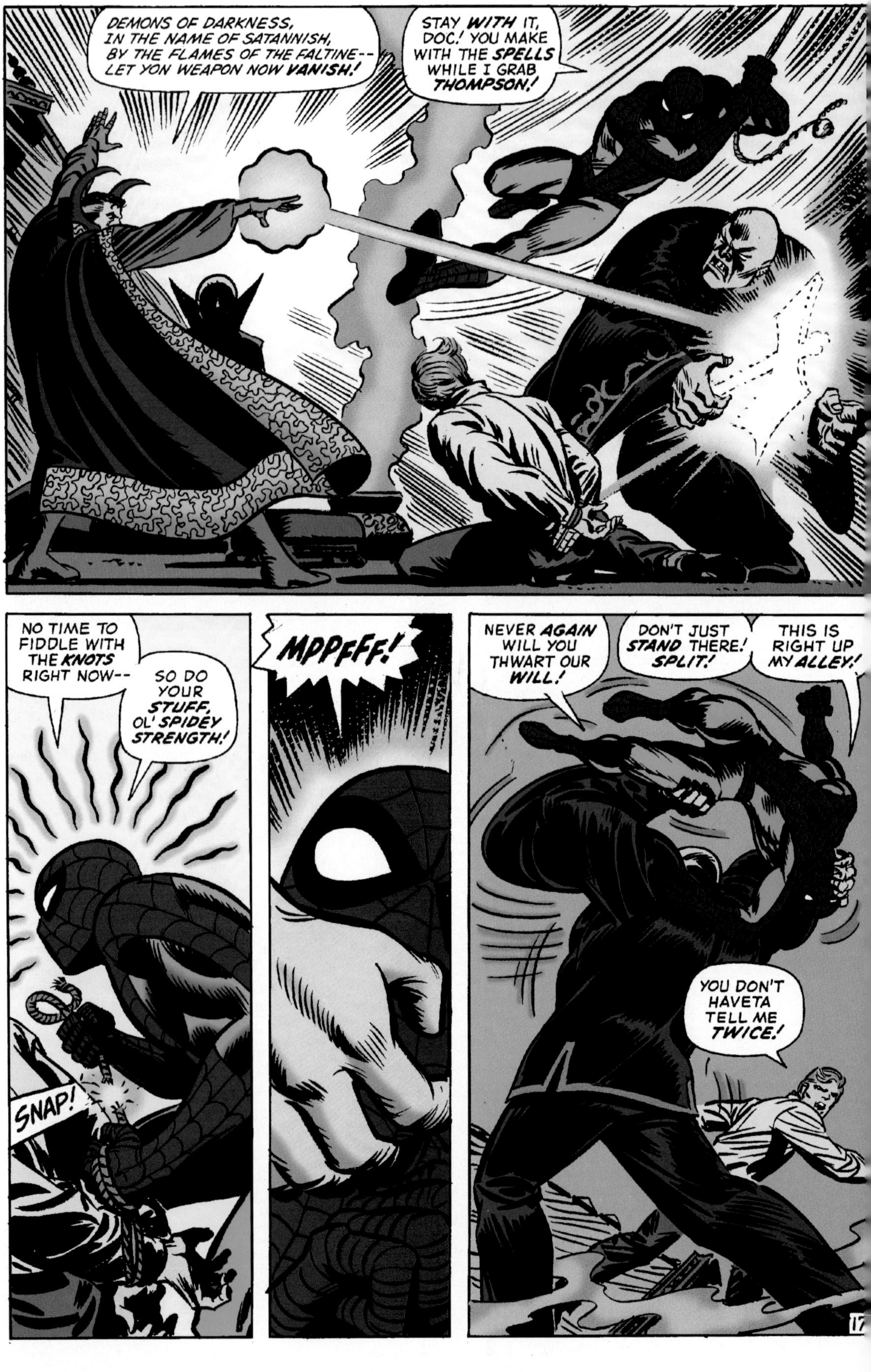
DEMONS OF DARKNESS, IN THE NAME OF SATANNISH, BY THE FLAMES OF THE FALTINE-- LET YON WEAPON NOW VANISH!
STAY WITH IT, DOC! YOU MAKE WITH THE SPELLS WHILE I GRAB THOMPSON!
NO TIME TO FIDDLE WITH THE KNOTS RIGHT NOW--
SO DO YOUR STUFF, OL' SPIDEY STRENGTH!
SNAP!
MPPFFF!
NEVER AGAIN WILL YOU THWART OUR WILL!
DON'T JUST STAND THERE! SPLIT!
THIS IS RIGHT UP MY ALLEY!
YOU DON'T HAVETA TELL ME TWICE!

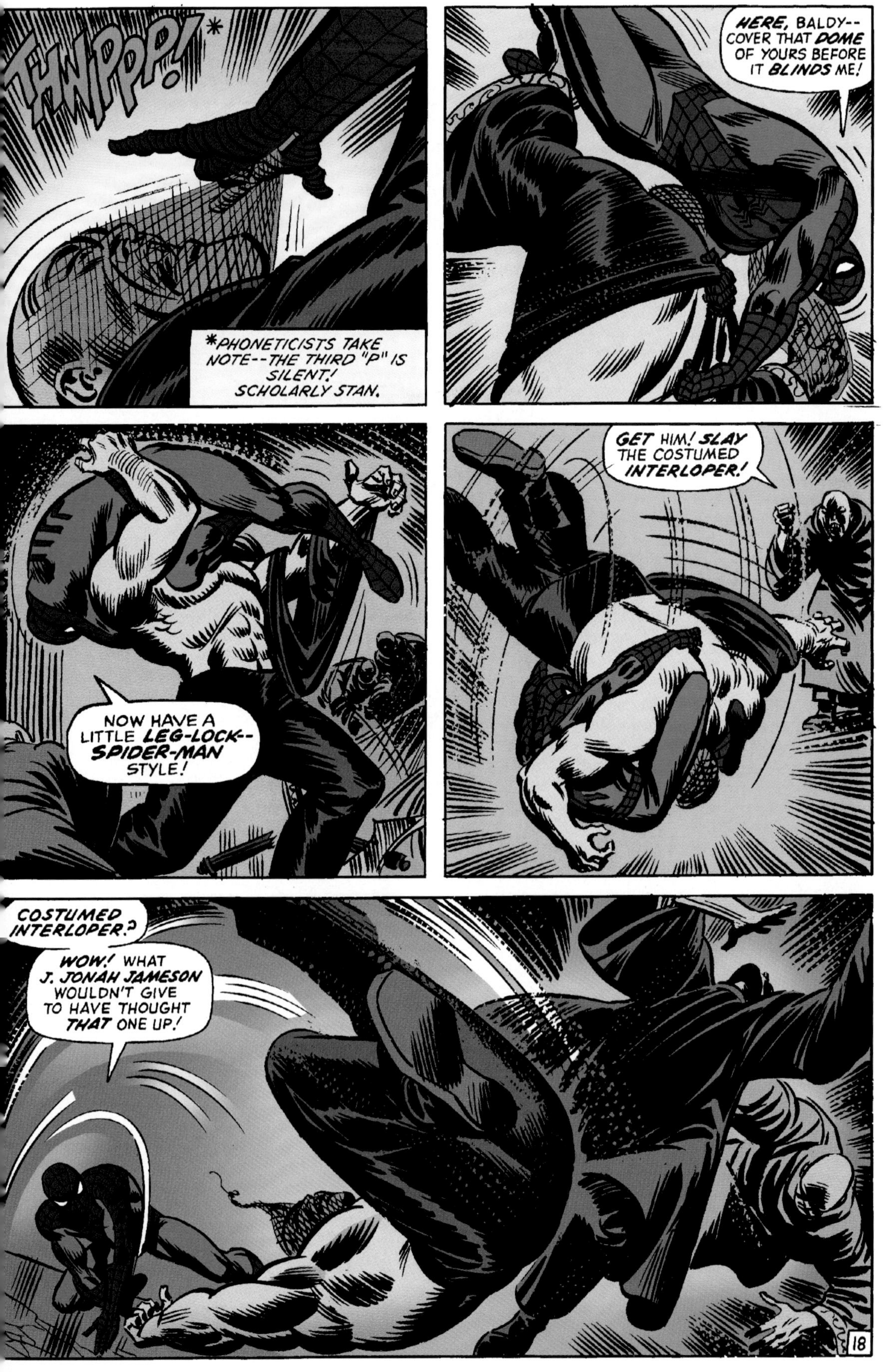
THWIPPP!*
*PHONETICISTS TAKE NOTE--THE THIRD "P" IS SILENT! SCHOLARLY STAN.
HERE, BALDY-- COVER THAT DOME OF YOURS BEFORE IT BLINDS ME!
NOW HAVE A LITTLE LEG-LOCK-- SPIDER-MAN STYLE!
GET HIM! SLAY THE COSTUMED INTERLOPER!
COSTUMED INTERLOPER?
WOW! WHAT J. JONAH JAMESON WOULDN'T GIVE TO HAVE THOUGHT THAT ONE UP!
18

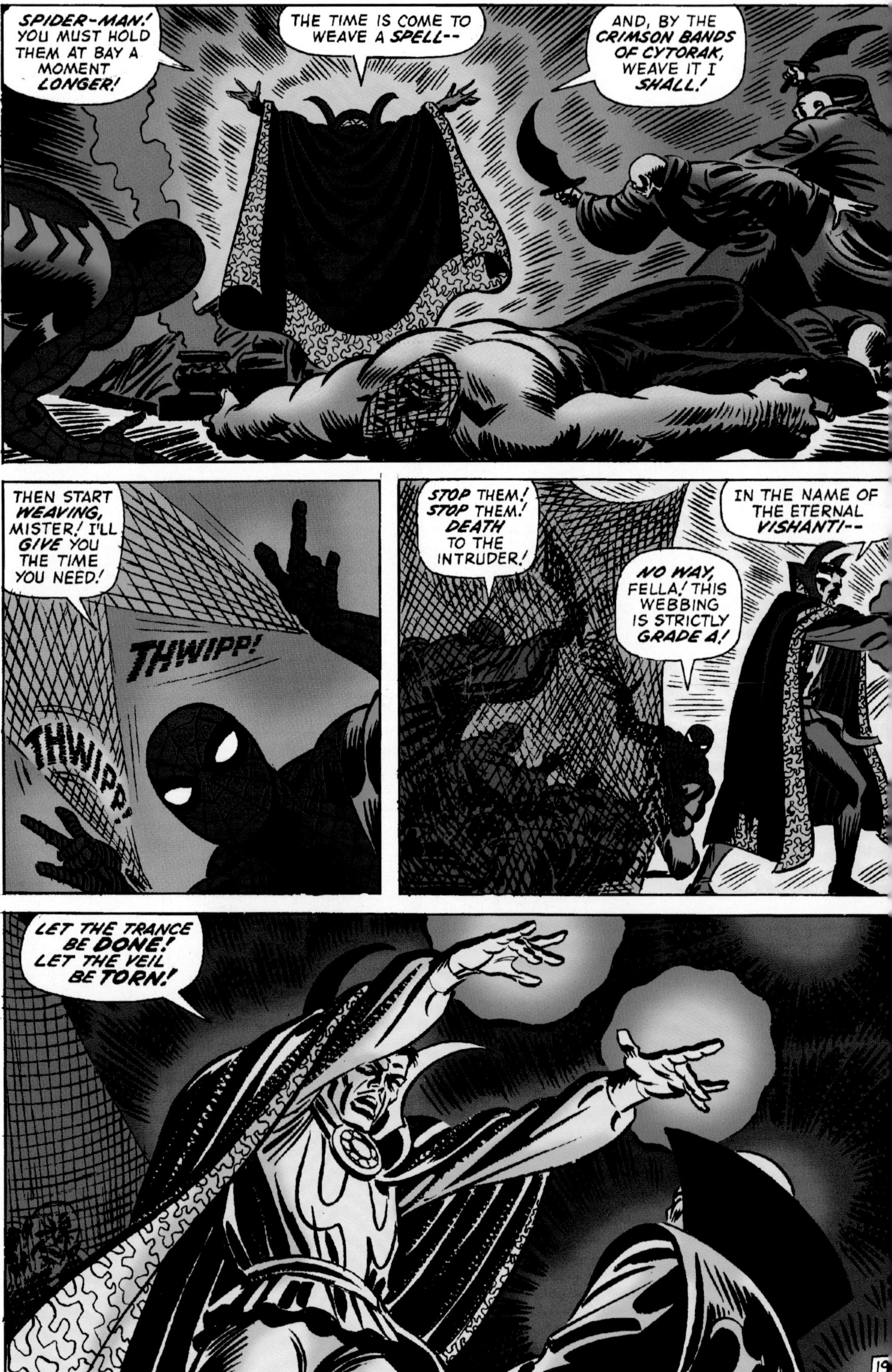
SPIDER-MAN! YOU MUST HOLD THEM AT BAY A MOMENT LONGER!
THE TIME IS COME TO WEAVE A SPELL--
AND, BY THE CRIMSON BANDS OF CYTORAK, WEAVE IT I SHALL!
THEN START WEAVING, MISTER! I'LL GIVE YOU THE TIME YOU NEED!
THWIPP!
THWIPP!
STOP THEM! STOP THEM! DEATH TO THE INTRUDER!
IN THE NAME OF THE ETERNAL VISHANTI--
NO WAY, FELLA! THIS WEBBING IS STRICTLY GRADE A!
LET THE TRANCE BE DONE! LET THE VEIL BE TORN!
19

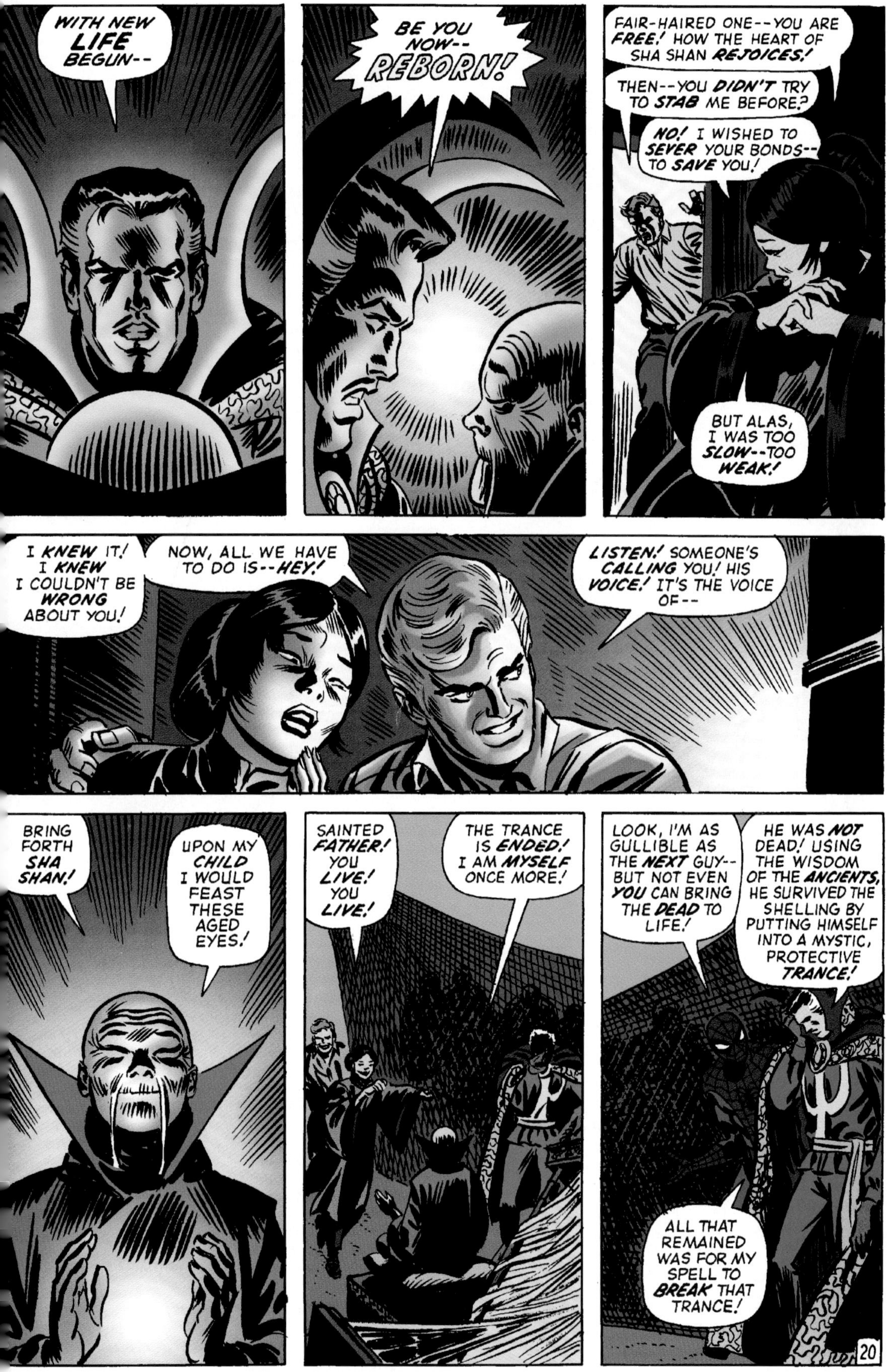
WITH NEW LIFE BEGUN--
BE YOU NOW-- REBORN!
FAIR-HAIRED ONE--YOU ARE FREE! HOW THE HEART OF SHA SHAN REJOICES!
THEN--YOU DIDN'T TRY TO STAB ME BEFORE?
NO! I WISHED TO SEVER YOUR BONDS--TO SAVE YOU!
BUT ALAS, I WAS TOO SLOW--TOO WEAK!
I KNEW IT! I KNEW I COULDN'T BE WRONG ABOUT YOU!
NOW, ALL WE HAVE TO DO IS--HEY!
LISTEN! SOMEONE'S CALLING YOU! HIS VOICE! IT'S THE VOICE OF--
BRING FORTH SHA SHAN!
UPON MY CHILD I WOULD FEAST THESE AGED EYES!
SAINTED FATHER! YOU LIVE! YOU LIVE!
THE TRANCE IS ENDED! I AM MYSELF ONCE MORE!
LOOK, I'M AS GULLIBLE AS THE NEXT GUY--BUT NOT EVEN YOU CAN BRING THE DEAD TO LIFE!
HE WAS NOT DEAD! USING THE WISDOM OF THE ANCIENTS, HE SURVIVED THE SHELLING BY PUTTING HIMSELF INTO A MYSTIC, PROTECTIVE TRANCE!
ALL THAT REMAINED WAS FOR MY SPELL TO BREAK THAT TRANCE!
20

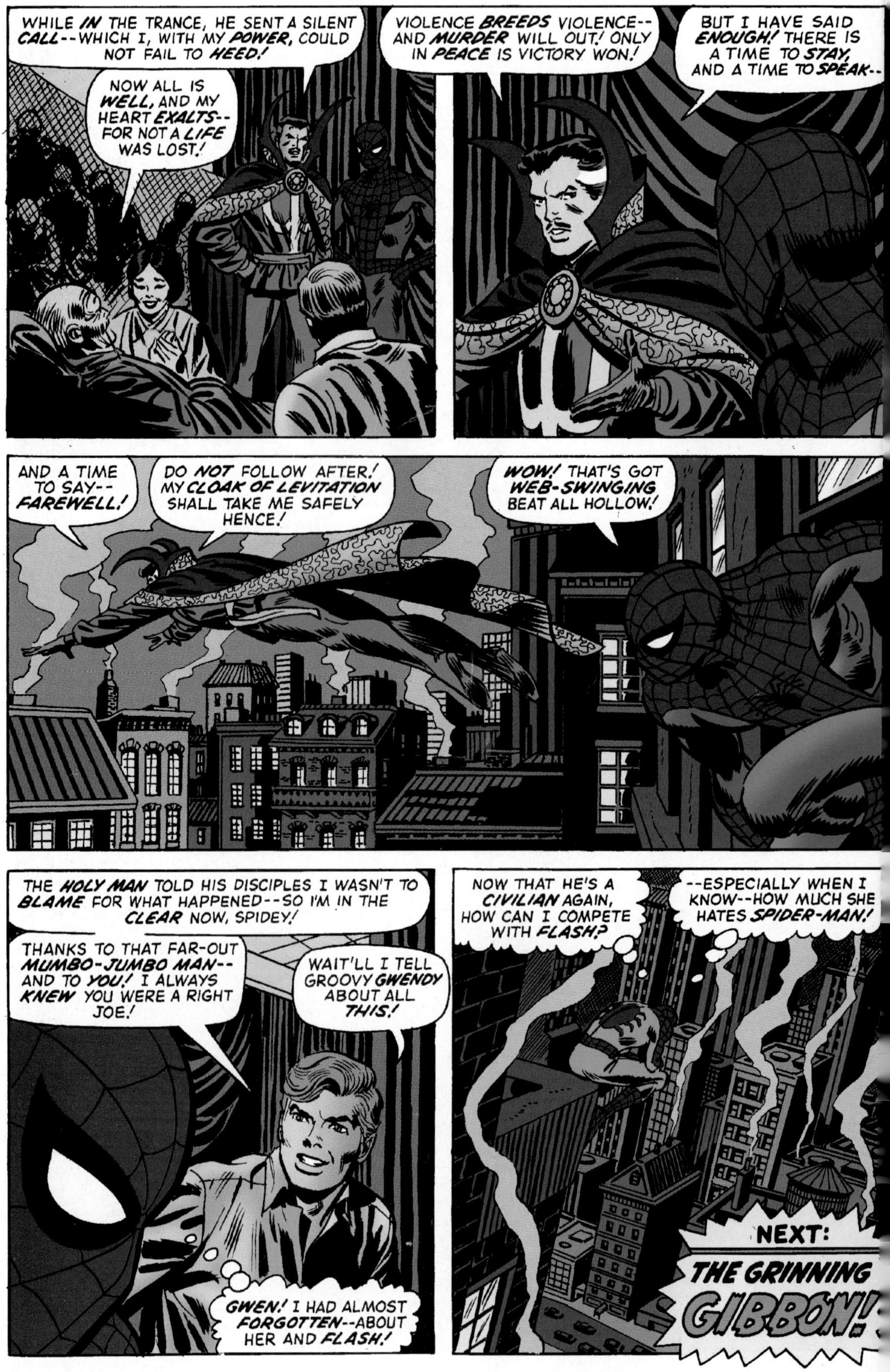
WHILE IN THE TRANCE, HE SENT A SILENT CALL--WHICH I, WITH MY POWER, COULD NOT FAIL TO HEED!
NOW ALL IS WELL, AND MY HEART EXALTS--FOR NOT A LIFE WAS LOST!
VIOLENCE BREEDS VIOLENCE--AND MURDER WILL OUT! ONLY IN PEACE IS VICTORY WON!
BUT I HAVE SAID ENOUGH! THERE IS A TIME TO STAY, AND A TIME TO SPEAK--
AND A TIME TO SAY--FAREWELL!
DO NOT FOLLOW AFTER! MY CLOAK OF LEVITATION SHALL TAKE ME SAFELY HENCE!
WOW! THAT'S GOT WEB-SWINGING BEAT ALL HOLLOW!
THE HOLY MAN TOLD HIS DISCIPLES I WASN'T TO BLAME FOR WHAT HAPPENED--SO I'M IN THE CLEAR NOW, SPIDEY!
THANKS TO THAT FAR-OUT MUMBO-JUMBO MAN--AND TO YOU! I ALWAYS KNEW YOU WERE A RIGHT JOE!
WAIT'LL I TELL GROOVY GWENDY ABOUT ALL THIS!
GWEN! I HAD ALMOST FORGOTTEN--ABOUT HER AND FLASH!
NOW THAT HE'S A CIVILIAN AGAIN, HOW CAN I COMPETE WITH FLASH?
--ESPECIALLY WHEN I KNOW--HOW MUCH SHE HATES SPIDER-MAN!
NEXT:
THE GRINNING GIBBON!